MISSION TO CIVILIZE

MISSION TO CIVILIZE

THE FRENCH WAY

MORT ROSENBLUM

ANCHOR PRESS
Doubleday
NEW YORK
1988

Library of Congress Cataloging-in-Publication Data
Rosenblum, Mort.
Mission to civilize.
Bibliography: p.
Includes index.
1. France—Relations—Foreign countries.
2. Civilization, Modern—French influences. I. Title.
[DC59.R67 1988]   909'.097541   87-15276
ISBN 0-385-24365-0 (pbk.)

Published by arrangement with
Harcourt Brace Jovanovich, Inc.

FOR GRETCH AND O.B.
la famille, quoi

Contents

Author's Note

THIS IS A reporter's book on a passionate subject. Reporters pick one of three roads, and they owe their readers some signposts. They can report facts, filtering out any point of view. They can write as editorialists, selecting an argument and then marshaling the facts to support it. Or they can analyze, looking at facts as they find them, and then saying what they think. My choice is the last.

The French like to say *qui aime bien châtie bien*. He who loves well punishes hard. My attraction to France might qualify me for shelter under such a formula. But my purpose is neither love nor punishment.

As a journalist and not a historian, I am tortured by the inability to ring up Richelieu and say, "Come on, you didn't say that?" I have borrowed liberally from historians, with careful adherence to the two-source rule and attribution where possible. For current sources, I have omitted some last names, and some names altogether. I chose their absolute candor over full identification; often, both are not possible. All characters are real.

In the reporting for this book, and over the past nineteen years, I have traveled to nearly every bit of real estate that flies—or flew —the Tricolor. My interest in the French civilizing mission ante-dates my move to France in 1977: a French mercenary officer taught me how to open a wine bottle without a corkscrew a decade earlier, in the Congo jungle.

Some of the reporting has overlapped my main purpose in life as a correspondent for The Associated Press. Nothing within these

covers engages the AP in any way; this work is my own. But I thank
Louis D. Boccardi and Nate Polowetzky for having the good sense
to keep me on the road.

No one reaches deeply into France without an invitation and a
guide. With deep affection, I thank Annie Amirda, Michel Lavollay,
Jean-Claude Nuti, Paul Chutkow, Jean-Jacques Sempé, and Hélène
Weigand, among others, for sharing the best of their France with
me, and occasionally rubbing my nose in it. Sempé, especially, for
the cover. And Annie, for the trickier translations and hard work
on the galleys.

On the subject of thanks, there is Marie Arana-Ward, for whom
my admiration and affection break all rules about how writers are
supposed to regard editors; Carol Mann, friend and agent who
started me on this project; Joel Donnet, Sylvie Gueyne, Kate Kins-
tler and others who helped; George Whitman of Shakespeare and
Company, for patience. Generous colleagues include Edward Behr,
Pierre Haski, Axel Krause, William Pfaff, Jonathan Randal, Scott
Sullivan, Paul Treuthardt and, of course, others.

And most especially, for every reason I can think of, there is
Gretchen Hoff.

                                                        M. R.
                                                        Paris

PART ONE

THE MISSION

Civilize: [Fr. civiliser, *1601] To bring out of a state of barbarism, to instruct in the arts of life and thus elevate in the scale of humanity.*

—*Oxford Historical Dictionary*

France, France, without you the world would be alone.

—*Victor Hugo*

CHAPTER ONE

France

THE CRUMBLING LITTLE town of St.-Paul clings, half
lost in a tangle of lush vegetation, to the western fringe of l'Ile de
la Réunion, itself only a tiny patch of volcano and canefield at the
bottom end of the Indian Ocean. It might be one of those forgotten
cornerstones of empire, essential to a time of sailing ships and
steamers but a costly nuisance cast off to the Third World in a
jet-powered postcolonial era. But it is blessed with a peculiarity
bestowed only upon the most enlightened of settlements. It is among
the chosen. L'Ile de la Réunion is France. And St.-Paul is French.

"Ah, but you must not make the mistake of calling this a colony,"
the political counselor tells visitors to the *préfecture.* "Réunion has
never been anything but French territory." The rationale might
differ in Guadeloupe, Tahiti, or elsewhere in France, on which, in
contrast to Britain's diminishing empire, the sun is not setting. But
any Frenchman can tell you the real key: France did not colonize,
it civilized.

France itself is strewn across the globe with four overseas *départements,* like American states, and six territories. General Charles de
Gaulle, visiting the Caribbean island of Martinique in the 1960s,
looked out over a cheering crowd of black and brown people and
shouted, "*Mon Dieu! Mon Dieu!* How French you are!"

And in much of Africa, the Middle East, and Asia, former
colonies, now independent states, still speak French and glance back
toward Paris to check their inflection.

Wherever the French have been and gone, the Gallic stamp

remains indelible. Take Pondicherry, a fleck of palm-fanned seacoast south of Madras which France kept for 250 years. The enclave was a toehold on the Indian subcontinent, just big enough to allow thriving trade and to enrage the British by offering asylum to dissidents of the Raj. France ceded Pondicherry to India in 1954. But they took away only the Tricolor, not Voltaire or Valéry. A recent visitor watched two elderly Indian gentlemen settle comfortably into a ricksha. As it nosed into the throng, a snatch of their conversation wafted back: ". . . *Mais, ils sont des barbares, voyons.*"

Or Mauritius, les Iles Maurice. After 158 years under the Union Jack, and another seventeen years of independence, its foreign minister calls it "a little France in the Indian Ocean." A community of French-descended aristocrats clings tenaciously to every last preposition in their surnames. Planters and businessmen, they own the best land, frequent exclusive clubs, and marry within their class. They are Mauritian by nationality, but French by nature.

Today a subtly structured empire, as rewarding as any in history, maintains France as a world power, perhaps the only cultural superpower, one that is based firmly and squarely on illusion. Freed of its colonies, it is master. Having killed hundreds of thousands in colonial wars, France is a Third World symbol of liberty, equality, and brotherhood.

That the French can find glory in the irony is the basis of their genius: One can assume any pose, and command any priority, if it is done with conviction and flair.

A FRENCH VIEW of the world is shared by aristocrats, peasants, technocrats, and communists. Gustave Flaubert, in his *Dictionnaire des Idées reçues,* defined the French: "The first people in the universe." Charles Péguy, the Catholic poet who took himself more seriously, observed, "God loves the French best." And Charles de Gaulle put it simply enough: *"La France est la lumière du monde."* France is the light of the world.

In his memoirs, de Gaulle wrote: "Any large-scale human edifice will be arbitrary and ephemeral if the seal of France is not affixed to it." And having created his Fifth Republic in 1958, he pronounced: "France must fulfill her mission as a world power. There is no corner of the earth where, at any given time, men do not look to us and ask what France has to say. It is a great responsibility to be France, the humanizing power *par excellence*."

Lest anyone think a Socialist government might abandon these cornerstones of Gaullism, François Mitterrand said in his 1981 inaugural address: "A just, generous France . . . can illuminate the path of mankind."

If not always fond of the gaggle of Oxford historians poking around in their psyche, the French received Theodore Zeldin's view warmly enough: "No nation, no democracy can write its own history without acknowledging some debt, or some direct influence to France."

The French world view brooks no self-doubt or diffidence. That niggling analysts might point out that France is no longer a major power is beside the point. France's nuclear arsenal is small but convincing enough. Its Foreign Legion and paratroop units show up regularly to calm other people's unruliness. Only the United States and the Soviet Union supply more arms to the world, and French salesmen penetrate markets of every sort. But true power, as seen from Paris, is not measured in megatons or trade figures but rather in the privileged dialogue among nations.

France illuminates *la bonne voie*. The right way. Moral conflicts, the confounding contretemps that the ungenerous might call hypocrisy, can be set aside for expediency. The greater goal outshadows all. France is the country of choice for nations wishing to distance themselves from superpowers; it is western but not the West. "French is the language of non-alignment," Egyptian foreign minister Boutros Ghali once remarked. It is also the first—or at least second—language of forty nations. Besides the French, 100 million people use it in their daily lives.

The French can find a way to be friends in need to any warlord who does not mind sharing their attentions with his foe. In the case of Muammar Qaddafi's Libya, for one, France has managed to remain friendly with its enemy.

And who is to call that wrong? It is the French way, right there in Descartes. For more than three centuries, French children have been taught to doubt everything but doubt itself and, at the same time, to stack their perceptions in neat little piles. "Descartes made a philosophy the way a good novel is made," Voltaire wrote.

"Everything was plausible but nothing was true." That tends to leave a clear field.

By Cartesian method, what can be seen very clearly is accepted as true. What is not very clear is not very true. "Very" is open to discussion; *donc* anything is negotiable if the goal is worth devising the principles necessary to reach it with integrity.

If you want a dog to look at something and you point at it, the dog will look at your finger. So will the French. France can be led by a logically moving finger to all but the most egregious objectives. Others might forgo their objective if they cannot find the way there among their repertoire of principles. Or they might ignore their self-inflicted restraints which, to the French, would be hypocrisy.

The *Christian Science Monitor* carried an article in 1985 on how the French manage to escape United Nations censure despite bald double-dealing. But it also quoted a senior British diplomat: "Nonsense, duplicity is the very stuff of diplomacy. Every country invokes high principles precisely when it looks after its own material interests. The French are simply more successful at this game than we are."

The view from London has been less charitable on occasion. When Argentina and Britain fought the Falklands War in 1982, each side appealed to France. The Argentines had five French-made air-to-sea Exocet 39 missiles. But they were not able to fit them to their French Super Etendard aircraft. French interests—which is not to say the French government—found a shadowy way to solve that problem for Argentina, well-placed British officials told me. As a result, thirty-six British lives were lost. The missiles sunk two ships. But only two. Being good allies, the French gave the British all the data they needed to defend themselves against the Exocets.

At the height of hostilities, France prepared to send Peru Exocets which, Britain feared, would end up in Argentina. The French desisted, but only after an appeal from Prime Minister Margaret Thatcher to President François Mitterrand. The British ambassador, in his pyjamas for a last-ditch 4 A.M. meeting, had not managed to dissuade top French officials. Immediately after hostilities ceased, despite a lingering climate of tension, France resumed arms shipments.

These are details of history. The weight and the glory of France elude the trifling measures of geopoliticians or the acts of individuals. The nation adds up to more than the sum of its parts. France is an end, says Jean Dutourd of the Académie Française; Frenchmen are merely the means. What really counts is the charge of electricity felt by all benighted non-French, whether Rwandan tourists or American presidents, who approach Versailles to rolling drums. Diplomatic setbacks and fleeting moments of ignominy fall away before an enduring grandeur.

IN PEKING, THERE is a Maxim's, a ludicrous parody of the real thing, opened with a flourish by Pierre Cardin to accompany his implantation of haute couture in the People's Republic. With its sumptuous art nouveau salons underused, it suffers from that most devastating of afflictions that might befall a French restaurant: it is *triste*. But it is Maxim's, and it is approached with reverence. At lunchtime, I asked the Chinese sommelier what wine was featured. He mumbled an inaudible reply. Pressed, he struggled gamely with the booby-trapped *r*'s and silent *t*'s of the long Burgundian name. Finally, he straightened, smoothed his black tails and breathed deeply beneath a starched shirt front. In a voice choked with emotion, he delivered the words that precluded all further discussion: "It is French."

FRANCE FIRST FORGED its overseas empire in an age when it was only natural that it should rule half the globe. Paris had been the capital of the world since the 1600s, for political thought and philosophy, for literature and art. Frederick the Great wrote his bad poetry in French; seeking a name for his Potsdam palace, he chose Sans Souci. French peasants stormed the Bastille in 1789, firing imaginations across Europe. Napoléon added an ironic twist to the new democracy, but he demonstrated the pure power of his nation. However much the French were feared or hated, they were admired. At Napoléon's approach, Russian generals fretted aloud in French.

England set up colonies to expand markets and secure raw materials for its revolutionized industry. France, while also seeking profits, had a different revolution to fuel. With legions of priests and poets,

France ordered itself on a *mission civilisatrice,* a mission to civilize. From Moorea to Mali, redeemed savages learned the stations of the cross and Rabelaisian ribaldry. Black, yellow, and brown school-children studied from books that began, "Our ancestors the Gauls were big and robust."

The word for this is still energetically in use: *rayonnement.* It comes from "rays," the bright beaming of the light of the world. The mission has changed, but it has not diminished.

"La France, c'est la langue française," pronounced Fernand Braudel, the historian of his century, shortly before dying in 1985. Lesser lights belittle the *chien chaud* syndrome, a supercilious mania for translating into French such staple foreign terms as "hot dog." One must not be misled.

Hardly anything is more serious in France than *francophonie.* The word means The Speaking of French. Its pope is the president of the republic and its college of cardinals, the Haut Conseil de la Francophonie. There is a secular arm, the Commissariat général de la Langue Française and a global Holy See, the Agence de Coopération Culturelle et Technique. Missionaries of the Alliance Française work in almost every country. Another 250 separate organizations, some heretical, propagate the word. And nine times since 1635, its bible—a dictionary—has been written and revised by a continually replenished body of forty saints: l'Académie Française.

The watchword is a verb that entered the language in 1568: *civiliser,* to oppose barbarity. Two centuries later, the French coined *civilisation* and never gave up rights to it.[1]

Jules Michelet, the prodigious historian of the last century, defined the French mission:

> The love of conquest is the pretext of our wars, something we ourselves have not realized. Yet proselytism is the most ardent motive. The Frenchman wants to superimpose his personality on the vanquished . . . he thinks he can do nothing in the world more profitable than to give him his ideas, customs, and fashions . . . this is a sympathetic instinct for intellectual fecundation.[2]

French object lessons included how to find victory in defeat. That came in handy after the Plains of Abraham and Waterloo, and subsequent encounters with the Germans. The empire strengthened, oblivious to humiliations of lost battles and the price exacted on colonies to help wage them.

By the 1930s, every French school displayed a world map proudly ablaze with deep pink blotches, marking an empire twenty-two times the area of the *métropole,* Mother France. The colonies' total population of sixty million was half again that of France. From the age of ten, children knew about the Gauls, Charlemagne, the Crusades, and the other past epochs that made France's civilizing role a natural state of affairs.

A textbook from 1926 tells fourth graders:

> France is one of the world's greatest powers. . . . Heroism shown and services rendered to humanity have enriched its national patrimony and radiance. And yet, in population France is very inferior to the great rival nations. If, in spite of this very grave inferiority, we could keep a considerable place on the earth's surface, it is because of the admirable vitality of the race exhibited in a *brilliant manner,* the expansion of the language outside of France, and the successive formation of two colonial empires. French is the auxiliary tongue of all civilized peoples. Among Europeans, it remains the preferred language of cultivated society. . . .
>
> It is every French person's duty to contribute to his full power in propagating our language by which are spread throughout the world the *generous ideas* that make people love France and increase her moral authority. Beyond that, the spread of our language helps greatly the spread of our products.

The textbook proclaimed: "Modern France cannot do without colonies." But after World War II, shaken by defeat and occupation, France set about dismembering its empire. In a long and bitter war it lost Indochina in 1954. African colonies were turned loose without a fight. Algeria won independence in 1962 after a vicious war of massacre and torture, which brought France to the edge of civil war. Yet officials in Vietnam, Cambodia, and Laos still study the West in French. Independent Algeria is a client and a friend.

In late 1984, in the garden of the French school in Bujumbura,

Burundi, I heard President François Mitterrand fire his countrymen with the message delivered to fourth graders sixty years earlier: "You are projecting the *rayonnement* of our culture, our society, our civilization."

Today the formal structure of *la France d'outre-mer* (overseas France) contains what a Parisian writer dismissed as "confetti of the empire." They are the DOM-TOM: *départements d'outre-mer* and *territoires d'outre-mer*.

The DOM are Guadeloupe and Martinique, in the Caribbean, near Puerto Rico; French Guiana, next to Venezuela on the shoulder of South America; and Réunion off southern Africa in the Indian Ocean. St. Pierre and Miquelon, near Nova Scotia, and Mayotte, near Réunion, are virtually departments, save for a few technicalities. The TOM are French Polynesia, a string of Pacific islands including Tahiti; New Caledonia, a large island, rich in nickel, east of Australia; Wallis and Futuna, a pair of nearby specks; and French Antarctica, an expanse of islands and mainland populated by 200 scientists and a lot more penguins.

The smallest piece of France is enclosed in a four-mile-long stone wall on the British island of St. Helena, southeast of Ascension Island on the way to Cape Town. It is Longwood, where Napoléon fought his last battles on maps of Europe spread over an inlaid billiard table. Queen Victoria designated the estate French property after sending home the emperor's remains, in 1840.

Altogether, they total 1.5 million inhabitants, 2.5 percent of France's population. Discounting the frozen wastes of Antarctica, their land mass is about the size of Pennsylvania, a quarter of the area of France itself. In cold accountant's terms, they are a drain on the treasury.

But, scattered handily about the globe, they are the lynchpins of the new empire. Each is a permanent flagpole for a nation that has grown great by showing its colors. Without asking first, France is free to station troops, refuel aircraft, launch spacecraft, and test nuclear devices. "I was in a cabinet meeting once when a staff researcher announced he had increased French territory by ten times," a senior official told me. "He had worked out how many square miles the DOM-TOM added to France, figuring a 200-mile offshore limit."

And in today's world, the French understand better than anyone the advantages of suzerainty over sovereignty. Twenty-five years after France set free its black African colonies, there are twice as many French in Africa: 300,000. Their currency then was the French African Colonies' franc, the CFA. Today, still freely convertible with the French franc, it is the African Financial Community franc, the CFA. The only two countries that shunned the franc zone, Mali and Guinea, came back to hammer on the door for entry. Spain's only African colony, now Equatorial Guinea, negotiated the right to use the CFA. The countries of Belgium's former empire, Zaire, Rwanda, and Burundi, are members in good standing of the French African Community. English-speaking states attend the annual French African summit as observers. Liberian president Samuel Doe, bemoaning his country's economic chaos, observed that Liberia's worst stroke of bad luck was that it was never colonized by France.

In the late 1960s, the French aided secessionists who nearly tore apart Nigeria, Britain's rich former African colony. In 1986, France, not Britain, dominated the Nigerian market.

France left Syria and Lebanon at the end of World War II, but almost every facet of Middle Eastern politics has its reflection in Paris. French jets and missiles destroy French technology on the ground. The dramas played out in Iran are, more often than not, produced in Paris, by factions loyal to every extreme. Ayatollah Ruholla Khomeini directed his revolution from a sedate village outside Paris. The shah's family fled to the Riviera. And each segment of the Iranian resistance has its French *quartier général*. When Beirut was too charred and cratered to be the Paris of the Middle East, Lebanese moved to the real Paris.

By custom, cities pretending to sophistication and charm were called the Paris of someplace or other. Saigon is no longer the Paris of the Orient, but Vietnamese aristocracy—the cultured class, not the war-enriched officers now in the United States—relocated to the source. The Cambodians and Laotians came as well, often with French spouses. Prince Sihanouk resides in Peking, but in France, he is home. Miniature versions of Southeast Asia, with borders and ancestral homes, have risen on the Left Bank.

Haiti fought off France in 1804 and went its own way. In 1986, Haitians rose again, and the dictator fled. To France.

France did not colonize Eastern Europe, but Poles, Romanians, and Czechs stand against the Soviet Union from the boulevard St.-Germain. Nor were the French in Latin America, but from Paris guerrillas speaking Spanish and Portuguese mounted revolutions against a half-dozen military governments. No self-respecting terrorist group or peace movement is without its French connection.

The literary tradition of Americans in Paris is slipping into history. But Poland's finest literary review is published in France. Eastern European, Latin American, Asian, and African writers work in Paris. When Mitterrand visited the Academia Brasileira on a trip to Brazil, members were upset that he brought a translator. "It is an insult," observed one senior academician. "Any cultured person here learns French as a child."

The British Council estimated in 1985 that France spends 2.3 times more than Britain to spread its culture abroad, nearly $450 million a year. That is well over what the American government spends.

The mission extends to French itself. In a television commercial between "Starsky et Hutch" and "Magnum," a suave gentleman murmurs to his chic companion, *"Un drink dans mon living?"* She slugs him so hard the fenders drop off his Renault. Then he tries again. *"Un dernier verre au coin du feu?"* Success. And a man's voice purrs, "The French language, the pleasure of understanding one another."

Le Haut Commissariat de la Langue Française, the ad's sponsor, uses the slogan: "The common language of 200 million people on five continents." That is pushing it. The number comes from totaling the population of every country with some official French at the top; many of those 200 million can barely manage: *"Oui, patron."*

But in February 1986, presidents, premiers and ministers from thirty-nine nations met in Paris for a festival of *francophonie,* twenty-five years in the planning. They gathered in the splendor of Versailles: Mitterrand and three Canadian premiers in well-cut wool; Africans and islanders in flowing robes, pinstripes and leopardskin; a natty Lebanese president in a silk suit. The audience was postrevolutionary nobility stiffened by republican roughage. And toward the front were a dozen Immortals of the Académie Française, like prehistoric salamanders in green-braided, long-tailed ceremonial cutaways.

Speeches revealed a certain defensiveness. Mitterrand had written only months earlier, "No one continues to listen to a people that loses its words." English was encroaching, and the watchword was neither French nor English: *Angst.* The concern was not without foundation. Reporters asked foreign minister Roland Dumas who would be charged with implementing any decisions taken. He replied, *"Un task force."*

By the numbers, French is not such a major language. A billion people speak English, and 800 million speak Mandarin Chinese. And then come Spanish, Hindi, Arabic, Bengali and Russian. Eighty-five percent of international telephone conversations are in English. The number of articles in French in leading scientific and technological journals dropped from 12 to 7 percent between 1980 and 1984. More people, in fact, speak good German than good French.

But it was *rayonnement,* not numbers, that France was after. Mitterrand reminded colleagues they were each part of a community of equals, free of any "nostalgia." That is, colonial taint. And he set the tone: "We are carriers of a culture that can have the ambition of being universal."

And then President Didier Ratsiraka of Madagascar, a nation that chose Marxism as an antidote to lingering French influence, took the floor. He asked, rhetorically, what he was doing there. And he answered:

"I am French-educated and proud to speak French, and my country uses French to communicate with the outside world, and as the teaching language of our university. . . . I address the French in general, and to the supporters of racism and xenophobia in particular: Know that, whatever you may think, in the four corners of the planet there are people who speak your language, who love your country and who are your friends. The people of Madagascar are among them, despite the ups and downs of history and the vicissitudes of events."

No Algerian was there to echo that message. But it was Cu Huy Can, Vietnamese minister of culture and a poet who spent his early life fighting to eject France from Indochina, who recalled that the first great encyclopedia was written in French. Saint Exupéry described the earth as *"la terre des hommes,"* Cu said, and French promised to be the language of world reconciliation in the next century.

Thomas Sankara of Burkina Faso did not attend, but he sent word. In French, he said, he could sing the "Internationale" and speak to oppressed peoples in New Caledonia. His rhetoric excoriates France but not French. For those directing the mission to civilize, that is good enough.

FOR THE ROMANIANS, among the most avid of Francophiles, the cultural lure of France is only nostalgia. Closed borders keep them from Paris, but memories are undiminished. In Bucharest, I poked among the back streets looking for a young dissident whose address friends had given me. He was gone, but I found his mother, seventy years old and elegant in a threadbare housecoat. She took my card, with its address on the rue du Faubourg St. Honoré, and she stared at it for a full minute. Her eyes misted. *"Ah, monsieur,"* she said, savoring the vowels and consonants which she commanded perfectly, *"c'est comme si vous veniez d'un autre monde."* I had come from another world.

IT CAN BE argued convincingly that France is on the wane, that too many people are looking behind its pretensions. Young Frenchmen commit the unthinkable sin of expressing doubts aloud. An Atlantic omniculture, with a strong American accent, is moving in as the new expression of Western civilization. Japan and Germany eat away at the markets. Only Washington's and Moscow's doomsday buttons matter in the power balance. Former colonies feel exploited. French-trained leaders are retiring, replaced by products of the University of Colorado. Racism is growing, and French overseas territories are buffeted by currents that are growing violent.

Flexible principles at times humiliate France. In July 1985, two explosive charges sank the *Rainbow Warrior,* flagship of the Greenpeace movement, moored in Auckland harbor preparing to protest French nuclear tests at Mururoa. The chief engineer, a Portuguese-born Dutch photographer named Fernando Pereira, died on board. Few people suspected France; that would have been too obvious. And, after all, France condemned international terrorism and regarded the peaceful little state of New Zealand as a friend. French Defense Ministry officials suggested to selected reporters that the British did it to besmirch France, in revenge for the arming of the Exocets.

Suddenly French papers found a whole chorus of deep throats leaking details. Cartesian logic tends to backfire when individuals see different very clear truths from those up the chain. And an internal war was raging among French secret services. We will get back to the *Rainbow Warrior.* But, briefly, it went like this:

After silence and denials, Prime Minister Laurent Fabius admitted that France was responsible. The head of intelligence was fired. Defense Minister Charles Hernu took full blame and resigned. Two arrested French agents were tried and each was sentenced to ten years in prison. And that was it. Reporters wrestled with the unanswered questions. The world wagged its collective finger. But France was prepared to take only so much. Despite a heated run up to the legislative elections, the opposition all but ignored the subject. No more questions were asked or answered.

Without French help in the investigation, New Zealand prosecutors had to drop the charge from murder to manslaughter. Most French believed that meant their government had negotiated a deal with the judges. When the Wellington government asked for reparations, French papers called it "ransom" and predicted their spies would be home for Christmas. Commentators decried Prime Minister David Lange as a political opportunist for refusing leniency to two officers simply following orders in their nation's interest.

The nuclear test, meanwhile, went off as scheduled; in fact, Mitterrand himself flew out to watch. Greenpeace found another vessel to send to Mururoa. But it broke down and headed for the French port of Papeete in distress.

Hernu, who is supposed to have lied about the bombing to his old friend, the president, did not go to jail. Instead, he received the loudest and longest applause of anyone at the Socialist Party congress shortly afterward. He outpolled everyone in his district for the National Assembly in March 1986, and was mentioned as a presidential candidate for 1988.

The opposition did not drop the affair entirely. Alain Madelin, a deputy and a leader of the Union pour la Démocratie Française, told a television reporter: "I am very sad for France, a France which haggles, a France which has set an example of terrorist action, a France which has lied, a France bogged down in deceit to the point where a foreign minister, speaking in the United Nations, has to erase in his speech the mention of human rights for fear of making the entire world laugh."

But for most French, there was far less remorse than chagrin that their government had made them look stupid. My greengrocer, a warm and generous man, summed up opinion nicely: "Those jerks, why didn't they wait until it was in open seas and then hit it with an Exocet? *Paf*, gone without a trace, and no one is the wiser. And to make a war minister quit, what for? That's like if I sell a rotten tomato, and they tell me I'm incapable of selling vegetables. I should have known, but so what? Like Watergate, to make Nixon quit. Ha. The *Rainbow Warrior?* That's only the press and some politicians. It doesn't concern the people."

But, I asked, what about the loss of life and the hostile act in an allied country? He looked at me as if I were a questionable tomato and emitted that classic French sound, like a gas bubble escaping from under a lily pad: *"Bofff."*

The whole episode had lacked flair, and it irritated him. But he is forgetting it with conviction.

Proper French style would have been to say nothing, to wait until people just dropped the subject. The columnist Georgie Anne Geyer found out how well that works for France on a trip to Africa. In socialist Tanzania, once a British colony, an editor berated her for American meddling in Africa. After a while, she broke in. The Americans have no African bases, she said. But the French have 8,500 troops and regularly overthrow governments. Why didn't he pick on them? He thought for a moment and replied, "Because they don't answer."

For the French, it is *présence* that counts. One need only look around, on any continent. In Paris, for a start.

PLACE ALIGRE, minutes from the Bastille, is as North African a market as in any casbah on the southern Mediterranean coast. Men with olive faces and flowing moustaches sell overripe figs, comparing them in leering terms to the undulating hips of housewives passing by. It is also the Caribbean, the slightest breeze redolent of mangos and cinnamon. And Black Africa, and Indochina and the South Pacific. Eyes and noses of every shape and hue take in the bustling activity. Only the language is the same.

In the center is old France, an antique market of brass coffee grinders and yellowing prints of ships at rest along Brittany quais. One Sunday morning at Aligre, I picked up a book from the pile on a groaning old card table. It was entitled *Visions d'Afrique,* from 1925. The author, Louis Proust, member of the Conseil Supérieur des Colonies and national assemblyman, described in the tone of his time daily life in the Ivory Coast:

And thus is the marvel of our colonial effort. It is not having made cities spring forth from deserts, nor having cast across the bush and the forests the long ribbons of railway, nor having installed in this virgin country prosperous industries and superb scientific establishments; it is not even having tamed ferocious races and having imposed our peace. That, any European nation could have done; but it is having, in 10 years, by our joyous activity, by our serene justice, by our benevolent firmness, by that powerful attraction that belongs only to France, reached deep into these childlike souls, of having gently steered them from the mists of their savagery to the light of civilization, of having, in the end, made of these indolent and bloodthirsty populations a real people of merchants, artisans and farmers.

By our exhortations, by our encouragements, and above all by our example, we have revealed to them the richness of the land, we have wakened in them a fecund curiosity. To see us, peaceable, hard-working and gay, to hear us speak of order, of work and of providing for the future, new ideas stirred among these slumbering intellects. The spears and hatchets, now powerless, are rusting at the back of straw huts, and everyone is at work planting. . . . and when one looks upon these thousand black silhouettes stop[ping] at the foot of each vine to carefully pour water carried in a calabash, one can already imagine an immense harvest germinat[ing] and flower[ing] under the radiant smile of the sweetness of France.

Proust recalls how the French African empire began. The first sixteenth-century trading posts were too vulnerable to attacks by natives and European rivals, so France built an impregnable (except for successful British and Dutch assaults) fortress on the Ile de Gorée, off what is now Dakar in Senegal, in 1677. Proust describes the quaint beauty of the island, its charming stone houses, asymmetrical little squares gay with laughing schoolgirls, like a Normandy village but for the fierce African sun.

He neglects to mention the rank stone cells that filled with water at high tide, where slaves in irons awaited transport to America. Slavery comes up only once in *Visions d'Afrique,* in a reference to Moslem explorations, "somber and destructive," that visited on Africa uncivilized empires which France was forced to strike down.

Nor does he detail the exhortations and encouragements he mentions. During 1927, for example, of 2,850 Africans "requisitioned" for the Sotuba Dam in Mali, 13 percent died, 32 percent were disabled and 24 percent managed to run away.[3]

But why be churlish? If the random glance around falls on Africa today, slavery is not a theme. Rather, the radiant smile of the sweetness of France, or at least the largesse of its coffers, enlightens half the continent.

Time and again, I have watched the colorful clash of symbols —the Tricolor, the Gallic *coq,* the Music of History—reorient those who stray from the natural order of things. In 1979, for instance, I went as a reporter when President Valéry Giscard d'Estaing flew to Guinea to call on President Ahmed Sékou Touré. No one missed the significance of this first visit to Guinea by a French leader. When, in 1958, de Gaulle offered French African colonies the option of total independence or association within a French community, only Guinea chose the former. Livid, departing French technicians took everything they could carry. They ripped telephones and light fixtures from walls. They left machinery too awkward to move, but carried off the instruction manuals. Sékou Touré led his people into a socialism that devastated the economy, isolated Guinea from the West, and filled the jails. Two decades later, he was ready for reconciliation. Giscard d'Estaing was coming down to do the honors.

Half of Guinea waited at Conakry airport, a ramshackle cluster of buildings in a coastal rain forest. At the foot of a red carpet, Sékou Touré stood with his cabinet, his high command, the party leadership, tribal chiefs, and assorted dignitaries. An honor guard, a band, and dancers flanked the officials. In the distance, huge crowds waved the brother nations' flags in the sun.

At the appointed minute, a sleek shape pierced the clouds, flashed in the sun, and settled gently on the runway. The aircraft slowed and wheeled toward the reviewing stand, and an audible gasp rose over the engine whine. Guineans had seen enough airplanes but never a Concorde, let alone one carrying a president of France. The svelte little jet rolled up, its nose sloping elegantly downward. A blue, white, and red flag flew from the cockpit window. Everyone, soldiers, witch doctors, and president, watched transfixed. The plane could have kept on rolling and taken Giscard d'Estaing back to Paris without even a wave. The message had been delivered. *Vive la France.*

Valéry Giscard d'Estaing was defeated two years later by an electorate fed up with aristocratic airs. France brought in the Socialists, men of the people, egalitarians. In 1984, President Mitterrand made a trip to Africa, and I went along to see the difference in style. At the airport in Kinshasa, Zaire, the crowds were waiting. Mitterrand was forty-five minutes late, as was his habit, and people grew restless in the steaming heat. Dancers dragged a bit, and soldiers wavered under the sun. Then a glint of sunlight caught the approaching aircraft. Same Concorde. Same blue, white, red flag in the cockpit window. And same reaction among the crowds. Socialist, schmocialist: *Vive la France.*

Freed of the burden of subduing colonies, France can afford the high road. In the new empire, the president of France arrives not as master but as colleague and friend, a dazzling accoutrement to the image of any Third World leader. And almost any week of the year, France is welcoming at home one of its own to whom civilization was brought as a total package. An army colonel who learned to polish buttons at St.-Cyr, who absorbed Molière for his school play, and whose blood courses at the flash of blue, white, and red snapping to the "Marseillaise," does not stray far when he takes over his country. If his economy collapses, there is the Ministère de la Coopération and the Elysée slush fund. And he never forgets, if he oversteps the bounds of decency, there is always the 2me REP of the French Foreign Legion.

The substance of France in the world, for better or worse, is measured in figures and analysis in later chapters. But, among the French, substance pales against a feeling that is as overpowering as it is intangible.

No visitor to France on a day of national effusion can possibly miss the feeling. Blue, white, and red banners the size of schooner sails hang criss-crossed in the Arc de Triomphe and up the vast sweep of a boulevard, the Champs-Elysées, that only the French could have built. In perfect cadence, strutting and prancing, a phalanx of horses carries the Garde Républicaine, each guardsman in gleaming silver helmet and rich plumage. At some point, unfailingly, brass instruments send the rousing strains of the "Marseillaise" upward into the air, and along the tingling spine of every French person within earshot.

The British might match the ceremony, but it is somehow different, an emotion that turns inward among people who seem reticent to show their pride. The Germans might have, but no longer; anything close would send shudders of past trauma among neighbors and Germans alike. American grandeur seems somehow too parvenu, too brassy, too conscious of the cameras, with too many on the sidelines feeling a nervous embarrassment when their eyes moisten.

I first felt it the night Giscard d'Estaing welcomed Jimmy Carter to Versailles. Guests arrived in their Citroëns, hair worked to exhaustion by master coiffeurs, silks brushed and furs fluffed. They walked across crunching gravel to the rumble of kettledrums slung across the saddles of horses draped in blue, white, and red. On the ornate facade of the Sun King's palace, an engraved legend could be clearly read by all who approached: *"A Toutes les Gloires de la France."* Amid the splendor, President Carter's security guards fidgeted uncomfortably, glancing surreptitiously at the awkward spaces between the cuffs of their trousers and the tops of their shoes.

And I saw it on the summer Sunday in 1984 when a million French marched on the Bastille to protest an attempt by the government to control the curricula of church schools. Under fleecy clouds, Tricolors snapped and unfurled against the tarnished copper of the

Bastille column. Parents, priests, politicians from all over France marched to Chopin and Beethoven, and throngs in the square sang Verdi's "Song of Slaves."

At the edge of the crowd, a short, stocky Frenchman stood at unconscious attention, the creases and puffs of his gray face revealing nothing. He wore a three-quarter-length tan raincoat. On his head was a newspaper folded into an admiral's cocked hat, the word *Prix,* in black letters, emblazoned on the side. His wife silent next to him, he watched, the corners of his mouth turned down slightly in satisfied discontent. The music stirred, 50,000 voices rose, and, in a subconscious natural gesture, he slipped his right hand into the front of his raincoat and held it there. Napoléon.

THESE ARE THE people who set out to civilize the old empire and who are hard at work bringing light to a new one. There are only fifty-five million of them altogether, with perhaps 1.5 million scattered abroad; 200,000 in the United States and about that many in West Germany. But they are French.

In the end, it is as Louis Proust put it in 1925, describing St.-Louis, Senegal, the seat of France's emerging African empire: "In a shiver of admiration and pride, one feels all the profundity and eternity that the word, *la patrie,* can express, as it is always the same soul which spans the generations, constantly rejuvenating but always the same, pursuing the same ideal, committed to the same task, and, at every moment, under whatever sky, burning with the same love for France."

CHAPTER TWO

The French

AN ENGLISHMAN APOLOGIZES when you step on his foot. A Frenchman berates you when he steps on yours. Beyond that, generalizing about the French is risky business.

It is easy enough, in France, to base your prejudices on fact. I had resolved to write this book without Alexis de Tocqueville. But here is this, from *l'Ancien Régime et la Révolution:* "France is the most brilliant and dangerous nation of Europe, best suited to be, in turn, an object of admiration, hatred, pity, terror, but never indifference." There are grounds enough for any of the abuse and adulation outsiders heap upon France. But the French, fifty-five million individuals who touch every extreme, defy generality.

Just when you devise nine new circles of inferno for Parisian taxi drivers, a cabbie returns your wallet and waves off a reward: "But it is only normal." A stranger throws open his home to you, and then invites your wife to lunch when you are at work. If France is so mean, where do you place Hélène and Jean-Claude: generous, open-hearted, broad-spirited, and very French? If it is so grand, who is making those raw, greasy, fast-food hamburgers on the Champs-Elysées?

And after centuries of shaping a society from empire, what is French? Annie Amirda, small and brown with an Indian father born in Vietnam, is French to her cuticles. Léopold Sédar Senghor, a poet who expressed the concept of negritude among African writers, was a French national assemblyman and is a member of the Académie

Française. He was also president of Senegal for its first twenty years of independence.

But distinct traits, habits, and patterns of thought shape the French into a society. They explain how France cast itself upon the world as civilizer, for better or worse. Ask any French person who has stepped far enough back to take a look.

My friend Claude, for example. A journalist for fifty years, he has lived in the United States, roamed the world, and observed the French empire from the outside with an insider's eye. Over asparagus in brown butter and *confit d'oie,* with a decent Cahors, he pronounced judgment:

> The Frenchman has to detest someone or something . . . his boss, his work, the state, the Socialists, the capitalists. Nothing is ever one's own fault; someone else is always to blame.
>
> And France lacks the sort of consensus needed in a country that is well off. The spirit is not ample. It produces people who are hostile. They drive like lunatics. Young people glower at the elderly. In the metro, you see old women who can hardly stand. Young men look them in the eye and won't get up to offer a seat. The French are xenophobic, very xenophobic, even among themselves. Many are racist. The famous French tolerance, the ideals of the French revolution: *Liberté, Egalité, Fraternité.* That is pure literature.
>
> When he had money, the Frenchman was the most ignoble tourist in the world. Looking at himself in the mirror, he knows he is the best. But when he goes abroad, and he sees he is not, it vexes him. But he won't say it, covering it with aggressiveness. It is very hard for him to admit that he is not the best. If you tell the French they are the most important, the most intelligent, as de Gaulle did, they tremble with pride. In fact, de Gaulle used to say all Frenchmen are sheep. But never in public.

Claude told me about an aging mechanic living so close to the Swiss border that the road to most of the rest of France went through Switzerland.

I asked him if he had ever been to Switzerland and he got angry. "Me? Those people? Never." It was very simple. Right next door was a wealthy country, where everything worked, clean, orderly, peaceful. It was constant proof to the garageman that his world might not be the best, and he cannot stand it.

He paused, saddened at the hard look I had invited him to take, and he reflected a moment to consider whether he had been too harsh. Then he concluded:

> These are a people I love. I was reared among them, and I am one of them. But there are moments when I am so disappointed. I find my compatriots so self-absorbed, so selfish, I am sickened by them. And I want to go somewhere else.

Another friend, Philippe, sees a similar view in a brighter light. A dentist, he keeps track of teeth on a slim Olivetti computer; Bruce Springsteen is piped into his office. He works hard and late, but is always just back from hiking in Scotland or rafting in Utah. He is young, smart, amiable, *branché*—plugged in—and ready to look over borders for inspiration. He separates himself from a not very silent majority stuck in patterns and prejudices dating back to the Middle Ages: *les Français moyens.* The label means average, or middle. But in a language where *pas mal* (not bad) means "pretty good," *moyen* smacks of mediocre. Philippe sums it up neatly: *"Le Français moyen, il est vraiment moyen."* The middle-class Frenchman is decidedly *moyen.*

ALAIN DUHAMEL, A popular French commentator, calls his countrymen narcissistic and vain but not insensitive. "They know well they are not the . . . navel of the world, only a medium-sized power, weakened, but which still matters and does not give up." But, he wrote, they are grandly wrong on one point: "They believe themselves to be loved and respected everywhere. What a mistake! Foreigners prefer France to the French and admire more the past than the present. The 'great nation,' as it named itself before in all modesty, has lost much of its luster and its attributes, its feathers and its clasps."

But many foreigners pass judgment before taking the trouble to know the French.

Outsiders go wrong by looking at France through their own optics. It is always a jolt for veteran travelers to find that culture shock in France is more severe than in Saudi Arabia or Bolivia. Elsewhere, things look and sound different, so you expect them to be different. France looks like home, or at least like familiar old postcards and paintings. Surprise.

French society, even at the ends of the earth, is made up of little overlapping circles. With luck, timing, and patience, an outsider can fall into one of these circles, and hardly anything is more pleasant. In Paris, some years ago, we found ourselves in the Ile St. Louis microcosm a few days before Christmas. We had a turkey and no oven big enough to cook it in. "But, see the baker," offered the cheese lady. "But of course," replied the Martins, the bakers, waving aside effusions of thanks. "It is only natural." Our outlook changed and so, it seemed, did the island's. The lady who howled every time our dog lifted his leg began asking after his health. The fruit and pheasant man told us dirty jokes as he personally selected each tangerine. The butcher spent twenty minutes hand-chopping the beef whenever I made a pot of chili. We met Mimi, the traffic cop, who had given up her job stamping passports at the airport to be posted on the Ile St. Louis, her circle. No kid on the island crossed the rue des Deux Ponts without a kiss on Mimi's cheek and a piece of candy from her purse.

When I first went to the bustling Café St. Louis, I ordered fried eggs and then left the yolks: a peculiar mania of mine. Three weeks later, I went back a second time. "Listen, you don't like the yolks," the owner said. "Shall I make your eggs with only the whites?" Only a Frenchman could do that.

But when a Frenchman strays out of his circle, or encounters an untested outsider, he acts defensively. In France, defensiveness is no more a simple state of unease than cooking is the throwing of a piece of meat into a pan. It is a sport, a high art form, a spiritual fulfillment.

Among the more accomplished, defense joins offense in a dazzling pas de deux worthy of standing ovation. A basic component is *mauvaise foi*, which translates not so much to bad faith as to wrong-footing. The idea is that, whatever the evidence, the other person is wrong.

For example: I was once in a Paris hospital for something requiring rest. At 4 A.M., two nurses, gossiping loudly in the hall, woke me up. I asked if they could please hold it down. One replied, outraged, "We are discussing supplies. If we don't get the necessary supplies, we can't take care of you." It was my fault.

Or: I got into a taxi with the "in service" light on and asked, please, to go to the Ile St. Louis, which was not far away. The driver whirled around. "What?! You don't ask my advice first? This is no longer a republic? Anyone can get in my cab and give me orders? Don't I have the right to eat, too?" He would have preferred another direction, toward his house. But his light meant he was working; by heading toward his cab, I had missed the only other one I had seen in fifteen minutes. Driving off toward my destination, he resumed, "Do I walk into your dining room and sit down and eat? I should have locked the door. Next time, I will, you watch. Do I . . .?"

Mauvaise foi does not necessarily mean *mauvais caractère*. It is a conditioned response, learned in self-defense. Once at Les Arcs, in the French Alps, I left an empty ski bag in the hotel's locked luggage room. A week later, it was gone. I mentioned this to the desk clerk who replied, without a pause, "Well, why did you leave it there?" His lip curled slightly to discourage further comment. According to the game, I should then have demanded to see the manager who would have found another means of proving me wrong. Instead, I said, "You are perfectly right. I was a fool to entrust anything to your care. I won't make a claim. But I'd like you to say, 'Monsieur, I am sorry you suffered this loss in our hotel.'" He thought for a moment and apologized. As I drove away, he trotted along in the snow repeating his apology. Forced beyond his reflex action, he responded in good faith.

Wrong-footing can be harmless. A Californian discovered in his Mexican restaurant in Paris that most French never considered asking for guidance. "People would just point to tacos on the menu and then eat them with a knife and fork as if they had eaten tacos that way all their lives," he told me. Any nearby Mexican who ate with his fingers was pierced with the look of scorn he deserved.

But *mauvaise foi* and *mauvais caractère* can blend into the poisonous mix that so discourages Claude. Late for a meeting, I turned up
a side street that was blocked by a truck unloading boxes. Five cars
behind, in mid-block, I could only wait and stew. At my back
fender, a woman in costly furs and a Citroën CX was trying to pull
away from the curb. My front bumper was touching the car ahead,
and I gave what was meant to be a friendly shrug of helplessness.
She gunned her engine, edged up until she bumped my car and
blasted her horn. The noise shot along raw nerves, and I covered
my ears in another gesture—still friendly; I hadn't caught on—to
ask for a little consideration. With an evil scowl, she leaned on the
horn until I got out, and she suspected I might not share the French
male's penchant for forgiving anything of a woman in makeup.

The contradictions can be unsettling. At one extreme, there is
la politesse, courtesy and manners polished to a blinding sheen. The
old treatises wax on for pages about when a hand should be shaken
firmly, brushed lightly with the lips, squeezed, or waved aside. At
the other extreme, there is the postrevolutionary tradition of asserting one's equality by acting with unbelievable rudeness. In *The
French,* Sanche de Gramont argues that this does not mean some
Frenchmen are polite and others are not. "It means that the same
man who kisses a lady's hand in a drawing room will half an hour
later be grossly insulting to a fellow motorist at a red light. Such
inconsistency is only possible because good manners are considered
a form of currency . . . and thus should be used thriftily and not
on strangers."

IT IS EASY enough, at this point, to slip into 1,001 Reasons to
Hate the French. (The *Village Voice* did it: "For *quiche* alone they
should be shot.") That is too easy. The society's harshest critics are
those French who live daily with its foibles but who also see its
balancing style and richness.

As I was writing this chapter, a friend handed me two letters
clipped from the *New York Times.* A Leonore Kuhn of Queens
described a pleasant trip to France. Someone had stolen her mother's
wallet in Nice but the police were helpful and assured: "In Nice they
rob, they don't mug." Later, someone returned the wallet and
papers, less the cash. She added, "French civilization also exists on

the roads. Although traffic always moved fast, no one tailgated, cut us off, used insulting sign language, blew the horn or ran red lights." And two people named Sneider noted kindnesses by French people who acknowledged their war debt to America. "I think it's pretty marvelous that we have run into two appreciative and gracious people, and write this letter to disprove the myth of the anti-American French."

Few French are surprised to learn, from foreigners rising to their defense, that they are actually human beings like everyone else. (And any Frenchman who drives the *autoroutes* is likely to wonder whether Ms. Kuhn had mistakenly crossed into Switzerland.)

But the French notion of civility helps to define France's place in the world. And there is no arguing the basic point: the French evoke in any outsider in their midst a mixture of admiration, outrage, and often awe. Therefore, back to the generalities.

UNLESS AN ADVANTAGE might be gained by *politesse,* the concept of me-first is defended with elbows, ski poles, bright beams and horns, and studied indifference to anyone already waiting. Lines work only in small confined spaces where crashers cannot avoid eye contact—and possibly scandal—with those they inconvenience.

Airport strikes are seldom prolonged, so as to disadvantage the strikers, or held during the week when businesses are most affected. They come on peak holiday weekends so the people who suffer are other workers' families whose vacations are ruined. A wildcat metro strike over petty grievances paralyzed Paris for eight hours late in 1985; ambulances sat immobile, heating fuel went undelivered, and mothers walked for hours with tiny children. That night on television, a union leader smugly blamed "the bosses" for causing such hardship.

Such obsequious Anglo-Saxon and Germanic standards as "the customer is always right" often fall away as needless obstructions. Witness, for example, my American friend Butch, coming home from university in New York, ecstatic to be revisiting the bakery in the Paris neighborhood where he was reared.

"May I please have three croissants, two *pains aux raisins* and one *pain au chocolat?"* asked Butch, as pleasant a human being as might be found anywhere.

The woman assembled his order, wrapped it in paper, and picked up a pencil stub. "Okay, what did you have?"

When he stopped to remember, she ripped open the paper and angrily enumerated the items: "Three croissants, one *pain aux raisins,* two *pains au chocolat."*

No, he said, gently. "I wanted one *pain au chocolat."*

She flung one chocolate bun back into the glass case, muttering darkly. The lady in line behind, shaking her head at Butch's atrocious behavior, sniffed her judgment: "After all . . ."

A repairman who came to fix my stereo fouled up the wiring. When he finally returned, I was out, and a friend let him in. He deceived her into thinking he fixed it (he fixed nothing) and tried to convince her to sign a paper reading, "The customer does not know how to work his machine."

Such behavior is capricious, not necessarily to be taken as personal or permanent. My friend Jeff bought an expensive piano for his house in Normandy. The distance is nothing, the salesman assured him, organizing a hasty delivery—and payment in full. When a key broke, however, Jeff was much too far away. We are too busy, the salesman sniffed, call back next month. Later on, I asked Jeff about the piano. "Great," he said. "We raised so much hell they came on Christmas Eve to fix it."

In Paris, especially, there is the *engueulade,* the art of pointless quarrel. Visitors who do not encounter it should not boast; it is likely that they are considered too wimpish to play. The Parisian *code incivil,* explained Stephen O'Shea in *Passion* magazine, is that the ruder you are to people, the greater value you give to their existence. "Thus," he wrote, "Parisians who respect you will shower you with pleasant little incivilities from time to time—but only after you've shown yourself worthy of insult." Responses are standard but varied, graduating up to *"Allez vous faire soigner!"* Go have yourself looked after.

"Do *not* stand on the principle of customer service," warns O'Shea. "For most Parisians, Swahili is more easily understood than this principle. Selling in France is an act of charity which a seller performs for a buyer. . . . Nor should you argue from the notion of graduated hierarchy. Parisians work *at* a company, not *for* it."

What counts in France is not one's designated function but rather one's self-conception. Do not, for example, push a gendarme too far. You may think he is a public servant, paid to protect you. He may think he is Robespierre.

A touch of avarice darkens the picture. At the Brasserie Lipp, the menu scolds in advance: "A salad is not a meal." Café owners often refuse to sell tokens for their public telephones to anyone but their customers. "I passed a serious accident the other night, with a guy lying there bleeding, and went to a cafe to call an ambulance," a cabdriver told me. "The guy wouldn't let me use his phone. It was midnight, and everything else was closed. When I told him I would report him to the police, he got real nice."

Me-firsting and wrong-footing are learned early. Competition is fierce at kindergarten, the first elimination heat toward the narrow gates of *les Grandes Ecoles.* A narrow aristocracy runs French government and business. Well-born or not, aspirants need ennoblement from the Polytechnique, a fine engineering school run by the Defense Ministry; the Ecole Normale Supérieure, a teachers' college and seminary for great thinkers; or the Ecole Nationale d'Administration, l'ENA, a boot camp for top civil servants. Few get in, and only the best survive.

For butchers or brain surgeons, there are *brevets, permis, concours,* and *patentes.* A lifeguard is no beach bum on part-time wages; he must qualify as a *maître nageur.* A notary goes to law school, buys a thick carpet for his suite of offices, and acquires a lofty air of importance. There is competition at each of these stages. Once ascended to his chosen goal, a Frenchman then competes for honors to set himself above his peers.

Napoléon created the Légion d'honneur and, with great fanfare, awarded nearly 40,000 little ten-pointed stars in twelve years. More recent presidents have slowed the pace, but there are medals of merit for postmen and healthy children. At Verdun, the army decorated a carrier pigeon gassed in the line of duty. At cocktail parties, any senior official with no rosette or ribbon in his lapel is apt to huddle in lonely mortification back among the canapés.

Who's Who in France weighs seven pounds, with 20,000 entries.

Among the higher levels, every encounter involves a clash of *esprits*. Sanche de Gramont defines *esprit* as "a verbal spark, quick, bright, and ephemeral. It serves, like courtesy, to deflect the thrust of all that is unpleasant in life." If you are particularly good, or tongue-tied, you can do it with the eyeballs.

With so much competition, someone has to lose. But the society takes care of that with a keenly developed sense of self-delusion. To win in the face of clear defeat, one merely stakes claim to the high road, whatever road is actually taken. Self-delusion obliterates any attendant contradiction. This applies not only to individuals but also to the society at large.

A selective view of the past filters out lower moments. Echoes of Charlemagne, Louis XIV, and Bonaparte drown out the small-minded politicians in between. *L'affaire Dreyfus* evokes a tenacious, courageous defense, and eventual clearing, of a Jewish officer wrongly accused of spying for the Germans. Not so many recall why the fight was necessary, that Dreyfus spent eight years on Devil's Island because anti-Semitic officers, too proud to admit error, falsified evidence. He never did get his back pension. Ferdinand de Lesseps is the hero who built the Suez Canal, not the man whose backers in Panama squandered lives and treasure and then hid the facts for years by buying off journalists and politicians.

World War II remains a dull, aching memory in some nations Hitler subdued. But, looking back, the French remember André Malraux's reedy voice etching a portrait of heroism over the remains of Jean Moulin. That the few *résistants* Moulin led were often betrayed by Frenchmen is beside the point. France, in the end, won the war.

These filters apply equally to the present. France is hardly alone in defending its own perceived values. But, whatever the fine points of fact, a woman scorned hath no fury like the French public defining—and then seizing upon—a principle.

In 1984, Jacques Abouchar, a reporter for the state-owned television network Antenne 2, was captured in Afghanistan. He had sneaked into the country with rebels, carrying a letter he could not read urging the resistance movement to intensify its fight. It was a journalist's nightmare. Reporters, in fact, have no right to break laws even though professional canons dictate that they must take risks to cover the news. (In Uganda, reporters have been shot on the spot for clandestine entry.) As Abouchar admits, to his credit, a reporter captured in such circumstances can claim only leniency. But France decided that freedom of the press—and the rights of Frenchmen—were under assault.

For forty days, up to ten minutes of evening newscasts were devoted to *l'affaire Abouchar*. Each night on Antenne 2, a large numeral marked off the days. Fifty thousand letters poured in, and huge crowds marched on the Afghan embassy. Prime Minister Fabius canceled his appearance at a Soviet embassy function, and the French Communist Party admonished Moscow. When Abouchar was freed, a national assemblyman flew to Kabul to bring him home in Mitterrand's personal jet. Fabius greeted him at the airport, with live coverage.[1]

Interviewing Abouchar, a colleague broke into tears, saying, "This is a man whose profession is liberty." Across France, Abouchar's release was heralded as a victory for press freedom. The theme of press freedom dominated the papers and airwaves for days. In a ninety-minute special, a young moderator noted that the Afghans observed that Abouchar's passport listed another profession besides journalist. "After all, all of us who brave such conditions give our professions as anything but journalist: businessman, art historian," he said. Abouchar, again to his credit, broke in to note that such deception was ignoble, and that his passport had been issued before he became a journalist.

Days later, a more practical application of press freedom was quietly ignored. Britain announced that, like the United States, it would leave the United Nations Educational, Scientific, and Cultural Organization, largely because of Soviet and Third World attempts to muzzle reporters. Britain was an outspoken critic of moves within UNESCO to "protect" journalists by issuing them credentials, i.e., licenses. Under such international arrangements, Abouchar would have needed a government-issued press card to prove he deserved protection. But UNESCO's headquarters are in Paris, a source of income and local pride. A Socialist government had seized upon UNESCO as a forum for expressing French solidarity with a Third World oppressed by superpowers.

For the most part, French television and press comment reported

Britain's decision with a note of sarcasm: Britain, a shameless ally of the United States, was simply following the master.

The French press reflects well how France looks at itself and the world. It is the filter the French rely upon to comfort themselves in self-delusion. Some fine journalists are quick to point out when the emperor is wearing fewer clothes than advertised. But they are few enough to be folk heroes on the fringe. Most delight in helping France find faults in others it somehow misses in itself.

Reporters at the Los Angeles Olympics sneered at ABC for focusing its U.S. coverage on American medalists, although pool footage was available on all events. "This only proves that this young nation must call attention to itself," one television commentator explained. Then his ten-minute Olympic report dealt exclusively with fencing and show jumping, the events in which France excelled.

That sort of blind aggrandizement is known among the French who laugh at it as *cocorico,* the sound of a cock crowing. Since the heyday of the Gauls, 2,000 years ago, the rooster has symbolized France. It is fitting enough. The rooster preens and struts and picks fights he thinks he can win. He puffs up and announces his accomplishments loudly enough to dispel any doubts. He dominates his hens. And, in any barnyard, he determines a pecking order and moves as far up the line as he can manage without grievous injury to himself.

Some journalists crow a great deal. Recently, French and American doctors, working separately, isolated the AIDS virus. News reports in Paris dealt as much with the glory attached to the French role as the breakthrough itself. Pasteur was recalled. And there was a fleeting reference to additional work by "certain researchers of other nationalities."

But that is not universal, and French journalists who reject *cocorico* do it with a vengeance.

Once in the Central African Republic, I chatted with a French reporter at a reception behind the Résidence de France. He surveyed the six acres of mango trees and flowering plants and the ambassador's terraced home, guarded by some of the 3,000 French troops based in the former colony. "We are always writing about how other countries act like masters around the world," he said. "You know, 'Hey, have you seen the Russian embassy in Kabul?' or 'Look what the Americans put up in the Philippines.' Hah. Look at this."

We were with the press corps covering Mitterrand's African trip in late 1984. He had attended the annual summit France organizes for its former African colonies—and independent states whose history deprived them of French colonization.

It was to have been a stormy summit. Weeks earlier, France and Libya had announced a mutual withdrawal of their opposing forces in Chad. Foreign Minister Claude Cheysson laid the honor of France on the line: "If they stay, we will stay. If they leave, we will leave. If they return, we will return." Then, his voice tinged with pride, he declared on television, "The French operation in Chad is not the American operation in Grenada nor the Soviet one in Afghanistan. The purpose of the operation was to make the foreigner leave. He has left."

But American officials revealed satellite evidence showing that more than 3,000 Libyans were still in Chad. Mitterrand, after a roundly criticized meeting in Crete with Qaddafi, admitted that the Libyans had not, in fact, gone. The Opposition howled, blaming the government for soiling the image of France. African leaders worried aloud that the French could not be trusted to save them should they face outside attack.

Mitterrand stood firm. He told the African summit that France had no obligation to defend Chad; it was not one of the African nations that had comprehensive defense pacts with France. Privately, Africans called that hair-splitting. They noted that France had promised to drive Libya out of Chad. But discord was masked by civility. The storm was supposed to come when Mitterrand met the press.

The French press corps jostled for seats, and Mitterrand opened the news conference. No hands went up. An American reporter asked about Mitterrand's talks with Chadian leader Hissène Habré, known to be furious that France had acquiesced to de facto partition. "Very interesting," the president said. A French reporter noted that the summit had been forecast to be tense; what was Mitterrand's reading? "Excellent." Another reporter asked about the conflicting numbers of Libyans in Chad. "I did not take my camera and see for myself," the president said. Little more came out of the questioning.

Not only the president was contemptuous of the press. In six days, there were two official briefings, both short and without substance. Minutes into the first, Guy Penne, Mitterrand's chief adviser on Africa, banged the table and stood up. *"Bon,* if you're going to ask questions like that, I am leaving." A reporter had asked whether Mitterrand would exchange toasts with his host, an apparent reference to the possibility of frostiness. Penne stayed but did not answer the question. In the second briefing, he offered a few generalities and announced, *"Voilà,* I've told you everything." Someone asked about Zairean president Mobutu Sese Seko's remarks. "Oh, I don't know, the usual." Pressed, he finally added, "Oh, I forgot. Mobutu asked for a formal declaration on Chad." The only news.

French officials are used to looking downward at the press. With others' leaders, French reporters are aggressive to the point of abusiveness. With their own, they exude gentleness. This allows French policy to exist on the separate levels of image and reality. Accountability to the electorate is a needless obstacle to expedient policy, and few French expect it. At the height of the Chad crisis, a television anchorman remarked, "The Americans have announced intelligence reports that Libyan troops have remained in Chad. French intelligence knew this, too, but it was supposed to be a secret. Why would the Americans reveal this? That is the mystery."

At the summit, a senior official denied that France had agreed to a partition of Chad. "We would never sign such a paper," he said. "And if we did, we certainly would not tell the press."

The arrangement is cozy. The press can raise hell when it counts. Reporters threatened to boycott coverage of Mitterrand's visit when Syrian customs inspectors wanted one of their number to remove his false teeth. If belittled by officials who use them ignobly, they are well treated. On the trip down to Africa, wracked at the time with famine, our menu was: *foie gras de canard truffé du Périgord, chaud-froid de bar sauce Roquefort, magret de canard aux deux poivres, cèpes sautés, pommes cocotte, fromages de France, gâteau Louisiane, corbeille de fruits,* and, need it be added, fine wines and champagne.

And consciences are salved by *Le Canard Enchaîné,* an iconoclastic weekly that is far enough off the wall to be ignored when convenient. A feisty daily, *Libération,* often separates itself from the pack. *Le Monde* has its moments of glory. But the state dominates television, and independent papers, with their own interests, often pull punches.

In 1986, when an *International Herald Tribune* reporter resisted the Elysée's efforts to edit Mitterrand's remarks in an interview, a veteran colleague from *Le Figaro* scolded him: "You don't understand. These are the rules, and things are always done that way here."

That is how Valéry Giscard d'Estaing fended off what might have been a major scandal about diamonds he received from Emperor Bokassa I. He sniffed regally at anyone who raised the subject. And it is why so many of the French wonder to this day how the Americans could turn out of office such a great president, in their estimation, as Richard Nixon.

For those charged with protecting French leaders, the press is just another part of the obstructive rabble. France, explains a range of modern thinkers, has never ceased being a monarchy. Petty officials serve their sovereign and thrill in the reflected glory. Perhaps not, but the wise Frenchman seeks not to give the police a chance to demonstrate their powers. As for the presidential guard, it might as well be protecting the Sun King. I had a reinforcing lesson in this on the African trip.

In Zaire, I joined French photographers taking pictures of Mitterrand with Mobutu. As a reporter, that was not my usual pursuit, but I wanted to illustrate a story I was working on. National photographers who regularly follow a head of state move like a well-rehearsed ballet troupe. Newcomers are slightly out of step, but that presents no problem. Security guards, by international custom, nudge them along. I photographed on the move, sticking with the group, well ahead of the two stationary presidents. Suddenly, everyone else leaped to the left on a subtle cue, and I was a split second late. The beefy Elysée security team leader grabbed me in a manner most civilized societies reserve for mass murderers caught red-handed.

"You don't understand anything, you stupid . . ." he said, using the *tu* form used only to show familiarity or contempt. He gouged my arm, shoved me hard enough to break a pair of glasses, and threw me diagonally between the crowd and the pavement. With a parting shot, I was apprised of my crime: "You are in front of the president."

That is what happened with *Warrior* gate. French journalists dug
and probed, printing leaks and raising questions, until Fabius admitted France had sunk the *Rainbow Warrior*. Key questions remained
unanswered. For example, what happened and who did it? Who else
was involved? Suddenly, the case was considered closed. The day
before the two French spies were sentenced in Auckland, Mitterrand
gave a two-hour news conference. He spent forty-five minutes
discussing an additional state-authorized television channel. Finally,
ninety minutes into the questioning, someone asked about the trial.
He was brief and vague, and the subject was changed. Later, someone asked what his defense minister had told him. "Monsieur Hernu
has been my friend, and he continues to be. . . . He bears objective
responsibility." Without elaboration, or elucidation, he dropped the
matter.

WHAT OUTSIDERS might call cynicism permeates French
thinking. I tried to explain at a dinner party why foreigners were
upset by the *Rainbow Warrior* affair. An eminent guest fixed me
with that gaze meant for children, morons, and Anglo-Saxon moral-
ists. In France, power and self-interest are respectable goals. That
explains why it is not necessarily corrupt to decide beforehand who
should win a competition or, at times, even a court case. If money
changes hands, there may be dishonor. Otherwise, a sort of cosmic
justice applies. In France, power and self-interest may come about
as omelettes do. They may require breaking eggs. At the level of
l'Etat, state services are given the power to break eggs in the interest
of France. What they must avoid, at all costs, is a *bavure*.

A *bavure* is a hitch, a foul-up, notably by officials or police, and
it is so common that a smooth operation is referred to as *"sans
bavure."* At times, *bavures* can be blamed on bad luck or innocent
incompetence. Captain Paul Barril, in *Missions Très Spéciales,* recalls
his first challenge as a commander of the elite GIGN gendarme force
in 1981. Pope John Paul II was in Paris about to say mass in front
of Notre Dame. Police had learned that some students planned to
set loose over the pontiff and his flock a giant helium-filled doll—
with an enormous penis in its mouth. Barril and another sharpshooter perched in the towers with .22 rifles and silencers to deflate
the prank. He confided the plan beforehand to a prominent televi-

sion reporter who did not break the story but had this to say: "You guys are such bunglers you'll end up murdering the pope on live television." Police found the students in time. No shots were fired.

Other times *bavures* stem from the inertia of French officialdom. In Paris, during 1985, a bandit shot a bank manager in the stomach and fled with a bag of money. He forced a passing woman to drive him away. Across town, they were caught in a traffic jam, and he turned her loose. She rushed into a nearby police station; the sergeant there only shrugged his shoulders. If the robbery was on boulevard Voltaire, he said, she would have to go to the Beaubourg station to report it. But you can still catch the man on foot, she pleaded. Lady, he replied, that is not our business.

Often, however, *bavures* are the result of a *guerre des polices*. National police forces, the gendarmes, regional units and security services fight among themselves for power and glory. Sometimes there is tense peace. More frequently, criminals and terrorists are the incidental decor of the battlefield. Barril was a major casualty.

In August 1982, in the midst of murderous terror bombings and machine gunnings in Paris, Barril got an enticing tip: two leading Irish terrorists with Palestinian links were hiding in Paris. His elite gendarmes arrested them, and he preened for glory. The first hitch was that an antiterrorist squad formed nine days earlier at the Elysée wanted credit. Barril, fuming, handed over his prize. Mitterrand's office announced "dangerous terrorists" had been caught in a daring action of exceptional importance. The suspects, however, turned out to be minor actors. One was a British informer. Second hitch: Barril and his gendarmes had been set up in a *piège à cons* (a trap for fools) by rivals in the secret services who had passed along exaggerated information.[2] Barril was not short of evidence against the terrorists. But that was the third hitch: he was found to have planted two pistols and explosives on the prisoners. The Irish terrorists spent nine months in jail, despite the fake evidence, while rivals argued over their import. They were released, but four years later police were still fighting over the case.

Bavure is also a Cartesian euphemism for police brutality. In 1986, a new conservative legislative majority set out "to terrorize the terrorists." And a lot of other people. Police swarmed through cities, making random identity checks more befitting Bulgaria than the reputed cradle of human rights. During the incidents, Paris police held ten minors, mostly girls, incommunicado overnight, treating them roughly; parents who came looking for them were turned away at the door at submachine gun point. A black plainclothes officer was slugged before officers noticed his badge; a 63-year-old man was roughed up for hours. Two journalists and their lawyer were kicked around and told by one policeman, "We don't give a damn about the regulations." On television, the Paris police chief explained, "These incidents have always occurred. Now there is a press campaign, and they are being reported."

But polls suggested a majority of Frenchmen approved of the new measures. Their personal interest was order.

Some call cynical official actions that place a narrow reading of national interest ahead of broader responsibilities. The French closed their airspace to U.S. F-111 aircraft en route from Britain to attack Libya on April 15, 1986. France, critics say, could have disassociated itself from President Reagan's dubious venture without enfeebling the Atlantic Alliance it relies upon for survival. Not that long ago, after all, the French were happy to see American warplanes overhead.

Among other things, the government wanted to protect eight French hostages kidnapped in Lebanon. They did; three Britons were executed instead. French relations with Libya are delicately balanced. The Crotale air defense system that U.S. aircraft had to avoid was maintained by Thomson-CSF, owned by the French government. Libya's public thanks did not help.

Americans brought up France's past humiliations, and mockery of the French was returned in kind. The magazine *Le Point* asked: "Could the Americans have an inferiority complex toward us? Could they be jealous of our culture, our sophistication, our taste, out subtlety?"

Some French politicians objected to the refusal. Mitterrand let it slip that France would have supported a tougher move if it was certain to topple Qaddafi. French sources floated the version that the plane, in fact, did fly over the French Pyrenees. Prime Minister Jacques Chirac explained that France had already helped the Americans by foiling a Libyan plot to massacre people waiting for visas at the U.S. consulate in Paris. No one mentioned that no Americans wait in that line; Frenchmen do.

Little was made of a detail that might have stirred major outrage. Among the buildings damaged by the U.S. bombing—indirectly but substantially—was the French embassy.

The next month, French authorities sought to ban a radioactive cloud from the Soviet Union. While surrounding countries reported alarming increases in radiation from the Chernobyl accident —and took vegetables, milk and meat off the shelves at heavy cost —France remained miraculously untouched. And then it came out that radiation had been up to 400 times normal in some parts of France, though still below what was considered the danger level. Pressed for an explanation, Pierre Pellerin, director of the Service of Radiation Protection, said, "Quite simply because there were two holidays in two weeks, and it was very complicated to transmit the data." Others added that the government did not feel it necessary to alarm the French public with technicalities it could not understand.

With forty-four nuclear power plants supplying 64.8 percent of its electricity, France is touchy on the subject of radiation. More, the farm lobby is large and loud. On a popular talk show, a French nuclear engineer said specialists around France knew of the high levels but were told, essentially, to mind their own business. A Belgian member of the European Parliament, Anne-Marie Lizin, said she was not surprised. The European Economic Community had been after France for years to supply nuclear data that EEC countries felt they needed in their own national interests.

BUT THESE characteristics of France, even the least admirable ones, reinforce amazing recuperative powers that allow the nation to spring back in full force from the deepest of defeats. France rests on the same old stones and slow-cooking sauces that have survived war, occupation, and economic depression. Its language, rooted in Latin, rich and resonant, carries far when spoken softly. The French way of looking at things—obliquely direct, judgmental from clear but unspoken baselines—is why France remains a seat of empire.

Well past closing time on Christmas Eve, a guide named Gervette

speared his failing flashlight at every last rock and niche to show
us Fontenay Abbey. It was not for the substantial tip he was surprised to receive. He was simply a nice man. And, mainly, he felt
a duty to St. Bernard, who built the place during the Crusades.

France is admired for outstanding service to the palate and the
nostrils, a sophisticated purveyor of luxury, class, and style. The
French tongue is fabled for wrapping around run-on consonants to
pleasing effect and, in private moments, for darting into intimate
places with accomplished accuracy. To the outside, France is slightly
effete, lacy at the cuffs—or red-nosed, walrus-mustached, and ber-
eted behind a thumbprinted bottle of Pernod.

Less known are solid, stalwart qualities that allowed France to
spread itself across the world. Colonial civil servants and settlers
have always represented a small segment of French society. They
brought their civilization in layers, steadily, with increasing numbers to replace those who died along the way. They simply placed
themselves above hardship. For example, malaria, or *paludisme,* was
nicknamed *palu.* The French diminished the disease by familiarizing
it. That it killed many of them was a mere setback.

The technology of empire was the simple, effective method of
the French heartlands. In Paris, researchers probed into biomedical
mysteries, but malaria was beaten by dumping pesticide out of light
aircraft. French aerospace engineers fashioned a supersonic jetliner,
but Upper Volta and Bora Bora, like the Charente Maritime, traveled in tough old Peugeot 404s. Citroën sedans flash down French-
built superhighways in the Ivory Coast, but the back roads depend
on the Citroën Deux Chevaux, which you can repair with a hairpin
in the middle of the desert. Others shaped the mechanics of their
empires in a similar manner, but not the people.

"The Americans go abroad and say, 'Hey, hurry up, watch, and
do it like us,' " Vincent, a French friend, remarked once in Africa.
"We say, 'Take your time, and be us.' "

Where others tried to suit themselves to local mentalities, until
they departed in frustration, the French reshaped local mentalities
to their own way. As a result, new generations see France as the
standard. African students might attend the University of Texas, but
they stop over in Paris on the way home.

For most French, settling the world is merely a noble role they have been called upon to perform. Outside the Chadian capital of N'Djamena, once named Fort-Lamy, a statue of General Lamy is inscribed, "He died for civilization."

The mission to civilize has never ceased. On trips to Africa, Mitterrand makes a stock speech to the local French communities, invited to watch their president up close and tingle to a recording of the "Marseillaise": They are France, and it is up to them to spread the word.

The "Marseillaise" gets 'em every time. Rouget de Lisle, thirty-two at the time, wrote it in 1792. It fit the mood of the French Revolution; but for all its stirring melody, it is drenched in blood. Sanche de Gramont wrote:

> It has always amused me to watch otherwise mild Frenchmen, the kind who wear long underwear in June and droopy cardigan sweaters to warm their livers, grow red in the face as veins in their necks bulge and their voices roar out about throat-cutting, outrage, parricidal projects, sanguinary despots, vengeance, expiring enemies, and impure blood soaking French furrows.

In an audience at Bujumbura, Jean-Marc, a paratroop sergeant-major, stiffened with pride at Mitterrand's words. He was no Socialist, but he was French. Jean-Marc was the archetype of the best in France abroad. Tall and straight, ruggedly handsome with a full black mustache, he spoke of duty and sacrifice with no trace of self-consciousness. He was unhappy that French troops were pulled out of Chad, but orders were orders. He missed his wife and family, he said, but that is life. Two minutes after meeting him, I had the impression he would step in front of a poisoned spear to save my life. He was the sort who would gently pick a fly out of his boeuf bourguignon without killing it but spray machine-gun fire into a crowd if ordered to do so.

I asked him how he felt about fighting to support African presidents who murdered their opponents and robbed their people blind. "Bof," he said, with an easy shrug. "None of them is a saint. This is Africa."

Like most French, Jean-Marc took a pragmatic approach, extracting reality from rhetoric. His line of thinking recalled conversations

I had had with French officials when the United States invaded Grenada in 1983.

American concern in Grenada was symbolized by an airfield the Cubans were building on the small Caribbean island. Prime Minister Maurice Bishop denounced U.S. values with Marxist-Leninist catchphrases. Bishop, trying to see Reagan, was kept waiting for a week and then palmed off on a low-ranking State Department officer. His ambassador approached the U.S. envoy to Cuba, Wayne Smith, who pleaded in vain for permission to listen. Isolated, Bishop was toppled by hard-line associates and then shot. Reagan, on the excuse that American medical students were in danger, ordered an invasion.

The French saw the airfield as a long strip of blacktop necessary to any country, particularly an island. Whether it was to be a civilian airport or an airbase would be a political decision, not a technical one. Had Grenada been in the French sphere and the Cubans had beat them out for an airport contract, they would have cashed in by selling jetways and microwave ovens. Quai d'Orsay strategists noted that for all Bishop's speeches, free enterprise thrived and tourists needed no visas. They have seen the Soviet Union fail time and again in attempts to rent friends. In Grenada, the French would have done what they do in the Congo and Benin, two former colonies. When leaders espouse Soviet-type rhetoric, they roll their eyes in amusement. Whenever those leaders come to Paris, they are paraded down the Champs-Elysées. And French influence prevails.

The French world view fixes Paris squarely at the center. When Lawrence Eagleburger, an American diplomat widely respected for a knowledge of Europe, criticized Atlantic allies, the French daily of record, Le Monde, reported in its news columns, ". . . and he does not even have the excuse of being one of Reagan's inexperienced conservatives." No room was left for the possibility that Eagleburger might have had a point worth considering.

For France, expediency counts, and diplomacy is the art of making it palatable. Suggestions that such pragmatism might include an element of hypocrisy are dismissed with a wave. What, a French diplomat might ask, about the democratic principles of such American friends as Mobutu Sese Seko and Zia ul-Haq?

However they might bristle at real or perceived insult, the French skin is not thin. Foreigners have bashed them for centuries. In *Henry VI,* Shakespeare had Joan of Arc observe, "Spoken like a Frenchman, turn and turn again." Benjamin Franklin wrote, "I know not which are most rapacious, the English or the French, but the latter have, with their knavery, the most politeness."

Obviously enough, such characterizations do no justice to the vast number of individuals who display kindness and loyalty that confounds outsiders who thought they disliked the French. But in the end, whether it is applied with politeness, principle, or arrogant duplicity, the French excel by *savoir faire.* That takes in such vital details as using the right knife. But, more, it means knowing which things are important in life and seeing to it that the lesser orders at least make an attempt to appreciate them. The French are at their best at home, or in spheres abroad still regarded as *chasses gardées:* exclusive reserves. Around the edges, things can get touchy.

MADAME THONG'S Vietnamese restaurant is a hole in a Latin Quarter wall, one room with a tiny kitchen in back. The paint is flecked and the floor, though swept clean, is marked by years of use. Sauces come in cracked saucers and chipped crocks. The food is fabulous and dirt cheap. American friends showed us the place after reflecting carefully on whether to share the secret. Our third time back, something instantly felt wrong. The air was heavy with judgment. Madame Thong was all smiles. But a French civilizing mission had taken charge of the place.

At the large center table, seven people sat around the governor-general, whose lofty gaze commanded the room. He was standard-issue petit bourgeois, but this was his empire. I could hear him organizing the party. "Ah, *mon petit,* I have found the most excellent little *resto, typique mais splendide,* totally undiscovered, only the Vietnamese truck drivers know about it." He sat at the head of the table, burgundy-tinted cheeks puffed, neck slightly back to give his nose sufficient elevation. His voice filled the farthest crevices of the room, the perfect host-raconteur for the masses who oohed over dishes he had selected. "And nothing is more disagreeable," he had just pronounced about something or someplace, in an impressive blend of condescension and pomposity. Just then, an invasion, foreign interests in the colony, and Americans, *en plus.*

His gaze followed us to the small back table, expressing minor outrage and some wonderment that we were seating ourselves without a visa. Every few moments, he glanced over to see if we were preparing to leave. Finally, his eye fell on a copy of a book I had laid on the table, Theodore Zeldin's *France 1848–1945: Anxiety and Hypocrisy.* That was the final straw. He decided on heavy artillery.

"Ah, the Americans," he began loudly to his friends, but in slow distinct French just in case we were still on the phrasebook. "You can find nothing to eat in the United States except fried shrimp." The "fried shrimp" came out in the sort of flat-accented, smeared English of someone who thinks he is imitating an American dialect. At that, he glanced over to check where the shot had landed. I laughed. He paused a moment. Anything further would require direct confrontation. No, this would be too much. And what if he lost? Suddenly, he tossed his head to his friends in a silent declaration of victory.

Peace fell upon the room.

CHAPTER THREE

France d'Outre-mer

CLOCKS ARE NO obsession with the French; there is no Big Ben, no Greenwich from which to fix a mean time. The Eiffel Tower has only restaurants and aviation warning lights. Notre-Dame Cathedral marks time with bells. The eight o'clock television newscasts start whenever the commercials finish. Time is money in France, all right. But clocks don't define life the way they might elsewhere any more than maps do. Wherever the hands might fall on a clock face, night or day, some Frenchman is standing in the sun in his neighborhood park, playing *pétanque*.

When the clocks note dinnertime in Marseilles, the *pétanque* balls are clacking in Réunion. The sun sets in Réunion, but the game picks up in Pondicherry. Some time after, the matches begin in New Caledonia. Then across Polynesia in the South Pacific, into the Caribbean and the edge of South America. By the time the *boules* roll to a stop in Miquelon, players are limbering up in Marseilles.

The game, rooted in southern France, blends bowling with horseshoes. It is taken seriously enough to be a blood sport, but it requires a subtle finesse. Small iron balls are thrown toward one another, launched with the elaborate care a Frenchman uses to deliver an adverb from his palate. But in mother France and the empire, the players have in common only their blue, white, and red *cartes d'identité*. And a state of mind.

In St.-Denis, capital of Réunion, the teams are diverse: tough-looking Malagasys in torn shirts, dark Tamils in red baseball caps and gold earrings, huge Africans from the coast, Chinese in aviator sunglasses. There are also, often in separate clusters, *les z'oreilles*. A *z'oreille* (from "ear," in French) is a Frenchman from the *métropole;* not to split hairs, a colonizer. Creole populations across the empire use the term with varying degrees of affection and scorn. It comes from the newly arrived Frenchman's habit of extending an ear to better capture the colorful distortions of creole dialects.

Creole is a sweeping term for people descended from early settlers. But the French, unlike the English, were hardly reticent about fraternizing with the locals. Their anthropological lexicon is vast. In every corner of the empire, strikingly handsome people emerge in shades from ebony to cream, with eyes and hair that confound categorization.

As it happens, Réunion has no "natives," no descendants of people living there when the colonizers first arrived. The island was uninhabited, and all local residents trace themselves back to Asians and Africans brought in by the French. Similarly, Guadeloupe, Martinique, and Guiana were peopled mainly by Africans shipped over to cut cane. In the Pacific, large native populations remain. Each *département* and territory is a singular microcosm with characteristics all its own. But transfers within the civil service and the military, refugees from former colonies, and free movement have shuffled the ethnic deck completely.

Technically, it doesn't matter. Everyone—Creole, native, and *z'oreille*—is French. But views differ on what that means.

For the black, brown, and yellow French who grew up believing in their ancestors the Gauls, all the pieces are part of the whole. "In Guadeloupe, we say everyone sees midday from his own doorway," a black nurse in Paris told me, meaning France is simply how you see it. That is, in fact, an old French saying. Outsiders who try to use "French" as a euphemism for white risk a reproachful stare.

But for many *z'oreilles,* far from home, each little piece of *France d'outre-mer* is a reductio ad absurdum of France itself. The DOM-TOM are, in effect, bush league training grounds for perfecting those inimitable traits that Francophobes and Francophiles love to seize upon. Distance from Paris seems to exaggerate attitudes and actions, whatever they are.

Réunion is a splendid example. I flew into St.-Denis one afternoon from Johannesburg, after three weeks among people who defined their colors sharply and defended social barriers as though their lives depended upon it. Here was France in shorts and knee socks, racially broadminded yet broadly racist, with social mores that blended modern with medieval.

Driving around, I might have been anywhere else in the country: down rue Pasteur to avenue Charles de Gaulle and rue de Paris, all marked in green-bordered blue and white street signs. The usual cast of characters was enshrined in pompous stone statues, plus the local hero, Roland Garros, pioneer flyer, who is honored in Paris by a tennis stadium. There was, as expected, a somber stone monument reading: "From l'Ile de la Réunion, to its heroic sons in the Great War, 1914–1918. They were worthy of France." Altogether, 607,000 soldiers from the colonies fought for France in World War I.

St.-Denis was clearly built for people who came to stay, by people who had erected other such towns in similar climes. The governor's mansion is handsome and huge, porticoed, white, and spectacularly landscaped. It is near the water, commanding the beach, with walls thick enough to bounce back the heaviest cannon-ball a Dutch fleet might muster. Straight, narrow streets mark out blocks of what is loosely known as French colonial architecture. Stone rowhouses are painted in light pastels, with a patina of mildew and weathering that obliterates centuries of differences in construction dates. Second-floor balconies hang in front of tall, louvered wooden shutters, fastened by elaborately scrolled iron fancywork. Blazing red and deep purple bougainvillea spill over walls. Palms wound in shiny green vines rise to roof levels.

The oldest buildings show graceful, almost delicate facades; but gates are high, carved doors are solid as iron, stone walls are massive. They were designed to stay cool under the sun, remind civil servants of home, impress the locals, and withstand the odd volley of paving stones should things turn nasty. Not surprisingly, the cathedral and the university were built to last.

The British, in their outposts, leaned toward wood-frame buildings and corrugated tin, as if they did not want the overhead to cut into profits. They were, in essence, camping out. Not the French.

As in any *arrondissement* in Paris, St.-Denis shop fronts bear the large green crosses of pharmacies, the red signs reading *Tabac,* and the usual run of Prisunic and Félix Potin chain stores. And, as in

Paris, there are the slightly skewed manifestations of a U.S.-accented omniculture of self-service boutiques and restaurants: Le Maryland, Big Burger, Kick Self.

From St.-Denis, I drove west, following Highway N1, marked as though it were exactly the same road I would stay on to Paris, if my Renault 12 had pontoons. Off to the left, cracked asphalt snaked over rusty trestle bridges and through rock tunnels, engineering marvels of their time that would serve well on a Third World superhighway. But this was France, and that was an abandoned old road. A new, four-lane divided *autoroute,* smooth as a dinner plate, was built out over the water. And I was battling an afternoon traffic jam of drivers in Peugeots and Renaults, each flashing his lights in the sun, delivering that lovable signal which translates roughly to: move your ass, *connard,* don't you realize *I* am on this road and I don't care if you are already over the speed limit and have engine trouble and don't want to upset your aged grandmother and are caught in this lane by trucks on your right; you are blocking the path between me and my *gigot d'agneau.*

People are not normally at their best behind the wheel. Down the road, at St.-Paul, I stopped to take a closer look. A twenty-four-year-old named Jean-Marie, a dark Creole with Negroid hair, hitched a ride.

"How's life? Awful. I'm a mechanic, but no work. Maybe I get an odd job, a few francs, and then nothing for months. It's bad in France but worse here. No one cares about us. This is no life."

Did anyone consider independence as an option? He smiled uneasily and then seemed to relax, deciding I was merely a harmless simpleton.

"I don't think so."

Had we been in Brittany, or Corsica, the idea of separation from France would have been no more likely, but the question might have provoked discussion. In Réunion, however, such issues are magnified by the distance; you stand squarely on one side of it or the other.

On the next stop down the coast, I had a look at the extremes to which Frenchness can be amplified in the outposts of empire. A lingering sore throat worsened, and I wondered where I could find someone to prescribe antibiotics on a raw, jungled coast in the

Indian Ocean. After St.-Paul, the road narrowed to two-lane black-top and led back in time. It meandered past thatched huts and coconut groves. Then a ubiquitous French stone town marker appeared: St.-Leu.

In a gleaming glass-fronted shopping complex, I spotted the large green cross of a pharmacy. Next door was a clinic; its neon sign offered therapeutic massage and a range of paramedical treats. A lovely blonde in hospital white sat at the receptionist desk inside. Ah, joy, I thought. Hope.

She heard me approach and, with evident pain, wrenched her eyes away from the latest issue of *Marie-Claire*. Her glance would have taken Flaubert a page to describe. That a receptionist's function is to receive is beside the point; I had barged into her circle. She deduced instantly that I had nothing to offer that she might want. And I obviously wanted something from her. Well, okay, dammit, there I was, and there was no escape short of getting up and leaving, which would be unacceptably direct. I would be permitted to have my say. But it had better be good.

Was there a doctor in the neighborhood? I asked, with elaborate courtesy, taking care not to leer at her breasts or the makeup she had elaborately applied to attract attention.

It wasn't good enough. She looked through me as if I were made of glass, and not particularly clean glass, and scowled slightly.

"The other side of the pharmacy," she said, dropping her eyes back to the magazine without bothering to add, "Can't you read, you nitwit?"

It was not, by the way, because I was a foreigner. Thin-skinned Americans tend to make that mistake. I was an intrusion, like some noisome insect to be swatted peevishly aside. Such displays of *mauvais caractère* can be reversed with volleys of gradually lessening hostility. For that, French is essential even if your adversary speaks perfect English. It is not a question of communication but of civilization. Learning French implies that one has sought to be civilized, and learning good French means one has taken it seriously. It gets worse. By speaking a strange language, the Frenchman risks the calamity of making awkward, funny noises or falling short of words, seeming somehow silly. And, symbolically, he—or she, in this case—would be handing you the advantage. For that, you must offer some motivation. A belt in the chops is fastest, but the Napoleonic legal code is even more complex.

The next stop, as often happens, was the other extreme.

"Of course the doctor will see you," replied a cheerful nurse, warmth coloring her features. "Make yourself comfortable there, and it will be just a moment." She said, in fact, *"une petite minute,"* meaning a lot of minutes, but the intention was that it would be as soon as it could possibly be done.

Dr. Bernard Bouchara smiled broadly. He briskly finished the medical business and wanted to chat. I decided to try my independence question. He was pleasant but firm.

"We're in France, only 10,000 kilometers away. No one wants it to be any different. Oh, maybe 1 percent, people who don't have this or that. But this is France and without that, there would be nothing."

He warmed to the theme and grabbed a pile of booklets from his desk. "Look, health cards. Where do you see such medical care anywhere around here? France is doing everything. I came here fifteen years ago, and it is incredible what they have achieved just since then. From Marseilles, for instance, there is very little difference."

Intangibles aside, he had a point. Back up the road at St.-Paul, the island's first capital, the process was obvious.

Outside St.-Paul are a cluster of simple caves where French settlers first sheltered in the 1600s. Nearby, a graveyard of moldering stones and wrought iron-railed monuments traces their history in chipped inscriptions.

"Evaste Feuille, captain of long voyages, killed in a duel." "Olivier Le Vasseur, called La Buse, pirate, Scourge of the South Seas, executed at St.-Paul in 1730." "Leconte de Lisle, poet." Small graves, with legends recalling short life spans, attest to the fevers and epidemics. Ornate mausoleums pay tribute to governors, commandants, and merchant kings.

A colorful poster tacked to the moss-covered wall outside bears a new inscription: "Vote for Paul Bernand, to build the future."

Back in St.-Denis, I met Pascal, a young French disk jockey in a local disco and acknowledged master of the few ceremonies of Réunion evenings. A friendly cook at the pizzeria introduced us.

Pascal started sketching maps for me and then grabbed my elbow. "What the hell, come on." He weaved through the darkened streets in his rattling Cadillac, pointing out every public house that wasn't locked past 11 P.M.

"Anyone looking for a good time has got to go somewhere else," he said. Somewhere else meant Paris. "There's not much for young people to do around here. A few parties, maybe, but it is boring. The local French are very racist. They don't mix much." I asked if local people wanted to separate from France. "Oh, there's an independence movement but it's not ripe. You've got to reflect. If they go independent, then what? There's no industry, nothing."

He wished me luck and went back to his buddies.

I tried the Milord, a dismal basement nightclub. It reeked of the tropical mildew that attacks any establishment that fights its surroundings by laying carpet and overdoing the plush sofas. I was joined instantly by a Swiss lady with skin like a crocodile and teeth to match. Her conversation revolved around a thirst for champagne. "A glass?" "A bottle." I steered her toward beer. Minutes later, I asked for the bill. Just like Paris: two drinks, listed at the equivalent of ten dollars each, somehow came to forty-five dollars.

A few days later, I took my political questions to the politicians.

In the town of St.-André, I found Serge Sinamalé, a dapper little Indian, pottering in the courtyard of his ramshackle home. A former leader of the Réunion Communist Party, he turned in his card and became a founding director of the Réunion Independence Movement, the MIR.

"We never try for big demonstrations, or push for high membership," he said, "because there is too much repression. If a militant works in a garage, or is a domestic servant of a Frenchman, he is kicked out the door. That is economic repression. We are not thousands and thousands. All colonial elections are rigged, anyway."

If there were a free referendum, how many people would choose independence? Ten percent, Sinamalé guessed. Then he thought again. "Well, maybe 5 percent. The colonial situation is in place, and people don't know the truth."

He drew a simple picture. France built a colony to tend the ships plying the spice route to Asia. When that role diminished, the economy was converted to agriculture, and indentured labor was

ferried in. Eventually, agriculture was neglected. Réunion, he concluded, was a client state of 550,000 inhabitants, 40 percent Indian,
40 percent mixed blood, and 20 percent *z'oreilles.*

"Now we are only a captive market for the French to unload
their finished products," he said, emotion speeding his words along.
"We import milk and honey, animals, plants, fruits, coffee, tea,
spices, straw. This is a tropical country, and we import straw."

He reeled off numbers from memory and then dug out sheaves
of papers to make his points: in 1945, exports equaled imports; by
1977, exports were 23 percent of imports; in 1983, 10 percent.

"Small producers buy animal fats and oils, byproducts, and we
spend good money for nicely packaged cooking oil from France in
the supermarkets," he fumed. "Rum is sold in bulk here at five
francs a liter, cut three times, and comes back at nineteen and twenty
francs a bottle. We produce a fine quality of brown sugar that
people love in Paris. But they buy it from us at two francs a kilo,
refine it to white sugar in France, and then sell it at 12.82 a kilo here.
Kids see on television and are taught in school white sugar is better.
That is colonization."

Sinamalé had other themes.

"They teach us Europe, the French language, but not what is
ours. That is colonialism, even if it is more subtle than before. The
form has changed but, at the bottom, it is the same. Some 150,000
Réunion people are in France. They have seen it is not El Dorado.
People say, 'Dirty nigger, go home.' They are learning."

Switching the subject, he sprang to a huge map of the Indian
Ocean. He jabbed his finger at dots of islands.

"France maintains Réunion as a military base. They have 3,500
men, in all services, ready day and night. Whoever controls the
Indian Ocean controls the world. While the U.S. battles for rights
on Diego Garcia, France has Réunion, Mayotte, and islands no one
knows about. What do we get? They pollute the waters, and we
can't even eat our own fish."

He said his movement had expected a change with a left-wing
victory in France in 1981 but instead found the situation worsening.
At a "point of no return," he said, strategy rests on spreading the
word and raising consciousness. The MIR is the only independence
movement that operates legally, in the open, he said, but other

groups were working clandestinely. An Air France vacation village was burned in 1984, and the odd explosion echoes loudly on the peaceful island. Would the MIR condone violence as a last resort? He shrugged. "If imperialism obliges us, that will come."

An hour later, I was hearing the other extreme, surrounded by the polished wood paneling and tapestries of Government House. Sinamalé seemed farther than twenty miles away.

"Oouuuf, you know there are arsonists everywhere in the world; it is a little premature to refer to an organization, is it not?" said the political adviser to the *préfet* (governor), adding a slight reverse spin of irony to the word "organization." The adviser, Adolphe Colrat, was in his thirties. But he was an ageless, seamless product of a fast-track civil service leadership system which is one of France's highest achievements. His uniform was a well-cut gray suit, with a Bordeaux silk tie. Smooth, charming, assured, he left his interlocutor room to question, but only on pain of severe self-doubt.

Asked about Sinamalé's economic statistics, he flicked an immaculate fingernail.

"You understand, we do these figures somewhat artificially as if there was really a balance to be measured. You cannot categorize these things, from the *métropole* to la Réunion. It is the same economy. We should do more to provide economic activity, I agree, perhaps in meat, cattle, pigs. We are self-sufficient in pork. We must create a new generation of agriculturists, revitalize the higher elevations of the island."

Education is strictly the same in the departments and territories as in France, he said, but in 1983 they added an optional course in creole language and civilization. They might, in fact, welcome new kindergarteners in creole.

Colrat had no figures on movement from Réunion to the *métropole*. "We know 500,000 people a year fly in and out of the airport, to all destinations, but it is, after all, a domestic flight to Paris."

The word "colony," he stressed again and again, was absolutely inapt. Réunion was settled as part of France and was never anything else. And as for separatists, they hardly totaled 100 votes in recent municipal elections. "Here," he concluded, "it is completely different from the atmosphere in the Antilles [Caribbean]."

OR IN THE South Pacific. Whatever Réunion may typify among the departments and territories, it is among the least explosive. All the DOM-TOMs keep French authorities occupied poring over the extensive files of secret services charged with keeping discreet order. When Colrat spoke, the ferment was in Guadeloupe where *indépendantistes* had killed a few people with random bombs to make their point. Caribbean independence leaders organized a meeting for separatists from the DOM-TOMs, Sinamalé included, to jointly denounce French rule. But the real crisis came in New Caledonia.

At the end of 1984, Melanesian natives and white settlers went to war. Before the hard-minded gendarmes from Paris could impose a tense quiet, a score of people died. A few Frenchmen were shot on isolated farms and back roads; ten Melanesians, Kanaks, were massacred in a vigilantes' ambush; police shot dead several *indépendantiste* leaders.

For nights on end, French families sat over their braised endives watching on television wild-haired brown youths stamp on all they held dear. It was Algeria all over again, ran the comment in the cafes. *Alors, ça recommence.* It was not close to being Algeria. But here, twenty-five years later, scenes were repeating themselves. Once again, it was suitcases or shotguns. In living color, frightened housewives loaded bedding, cooking pots, and small children into battered station wagons. French farmers, lean and leathery, declaimed in earthy backcountry accents: "We've been here three generations, and we're not going anywhere. If blood has to flow, let it flow." "Me afraid? I'll cover that fucking roadblock all alone—with my rifle."

And all around the empire, dark-skinned French watched the militant Socialist Kanak National Liberation Front—the FLNKS— win concessions from Paris. With a schedule of referendums and increasing autonomy, the future suggested a choice between independence or bloodshed.

But that was New Caledonia. In Mayotte, not far from Réunion, voters fought to stay closer to France than Paris wanted. With all the feared "contagion" from the Pacific, independence movements elsewhere made modest gains. And even in New Caledonia, Article

88 of de Gaulle's constitution could turn, once again, a French defeat into victory. It stipulates, "The Republic or the Community may make agreements with states that wish to associate themselves with the Community to develop their civilizations." France, freed of responsibility, might continue its mission.

It is not simple. After New Caledonia, partly as a result, the situation worsened in Guadeloupe and Guiana. The threat and the response vary widely; each of the DOMs and TOMs is examined farther on, along with former colonies only figuratively in the empire. Few separatists expect Paris to turn loose the far-flung bits it describes as inseparable parts of France. But those sensitive to the themes of decolonization and peoples' rights see danger ahead. Violence at barricades and noisy strikes tarnish the French image as a champion of developing nations. Bombs in remote marketplaces are heard around the world.

L'Expansion magazine tried to put a price tag on the DOM-TOM in 1985. Together, their trade deficit came to about twenty billion francs. With nickel, New Caledonia's export earnings came to half of its import bill. In Polynesia, however, exports covered 6 percent of imports. Of course, most imports were from France. Education, defense, and government services cost twenty-three billion francs in 1985. And social security taxes from the DOM-TOM cover only 30 percent of what the state pays out. Capital investment and bank loans added billions more to the bill. So did subsidized losses for services such as Air France.

With 2.4 million French out of work, 400,000 people from overseas territories in the *métropole* might be regarded as an expense. The rate of immigration is unsettling. In 1954, mainland residents from the DOM-TOM numbered only 24,200.

Even on Clipperton, where no one lives, the costs are high. The speck of land, named for an English pirate, is 900 miles off Mexico at the center of rich tuna beds. The Mexicans took it from France in 1858 and occupied it with seven men and their families. Then, caught up in a revolution, Mexico forgot they were there. One by one, they died off. Finally, the garrison dwindled to a single man, a tyrannical Indian. The three surviving women murdered him with a hammer. That same day, by coincidence, a passing American ship stopped by, looking for secret German bases. That was in 1917. The

French reestablished their claim in 1931 and now are building a port.

As finance minister, Giscard d'Estaing once murmured, "These are expensive little dancers." But as president, and in the opposition, he argued loudly that each territory is vital to the glory of France.

The return of the right in 1986 brought new emphasis on overseas France. The DOM-TOM Secretariat was given full cabinet status under Bernard Pons, a confidant of Chirac's. He reminded reporters that no other European country was situated in the Americas, the Indian Ocean, and the South Pacific. And he exulted: "Our overseas departments and territories are France's joker in Europe for the twenty-first century."

Pons, just back from the South Pacific territory of Wallis and Futuna, promised changes. For one thing, Wallis would get television. And Futuna would get electricity.

Until further notice the Tricolor goes up every morning. In spite of striking differences, small scenes, vignettes, and recurrent casts of characters stitch the DOMs and TOMs into a single sprawling patchwork that is France in the extreme. Everywhere there is a Restaurant Tonkinois, or Mandarin, or both, featuring red flocking, cheap rosé wine, and *soupe chinoise:* transparent noodles, shrimps, and sliced pork, served up by someone whose roots in Vietnam were severed in the 1950s. There is always a hard-eyed blonde, skin tanned to the texture of a grapefruit, wearing an immodestly short sundress and walking a small gray dog. You can bank on a Café de Paris, most likely frequented by multihued hookers and youths of proven skill at *le windsurfing.*

The pace is always slower than in the *métropole,* but not by much. Direct-dial telephones, daily flights, and satellites swallow up the space in between. A global "regional" television network links all bits of the empire. And life has changed. There is less time for the old colonial qualities of bonhomie and hospitality to ripen under the sun.

In the past, only a small percentage of Frenchmen ever ventured out to live in the empire. When it was tough, the washouts went home or slowly dissolved in their Pernod. They came out by choice, or they were driven overseas by motives strong enough to make them stay and try to like it. Settlers raised families, and each new generation dug in more deeply. The hard, simple life required a strong reliance on neighbors. People often felt a sense of mission, if not to civilize, at least to stand by the land they made flourish. People who came out from the *métropole* for a tour of duty felt a part of their commitment.

Much of the old settler stock remains across the empire. But life is easier now, and *z'oreilles* are likely to be disgruntled city folk who can find no work elsewhere, or who were rotated out by the luck of the draw.

HEADING BACK TO Paris from Réunion, I encountered one guy who did not want to be working on a sunny Sunday in some outpost of the empire. Unfortunately, he was a cop, assigned to airport security. Those who wonder why foreigners do not always rank the French among their favorite people would do well to consult him.

He was short, with a mousy mustache lounging under dark sunglasses. He looked me over with the light smirk of a French bureaucrat anxious to wield his small allotment of power, and I knew I was in trouble. A dull stare and passive resistance would have ruined his fun. But I needed something.

I had brought a dozen rolls of exposed but unprocessed film from southern Africa, along with a few dozen fresh ones. Please, I asked, could he check them by hand? It was a simple courtesy granted in such relaxed places as India, China, and Bulgaria. In fact, only at Roissy Airport in Paris (and once in Vienna, to be accurate) had I been refused before. His smirk widened, and he pointed to the sign over the X-ray machine promising no harm to film.

Yes, I explained, it should not matter one time, if the machine was working properly. But I traveled a lot, and every X-ray built up a cumulative effect. That was what a Kodak engineer had explained once, and I had lost irreplaceable pictures to an X-ray before.

"In there," he said, pointing to the machine, beaming with pleasure at my growing concern.

Look, I explained, I'd love to risk it, but I can't really go back to Botswana and hope that a lion leaps up just when my camera happens to be lying at hand on the breakfast table.

"In there."

The more I insisted, the worse it got. People began to back up in line.

"Listen, I have had film ruined before," I repeated. He lunged for the kill.

"In France?"

Herein was the game. He was playing *mauvaise foi*. I could say, "Yes, France," and prolong the play. I would then demand his superior, who would support him. And they would both amuse themselves all afternoon by sifting through my mountain of hand luggage.

"No," I admitted. "It was not in France."

"Aha," he exclaimed, managing somehow to double the size of his chest. I half expected him to crow *cocorico* and flap his arms. "This machine . . ." with a pause to deliver the word that would brook no further discussion, "is French."

I, like every other passerby and freebooter who had rashly considered making a dent in Réunion, gave up.

CHAPTER FOUR

Corsica: Empire at Home

A FAVORITE THEME of authorities explaining the inherent Frenchness of the overseas *départements* is, "But Guadeloupe (or Réunion) is as French as Corsica." You hear it often. You do not, however, hear it in Corsica.

That little island of breath-catching beauty and blood feuds has flown French colors since 1769. Illustrious Frenchmen have emerged from its ancient stone ports; Napoléon, for one. Corsicans built much of France's empire and died in its wars. The island is ninety minutes' flight from Paris, an afternoon's sail from Marseilles. Everything is there: Prisunic and Monoprix, perfumed poodles, and the kiosks papered in magazine covers of the nation's luminaries of the hour.

But Corsicans in the north revere a man from their mountains, exiled two centuries ago: Pasquale Paoli, who led the island during its only fourteen years of independence in two millenia of resisting outsiders. In the south, they like Napoléon because he colonized France from Corsica.

Corsica is neither a DOM nor a TOM. It is France, pure and simple, as though the 100 miles of Mediterranean between its north coast and the mainland were a bridged river. But it is not French. To test this, drive around in a car with a license plate ending in "75," for Paris. For years, an average of two bombs a day have ripped the fronts off businesses owned by continental Frenchmen.

It is not that most Corsicans want independence from France. But even conservative dyed-in-the-flannel Francophile politicians do their ward-heeling in the blend of Italian, Arabic, Latin, and Catalan that Corsicans speak with towering pride. All parties display the same symbol of Corsica: the black Moor's head—a slave demanding freedom—with a white blindfold pushed up onto the brow, ready to look any executioner in the eye.

Corsica is the most clearly defined of a handful of regions of heartland France where people consider themselves more than just French. Before France was diced into departments, regions grappled with Paris for power. In Brittany, the Basque country, Languedoc, and Alsace, aging farmers and young intellectuals argue their right for a separate identity. They take the issue with dead seriousness. Some want "Basque" or "Breton" written in their French passports; or they insist that their children learn history and arithmetic in their own disappearing languages. They want regional assemblies with more control—and especially more of the taxes they pay to Paris —to settle local issues.

Within these mainland regions, families link themselves tightly together, preserving traditions, cuisines, and languages. Occasionally, Breton terrorists will bomb Versailles Palace or a television relay station so France does not forget they are out there, unsatisfied. Cultural Minister Jack Lang set up a national council for languages and cultures to protect minority tongues. The right wing howled that French was imperiled. But Lang argued the reverse: by preserving disappearing languages, France might encourage other European nations not to dump French as a second language in favor of English.

Mitterrand visited Basque territory and applauded efforts to seek an identity. He said, "I will always be at the side of those who wish to exist at their deepest levels." But, he added, if the question is autonomy, or independence, "I say clearly, face to face, with conviction: No!" He was treated to whistles and a snatch of the Basque tongue: *"Mitterrand kamporat."* Mitterrand out. (And someone stole a police car from his guards, with a secret route map, itinerary, and list of radio frequencies lying on the front seat.)

The Basque problem is bitter and bloody. In two years, the *Groupe antiterroriste de libération* killed twenty-three people in French Basque country, including eight who had nothing to do with the lingering dirty war. The GAL, mainly demobilized French veterans of Algerian War terrorism, fight against the clandestine Basque organization, Iparretarrak. Early in 1986, Iparretarrak set off a fresh round of bombs and promised to pursue an "armed struggle" for independence.

But even with the Basques, identity issues on the mainland have an air of unreality. In a fast-traveling Citroën, Basqueland has no borders. Normandy blurs into Brittany; ancient political and cultural borders are marked by little more than flags in ancient colors or stylized signs on the *autoroute*.

But there is no mistaking Corsica. Its mountains loom straight up out of the water. Vineyards climb up the slopes to villages carved from the rocky peaks, with gates that have slammed shut behind every transient occupier: Phoenicians, Etruscans, Carthaginians, Romans, Byzantines, Saracens, Moors, Genoese, Pisans, Iberians. Its ports are redolent of juniper and oleanders, ripe nectarines, spices and salt breezes, the smoky sweet scent that attracted so many invaders.

In Paoli's old capital of Corte, perched up high at the dead center of the island, computerized tellers dispense 500-franc notes to the passing *pinzuti,* the continental Frenchmen. But up the narrow streets of rough paving stones, the old life goes on. Corsicans smoke their hams, splash out hearty red wine, comment on the sky, and wait to see what new surprise the Mediterranean will pitch up on their shores.

I HAD BEEN fascinated by the idea of Corsica since my first day as a correspondent. I shared a tiny Congolese hotel room with a fearless and good-hearted Corsican photographer named Bodini who ate garlic cloves as if they were apples. "Me, I like fishing, tranquility, and women," he announced, suggesting that that was the first line of the Corsican national anthem. My kind of place.

I flew down next to an immense Frenchwoman in a flowered muumuu who cuddled two Yorkies in a padded basket on her lap. On landing, the steward announced, *"Bonnes vacances,"* as if there were no other reason for being in Calvi. But we had flown far beyond Cannes. The man at the car rental desk wore only satin jogging shorts in Hertz yellow. "This island has produced three great men: Napoléon, Tino Rossi, and Domé," he said, tapping his dark brown bare chest. "Me." Joking over and business done, he stopped a moment to size me up, with sharp gray eyes set among deep crags. "Here," he said, "is a map of Corsica. That way, you also have a portrait of my face."

With Domé's map, I found the village of Pigna. Its little stone plaza hangs off the brow of a mountain, and a wide, fragrant valley sweeps off to the sand beach far below. Toni Casalonga, master engraver and painter, runs a gallery in a medieval house up a twisting cobbled lane from the square.

"In fact," he explained, with a slight chuckle, "we are absolutely like an overseas department, and we don't even have any distinguishing marks to set us apart: no black skin, no unusual way of dressing. . . . But am I against being in France? That is like being against the handbrake in a car. You don't want it until you need it."

Casalonga is an aesthete, dapper and gentle, far from the stock stereotype of the rough, mustachioed Corsican. He has given a lot of thought to his people's dilemmas. "Is someone here first Corsican or French?" he began, repeating my question. "It depends on how you put it to him. The Corsican is highly sensitive to being regarded a traitor, as somehow unreliable or unpatriotic. If he perceives a challenge, he will answer defensively, 'Of course, I am as French as the next guy.' But, in the end, it will come out: he is Corsican.

"These are questions a Corsican must never put to himself."

More to the point, he said, is the question of dependence. With its agriculture crippled by lack of field hands and high transport costs, Corsica depends on France for virtually everything: food, clothing, fuel, even refrigerator repairmen. Economically that is bad; psychologically, it is disastrous.

Casalonga is not bothered by the more than one million tourists who come to the island each year, mainly from the continent. Tourism, he said, might push Paris finally to spend the money necessary to lift Corsica out of its lingering stagnation. "We have a choice between that or nothing at all," he said. "We are not closed to the outside. Among the young, there is more than unemployment; there is social despair. They see no future, no challenge, and they are ripe for extremists." He added, "But we have to be careful to preserve a balance, not to let the numbers become so overwhelming that they destroy the past."

The past in Corsica is the present. The Genoese, driven out in the 1760s after four centuries of occupation, are reviled as though they left last month. Two clans dominate the island, drawing strength from family alliances dating back uncounted generations. But the history books piled high in Casalonga's gallery describe a Corsica that is going fast.

Early accounts describe how islanders resisted when the king of France answered a plea from Genoa to help suppress rebellion. When the French established control, they took over sovereignty. By now, it doesn't matter whether historical incidents are exaggerated. They are the patrimony.

In his pamphlet, *Life of Pasquale Paoli,* illustrated by Casalonga, René Emmanuelli writes: "This is the response of a militiaman, fallen gravely wounded into the hands of the French who, surprised at the lack of any organized medical corps, asked: 'How do you save yourselves without ambulances or doctors?' The soldier replied: 'We die.' "

In the early 1800s, when the winds were contrary the island went months at a time without a single vessel from the mainland. The first steamship arrived in 1830, an event marred only by an attempt by Bastia sailors to set it afire as a threat to their jobs. Three years later, with regular service to Toulon, 2,899 travelers got off in Corsica.

One early visitor was Alexandre Dumas. He wrote:

> A traveler arrives in a village, walks down the length of the main street, chooses the house that pleases him most and knocks at the door. An instant later, the master appears, invites him to come in, offers him half of his dinner and all of his bed, if he has but one, and the following morning, on accompanying the visitor out, thanks him for the preference shown. There is, of course, not the slightest question of compensation, the master regarding as an insult the merest word on the subject.

Such welcomes still apply, or nearly so, in remote parts of the island. But it is clear that they are reserved for people not intending to take charge of the house.

A dusty document puts into clearer focus the repeated assertion of modern French administrations that Corsica has been an equal part of the whole since it became a department in 1790. In an 1836 report to Paris, a departing prosecutor general named Mottet noted that Corsica cost France three times what it contributed despite rich agricultural potential.

He warned of a material problem and a moral problem, each linked to the other. Once, Mottet said, he asked a landowner why a river was allowed to run across a wide plain without watering it.

"A canal would be easy," he told me, "but sharing the water would be impossible."

"Why? You could make an ordinance."

"We could never agree to it."

"The authorities could impose it for you."

"Yes, but who would enforce it?"

"The courts."

"The courts!" he said with a bitter smile. "No, *monsieur*, sharing the water would be done by rifle fire."

Mottet continued:

There is the real state of Corsica. Everything is done by rifle fire. Law is nothing; force is everything. . . . Need we have statistics to resume the moral state? I knew of, in 1834, 416 attacks on individuals, including 188 murders, assassinations or attempts and 228 injuries, more or less grave. That is 20 times, 30 times more than in any other area and the population is only 196,000 souls. . . .

The state must not depend on the use of force; experience has shown that 20 times. . . . The Empire and the Restoration have sent generals with full powers: arbitrary arrests, detentions without trial, repeated executions. The Corsicans have seen it all, have suffered it all with impassivity and have remained the same. . . .

It would be folly to expect the country to improve by itself, without the help of money or a modified administration. If nothing is done, Corsica will be in 50 years what it is today, and we will have spent a hundred million francs more with no profit, even for the island. One can discuss the system to follow, but one

point remains beyond discussion: It is that we must occupy this
unhappy country and occupy it as soon as possible.

Ajaccio, for better or for worse, is occupied. In the palm-fringed
capital, wedding cake apartment blocks and office buildings muscle
in on the medieval quarter. Traffic chokes the cours Napoléon, a
standard-issue Main Street France. But the boom came 125 years
after Mottet's report. As predicted, Corsica stayed the same for half
a century. Then World War I killed 40,000 Corsicans, one of every
five. Thousands of others stayed on the continent or shipped out to
the colonies. The island struggled along, moribund.

Then France lost Algeria, and thousands of *pieds-noirs* settled in
Corsica. They received the subsidies and credits for which Corsicans
had been pleading. Newcomers prospered, bought land, and built
businesses. The bad blood still circulates. Today, the ratio of what
Paris spends on Corsica to what it earns is perhaps twice the figure
of Mottet's time. But Corsica is an assured market, and that is part
of the problem.

In Ajaccio today, points of view are as extreme as the architecture.

Paul Bernard, the prefect, was frank but reassuring in a comfortable French prefect's way. He recalled that the Socialist government
passed a Special Statute for Corsica in 1982, setting up a regional
assembly and offering economic incentives. That, he said, passed its
difficult period of apprenticeship and was taking hold. In 1985, Paris
contracted to spend one billion francs to the region's 300,000 for
specific projects in agriculture and fishing, infrastructure, youth
training, housing, and tourism.

"People here have rejected separatism and terrorism," Bernard
said. "They have shown their will to manage serenely the affairs of
the region."

In December 1984, when mysterious terrorists sprayed machine-
gun fire at an elite CRS police unit and killed three officers,
30,000 Corsicans of all parties marched against violence. At 10
percent of the population, the prefect noted, that was equivalent
to five million people in the streets on the mainland. Union leaders painted "Jobs, not bombs" on the side of a bullet-riddled van.
Separatists and autonomists polled less than 15 percent of the vote

in 1983, and they hold six of the regional assembly's sixty-three seats.

But young Corsicans are still discouraged by political and social mores of the past, Bernard acknowledged. Hard hit by the economy, some are attracted to violence.

"Our goal is to demonstrate to the youth that if they work hard and honestly, they will gain from it," he said. "The youth are afraid. But if we can show the state is no longer an accomplice of the system, and it supports the honest citizen, this will disappear."

Also, the prefect added, "We have made the wager of democracy. We preserve essential liberties, no repression, no undue police presence. In the end, democracy will carry the day."

I had already noticed a relaxed approach to security. At the gate, a bored gendarme did not even glance at my ominous-looking black bag. Departing later from Calvi was a refreshing break in my running war with French airport security inspectors. An officer briefly surveyed my huge pile of hand baggage and frowned on finding my portable computer. With sincere concern, he asked, "How can you take work with you on vacation?"

Across the street from the prefecture, however, Jean-Pierre Arrighi had a different view entirely.

"The French colonizers here are at the level they were when taking over the Middle East, as unwanted occupiers. They must come into modern times. People here will sabotage their colonialism, and they cannot stop the steam from escaping. If they try, it will explode, and independence will be inevitable under the worst possible circumstances."

Arrighi speaks for the Corsican People's Party (PPC), a small left-leaning (and legal) group that espouses "armed propaganda" rather than the armed struggle of the clandestine FLNC (National Front for the Liberation of Corsica).

The PPC wants increased autonomy for Corsica, with separate passports and bank accounts, leading to eventual independence. Arrighi is not deterred by the economics.

"When you have this sun and water, and this strategic position, you don't worry." If France paid back what it took from the Corsican economy, he said, the island could balance its budget for a decade. There is the Carbo Sarde deal, for example: France allows

Italy to run power lines across Corsica to its island province of Sardinia, twelve miles to the south; Italy pays off with electricity in the Alps. Corsica, Arrighi says, gets nothing.

"Corsica was rich," he insists. "Not only rich, but happy. That is why we are so angry."

Pierre Poggioli heads the Corsican Movement for Autodetermination (MCA), the leading separatist party. With 7,000 votes in 1983, it outpolled the more moderate Corsican People's Union (UPC), for years the most popular rejectionist front. For Poggioli, that means Corsicans are fast growing fed up not only with French domination but also with the island's internal politics.

"Our experience in the regional assembly shows the state has no solution that can interest us," he said. "Nothing works. Unemployment is increasing, and we are ever more dependent. The two clans run Corsica, and they need dependence, status quo, as the basis for their power. If the clans continue to dominate it is because Paris wants them to."

Poggioli maintains that only one voter in three actually went to the polls. The clans, he said, collected proxies from people who owed them favors: jobs, pensions, loans, court decisions, land. And they can afford to dispense favors, he continued, only because state grants and loans and commercial monopolies are dispensed through clan leaders.

People disagree on the numbers, but even French authorities identify electoral fraud and clan domination as a crushing problem in Corsica. In the old days, small groups took charge of the land and built up loyal followings to defend it. Vendettas kept accounts straight and borders clearly drawn. Today, critics say, the clans operate like Mafia families, but with less bloodshed. François Giacobbi in Bastia and Jean-Paul de Rocca-Serra outside Ajaccio divide their territory carefully and work in harmony. Both deny any wrongdoing, but each acknowledges personal followings. Party labels mean little compared to the name on the ballot.

"The state does nothing to destabilize the clans," Poggioli said. "If they had no resources, they would wither on their own. They have no interest in Corsica's development. If there were other economic means available, people would owe them nothing."

MCA headquarters is in a new apartment block, its walls plastered with posters extolling separatists from Pasquale Paoli to Bobby Sands. Poggioli does not think much of the prefect's idea of liberty. His phone is tapped, he said, and the newspaper he puts out is regularly prosecuted for condoning violence and publishing false information.

The party is widely known as the legal arm of the FLNC, a status Poggioli rejects. "We are a political organization, and we do not feel we can condemn another organization for the means they choose."

What worries the separatists most is numbers. Census figures show that of the island's 240,000 inhabitants, 166,600 are Corsican, 33,600 are continental French, and 39,800 are foreigners. Of the Corsicans, one in three is older than sixty. The MCA argues that the real situation is far worse: 120,000 to 130,000 Corsicans at the most. Uncounted others are scattered from Toulouse to Tahiti.

From the beginning of the empire, Corsica was a reserve of manpower used to hard, hot work. Each time clan leaders placed someone's son abroad, they ensured a whole family's loyalty for a decade. Now that it is time to build a computer-age state in Corsica, others are coming in to do it.

With a million tourists, there is no hotel training program on the island. Civil servants and technicians come from the mainland, sometimes to return home grumbling that Corsicans forced them out.

"Immediate independence would be the worst catastrophe we could have," said Poggioli, the separatist. "First we must put in place a structure. The government's plan to spend money will not work. All that money will be deflected to the clans."

Like separatists elsewhere, Poggioli acknowledges that his is a minority view because people are not aware of realities. "We had 10,000 gather for a rally—in secret, because the television and the papers did not cover us."

There are, it is true, only two significant dailies in Corsica, local editions of papers from Nice and Marseilles. I had asked one local correspondent if he had a telephone number for Poggioli, who was, after all, leader of a key bloc in the regional assembly. "Not really," the reporter shrugged. "I don't know him too well, and it's not the policy of the newspaper."

In the 1986 elections, the MCA kept its six seats in the regional assembly, but its share of the popular vote dropped from 12.73 percent in 1983 to 9.05 percent. Observers from several parties complained of irregularities; in Bastia, some contended, electoral lists used for registration were not the same as those delivered for counting.

"The *autonomistes,* the *indépendantistes*, they are finished," remarked a French reporter who knows Corsica well. But who knows Corsica well? On May 16, thirteen hooded terrorists took over a holiday camp at Cargese, tied up the thirty customers and the owner and set fire to bungalows. The owner got loose and tried to dismantle a bomb they left behind. He was killed, along with a gendarme. Such deaths were unusual, but bombings continued at their regular pace.

IN AJACCIO, NAPOLÉON Bonaparte is everywhere. A lot of Corsicans are bitter at the memory of the little emperor, blaming him for nailing down all hopes that Paoli's republic might be restored. But an active Bonapartist Party argues that it was not a matter of a Corsican helping France to colonize Corsica. It was a Corsican who colonized France.

After lunch at Le Petit Caporal—the Little Corporal—next to Le Premier Consul bar and across from an enormous statue of who else, I walked through the medieval quarter to Napoléon's big but undistinguished house.

The tour was fascinating, through a bourgeois house where roomfuls of young Bonapartes grew up, forming their view of a world one of them would soon command. But on a sultry sunny afternoon, the guide could hardly keep his eyes open. In room after room, he droned out his spiel in deadening monotone. "Here is where his mother, returning from the cathedral next door, gave birth to Napoléon. . . . Here is Napoléon's inkstand, Napoléon's documents, Napoléon's sword." Finally, he directed us down the stairs, or so I thought, and I moved toward the exit.

"Halt," ordered a pinched little guide at the bottom, fixing me with a violent stare. "Where is your escort?"

"He is coming, but . . . "

"You must remain at all times with your guide," he sputtered, the Napoléon in him rising with his voice. "When you reach the end of one part, you must wait."

"Forget it, it's not worth the trouble," I said, heading toward the door.

Having paid my eight francs, I had placed myself under his orders until he granted me leave. His face purpled at the outrage; desertion in the ranks at the hallowed shrine. He made a brief move in my direction. But then he stopped and accepted his Waterloo, looking as if he had swallowed Napoléon's cocked hat.

MOST CORSICANS SEEM convinced that the future will make a sharp break from the past and present, but few agree on what shape it may take.

In Pigna, Bill Graham, an international lawyer from Canada who bought a home here in the early 1970s, sees steady progress upward.

"Oh, I suppose the quality of *lonzo* [raw ham] is not as good because the poor peasants don't have to spend their lives slaughtering pigs up in the mountains, but I have seen a better life for people over the past twelve years, with increasing prosperity and respect for the past."

Residents of Pigna got together to save the crumbling facade of their church, for example, doing it on their own with money earned from new economic activity.

Casalonga muses at the outside possibilities.

"You know, there may be a completely new social and political experiment here, something to be tried in a small place and kept if it works or rejected if it doesn't," he said. "Every 200 years, that has been the case, it's a pattern." He ticked them off. In 1133, Pope Innocent II split the island between Pisa and Genoa; the Genoese set up a state in the 1300s; then Sampiero Corso tried something else until Genoa crushed his rebellion. And there was Paoli's republic. "Did you know Jean-Jacques Rousseau drafted a constitution for Paoli? Never put into practice, of course. It is time again, and perhaps the French will try something new."

Not likely.

Buses full of *pinzuti* tourists grind up the mountain, obscuring in diesel smoke the red letters scrawled on rocks: *"Français dehors"*
—French go home. At a nearby convent, a priest worries aloud at

how Corsican children are losing their values, corrupted by naked bathers on the beaches and television waves that reach isolated mountaintops invaders did not approach.

At San Antonino, another storybook Corsican mountain settlement, Sunday afternoon *pétanque* games are no longer village affairs. Snapping shutters distract the players and braying tourists drown out their patter. Up to now, Corsican hospitality is holding. "Eh, oh, we're going to be on TV tonight," a young player joked when someone's Pentax recorded his pitch. Felix Marcelli, in a blue-striped mariner's jersey, with skin the texture of an overused football, just laughed. I asked if he minded the influx.

"C'est très bien, très bien."

But in Calvi, Les Aloès Hôtel closed its kitchen in 1984, giving up in the face of fifty-seven new restaurants where tourists can eat fast and nasty. These days it is not the menu that counts but the notations on top: "English spoken." *"Mann spricht deutsch."* Maître d's are often rude to young outsiders. Prices are Champs-Elysées. That, many Corsicans fear, is a sign of the times.

All is not lost. At the Aloès, bar talk is still running 1,000 years behind the times. "You know, it wasn't the Saracens who killed Roland [Charlemagne's son], as it says in the *Chanson de Roland,"* the bartender confided to me one night. "It was the Basques."

But the centuries are advancing fast. In Casalonga's stacks in Pigna is a fragment of Flaubert's diary from 1840:

> All this is so far from France, so far from our century, frozen in an epoch we dream about now in books, and I asked myself, as I rubbed oil onto my reddened legs, when one travels in stagecoaches, when there will be, instead of these crumbling houses, restaurants à la carte, and when all of this poor country will be miserable thanks to the cupidity that will be introduced, if all of that will be worth more.

PART TWO

THE OLD EMPIRES

Gaul united, forming a single nation, fired by a common spirit, can challenge the universe.

—Vercingétorix, quoted by Caesar,
embellished slightly by Napoléon III

CHAPTER FIVE

From Gauls to Franks

THE FRENCH, MASTER civilizers, started out at the other end of a mission to civilize. Roman envoys crossed the Alps and declared themselves appalled at the barbarity they found. Cicero's remarks to the Senate might have been Louis Proust's report on West Africa to the French Assembly nearly two millenia later. "What could be more filthy than their towns?" the Roman orator sniffed. "What is cruder than their farms?"

Historians quibble over whether France was France back then. But for a century now, schoolchildren have thumbed through primers showing warriors in long blond braids and winged helmets: their ancestors, the Gauls. Ferdinand Lot brooks no waffling. "Before France was Gaul, or to put it better, France continues on from Gaul, and Gaul precedes France. To write the history of Gaul is to write the history of France."

Gaul—France—was peopled first by diverse Celtic tribes, restless and cantankerous enough to move west to the edge of the continent but not driven to build boats and keep on going. By the end of the Stone Age, France was the heartland of Celts whose territory stretched from east of the Danube to the British Isles.

Cicero, in fact, was a little hard on them. The Celts were rough around the edges, but they were in touch with the times. Phoenicians brought their civilization along the Mediterranean coast. Marseilles was colonized from Asia Minor by 620 B.C., and Greek culture filtered northward from the thriving port. Three centuries before Christ, the Celts sacked Rome and invaded Greece.

The Celts lived in timbered clay huts, with elaborate iron cook-ware, forged weaponry, and tanned leather clothing. But the early tribes, too jealous and suspicious to forge any institutions beyond changing military alliances, formed no nation. Gaul—*Gallia*—was the Roman name for their geographical confines. In Latin, the Celts were *galli.* So were roosters.

While the Romans pursued architecture, philosophy, engineer-ing, military science, and belles lettres, the Celts hunted wild pigs and foretold the future by stabbing prisoners and reading the blood flow. The Romans, more civilized, also spilled prisoners' blood and guided their lives by superstition. That posed the obvious question: What is civilization? As in the case of the Romans, and later the French, those with the power to export civilization brought along their own definition.

The Romans colonized southern Gaul by 120 B.C. They built roads and massage parlors and sports stadiums; their ruins today are sprinkled across Provence and the Mediterranean coast. And from fortified outposts, the Romans kept an uneasy eye on Celtic politics to the north.

By 70 B.C., balances began to shift among the Celts. The Se-quanes, to overpower the Eduans, courted a calamity the French would suffer again and again: they brought in Germans. Ariovistus's troops crossed the Rhine and subdued the Eduans—and then the Sequanes who had hired him. The Eduans appealed to Rome for help.

The Senate demurred at first. Ariovistus was an official Friend of Rome, having signed a mutual defense pact. But the Helvetians were also pressing in on Gaul. Hungry German and Swiss warlords meant a threat to Rome's southern colonies. The Eduans, like the Sequanes, received more help than they wanted. They got Julius Caesar and a Pax Romana that lasted four centuries.

Caesar, an able enough general, was a prodigious war correspon-dent. Untroubled by censors, press credentials, or inconvenient facts, he reported his own campaigns in the third person. Today, his *Commentaries* remain the basis for what historians know about the Gallic Wars. He depicts himself as the prudent mediator, driven reluctantly to arms to enforce diplomacy. But his actions suggest a ruthless soldier-politician for whom Gaul was virgin ground for enough glory to earn his next promotion: emperor of Rome.

A first wave of Germans had ventured over the Rhine, Caesar reported. "When the uncivilized Barbarians had acquired a taste for residence in Gaul, with its good land and high standard of life, more were brought over, and there were at present about a hundred and twenty thousand of them."

Ariovistus, brusque and arrogant, challenged the Romans to force him out. They did, handily, and grateful Gauls prevailed upon Caesar to stay, as the *Commentaries* tell it. He was staying in any case, as proconsul. His purple mantle conferred the powers of viceroy, military governor, and tyrant-at-large.

His first news analysis has held up rather well:

> In Gaul, not only every tribe, canton, and subdivision of canton, but almost every family, is divided into rival factions. At the head of these factions are men who are regarded by their followers as having particularly great prestige, and these have the final say on all questions that come up for judgment and in all discussions of policy. The object of this ancient custom seems to have been to ensure that all the common people should have protection against the strong; for each leader sees no one gets the better of his supporters by force or cunning—or, if he fails to do so, is utterly discredited.

The Gauls, he noted, were happy to barter for wine at one slave per jug. They were extremely superstitious, given to human sacrifice, and their lives were governed by a mystic fraternity of druids.

Caesar conquered by dividing, playing tribes off against one another. A Friend of Rome was protected and rewarded. Foes were crushed and packed off to the lions. Resisting settlements were razed, and survivors enslaved. The Romans seized hostages to ensure that subdued leaders did not change their minds later. When short of legionnaires, Caesar relied on Gallic collaborators and German mercenaries.

The French today trace the taproot of their glory, the indomitable Gallic spirit, to Caesar's occupation. There is Astérix, a feisty little cartoon character who drinks a magic potion the way Popeye eats spinach. Thus fortified, he and his brawny sidekick, Obélix, dislocate outsized Roman noses, sending legionnaires flying out of their leather-thonged sandals, to the inevitable pronouncement: "They're nuts, these Romans."

Astérix, argues Alain Duhamel in *Le Complexe d'Astérix,* personifies the Frenchman's image of his own political temperament: rebellious, mercurial, courageous, sarcastic, grumbling, generous, individualistic, hungry for adventure and glory, mocking of the powerful, allergic to conformism, sentimental, misogynistic, with condescending scorn for the rest of the world.

And there is Vercingétorix, a Gallic commander whose ten months of glory are celebrated in France 2,000 years after his defeat. Caesar, likely for his own purposes, painted Vercingétorix as a fiery guerrilla chieftain who inspired the colony to rebellion. Events suggest another reading. The Gauls chafed under the Roman proconsul and the Latin civilization he imposed. Their culture was endangered. Bards no longer sang of their ancestors' revered free spirits. Druids could not skewer prisoners for their gods. And the Gauls did not like paying taxes.

Caesar tried to consolidate Gaul by convoking all tribal leaders to Paris, called Lutetia at the time. Some did not turn up. Instead, bitter enemies met deep in the forest to ally secretly against Rome. Among them was Vercingétorix, chief of Arvernes, the son of a leader executed by rivals who feared he would be king of Gaul. Vercingétorix learned early from his father's mistakes. At about twenty, he was a barn-burning orator who could draw first blood whenever challenged.

In 52 B.C., Caesar wintered at Ravenna in northern Italy, fretting over Roman politics, which menaced his position. At the same time, he worried about a restive Gaul. Snow blocked the Alpine passes to France, and most of Caesar's legions were with him on the wrong side.

Gaul seized the moment and arose. The Carnutes stormed Genabum (now Orléans) and massacred Roman civilians. Other tribes followed, united behind Vercingétorix.

Historian Camille Jullian saw this unity as "the result of a universal sentiment, of a desire for the liberty of all, of an accord for the love of Gaul. . . . A collective spirit formed the ferment of a civilization of empire."

Jullian notes, however, that Vercingétorix lavished gold and promises of power on his recalcitrant allies. He commanded loyalty; but, just in case, he kept hostages.

Caesar, ignoring the winter, drove his men into Gaul. The campaign was vicious. Seasoned centurions used javelins and long daggers, attacking with precision strategy. But the Gauls howled down on them with bloodcurdling yells, swinging heavy swords and protected by leather shields. They adorned their horses with the heads of Romans who did not get out of the way.

The Gauls' alliance held, and they built up defenses. Caesar had to besiege Avaricum (now Bourges) until his men finally stormed the ramparts. They were so enraged by then that they slaughtered 40,000 men, women, and children before taking the time to loot. The Romans marched on Lutetia, but it burned before they could take it. At Gergovie, near what is now Clermont-Ferrand, Caesar lost patience with siege tactics and charged the walls. Vercingétorix inflicted so much damage that Caesar fled. It was his first defeat.

Each side craved vengeance, and they squared off for a showdown at Alésia.

For the Gauls, the town of Alésia, 125 miles east of Paris in the Burgundy hills, home of the Mandubiens, was their spiritual center. Legend described it as unconquerable, the cradle of their race. At the fall of Avaricum, Vercingétorix had rallied the tribes with the promise of a united Gaul. They would win the next battle and rule the world. But if they lost at Alésia, it was clear, Gaul would be crushed forever.

For the Romans, heavily outnumbered and far from home, Alésia meant all or nothing. Caesar knew that if he lost the advantage and his dwindling Gallic allies deserted him, his army would be slaughtered to the last man. Triumphant hordes would obliterate the traces of Roman civilization in Gaul, blotting out not only his life but also his place in history.

For both sides, the site was a majestic sweep of a battlefield, designed by the gods for glorious victory. Alésia perched atop Mont Auxois, 1,300 feet over the Plaine des Laumes, behind solid ramparts of hardened logs and earth. Caesar's camp was pitched on facing hills, and he gazed straight across the rolling meadows at his enemies' watchtowers.

Caesar's 50,000 legionnaires faced 80,000 Gauls encamped within the city's walls. He chose science rather than strength. For three weeks, his muscled veterans dug two parallel trenches, each twenty feet wide and nine feet deep, in an eleven-mile circle. Behind them, sharpened branches like barbed wire were rooted in the earth. Then he laid down buried minefields, one of fire-tempered wooden stakes and the other of iron spikes, both masked by leaves and grass. If he could not get in, no one would get out. And then, to defend his men from any rescuing force, he built a second circle, fourteen miles around, with the traps pointing outward. In between, he erected wooden terraces as high as the walls of Alésia.

Vercingétorix was confident. He had food and fodder for at least a month. His cavalry sneaked through the unfinished Roman lines to ride for help; all Gaul was resolved to support him. After three weeks, however, he was nearing desperation. No aid came, and some lieutenants pleaded for surrender. Others urged a frontal assault, preferring impalement to starvation. The relief column was long overdue. But each day the horizon was empty, and the foreground was thick with Romans.

Caesar's nerves were no calmer. Daily, chances increased that reinforcements would thunder over the hills. If Vercingétorix broke out, the Romans would be trapped between two fronts.

Desperate, Vercingétorix emptied Alésia of the people he had come to defend. Civilians at least would eat as Roman slaves; he needed all the food for his troops. The women and children, the sick and weak, streamed out of gates that slammed shut behind them. But they were trapped in the middle. Caesar had enough slaves. Tens of thousands died slowly of hunger.

Just as the besieged troops came to terms with cannibalism, the surrounding hills blackened with 250,000 armed Gauls. The battle, begun the next day, lasted a week. At daybreak, Vercingétorix attacked from the inside, but the relief force hung back. Only the cavalry charged, and the Gauls' best horsemen rode straight into Roman steel. Vercingétorix was beaten back.

The next day, Vercingétorix's allies waited at a safe distance, making only a minor dent with rudimentary artillery. They tried a bumbling night attack, which fell on the strongest part of the Romans' defenses. Gauls fled in terror, seeing comrades lying impaled on the hidden spikes. In a belated council of war, the Gallic generals finally located a weak spot: Caesar's command post on a rock outcropping. They attacked and breached the line. At the same time, Vercingétorix broke through from the other side.

Caesar's lines were cut at two points, and the Romans were outnumbered five to one. Centurions fought on by reflex, convinced that the battle was over and all was lost. But the Gauls' main force still held back, leaving combat to frontline units and the remaining mounted troops. Caesar sensed a turn in the battle. He ordered a massive counterassault behind his German cavalry. The Teutonic horsemen mauled the attacking Gauls. They charged into massed troops and refused to retreat, bellowing war cries and flailing sabers. The bulk of the relief column fled, and Vercingétorix retreated into the Alésia gates.

The next day, the commander of united Gaul threw his broadsword at Caesar's feet. It took six years for Caesar to return to Rome; the proconsul trundled Vercingétorix across Gaul as he accepted the obeisance of chieftains who had vowed to resist him to the death. Finally, Vercingétorix was paraded into Rome in chains as a symbol of Caesar's glory. Then he was quietly executed.

TODAY, VERCINGÉTORIX stands twenty-one feet tall on Mont Auxois, his sword at his side, gazing at the empty space where Caesar camped. French fathers take their children to see him, sweeping by without a look at a smaller Joan of Arc on a horse in the town square below. The statue was commissioned in 1865 by Napoléon III who, in his thick German accent, reminded the French of their ancestors the Gauls.

Not far away, along the *autoroute* to Lyon, expert hands have duplicated the siegeworks that defeated Alésia. An Archeodrome depicts daily life among hearty Celts (Gauls) going back 6,000 years. But visitors head straight for the *pièce de résistance:* the cut branches, the rusty spikes, and the towering ramparts. The replicas are impressive, but the accompanying history lesson is left a little vague.

France's Gallic content is open to question. The Franks, who later overran the terrain and gave it their name, were German, but the

French cling to the glory of Gaul. And if an indomitable Gallic spirit exists, the aura of Vercingétorix exemplifies it. Humiliating defeat converts easily to noble victory. The trick is in how you choose to remember it.

Rome obliterated Gaul. Occupied, it was a prosperous model colony. The Celtic language dissolved into Latin, and traditions melded into what historians call a Gallo-Roman society. Subdued, the Gauls poured wealth into Rome and fought in its legions. In return, Rome held off Germanic forces and kept peace among fractious clans.

In the third century, invaders poured over the Rhine, settling as far west as the Pyrenees. Rome restored peace, but the empire declined and fell. Gallic provinces were left as a loose amalgam of odd-shaped fiefdoms, open to the east. Franks moved in. Their name meant "free"; they were never conquered by the Romans. Frankish and Gallic blood, at first spilled in battle, was mixed in marriage.

And in the late 400s, a Frankish chieftain named Clovis created France.

Clovis murdered rivals, friends and relatives included, to consolidate power. Specializing in deceit, treachery, and military prowess, he forged a kingdom from the Rhine to the Pyrenees. Although a pagan, he acquired a Catholic wife of noble standing and the blessings of a steadily more powerful church. Over thirty years, he sank the roots of unity and order in what is now France. But, after Clovis, three centuries of Merovingian kings tugged hard at these fragile roots.

André Maurois, like most classical historians, depicts the Merovingian period as a black age during which men were at the mercy of their passions. Brothers poisoned one another for succession. Blood poured for bits of land. Bishops were murdered at their altars. Concubines schemed against queens, slaves against masters. Enemies were skewered on the spot. Indeed, Maurois notes with some horror, "Warriors broke into a church in the midst of a council, bellowing at the top of their voices." Other historians say the Merovingians were merely in tune with the times.

The idea of France, in any case, was kept fresh by the church, by culture and tradition, and by diverse branches of the aristocracy. At the end of the eighth century, France approached glory. It was the seat of empire, under a Germanic king known as Carolus Magnus Charlemagne.

For forty-three years, until he died in 814, Charlemagne shaped a cultivated society, faithful to the pope. "The Merovingian dynasty had lost all moral sense," wrote Fustel de Coulanges. "Charlemagne took it as his task to better souls and to make virtue prevail." Maurois thoughtfully advises caution in reading official rave reviews by Charlemagne's official biographer, Einhard. But he allows that Charlemagne "elicited respect through his dignity of bearing, and affection through his friendliness of manner. . . . He was pious, well-meaning, and a hard worker." The church was not enthusiastic about his five wives and four concubines. But his conquests of pagans swelled the Roman Catholics' ranks.

Charlemagne inherited a loosely knit kingdom and a ragtag army to defend it. Frankish troops, allied with the papacy, had driven Moslem raiding parties from the French heartland. As their new commander, Charlemagne chased pagans across the former Roman Empire. He conquered Lombardy and Aquitaine and then pursued barbarian invaders: Saxons, Slavs, Avars, Saracens, and Norse Vikings. He marched on Spain but, sidetracked elsewhere, gave up on Iberia. His empire extended from the Pyrenees to the Vistula, the river Warsaw straddles.

Charlemagne's blood was German, but his court was in France. The seat of the world had shifted from Rome to Aix-la-Chapelle. In 800, Pope Leo III called on Charlemagne, as temporal master of Europe, for help in a power struggle. Charlemagne pronounced the pope innocent of any wrongdoing. The grateful pontiff crowned him Charles Augustus, Emperor of the Romans. The Western Empire was revived, and a Roman pope established the right to crown as emperor a loyal soldier. The Vatican, as a result, had a considerable number of divisions.

Charlemagne's Europe was shaped to his personality. He was not rich; Moslems blockaded eastern routes to gold, spices, and luxuries. Jewish counselors ran his foreign affairs; no one else would treat with Mohammedan infidels. Dukes, counts, marquis, and assorted warlords collected taxes. When nudged by Charlemagne's roving inspectors, they passed some revenue upward. Lacking a civil service, the emperor let personal retainers handle government affairs.

Twice a year, notables gathered outside the Aix-la-Chapelle palace to debate problems of the realm. Charlemagne's scouts and spies signaled wrongs needing redress.

The emperor had Saint Jerome and Saint Augustin read to him at mealtimes. The scholar Alcuin, whom he hired from York to establish an academy, wrote, "During the morning of my life I sowed in Britain the seeds of knowledge; now, toward its evening, though my blood may be chilled, I sow these seeds ceaselessly in France, and I hope that, with the grace of God, they will prosper in both countries."

The empire collapsed after Charlemagne's death. Barbarians gnawed at its edges, and the few ships and troops could not protect long lines of communications. Families partitioned the rest, and the upheaval resembled the bloody days of the Merovingians.

But Charlemagne's roots held. He had nourished a Latin-based Western culture, with a landed aristocracy, a permanent military, and a union between the pope and the king of the Franks. The empire broke up into separate states. Nonetheless, Ferdinand Lot observed, "The imprint was so strong that within the bosom of each new state there would remain, in its institutions, in its law, and in its ecclesiastical organization, enough common elements for a European civilization to survive into the Middle Ages."

A king of France, 1,200 years ago, had gone far on his mission to civilize.

CHAPTER SIX

Spreading the Word

BY THE YEAR 1000, France was stitched into a patchwork of fiefdoms and assorted domains. Dukes, counts, and barons ruled wide sweeps of land. At the edges, small-time lords fortified their castles against bandits and tax collectors. Kings ruled in Paris but took along armies when they ventured down the road.

Western migrations had stopped. The Normans, Vikings from Scandinavia, were the last to come, muscling their way in from the north coast as far south as the Loire. They had their own views on royalty. Territorial warfare was constant. The aristocracy chose their king among pretenders who lobbied for support. Noblemen were as much allies as subjects of the king. They wanted a monarch with a generous spirit and a sharp sword.

In 987, Louis V died, the last of the Carolingians. His closest heir was excessively brutal and the crown went instead to the Capets. Hugues Capet descended from Robert the Strong who beat back a Norman advance in 866. He ruled with his son, Robert II, the Pious. They began a 300-year dynasty that sent French knights beyond the edges of Christendom, civilizing infidels at sword point.

Robert II was just, devout, and cultivated. Intellectuals loved him; generals respected him. He ruled for thirty-five years, outlasting rivals in Flanders and Germany. He balanced the independent dukes in Normandy and Aquitaine. But his three sons bitterly contested the succession.

Henri I, the eldest, won the crown. But he owed political debts across France. He split off Burgundy as a duchy for his brother

Robert. The real problem was Normandy, whose duke supported Henri but demanded Vexin in exchange. When he died, the king took it back. And then the fragile structure collapsed. Normandy fell under the control of a new duke, a gentleman known then as William the Bastard.

THE NORMANS, pagan marauders two centuries earlier, had settled comfortably in little stone ports and farms. They brought their own character to the language: *écraser,* to crush, is from the Norse. But they learned French, and they embraced the church. William's father, Robert the Magnificent—Robert the Devil, to some—died on a pilgrimage to the Holy Land.

Faith did not wipe out greed. Armed tourism remained their favorite sport. Norman bands seized Sicily and chunks of southern Italy, establishing duchies. Norman mercenaries fought in Byzantine armies, sharing in the spoils and broadening their horizons toward the east.

And in 1066, William the Bastard crossed the English Channel and stamped himself into history as William the Conqueror.

After Edward the Confessor died, William said he had been promised the English crown. However, Edward later chose Harold, of the family of earls who owned most of England. A tattered tapestry at Bayeux, narrow but long as a football field, recounts how it all happened. William had rescued Harold from a warlord up the coast, and in return Harold had promised to support him in England. But now Harold was stealing his crown. He was going after it. Just after Easter, a star trailing fire lit the skies over the Channel. Halley would identify it 700 years later. At the time, it was an omen of upheaval among kings.

Like the Allied assault in the other direction, nine centuries later, William's invasion was carefully prepared. Italian Normans, allies anxious for spoils, and freelance adventurers streamed up the roads to Normandy. The latest technology was taken aboard a fleet at Saint-Sauveur, near Cabourg, a tiny port named for an ancient miracle.

William packed his men on oversized gondolas, powered by bedsheet-type sails, on a narrow little stream called the Dives. The winds were wrong, and his fleet nearly had to conquer Belgium instead of England.

Harold was elsewhere in England when William finally landed and dug in at Hastings. When Harold approached, William rode out to attack. Three horses were killed beneath him; finally, he fought on foot, flailing the English with sword and shield. He broke up massed English forces with a stratagem that has served French legions since: his troops fell back in feigned retreat and then rounded on disorderly pursuers. Harold was killed; God had chosen.

William was crowned at Westminster in tumult; rioting English soldiers burned the town. Over two decades, he imposed his order with brutality and cunning. In the warring French principalities, aristocrats bullied the king. In England, the king was sovereign, and noblemen served him faithfully. William drew up tax and census rolls, taking charge of the island's riches. He seized land and paid stipends to the nobility. Peasants were locked into serfdom, but royal justice reached remote farms. Norman clergymen reorganized the church in England.

When William died in 1087, England and Normandy were split among two of his sons. But the Norman invasion had grafted more branches of French society and culture. The Anglo-Saxon aristocracy held only 6 percent of English land; the old noblemen were mostly dead or in exile. A cluster of Anglo-Norman barons owned land on both sides of the channel. During the next 800 years, England and France would fight interminably, and often English admirals and generals would humiliate the French. But each English sovereign would go to battle under a standard emblazoned in French: *Dieu et Mon Droit*.

SIX YEARS BEFORE William conquered England, Togrul Beg, the Seljuk, captured Baghdad and imposed Turkish rule on the vast Arabic empire. And in 1071, the Turks pushed the Byzantines from Christian Armenia at the battle of Malazgerd. They took Jerusalem from the Arabs. Within the decade, Turks ruled most of Asia Minor. Suddenly, Christian pilgrims could no longer pass among the Moslems to pray at the Holy Sepulcher. By 1090, survivors were telling of atrocities. Infidels rained arrows on them, sweeping from the hills to carry off the women and the pilgrims' meager belongings. Christians were banned from holy places, arrested, or expelled. The sanctified relics of Christ were imperiled.

On November 27, 1095, a French pope, on a visit to the French town of Clermont, demanded holy war. "God wills it," Pope Urbain II shouted to an enthusiastic crowd. He toured France eliciting support. The response was overwhelming.

Crusades had already routed the infidel in Spain. French noblemen made twenty-one forays as part of the *Reconquista,* restoring Christian civilization to the Iberian peninsula. They had discovered a side benefit of God's fight. As historian Jean Favier notes, "Of course, the combat for faith fits in quite well with conquest in that the soldier of Christ can install himself in places he has taken from the infidel."

Urbain II's idea was different. Crusaders were to deliver the Holy Land to Christianity at large and to free the faithful trapped under Islamic hegemony. This was the pope's war; kings were discouraged from attending. In any case, Philippe I of France had been excommunicated for an illicit marriage. And in medieval Europe, noblemen commanded the armies. A monk named Pierre the Hermit circled France on a mule and enlisted peasants for a poor man's crusade. They rushed on ahead, but were cut to ribbons barely east of the Byzantine borders. The pope's divisions were headed by aristocrats with enough holdings to pay for the campaign.

According to the few conflicting accounts of Urbain's appeal, the pope drove home his message of the need for purification. Baldric of Dol said that he thundered:

> You, girt about with the belt of knighthood, are arrogant with great pride; you rage against your brothers and cut each other to pieces. . . . You are the oppressors of children, plunderers of widows; you, guilty of homicide, of sacrilege, robbers of another's rights; you who await the pay of thieves for the shedding of Christian blood—as vultures smell fetid corpses.

But he apparently bolstered his spiritual appeal with the promise of reward.

"The possessions of the enemy will be yours, too, since you will make spoil of his treasures," Baldric quotes him as saying. Robert the Monk has him adding, "Wrest that holy land from the wicked race, and subject it to yourselves, that land which, as the scripture says, 'floweth with milk and honey.' " And, Robert adds, the pope reminded listeners that their land "is too narrow for your population; nor does it abound in wealth; and it furnishes scarcely enough food for its cultivators . . . hence it is that you murder and devour one another."

The first to stitch a cross to his shoulder was Raymond de Saint-Gilles, count of Toulouse, who had acquitted himself well in Spain. He was pious but impetuous. Urbain II gently resisted his efforts to be field marshal and, instead, balanced his power with that of other noblemen.

One was Godefroi de Bouillon, duke of Brabant, big, blond, and bearded, a hunter of extraordinary force. Arab chroniclers still marvel at the day a Syrian sheik started to challenge him to decapitate a camel with a single sword stroke. By the time the sheik finished his sentence, a camel's head rolled at his feet. Fellow crusaders had few reproaches. One was that he prayed so long at holy places, their dinner got cold.

The crusaders formed an international brigade, largely French but with elements from what are now Belgium and Italy. They chose the common name Franks, evoking the time when Gaul, Germany, and Italy came under the rule of Carolingian kings and the Roman church.

They set off in 1096, following what eight centuries later would be the route of the Orient Express. Within three years, they approached the walls of Jerusalem. Battle, intrigue, and Levantine summers had depleted their ranks. But they took Antioch in Syria and as they marched down the coast of Lebanon, terrified emirs sent out food to speed them on their way.

Franks and Turks quickly learned that neither were pushovers in battle. The crusaders clanked along slowly, encumbered by chain mail armor and heavy siege gear shipped in from Genoa. Mounted knights were the shock troops behind legions of foot soldiers. Preferring hand-to-hand combat, they regarded the infidels' arrows as cowardly, but efficient. Still, the more mobile Turkish horsemen melted away at iron-edged crusader charges. The Franks' smaller numbers usually carried the day.

At Jerusalem, the Franks faced Egyptians who had taken the city from the Turks. Fired with zeal, weeping from emotion, four crusader armies assaulted the ramparts. Arabs poured burning petroleum (the dreaded Greek fire of the Middle Ages) on wooden siege towers.

Godefroi made a bridge to the city walls, and crusaders raced in with flailing swords. "We advanced in blood to our ankles," wrote one soldier, describing the combat for the Al Aqsa Mosque, the Temple of Solomon. Carried away by the victory, crusaders wrought such havoc on the Arabs that Archbishop Guillaume de Tyr wrote, "The city offered such a spectacle of carnage among the enemy that the victors themselves were struck with horror and disgust." The coastal emirs, who had been prepared to negotiate, heard of the slaughter and slammed shut their gates to fight to the death.

With 1,200 horsemen and 9,000 foot soldiers, at odds with each other and facing Egyptian armies of five times their number, the Franks began what was to be nearly 200 years of occupation of the Holy Land.

The crusaders proclaimed the kingdom of Jerusalem and offered Godefroi a crown. He took the job but changed the title from king to guardian of the Holy Sepulcher. If Jesus Christ wore a crown of thorns, he said, he could hardly wear one of gold.

Godefroi died months after the conquest. His brother was crowned Baudouin I. He was an energetic warrior who rallied his men with simple logic: "If you lose, you have a martyr's crown; if you win, immortal victory. As for fleeing, that is useless. France is too far away." He died in 1118 and, by chance, his cousin arrived in Jerusalem on the day of his funeral. Baudouin II ruled well until 1123 when, out hunting with his falcons, he was caught by the Turks. Ransomed, he took back his throne. In 1131, he fell ill and died. The crown went to Foulque d'Anjou, one of the most powerful barons of France.

Foulque ruled for twelve years until the day he went rabbit hunting near Acre. His horse stumbled, and he crushed his skull. His eldest son, Baudouin III, was only thirteen; his widow, Melisende, was regent. In rapid attacks, the Turks seized Edesse, besieged Antioch, and harassed Christian columns.

By then, generations of Creoles (called *poulains*), although considering themselves European, were no longer fired by the zeal of Pope Urbain's words. The chronicler Foucher de Chartres recorded, "The colonist is becoming a native, the immigrant an inhabitant. Each day relatives and friends come from the West to join us. They do not hesitate to abandon there all they owned. In effect, who was poor there attains opulence here. Who in Europe owned not even a village finds himself in the Orient lord of an entire city. Why return to the West when the East fulfills our wishes?"

It was time for a new Crusade. Saint Bernard, a tireless French monk, preached renewed fire from a hillside at Vézelay. He was a giant of his age, a founder of 1,200 abbeys. Among others, he moved King Louis VII of France and Emperor Conrad III of Germany. Not a day too soon, they set off with separate armies for the Holy Land.

Conrad III went first, following Godefroi's route. Byzantine guides took him into Turkey, where he lost three-quarters of his army. The Christian emperor of Byzantium had sold him out because peace talks were underway with the Turks and, crusader or not, the meddling German was in the way. Louis VII fought his way through Asia Minor but had to continue by water. The Byzantines delivered few of the ships they promised. Louis's troops waited for the next transports; none came. Betrayed by the Byzantines, they were decimated by the Turks.

The two sovereigns eventually reached Jerusalem and charged off in the wrong direction. A Turkish force at Aleppo menaced Antioch, Jerusalem, and everything in between. Pressed to the wall, the crusaders depended on an alliance with the Arabs in Damascus.

Louis and Conrad attacked Damascus, on bad advice. Conrad was killed and Louis went home, leaving behind a fractured alliance, an outraged Creole aristocracy, and a strengthened Turkish threat.

"The failure of the second crusade brought a grave diminishing of the Francs' prestige in the Moslem world," historian René Grousset wrote. "The two most powerful princes of Christianity had come and gone, having done nothing."

Baudouin III grew up and saved the day. He fought battles,

forged alliances, chastised unruly barons, and restored the faith. He won over the Byzantines by marrying the Byzantine emperor's beautiful young daughter. He was a model king, but only for a short while. His physician prescribed too much medicine and he died in 1162, at thirty-three.

Baudouin's brother, Amaury I, made another mess. He tried to conquer Egypt and, in the process, allowed power to pass to Islam's greatest general, Saladin. Amaury died of typhus at thirty-nine, leaving his fourteen-year-old son as Baudouin IV. The young king, according to Guillaume de Tyr, was charming and remarkably talented, handsome, lively, open, agile in physical exercise, and a perfect horseman. He had an excellent memory, never forgetting a slight or a favor. He was also a leper.

As his body wasted away, Baudouin led his armies in stunning feats of arms. Near Ramallah, the seventeen-year-old leper took 300 knights on a wild charge that routed Saladin and thousands of Turks, Kurds, Arabs, and Sudanese. The Moslems fled to Egypt, tossing away baggage, helmets, and weapons as they galloped away. Baudouin consolidated the kingdom; but, with no heir, he left the succession in shambles.

The crown went to the vacillating commoner who married Baudouin's sister Sibylle, Guy de Lusignan. As Saladin amassed his strength, Guy allied himself with the greediest and cruelest of noblemen against the advice of his last few capable leaders. The end was swift.

Despite warnings, Guy led his entire army north to Tiberias. Their water ran out. Saladin, camped between the Christians and the water of Lake Tiberias, exulted, "Allah has delivered us." When Guy's army stopped to rest, collapsing under their armor in the baking heat, Saladin attacked. He set an arc of fire to the prairie, trapping the crusaders inside. Nearly all perished, burned alive or cut down by Moslem weapons.

The survivors, Guy included, reached Jerusalem. But soon Saladin was at the walls. He allowed the Christians safe passage to Tyre. With thunderous cries of *"Allahu Akbar"* (God is great), Saladin entered Jerusalem in 1187. The crusaders' kingdom of Jerusalem was reduced to a few coastal towns and scattered fortresses like the impregnable Krak des Chevaliers in Syria.

AS CHRISTIANS struggled to hold onto the Holy Land, the kings of France and England fought over real estate at home. Philippe Auguste, a Capet, ruled in Paris, using all the stealth, treachery, and artillery he could muster. What he could not win in battle, he won by playing off one English Plantagenet prince against another. In 1189, he broke Henry II by spurring the English king's sons against him. The English crown went to Richard I.

Richard Coeur-de-Lion, the Lion-Hearted, was nearly as French as Philippe Auguste. He was born in France, he spoke French, and he spent less than a year of his life in England. His main contact with the English nobility was to raise taxes for his constant campaigns and occasional ransoms.

Shortly after Richard was crowned, he and the French king, then allies, set off together on the Third Crusade. By the time they reached Acre, they were at each other's throats. Richard, insulted in Cyprus, had stopped to take over the island.

Their armies recaptured Acre, and Philippe Auguste went home. Richard stayed long enough to cover himself in glory. He stood fast against Saladin, raised the crusaders' morale, and then he also headed back to his kingdom. But the trip took longer than he planned.

Richard's lion heart was matched by a rhinoceros temper. When aroused, he trampled headlong over diplomatic niceties. After the crusaders took Acre, the duke of Austria flew his flag from the ramparts alongside the English and French banners. Richard snatched it down and flung it in the moat. Dukes' flags, he snarled, do not stand with kings'. The incident might have been forgotten had Richard not passed through Austria in a flimsy disguise.

The duke threw Richard in prison, and Philippe Auguste urged him to lose the key. In his colleague's absence, the French monarch seized chunks of Richard's land. That sat badly with the aristocracy and the pope, who recalled that crusaders' property was sacrosanct.

Richard bought his freedom. With his brother John he fought a five-year war with France in Normandy, beating the Capet king back to where he had started twenty years earlier. But Richard was pierced by an arrow near Limoges, and John inherited the throne. Philippe Auguste won back Normandy. John invaded France and spent so much money on a fruitless campaign that the English nobility rebelled. In 1215 John signed the Magna Carta, limiting the rights of kings in England.

LATER CRUSADES stirred political forces but did little to strengthen Western presence. From 1239, a scrap of verse by the knight-poet Philippe de Nanteuil recalls a campaign against Egypt:

> *Ah! France, douce contrée,*
> *Maudite soit la journée*
> *Où tant de vaillants chevaliers*
> *Sont devenus prisonniers!*

(France, sweet country, damned be the day when so many valiant knights became prisoners.)

An Egyptian sultan gave Jerusalem back to the Christians in 1240, in a political deal, but Turks grabbed it again four years later.

Then Saint Louis appeared. A Capet, king of France since 1226, Louis IX set off on a crusade from the French port of Aiguesmortes he built for the occasion. It was strictly a French operation: he took along his three brothers, and shiploads of dukes, counts, and barons. His goal was to capture the heart of Islamic power, and he sailed for Egypt.

Saint Louis fought his way up the Nile, but typhus and dysentery crippled his army. Captured, then ransomed, he led his forces to Acre. Jerusalem was too well defended, but the French legions pacified the Syrian hinterlands. Louis went home after four years, leaving the crusaders united, with their rear guards safe. But as soon as he left the Franks' colony began to collapse.

Crusaders fought a street war among themselves in Saint-Jean d'Acre for possession of a church between the Venetian and Genoese sectors. Armed quarrels spread to other towns. Meanwhile, the crusaders botched their foreign policy.

Mongol hordes from the Asian steppes had seized most of Syria. With a thin claim to Christianity and a respect for European swords, they sought an alliance against the Moslems. The crusaders, frightened at the idea of Mongol neighbors, instead banded with the defenders of Islam.

Mamelukes, Turkish slaves from the Caucasus who rose to power, reigned in Egypt. With the crusaders' help, they routed the Mongols; then they turned on the Franks. In lightning succession, Mameluke sultans attacked the last colonies. Prince Edward of England negotiated an eleven-year reprieve for Saint-Jean d'Acre, but crusaders used the time to carry on internal quarrels. Pisans and Genoese fought naval battles in the port.

In February 1289, 40,000 horsemen and 100,000 foot soldiers besieged Tripoli. A month later, Venetians and Genoese, whose conflicts had sapped the city's strength, slipped off with their riches at night in ships, leaving the French alone. Sultan Qalaoun stormed the city, slaughtering most of the men and taking women and children as slaves.

In Saint-Jean d'Acre, an Italian people's crusade sought revenge. Like Pierre the Hermit's army, it was formed of peasants, not soldiers. Zealots fell upon Moslem farmers and merchants, in the fields and markets, slitting throats with abandon. That was all the Mamelukes needed.

Sultan el-Ashraf Khalil sent 60,000 horsemen, 160,000 foot soldiers, and batteries of catapults to attack the city. Acre's population totaled 35,000, counting crusaders, Creoles, pilgrims, and Italian sailors on shore leave. Of that, 14,000 were foot soldiers and 800 were horsemen.

Saint-Jean d'Acre fell after a furious fight. A few Christians escaped by boat, but most were killed. The fortress-convent of the Knights of the Temple held for a month and a half. Finally, the sultan offered safe passage for the few defenders left inside. They came out, and he beheaded them.

Tyre, Sidon, and Tortose were evacuated without a fight. The Templars held out on the island of Rouad, facing Tortose, until 1303. Only in 1914 did the Franks—French forces—again reenter Syria. From the island of Rouad.

HISTORIANS, CHURCHMEN, and romanticists draw conflicting conclusions from the First Crusade and the five others that followed.

Paulin Paris notes how the Orient influenced Europe. Crusaders' chronicles were the first writings in French, which Dante had dismissed as "that language of wet nurses." Paris wrote, "People would have long seen Latin as the only written language had the Crusades not . . . made them feel the need to correspond with relatives and friends without having to call on an intervening cleric." From private letters later developed the great novels about the Round Table and Merlin, Arthur, Lancelot.

Contact with the East broadened the European medieval outlook. Tapestries, silks, and brass fittings found their way to dingy castles in Normandy. More than one crusader remembered Saladin's rosewater sherbets from the snows of Mount Hermon.

But Marshall Baldwin emphasizes Western impact on the Levant. "When their goal had been achieved some warriors elected to remain in the east, and they and their successors faced the manifold tasks of a 'colonial' administration. Vastly inferior in numbers to their heterogeneous native population, they created in an eastern environment a civilization which was fundamentally western."

Ships linked the Holy Land to Europe, and Italian merchants set up commerce.

André Maurois notes, ". . . the French tongue and civilization in the Near East acquired a privileged position."

Sir Stephen Runciman, the English authority, observes:

> The determination of the Westerner to conquer and colonize the lands of Byzantium was disastrous for the interests of *Outremer*. It was more disastrous still for his European civilization. Constantinople was still the center of the civilized Christian world. . . . Knights could not believe that so superb a city could exist on earth; it was of all cities the sovereign. . . . Greed and clumsiness led [the men of the Fourth Crusade] to indulge in irreparable damage.

Runciman argues that the crusaders broke Christian defenses and allowed the infidel to penetrate the Balkans. He concludes his three-volume work:

> To the Crusaders themselves their failures were inexplicable. They were fighting for the cause of the Almighty; and if faith

and logic were correct, that cause should have triumphed. In the first flush of success they entitled their chronicles the *Geste Dei per Francos,* God's work done by the hand of the Franks.

It was less surprising that the enterprise collapsed, he wrote, than that it lasted 200 years.

> In the long sequence of interaction and fusion between Orient and Occident out of which our civilization has grown, the Crusades were a tragic and destructive episode. . . . The historian . . . must find his admiration overcast by sorrow at the witness that it bears to the limitations of human nature. There was so much courage and so little honor, so much devotion and so little understanding. High ideals were besmirched by cruelty and greed, enterprise and endurance by a blind and narrow self-righteousness; and the Holy War itself was nothing more than a long act of intolerance in the name of God, which is a sin against the Holy Ghost.

René Grousset, the French arbiter of the period, drew similar conclusions. But he cuts straight to the center with an essential point: the crusaders established the first French colony abroad, and they were the early epitome of a mission to civilize.

FOR THE NEXT CENTURY, France was in conflict—against the English, the Spanish, the Flemish, the Italians, and among its own provinces. Philippe VI established the House of Valois in 1328. French ships took the Canary Islands in 1402. Black Plague was followed by a wave of anti-Semitism.

In 1415, France floundered in the hands of half-mad Charles VI and nobles warring to rule in his name. Henry V of England invaded Normandy with a thin claim to the throne. His small army killed ten thousand Frenchmen at Agincourt, one of the bloodiest of medieval battles. Treachery and assassinations among the French helped consolidate his position. Henry V died in 1422, and so did Charles VI. France had two kings: Henry VI, only ten months old and worse, not French, and the Dauphin, Charles VII of Bourges, who could not wrest Paris from the English regent, the Duke of Bedford.

Then a seventeen-year-old shepherd girl from Lorraine showed up at Chinon and asked to see the Dauphin. Her name was Jeanne d'Arc, and she heard voices. She amazed Charles by picking him out of a cluster of lords. He gave her some troops. She captured Orléans and then rallied Charles' followers under a cross and the *fleur-de-lis*. Bedford called her a witch—on his way out. Charles VII secured the throne. But rivals captured Joan at Compiègne. The savior of France was sold to the English who, after a decent interval, burned her at the stake in 1431.

A lot of Frenchmen since have regarded Jeanne d'Arc as proof that patriotism, faith and genius can produce a miracle whenever France needs one. Charles VII came around to that view fifteen years after her death. At the time, he did nothing to save her.

Crippled by the One Hundred Years' War, France floundered on. And in 1515, François I shifted the nation into another age.

France had taken its hexagonal shape, with a largely homogeneous people who saw common political and economic interests. And France was seen that way from the outside.

"The horizons are broadened," writes Jean Favier, concluding an exhaustive study of the period. "The history of France is from now on linked with a world that encompasses as much the Eastern Mediterranean as England and Scotland, where vital parts are played in the Germanic countries and Italy, where borders are before Granada and Budapest."

Favier adds, "But the French have missed the opening that others find toward Africa, toward the Atlantic. They have sought too late the silk road, and they have also missed the road to gold."

France, soon enough, would find its own roads.

CHAPTER SEVEN

Building an Empire

FRANÇOIS I'S FAVORITE passions, of many, were power and glory. His neighbors included Henry VIII of England and Charles V, a slack-jawed little monarch with brilliant eyes who ruled Austria, Spain, the Netherlands, Naples, and enclaves in between. France was the strongest nation in Europe but not the richest. It could use all the power and glory its king could muster.

Competition was bitter for Flanders. England wanted it as a commercial foothold on the continent; France needed a buffer to protect its northeastern flank. But Austria held Flanders tightly as a bargaining chip. Italy had long attracted French kings, but the new wealth and beauty of the Renaissance fired lust across Europe. Italian city-states, accustomed to invasions, made the best of them. They remained free by pitting one foreign power against the others. Sovereigns perched precariously atop shifting alliances.

In this climate, one of the first of many diplomats and travel writers tried his hand at describing the French character. He was Niccolò Machiavelli:

> These French are perfectly insupportable: always worried, preoccupied only with the moment, forgetful of others' good deeds as well as outrages, little concerned with their blood but terribly avid for money. . . . Since the time of Caesar, the French have hardly evolved: changeable and lightweight, weak in adversity, insolent in good fortune; you cannot count on them. They

keep their promises poorly and their own interests always predominate.[1]

In his *Rapport sur les Choses de France,* Machiavelli declares the French to be thieves. He wrote:

> They are by nature partial to the belongings of others. A Frenchman is capable of stealing coolly whether to give himself the stolen object, or to squander it, or to present it to the one from whom he stole it. As opposed to the Spanish, you will never again see what the French have stolen from you.

France was difficult to beat, Machiavelli wrote. England was but a shadow of its former self, out of practice at warfare. Spain could not muster the strength to cross the Pyrenees, nor could any Italian state attack across the Alps. Flanders depended economically on France, and Switzerland could manage only border raids. The counterweight, he concluded, was that the French were lousy soldiers:

> They are by nature more impetuous than resistant or skillful; and, if they encounter an enemy who can withstand the fury of the first shock, they lose their bite and lose heart, so much so that they are then more cowardly than women. They suffer so badly from fatigue and lack of comfort that, in the long run, discipline breaks down and it is easy, if one surprises them in this disorder, to triumph over them.

But François I was an imposing adversary, adept at the hard pragmatism Machiavelli later prescribed in *The Prince.* He was six-foot-six at a time when five-foot-five was not short. He stood as solidly as Henry VIII, with an intense stare and a powerful sword arm. He loved art, learning, and copulation. Louis XII had tried devious means to will his throne to someone other than his son-in-law and cousin once removed. But, just before dying, he threw up his hands, saying, "We busy ourselves in vain; that large young man will ruin everything."

Once crowned, François I hired 26,000 mercenaries and rushed off to conquer Milan. He also made permanent peace with the Swiss,

bringing the Swiss Guard into the French court and securing rights
to recruit soldiers in Switzerland. In Italy, he struck a deal with Pope
Leo X over naming bishops and taxing the French church. As a
result, France was able to resist the Reformation. André Maurois
observed, "Henry VIII broke with Rome in order to despoil the
monasteries; François I had despoiled them by previous agreements
with Rome."

François I wanted most the title of king of the Romans, emperor
of Christian Europe. By custom, seven archbishops and noblemen
elected the emperor. They were open to bidding. And Charles V
also wanted the job.

The Austrian monarch was the grandson of Ferdinand of Aragon
and Isabella of Castile, who had outfitted Columbus. He was backed
by the rich mine owners and merchants of southern Germany.
Ruling the Germanic empire, with his other domains, Charles V
would encircle France. If he lost the crown to François I, his vast
territories would be split in two. The heat was on.

Henry VIII parleyed with François I at Calais under tents stitched
in gold thread, but decided against backing the French king. English
merchants sold wool; Flemish weavers made cloth; and Charles V
was master of Flanders. Thus, England toppled the careful balance
of power in Europe.

With all Europe lined up against him, François I attacked, marching east against Charles's forces. He was beaten and captured but,
in fine French style, emerged triumphant. "All is lost, save honor,"
he wrote to his mother. Schoolchildren today study his verse: "The
body conquered, the heart remains the victor."

France remained united, and Charles V did not know what to do
with his prisoner. If François I died, a new king would come
looking for revenge. The Austrian could not pay off allies with
chunks of France, or keep any himself, without his prisoner's approval. Finally, François I agreed to give up Burgundy as ransom.
At home, he repudiated the deal and launched a world war.

The king found a new ally: the Turks. Only two centuries had
passed since Saint Louis had crusaded against Moslem unbelievers.
But it was no time for encumbering ideology; France was in peril.
François I relied on Protestants and Moslems to fight Catholic
Austria abroad while he put to death heretics at home. Such contra-

dictions worked out smoothly in France over the next centuries. Church and state remained close; principle and practice did not.

The war was punctuated by separate peaces and split alliances. By the time François I died in 1547, France was fighting not only in the Old World but also in new ones halfway around what only recently had been determined to be a globe.

Occupied close to home, François I had let upstart adventurers raise flags across the oceans in the names of Spain and Portugal. Iberians had the luxury of looking for easy ways to China and India. Portugal, with a million inhabitants, sent out the first probing voyages around Africa. The New World was beginning to speak the language of the ten million Spanish. France, the most powerful single nation of the age, with twenty-five million inhabitants, was out of the game.

It was a double bind. France could not afford to explore and colonize because wars and old war debts ate up most of its revenue. Yet weaker nations suddenly found themselves rich from transoceanic plunder.

Spain's galleons carried gold and silver. France brought back codfish, the catch of a few adventuresome Bretons and Normans off the Newfoundland Banks. Freebooting pirates carried French colors, but they did not always pay their taxes.

French intellectuals, unimpressed with new worlds, put little pressure on the king. They were building glory at home with such seats of excellence as the Collège de France. But François I was losing out on the title to much of the world, and he was not happy. After the Vatican's Treaty of Tordesillas divided all but the Old World between Spain and Portugal, he grumbled, "Show me the Act by which Adam made his legacy of the earth."

It must be noted, in the interest of sound journalism, that François I possibly said nothing of the sort. In fact, Louis XIV probably never said, "L'Etat, c'est moi." History has a way of placing well-turned phrases in mouths long silenced. More, colonial history was recorded largely by impassioned men, rich in ink and imagination, whose purposes were other than to reflect reality faithfully. A French seaman named Jean Cousin, off course from Africa, may have discovered America four years before Columbus, as some will swear. But historians, French and otherwise, have blown off a good deal of mist. Some sources are cited in text and notes, but readers are directed to the bibliography.

FRANCIS PARKMAN, a precise Bostonian of the last century, argues that France's early achievements in the Americas are little appreciated:

> While the Spaniard roamed sea and land, burning for achievement, red-hot with bigotry and avarice, and while England, with soberer steps and a less dazzling result, followed in the path of discovery and gold-hunting, it was from France that those barbarous shores first learned to serve the ends of peaceful commercial industry.

Breton and Basque fishermen steadily worked the cod banks off Newfoundland, perhaps from as early as the 1490s, and Norman explorers probed the St. Lawrence gulf in 1506, 1508, and 1518.

The king's character pushed France onward, Parkman concludes:

> Chivalry and honor were always on his lips; but Francis I, a forsworn gentleman, a despotic king, vainglorious, selfish, sunk in debaucheries, was but the type of an era which retained the forms of the Middle Ages without its soul, and added to a still prevailing barbarism the pestilential vices which hung fog-like around the dawn of civilization. Yet he esteemed arts and letters, and, still more, coveted the *éclat* which they could give. The light which was beginning to pierce the feudal darkness gathered its rays around his throne. . . . Among artists, philosophers, and men of letters enrolled in his service stands the humbler name of a Florentine navigator, John Verrazano.

France sent Verrazano west toward China in 1523, but America stood in his way. He poked around, left his name on the Narrows at New York, sailed north, and then came home to Dieppe.

Eleven years later, François I tried again with Jacques Cartier, from the ancient walled port of St.-Malo, bastion of pirates and traders who, for centuries to come, ranged the seas for France. Cartier explored the mouth of the St. Lawrence in 1534 and brought back two Indians. A year later, with three ships, he returned to sail up the St. Lawrence to China. Indians warned him that the god Coudouagny would visit freezing agony upon the French if they persisted upriver. Coudouagny, Cartier replied, had obviously not heard of Christ.

The explorers climbed an imposing hill named Mont Royal (as in Montreal), and saw that a great deal of narrow river and forest lay between them and Cathay. They turned back, but the river had frozen. Trapped in frail wooden ships, they relied on friendly Indians to deliver food. Friendship dwindled, along with the food stores, and scurvy killed twenty-five men. Miserable with cold and disease, the Frenchmen kept the Indians away for fear they might seize the advantage and attack.

Spring came, and Cartier took home the tattered remnants of his party. Bereft of other treasures, he kidnapped the Indian chief, Donnacona, and his chieftains, to testify to François I about riches yet undiscovered. The Indians died soon after reaching France.

Cartier found another adventurer smitten with the idea of Canada, a Picardy nobleman named Jean-François de la Roque, sieur de Roberval, with enough royal cash to outfit five ships. He set off again in 1541, and Roberval was to follow. The Indians were not pleased to see him without Donnacona. Cartier built a fort in which to sit out the winter. But then, mysteriously, he abandoned New France. Roberval, finally arriving, stopped Cartier on the way out. Against orders, Cartier sneaked away to France; Roberval soon followed.

Cartier's seven-year struggle in Canada left only a few flagstaffs and *fleur-de-lis*. And he added to the French language the expression, "False as the diamonds of Canada."

Samuel de Champlain and France's great conquering voyages were still years away.

HENRI II TOOK power in 1547 and shifted French attention back to the neighborhood. His defense strategy served for four centuries: keep Germany as divided and troubled as possible. France's interests lay along the Rhine; Italy was a luxury to be left alone. The Treaty of Cateau-Cambrésis, a reshuffling among sovereigns in 1559, shaped modern France. By renouncing designs on

Italy, the French secured Metz, Verdun, and Toul to the east and Calais to the west. France, more defensible, was knit more tightly together. And the French were happy. They did not necessarily love a king for winning foreign ground; but they were bitter about anyone who lost a square centimeter of French soil.

Henri II seemed about to be a great king, if a little bloodthirsty over heretics. But he insisted on jousting in a tournament with the son of the captain of his guard. A spear in the eye left France in the hands of his widow, Catherine de Médicis. For the next thirty years, while overseas empires were taking shape, France was ruled by three mediocre kings: a François, a Charles, and an Henri.

Under Henri III, in 1582, Norman merchants occupied the island of St.-Louis in Senegal. But it was only later that St.-Louis became the capital of vast African holdings. France had dealt in Africa as early as the 1300s when Normans from Dieppe set up three trading posts on the Guinea coast. Ships from Dieppe, funded by merchants but protected by the crown, were searching for a western route to the Indies a few years before Columbus. Under François I and afterward, however, the early momentum stalled.

The French were bled by wars of religion, at home and with neighbors, while the court was preoccupied with intrigue and financial chaos. The aristocracy rankled under the informal regency of Catherine, described by one as "that fat daughter of Florentine peddlers."

Frenchmen began shifting allegiance to an Henri from the house of Guise, which worried the Valois king, Henri III. Henri de Guise appeared at the castle of Blois, invited by the king for a council, and was chopped to bits by halberds. Catherine, appalled, knew grief would follow. It did. Soon afterward, a Dominican monk assassinated the king with a dagger, thus extinguishing the House of Valois.

That was in 1589. The France that François I had begun to shape fell again into capable hands.

As Henri III lay dying, he clutched a former enemy, Henri de Navarre, a relative only in the twenty-second degree. "I die happy at seeing you by my side," Henri III told him. "The crown is yours. . . . I order all officers to recognize you as their king after me."

Henri IV took the job. He was a Bourbon and a descendant of

Saint Louis. But he was also a Protestant in a country that bled half to death fighting to preserve Roman Catholicism.

The new king steered a careful course. At first, he rallied the French, saying, "We are born not only for ourselves, but above all to serve the country. Those who honestly follow their conscience are of my religion, and as for me, I belong to the faith of all those who are gallant and good."

He held out against the church. He would search his conscience, he said, but would anyone respect him for converting with a dagger at his throat? Those unwilling to wait could forsake him, he added. "Among the Catholics, I shall have with me those who love France and honor."

But the nobility of Paris hung back, refusing to follow the king unless he converted. Paris, in the 1590s, was already large and lovely, the heart of France. And completely Catholic. Elsewhere, dissension grew, and the council of nobles, the States General, was summoned to Paris.

Finally, Henri IV dressed in white and kneeled in Notre-Dame to embrace the religion he had renounced years before. "Paris," he said, "is worth a mass."

He put together a tense armistice, codifying tolerance under the 1598 Edict of Nantes. Then he threw himself into restoring French grandeur. He told the Rouen notables:

> You know to your cost, as do I to mine, that when God called me to the crown, I found France not only half ruined, but almost entirely lost to the French. . . . Through my care and toil I have saved the heritage; I shall now save it from ruin.

Parkman described his impact:

> To few has human liberty owed so deep a gratitude or so deep a grudge. He cared little for creeds or dogmas. Impressible, quick in sympathy, his grim lip lighted often with a smile, and his war-worn cheek was no stranger to a tear. He forgave his enemies and forgot his friends. Many loved him; none but fools trusted him. Mingled of mortal good and ill, frailty and force, of all the

kings who for two centuries and more sat on the throne of France
Henry IV alone was a man.

The king brought in an old friend, Maximilien de Béthune, later
the duc de Sully, who rebuilt France's crippled economy. Par-
simonious, hard-nosed, and a lunatic for work, Sully rose at 4 A.M.
to pore over intelligence reports in his office decorated with portraits of John Calvin and Martin Luther. He hunted down corrupt
tax collectors and slashed budgets. Steadily, he built up a reserve to
fund his other great love, beside penny-pinching: artillery. French
ramparts and marketplaces bristled with cannons under his command.

"Here was Calvin turned artilleryman and financier," Maurois
observed. Henri IV, more progressive, stopped him from setting up
an inspectorate of morals in each bailiwick to poke into families'
habits. But Sully blocked the king's hopes of reviving the French
manufacturing industry which, at the beginning of the seventeenth
century, was growing much faster than England's. He preferred
agriculture.

Neither the king nor Sully thought much of the New World.

"Tilling the soil and keeping flocks—these are France's riches, the
real mines and treasures of Peru," said the finance minister. He
resurfaced roads, lining them with elms, and built bridges. Transport
and irrigation canals were laid out across France. Forests and fields
were marked out; feudal lords were ordered to eliminate wolves and
wildcats. Breeding studs produced fine herds. Paris bloomed with
such triumphs as the Place des Vosges, admired across Europe.

Quebec was founded in 1608, but Sully was more interested in
the Pont Neuf over the Seine, inaugurated the same year. He counseled the king: "Things which remain separated from our body by
foreign lands or seas will be ours only at great expense and to little
purpose."

If Henri IV did not aggressively export France, he built French
civilization into an exportable commodity. In his name, sea captains,
merchants, and adventurers roamed the new worlds.

Champlain and Pontgrave charted the mouth of the St. Lawrence
up to the Great Lakes, founding Acadia and a handful of settlements.

To back it up, Henri IV claimed for France all American territory north of the fortieth parallel.

A French expedition settled Madagascar in 1601; three years later, La Ravardière claimed for the king Guyane—French Guiana—on the South American coast. In 1604, a company was formed to push trade with India.

Whatever else Henri IV might have done remains speculation. In 1610, a man named Ravaillac leaped onto the running board of the king's carriage and stabbed a knife through the window. Henri IV died instantly, his aorta severed.

Of all the French kings between 1515 and the French Revolution, only Henri IV reaches historian Jean Meyer's category of "good or very good"; François I and Louis XIV made it to "rather good."

Henri IV awakened a feeling of patriotism and a sense of unity that would never again leave France. During his reign, literature flourished, enriching the language. Thought and philosophy expanded, in French and throughout Europe. Henri IV had implanted firmly a Renaissance in which the mind and nature, rather than the Bible, would define the world.

Maurois concludes, "Henri IV remains, together with Charlemagne, Jeanne d'Arc and Saint Louis, one of France's heroes. He typifies not France's mystical aspect, but its aspects of courage, good sense and gaiety."

LOUIS XIII was king at nine, under the regency of his haughty Italian mother, Marie de Médicis. She, in turn, was dominated by a swarthy and mysterious Florentine, Leonora Galigai. And Galigai was married to a foppish schemer named Concini. They enlisted support from the clergy through a young bishop with an arched nose, a goatee, and a long cavalry moustache over thin lips: Richelieu. The young king, unsociable, a daydreamer, was left to his tutors.

One morning Louis XIII, at sixteen, announced that he was king. Concini had been put to death overnight on secret orders to the guard; Galigai was burned as a witch. Marie de Médicis was exiled to Blois. And the ambitious, proud prelate, Richelieu, went back to his diocese.

Before long, however, Louis XIII began to make use of Richelieu's skill at oratory, administration, and punishment. In 1624, already a cardinal, Richelieu was named chief minister. He grumbled that the French were hard to govern, with "more heart than head." He frequently bemoaned "the apathy of France," but he marveled at its recuperative powers. A writer and thinker, he founded the Académie Française and gave lasting form to French ideas of logic and tradition.

Richelieu burned to rebuild a strong army and a navy, but finances were short. Spain, flush with Inca and Aztec booty, was developing the strongest infantry in Europe. In 1636, Spanish armies penetrated deep into France. The king and cardinal appeared in the streets of Paris, and the French rallied. Money and men were thrown into the field. Spain retreated, and Richelieu was awash in glory.

Louis XIII's philosophy was not far from Henri IV's: what mattered was France's greatness within safe borders. Richelieu sought to trim "the great tree of Austria," not to build an empire but rather to keep a rival power from gaining enough strength to threaten France.

Like most French leaders, the king worried about sending abroad too many strong arms and agile minds needed at home. But the ambitious cardinal was not about to let France pass up wealth and glory.

Richelieu set up a system of state colonization through privileged companies. The Compagnie des Indes later built France's first colonies in India; the Compagnie des 100 Associés developed trade with Canada. Under the cardinal's aegis, merchants settled Martinique and Guadeloupe, St. Kitts, Grenada, the Grenadines, St. Lucia, and a string of smaller islands. He sent pioneers to Réunion, then l'Ile de Bourbon, and reinforced colonies in Madagascar and Guiana.

These early colonies were mostly collecting points for exotic riches: beaver pelts, cloves and cinnamon, silks and cottons. Some were plantations for sugar, tobacco, and coffee. But hard behind the traders and farmers, priests carried the word to whatever heathens they found. Montreal, founded in 1642, was a missionaries' outpost.

Moral judgments on these first missions to civilize reached absurd

extremes. In the 1940s, the Académie Française lauded Marius Leblond for a whole shelf of histories of the period. Some excerpts:

> Our action was dominated by the concern for evangelism
> infinitely more than commerce. . . . Our worthiness and initiative
> flourished in the Pacific Ocean which in the 18th Century was
> made *a French sea*. . . . Heroism is the dominant character of our
> action in the New World.

Writing on the Caribbean, Leblond notes that native Arawaks and
Caribs sometimes resisted French settlement:

> The indigenous problem posed itself immediately with as
> much instability and cruel drama as in Canada: our deep Christian
> genius was not the only quality summoned up against it; an
> incredible power of spirit, of invention, of flexibility and imita-
> tion pushed to the level of art was quickly demonstrated in our
> brand new mission of Colonization. . . . France, in its ensemble,
> tried to be soft with the Caraibes.

Except, of course, for the settlers who massacred Indians by the
thousands. Leblond skips over the decimation of the natives, amply
documented elsewhere. He mentions slavery as an economic fact of
life after carefully asserting that France did not start it. And piracy,
by his accounts, was a noble effort to adjust a balance of trade
skewed against France.

Like many, Leblond is fascinated by the buccaneers, *les boucaniers,* named for the spits on which they smoked their meat. "Since
Gaul the French have been great lords of the hunt and bleeders of
wild boar," he writes of the freebooters' main off-duty passion.
He describes their filthy, blood-caked tight breeches, pigskin shoes,
and pointed hats and adds, "The fantastic aspect is completed by
an arsenal of knives, bayonets, a long rifle made in Dieppe or
Nantes."

Their main base was Haiti, ". . . a very Great Island bristling with
rough and wild beauty, with ravines and powdery savannahs
. . . which we denuded before rearming with rich plantations of

coffee, sugar cane, and tobacco. We had to throw in millions of blacks with filed teeth, ferocious eyes, and calloused hands who quickly became one with the land, as sun-varnished, hard, and fecund as they were."

RICHELIEU DIED in 1642, Louis XIII a year later. Again, France was left with a child king. Louis XIV was an infant.

Queen Anne of Austria, a Spaniard of flaring temper, was regent. She convinced the Parlement of nobles to rescind Louis XIII's will, which subjected her to a council handpicked by Richelieu. Then she surprised everyone by naming as chief minister one of the dead cardinal's close cronies, an Italian named Giulio Mazarini, or Mazarin. He pursued Richelieu's colonial policy, setting up a company to trade with China and another to dig deeper into Cayenne, the capital of Guiana. But domestic affairs dominated the regency period.

Frenchmen were not thrilled at being governed by two foreigners. Finances were in shambles. The Parlement, an assembly of hereditary magistrates, wanted more power. Rumblings among nobles and common folk crystallized into the Fronde. A *fronde* is a sling for heaving rocks, David-style. And occasional whizzing projectiles kept Mazarin on his toes. The Fronde, a series of upheavals, was a dress rehearsal of the French Revolution. Most of the royal family fled Paris. Insurgents stormed the palace and demanded that the regent show them the king in his bed so they could be sure he had not sneaked away. Disorganized, half-hearted and sometimes cowardly, the Fronde never rose to revolution. After some compromise, tension subsided. By 1652, when young Louis XIV rode ceremoniously through Paris, the Fronde was quelled. But the prince never forgot the humiliation and fear.

Mazarin ran the government until 2:30 A.M. on March 8, 1661. Gravely ill, the cardinal was going over France's books with a favorite assistant, Jean-Baptiste Colbert. Then he died.

Louis XIV's nurse broke the news to him in the morning, and the king shut himself in his study to meditate for two hours. He never revealed what went through his head. But he emerged to begin a strictly personal rule. He was the Sun King. And the indefatigable Colbert, as everything but war minister and secretary of state, directed his rays.

VOLTAIRE CONCLUDED that for anyone of taste and reflection, world history produced only four centuries of note: those of Pericles, Augustus, the Médicis, and Louis XIV. "Europe has owed her manners and her feeling for social life to the court of Louis XIV," he wrote. True, novice footmen at Versailles knew twenty-seven ways to fold a table napkin, and guests at better French tables learned to turn their heads delicately when spitting, but Louis XIV ate with his fingers until he died in 1715, at which time Voltaire was barely twenty-one years old.

The king's reviews were mixed.

Like François I and Henri IV, Louis XIV devoted himself to the glory of France. He fashioned the pursuit of glory into such a high art form that the French of today still bask in his radiance. He also, as historian W. H. Lewis notes, "rode roughshod over Europe, sowing that crop of hatred which was to bring him fifty years later to the very edge of complete disaster." In the end, he survived by flanking his polished haughtiness with the finest military hardware and architecture of the age.

A year after taking personal charge, he set the tone. The French ambassador to Rome, the duc de Créqui, so antagonized the city with swaggering insolence that on August 20 the Corsican Guard fired on his coach. Louis received the news at dinner. He stalked from the table and ordered an assault on Italy. Later the king relented, on a few conditions: that the Vatican surrender Avignon to France, that the pope raise a pyramid in Rome bearing details of the crime and its expiation, and that the pope's nephew, Cardinal Chigi, come to Paris to read a full apology to the entire court. Finally, the pope disbanded the Corsican Guard. (A century later, Louis XV went his great-grandfather one better and took over Corsica.)

Louis XIV fashioned Versailles with such grandeur that every self-respecting monarch from Peter the Great to Roi Christophe of Haiti tried to copy it. Not the least of his motives was to leave downtown Paris, to make sure no more importuning masses barged in on royalty. He turned down plans by his genius military architect,

Vauban, to fortify Paris with concentric ramparts. Paris, he decreed, should be defended at France's borders. Instead, he developed the intelligence network inherited from Richelieu, planting secret agents, devising codes, and laying the groundwork for three centuries of French dirty tricks abroad.

And to underwrite the costs of glory and arrogance, Colbert built France's first overseas empire. His idea was simple: the colonies were to make money.

Colbert had the same thick wavy hair as Louis XIV, with similar puffy cheeks and hungry eyes. But he was a technocrat, a financial wizard and master organizer. He gathered together the ragtag bits of private enterprise around the globe under a single ministry at Versailles. He built ships to carry goods and fight off rivals.

In 1664, he commissioned the Compagnie des Indes occidentales and the Compagnie des Indes orientales. The first was to settle both Americas and the Caribbean; the second, to colonize Madagascar and dominate trade with China. He backed the first French establishment in India, at Surat, in 1668. Two years later, he created the Compagnie du Levant to import silk and cotton from Asia Minor. He revived Richelieu's efforts in the Indian Ocean, sending colonizers to Réunion.

Colbert encouraged adventuresome Frenchmen to poke around unmapped territory, especially that coveted by Britain. His governor in Haiti, Bertrand d'Ogeron, encouraged the *boucaniers,* "the brothers of the coast." The king commissioned some freebooters who roamed far to the south. Largely from St.-Malo, they were called *Malouins* (the French name for the Falkland Islands is still *les Malouines,* after its discoverers). Leblond, yet again, sings their praises:

> Les Malouins! Honor of French commerce. . . . Their Duguay-Trouin took Rio de Janeiro in one of the most sumptuous exploits of naval history and imposed a ransom . . . which helped save the Great King from bankruptcy and disaster . . . the ladies of Peru danced for them in golden capes and skirts embroidered in triple rows of lace; the Spaniards who they drubbed so many times revered them. . . . We find in them the most complete and creative genius, honored in all the Empire.

Colbert's crown company brought new life to Martinique and Guadeloupe, each settled in 1635 by Norman explorers who found it hard to keep the colonies afloat without help from Paris.

A globe-girdling empire was no mean feat, given the rigors of seventeenth-century sea travel. Fortunes were consumed by it and a fair number of voyagers never reached their destinations. An account from 1644 describes an effort to sail the queen of England across the Channel. After a nine-day gale, she was landed in Holland. During the voyage, she "suffered the terrors of almost certain death, tied down in a little bed, with her ladies tied down around her in theirs."

Robert Challes, quartermaster and "king's writer" aboard *L'E-cueil,* bound for the Far East in 1690, left an account of life at sea. The 500-ton ship, with 350 men and thirty-eight guns, was "a farmyard," the bullocks, ducks, and pigs making it all but impossible to walk on the deck. Wine was so short he had to sneak on deck at night to supplement his ration. The six-ship convoy sailed past the Cape of Good Hope. France was at war with Holland, and *L'Ecueil* ran up Dutch colors when an enemy fleet passed.

But the ship attacked the Dutch vessel *Montfort* off Ceylon. Challes rages for two pages at the boatman who did not get him across in time to pick over the spoils. Then, in an abrupt fit of morality, he notes that the dignity of his position as king's writer places him above looting. The admiral shared the loot with him nonetheless, and he is pleased. He observes: "So I keep my reputation as a man who does not loot, while I in fact get a reasonable share of the booty."[2]

ENTHUSIASM FOR EMPIRE was hardly total. America, for example, was no great prize. Père Jacques Marquette and Louis Joliet pushed down the Mississippi as far as the Arkansas River, but hostile Indians blocked their way. They returned in triumph to Quebec—bells pealed the entire day—and then everyone forgot about the Mississippi. Then Cavelier de La Salle located a channel through the delta. He found a dry spot and claimed the place with all the pomp of the era.

A stone column was painted with the king's coat of arms. La Salle's exhausted company sang a "Te Deum" and "Domine Salvum fac Regem," shouted, *"Vive le Roi,"* and blasted muskets into the trees. La Salle read a wordy proclamation and raised a cross. Everyone sang "Vexilia regis" and a lead plaque detailing the proceedings was buried in the ground. Finally, more shouts of *"Vive le Roi!"*

Then La Salle returned to France for his fame and fortune. But Louis XIV was not impressed. He received the explorer but turned down his request to go back. Later, the king changed his mind. La Salle went back to start a colony.

La Salle assembled a dozen gentlemen, 100 soldiers, a handful of priests, artisans and laborers, enough stores to start a small city, a frigate and three other ships. He set sail for the Gulf of Mexico, missed the mouth of the Mississippi, and spent two years lost in Texas.

Disease, despair, and desertion reduced La Salle's company to thirty-six. He took sixteen of them north to try to find Illinois. A few finally made it, but not La Salle. One of his last remaining lieutenants killed him during a mutiny.

France's start in Louisiana presaged its on-and-off tenure there and its ignoble end. It was a decade before anyone came back to add substance to the lead plaque and the royal standard left to remind the Indians that they belonged to France. Louis XIV, with most of Europe to fight, had other priorities.

The king still had France to unite, culturally as well as politically. The French language was refined during the splendid century, but it spread only slowly. Racine traveled to the southern duchy of Uzès in 1650. By Lyon, he said, he was intelligible only to himself. "My misfortune grew at Valence. As fate would have it, I asked for a chamber pot and a small stove was placed under my bed. You can imagine the results of this damned adventure when a very sleepy fellow used the stove for his night's needs. But in this part of the country things are even worse. I swear that I am as much in need of an interpreter as a Muscovite in Paris."[3]

Colbert himself slowed colonization, except in Canada, for fear of depopulating the *métropole*. France had twenty-two million inhabitants at the start of Louis's reign; at the end, after seventy-two years of war and epidemics, the figure remained the same.[4] The crown awarded 2,000 *livres* (about $5,000 today) to any nobleman who produced more than ten children.

By the time Colbert died in 1683, however, the *fleur-de-lis* flapped in Canada, the Caribbean, Guiana, Senegal, the Indian Ocean, and in India itself. Foundations were laid for commerce and farming, mining, trapping, and fishing. And he had set in motion a permanent wave of Frenchmen anxious to shine their light abroad. In exchange, of course, for some modest return for their efforts.

CHAPTER EIGHT

Into the New World

COLBERT LEFT BEHIND the most powerful navy in
Europe. And Louvois, who had taken over the War Ministry in
1664 at the age of twenty-four, transformed a corrupt and sloppy
militia into Europe's strongest army. Frenchmen were spreading
through the New World, Africa, and beyond, raising the royal
colors and fulfilling dreams of further glory. Louis XIV devised a
land-sea strategy to dominate the world.

It didn't work. English and Dutch ships ganged up on the French
off Normandy in 1692 and pounded Colbert's fleet to driftwood.
A year later, famine ravaged Europe, hitting France the hardest.
Enemies pressed on all sides. Louis XIV, his maritime power lost,
concentrated instead on his victorious armies close to home. Rather
than build colonies, he settled into a duel with England that would
last 120 years.

But the mission to civilize flourished, with the king's distracted
blessing. French freebooters, *les flibustiers,* prowled the Spanish
Main. Baron Jean de St. Jean Pointis relieved the Spanish colony of
Cartagena, Columbia, of twenty million pounds worth of assorted
loot. In northern waters, French pirates seized so much from English
and Dutch ships that Nantes merchants declared them the greatest
financial asset France had yet known.

Brisk trade brought slaves from Africa to the West Indies and
sugar back to France. Stone forts protected Louis XIV's island real
estate. To the north, trappers brought beaver pelts from remote

rivers, and a few troops defended France with scattered outposts and tenuous alliances with Indian chiefs.

If Louis XIV funded few settlements, his dubious statecraft sent French pilgrims around most of the known world. He revoked Henri IV's Edict of Nantes and proclaimed, once again, open season on Protestants. Non-Catholics were commanded to stay home and convert. Instead, huge numbers slipped away. Incorrigibles were deported en masse.

French Huguenots took their skills and fortunes to Holland and Germany, to England, and beyond. Today, their descendants are everywhere. In South Africa, an Afrikaner named Du Toit leaped to his feet on seeing a French address on my card, ecstatic to receive a visitor who might not call him "Doo-toyt."

Louis XIV forced thousands of the French to pay nominal homage to the church, and he proved he was king. But he lost 100,000 of his most industrious people, who smuggled out fortunes, along with trade secrets and specialized tools. W. H. Lewis estimates that 9,000 sailors, 600 army officers, and 12,000 troops left France. Lewis added:

> And what of the invisible items . . . of infinitely greater moment? Loss of honor and good faith on the part of the Crown, misery, fear, hatred, delations, bribery, savagery, the enmity of all Europe, the disapproval of the Pope—who shall say at what price these were estimated when the account finally came up for audit?

European sovereigns found their colonies to be useful pressure points for triggering responses elsewhere, like a global Japanese foot massage. Britain, for instance, routinely defeated France in some far-flung harbor and handed back the spoils for renewed trading rights at Antwerp. Colonies were not jewels of the crown but pawns on a chessboard.

But Louis XIV felt bound by his duties as leader of the world's most enlightened nation. Missionaries sailed first class in his vessels. He gave each one a mattress and bedding, a white suit and six shirts, a cassock, six pairs of drawers, twelve handkerchiefs, twelve night-shirts, twelve pairs of thread stockings, a hat, three pairs of shoes, a sea chest, and one spirit case for every two priests. And some pocket money.

He sent the Abbé de Choisy to convert the Siamese court—and to secure a French base and commercial ally in Asia. Choisy liked to dress richly as a woman, draped in jewelry, and gossip with the ladies. In Paris, as "la comtesse de Sancey," he kept mistresses but insisted they wear men's clothing. But he flung himself into Christianity after a serious illness, and he accepted the Siam mission.

More than Asia, the king concentrated on America. Long after La Salle's Louisiana fiasco, a Canadian-born officer named Lemoyne d'Iberville persuaded the court to outfit a small fleet to the Mississippi. On March 2, 1699, struck by the beauty of the site, he set up a capital at Biloxi.

The river was too shallow, the soil too sandy, and the sun too hot. Dysentery ravaged the settlers. Thugs and outcasts were rounded up in France to bolster the ranks, but a colony of 400 Protestant families, leaving the Carolinas, were turned away. The governor told them, "The Sovereign did not chase the Protestants from his kingdom in Europe to have them set up a republic in his American domains."

Biloxi was abandoned for Mobile. Louis XIV sent out twenty-three young ladies, "raised in virtue and piety," to help populate the colony. But by 1708 an outraged nobleman reported:

> The colony is composed of 279 persons, including six sick people, plus 60 errant Canadians who are in savages' villages along the Mississippi without permission of any governor and who destroy by their evil libertine life with the savage women all that the gentlemen of the Foreign Missions and others teach about the mysteries of religion.

Liliane Crété, in her *La Vie Quotidienne en Louisiane,* noted that Bienville, governor of Louisiana, complained that he was so short of food that he was obliged to give "the largest part of his men to feed the savages." She did not elaborate.

The king, busy with a lingering war of Spanish succession, ceded Louisiana to a merchant, Antoine Crozat. His meager earnings fed 100 infantrymen and seventy-five Canadians in five dirt and log forts spread over the vast territory. Crozat gave up his fifteen-year concession after five years.

Louis XIV died in 1715, ending the Splendid Century. Another Louis would follow; meantime, Philippe d'Orléans, as regent, governed France and the empire.

Suddenly, Louisiana was on everyone's lips. A Scottish financier named John Law swept away the regent with visions of a prospering colony. "The land abounds in gold, silver, copper and lead," Law's agents reported. His Compagnie d'Occident was given control of Louisiana. Law obtained virtual control of the French economy, which he intended to fuel with profits from the colony. Frenchmen lined up to buy his stock, which soared to dizzying heights. Adventurers and gold-seekers rushed west in 1718. But neither farmers nor entrepreneurs followed.

Two years later, the bubble burst. No one found gold or any other wealth; the stock plummeted, taking the fledgling Paris market along with it. Law's paper money was worthless. He fled France, while remnants of the company kept Louisiana limping along.

Planters were given land but they had to find labor. White farmers wilted in the sun, and most tended to cut corners on their employers' time. So the company brought slaves from the Guinea coast. By 1724, Bienville had a code for the blacks, with a first article banning Jews from the colony. It stayed on the books for more than a century.

Bienville decided the colony needed a decent capital. He picked a narrow strip where Indians had to portage their canoes and named it Nouvelle-Orléans, after the regent. The place flooded so often that a levee was built along with the first houses. It attracted such dregs that the court decreed, "Henceforth, no more vagabonds and criminals will be sent to Louisiana."

But the company dispatched *filles de cassette*—"hope chest girls" —who were educated by Ursuline nuns and then matched with husbands of good family. Their parting gift was a *cassette* containing a modest trousseau. Liliane Crété observes, "Judging from the number of Louisiana families who flatter themselves today by claiming to descend from these virtuous creatures, these girls must have been extremely prolific." Short of prospective wives, the company also sent over *ribaudes* gathered up on the streets of Paris. One governor complained that a dozen young women shipped out for marriage were "so ugly and so badly made" that local bachelors preferred Indian women.

The Indians were growing restive for other reasons. France and Britain both exploited rivalry among the tribes. Each had allies and enemies, and neither was above inciting Indians to lift scalps of the other European tribe.

Such tactics were a specialty of the French in Canada to discourage English forays north. Francis Parkman recounts an incident of 1694 on the Oyster River, near what is now Durham, New Hampshire. A French lieutenant, Villieu, and a priest helped 105 Abenaki Indians massacre 104 people, mostly women and children. Twenty houses were burned and twenty-seven prisoners taken. "This stroke," observed Villebon, the French governor of Canada, "is of great advantage because it breaks off all the talk of peace between our Indians and the English. The English are in despair, for not even infants in the cradle were spared."

An Abenaki chief, Bomazeen, taken prisoner in Boston, said missionaries had told him Jesus Christ was a Frenchman, the son of the Virgin Mary, a French lady, and the English had killed him. His death must be avenged to gain his favor, Bomazeen said he was told.

Parkman notes, in balance, that French Canadians often paid ransoms for English prisoners taken by their Indian allies. Some were made to work off the debt, he said, but "they were uniformly treated well."

In Louisiana, Bienville boasted that his Choctaws had razed three Chickasaw villages, bringing back 400 scalps and 100 prisoners. The Chickasaws had disturbed commerce along the river. He wrote, "It is an important advantage in the state of things, particularly since this result was obtained without risking the life of a single Frenchman by the care which I took to make these barbarians act against each other."

After a while, the Indians caught on. The Natchez, fed up with settlers taking their lands, massacred 200 Frenchmen on November 28, 1729. The French mounted a punitive expedition to recover their women, children and slaves. They took along 200 Choctaws and some blacks who did most of the fighting. The Natchez took refuge with the Chickasaws and, together, declared war on the French.

Allied, they harassed the river and the hinterlands. A wall went up around New Orleans, and settlers upcountry, at the least, lost sleep.

The Compagnie d'Occident finally collapsed in 1731, and the crown took over the colony. By then, the English were poring over maps with concern. French settlements formed a thin but unbroken line from the mouth of the St. Lawrence to the Mississippi Delta, and on down through the Caribbean. The thirteen English colonies were encircled. Increasingly, pioneers probing west found themselves hacked to bits by Indians inflamed by the French.

Louis XV, who had taken the throne, was no great empire builder but a proud king of a nation that believed itself the natural leader of the world. He knew that French holdings in Canada and the Caribbean islands disrupted Britannia's plans to rule the waves. But, since Cartier, France had been divided over Canada. Quebec grew slowly, partly stifled by jealous fur traders who feared competition. In 1664, Louis XIV had made the moribund territory a crown colony, and Colbert sent out 10,000 settlers to defend it. But enthusiasm was muted. Voltaire dismissed all of Canada as "a few acres of snow."

The 1713 Treaty of Utrecht, a crucial settling of accounts with Britain, had left the French Canadian map in tatters. France lost Newfoundland and Acadia at the mouth of the St. Lawrence as well as the vast Hudson Bay. The treaty also gave Guinea and West Indian islands to Britain, altogether four million square kilometers of Colbert's empire.

After that, French pioneers held fast in Canada against paralyzing winters, shortages of food, tools, and supplies, and a dubious regard from Paris. Louis-Antoine de Bougainville wrote home in 1754: "What a country, my dear brother, and what patience is needed to bear the slights that people go out of their way to lay on us here. It seems as though we belonged to a different nation, even a hostile one."

That year, five years from a final showdown with Britain, French Canadians numbered 55,009 against at least a half million in the thirteen English colonies to the south.

A SHORT SAIL from New Orleans was Saint-Domingue (Haiti), one of the richest properties of the New World. Its plantations produced sugar and tobacco. It had no minerals, but its ports sheltered pirates who mined gold and silver from boats headed back to Spain. And it helped protect France's other Caribbean islands.

France and England started off amicably in the West Indies, from 1627, sharing the tiny island of St. Christopher (St. Kitts to its friends). In one of their few successful joint enterprises, the French and English exterminated the Carib Indians on the island.

But each power moved off in a different direction. Belain d'Es-nambuc, a ruined Normandy gentleman turned freebooter, took to the sea "as one sets forth on Crusade." He settled Martinique from St. Kitts in 1635. That year, Liénart de l'Olive and Urbain du Roissey sailed from Normandy to claim Guadeloupe.

It was tough going. Of the first 550 pioneers to leave Le Havre, 350 died at sea; Richelieu's company had skimped on food. Later, of seventy passengers on Roissey's ship, the *Catholic,* sixteen landed, alive but barely strong enough to build shelters. When Colbert took over in 1664, Martinique and Guadeloupe had fewer than 8,000 white settlers between them. By contrast, Britain's Barbados, half the size of Martinique, had 10,000 inhabitants by 1640, as many as Massachusetts or Virginia.

The Compagnie de Rouen sent 400 men to Guiana in 1643; within two years, all but twenty-five had died. The population grew but dropped again with every British and Dutch raid. By 1670, it was 300 whites and 1,000 black slaves.

France had already lost out on the tobacco market. In 1540, the French ambassador to Lisbon, Jean Nicot, as in nicotine, sent Cather-ine de Médicis tobacco from Florida. By the time the crown decided to plant the crop, however, Spain, England, and Holland had cornered the market. That left sugar. From 1651 to 1700, the French brought 152,000 slaves to Caribbean sugar plantations. The British, ever pushing their advantage, brought 242,000.[1]

The Treaty of Utrecht gave St. Kitts to Britain but nailed down the French claim to a small string of islands. An economic boom had begun, punctuated only sporadically by the less figurative boom of naval guns. Real estate changed hands frequently. France sold Saint Croix to Denmark in 1733 but later relieved Sweden of Saint Barthélemy. Grenada, at first French, became British.

In the wars to follow, Britain sent a small party onto the imposing Diamond Rock just south of Martinique and for eighteen months blasted away at every French ship trying to negotiate the straits. To this day, the rock is commissioned in the Royal Navy as H.M.S. *Diamond Rock*. Passing British ships salute it, sending the French into fits.

RIVALRY EXTENDED around Africa, through the Indian Ocean, and into Asia, where European powers raced to establish permanent settlements. Had things gone according to Colbert's plan, France, not Britain, would have civilized India. Neither, of course, consulted the Indians.

Europe had craved Indian silks, precious woods, and spices since the Middle Ages. In the 1400s, Portugal and Holland set up trading posts on the subcontinent. The Parmentier brothers reached India for France in 1529, followed by navigators from Rouen and the ubiquitous *Malouins*. Henri IV organized a trading company, and Richelieu gave it form. But only under Colbert, twenty-six years later, was the first French *comptoir* (trading port) established in India, at Surat, north of Bombay. Five years later, Pondicherry was founded near Madras. Chandernagore, outside Calcutta, was ceded to France, and then Calicut, south of Bombay.

By 1701, the French governor had flags planted strategically along both sides of the Indian peninsula. By alternately wheedling and strong-arming, France broadened its hold. And in 1741, the new governor, Dupleix, went for broke. He artfully played off nabob against maharajah, shifting alliances and dangling promises. No general, he nonetheless picked fights with the British who wanted to expand their own *comptoirs* near Bombay, Calcutta, and Madras. Dupleix brought in La Bourdonnais, French governor of Mauritius, who had the nearest convenient fleet.

With the excuse of the War of Austrian Succession, France and Britain battled at Pondicherry. Dupleix lined up the Nabob of Carnatic, who threatened to besiege the British at Madras if they attacked Pondicherry. Meanwhile, La Bourdonnais scattered the Indian army and captured Madras with hardly a fight. Then he gave it back in order to ransom prisoners.

Dupleix was incensed. The admiral merely wanted to stamp out British interests in India; Dupleix wanted India. He had La Bourdonnais recalled to France, but his public relations suffered when the admiral got there.

Without a fleet, Dupleix defended Pondicherry against thirty British ships and an army of Indians. After fifty-eight days of bitter attacks, the English gave up. French historians call that victory, on October 18, 1748, one of the finest military episodes of the eighteenth century. The only problem was that on that same day Louis XV signed the Peace of Aix-la-Chapelle, which restored all conquered territory in Canada and India. He said he sought peace "as a king and not as a tradesman."

Although India was up for grabs, France and England had promised not to fight over it. Dupleix sought instead to conquer by diplomacy. With a crafty aide and a striking Creole wife, he amassed land titles by promising protection and collecting on political debts. His empire extended along 500 miles of coastline and totaled thirty million inhabitants—as many as in France.

The Compagnie des Indes, however, wanted profit and not power. Finally, Dupleix spread himself too thinly to neutralize his enemies in India and France. He was recalled in disgrace in 1754, and his successor signed trade accords with the English. Lord Clive, according to French historians, immediately put to good use the fallen governor's tactic of divide and conquer. Dupleix died in France, broken and miserable, and the fate of French India was sealed forever.

LOUISIANA, MEANWHILE, was still struggling. Into the last half of the eighteenth century, New Orleans' population numbered only 800. The upper crust wore powdered wigs and brocade to gala balls, stocking gilt-carved buffets with fine wines. The master dance instructor was a Parisian named Baby; authorities found it necessary to limit the cabarets to six. And, when it rained, the streets were ankle-deep in mud and alligators. The town was desperately short of carpenters and bootmakers.

Devastating tornadoes alternated with periods of drought. Yellow fever was endemic. Indian wars continued, and disgruntled Choctaws threatened to join the more generous English. The army was so ill-disciplined and cowardly, one local authority grumbled, that he would have sent blacks to fight if they weren't so expensive.

Governor Kerlerec asked for Swiss troops since Frenchmen had disgusted local inhabitants "for the horrors of which they are capable."

The colony might have prospered. One sixty-man French army unit performed so well that each was discharged and given land, a wife, and farm animals; they prospered. Acadians filtered into the colony, thriving after their exodus from Nova Scotia. But Louis XV, battered in Europe and elsewhere, ignored repeated pleas for help. By the time he noticed, Britain's western settlements cast a dark shadow over Louisiana.

France pushed Spain into helping to counter British advances. The Spanish immediately grabbed Cuba. Louis XV worried that Spain might desert him, so he tossed King Carlos III, "his very dear and well-loved cousin," another chunk of territory: Louisiana.

The act of cession was signed secretly at Fontainebleau on November 3, 1762, but it was not until 1764 that Louisiana settlers learned they were to pledge allegiance to a different flag. Frenchmen already had a great deal more to mourn.

William Pitt took power in Britain in 1757 and set out immediately to evict France from North America. His fleet seized the fortress at Louisbourg, in Cape Breton, and a land force overran Fort Duquesne in the Ohio Valley. In a third swift stroke, he sent troops against Montreal. But a smaller French army under Louis-Joseph, Marquis de Montcalm, blasted the British into disarray. Pitt ordered a final multipronged attack at the heart of New France. For the crucial assault on Quebec, he chose James Wolfe, a slight, untested, rheumatic thirty-two-year-old colonel with a weak chin and a receding forehead. Wolfe was given a general's commission, 8,500 experienced regulars, and a well-armed fleet of forty-nine ships.

At Quebec waited Pierre de Rigaud, marquis de Vaudreuil, born a French-Canadian and, at sixty, governor-general of New France and former governor of New Orleans. He was not modest. "My firmness is generally applauded," he wrote to the court in 1759. "It has entered all hearts and one and all say loudly, 'Canada, our native land, will bury us in her ruins before we yield to the English.' This is the course which I am firmly resolved upon and which I shall maintain inviolable."

He had at hand Montcalm, at forty-seven one of the most courageous and efficient officers of the French army. But Vaudreuil outranked Montcalm and did not let him forget it. Before the British appeared, Montcalm cursed in his journal the governor's "ridiculous, obscure and misleading orders."

In response to Montcalm's plea for reinforcements, Paris sent 400 men and some cargo, including brandy. Warships could not be spared. The court also directed Vaudreuil to defer to Montcalm on military matters. There is no evidence, however, that the governor advised the general of the order.

Quebec today, built up the side of dramatic cliffs like the prow of a ship, appears impregnable. In 1759, after a century of costly but bungled attempts at fortification, the badly designed and half-finished walls were less imposing. Corruption and jealousy among the engineers had taken their toll. The city was still more vulnerable because no one had fortified the south bank, 1,000 yards across the St. Lawrence River. In battles past, river currents had deterred the British, and complacent French strategists counted on similar future help from nature. With Wolfe nearly at their door, French commanders debated what should be done about fortifying the city.

"There had been much inefficiency and much dishonesty, and France—and New France—were to pay for these things now," observed C. P. Stacey in his account of the battle.

The French found, at the last minute, that they could not block the Traverse; the tricky channel was too long, and no one had yet charted it properly. "Our best seamen," Montcalm observed, "seem to me to be either liars or ignoramuses."

But Montcalm was able to deploy 15,000 regulars, militiamen, and Indians against the invading force. Wolfe had little intelligence about his objective beyond a faulty map drawn by his chief engineer, a former prisoner at Quebec. The French drew first blood, capturing a British cutter. Wolfe was bitter at what he called the timorous and somewhat uncooperative Royal Navy.

For two months, Wolfe maneuvered off Quebec to little effect. He bombarded the city and, in retaliation for past massacres of Britons by the French and Indians, he burned riverside villages. But he had only a month before winter threatened. He had already lost 850 men in battle, including fifty-seven officers, and more to disease.

Bedridden with kidney stones, dysentery, and fever, Wolfe was in a bind.

Montcalm, too, was hard pressed. Flour from France was exhausted, and Quebec lived on short rations from the local harvest. The British had cut the river above the capital, burning emergency stores.

Finally, in mid-September, Wolfe made his last move, what Stacey calls his eighth plan. At night, aided by the navy he had abused, Wolfe landed a heavy force at an undefended cove upriver. Officers scaled a cliff face the French thought impregnable. Warned of this eventuality, Montcalm had remarked, "We need not suppose the enemy have wings."

Sentries were dispatched in a brief skirmish, and troops scrambled up a steep narrow path. When dawn broke on the Abraham heights, the French-Canadians found an unbroken line of scarlet tunics advancing toward their capital behind the Highlanders' wailing bagpipes.

Wolfe formed six battalions and the Louisbourg Grenadiers, 4,441 men by British count, and sailors lugged two brass cannon up the path. The French had an equal force, with heavier guns, but they suffered from the surprise. Montcalm probably should have waited for help. But at 10 A.M., a hastily formed front unfurled silk banners, cheered, and ran at the British. Disciplined musket volleys cut up the French lines. Wolfe was shot dead in the chest; Montcalm was fatally wounded a few minutes later. The British lost 640 dead and wounded; the French, probably double that.

It was no more than a major skirmish, Parkman notes, but in terms of what it meant, it was one of the greatest battles in history. The French-Canadians held out for another year, besieging the British at Quebec and defending Montreal, but Louis XV sent little help. For France, Canada was lost on September 13, 1759, before lunch, on the Plains of Abraham.

THE TREATY of 1763 could hardly have been more galling. Signed in Paris, it excised in a single cut four million square kilometers of the French empire. It was the same territorial loss that the Utrecht treaty imposed a half-century earlier, but it was far more devastating. France lost Canada and Cape Breton; all of India but for five small trading posts which could not be fortified; Grenada, the Grenadines, and Tobago; and Senegal, its main foothold in Africa. Britain had humbled France.

For Fernand Braudel, French grandeur ended in 1763.

In the New World, France kept a tiny foothold in the far north: St. Pierre and Miquelon. The English could afford a slight flourish of magnanimity. After all, some day a stronger France might seek revenge. But elsewhere in North America, trappers and farmers would have to learn to love a new king or face very cold winters on their own. Along the Mississippi and in Louisiana, the French would have to start hardening their *r*'s and living without Bordeaux reds.

France stayed in the Caribbean, but its little island paradises bristled with cannon behind thick stone ramparts. Spanish and Dutch ships made occasional raids, official or otherwise. But the constant threat was British.

The remaining empire was strong enough in few places to resist a determined push from an English fleet. It comprised Madagascar, Réunion, Mauritius, and the Seychelles in the Indian Ocean; and in Africa, France held scattered slaving and trading posts on the western bulge.

In 1763, Choiseul, Louis XV's foreign minister, took charge of the navy and raced to rebuild the fleet. Bougainville, who escaped from Canada, sailed to Tahiti in 1768 and staked out the vast stretches of the South Pacific that France still controls. La Pérouse followed him five years later to solidify the French presence in the South Seas.

But scandal marred success.

Choiseul decided to build up Guiana as a southern American base to replace Canada, lost in the north. Jesuit missionaries had settled in from 1709 and, by the mid-1700s, priests counted 10,000 "civilized Indians." The colony had 1,200 whites, 5,000 black slaves, and 2,000 mulattoes. Gabriel Hanotaux noted that its promise of natural wealth was attracting "the attention of civilized humanity."

A colonist named Préfontaine fired Choiseul's imagination. The minister ordered a pioneer venture, down to thousands of straw hats with chin ribbons and tambourine players to entertain the settlers. To avoid attention, volunteers were sneaked out of Paris at night, in closed carts, and dispatched to ships. It was the most ambitious attempt France had yet made to people a colony.

At Kourou, Préfontaine cleared a town site and built fourteen rows of straw huts around a statue of Louis XV. Within months, 8,000 settlers arrived. Ship captains unloaded their passengers and left, stranding them without shelter in the pounding rain. Authorities at Cayenne, four miles down the coast, refused to help. Within two years, 10,996 settlers were landed; of those, 918 lived to go home. Scarcely twenty families remained to farm in the region. The exercise cost an estimated thirty million *livres,* about six million dollars in currency of the time.[2]

Abbé Guillaume Reynal brought harsh judgment in his classic work of 1772, edited by Denis Diderot, *Histoire philosophique et politique des Deux Indes:*

> When a prince, a minister, is guided by the public opinion of enlightened people, if he encounters misfortune, neither heaven nor earth can reproach him. But enterprises undertaken without the counsel or wish of the nation, events hidden from all those whose lives and fortunes are exposed—is it anything but a secret league, a conspiracy of a few individuals against an entire society? Up to what point does authority feel itself humiliated? To what point does it exhibit such scorn for men not even to seek to excuse itself for its faults?

LOUIS XV DIED in 1774 in a lingering climate of national humiliation, loss, and lust for vengeance. Yet another Louis took the throne. Soon afterward, his court received secret envoys from a national liberation front. Americans sought revolution against Britain and they needed help. Might France be interested? Might it, indeed.

Foreign Minister Charles Gravier, comte de Vergennes, reported to the king: "The inveterate emnity of [Britain] imposes upon us the duty to lose no occasion of weakening it, so that we cannot but gain by seizing the one now being offered; we must, therefore, give support to the independence of the insurgent colonies."

Before any American reached Paris, Louis XVI had already directed that one million *livres* be loaned through Pierre-Augustin

Caron de Beaumarchais, author of *Le Mariage de Figaro,* poet, salon star, and sometime secret agent. Beaumarchais had argued that if France did not help the Americans, it would lose the West Indies. He set up a phony mercantile company, Roderique Hortalez and Company, and bought munitions from the French arsenal. Spain matched the amount, and the next year, France paid out another million.

American freedom, orators of all extremes tend to forget, was paid for largely with clandestine foreign aid to the rebels.

In 1777, the French dispatched eight chartered ships with 200 brass cannons, 300 rifles, 100 tons of powder, 3,000 tents, heavy stores of bullets, mortars, and cannonballs, and clothing for 30,000 men. All but one ship made it.

Benjamin Franklin and Silas Deane, a Connecticut merchant, bought supplies under the unseeing gaze of a neutral French government. The Americans tried to pay for their arms, but their exports of tobacco and other crops were too bulky to avoid a British blockade. French subsidies and loans made up the difference. Deane worked the deals. Franklin solicited cash from the court at Versailles. The total ranged near 15,400,000 *livres*—worth $2,852,000 at the time—up to the beginning of 1781. That year, new grants added $1,000,000.

France was short of cash, but there was more: a further loan of four million *livres* and a gift of six million. The court guaranteed a Dutch loan of ten million. Spain sneaked some money to the Continentals but stayed out of the war until France promised to help get back Gibraltar and Florida. Spanish leaders feared an independent United States as yet another threat in the New World. Prussia, Austria, and Tuscany slammed the door on American envoys.

By the end, France had paid out an estimated $8,167,500—or $9,600,000, by some counts—compared to Spain's $611,328.[3] In addition, France paid heavy costs for deploying its army and navy. The difference, in the end, was not money.

American morale soared with the first tangible foreign ally. Gilbert du Motier, marquis de Lafayette, was only twenty in 1778 when he rushed to aid the rebels. At the time, he was chafing under garrison life in Metz, living elaborately on his wife's vast inheritance. And he hated the English, who had killed his father in battle.

Lafayette bought the vessel *La Victoire* in Bordeaux and prepared to sail. Louis XVI heard of his plans and forbade the voyage. But Lafayette slipped away a few steps ahead of the cops, helped by a French agent of Franklin and Deane's. As soon as he reached America, the Continental Congress made him a major general, without pay. Washington, at forty-five more than twice his age, adopted him as evidence of French support.

Soon afterward, Vergennes negotiated a "conditional and defensive alliance" which protected the French West Indies but gave up claim to Canada, Bermuda, and all of the United States east of the Mississippi. The minister met secretly with Franklin, who was loved in Paris despite his clumsy French.

Alexander Hamilton wrote in 1780, "Our countrymen have all the folly of the ass and all the passiveness of the sheep in their composition. They are determined not to be free and they can neither be frightened, discouraged, nor persuaded to change their resolution. If we are to be saved France and Spain must save us." Not Spain.

At first, a French naval force under Admiral Jean Baptiste, comte d'Estaing, accomplished little and sat sheltered in port. But in the spring of 1780, France sent 5,500 troops under Lieutenant General Jean-Baptiste-Donatien de Vimeur, comte de Rochambeau. Then Admiral François Joseph Paul, comte de Grasse, arrived with twenty ships of the line and headed for Chesapeake with 3,000 troops from the Saint-Domingue garrison.

They were welcomed warmly. One merchant wrote, "The French officers are the most civilized men I ever met. They are temperate, prudent, and extremely attentive to duty. I did not expect they would have so few vices." And another: "Neither Officers nor men are the effeminate Beings we were heretofore taught to believe them. They are as large & as likely men as can be produced by any nation."

The war was heading for a showdown. Britain's Cornwallis had massed his army of 7,200 at Yorktown. Washington moved 7,000 men, half of them French regulars, overland to Virginia. Comte de Barras broke out of a British blockade at Newport, behind Rochambeau's heavy guns, bringing a twelve-ship French squadron to the battle. De Grasse unloaded men near Yorktown and sent transport for Washington's and Rochambeau's forces.

Benedict Arnold, the traitorous American commander of West Point, nearly ruined the preparations. But the cooperation among generals, admirals, and colonial authorities was unparalleled in eighteenth-century military history. Britain was slow to send reinforcements and patrols, leaving a small French force in control of the Caribbean. At Yorktown, the British admiral, Sir George Rodney, assumed the French would melt away as they had in the past. He sent fourteen ships and found that de Grasse and de Barras had thirty-six.

The decisive battle for American independence was fought by 18,000 French seamen and 7,800 French foot soldiers against 8,000 British and German mercenaries. Only 5,700 Continental regulars and 3,200 militiamen took part. Today, in Bar-sur-Loup, not far from Nice, a statue of de Grasse is inscribed: "To our native son, victor of the Battle of Yorktown, who gave the United States its freedom." Yorktown, Pennsylvania, is the twin city of Bar-sur-Loup, and its mayor visits France occasionally to observe that the inscription is not far from correct.

Rodney, of course, later captured de Grasse in the Antilles. And France got little out of the war beyond heavy debts. The Americans' immediate gratitude was overwhelming. Not long afterward, however, Louis XVI's young ally was at the point of declaring war on France to preserve its right to trade with Britain.

The humiliating Treaty of Paris of 1763 was replaced by a new one—at Versailles. Signed in 1783, it gave Senegal back to France, along with five *comptoirs* in India and the islands of St. Lucia and Tobago in the Caribbean. The French navy, with its honor partially restored, was ready to try again to spread the *fleur-de-lis* around the globe.

But Louis XVI did not have long to weigh what he had won from George III. The French king was about to face his own revolution, and it would sweep away him, his throne, and a centuries-old idea of *la France*.

CHAPTER NINE

Revolution and the Emperors

JULY 14, IN PARIS or Papeete, is no day to miss. Aging couples ignore their swollen joints at neighborhood firehouse dances. Island bars, awash in rum, throb with drumbeats. Exploding lights color the skies over the Eiffel Tower. It is Bastille Day.

From the distance of two centuries, the French Revolution seems fairly simple. Fed up with a bloated aristocracy and a dithering king who ran up bad debts, France erupted. Parisians armed with pitchforks stormed the Bastille; lopped off the heads of Louis XVI and Marie "Let Them Eat Cake" Antoinette; chiseled *Liberté, Egalité, Fraternité* on coins and building facades; and then set off to beam light elsewhere in the world.

In fact, it took the Revolution three and a half years to execute the king, and fifteen years later he was replaced by an emperor. Before the Revolution wore itself out, after a decade, more than 40,000 people passed under the guillotine in Paris, or were drowned in the provinces, in the name of liberty, equality, and brotherhood. But the French Revolution changed the world in 1789. Some argue that it is still changing the world.

Historians spend lifetimes tracking the Revolution as it smouldered at the gates of Versailles and then burst into flame, consuming instigators, followers, and very nearly the nation it was meant to save. Jules Michelet's seven tomes on the Revolution alone augmented his seventeen-volume history of France.

The idea of change had been in the air. In England, a parliament, not God, determined the rights of kings. And John Locke rubbed it in with treatises on the rights of man. Voltaire brought Locke's views to France in 1734, adding his own appreciation of England, "where the prince, all-powerful to do good, has his hands tied against doing evil." His *Lettres philosophiques* were burned, but not soon enough. Jean-Jacques Rousseau evoked the noble simplicity of life without an idle class crushing the peasants. "Voltaire and Rousseau," declares historian Jean Tulard, "were responsible for the downfall of the monarchy." Among others. Diderot's *Encyclopedia* catalogued new concepts of equality. Montesquieu's *Persian Letters* ridiculed the king and his 600 pastry chefs.

Later, the Industrial Revolution lifted England with steam. The Americans threw off outside masters, building a nation on equality and freedom, with the French watching from ringside seats.

Feudal France comprised three *états*. The First Estate was the clergy; the Second, the nobility. Both ran up staggering expenses but paid no taxes. The burden fell on the Third Estate, the commoners. From 1604, anyone with enough money could buy into the nobility and, as an officer of the crown, steal back his investment with substantial interest. Purchased titles were hereditary, but they did not guarantee high breeding.

An intelligent aristocracy might have lightened up and eased toward reform. But in France, the privileged few squeezed harder, hoping to stamp out revolutionary tendencies before they grew dangerous. Caught up in the elaborate minuets at Versailles, they had little contact with the peasants who struggled to pay the bills. Louis XVI, meanwhile, hunted and puttered with locks.

The Etats généraux (States General) had represented all three sectors as a consultative body, but it had not been convened since 1614. After the Fronde, noblemen in the Parlement de Paris arrogated legislative power to themselves, so much that Louis XV abolished the body in 1771. Louis XVI reinstituted the Parlement four years later, thus bumbling headlong onto a slippery slope.

The Parlement blocked each attempt at reform and, at one point, lectured the king:

> Any system which, under the appearance of humanity and benevolence, would tend, in a well-ordered monarchy, to establish among men an equality of duties, and to destroy the necessary

distinctions, would soon bring disorder, the inevitable result of absolute equality and would produce an overturning of society.

They may have misread the causes, but they predicted the effect with stunning clarity. In his priceless *Story of Mankind,* Hendrik Willem Van Loon notes:

> It was the royal habit to do the right thing at the wrong time in the wrong way. When the people clamored for A, the king scolded them and gave them nothing. Then, when the Palace was surrounded by a howling multitude of poor people, the king surrendered and gave his subjects what they had asked for. By this time, however, the people wanted A plus B. The comedy was repeated. . . . And so on, through the whole alphabet and up to the scaffold.

An impasse forced Louis XVI to convene the Etats généraux, ignored for 175 years. The Third Estate demanded to meet jointly with the first two. The nobility objected, and the king ordered the commoners out of Versailles until they agreed to meet separately. Mirabeau, hero of the hour, told the aristocrat who brought the news: "Go tell your master we are here by the will of the people and will be expelled only at the point of bayonets."

That was on June 28. On July 8, the Third Estate, supported by most of the clergy and much of the nobility, formed a Constituent Assembly. Louis XVI refused to accept limitations on his power and amassed 25,000 hired foreign troops around Versailles; he wasn't sure of Frenchmen. On July 13, a crowd of demonstrators clashed with the Royal German Cavalry in the Tuileries Gardens. That went down badly among French commoners already chafing at the power of Louis XVI's Austrian queen, Marie Antoinette. A militia was formed. Within hours, it grew to 12,000 men.

On July 14, a group of the new guardsmen, along with stray workers and some irate *bourgeois,* seized rifles and cannons at the Invalides. Picking up supporters, they marched off to collect more weapons at the Bastille, a symbolic but disused political prison. They negotiated for arms but, as one leader joked later, the Bastille commander "lost his head before it could be cut off." Someone fired on the crowd and started the French Revolution.

FRANCE AT THE time was the strongest state in the world, with 16 percent of Europe's population: twenty-six million, compared to barely twelve million in England and eight million in Prussia. The French, victorious in the American war, had never been more powerful at sea and on land. French art and philosophy dominated the continent. France prospered from its colonies. At home, the fields and farms flourished. But national borders were vulnerable. Foreign powers controlled bits of the left bank of the Rhine, Savoy, Nice, and Avignon. The Revolution twisted and turned, weakening the state. Louis XVI, still on the throne, was made king of the French rather than king of France. The divine right was abolished. But his royal associates in Europe, worried by the precedent, negotiated in secret to come to his aid. Diehard aristocrats expected to rout the *sans-culottes,* revolutionary troops in raggedy breeches. The Austrians penetrated deep into France, but a people's army turned them back. Louis XVI's foreign dealings were discovered, and he went to the guillotine in January 1793.

Revolutionary leaders sought to strengthen the empire. In 1789, the Etats généraux declared itself in favor of colonial enterprise. Two years later, the legislature abolished all trade monopolies with India, the West Indies, Senegal, the Levant, and the North African Barbary Coast. "Commerce with the colonies," it said, "is commerce among brothers, commerce of the Nation with another part of the Nation." And in 1794, the government abolished slavery and decreed that "the colonies are an integral part of the Republic and are subject to the same constitutional laws."

But while France was in turmoil, England grabbed Tobago, Saint Pierre and Miquelon, and Pondicherry. In April 1794, Guadeloupe and Martinique fell. A black army under a former slave named Toussaint-L'Ouverture saved Haiti from the British. But that set in motion forces that soon brought the island independence from France.

Bordeaux, Nantes, and Le Havre were starved of colonial trade. French industry, spurred at first by war, stagnated. Invaders probed

French borders, anxious to pick over the spoils. By 1795, France was pressed to the wall.

Enter Napoléon. Three French armies headed east in 1795 to face Austria and the Italians. The army of Italy was commanded by Napoléon Bonaparte, a young general from Corsica. His victories were dramatic, based on strategy, speed, and surprise. He slipped between two armies waiting for him and crushed the Sardinians, winning Savoy and Nice for France. Then he chased the Austrians home, conquering northern Italy and bringing rich tribute back to the dwindling French treasury. He attacked again, reaching nearly to Vienna, and Austria capitulated. Pope Pius VI ceded Avignon to France. The revolution had passed to a Directoire of five men who began to consolidate France. They secured the left bank of the Rhine and signed peace treaties with Holland and Spain. By 1797, France was at peace, and largely in control, on the European continent.

But there remained England. French ports wanted peace so they could resume their lost colonial trade. In Paris, however, merchants argued that peace would give England a chance to trade in the European markets which the French monopolized. The only answer was war, but Bonaparte dared not try an amphibious landing. Britain's lord admiral of the moment had it right: "I do not say the French cannot come. I merely say that they cannot come by water."

The naval stand-off with England brought another complication: the Americans. At first, Americans had thrilled at the news of revolution. They saw Lafayette emerge to head a people's militia in his own country. The 1789 French Declaration of the Rights of Man read like their own Bill of Rights.

Not long before, Patrick Henry had recalled "a dreadful precipice from which we have escaped by means of the generous French, to whom I will be everlastingly bound by most heartfelt gratitude." He added, "Surely Congress will never recede from our French friends. Salvation of America depends upon our holding fast to our attachment to them."

But the Americans wanted to restore some goodwill with England, build an economy, and make some individual fortunes. The French wanted gratitude. It was not a period about which to write fulsome speeches about undying friendship.

"Dragon's teeth have been sown in France and came up monsters," John Adams observed. Americans were torn between deploring revolutionary excesses and standing by an ally. Commerce prevailed, and they chose strict neutrality, infuriating the French who needed American bases for their weaker navy. France's envoy, Edmond Genet, tried to bypass George Washington and appeal to the people. He was bundled back to Paris amid acrimony. The United States was caught in the middle: Britain confiscated cargo and impressed U.S. seamen in the French West Indies; France seized U.S. ships bound for England.

John Jay negotiated a treaty with Britain which France denounced as a willful sellout; to mollify the French, a U.S. commission went to Paris. They dealt with Charles-Maurice de Talleyrand-Périgord, the foreign minister, who had returned from thirty months in the United States convinced that Americans were crude, simple, and greedy.[1] The result was the XYZ affair.

The French flattered and bullied the Americans, seeking a loan while plundering U.S. commerce. As negotiations continued, the Directoire decreed that a ship's nationality would be determined by cargo, not flag; a pair of English-made boots on board was grounds for seizing a U.S. ship. One of Talleyrand's diplomats insisted on a *douceur*—a bribe—to ease along diplomacy. "No, no, not a sixpence!" retorted Charles Pinckney. (This, amplified by a South Carolina Federalist, was reported as, "Millions for Defense but Not One Cent for Tribute.")

The Americans refused to repudiate neutrality, so the French punished them for "betrayal" by threatening war. The commission reported back in full, detailing insults, and warning that weak, spiritless nations could expect to be trampled by France. Their dispatches were made public, called the XYZ cables, and they touched off a jingoistic storm. "At no time in America's national history have her people so heatedly denounced or so thoroughly detested France," historian Marvin Zahniser wrote.

The United States squared off for war with France. In subsequent years, harsh embargoes and seizures embittered merchants. In 1812, some Americans were surprised that it was the English, not the French, whom they fought.

TALLEYRAND, meanwhile, had an approach to England that suited Bonaparte well: choke the British empire by seizing Egypt. The ambitious Corsican suspected that France might be ripe for a military dictator. But he first needed more glory, such as a dramatic victory beyond Europe. He could block England's Suez route to Asia and mount an assault on India. Egypt, an important new colony, would replace lost territory. Bonaparte landed 35,000 men in Egypt, after seizing Malta on the way. He announced as his pretext: "It is long enough that the beys who govern Egypt insult the French nation and cover its merchants with affronts. The hour of punishment has arrived."

He explained he was there to liberate Egypt. "Is there good land? It belongs to the Mamelukes. Is there a hearty slave, a handsome horse? It belongs to the Mamelukes. If Egypt is their farm, let them show the lease God has given them."

Hostile Egyptians and dysentery left the French miserable. Admiral Nelson shot up the fleet, leaving Bonaparte's men no transport home. Then Turks amassed in Syria to counterattack. Bonaparte pushed north to meet them, but at Saint-Jean d'Acre, he was beaten by a French mercenary commander behind walls that once had protected French crusaders. France, meanwhile, was crumbling fast. Bonaparte delegated his command and rushed to Paris.

Austria, Russia, and Naples, with British funds, had armed 350,000 men. France clamored for a savior. Bonaparte arrived just after news of a French victory over the Turks. Crowds went wild. The Directoire made him first consul and then consul for life. In 1804, he changed his title to Napoléon I, emperor of France.

NAPOLÉON, a symbol of Gallic genius, grew up short and sickly on an island that fought to remain free of Paris, the son of a social-climbing notary public. His French sounded Italian, and he could hardly spell. His flash of glory lasted less than twenty years. But he conquered more ground and killed more enemies than Alexander the Great or Genghis Khan. Paris exalts his memory. He is even on brandy bottles, right hand fondling his sternum under a loose tunic, hat cocked jauntily over a furrowed brow. His code of law still prevails. Avenues radiate from his Arc de Triomphe, bearing names of his victories, his generals, and his Grande Armée. His noble *N* is emblazoned on the bridge to Notre-Dame. Les Invalides, where he is buried, is a museum to his splendor.

Van Loon, after cataloguing Napoléon's faults, muses:

> Here I am sitting at a comfortable table loaded heavily with books, with one eye on my typewriter and the other on Licorice the cat, who has a great fondness for carbon paper, and I am telling you that the Emperor Napoléon was a most contemptible person. But should I happen to look out the window, down upon Seventh Avenue, and should the endless procession of trucks and carts come to a sudden halt and should I hear the sound of heavy drums and see the little man on his white horse in his old and much-worn green uniform, then I don't know, but I am afraid that I would leave my books and the kitten and my home and everything else to follow him wherever he cared to lead. My own grandfather did this and Heaven knows he was not born to be a hero. Millions of other people's grandfathers did it. They cheerfully gave legs and arms and lives to serve this foreigner, who took them a thousand miles away from their homes and marched them into a barrage of Russian or English or Spanish or Italian or Austrian cannon and stared quietly into space while they were rolling in the agony of death.

Why? Van Loon admits that he can only guess:

> Napoléon was the greatest of actors and the whole European continent was his stage. At all times and under all circumstances he knew the precise attitude that would impress the spectators most and he understood what words would make the deepest impression. . . . At all times he was master of the situation. . . . Even at the end, an exile on a little rock in the middle of the Atlantic, a sick man at the mercy of a dull and intolerable British governor, he held the centre of the stage.

In sum, a French ideal.

Napoléon's ups and downs went quickly. He conquered in the name of *liberté, égalité, fraternité,* but he oppressed the masses with a talent Louis XVI never approached. Flushed with victories, he amassed ships to attack England in 1805. Lord Nelson annihilated the fleet at Trafalgar. Without a navy, France all but abandoned its colonial empire.

He took Louisiana back from Spain; the vast territory would supply his sugar islands. But he needed Florida in order to command the Caribbean, and the Spanish would not budge. In 1803, he sold Louisiana to Thomas Jefferson, and America went into the empire business.

The Egyptian campaign withered away. France had nowhere to go but east, by land. Czar Alexander I of Russia had tried five times to defeat Napoléon, aligning himself with any sovereign willing to fight. In 1812, a French army headed toward Moscow. Within two months, Napoléon seized the Kremlin. But he stayed too long. The city burned, and the French retreated into the Russian winter. Cossacks reduced the Grande Armée to a mob fleeing in panic.

Back in Paris, Napoléon raised an army of teenagers. He met the Russians at Leipzig, lost a bloody battle, and fled. Then he abdicated in favor of his young son, but victorious allies placed Louis XVIII on the French throne. The king sent Napoléon to rule the Mediterranean island of Elba. Within two years, he landed a tiny band of loyalists at Cannes. Soldiers deserted the indolent Bourbon king to serve him. France resented Napoléon's depredations, but he had made Paris the capital of the world.

Emperor again, Napoléon sought peace, but his enemies wanted war. His old fire was gone. He defeated a Prussian army in Belgium but let the main force escape. Two days later, about to conquer Wellington at Waterloo, Napoléon saw what he thought was his cavalry galloping up for the coup de grâce. It was the Prussians. The emperor was crushed again, 100 days after his triumphant return. He handed his crown to his son and made for the coast, bound for America. But Louis XVIII, back on the throne, expelled him from France. Napoléon knew the Prussians would shoot him so he informed the English court that the former emperor of France wished "to throw himself upon the mercy of his enemies and like Themistocles, to look for a welcome at the fireside of his foes." He got St. Helena, the rocky Atlantic island where he died seven years later.

The 1814 Treaty of Paris again reordered the Caribbean. France got back Guadeloupe and Martinique, along with Guiana and St. Pierre and Miquelon. But Tobago and St. Lucia went to Britain.

Haiti was lost for good. Toussaint L'Ouverture, after defeating the British, demanded a better deal from the French. Napoléon did not like his tone; in 1802, he sent his brother-in-law, Leclerc, with a huge army and secret orders to restore slavery. Napoléon told the Haitians that only France and its revolutionary ideals could defend their liberty. But France restored slavery in Guadeloupe, and Haitians suspected duplicity.

Leclerc invited Toussaint to meet him under a safe conduct. The Haitian leader, seized and deported, died miserably in a freezing stone cell in the Alps. But insurgents battered the French force. In months, yellow fever killed 29,000 men, including Leclerc. Napoléon promised another 35,000 troops but they could not penetrate a British blockade.

THE RESTORED Bourbons slowly rebuilt the colonial empire. The 1814 treaty had also cost France the Seychelles and Mauritius. But there was still Réunion (l'Ile Bourbon) and, farther east, Pondicherry and other Indian properties. France colonized the east coast of Madagascar, and kept African trading posts at St.-Louis and the Ile de Gorée. From there, they established rights far up the Senegal River.

And then a Barbary Coast potentate had the temerity to slap the French consul, and North Africa was on its way to becoming part of Europe.

Louis XVIII had died in 1824. An ineffectual but moderate remnant of the *ancien régime,* his imposed reign had caused no great unrest. But his brother, Charles X, was a religious zealot, anxious to reimpose an absolute monarchy. He made the theft of sacred objects punishable by death. Charles X was not nearly as widely loved as he would have liked to be. But he kept trying.

In 1827, Charles X's consul, Pierre Deval, guided his horse through Algiers up to the Casbah to salute Dey Hussein. Relations were tense. Since the Turkish occupation of the sixteenth century, the French had leased trading posts on the North African coast. But there was bickering over rent. Also, Hussein wanted the payment due an Algerian Jewish merchant whom he had backed in a grain sale to Napoléon. Twice he had written to King Charles X asking for settlement of the debt.

We have Deval's account of the meeting.

After paying his respects, the consul asked about a papal vessel under the French flag which had been seized by Barbary pirates. Hussein exploded.

"Instead of raising a subject that does not concern you, you had better hand me a reply to the letter I have addressed to King Charles. Has it arrived, this reply? When will you give me the money? If you do not, I will throw you in prison."

"Ah!" retorted Deval. "Don't touch me. If you touch me, you will be dealing with my government."

Hussein slapped the consul across the face with his peacock-feather fly whisk.

"It is not me you insult, but the king of France," Deval said. "The king of France will avenge it."[2]

The dey ejected him from the palace with unkind words for the king of France.

Six weeks later, France declared war and blockaded Algiers for three years. The effect was minimal. Two crippled French vessels drifted ashore; their crews were massacred, and the Sardinian consul had to buy back their severed heads in order to bury them. A French envoy, La Bretonnière, went to negotiate and Hussein's cannons fired at his ship.

It was all too much. Charles X sent 37,000 men. England objected vehemently, fearing a French colony between Gibraltar and Malta. French newspapers ridiculed the venture, warning of a debacle. Within a month, the *Provence*, which had evacuated Deval and then La Bretonnière, sailed into Algiers harbor. A French force landed unopposed and fought its way into the narrow, twisting streets of the city. The Arabs' guerrilla tactics confounded the commanders, used to orderly European formations. But firepower made the difference.

In his *La Vérité sur l'Expédition d'Alger,* Amar Hamdani suggests premeditation: Deval had proposed two weeks before his meeting with Hussein that Charles X should blockade Algiers. Eyewitness accounts, Hamdani adds, say that Deval was rude, provoking Hussein deliberately; the consul abused the purpose of the audience. And the fly whisk was not made of peacock feathers; it was straw from a date palm.

The king's purpose was as much survival as vengeance. Not long before, such victories had brought Parisians into the streets bellowing, *"Vive l'Empereur."* Charles X hoped something similar would shore up his sagging monarchy. But he went to Notre-Dame to celebrate in near silence. A few weeks later, Paris rose again. This time revolutionaries and king alike benefited from hindsight. The July Revolution took only three days. Charles X abdicated and Republicans averted civil war, naming the duke of Orléans, Louis-Philippe, as constitutional monarch, king of the French.

Louis-Philippe pushed on into Algeria. Alfred de Vigny reflected the predominant mood: "If one prefers life to death, one must prefer civilization to barbarousness. No people henceforth will have the right to remain barbarous at the side of civilized nations."

The war, however, was barbarous on both sides. General Thomas-Robert Bugeaud adopted *razzia* (scorched earth) as a tactic. One officer, Louis-Adolphe Saint-Arnaud, wrote, "We have burned everything, destroyed everything. How many women and children have died of cold and fatigue!" Another noted, "The carnage was frightful. Houses, tents, streets, courtyards littered with corpses . . . in the disorder, often in the shadows, the soldiers could not wait to determine age or sex. They struck everywhere."

The Arabs responded in kind, provoking the French to even greater excesses. One French officer lighted fires at the mouth of a cave, asphyxiating all but ten of the 500 men, women, and children seeking refuge inside. The incident raised a scandal in the Senate, and *Le Courrier Français* condemned "this cannibal act, this foul deed which blots our military history and stains our flag."

Two months later, Saint-Arnaud asphyxiated 1,500 people in another cave and sent a confidential message to Bugeaud: "No one went into the cave; not a soul . . . except myself." On Bugeaud's advice, the government hid the details from reporters, deciding that they were "evidently easy to justify, but concerning which there is no advantage in informing a European public."[3]

By 1837, France had imposed sovereignty over Algeria except for a part of Oran held by Abd-el-Kadar. Ten years later, Abd-el-Kadar surrendered. In 1848, Algeria was carved into three *départements* and absorbed into France. Arabs fought sporadically against French settlers taking their land, but peace held.

Few French knew how Algeria was subdued. Victor Hugo visited Bugeaud, then governor-general, and found him depressed. France could not hold its head high, the governor said, and Algeria would be hard to colonize. Hugo disagreed:

> Our conquest is a grand and happy thing. It is civilization marching against barbarousness. It is an enlightened people finding a people in the night. We are the Greeks of the world; it is up to us to illuminate the world. Our mission accomplished, I can only shout, Hosanna. You think differently from me; it is simple. You speak as a soldier, a man of action. I speak as a philosopher and a thinker.

Later, Hugo described a peaceful dockside scene interrupted by hubbub around a mysterious cargo, with a long frame and a heavy iron blade: "A spectacle more interesting, in fact, than the palm trees, the aloes, the fig trees, than the sun and the hills, the sea and the sky: it was civilization arriving in Algiers in the form of a guillotine."

The Arabs were mystified. Here was an occupying power that might fall upon a suspect, arrest him and, after trial, release him for lack of evidence. But attacking officers might wipe out a score of Arab men, women, and children without a second thought.

"The Arabs . . ." reflected Alphonse Daudet, "a people we civilized by bestowing our vices."

PUSHY AMERICANS limited French movement in the Western Hemisphere. James Monroe enunciated his Doctrine, prompting L'Etoile in Paris to reflect on the cheekiness of a temporary president of a poorly armed republic, independent for only forty years. Tension grew serious over compensation for shipping seized by Napoléon. France agreed to pay but didn't. Charles X, short of cash, delayed and came up with counterclaims. Finally, Andrew Jackson blew his stack. "I know them French," he was quoted as saying. "They won't pay unless they're made to." Paris agreed to settle but only with an apology. "France will get no apology," thundered the *Washington Globe*. In 1835, envoys were recalled and navies were put on alert. Jackson finally came up with something close enough to satisfy France.

"These people seem to me stinking with national conceit," Alexis de Tocqueville wrote to his mother. "It pierces through all their courtesy."

LOUIS-PHILIPPE FACED pressure to expand the empire. Alphonse de Lamartine pointed to England's successful colonization which, he said, "has given birth to children who will perpetuate her name and her influence." The king colonized slowly, anxious to avoid conflict with Britain. But he pushed ahead, nonetheless. "What does it matter if 100,000 shots are fired in Africa?" he remarked. "Europe does not hear them."

Missionaries clashed over who would civilize souls in the South Pacific. Admiral Dupetit-Thouars planted French colors on the eastern Society Islands, the Marquesas, Gambier, and Wallis. French forces occupied the Gabon estuary and the Ivory Coast in 1838 and, later, northwest Madagascar, Mayotte, and scattered Indian Ocean properties. Intrepid Frenchmen set out on their own. René Caillié, obsessed with the ancient desert city of Timbuktu, walked there alone in 1838, disguised as a pilgrim.

In 1848, Louis-Philippe's July Monarchy melted away. "It died," observed Maurois, "for lack of *panache.*" Accustomed to glory, France found the complacent, peace-loving regime dull and ridiculous. People seized on Lamartine's judgment: "France is bored."

And nothing cuts boredom like another Napoléon.

NAPOLÉON I had left his crown to his son, but Napoléon II, the duke of Reichstadt, disappeared into history. It was Louis-Napoléon who took the name Bonaparte most seriously. His mother, Hortense, was the daughter of Joséphine de Beauharnais and Napoléon's stepdaughter. Hortense married Louis Bonaparte, becoming at the same time Napoléon's sister-in-law. No one is certain if Louis was actually Louis-Napoléon's father. But the blood lines were clear enough for royalty.

Louis-Napoléon studied in Switzerland with an affable but indolent tutor and nearly ended up as yet another Bonaparte wastrel. But at the age of twelve he came under the tender mercies of Philippe Le Bas. From dawn to late at night, he absorbed Latin, German, Greek, history, science, mathematics, and the rights of kings. Le Bas cured his nightmares by cutting out the more violent subjects: riding and dance.

Banned from France as a Bonaparte, Louis-Napoléon sneaked into Strasbourg and instigated a few officers to mutiny. Louis-Philippe laughed it off and sent him to the United States. In 1840, however, Louis-Napoléon invaded France. It was not the way his uncle would have done it. He landed at Boulogne in a fragile boat with a few followers. Officers on shore had been bought off, but not very effectively. The garrison was waiting. Louis-Napoléon fired a pistol shot at the commander but fortunately, and probably deliberately he missed. This time, he was locked up in a humid stone cell near the Belgian border.

In prison, he wrote books on Bonapartist ideology. By 1846, fearing for his health, he sneaked out of his cell disguised as a workman. He fled to London to wait.

Then thirty-nine, the "Little Eagle" was short but ponderous, with drooping mustaches, a red beard, and dull grey eyes. He spoke French like a German and weighed each word. "At first glance, I took him for an opium addict," one visitor remarked. "Not a bit of it; he himself is a drug, and you quickly come under his influence." He had wit. His cousin, Prince Napoléon, once remarked, "The Emperor? But you are like him in nothing." He replied, "You are wrong, *mon cher;* like him, I am saddled with his family."

Louis-Napoléon came back to be elected first president of the Second Republic by a landslide. When his term expired, the law forbade reelection. So he rallied the army to demand that he stay on as president. Mysteriously, crowds began chanting, *"Vive l'Empereur."* By popular acclaim, as he explained, he had himself crowned Napoléon III.

"THE EMPIRE means peace," Napoléon III declared, and he fought half of Europe to prove it.

He courted the English, who had quashed the First Empire and still commanded the seas. Britain vowed to defend the Ottoman Empire against Russia, and he proposed an alliance against the czar.

After a disastrous start to the Crimean War, Britain and France won. But even the emperor's victories brought him grief.

In Italy, he reversed his loyalty to nationalists and sent troops to defend the pope's temporal powers. But after Italian patriots fire-bombed his carriage, nearly killing him and Empress Eugénie, he backed their cause to push Austria out of Italy. The Italians triumphed, with Napoleonic aid; they gave France Nice and Savoy as spoils. But they then rose against the pope. The French clergy, and even the devout empress, rounded on the emperor.

Prussia, showing no gratitude for Napoléon III's help against Russia, joined his enemies. Then the emperor made peace with Austria, infuriating the Italians. He advised the pope to yield, outraging his own clergy. By the time he yielded to pressure to back the Vatican, Pope Pius IX was allied against him. King Victor Emmanuel united Italy and seized most papal lands. Napoléon III had lost all over the board.

At home, he enraged capitalists and conservatives by signing a free-trade accord with England. He secured lower tariffs, fewer embargoes, and more concessions for French products. But industrialists were angry that he did not consult them first, and many cursed the emperor for bringing their ruin. That was the pattern. He brought France to a state of unparalleled wealth; railroads, ports, and factories were built. New banks encouraged people to save. He brought prosperity to the colonies and abolished most of the remaining slavery. But people rankled at his heavy hand and his ubiquitous secret police.

Overseas, the empire expanded. Napoléon delivered from the throne, in November 1863, the watchword of his lucid if erratic march toward free trade: "To civilize the world with commerce."

From 1853, France peopled New Caledonia with gold seekers, smugglers, deserters, and other hard cases. Despite objections by native Melanesians, a penitentiary was built. One of the first inmates was a terrorist named Berezowsky who had shot at Czar Alexander II as he and his host rode through the Bois de Boulogne to the 1867 World's Fair.

The emperor moved into Indochina. French priests had cast about the area for souls to save since the sixteenth century, and French traders probed the coasts. Annamese rulers resented the meddling.

The court at Hue beheaded two missionaries; one was French. Napoléon III sent ships to fire on the city, but two more Europeans were executed. So Admiral Rigault de Genouilly, fresh from bombarding Canton, shot his way up the Saigon River and demolished the local citadel. French sailors were still carrying loot from Peking where, in rare concert with the English, they had burned the Summer Palace and blackened their names for generations to come.

One officer described the 1859 Saigon assault:

> Major Delavau bashed in a door with a rifle butt and bayonet, and I did the same at another side. We penetrated the enclosure but we were stopped by a structure inside, three meters from the door from where they rained down on us a hail of firepots and rockets which, plunging us into a chaos of flames, smoke and explosions, forced us to retreat. I changed my plan of attack.

A city was shaped by men in wool and boots, protected only by funny-shaped sun hats from the steaming humidity and insects. Ten percent of Saigon's early settlers died from dysentery, malaria, cholera, or mysterious causes. At first men slept in open huts. Wrote one: "All animals of creation enjoy easy access, and you must grow accustomed to the sound at night, around you and over you, of innumerable reptiles, rats, and bats reaching sometimes an incredible wingspan." And another: "We slept in barns with no lack of scorpions or snakes, not to speak of an evil-doing insect that no one ever caught, nor saw, whose bite swells the skins and causes fever."

But there was mosquito netting and red wine. Within three years, French Cochin China covered three provinces of southern Vietnam, with 260 miles of telegraph line and a lighthouse beaming radiance into the South China Sea. Saigon had a girls' school, sidewalks, a decent hotel, and an urban plan for a city bigger than Paris. In 1860, 110 European trading vessels called at the city, along with 140 Chinese junks.

Steam had made the difference. Of 120,600 Frenchmen who embarked on Compagnie des Indes ships from 1644 to 1789, about 35,000 were lost at sea. But by 1862, the Messageries impériales began bimonthly service east with a railroad link across the Suez.

The trip from Marseilles to Saigon took five weeks, instead of thirteen around the Cape of Good Hope.

The French had found Indochina divided among ancient peoples who defended their borders with armies and diplomacy. The Annamese (Vietnamese) controlled what is now Vietnam from the Citadel at Hue. China cast a shadow over the northern Annamese in Hanoi and surrounding Tonkin. The Khmer, pushed across the Mekong to Cambodia, kept a fragile independence from the neighboring Siamese. The Lao court sat at Luang Prabang.

Cambodia soon slipped under French protection; King Norodom preferred Napoléon III to the closer-to-home perils of the king of Siam. A young officer named Francis Garnier, as worthy a candidate for the label "intrepid" as history might produce, explored the Mekong River and routes to China. He brought France to most of Tonkin.

Meanwhile, yet another French officer-explorer began settling vast tracts of African hinterland. Louis Faidherbe, with a stiff collar and a huge mustache, sank French roots on the little island of St.-Louis; it is now connected to the mainland by Pont Faidherbe. Senegal, no longer exporting humans, needed cash crops. He developed agriculture and administration so prosperity could follow.

And on November 17, 1869, the Suez Canal was opened, a triumph of French diplomat and engineer Ferdinand de Lesseps, linking Europe directly to the East.

As soldiers and traders established outposts of empire, Roman Catholic missionaries settled in to civilize them. From 1822 to 1870, twenty-two new missionary orders were organized in France. By 1870, the French colonial empire covered 900,000 square kilometers, with 2,820,000 inhabitants. Napoléon III had some cause for pride. But there was also Mexico.

IN THE 1850s, French and English residents had been harassed—robbed and raped—by troops under the latest Mexican revolutionary, Benito Juárez. Lord John Russell proposed an Anglo-French force to stabilize Mexico and set up a government that would pay off its debts. Napoléon III was anxious to fight again alongside England. And he was fascinated by the idea of a canal across Central

America. But, under the Monroe Doctrine, the American president would likely object. Then the United States went to war with itself, and the picture changed.

France needed cotton from Mexico since the South stopped its exports, and it was desperately short of silver. Mexico had both. A Mexican victory would have foreign policy benefits. Napoléon III could share spoils with Austria to ease enmity over Italy. By taking along Spain, he could open the Spanish market to French merchants. And he would satisfy his Spanish wife, whose Mexican monarchist friends badgered him for support.

Also, Napoléon III saw Mexico as vital to the balance of what he called "the current state of civilization of the world." A strong United States fed European commerce and industry, he wrote. But if Washington controlled Mexico and Central America, it would be too strong. The balance would shift, endangering French interests.

Napoléon III wanted to conquer Mexico. The English, though less ambitious, made no objection. If the emperor succeeded, they would also benefit. If not, he was on his own.

The invading army melted under the coastal heat, battered by guns sent from the United States. Juárez agreed to pay his debts, and England and Spain were ready to go home. Napoléon III had named Maximilian, the brother of Emperor Franz Joseph of Austria, to be emperor of Mexico. But Maximilian agreed to the job only if backed by all three allies.

France, however, was not deterred. Marshal Bazaine pushed on with 23,000 reinforcements and the only map of Mexico he could find in France. The French waited five months before attacking Puebla, en route to the capital. There French forces gave Mexico its beloved Cinco de Mayo by getting themselves clobbered on May 5. But the French finally marched into Mexico City. A general reported back: "Sire, soldiers are literally crushed under flowers and wreaths. . . . The return of troops to Paris after the Italian campaign can alone give an idea of the triumph."

Maximilian and Empress Carlota took the throne in May 1864, and French troops were soon covered in more than flowers. Mexico needed an emperor even less than France did, and resistance was violent.

Napoléon III, in the meantime, had backed the Confederacy, confident that it would win. He needed Southern cotton and he preferred a divided America. In nearly a century of French-American friendship, the alliance had twisted and turned. But this was a severe blow. When Washington won the war, it threw its full weight behind Juárez.

The situation deteriorated fast in Mexico City. Bazaine mocked Maximilian and talked of taking the throne himself. Finally, Carlota made a desperate trip to Paris to plead with Napoléon III for more help. He refused. She then went to the pope and, after that, went mad. Soldiers deserted until the garrison shrank to 5,137 men, and Maximilian surrendered to Juárez.

In May 1867, Napoléon III received the crowned heads of Europe and huge crowds at the *Exposition universelle* of French industrial and technological triumphs. Moments before awarding the prizes, he was handed a telegram from Vienna: "Emperor Maximilian has been shot."

BISMARCK DROVE in the last nail. He annexed Danish provinces and dominated Germany. Napoléon III acquiesced, expecting a close alliance in exchange. Bismarck promised he would expel Austria from the German Confederation and take sides with Italy. If France remained neutral, he said, it could expect territorial compensation. Bismarck marched on Austria, leaving Germany exposed, but the French did not cross the Rhine. When the German prince returned, victorious, Napoléon III claimed his rewards, but Bismarck laughed him off.

The emperor demanded Belgium; Bismarck informed the English, who threatened war to keep Antwerp. Luxembourg and Mainz were German, Bismarck said. Venice went to Italy.

Napoléon III lost out, and the French do not like losers. The emperor admitted to "black spots which darken the horizon." Adolphe Thiers told the imperial ministers, "There is no mistake left for you to make." There was, of course.

The Spanish throne fell vacant, and a Prussian was invited to occupy it. But Napoléon III objected, and the Prussians informally deferred. The French emperor wanted a more formal renunciation of the throne, and sent an envoy to Wilhelm, the Prussian king.

Bismarck, who knew his media, issued separate communiques on that encounter. He told the Germans that an arrogant little Frenchman had insulted their king. At the same time, he told the French that the German monarch airily dismissed their envoy. It was clever news management. Bismarck provoked a war that Napoléon III half wanted anyway.

"Never," said Maurois, "had an international cataclysm been set in motion on a flimsier excuse."

Germany was ready; France was not. In two days, the Germans won two decisive victories. Napoléon III, suffering from bladder stones so painful he could barely walk, led an army toward Sedan. Bazaine, weak and indecisive, lost a main force. Within a month, on September 2, 1870, the emperor was a prisoner. He was allowed asylum in England, where he died in pain and was buried.

The Germans took Versailles and surrounded Paris. But a new Third Republic held the capital. Léon Gambetta floated out of Paris in a balloon and raised an army in Tours. Parisians, under siege, were reduced to eating zoo animals and rats, and by January they gave in.

Bismarck negotiated a humiliating peace, accepting huge indemnities—and Alsace and Lorraine. Just for good measure, a German army marched down the Champs-Elysées. The broad avenue, leading from the Arc de Triomphe of Napoléon I, was silent and draped in black.

CHAPTER TEN

Mission in Full Glory

AS USUAL, THE recuperative powers of France turned doom into triumph. Beaten badly, the French had no prospect of European adventure. Instead, they set out to colonize whatever real estate was left unclaimed—and some that wasn't—in the rest of the world.

For the first time, colonial policy was more than a haphazard, often reluctant reaction to circumstances. Colbert might have attempted more with swifter ships and telegraph; Napoléon III was headed in that direction. But it was the Third Republic that marshaled bankers and bandits, masons, teachers and preachers, public relations experts, soldiers of fortune, and soldiers of every other sort.

France flung itself headlong into its mission, with all its extremes. Some men and women died miserably pushing through the puff adders in pursuit of lofty goals. Others grew fat at home on the profits of mercantilism based on colonial monopolies. French ingenuity, sacrifice, and greed during the seventy years of the Third Republic shaped vast tracts of modern Africa, Asia, and the oceans.

A best-seller of 1874 was *De la Colonisation chez les Peuples modernes* by a thirty-one-year-old economist named Paul Leroy-Beaulieu. "The foundation of colonies is the best business in which one might engage the capital of an old and rich country," he wrote. Colonization, he added, was "one of the highest functions of societies which have reached an advanced state of civilization. . . . Colonization is the expansive force of a people . . . the submission of a universe, or a vast part of it, to its language, its mores, its ideas, and its laws. A people that colonizes is a people that casts the bases of its grandeur into the future and assures its future supremacy."

Others disagreed. Gustave Flaubert defined the subject in his *Dictionnaire des Idées reçues:* "Colonies (our): To be afflicted when one speaks of them."

Enthusiasm grew slowly. Admiral François Page, laying out the streets of Saigon, wrote:

> This country is strange, but full of resources. If France had a shadow of common sense, it could found here a magnificent colonial establishment, which would bring in money, a great maritime movement, and jobs for a multitude of layabouts who know only how to waste their time and degrade themselves. But these are dreams I don't wish to pursue. *Gaulois,* my friends, I know you too well; stay under your gray or blue sky, chat, gossip, and we'll let the earth turn.

Soon after Cochin China was established, Paris nearly gave most of it back, including loyal Annamese who would be punished for having accepted French protection. Prosper Chasseloup-Laubat, minister of the navy, spiked the idea with a memo that set the tone for colonial policy to come. He weighed potential income and money already spent. African slavery was finished, he noted; low-paid Indochinese could replace them throughout the empire. He pinged lightly on the triangle of glory, the Cap Saint Jacques lighthouse shone as "a dazzling symbol of the possession of France." Then he rose to a crescendo:

> France alone was absent (in Asia), but Providence seems to have reserved . . . not only one of the most beautiful and richest countries in these parts, but even more the one most prepared to receive the seeds of our authority . . . to be the center from which will radiate Christian civilization in the Far East.

Francis Garnier, the soldier-explorer, echoed his appeal:

> This generous nation, whose opinion rules civilized Europe and whose ideas have conquered the world, has received from Providence the highest mission, that of emancipation, of calling to the

light and to liberty races and peoples still slaves to ignorance and despotism.

Providence carried the day. In 1867, the French seized three more southern provinces, explaining that they were a refuge "for all the malcontents, all the agitators, all the enemies of our authority."

The war in Europe left the colony to fend for itself. News of Napoléon III's downfall reached Saigon September 27. But, just to be safe, the governor left his picture on the wall until official word arrived October 21. Six weeks after France, Cochin China left the Second Empire for the Third Republic.

In desperation, Empress Eugénie had offered Bismarck the young colony in return for Alsace and Lorraine. He laughed. "Oh! Oh! Cochin China. That is a big piece for us. We are not rich enough to afford the luxury of colonies."

Garnier found that the Saigon River went nowhere. For an access to China, France would have to go farther north, and the opportunity soon arose. A merchant named Jean Dupuis had set up shop in Hanoi to trade with the Chinese on the Red River. Tu Duc, the emperor at Hue, asked the French to remove him. Garnier took a small force to Hanoi to bring back Dupuis. But his secret orders were to open the river for the French.

Garnier blasted into the Hanoi citadel and seized Tonkin. But local mandarins hired the Black Flag, Chinese bandits, to murder him. Garnier chased a Black Flag band to the outskirts of Hanoi and ran headlong into an ambush. He emptied his pistol into the Chinese but was cut to ribbons.

In 1874, France agreed to abandon Tonkin and the Mekong Delta; in exchange, Hue granted a clear title to Cochin China and Annam was made a protectorate.

A college in Saigon trained colonial administrators. Later, moved to Paris, it grew to be the prestigious Ecole Nationale de la France d'Outre-mer. Eliacin Luro, the first director, defined its goals:

> In the matter of colonization by domination, by assimilation, one must not go too quickly; one must count on time. Mores, languages, laws cannot be changed in a few years, under pain of disaster. One must understand, penetrate the civilization of the

conquered, know their language, let them function first as they functioned before, then, little by little, patiently direct their steps, modify their pace. Finally, to the degree that an exchange of ideas among peoples has been made, that an economic revolution born of free competition has come to change mores, one must slowly modify and change laws.

First, of course, one must conquer. The Chinese did not recognize Tu Duc's treaties with the French and continued to massacre French traders and travelers.

Paris was in no timid mood by 1882. Pushed by Minister Jules Ferry, the navy dispatched Commandant Henri Rivière with orders to seize Hanoi and hold it while the diplomats did the rest. He took the city easily and then calmly wrote novels. At fifty-five, he wrote to his friends Flaubert and Alexandre Dumas *fils,* he was getting a little old to be a conqueror.

The Chinese sent more troops to Tonkin and refused to give way. Like Garnier, Rivière sallied forth after Black Flag thugs. He did not bother with forward patrols. When an aide advised caution, he replied, "Bah! You are made for the great wars. Me, I know about this. Let me take care of it. You will see." He was ambushed at the Bridge of Paper, where Garnier died. Rivière leaped from his carriage and charged with a cane. A bullet dropped him, and he was beheaded.

The French held Hanoi, but a hothead commander moved north toward the Chinese border. At Lang-Son, a messenger handed him a dispatch he could not read. He attacked, and his force was decimated. Later, it was learned that the Chinese were leaving; the message asked only for a few days to pack.

In Paris, reaction was violent. *Bon,* the Chinese were advised, no more Mr. Nice Guy. The French Tonkin force, totaling 3,750 men in 1883, swelled to 40,000 by July, 1885. France called out the nastiest of the Foreign Legion: the Turcos, sharpshooters from Algeria; the Zéphyrs and Zouaves, hard veterans of Africa. And there were regulars from the *métropole,* sweating in heavily ornamented parade uniforms under giant campaign sacks.

The French learned Vietnamese jungle tactics the hard way. Buried bamboo staves took a toll. Fast strikes surprised men used to orderly conduct of battle. But a bitter, brief war settled the Tonkin affair by treaty in 1885. War erupted again and then subsided. France still had to fight for trading posts in China, but it was master of Tonkin, Annam, Cochin China, Cambodia, and Laos.

IN PARIS, the political war was just as bitter. Jules Ferry, called *le Tonkinois,* fell over Lang-Son in a national upheaval over the whole policy of empire. Ferry, premier and then foreign minister, imperious and cutting, was not widely popular. Some thought he was too close to Germany. Catholics resented his sectarianism. His zealous defense of colonization had a following. But from November 1883 to late March 1885, he was called to the legislature twelve times to justify his Indochina policy.

During a heated exchange in the Chamber of Deputies, in July 1885, Ferry said: "Gentlemen . . . it must be openly stated that the superior races have rights in relation to inferior races. . . . I repeat that they have rights because they have obligations—the obligation to civilize all inferior races." To shouts that he was justifying slave trade, Ferry replied that the French Declaration of the Rights of Man was not written with African blacks in mind.[1]

Ferry's nemesis was Georges Clemenceau, spokesman for the left with a personal grievance against the minister. He said France was sinking into war with China, a nation of 400 to 500 million inhabitants. "While you are lost in your colonial dream, there are men here at your feet who demand useful expenditures to develop the genius of France," Clemenceau said in the National Assembly. He saw no predestined role for France. Germans, he said, tried to crush France to prove themselves a master race. "Since then, I must admit, I look twice before turning to a man or a civilization and pronouncing: inferior man or race."

Economist Frédéric Passy railed against spending "the blood and the gold of France" in fruitless global enterprise. If France seeks to radiate greatness, he argued, it can only do it by growing strong.

After the Lang-Son debacle, Ferry had to ask the National Assembly for more money to win the war.

"We need it . . . for our honor," Ferry started.

"Who compromised our honor?" demanded Georges Périn.

Things went downhill from there. At one point, Clemenceau thundered:

"We do not wish to hear you any longer; we do not wish to discuss with you the greater interests of *la patrie*. . . . We do not know you anymore, we do not wish to know you. . . . These are not ministers before me, but men accused of high treason."

Funds were approved—it was too late to back out—but Ferry had to sneak out the back to avoid crowds outside waving fists and yelling, "Get out, *misérable!*" "To the gallows!" And, "Into the water, Tonkinois, Prussian!" Some saw Ferry cry.

Léon Bloy, in his gutter style, fumed: ". . . This man would turn, by the urine stink of his tears, more fetid than the sexual impurity of the Whore of the prophet, the fertilizing mayonnaise of the sewers of Pantin and Bondy."

"And all of this for Tonkin?" reflected Guy de Maupassant. "It is written therefore that our colonies will be, for us, always fatal."

De Maupassant reasoned that some lands should remain uninhabited by Europeans. "The human seed grows like that of plants in land that is good for it," he wrote. ". . . I would put all our colonies in a suitcase, Senegal, Gabon, Tunisia, Guiana, Guadeloupe, Cochin China, the Congo, Tonkin and the rest, and I would find Mr. Bismarck. I would say, 'Sir, you're looking for colonies . . . here is a complete assortment, of all types, of all nuances. . . . I ask of you, for each, one kilometer of Alsace and one kilometer of Lorraine."

Right-wing deputies also insisted on recuperating Alsace and Lorraine as a first priority. Paul Déroulède thundered, "I have lost two sisters, and you offer me twenty chambermaids!"

But the race was on. Gambetta and Ferry had already planted the flag in Tunisia in 1881, with the treaty of Bardo. Troops went to Madagascar in 1883 for the ostensible purpose of protecting missionaries. The French obtained a protectorate accord two years later, but only a decade of blood and bitterness brought the island firmly under control.

Pierre Savorgnan de Brazza, an Italian count of dash and endurance, explored the rain forests of central Africa. He was a naturalized French army officer who funded much of his own expeditions. He had claimed Gabon. Then, marching barefoot with Senegalese troops, he raced to the Congo River ahead of Henry Morton Stanley and his Belgian flag.

The Bateke king, Makoko, chose the French. He handed Brazza a sack of dirt destined for "the great white king" (a president, in fact) to remind him that he owned the Batekes' land. Makoko dug a pit for his chiefs' arms. Brazza planted a tree on top and declared, "May peace last until this tree gives forth iron and powder." He left behind three Senegalese to protect a new settlement called, not surprisingly, Brazzaville.

Brazza wrote, "The Moslem element being unknown in the region, European civilization need not expect to encounter the hostility, hatred, and fanaticism which oblige the French to advance only with armed force from Senegal to Niger. There is nothing to be feared except the natural opposition to whatever is new."

But farther north, Frenchmen in growing numbers were buried beneath the sands, their bodies tilted toward France. Expeditions pushed up the Niger River into the Sudan, now Mali. Joseph Galliéni, a hero of Indochina, led the way. After two years on campaign, his kit was so ragged that he had to borrow pants from the surgeon and boots from a gunnery lieutenant in order to negotiate with an emir. There was also Aimé Ollivier, who never took off his gloves, bathed each morning, dined with flatware, armed himself only with an umbrella, and regarded as essential survival gear his library of Racine, Montaigne, Plutarch, and Ronsard.

In 1888, a Peul emir, Almamy Hamadou, signed Guinea over to France and then chortled to aides about the European mania for meaningless treaties. He would accept arms and gifts and let the termites take care of the paperwork. It took more blood, but France made the treaty stick.

Pieces of the patchwork were sewn into place. The Foreign Legion, fresh from Tonkin, marched into Dahomey. They took literally their slogan, "March or Die." Bullets and spears killed 100; dysentery and malaria killed 200. But they hunted down Zinc-Beak, the "Shark King," and replaced him with a friendlier monarch. Other parts of the coast and the desert were brought under the French flag.

In most of West Africa, France aligned friendly tribes against hostile ones, mainly northern Moslems who trafficked in slaves.

French protection meant lost independence but a certain freedom from slave raids and looting.

Timbuktu had been terrorized for centuries by Tuaregs, the fabled "blue men" of the desert. René Caillié, a lone Frenchman, had smuggled himself in and out of the ancient Islamic center, disguised as a pilgrim, but until 1893 the city was forbidden to Europeans. That year, a young naval officer named Boiteux sailed up the Niger under orders to do no more than look around and leave.

Boiteux tied up at Kabara, the port five miles south of Timbuktu, and sent a message to town authorities. Their promised emissaries did not appear; Tuaregs on camels ranged the dunes between port and town. French guns routed a Tuareg assault, and Boiteux could wait no longer. He fought his way to town and dug in on the outskirts. Local leaders, meanwhile, were frantic. If they leaned to the French, the Tuaregs would sack Timbuktu the moment the foreigners left. If not, the French would do the sacking. While they waffled, word came that Boiteux had better return to his boat.

Tuaregs had killed twenty Frenchmen, the worst debacle yet in West Africa. Boiteux faced excited Tuaregs and 10,000 restive townsfolk with fourteen men. He pleaded for help from Colonel Bonnier downriver. Across the shimmering dunes, he could see the billowing robes of nomads gathering for the kill. The French position grew desperate. Then Bonnier rode in with the cavalry. Boiteux ran to greet him; the colonel cursed him as a dolt and sentenced him to forty-five days' arrest on his own boat.

The battle was bitter. Evaporating and reappearing over the dunes, the Tuaregs dispersed Bonnier's straggling column into disorder. They swept in on camels, thrusting swords and firing at close range. A third of the French force was killed: eleven officers, two sergeants, and seventy-four riflemen. Bonnier, shot square in the chest, was among the first.

A fresh column arrived under Joseph Joffre and methodically subdued the nomads. The French governor, seeking news, dispatched message after message into the void; he recalled Bonnier, already dead; he reassigned Joffre to the railroad as punishment. Joffre fought a last battle, leaving sixty Tuaregs dead without losing a man, and returned to find a frantic request for news. He dictated a response to the governor: "All is quiet in Timbuktu. The sanitary situation is satisfactory."

He reflected a moment and added, "Satisfactory enough."

There was more desert to pacify. For thirty years, an emir named Samory pillaged farming tribes and eluded French forces. Finally, in 1899, he was on the run. The French knew if they killed him in battle he would live on as a martyr. They caught him and paraded him in chains.

That left Chad. The reigning emir, Rabah, wanted Europeans out of his vast desert at the center of Africa. But France needed Chad. A freelance colonizer named Ferdinand de Behagle attacked but fell into Rabah's hands. A 1941 history, *Sous le Casque Blanc,* by Roland Dorgelès of the Académie Goncourt, gives these as Behagle's final words (without indicating how he happened to know them): "I must die, *c'est bien.* A Frenchman does not fear death. But remember I will be revenged."

There is no disputing the last part. Emile Gentil, from the French outpost of Fort-Archambault, dispatched forces to chase Rabah across Chad. Major Lamy ran him to ground. But the emir's men fired from hiding, killing Lamy on his horse, and then fled. Later the French found Rabah's body. A bullet fired at the disappearing nomads had struck him in the head.

The skirmish was on the Chari River, where Gentil situated the new capital of French Chad. He called it Fort-Lamy, and a statue to Lamy was inscribed, "He opened the way for civilization. . . ."

That last piece in place, France had an unbroken stretch from the Mediterranean across the Sahara to the Congo. With enough stamina, you could travel 4,565 kilometers, from Algiers to Brazzaville, without leaving French territory.

EUROPEAN POWERS met at Berlin in 1884 and for a year they drew arbitrary lines on an African map, dissecting ancient tribes, separating arid hinterland from potential farms, and ignoring natural divisions. Geographers could only guess at the terrain. Philosophically, the dominant approach was Victor Hugo's: "What a land, this Africa! Asia has its history, America has its history, even Australia has its history; Africa has no history." Colonizing powers divided up the continent with every intention of bestowing history.

Bismarck encouraged French colonial adventure, reasoning that an otherwise occupied France would not threaten him on the Rhine. Morocco, as a result, joined the French sphere.

Conflicts were numerous. France battled over the Congo River where Brazza and Stanley, in the pay of King Leopold of Belgium, glared at one another across the water. But the last great standoff was on the Nile.

Britain planned to lay a railroad track from Cairo to Cape Town, marking in iron their mastery of Africa. France wanted a road from Dakar to Djibouti. An east-west axis, with a spur to Brazzaville, would give the French domination. Both sides felt they had earned the right to command the continent. For each, the missing central link was Sudan.

Paris sent Captain Jean-Baptiste Marchand to Sudan in 1896. His minister's last words, he noted, were, "Fire a pistol shot over the Nile; we will take care of the rest." Almost immediately afterward, London dispatched Sir Herbert Kitchener up the White Nile in the first attempt to reoccupy Sudan since the Mahdi overran Charles "Chinese" Gordon at Khartoum twelve years before. From opposite directions, Marchand and Kitchener were racing for an abandoned, swamp-bound little outpost called Fashoda.

Kitchener moved down from Egypt with one major obstacle ahead of him: he had to subdue a vast desert full of Islamic fanatics who had already slaughtered a British army entrenched behind walls. Marchand, meanwhile, only had to walk across Africa from the Atlantic through the nastiest bit of jungle on the earth's surface, carrying 500 tons of baggage.

The proud and prickly French captain cut 120 miles of road through impassable rain forest, spanning ravines with logs. He commandeered the river steamer *Faidherbe* on the Ubangi; for most of the trip, the boat had to be broken into sections and rolled along over tree trunks. Hostile tribes ambushed his column; porters deserted; disease decimated his ranks. Finally, on the Nile, his ragtag band bogged down in the mud, moving scarcely 500 yards a day. Supplies dwindled and mosquito nets were in shreds. His men awaited orders.

The moment is described in Dorgelès's paean to French explorers: "He raises his eyes. This illuminated gaze which penetrates you.

'They have asked us the impossible. *Eh bien.* We will give them the impossible, or we will give our lives. God will decide.'"

It took the French two years to reach Fashoda, and they won the race. Kitchener, pinned down by Dervishes, had to await reinforcements from Egypt. Marchand found a gun platform in the crumbled old citadel and ordered the flag raised. In mid-ceremony, a rotten rope broke and the Tricolor tumbled to the ground. "At that omen," remarked a French officer, "Romans would have turned around and gone home." But Marchand rebuilt the old walls and held off Mahdist attacks, using 12,000 cartridges. He had 28,000 left when Kitchener's huge force steamed up the Nile.

The meeting was gentlemanly. Kitchener had orders to raise an Egyptian flag for the khedive at the fort. Over our dead bodies, Marchand said. Given the numbers, that was likely, Kitchener replied, not to speak of certain war between England and France.

Marchand had sent a flash message to Paris for instructions and expected an answer in ten months. Kitchener had better communications, but the French did not trust them. The Tricolor still hung limply in the humid air, and Doctor Emily's zinnias bloomed. "These French," muttered an English officer. "Flowers at Fashoda."

The atmosphere was icy cold on the White Nile, but in Paris and London it was scorching. Newspapers screamed for war, evoking national honor, manifest destiny, and every other Anglo-French issue back to William the Conqueror. Fleets were mobilized. But Foreign Minister Théophile Delcassé knew the real threat was Germany; a war with England would be fatal. King Edward VII and his minister, Lord Lansdowne, were no enemies of France.

Delcassé ordered Marchand home. The captain, seeking confirmation, sent his deputy, Baratier, to Paris. It was true. Dorgelès reports this exchange:

"And the minister?" asked Marchand.
"He asked me why we were still at Fashoda."
"What?"
"Yes, he greeted me with those words. . . . He then said that if England declared war, our mission was lost."
"What does that matter, our lives!" Marchand said.
"That's what I told him. That our fate should not count if the

honor of France was at stake. He replied, 'You don't understand very well the honor of France.' "

The French backed away not only from Fashoda but from all of Egypt and Sudan. Colonial rivalry ended, more or less, all over the globe. England and France reached an entente cordiale, an informal friendship that, so far, still holds. It was finally the swamp itself, not the French, that blocked a link from Sudan to the south.

THE FRENCH set about consolidating the empire they had staked out. But they were thin on the ground almost everywhere.

"The truth is that in the Congo our authority stops at the range of the rifles of our outposts," wrote Pierre Mille in 1899. The Belgian Congo colonial army numbered 12,000, he said; the French Congo army, in an area four times the size of France, had 1,400. "In this sense, the word 'impossible' continues not to be French," he said. "Individual initiative is, in our country, admirable. It is the collective initiative and the practical sense of the utilization of effort that is lacking."

An entertaining account of travel in French Africa comes from Mary H. Kingsley, a Victorian lady of ineffable pluck, whose 1897 diary includes advice on how to negotiate a mangrove swamp in a hoop skirt. She wrote:

> The French officials in Congo Français never hindered me, and always treated me with the greatest kindness. You may say there was no reason why they should not, for there is nothing in this fine colony of France that they need be ashamed of any one seeing; but I find it customary for travellers to say the French officials throw obstacles in the way of any one visiting their possessions so I merely beg to state this was decidedly not my experience.

In Gabon, she said, a customs officer

> is courteous and kindly, but he incarcerates my revolver, giving me a feeling of iniquity for having had the thing. I am informed if I pay 15 shillings for a license, I may have it—if I fire French

ammunition out of it. . . . My collecting cases and spirit, the things which I expected to reduce me to a financial wreck by custom dues, are passed entirely free, because they are for science. *Vive la France!*

The people are seminomadic:

So when a village of Fans has cleared all the rubber out of their district, or has made the said district too hot to hold it by rows with other villages, or has got itself very properly shelled out and burnt for some attack on traders or the French flag in any form, its inhabitants clear off into another district.

Up the Ogooué, past the place where Albert Schweitzer later built his hospital, a French official refused to take responsibility for her traveling the rapids unaccompanied. The last woman through had had a husband. Her Igalwas guides are as good at rapids as any mortal man, she said,

and as for the husband, neither the Royal Geographic Society's list, in their "Hints to Travellers", nor Messrs. Silver, in their elaborate lists of articles necessary for a traveller in tropical climates, make mention of husbands.

She proceeded onward. Praising Brazza, she wrote:

It is impossible for any one to fail to regard him with the greatest veneration, when one knows from personal acquaintance the make of the country and the dangerousness of the native population with which he has had to deal.

She recounted Brazza's speech to Makoko on the glory of the French emblem.

I have no hesitation in saying . . . this high-flown statement is true; and although Brazza did a good thing for France that day, Makoko also did well, for he saved himself from the [Belgian] Congo Free State.

Gradually, needs were met, order was imposed, and roads were built. With the last pieces in place, France established French West Africa, administered from Dakar, and French Equatorial Africa, from Brazzaville.

NEW CALEDONIA had a rocky start. It was designated a penal colony but its energetic and somewhat bizarre governor, Admiral Charles Guillain, wanted more for the place. He designed an emblem featuring a convict, a native Kanak, and the motto "Civilize, Produce, Rehabilitate." He lured settlers from Réunion and elsewhere and urged them to form tight-knit little cooperatives in the manner suggested by his *maître-à-penser,* socialist reformer F. M. C. Fourier.

Arrivals included 5,000 deportees from the Commune of Paris, leftists who had held the capital for a month during the turbulent early days of 1871. They stayed for nearly a decade in a stone village on the luxuriant little Ile des Pins, just off the end of New Caledonia. Most left with an amnesty, and the jungle took back their camp.

And then the Kanaks arose in 1878, in a bloody first act to sporadic rebellion. The Kanaks, native Melanesians, were led by a bearded chief named Atai, remembered now as *le Vercingétorix noir.*

They had welcomed Captain Cook, who discovered and named the island, and the first missionaries. But shiploads of settlers upset the balance. The French took the best land and ran 80,000 head of cattle over sacred places. Missionaries slipped in esteem; they did not want the Kanaks to eat human flesh, but the Catholic God had a poor record for granting miracles. And European men had ungainly appetites for Melanesian women. Guillain, intending to protect Kanak land, had thrown traditional tenure into chaos with a system of titles.

The spark was the murder of a white ex-convict who lived with a Kanak woman. Some chiefs were arrested. Guerrillas attacked a military post at La Foa and killed four gendarmes. Another thirty-nine white settlers were massacred. Commandant Henri Rivière moved in heavy guns. Accounts are grim on both sides. Atai was betrayed; French soldiers overran his camp, cut off his head, and packed it off to Paris for anthropological study. Revolt spread across the island. The *Encyclopédie de la Nouvelle-Calédonie* estimated that 1,000 insurgents and 200 Europeans died. About 200 farms, settlements, and native villages were razed. The revolt ended in 1880 when 110 Kanak warriors from six tribes surrendered.

France now occupied colonies across the Pacific. The Loyalty Islands off New Caledonia were settled, along with other remote bits of coral and volcanic rock. But the prize was Tahiti.

Parisian geography still tends to lump Melanesia with Polynesia. It may be true, as claimed, that the Ministry of Colonies in 1860 refused to build a bakery in Nouméa, New Caledonia, since people there could buy their bread in Tahiti. It was only a 3,000-mile swim.

The first European to sight Tahiti was Samuel Wallis, the Englishman after whom, following colonial logic, the French island of Wallis (pronounced Valees) is named. That was in 1769. Then came Bougainville, the French Quebec veteran, who was pioneering for Choiseul. The next ships were English, including Cook's. In 1789, Tahiti saw Captain Bligh's *Bounty,* more of it than most Tahitians wanted to see. Along with Union Jacks and *fleurs-de-lis,* the ships brought missionaries, habit-forming luxuries, and murderous microbes.

An English missionary, Pritchard, arrived in 1824 and grew close to Queen Pomare IV. He counseled against perfidious Frenchmen, and had two French missionaries arrested and bounced off the island in 1836. Admiral Dupetit-Thouars settled that score in 1838 and gave the queen a treaty to sign. Five years later, Tahiti agreed to be a French protectorate. But Louis-Philippe backed away from the agreement. Thus encouraged, Tahitians rebelled against the French. Blood was spilled, but calm returned in 1846, with a new accord.

Troubles lasted until 1880, when France moved in permanently. Colonial officials divided up the island and gave titles to individual Tahitians, overturning an elaborate structure of common land owned by ancestors. The Marquesas Islands had been French since 1858; the rest of the Society Islands followed.

Glancing today at a Gauguin, or a postcard, it is clear how Tahiti got its reputation as a paradise. But Henri Lebeau, traveling there in 1910, reported, "In this splendid place . . . all is ruin, misery, human decrepitude."

Tahiti, then ravaged by epidemic, would eight years later lose perhaps a quarter of its native population to Spanish influenza. In the Marquesas, according to historian Pierre-Yves Toullelan, the population fell from 60,000 in 1800 to 20,000 in the 1840s and 6,000 by 1874. Half of those survivors died by 1900.

French-born colonists in Polynesia totaled 477 in 1902. By 1926, 1,697 Europeans lived among 35,862 islanders throughout Polynesia.

FROM 1880 TO 1895, the French overseas empire grew from one million to 9,500,000 square kilometers. The population expanded from five to fifty million. The empire was far more than a string of primitive outposts manned by lonely men in scuffed boots. Saigon, by 1887, had already inspired a traveler to write:

> The rue Catinat, with its arcades, is the rue de Rivoli; the quai de Commerce is the quai d'Orsay; our delicious little theater, it is the ex-Folies Marigny. If you have no Bon Marché, here is Civette. The tour d'Inspection, the promenade of the Champs-Elysées. Spend the evening before the cafes of Saigon: the *terrasses* are as thick with people as on the *grands boulevards*. The sound of a piano brings you memories of the absent motherland and evokes sweet impressions in the soul.

Local cooks learned ancient Norman recipes, and added traces of curry and citronelle to develop a cuisine few cultures can match. The cathedral filled on Sunday mornings, but not nearly so regularly as the hippodrome.

In October 1912, Albert Sarrault, later to be minister of the colonies, addressed the Government Council at Hanoi. He was governor-general of Indochina, but he spoke for all parts of France d'outre-mer:

> The work accomplished is really grand, useful, fecund, and it deeply honors the nation that has conceived it. We came here charged with a high mission to civilize; we have now, by far, honored our engagements. We can without boasting, but without fear, face any comparison with other nations that ceaselessly oppose us in the work of colonization. And despite the few certain faults of our action, the few errors, the few organizational

vices, even the abuses not yet completely corrected . . . with what tranquility, nonetheless, can we turn to the indigenous person entrusted to our tutelage to tell him: "Compare your present state with what it was, before the radiance of the French soul in your country."

Sarrault boasted of peace and security, justice, flourishing fields, ports and bridges, schools and hospitals. He concluded, "Look at all this and ask yourself if French protection is an empty phrase, if any other nation of the world could have given you more, and if you, if left on your own, could have achieved this ensemble of progress and benefit."

Twelve years later, a Vietnamese nationalist named Ho Chi Minh took a different view: "Taxes, forced labor, exploitation; that is the summing up of your civilization."[2]

Léon Bloy put it this way:

The history of our colonies, especially in the Far East, is but pain, unlimited ferocity, and unspeakable turpitude. I have heard stories to make the rocks sigh. The one example suffices, of a poor young man who tried to defend some Moi villages, unbearably oppressed by administrators. The account was soon settled. Seeing him without support or patronage of any sort, the generals set a simple trap . . . and led him by the hand to activities described as rebellious.

Bloy referred to his own brother, Georges, imprisoned in 1886 after defending Indochinese against the administration.[3]

Anatole France, less personally involved, was more to the point: "Will this colonial folly ever end? . . . Colonies are the scourge of peoples."

In a study called *La Décolonisation*, Henri Grimal cites an unnamed French jurist's definition of the phenomenon:

To colonize, is to establish relations with a new country to profit from its resources of every nature, to develop it in the national interest, and to bring the endowments of a superior race to its primitive peoples, deprived of the advantages of intellectual, social, scientific, moral, artistic, literary, commercial and industrial culture. Colonization is therefore an establishment founded in a new country by an advanced civilization for the double advantages we have thus described.

The greatest colonial figure of his age, Hubert Lyautey, reflected a main current of French thinking for fifty years. As a young officer in Tonkin, in 1895, he advised a friend in Paris to visit England and the United States:

> For what is the ensemble of questions of the Far East, whether Japan, Laos, Siam or Afghanistan, it seems that you are in a position to know them as well in Paris as on the spot. There remains only the people to see, but these are no more than curiosities, and in their present slumber, from which they will certainly be awakened, they have nothing to teach us.

Lyautey found the Indochinese ugly but worth saving. At least, he wrote, colonies benefit the army: an ambitious officer learns more abroad in six months than during a whole career in France. He was upset that France messed with the dregs of Indochina but passed up the richest part: Siam. He enjoyed the pomp of colonial office, but was happiest chasing Chinese pirates with the Foreign Legion. At rest, he wrote his brother for a copy of Baudelaire's *Les Fleurs du Mal* and a *Figaro* review of the season's events on the Champs de Mars.

Two years later in Madagascar, he wrote: "It is not the Frenchman that lets down France but rather France that lets down the Frenchman. The *métropole* is decidedly a pain. Parliament seems to see our colonies according to the old Spanish method rather than the good old English method. One depletes and kills colonies by wanting them to be immediately remunerative; one prepares colonial empires for the future in letting them develop freely."

Lyautey decried an "absurd" customs regime, a premature tax system and a corps of officials and magistrates that were not only useless but also damaging. Governments had to invest heavily to earn from their colonies, he wrote, concluding: "Colonial policy is not for the poor, and we are poor."

France paid some heed. Between 1896 and 1900, only 9.8 percent of French exports stayed within the empire; colonial imports were 7.8 percent of the total. But investment was heavy. In 1914, 2,500 miles of road were built in Tunisia alone.

But in 1925, as governor of Morocco, Lyautey made a speech in Rabat that more Frenchmen should have heard:

> It is to be foreseen—and indeed I regard it as a historic truth —that in the more or less distant future North Africa—modernized, civilized, living its own autonomous life—will detach itself from metropolitan France. When this occurs—and it must be our supreme political goal—the parting must occur without pain and the nations must be able to continue to view France without fear. The African peoples must not turn against her. For this reason, we must, from today, as a starting point, make ourselves loved.

THOSE WHO DEFENDED colonialism as noble, and those who rejected it as immoral, each saw their view vindicated. At war with Germany, one Frenchman died every minute from August 1914 to February 1917. In four years, 75,000 Senegalese, Algerians, Indochinese, and others died for France, along with 1,126,000 Frenchmen. They were heroes rallying to the motherland—or luckless dupes forced to fight. Altogether, 607,000 colonial soldiers took up arms: 294,000 North Africans, 189,000 black Africans, 49,000 Indochinese, 41,000 Malagasys, 23,000 from the Caribbean, and 11,000 others.

The war bled France almost to death, but the allies won. Germany was stopped short of Paris this time. The Third Republic survived the war, and the empire emerged stronger than ever. Alsace and Lorraine were restored to France. The German colonies of Togo and Cameroon were absorbed into French Africa.

And in 1919, the League of Nations gave France trusteeship over Syria and Lebanon, which became the first French holdings in the Middle East since the Crusades. Almost immediately, France was at war with Moslem Syrian nationalists, and skirmishes continued off and on for years. But many welcomed the Tricolor. Before the war, France had 500 schools in Syria, with 50,000 students, from an "intellectual protectorate" dating back to Père Joseph in 1617.

Debate has been constant—and it rages still—over the cost of empire. A colonial zealot can show that France might have sunk into bankruptcy without assured markets and raw materials; a hostile legislator can demonstrate how colonies dragged France into a fiscal quagmire. Accounts are likely to be in the black, taking in the indirect returns. By 1933, a third of French exports were sold in the colonies, which produced a quarter of France's imports. But all of that misses the point.

Under Louis XIV, the population of France was twice that of any European power. In 1800, only the Russians outnumbered the French. A century later, there were more Austrians, Germans, and Britons (and, by 1933, Italians) than French. *La Grande Guerre* had killed 10.5 percent of the active male population, and it disabled nearly as many. Farms and industries were wrecked, peasant families shattered.

To a large degree, France owed its freedom to officers trained in the colonies. Galliéni, who tamed Tuaregs and *Tonkinois* with an agile wit, held off the Germans by sending troops in taxis to the Marne.

France could not have purchased the 1931 Colonial Exposition at any price. At the edge of Paris, workmen recreated the empire: Angkor Wat, Tunisian souks, an African village, and more. French people of every shade, in every costume, were brought to the capital. Children's imaginations were fired; chests swelled. Visitors from all over the world watched in envy the fruit of French cultivation.

A handsome *Atlas Colonial Français* was published for the occasion. Its introduction, set in type reserved for formal dinner invitations, was signed by Lyautey, by then Marshal Lyautey, member of the Académie Française, soldier, governor, historian, and empire-builder *par excellence.* Not only were the colonies essential to French grandeur, he wrote, but the war had proved them also vital to French survival. "What would have become of us if we had been reduced to our own means? The colonies are a reservoir where we can always find whatever we need." He concluded:

Must one add these are not the only reasons? Colonization, as we have always understood, is but the highest expression of civilization. We help backward peoples raise themselves up the ladder of humanity. This mission to civilize we have always fulfilled in the *avant-garde* of all nations, and it is one of our most handsome titles to glory.

Leafing through [this atlas] is a veritable voyage around the world, a world where one finds everywhere the flag and the face of France.

Within a generation, the titles to glory would be called into question. But before then, within the decade, France would need every drop it could draw from the rich reservoir in Lyautey's metaphor.

CHAPTER ELEVEN

End of Empire

ADOLF HITLER'S BLITZKREIG swept over the Rhine toward Paris before France recovered from the shock. France, like England, had bent double to appease Hitler, but when Germany invaded Poland, no choice was left. At 5 P.M., September 3, 1939, France declared war. More than with any war since the Gauls resisted Caesar, there were irrefutable reasons of principle. But there was no way to win. On June 22, 1940, France signed an armistice. The Third Republic was dissolved, replaced by the Third Reich.

France was more vulnerable in 1939 than in 1914. Despite all the lessons of World War I, the country was better equipped with glory than guns. European wars would be fought with steel and technique. But in 1927, France spent more on fodder for cavalry horses than it did on higher education.[1]

Sanche de Gramont noted that France, as usual, was one war behind. He blamed the debacle partly on the French penchant for taking words as deeds. Six months before the invasion, he wrote, novelist Jules Romains visited the army's supreme commander, General Maurice Gamelin, in the ancient Vincennes fortress where he sat "like a chief friar in a monastery." The general disliked going to the front, where he might see things that interfered with his opinions. In fact, Gamelin told Romains that the Germans would amass their total power for a swift and horrible assault. "When will it happen? May. Yes, May, it is almost certain." It was then May.

"Here was the French army chief predicting the date and the outcome of the German spring offensive for which France was totally unprepared," de Gramont observed. "For him, it was enough. He could go back to reading Einstein and art books. What did it matter that France did not have the planes or tanks to meet the German offensive so long as he, Gamelin, had an intellectual grasp of the situation?"

France had few friends to count on. Italy was hardly an ally; Mussolini's cheerleaders had crowds chanting, "Nice! Savoy! Tunis! Corsica!" Italy gave Germans access to the southern Mediterranean and North African colonial armies were needed to defend their own coasts. Russia had signed a nonaggression pact with Germany. Belgium was neutral. England, strong at sea and in the air, had few ground troops to offer. That left the United States, which meant almost nothing.

American neutrality laws tied the hands of suppliers who might have sold arms to France as they did in World War I. The antiquated French air force was outnumbered; the impenetrable Maginot Line was outflanked. And no one probed the Siegfried Line to take the war to Germany while Hitler was nailing down Poland. German armor punched through from the north and raced down along the Somme and the Aisne toward Paris. Dive-bombing aircraft softened what little defense could be swung into place. "Not even Joan of Arc could have stopped tanks with a peashooter," an American correspondent observed.

French 75s, admirable artillery pieces though they were, were no match for Panzers. Defending forces enabled Britain to pull 260,000 men back across the channel from Dunkirk. But Hitler boasted, with some reason, that he had captured 1,200,000 French, English, Belgian, and Dutch prisoners during that delaying action. Paris was obviously lost, and so was the war. At that point, Mussolini displayed characteristic courage and declared war on France.

The French government retreated to Tours, afraid that a battle for Paris would demolish the city. Then the bombs rained on Tours. The cabinet, not surprisingly, was divided. No one wanted the French fleet or the air force to fall to Germany; with that extra strength, Hitler could conquer England. Then who could eventually pick up the pieces of France?

Americans, perched squarely on the fence, were in any case short of hardware. Cordell Hull dismissed what he called "extraordinary

. . . hysterical" appeals. France made a final plea to Franklin D. Roosevelt; he said no. Britain would fight to preserve France on one of two conditions: the French fleet must be delivered to English ports; or France could join England in an "indissoluble Franco-British union."

But the French government, already evacuated to Bordeaux, was running out of territory. Algiers was considered but rejected as too far away and with no industrial base for supplying an army. Millions of refugees choked the roads meanwhile, including remnants of shattered armies fleeing the Germans. "Men living in that atmosphere of confusion and horror, had they been hard as flint, could not have remained calm and serene," said President Albert Lebrun.

France surrendered. A "free" zone established a capital at Vichy, and ministries settled into hotels built for ailing tourists coming to take the waters. Marshal Philippe Pétain, a hero of past battles, was head of state. Germany occupied Paris and three-fifths of France.

But in London, two days after the armistice took effect, Winston Churchill recognized Charles de Gaulle as "leader of the Free French."

DE GAULLE WAS the serious-minded son of a family that traced its roots to the medieval sword-bearing officer class. He rose through the ranks of the French army, lecturing at St. Cyr and publishing his thoughts in slim volumes. At the end, he commanded a division and then a cabinet post, seeking to head off the inevitable. Finally, he scrambled into an RAF plane at Bordeaux and went to London. Churchill wrote later, "De Gaulle carried with him, in this small airplane, the honor of France."

There are excellent biographies of de Gaulle, Jean Lacouture's and Don Cook's, among others. The general himself was neither brief nor modest in his memoirs. For quick reference, a glance at his photograph in profile is sufficient. His eyes, wise and worried, gazed loftily over an Alpine nose. He was the picture of immovable France in deep trouble.

De Gaulle spoke of his *certaine idée de la France.* He said he imagined France as the princess of fairy stories, or the Madonna in frescoes, dedicated to an exalted and exceptional destiny. He wrote,

Instinctively, I have the feeling that Providence has created her either for complete successes or for exemplary misfortunes. If, in spite of this, mediocrity shows in her actions, it strikes me as an absurd anomaly to be imputed to the faults of Frenchmen and not to the genius of their land. But the positive side of my mind also assures me that France is not truly herself unless in the front rank . . . that our nation . . . must aim high and hold itself straight, on pain of mortal danger. In short, France cannot be France without greatness.

In London, the general spoke on the BBC, appealing to the French to rally against occupation. Shortly afterward, a telegram arrived from Fort-Lamy, Chad, in the heart of France's African empire. Félix Eboué, the Caribbean-born governor-general, had rallied French Equatorial Africa behind de Gaulle. Bits of the empire followed.

By the terms of title of French overseas property, Eboué's gesture gave de Gaulle a piece of France. The general could argue his legitimacy on firm ground. That was a fine point, however; de Gaulle was not in the habit of arguing.

The general's manner provoked the stiffest of British upper lips to curl in fury; American leaders liked him even less. Roosevelt wrote to Churchill in 1943:

The continual intrigues of de Gaulle upset me more and more. When we actually enter France, we must consider the action as a military occupation organized by English and American generals. . . . I do not know what to do about de Gaulle. You perhaps might want to name him governor of Madagascar.

Churchill, in turn, called de Gaulle "a vain and malicious man" and told Roosevelt, "One cannot truly leave this fool to continue his pernicious activities."[2] De Gaulle placed the cross of Lorraine on his Free French flag. Churchill later grumbled, "The heaviest cross I have to bear is the *Croix de Lorraine.*"

De Gaulle observed that he had no choice. For the survival of his nation, he was destined to act as the perfect symbol of France, of French civilization, and of the French character. His admirers said he was correct. His detractors said yes, that was exactly what Roosevelt and Churchill were talking about.

Brazzaville and then Algiers served as Free French headquarters, along with London. At every stage, de Gaulle made it clear that he was a head of a world power, temporarily dispossessed of his national palace.

Bearing French honor, during World War II, took a strong back. French armies had fought better. A heroic resistance organization harassed the Germans, saved Allied pilots, and laid the groundwork for D-Day. Many paid with their lives. But the hated term collaborator was spoken with grim frequency. Degrees of collaboration varied widely. Many French hated the Germans but silently accepted occupation in fear that their own families might suffer. Nazi records show that 2,200 German Gestapo agents were sent to France. The French working for them were more numerous and, in some cases, more zealous. Forty percent of the industry in Vichy France fed Germany's war machine. De Gaulle was not only disavowed, he was sentenced to death *in absentia.*

A scattered Resistance, later unified under Jean Moulin, sabotaged the occupation. No one's figures are accurate, but activists were few in the dangerous early period. At the height of the war, hard-core *résistants* probably numbered fewer than 75,000, or 0.2 percent of the adult population. At liberation, the total suddenly swelled into the hundreds of thousands.

Jean Dutourd captured the mood in *Taxis de la Marne,* a poignant recollection of his surrendering to the Germans as a young soldier. His ironic title referred to France's moment of glory in the earlier world war, stopping Germany by ferrying troops to the front in taxicabs. He wrote:

> The name de Gaulle seemed bizarre; I did not at all grasp the weight of his proclamation and his decision to pursue the war in the name of our country. My comrades shared my indifference: we were much more interested in Pétain who had ended an untenable situation by signing an armistice. Thanks to him, all was okay and soon our treasured civilian life would be restored. In short, we were, according to the word that had such success

later, realists. We preferred to accommodate to reality rather than change it.

And then he added:

> The word realism is mainly a polite translation for cowardice . . . In the best of cases, realism leads to mediocrity; in the worst (the more frequent), it leads to the grave. There are circumstances where prudence is the worst of follies. Almost nothing done by great men is realist. It is by realism—lack of imagination—that men accept slavery. By the maxim, 'Better to be a live dog than a dead lion,' one descends to the rank of dog, which is precisely our case today. . . . One consoles oneself thinking if dogs wear collars and are kicked in the ribs, they are at least fed and sometimes petted. But that is deception, since not all lions die.

Passions distort memories, but facts are established. I discussed them in early 1986 with Serge Klarsfeld, a French lawyer who has painstakingly documented the period. His clinically precise treatment tends to surprise those who know his background. Klarsfeld escaped the ovens because his mother hid him in a wardrobe when police carried off his father. He spent the night listening through the thin wall to French officers torturing two little Jewish girls, neighbors, for information about their family's whereabouts.

Frenchmen delivered 76,000 Jews to the Germans, in cattle cars, along with thousands of Gypsies; only 3 percent came back after the war.[3] Vichy laws were virulently anti-Semitic. Some French risked a great deal to shield Jews; others, however, denounced Jews and then looted their belongings as soon as the police arrested them and took them away.

In a bitter television debate recently, a former French *résistant* quoted a remark of Hitler's: "Pétain, with his police, replaced fifteen divisions for me." At the time, the King of Denmark insisted on wearing a yellow Star of David to symbolize his resistance.

So raw were the wounds that Marcel Ophuls's epic film, *The Sorrow and the Pity,* was banned from French television for half a generation. Certain myths must be preserved, officials argued. It was only in 1981, after an energetic campaign by Klarsfeld, that French schoolbooks began to discuss the Vichy government's treatment of Jews. Later, Klarsfeld helped France to persuade Bolivia to hand over Klaus Barbie, the Gestapo officer in Lyon who tortured to death the Résistance hero Jean Moulin and sent hundreds of Jews to death camps. His trial was delayed repeatedly, to the relief of some Frenchmen not anxious to hear details he might reveal.

Leaks and personal feuds within the Free French organization hurt the war effort. Roosevelt and Churchill made a point of organizing D-Day without de Gaulle, keeping him out of most of the plans for the landing at Normandy. But the token French participation was enough for history: Captain Philippe Kieffer's 177-man commando team upheld France's honor on the Normandy beaches. Soon after, French land forces were again fighting to liberate France.

With Paris delivered, no force on earth could keep France's symbol of the hour, in his khaki kepi, from striding down the Champs-Elysées in a dazzling swirl of blue, white, and red. That de Gaulle was not invited to Yalta to help shape the postwar world was simply one more slight to rise above.

THE COLONIES played more than a strategic role. "Without her empire, France would be today nothing more than a liberated country," Gaston Monnerville said in 1945. "Thanks to her empire, France is a victorious nation."

In 1944, before the war ended, de Gaulle had convoked a meeting in Brazzaville of governors of the African colonies. He praised Brazza for winning Africans' friendship and using that "to advance at the same time the authority of France and civilization." That, de Gaulle said, was France's goal: "It is France, the nation designated by its immortal genius, whose initiatives are steadily raising men toward the summits of dignity and brotherhood where someday we all might come together."

The colonies' loyalty established a permanent link between *la Métropole* and *l'Empire,* he said. The meeting was to discuss carefully measured tangible gratitude. "There would be no progress . . . if men could not lift themselves little by little to a level where they would be capable of taking part in the management of their own affairs."

But no Africans were invited, and the ground rules were clear: "The goals of France's work of civilization in the colonies excludes any idea of autonomy, or any possibility of evolution outside of . . . the Empire; the eventual constitution, even distant, of self-government in the colonies is to be excluded."

Resolutions suggested that forced labor be abolished within five years and discouraged polygamy, among other things. They affirmed the Africans' right to education and advancement.

The Brazzaville meeting had shifted away from the term empire. The United States and the Soviet Union each inveighed against empires in the post-war world, and France saw potential heat coming from both extremes. The word, in any case, was not particularly popular since Napoléon III. Instead, de Gaulle laid plans for a French Union.

In Paris, a freshly reconstituted Fourth Republic began putting France together again. One of its first moves was to define the parts of the French Union.

Réunion, Guadeloupe, Martinique, French Guiana, and St. Pierre and Miquelon were folded into the motherland, like the three departments of Algeria. The water separating them from the continent was juridically beside the point. They were not colonies; they were France. The rest of *France d'outre-mer* was divided into various categories of association with futures yet to be defined.

But some leaders in the colonies had already defined their futures without France. Syria and Lebanon, loosely tied to Paris, broke free after some struggle. French troops put down a nearly unreported rebellion in Madagascar, killing anywhere from 10,000 to 100,000 insurgents in 1947. The respected political scientist Alfred Grosser noted in *Affaires Extérieures* that authorities did not acknowledge reports of systematic torture in Madagascar. "But the accounts are precise and not refuted, and the Tananarive prison is certainly not the only place where one inflicted tortures very similar to those used by the Gestapo in France," he wrote. No one was prosecuted, Grosser said, not even a lieutenant who ordered the prison massacre on May 8 of 107 hostages, including sixteen women and four children.

France had a bigger problem with Vietnam. The Japanese seized French Indochina early in the war; it was their granary throughout the Southeast Asian campaign. French colonial administrators helped. Paul Mus, former director of the Ecole Nationale de la France d'Outre-mer, was with French intelligence in India at the time. He described in *Politique étrangère,* how Japan could not have exploited the vast network of isolated hamlets without France's help. In exchange, he said, the French were able to seem masters of their own situation, saving face among the Vietnamese. Collaboration might have gained time, but it was not enough.

Within a year of Germany's surrender, France was at war again. Britain set a precedent by freeing the Indian subcontinent, but France and Holland sought to hold their Asian colonies. According to Swedish economist Gunnar Myrdal, the French and Dutch "did not see their own interests with as much intuitive intelligence." France argued that war was essential in Indochina to hold the line against communism.

Ho Chi Minh, a committed communist since 1917, wanted complete and immediate independence for Vietnam. France refused. Before the war, colonial administrators in Indochina numbered almost 5,000, as many as in British India with fifteen times the population. In 1930 alone, there were nearly 700 summary executions.[4] Had Gandhi tried passive resistance in Indochina, Ho wrote, "he would long since have ascended to heaven." After the war, the Viet Minh pushed hard. Provoked by a series of minor incidents, French naval guns pounded Haiphong harbor on November 23, 1946. Thousands were killed. A month later, General Vo Nguyen Giap waged war on Hanoi. France tried to compromise. In a speech, governor Emile Bollaert promised independence. But he used the words *Doc Lap,* which translate equally to "independence" or "liberty."

France replaced Emperor Bao Dai on the throne in Vietnam, to the satisfaction of few. At an earlier moment of empire, flair and style might have calmed resistance. But the French had not merely lost face, they had had their faces rubbed in mud for four years. The Japanese had pitched aside the Tricolor in Asia.

Vietnamese who fought for France in World War II were infants, or yet unborn, when Albert Sarrault waxed eloquent about the gratitude they should feel. Many of them felt that domination by a capital halfway around the world was not worth a long list of material benefits.

La Guerre d'Indochine was the same sort of bitter, desperate quagmire that the United States stumbled into a generation later. But, in important ways, it was worse. At one extreme, France was at war with itself, committed to bleeding heavily yet again to preserve honor and territorial integrity. At the other extreme, France pursued a vicious colonial war, visiting genocide and torture on a people seeking only to be free. More toward the center, the French were suffering yet more war to hold back communism, spending American money but their own blood.

The war spread quickly in the late 1940s, and Ho Chi Minh sought to negotiate. France pressed on. The Korean War ended, and the Chinese diverted large amounts of aid to the Viet Minh insurgents. French morale flagged badly.

Until 1950, allies considered the French campaign a colonial war. Then China recognized Vietnam. American aid to France began paying for 80 percent of the war costs.

France was disturbed by what was known as the "dirty war," guerrilla tactics answered in kind. Lucien Bodard, in *The Quicksand War,* wrote:

> So often I wanted to ask a French officer, man to man: "Can you defend civilization while you let yourself slide toward everything most inimical to it—violence, deliberate cruelty, torture?" But for months, for a year, I could find no one who would talk. The younger officers of the Expeditionary Force were aware that in France, in their own country, they were unpopular, even detested, and they bore the condemnation in silence.

He found one, however, who talked all night. The officer had been a resistance fighter and hated the idea that the French were acting as the Germans had. But he realized torture was the Asian way and, however Europeans might misunderstand, it saved lives in the end. He said:

> The Viets push us into atrocities. Yet we kill infinitely less than the Viets, and infinitely less than the Americans would. They wouldn't bother to go into details, they'd just bomb whole "zones." Liquidate the population and liquidate the problem.

And at that, international opinion puts up much better with the most lethal wholesale hammering than with the torture of a single assassin.

French efforts renewed under a new commander, General de Lattre de Tassigny. In 1951, he urged escalation of the war, saying, "Nations never die a violent death; their heart continues to beat as long as faith animates it, and it stops only when they refuse to fight and they give up wanting to live."

But, sick and aging, he retired to Paris. The war widened. By 1953, the communist Viet Minh controlled two-thirds of Vietnam. An eager new French military command devised a plan to lure their enemy's main force into a direct assault. The site they chose was a fortified camp deep inside Vietnam, near the Chinese border: Dien Bien Phu.

The camp was in a hollow, dominated by hills. French generals misjudged the guerrillas' ability to muster firepower, and they assumed their air force could keep them supplied. General Giap blasted the camp for fifty-six days, pounding it to rubble with guns his men lugged in on their backs. Dien Bien Phu fell on May 7, 1954, at a cost of more than 1,800 French lives.

With Dien Bien Phu, the government of Joseph Laniel fell. He was the twentieth premier since liberation. Pierre Mendès-France took power June 17, and signed a ceasefire on July 21.

Bodard recalled a conversation with a paracommando captain at the Normandy Bar in Hanoi, when it was all over.

"It was all for nothing," [the captain] was saying. "I let my men die for nothing." His glare was as blind as a sleepwalker's. . . . "In prison camp we faced the reality of the Viet Minh. And we saw that for eight years our generals had been struggling against a revolution without knowing what a revolution was. Dien Bien Phu was not an accident of fate, it was a judgment."

[Bodard added:] In Hong Kong, an American journalist said to me, "You have the most rotten army in the world, but we could have made you win at Dien Bien Phu, and I think we should have." One of his friends said hastily, "But I admire your army. They know how to make a *beau geste.*" It was kind of him, no doubt, but he really meant the French army, like a Louis XV armchair, was the masterpiece of an extinct civilization.

What could I answer? The Americans would never have fought as we did. They would have fought a different war. And by crushing the country and the people under a hail of bombs and dollars, they might well have had more success than we did.

Maybe not. Over eight years, the number of French dead and missing surpassed 50,000, more than American casualties later. Perhaps a half million Viet Minh were killed, along with an estimated 800,000 to two million Vietnamese civilians. The war consumed more than the $2.7 billion France received under the Marshall Plan. War costs each year amounted to 10 percent of the national budget.

France was forced to abandon loyal Vietnamese to their fate, along with a way of life it had sworn to preserve. And there was much more to pay. Less than seven months after the fall of Dien Bien Phu, and in no small way because of it, the Algerian War began.

AS FRANCE FIRST struggled in Algeria to subdue Abd-el-Kadar, Franciade-Fleurus Duvivier wrote: "In spite of the savage war we are waging against them, all natives will be with us in thirty years' time. Let us therefore adopt a policy not of containment but of confidence."

But the more prophetic voices were ominous. Baron Lacuée warned in 1831: "As long as you keep Algiers, you will be constantly at war with Africa; sometimes war will seem to end; but these people will not hate you any the less; it will be a half-extinguished fire that will smoulder under the ash and which, at the first opportunity, will burst into a vast conflagration."[5]

Not long afterward, a conquered chieftain told his captors, "You are merely passing guests. You may stay three hundred years, like the Turks, but in the end you will leave."[6]

In its self-defined mission of bringing civilization to Barbary, France sought to assimilate a new class of brown French. Napoléon III, on a five-week visit to Algeria, had ordered, "Treat the Arabs, in the midst of whom you must live, as compatriots." Since 1847, Algeria had been divided into three departments. Each was just like

Savoy, Corsica, or Bouches-du-Rhône, the history books insisted. By 1954, it was hard to make that point with a straight face.

Boundless energy had been expended. Algeria is the world's tenth biggest country; France built roads and telephone lines across an area four times the size of the *métropole*. Tall white buildings rose over modern harbors. Teachers and doctors reached remote outposts. Marshes and deserts were turned into productive land. Algeria was developed, or as the French would say, *mise en valeur*. But the result was that Europeans streamed in—more Italians, Spanish, Corsicans, Maltese, and Greeks than mainland French—and Arabs and Kabyles were contained ever more tightly.

The native *indigènes* were exhorted to accept full French citizenship and rise to new heights as *évolués* (those who had "evolved"). There was a catch, however. Algerians were Moslem, and accepting French law meant rejecting the laws of the Koran. By 1936, only 2,500 Moslems had applied for French citizenship.[7] Léon Blum urged a new statute to resolve the conflict; the National Assembly refused. In contrast, foreign settlers received French nationality easily, forming a ragbag nobility of cultures with no particular loyalty to Paris. Algeria first stood behind the Vichy government; de Gaulle nearly had to fight his way ashore to set up headquarters in Algiers.

Unlike other *départements,* Algeria came under a governor-general who reported to the Interior Ministry. Legislators were elected by a system heavily skewed toward the *pieds-noirs,* the white settlers. The local assembly was divided into two colleges, one of them all French. Mayors and commanders of outlying districts were also French. Some rich and socially accepted Moslems were active in community affairs. But "assimilation," official policy since 1847, was a standing joke.

Edward Behr, there as a correspondent, noted in *The Algerian Problem* that the majority was dominated by a "a poor white minority, insecure and vociferous." He observed, "It seems to have been a thoroughly evil, as well as a thoroughly inefficient system."

French administrators rigged elections, installing their own Moslem candidates over leaders they considered dangerous. Jacques Soustelle, governor-general and dominant figure of the period, reported to the government in May 1955:

The pseudo-deputies . . . put in office thanks to the electoral fraud, most often illiterate and frequently dishonest, representing nothing and nobody, have no influence in their voting areas and do not even repay the administration for having created them. Few mistakes have been more tragic than that which consisted in distorting our own laws to bring into prominence discredited personalities without any intellectual or moral value.

The argument of Plato's *Republic* was convenient: The masses were not prepared to share power. But little was done to alter the balance between Moslem masses and the Europeans.

In 1954, a group of senior officials and economists under Roland Maspétiol drew a picture of the inequality between 1,070,000 Europeans and more than eight million Moslems.

Ten percent of the population held 90 percent of the wealth. Almost one million Moslems had no work; two million more were seriously underemployed. Eighty percent of Moslem children did not go to school. Three-quarters of all Moslems were illiterate in Arabic; 90 percent could not read French. Yearly income per head of family in Moslem rural areas was sixteen pounds sterling; in the cities, it was forty-five pounds. Official spending, adjusted to inflation, was at the same level as in 1913.

The average European farm was eleven times larger than an average Moslem farm, and it brought in twenty-eight times more revenue. Algeria's main wealth came from wine, which Moslems did not drink.

A second study in 1961 divided the population into three categories: 16 percent had living standards comparable to Western industrialized nations; 26 percent lived at "Mediterranean" standards, those of Greece, Portugal or southern Italy; and 62 percent—all Moslems—were comparable to the rural masses in Egypt or India.

For many Moslems, economic imbalance was not the worst part. Individual attitudes toward Moslems ranged, most often, from condescending to insulting. Back in 1892, Jules Ferry decried the white settlers' discrimination against Moslems:

We have taken a close look at him, and have studied his private and public behavior. We have found him very limited. . . . He lacks what may be described as the virtue of the victor, the balance of the spirit and of the heart, and the regard for the weak which is in no way incompatible with firm leadership. It is difficult to try to convince the European settler that there are rights other than his own in an Arab country and that the native is not a race to be taxed and exploited to the utmost limits. . . . the settlers proclaim that [they] are totally incorrigible and utterly incapable of education, without ever having attempted, over the past 30 years, to do anything to drag them out of their moral and intellectual misery. . . . They fail to understand any other policy than that of containment. To be sure, there are no thoughts of destroying them; it is even claimed that there is no urge to drive them back. But there is no concern for their complaints, or for their numerical growth which seems to increase with their poverty.[8]

The years brought little improvement. The first Moslem colonel to command a regiment was announced with fanfare only in 1959. The races lived in loosely defined separate areas. In Algiers, the European city fronted the sea, with the same terraces and chic store windows found on the opposite rim of the Mediterranean. The Arab quarter, the Casbah, was a medieval rabbit warren of stone lanes twisting up the hills. The fabled invitation, "Come wiz me to ze Casbah," clearly was issued by someone who had never been there.

Germaine Tillion, a liberal sociologist who knew Algeria well, acknowledged France's good intentions, but she tore into the failings of policy which amounted to separate development. In *Algérie en 1957*, she quoted an old man from Kabylia: "You've taken us halfway across the ford and left us."

Resistance rippled from time to time. But the guillotine which Victor Hugo saw arrive tended to discourage troublemakers.

The Algerian time bomb exploded the day after Germany surrendered. While France celebrated liberation, a crowd of Moslems demanded their own freedom in the market town of Sétif, west of Constantine. Crop failures and wartime shortages left people in Sétif miserable. Rich harvests on Europeans' prime land nearby did not help their spirits. The undercurrents smacked of imminent rebellion.

Eight thousand Moslems began to march, ostensibly to lay a wreath for Algerians fallen in the war. The French subprefect decided not to intervene, especially since he had only twenty gendarmes. But the crowd unfurled the green and white standard of Abd-el-Kadar and chanted, "Free and independent Algeria!" He ordered police to stop them. Warned there would be a fight, he replied, "All right, then there'll be a fight."

Someone shot first. A Moslem was killed, and the cry of *jihad*, holy war, arose. Crowds overran the police and fanned out, slaughtering any Europeans they found. On small farms, faithful servants turned on their lifelong masters. In five days, 103 Europeans were murdered. Another 100 were wounded, and the rape victims included an eighty-four-year-old woman. Breasts were slashed off; men's sexual organs were stuffed in their mouths. Then the French army arrived.[9]

A systematic *ratissage* left Moslem villages in ashes; suspected culprits were shot dead on the spot. Bombers flattened at least forty remote hamlets. Gunboats shelled the coast. European vigilantes attacked at random, lynching and stoning Moslems. Official French figures put the Moslem death toll near 1,100. Thirty years later, President Habib Bourguiba of Tunisia insisted it was over 50,000. Objective estimates range between 6,000 and 16,000.

Historian Charles-André Julien described the repression as "ferocious, pitiless, in truth inhuman by its lack of discrimination."

The uprising was barely reported in France, but in Algeria everyone knew about Sétif. A steamy calm prevailed for the next nine years, but nationalist leaders, each fired by memories of Sétif, were preparing the moment. It was to be 1 A.M. on All Saints Day, November 1, 1954.

Rebels targeted the bleak Aurès mountains, bastion of the traditionally fractious Chaouias. They shot two French army sentries in the garrison town of Batna and then two more soldiers. Insurgents stopped a bus and fell upon two French teachers, Guy Monnerot and his twenty-one-year-old wife. The Moslem *caid* of the nearby village of M'Chouneche tried to stop them. In *La Guerre d'Algérie*, Pierre Montagnon records this exchange.

"You cannot kill these young people, come from so far to teach our children."

"Who cares? Our civilization is the Koran, not that of these *Roumi* dogs."

The *caïd* was shot dead with a machine-gun burst. Monnerot was executed; his wife was assaulted and left for dead.

In all, separate bands struck in seventy places across Algeria, with little material damage. But Cairo radio broadcast the first proclamation of the *Front de Libération Nationale,* the FLN. It insisted on independence, with or without the accord of France.

Rebels organized in cells almost impervious to infiltration; no guerrilla knew more than four or five others. Algeria was divided into seven military zones. Scrounged weapons, hidden away, probably totaled fewer than 400 aging rifles, with nothing bigger than a machine gun. Communist and Arab help would not come for two years. An amateur factory in the Algiers Casbah produced 200 bombs from oil cans and jam jars.

The French were hardly better prepared. Officers could muster only 3,500 fighting men; most of the 57,000 troops were needed in garrisons or were still earmarked for Indochina. Two days before the war started, a headquarters colonel snorted when told 100 armed rebels had been seen in the Aurès mountains: "Monsieur le Préfet, I've been patrolling these roads for a very long time and have never seen a *fellagha* in front of my jeep." When the assault came, he insisted on waiting for written orders to sound the alarm. At Batna, two soldiers were killed even though they saw the rebels approach. Under peacetime orders, their rifles had been unloaded and their ammunition had been sewn into their tunics.

In Paris, the first top official to warn of trouble was François Mitterrand, the minister responsible for Algeria. "I sense something . . . the situation is unhealthy," he said in the summer.[10] But he did little about it. Later, Jacques Chevallier, secretary of state for defense and a *pied-noir,* former (and future) mayor of Algiers, took a long weekend to go have a look for himself. He chose All Saints Day.

The world mood was against France. The French had already set free Morocco and Tunisia, after minimal armed conflict. Britain had given independence to India; Ghana's would follow soon afterward. The French Union was edging toward new flexibility.

But France rebounded quickly: Algeria was different.

A million white Algerians argued, as other whites did in South

Africa, that their enterprise and achievement outweighed the simple dictates of majority rule. They were not colonizers who could go home; they were home. Governments in Paris were too busy sweeping up debris from fifteen years of war to read the writing on the wall. And many French, along with most *pieds-noirs,* were in no mood for yet another humiliating retreat.

Mendès-France sent Soustelle to be governor-general. Later, Soustelle wrote:

> Algeria! Divided most profoundly within herself, torn between the past and the future, quartered by desires and rancors, she discharged into my face, when I leaned anxiously over her, the ardent and heavy breath of a sorcerer's cauldron. How could one not love her, especially in that ordeal. "When your son has grown up, treat him like your brother," says the Arab proverb; it was certainly painful, but the son had become a man, our equal, our brother. That was what one had to understand.

At first, the *pieds-noirs* hated Soustelle for his liberal approach. He tried to attack the causes of Moslem discontent. His corps of Sections Administratives Spécialisées, the SAS, brought help to neglected areas. School budgets were doubled, and Arabic was accepted along with French. "Assimilation" gave way to "integration," urging Moslems to live side by side with Europeans as Frenchmen.

But attitudes remained basically unchanged, and FLN units grew steadily. The war widened in a series of "incidents." Soustelle issued orders to adhere strictly to Mitterrand's policy: suspects must be handed over to qualified authorities; brutality or any "offense against human dignity" was "rigorously forbidden." But army commanders secretly short-circuited the system. An unofficial policy of "collective responsibility" grew common.

In his *Les Français d'Algérie,* Pierre Nora gave an example. Near Sidi-bel-Abbès, a Foreign Legion patrol executed nine farmhands suspected of helping rebels. The *pied-noir* farmer was outraged. "How could you shoot down workers who saw me born! Without warning me? . . . Assassins, vandals, is this how you pacify?"

The FLN adopted the tactics of Brazilian guerrilla leader Carlos Marighela. They terrorized civilians, bringing widespread repression which, in turn, radicalized the Moslem masses. In August 1955, the little port of Philippeville was awash in blood. Screaming Moslems slashed the throats and bellies of European women and smashed infants' heads against walls. Entire families were massacred. One was the Mello family: the father, the seventy-three-year-old grandmother, and the eleven-year-old daughter were killed in their beds, their arms and legs hacked off. The mother was disemboweled and her five-month-old baby, slashed to death, was placed in her opened womb.

Frenzied revenge killing followed. Official tolls say 123 people were killed by mobs that day, including seventy-one Europeans. The French said they killed 1,273 "insurgents." FLN officers estimated their dead at 12,000.[11] Soustelle surveyed the carnage and decided that his only course was to crush the rebellion.

"A somber harvest of hatred sprouted in the bloodshed," he said. "Far from being brought together by the ordeal, human beings were going to divide themselves and tear themselves to pieces."

The situation worsened at a tumultous pace. Albert Camus rallied Jean-Paul Sartre, Simone de Beauvoir, and other left-leaning intellectuals to push—in vain—for the liberal reforms Soustelle could not accomplish. In Paris, Mendès-France fell after losing a vote of confidence over his North African policy. Edgar Faure, the new premier, called early elections in hopes that a new National Assembly could be steered toward a solution. Guy Mollet, a Socialist, emerged as premier but two and a half million votes went to the militant champion of the extreme right wing, Pierre Poujade.

Mollet recalled Soustelle, but so many *pieds-noirs* thronged the port to keep him in Algiers that it took him an hour to cover 200 yards. Soustelle's replacement was General Georges Catroux, seventy-nine and a liberal. He was regarded as the man who sold out France in Syria and Morocco. Mollet went to Algiers to install Catroux personally, but the premier had to retreat under a barrage of tomatoes and cabbages. Catroux "resigned" in favor of Robert Lacoste, and Mollet brought French troop strength in Algeria to 500,000.

It was a bad year all the way around. The United Nations debated the Algeria problem, and the FLN's support grew in Asia and elsewhere among new leaders of what would be called the Third World. The French hijacked FLN leader Ahmed Ben Bella on his way to a summit in Tunis, infuriating Bourguiba and Moroccan King Mohammed V. In Morocco, French settlers were killed in bloody reprisals. Fragile attempts to negotiate with the FLN went out the window. And then there was Suez.

Gamal Abdel Nasser nationalized the Suez Canal in 1956. The world, at the time, was in uproar. The Soviet Union crushed an uprising in Hungary and nailed down its bloc. War broke out between Israel and Egypt. The United States was reelecting Dwight D. Eisenhower. France was worried, above all, that Nasser would arm the FLN; a shipload of weapons had been seized already in the Mediterranean. With Britain, France invaded the Suez. General Jacques Massu, with troops hardened in Algeria, was nearly at the canal. But the British, wavering from the start, backed out under Soviet pressure. Then Eisenhower obliged France to retreat—and not happily.

Mollet insisted that his aim was to help Israel, but Algeria was at center stage. Nasser was left free to help the FLN. French relations with Britain, strained since the war, turned acrimonious. London had fallen under the sway of Washington. French politicians ex-coriated the United States for not helping them fight communism in Algeria.

And, to top things off, there was the Battle of Algiers.

Until mid-1956, the war was mostly in the *bled,* rural mountains and remote plains. Then the FLN murdered French gendarmes in Algiers. A prime suspect's house in the heart of the Casbah was mysteriously blown up, killing civilians. In reprisal, guerrillas used young Arab women to sneak explosives past checkpoints. On September 30, bombs obliterated the Milk-Bar and a popular cafeteria, strewing torn limbs and panic in the heart of European Algiers. Massu's paratroopers, facing a war of urban terror, fought back with interrogation by torture.

The Battle of Algiers was won within a year, but some French are still agonizing over how it was done.

At the time, little was reported about torture. Some—not all— French reporters neglected to pass along what they knew. Foreign correspondents heard stories, but had trouble pinning down names and places. *Les paras* and the police issued no invitations to interrogation sessions. Later, no doubts were left.

Recently, a French journalist I know well told me, "I went in the wrong door at police headquarters [in Algiers] and saw a guy with his hands cuffed behind him. A long tube down his throat was attached to a faucet so they could force water to distend his stomach until he was ready to talk. I didn't say anything about it because it wasn't my business. And besides, I was a *pied-noir*. Of course, the police tortured. They were up against fanatics who were planting bombs. Everyone agreed it was the only way."

A favorite device was the *gégène,* a hand-cranked magneto used for powering field telephones. Attached to ear lobes or testicles, it also powered reluctant tongues. Suspects were sometimes beaten or lashed to poles and left suspended. There were water tortures: prolonged dunkings and water forced down the throat through a funnel. Occasionally there were summary executions.

No one has accurately determined the extent of the practice. Ministers and ranking officials insist that no one ordered torture, but officers privately acknowledge that it was systematic. Some argued that it was a noble necessity: without it, paratroopers could not have stopped the random bombing. Torture, by that reasoning, saved innocent lives. When Paris objected, Behr said in an interview, excesses were simply moved farther out of sight. Jean Lartéguy recalled that one officer told Mollet, "If everything has to happen in the basement, it is because of you."

The result was what the FLN sought in using terror; sympathy for their cause grew in proportion to the repression. Paratroopers broke an eight-day strike by smashing open closed shops and forcing people back to work. With the battle over, they exercised virtually unlimited control over Moslem Algerians. But they won few hearts or minds.

Beyond torture, and beyond the Battle of Algiers, was the general conduct of the war. Jean-Jacques Servan-Schreiber jolted the nation in 1957 with a personal account, *Lieutenant in Algeria.*

As an example of day-to-day excesses, he started with a random communique: "Yesterday at Brahim, the occupants of a truck machine-gunned people in the street. Fortunately, only one man was wounded." Then he explained what happened.

A young Arab, nearly run down by an army jeep, started to yell at the soldiers. One pointed a machine gun at him. An old man tried to calm down the youth. In his tension, the soldier shot the old man. The soldiers drove off. A "territorial unit" of local settlers saw the body; they decided the old man had been executed by Moslem terrorists for being pro-French. Just then, a truck rolled by carrying five Arab mineworkers. They stopped it; the driver was too frightened to speak French, and they beat him up. An army truck roared up, and the Arabs, in the momentary confusion, fled. The army patrol was led by a sergeant named Maure, a young married railway accountant from Limoges. His men thought him soft because he didn't get drunk or screw around. Pressured to act quickly, he ordered a chase. His patrol caught the Arabs and shot them all dead.

"Maure thanked God that everything had gone so well, and that his men—reservists like himself—had been able to do their duty as soldiers without a single one being killed or wounded," wrote Servan-Schreiber. "His nightmare was that he might one day have a dead man or a disabled man on his conscience. Good old Maure."

At headquarters, however, a problem developed. No weapons were found on the victims, and a young lieutenant asked his captain, Martin, what to do. What do you think? scolded Martin. But if the report said there were arms, it was decided, they might have to be produced later at an inspection. Sometimes captured arms went unreported and were saved for such occasions, but none were available. Instead, no mention was made of the dead Arabs. Then a Captain Julienne broke in. The dead men would be missed, he said, and Moslems would hate the French for the injustice. "I'm suggesting that it's bad business to kill people who may be innocent, and that it is not what we are here for."

In a condescending but friendly manner, Captain Martin explained that Julienne was right—in theory. Unfortunately, he said, there were two choices. He could risk having his men killed, and people would write to their deputies complaining that he was a butcher. "Or you do your duty honorably, which is to say you put the *fellagha* out of commission and look after our men the best you can. In that case, there's only one way: treat every Arab as a suspect, a possible *fellagha*, a potential terrorist—because that, my dear sir, is the truth. And don't come back at me with words like charity and justice. . . . You can talk about that in Paris with the politicians who got us into this mess."

Later, Julienne told Major Marcus, "I've seen enough here to be convinced that what they're making us do here is leading straight to the loss of Algeria—not to speak of our honor as Frenchmen." Weren't there commanders and leaders who saw that? Marcus replied,

> There are, more than you'd think. It is not stupidity that is destroying us, it's cowardice. They understand, but they don't turn a hair. People are lying, Julienne, they're lying from the top to the bottom of the ladder. . . . People lie so much that they don't know they are doing it. You lie from a sense of duty, you see. Once you've got that far, there's no way out. . . .
>
> What the Arabs hated was the colonial set-up; they didn't really hate France. The army should have been independent of the colonial establishment, separate from the rottenness of the administration, from the settlers, the policemen, the mayors, from everything that the colonial attitude has represented for a century now. . . . It did the very opposite.

Servan-Schreiber describes attempts among the extremists to murder radicals like Marcus and himself. More generally, he was vilified as a traitor by brothers in arms. A great many Frenchmen agreed with him. But little changed.

An English foreign legionnaire, Simon Murray, wrote later:

> The effectiveness of torturing people to make them betray their cause cannot be disputed. But with all the good results . . . was a steady buildup of hatred against the French. And this antagonism drew the Arabs, so often divided among themselves, into a common cause; it made them feel the necessity of combining for survival and it made them finally aware of their own strength. The French became the foreign intruder. . . . I wonder how many more crosses must be struck before the end comes—the end for

the French, when a new nation will be born, conceived entirely through French misunderstanding.

Along with torture in Algeria was the scorched earth policy. As Behr suggests, anyone doubting the ravages of random destruction need only have flown low over mountaintops to see village after village, flattened, burned black and lifeless.

Behr noted that he had seen earlier sporadic examples of French excesses in Morocco and Tunisia. But, he wrote, "it was not until the Algerian rebellion spread that people and army brutality became a permanent and quietly efficient instrument, a weapon of war of the same calibre as the grenade or the mortar-bomb."

In late 1985, a Foreign Legion colonel who was in Algeria told me, "No one ordered torture, but it is impossible to control all individual units. And what is torture, anyway? If you kick in a door and fire off a burst without looking first, it is torture if there are women and children inside, but war is like that."

What about the *gégène?* He snorted.

"The *gégène* is not torture, it is a *rigolade.*" That means, a laugh. "I've tried it myself."

He did not attach the electrodes to his scrotum, of course. And he knew when the crank would stop turning—and what would not come next. Psychological torture, victims say, can be worse than outright pain.

A Frenchman who was a senior civilian official in the late 1950s was blunt:

Of course, torture was widespread, institutionalized, severe. How could you order an army to win a war and not fight it? We tried to control it after 1958, to fight a cleaner war, but it was impossible. The government sent thousands of letters to local commanders: "We understand Mohammed So-and-So has disappeared in mysterious circumstances. . . ." That sort of thing. It had some effect. Look, we managed to slow down torture. But stop it? Impossible.

At one point, a young official in Algiers named Eric Westphal energized a government review committee to investigate human rights abuses. Disgruntled military officers dynamited his house.

The issue burned in 1985 after Paris newspapers quoted Algerians as saying National Front leader Jean-Marie Le Pen, as a lieutenant, had tortured them. Mohammed Mouley said Le Pen commanded a patrol that tortured and killed his father. Le Pen denied personal involvement but defended rough treatment to obtain information. And then his longtime friend, Dr. Jean-Maurice Demarquet, spoke out. He said Le Pen asked him to testify in his favor. That offended his honor.

> I didn't want to lie [he told *Le Monde*]. I even told him we have brothers in arms who have a perfect memory of what we did with them. I said, it had to be done; you have no cause to blush. It is absolutely evident that Le Pen was a member of teams that tortured personally. Personally. It is like that. I must say that we shared the same episodes. That one tries to pretend that it did not happen when the context changes, I don't accept that.

The revelation, among others, did not seem to affect Le Pen's standing with the extreme right. In fact, a poll conducted by the Louis Harris organization and the magazine *Evénement* among 1,-000 adults showed that 20 percent approved of torture in Algeria if it saved the lives of Frenchmen or friendly Algerians. And 40 percent said that if Le Pen were proven a torturer, it would not affect his qualifications to be a French public official. Apparently not. In the March 1986 legislative elections, his National Front won 9.72 percent of the vote. Le Pen and thirty-four Front members took seats in the National Assembly, equalling the Communist Party's bloc.

Answering another question in the Le Pen poll, 72 percent rejected the use of torture under any circumstance. In an interview with *Libération,* General Massu dismissed the Algerians' testimony against Le Pen:

> There is torture, and there is torture. They weren't so badly tortured because they are doing well twenty-eight years later. If they had been horribly tortured, they would not be in that condition. If we had conducted a classic war against them, and

if they had been wounded by machineguns or artillery, they surely would not be talking like that. Now don't come telling me your stories with your tortures. That is a big word.

Assembling notes for this chapter, I clipped an article headlined "Confessed Torturer." It was, in fact, about an Argentine officer who took part in the torture of two French nuns. France and the French energetically condemned the Argentines' "dirty war" against terrorism. I missed the Battle of Algiers but not the Battle of Buenos Aires. Comparisons are risky, and degrees are always different, but some parallels are inescapable. Argentines are not inherent torturers any more than the French are. But in each case, a certain carte blanche was built into the system and overlooked by those who could revoke it.

Some would take Cardinal Newman's approach of the last century: "A gentleman is one who never inflicts pain." Others might answer that the British prelate never raced against time to find an FLN bomb cache. But extreme methods were used even when time was not particularly of the essence. That French officers tortured does not condemn a society. But, unlike in Argentina, there was no clamor for justice after the dirty war, nor did there seem to be much concern at all.

In late 1985, I met Gisèle Halimi, a lawyer who built a reputation defending torture victims during the war. Simone de Beauvoir wrote a preface to a book Halimi wrote describing the difficulties of making French justice work. I asked her about the period, and she cut me off with a sharp look. "Do you think, Mr. Rosenblum, that twenty-five years later is the time to speak about Algerian torture?" By coincidence, that was the day Argentine courts sentenced five generals and admirals for their depredations of a decade earlier. And in Lyon, Klaus Barbie awaited trial for World War II crimes against the French.

I asked three people why no postwar investigations were made. A former civilian official in Algeria said, "It is a great hole in the memory of Frenchmen. There is a collective guilty conscience, and most want it forgotten. My twenty-four-year-old daughter is just now reading her first book on the war in Algeria."

Barry Goodfield, an American who has spent ten years training

French specialists in psychotherapy and who has examined the effects of war on European societies, was more clinical.

"It is unconscious behavior relating to an identity. The French do not see themselves as being capable of that sort of abuse. You can't try someone for something that could not have been done."

But my friend Claude, the elderly French journalist cited above, responded passionately.

Look, France had just emerged from four years of occupation, where Frenchmen were shot in the back. Twenty dead, fifty dead, in reprisal for one German soldier killed. And then Frenchmen were shot in the back by Algerians. After all that, you think anyone got worked up about a little torture? Besides, no one really knew. They didn't absorb what happened. These are not things that Frenchmen do, torture, murder. . . .

Eh bien, oui, this is a bloody society. Look at the Commune [in 1871]. In six days, no, five days, they killed 37,000 people. The army admits to 17,000. The *communards* say 37,000. Believe me, the French are already immunized against violence. What makes me sick is the hypocrisy, the false principles, with which we cry over abuses in Argentina or Chile. We did the same thing, and I am convinced that we would do it again. It is sad, but *c'est comme ça.*

B Y 1 9 5 8, Habib Bourguiba and Mohammed V were pushing hard for negotiations, but French commanders suspected them of helping the FLN. On February 8, 1958, for a second time antiaircraft fire hit a French plane from the Tunisian border village of Sakiet. Three hours later, a B26 squadron flattened the place. It was a market day. About eighty people were killed: children in a school, patients in a hospital, marketwomen. Bourguiba expelled French troops who were in Tunisia under treaty. Premier Félix Gaillard accepted a "good offices" mission from the United States and Britain to heal the rift. But Paris papers sneered at *"Messieurs les bons offices"* meddling in domestic matters.

An anti-American chorus grew; clearly, it was argued, Americans wanted oil from an independent Algeria. On April 15, the Gaillard government fell and, not long after, so did the Fourth Republic.

René Coty was president without a government. *Pieds-noirs* and Moslems alike rebelled against Lacoste, the lame-duck governor. When Lacoste had three terrorists guillotined, the FLN executed three French prisoners. That pushed the army over the edge.

General Raoul Salan telegraphed Paris that unless a clear commitment was made to keep Algeria French "one cannot predict how it (the army) will react." Salan, in effect, ran Lacoste out of town. The *pieds-noirs,* meanwhile, surged through the streets in cars, bleating out a five-note slogan on their horns: *"Al-gér-ie Fran-çaise."* Housewives rapped out the same rhythm on pots and pans. They mobbed the Forum, a vast plaza in front of the governor-general's offices. Then they seized the building itself, burning files and occupying offices. Salan addressed crowds from the balcony, ending his speech, *". . . et vive de Gaulle."* After that, crowds had a new chant: *". . . de Gaulle au pouvoir."*

For twelve years, de Gaulle had sat out events quietly at his modest home in Colombey-les-Deux-Eglises. In 1948, Janet Flanner wrote, "Time, weight, and, evidently, the general's glands are giving his visage a heavy, royal outline; he looks more like a man of dynasty than of destiny." In April 1958, he told a Gaullist deputy, "They will create a burnt earth, they will wait until there is nothing left before calling for de Gaulle! I shall never come back to power in my lifetime." But a month later, at sixty-seven, grayer, heavier, with failing eyesight, he answered the call.

Coty named de Gaulle premier with wide powers, threatening to resign if the National Assembly did not agree. The vote, on June 1, was 329 to 224. He would rule by decree for six months; the Assembly would recess for four months; and he would submit a new constitution for France.

De Gaulle hurried to Algiers and appeared on the balcony where his name had been shouted repeatedly. Salan said, "Our great cry of joy and hope has been heard!" The crowds roared for three full minutes. De Gaulle stretched his arms to a great *V* and thundered, *"Je vous ai compris . . . !"*

De Gaulle had yelled, "I have understood you," and he likely did. But few understood him. Men and women weeping for joy heard him say that all Algerians would live together as Frenchmen, with full and equal rights. They heard him offer the FLN reconciliation:

"Never more than here, nor more than this evening, have I seen how beautiful, how great, how generous is France!" But in that crucial speech, no one heard him say, *"Vive l'Algérie Française!"* And hardly anyone translated full rights to majority rule.

It was a ruse, pure and simple, to gain time, de Gaulle acknowledged later in his memoirs. That was plain at the time to those around him. On his return to Paris, he muttered to an aide, "Africa is finished, and Algeria with it."

The war had split apart the nation. "France is headed toward a great destiny, " de Gaulle declaimed. "We are all murderers," wrote Sartre.

Later that year, de Gaulle called a referendum on a constitution that would give the president of France sweeping power. Later, he would run for president. Sartre remarked that he would rather vote for God: "He is more modest." But 85 percent of metropolitan France voted, giving the Fifth Republic constitution an 80 percent backing.

Colonies in the French Union were invited to remain associated with the new France as independent nations. Every African state but Guinea voted *oui* by a landslide. De Gaulle reminded Ahmed Sékou Touré that France had lived long without Guinea; he pushed the colony out of the nest that same year, without a franc, and recuperated everything French that could be packed onto ships. The others took independence within the "community" in 1960, in an orderly manner.

Algeria, being France and not a colony, could only approve or reject the constitution. Moslems voted overwhelmingly in favor, trusting de Gaulle to find some end to the war.

In a press conference on October 23, de Gaulle offered his *paix des braves,* a noble peace, with a white flag of truce. Jacques Fauvet of *Le Monde* lauded "the nobility of tone, the harmony of thought." Alain de Serigny, in the *Echo d'Alger,* put it this way: "The white flag means surrender."

The FLN rejected the offer, saying they wanted a political solution, not peace. The left agreed that a cease-fire would mean their capitulation. The army and the *pieds-noirs* saw it as capitulation by France. Projecting the demography, many feared that total integration would change the white-Christian nature of France. But then, turning Algeria loose meant losing yet another war.

De Gaulle pushed ahead. He transferred Salan to Paris and purged other activists. He named a forty-four-year-old technocrat, Paul Delouvrier, as civilian administrator, and a tough general of fifty-three, Maurice Challe, as military commander. When appointed, Delouvrier warned de Gaulle that he felt independence was inevitable. "That is not to be excluded," the general replied.[12] And he let the world know that France was back on the world stage. He told the Americans and the British that unless he had an equal part in running NATO, "France will take no further part." He laid out plans for an independent nuclear force. He rejected Britain's idea of a Free Trade Area. The economy braced for growth; new buildings in Paris reflected a confident new mood.

But the FLN brought terror to Paris. In one month, 423 attacks and bombings in France killed eighty-one people. Countermeasures brought the disquieting feel of a police state. Troop trains, too long a feature of French life, weighed on the spirit. Ted Joans, a black American poet who might be mistaken for an Algerian, remembers bitterly how the *garde mobile* regularly rammed gun barrels in his stomach and insulted him at Paris checkpoints. Real Algerians suffered worse fates.

In *Force of Circumstance,* Simone de Beauvoir wrote:

> The police waited for the Algerians to come up out of the metro stations, made them stand still with their hands above their heads, then hit them with their truncheons. He'd [Claude Lanzmann] seen with his own eyes teeth smashed in and skulls fractured. . . . Corpses were being found hanging in the Bois de Boulogne, and others, disfigured and mutilated, in the Seine.

She said scores of bodies were being found and thousands of Algerians were rounded up "like the Jews at Drancy before." When she and friends sought to demonstrate, she said, police pushed them around. She quoted one as saying, "Ah, you cocksuckers! The cops can go out and get themselves killed and you don't give a shit, but if it's those Algerian bastards who get it, then you start screaming."

Later, she wrote, "De Gaulle spoke on New Year's Eve, and I turned the radio off after two minutes, sick to my stomach with that neurotic narcissism and empty grandiloquence." Then, embittered by Parisians honking horns in joyful abandon despite the tragedy, she added, "I took some belladenal to escape all that hateful gaiety, the gaiety of the French people, of murderers, of butchers."

In 1985, Michel Lévine published a book on the episode she describes. In October 1961, he wrote, 200 Algerians were found dead in Paris and another 400 disappeared.[13] Among others, Lévine quoted a survivor named Khebach who described how police beat him and others and threw them in the Seine. Official records and history books reveal almost nothing about the killings, he said, and no law officer was prosecuted.

MEANWHILE, Cold War tension heightened. China and some Eastern bloc states recognized a provisional Algerian government. The Soviet Union remained aloof, helping de Gaulle just enough to strain the Western alliance. Neither the United States nor Britain took a clear stand for France.

Then terrorism ceased in Paris. Challe hit hard in the mountains —the *djebel*—and ran down broken fragments of FLN forces. *Les paras* and legionnaires pressed a relentless campaign, putting the rebels on the defensive. In response, the FLN again terrorized *pied-noir* civilians. It was clear that even a military victory would not resolve the political crisis.

On September 16, 1959, de Gaulle pronounced the fateful words *self-determination*. Holding the nation spellbound, he said Algerians could choose among total separation, integration with France, or associated independence. He wanted the last. Reaction built slowly but grimly. Challe argued that his men could not die to no purpose. Massu was yanked out of Algeria for criticizing de Gaulle's shift to a German reporter. That touched off yet more reaction.

In January 1960, militant *pieds-noirs* mounted barricades in Algiers. French gendarmes sought to control them. A shot was fired, and the crowd began murdering gendarmes. The 1er REP of the Foreign Legion—a paratroop regiment—and other paratroop units mysteriously failed to protect the gendarmes—or to retaliate.

Frenchmen had shot Frenchmen, and ranking officers were dangerously linked with rebelling civilians. Jo Ortiz, a *bistrot* owner who
led crowds, was heard to boast, "Tomorrow, in Paris, I will be the
ruling power." Premier Michel Debré, visiting Algiers, found what
he called "a soviet of colonels." One of the colonels told him de
Gaulle could either renounce self-determination or be replaced by
Challe.

Military censorship muffled the impact in Paris. But coup d'état
rumors bounced among the circles of power. De Gaulle put on his
general's uniform and addressed the television cameras.

"Well then, my old and dear country, here we are together, once
again together, faced with a harsh test." Who, he asked, could
believe the lies that he planned to abandon Algeria?

Horne recalls watching a bistro crowd breaking into tears at the
"hypnotic wizardry." He wrote, "I do not remember any fighting,
wartime broadcast of Churchill's having a greater effect."

Rebelling *pieds-noirs* dismantled their barricades, dejected and
bitter. De Gaulle had France thoroughly confused. In March, he told
officers in Algeria that independence was "a monstrosity . . . France
must not leave. She has the right to be in Algeria; she will remain
there." But he did not renounce self-determination.

Privately, his memoirs say, he felt that prolonging the status quo
would mean a bottomless quagmire, with a "futile and interminable
task of colonial repression."

During 1960, de Gaulle negotiated clumsily with the split Algerian leadership. Provisional leader Ferhat Abbas agreed to meet
him but talks broke off. The rebels won political advantage, and he
further alienated the army and *pieds-noirs*. Challe, transferred from
Algiers, resigned.

In December, de Gaulle told officers at Blida:

> The work of France in Algeria must go on, and it is only too
> evident that it cannot go on under the conditions of yesterday.
> There is—you are all aware of this—the whole context of eman-
> cipation which is sweeping the world from one end to the other
> . . . which has swept, without exception, over all those which
> once were empires, and which cannot but have considerable
> consequences here.

Assassination plots were hatched. And then former officers and civilians set up the Organisation de l'Armée Secrète, the OAS, to force de Gaulle's hand with French terror against France.

Algiers, at the time, was in chaos. Robert Quiriconi, a *pied-noir* journalist now working in Paris, recalled recently:

> It was absolute madness. The French army went after weapons in French homes. All along the enemy had been the Arab, and people were angry, confused. There were curfews; all night long patrols clanked by. Cars caught in traffic jams honked: *Al-gér-ie Fran-çaise.* On starry, balmy nights, housewives on every balcony banged out the slogan with spoons on pans. There was a constant beat. It was the cry of a people that didn't want to die, and it came from the gut.

In April 1961, Salan and other officers tried a coup d'état.

Challe hesitated until he heard de Gaulle tell reporters: "Decolonization is our interest and, therefore, our policy. Why should we remain caught up in colonizations that are costly, bloody and endless when our own nation must be renewed from top to bottom?" France, the president said, would put no obstacle in the way of Algeria's sovereignty.

D-Day was April 20. The coup was hastily planned, leaked to French intelligence, badly coordinated, and generally improbable, and it went into action a day late.

"It seemed like a million people surged into the street," Quiriconi said. "Their hearts had been gripped by desperation, and suddenly they were free. Like a huge weight had been lifted. It was spring, *la fête,* and everyone was smiling. They couldn't believe the army would not pull it off."

Simon Murray's diary describes the heady feeling of being trucked through the night to Algiers, with legionnaires fully expecting to land on Maxim's in Paris as conquering heroes:

> The prospect of being involved in a putsch, a civil war, has a certain fascination almost. . . . De Gaulle's voice orders the army back into line as it thunders over the French radio—and we wait

for orders, sitting on the fence. Sunday approaches. It looks like a long weekend. . . . We were to occupy the airport, which was held by French marines, and they weren't having any of it. So we were given wooden batons, heavy, with sharp points, and in one long line we slowly eased into the marines, pushing them forward like bolshie rams. They frequently turned and attacked with aggression. This was met in many cases with savage beatings and it became a sad and shoddy business. . . . We were in control of the airport from which we will apparently make the drop on Paris.

It was a delicate balance. Old Sherman tanks had clattered up to protect the National Assembly in Paris, but no one was certain there were enough troops in town to save France. Challe insists he never planned to attack France. In any case, de Gaulle again stared down the opposition. He told the nation:

"Françaises, Français! Look where France risks going, compared to what she was about to again become. *Françaises, Français! Aidez-moi!"* De Gaulle had heard the news after watching a performance of *Britannicus,* a play by Racine about treason at the court of Nero. After his speech, Flanner observed: "When he cried three times 'Hélas! Hélas! Hélas!' it was the male voice of French tragedy, more moving, because anguished by reality, than any stage voice in *Britannicus."*[14]

Rebelling officers had seized all communications. But by then it was the transistor age. Glued to tiny radios, the soldiers knew most of France was against them. Career men tended to lean toward rebellion, but drafted troops doing their time heard their commander-in-chief order obedience. Key units hung back in Oran and elsewhere.

In the midst of rebellion, France detonated its first nuclear device at Reggane, its Algerian Sahara test site. De Gaulle now led an atomic power, not some banana junta to be overthrown by retired generals.

The putsch collapsed. It lasted four days and involved about 14,000 officers and men to one degree or another. Five generals and 200 officers were arrested. Conscripts denounced officers, and officers denounced one another. "It was all a thoroughly nasty episode, bringing out much of the worst in human nature, and for many months its poison lingered in the body of the French army," Horne wrote. The coup leaders were sentenced to fifteen years in prison, or less, and all were given amnesty in 1968. Those who fled were sentenced to death *in absentia.*

The 1st REP, squarely behind the coup, was disbanded. The headquarters its legionnaires had built, brick by brick, was dynamited flat.

France was defeating the FLN militarily, but its will to continue was effectively crushed, and the FLN knew it. De Gaulle negotiated from weakness in the black mood of a world chilled by Cold War. Pushed too far, de Gaulle threatened partition. The FLN reacted violently, and fresh waves of terrorism brought more slaughter among Moslems and *pieds-noirs.* In a speech on July 12, de Gaulle said emphatically that France would accept "an entirely independent" Algeria.

A bitter interlude with Tunisia darkened the atmosphere. Bourguiba suddenly demanded that France abandon the key naval base it had leased at Bizerte. Also, he asked for an important Sahara border adjustment near the Algerian oil fields. De Gaulle rankled at what he called "a threatening letter." After waiting two weeks for an answer, the Tunisians attacked the base. France sent 7,000 paratroopers; aircraft strafed and bombed Tunisian positions; three French warships blasted through the blockade. After three days, Tunisian casualties were 700 dead and 1,200 wounded; for the French, twenty-four dead and 100 wounded. De Gaulle made his point but infuriated a vital North African ally.

Meanwhile, army and Foreign Legion officers in hiding and assorted frustrated extremists fortified the OAS. They tried to kill de Gaulle and break French will with terror. De Gaulle's agents, *les Barbouzes,* tried to infiltrate the OAS, and their war was brutal. OAS squads bombed leftist homes in Paris. When they blinded a four-year-old girl, even French papers that supported *Algérie Française* carried huge photos of her bloody, disfigured face. By then, the OAS had killed 553 people.

Paris crowds demonstrating against the OAS clashed with police, leaving eight dead and 100 injured, and 140 police officers injured.

At the mass funeral, the biggest turnout in Paris since liberation, Simone de Beauvoir remarked, "My God! How I hated the French!"

As the end drew near, Salan committed the OAS to its own war in Algeria. Killings on all sides averaged up to forty a day in Algiers. The OAS executed such moderate Algerians as Mouloud Feraoun, a prize-winning Kabyle author and friend of Camus. He had symbolized a bridge of hope, writing at one point:

"There is French in me, there is Kabyle in me. . . . When Algeria lives and raises its head [again] . . . it will remember France and all it owes to France."

In eleven days of talks at Evian, de Gaulle reached an agreement with the FLN. He had hoped to retain petroleum rights, military accords, and other concessions, but it was too late. A cease-fire began on March 19; a month later, Salan was captured. After a last orgy of terror, the OAS gave up. On July 1, Algerians voted massively for independence in a referendum.

The *pieds-noirs* were left with a symbolic choice: the suitcase or the coffin. An exodus of 1,380,000 Europeans and pro-French Moslems hurried to France, many destitute and broken. Others streamed out to Spain or Canada or Israel. Only 30,000 Europeans stayed behind.

As Challe had feared, *harkis* (Algerians who fought for the French) were massacred by the thousands. Under the Evian terms, French units stood by while *harkis* were taken off to slaughter. Some Frenchmen risked their own lives to protect Moslems who had been loyal to them. In other cases, Horne wrote, French officers disarmed the Moslem troops with the promise of providing better weapons "and then sneaked away in the middle of the night, abandoning them to their fate." He added:

"It was a tragedy even more odious than that of the Russian prisoners of war handed back by the Western allies in 1945. Estimates of the numbers of Algerians thus killed vary wildly between 30,000 and 150,000."

Those who made it to France, he said, "were, for the most part, to live lives of poverty, unappreciated and unassimilated." Some have done well in France, but many still live today in wretched camps, targets of growing racism.

One Algerian deputy, who lost ten family members to FLN reprisals, warned de Gaulle his people would suffer. *"Eh bien,"* the general replied, *"vous souffrirez."*[15]

The war lasted seven and a half years. French figures list their dead at 21,600 (including 7,000 killed "accidentally"); more than 65,000 wounded and injured; and 1,000 missing.[16] For Moslems, they estimate 141,000 male combatants killed by security forces; 12,000 FLN members killed in internal purges; 66,000 Moslem civilians killed or abducted by the FLN. In 42,090 listed acts of terror by the FLN and the OAS, 2,788 European civilians died and 500 disappeared, official figures say. Algerians now put their death toll at a million. No one really knows.

To the French as a people, the war was devastating. *Petits blancs* showed what cruelty they would accept for personal gain or political ideas. No one was equal, a brother, or entitled to liberty if he stood in the way of *l'Algérie française.* Democracy and its institutions were needless obstacles. The society showed itself prepared to condone excesses, willing to look elsewhere until left with no choice. For a France immersed in defeat and dejection for most of twenty-three years, it was a heavy blow.

ON JULY 5, 1962, French colors were hauled down and taken home. Some military units stayed behind for a while. But de Gaulle gave up Algeria completely; he was moving France out of the colony business. A modern empire, he understood well, worked in different ways.

PART THREE

THE NEW EMPIRE

France will be swept from the face of Africa.
>   —*Ahmed Sékou Touré of Guinea, at
>   independence*

But of course we take francs, madame. This is France.
>   —*Gabonese shopkeeper, twenty-five years
>   after independence*

CHAPTER TWELVE

Africa I: Trompe-l'Oeil

WHEN IT CAME time to disassemble the African empire, France went home with all the panache it could muster, which is a great deal of panache. Troops in crimson shakos paraded, sun glinting off their cornets. Snapping flags were lowered and ceremoniously folded away. Brand-new national anthems wafted over the flame trees and bougainvillea in the capitals of brand-new nations. French mills spun out acres of bunting in a dozen bright colors. Cargo flights from Paris shuttled out delicate pastry puffs, choice *foie gras* and ball gowns to the heart of darkness. Freshly installed presidents, stiff with pride and the starch in their immaculate formal shirts, rhetorically turned the page of colonialism toward glorious new chapters of independence.

Then calm settled again on the sleepy capitals, and the sign painters took over.

At each new government headquarters, a door was labeled *Ministre des Finances,* and an African moved in. The office's former French occupant shifted to a smaller, adjoining room behind his own new sign: *Conseiller Technique.* And so on in virtually every important department, including the armed forces and secret police.

France thus went from colonial power, at a time in history when that status inspired no admiration, to mentor and friend of an emergent continent. Territories that had begun to besmirch French grandeur formed the basis of a new overseas empire in which each state was bound to Paris by its own free will. More or less.

The theme of African decolonization was "winds of change,"

from a speech by British Prime Minister Harold Macmillan. Britain
nudged its colonies out of the nest, equipping them with cash
reserves, well-trained civil services, parliamentary democracies, and
best wishes. And the wind currents dashed most to the ground.
Ghana went bankrupt and jolted from one military coup to another.
Nigeria exploded in civil war and then paralyzed itself with corruption. Uganda fell under the bloody depredations of Idi Amin.
Tanzania, Zambia, and Sierra Leone suffered economic chaos.
Malawi, abandoning the niceties of Westminster democracy, was
known as a "one-man Banda," in the tight grip of President Hastings Kamuzu Banda. Kenya, a relative success story, was fraught
with problems. After twenty-five years, some hearts may belong to
Britain's Commonwealth but a lot of hard assets are mortgaged to
international bankers.

France shielded its colonies from the winds of change with an
elaborate *trompe-l'oeil*. It only looked like independence. In fact, it
was a windbreak. Africans took cover from the buffeting of world
currents. And France made sure its windfall did not blow out of
reach.

New governments were in charge. France simply shaped the
decisions, made up the deficits, warded off coups d'état and invasions, stabilized the currency, controlled imports and exports at
preferential rates, locked up the oil and strategic materials, moni-
tored the politics, stood by during bleak years, and drained profits
from the private sector in both good years and bad.

The *trompe-l'oeil* was a masterwork of modern statecraft. On its
face, it was decolonization on a grand scale, a lasting monument to
the French principles of *liberté, égalité, fraternité*. It was not really
a sham; each state is, in fact, independent. "Association" is legally
seated in Article 88 of the French Constitution, which allows states
to link themselves to France "to develop their civilization."

During a state visit, President Georges Pompidou remarked to
Léopold Sédar Senghor of Senegal, "We both come from the same
culture." Senghor corrected him: "I come from two cultures, and
I would not forsake either one."

Two huge blocs, French West Africa and French Equatorial
Africa, were broken into fourteen small states, easily manageable if
not each homogeneous. Britain might have done better had it done

the same in Nigeria and the Sudan. Or Belgium, in the Congo.

Whether they believed it or not, the French packaged decolonization as a voluntary step toward a better future. As de Gaulle put it, "If I did it, it was above all because it seemed to me to be contrary to the interest and new ambition of France to hold itself riveted to obligations, to burdens which no longer fit with what its power and its glory require."[1] The arrangement served the needs of practically everyone: the French Africans gained independence with a safety net below; the Americans could rely on stability in vast regions of potential upheaval; other Africans could vilify the French, or plead for their help, as domestic politics demanded.

And France, with a faithful bloc, assured its political *rayonnement* in world affairs. Louis de Guiringaud, a former foreign minister, put it bluntly: "Africa is the only continent which is still the right size for France, still within the limits of its means. It is the only one where France can still, with 500 men, change the course of history."

A degree of nobility infused French motives. But order has been preserved by the frank pragmatism and subsurface maneuvering that characterize French diplomacy. Coups d'état not first cleared in Paris face a limited life expectancy. In public, the Elysée listens politely and silently to routine floggings of the three weird sisters of emergent Africa: colonialism, neocolonialism, and imperialism.

France reduced the risk of unpleasant surprise by maneuvering friendly leaders into place before independence. Elections were tailored to suit the circumstances. One-party states emerged, and elites in power made sure no one would unseat them, with little objection from Paris. Sympathetic leaders were easy to find; for example, Senghor and Félix Houphouët-Boigny of the Ivory Coast had served in French cabinets.

And then, to make sure things stayed on course, de Gaulle entrusted Africa to Jacques Foccart and to SDECE.

Foccart, who grew up in Guadeloupe and knew the empire well, was legendary for the twenty minutes every day he spent with de Gaulle. He ran Africa for the Elysée, short-circuiting ministers and military commanders, placing his own agents in sensitive spots. He filtered access to the president and dispensed favors in his name. Little happened that he did not know about. Often things happened because of him.

SDECE (pronounced "ez-dek") was the Service de documentation extérieure et de contre-espionnage. Later, it became the DGSE
—Direction générale de la sécurité extérieure—of *Rainbow Warrior*
fame. France helped each new state set up its own intelligence
agency. Maurice Robert, SDECE chief for Africa, then linked them
to France through the PLR (Postes de Liaison et de Renseigne-
ment). "That permitted me to weave very privileged relations in all
French-speaking African countries," Robert said later.[2] The Africa
section, which began the 1960s with 150 agents, became one of the
most active branches of SDECE.

France also signed military accords with each of the new states.
Terms varied, but most governments were in a position to call on
Paris for help, and all allowed transit rights. The French closed
down almost all of their 100 garrisons in Africa but left well-armed
mobile units at strategic points. And all final military decisions were
left to France.

The idea was to protect French interests and keep out the Soviets.
SDECE tried to work closely with the Bureau of State Security—
BOSS—in South Africa, but the French government kept contacts
to a minimum.[3] In Cameroon, the first test came even before independence. French troops fought for five years before putting down
the Union of Cameroonian Peoples (UPC), bitterly opposed to
Ahmadou Ahidjo. Maurice Delauney, the French commander,
boasted in his memoirs: "The most spectacular operation permitted
me to entirely destroy the UPC headquarters at Bamenda [in British
Cameroon]. One fine night, French and Camerounians, all volunteers, crossed the British border . . . and burned all the buildings,
placing out of action several leaders of the party. Moumié, unfortunately, was not there." Not to worry; SDECE was prepared.

In their book, *La Piscine,* Roger Faligot and Pascal Krop give
this version of events, based on interviews with French agents.

Félix Moumié, the UPC leader, was in exile, often in Europe.
One evening a gentleman known as "Grand Bill," who had a phony
press card, took him to dinner in Geneva. Moumié was called to the
phone, a little surprised because no one knew he was there. Grand
Bill slipped a little thallium in his Ricard. Back at the table, Moumié ignored the aperitif. Ever resourceful, the agent laced his guest's

wine. At the end of the meal, having drunk his wine, Moumié also knocked back the Ricard.

Disaster. The dose was supposed to be small. Moumié would have gone to his exile home in Guinea and died there, where Sékou Touré would be accused of murdering him. Swiss doctors diagnosed the poison, and Grand Bill hid out on the Riviera. Fifteen years later, he was arrested in Belgium and extradited to Switzerland, but France managed to quash the proceedings.

Sékou Touré, in fact, was a favorite French target. He went to war with de Gaulle because of what seems to have been a tropical temper tantrum. When de Gaulle toured African colonies to campaign for "association," Sékou Touré considered himself close to France. In his major address, he said: "We intend to exercise with sovereignty our right to independence, but we intend to remain tied to France. In this association with France, we will become a proud, sovereign and free people."

But he went overboard on hyperbole. He hammered away at the theme of independence, to the wild cheering of crowds, as de Gaulle sat stonily behind him, his glower as purple as Sékou Touré's rhetoric. The Guineans had sent de Gaulle the speech, but an aide had not wanted to wake the general to show it to him. Things went downhill from there.

When it came time to vote, Guinea registered a thundering *non*. Guinea took independence immediately and first the Soviet Union, then China, recognized it. France scooped up everything and went home: light fixtures, instruction manuals, civil records. They smashed crockery in official residences. Then SDECE set about sabotaging the new government. When Sékou Touré ordered new currency, secret agents flooded Conakry with counterfeit bills. A string of coup d'état attempts failed, despite help from the Portuguese and West Germans. Guinea expelled all French diplomats in 1965. Sékou Touré grew steadily more autocratic, filling jails in which people often disappeared without a trace.

In 1983, a year before his death, Sékou Touré received Foccart in Conakry; he had already made peace with Giscard d'Estaing. Foccart wanted to talk about the past, Faligot and Krop recount. They quote Sékou Touré as saying, "France had an unqualifiable attitude. Why, on purpose, leave to rot in Marseilles important shipments of food for my people? Not to mention the plots."

MONGO BETI, a noted Cameroonian writer, was not among those dazzled by the *trompe-l'oeil*. He wrote:

> A decolonization which establishes an indigenous tyranny based on the silence of cemeteries or the desert of an indentured population, which is shielded from indiscreet scrutiny of the outside world, cannot escape skepticism. . . . The stability of a Camerounian regime deceives only the village idiots.

Other African nationalists berated Francophile leaders as toadies of a lingering colonial presence. Houphouët-Boigny caught the brunt of their derision, but he laughed it off. In 1968, President Mobutu Sese Seko of Zaire (he was Joseph-Désiré Mobutu of the Congo then, before "authenticity") visited the Ivory Coast for the first time. He was dumbstruck by the smoothly clicking wheels of government and business in Abidjan, a capital of glass, steel, and flowers that would do credit to the Riviera. Ah, he asked his host, but how many Frenchmen are here to make it work? "Fifteen thousand." And how many will you have in ten years? "Thirty thousand."

In fact, there were nearly 60,000 Frenchmen in the Ivory Coast ten years later, six times the number at independence. Eventually Mobutu called in French military officers and financial advisers. Zaire, which was colonized by Belgium, is a member in good standing of the club of former French territories.

AN ENDURING piece of African lore is the bet at independence among Kwame Nkrumah of Ghana, Sékou Touré, and Houphouët-Boigny over whose system would come out ahead.

Nkrumah, champion of Pan-African unity, bartered away wealth for useless Soviet hardware and monuments to his own glory. He was overthrown by the military, and Ghana has suffered economic catastrophe for most of its life as a nation. Sékou Touré's rhetoric went nowhere. Although Guinea is rich in bauxite, iron, diamonds, gold, and fertile land, its Soviet-plundered socialist economy fell into ruin. By 1979, Sékou Touré edged back toward France. When he died in 1984, military leaders who took over urged France to help the country to its feet. Houphouët-Boigny's Ivory Coast, with few minerals and mediocre soil, was a thriving modern state, boasting a capital of twenty-story office towers and fast lanes, rich from cocoa, coffee, and palm oil. (The political and social arguments, of course, were another matter.)

After Sékou Touré died, military rulers turned immediately to France. They negotiated to dump their currency, the syli, for the CFA. France demurred; the syli was so weak it was devalued by 93.7 percent, to a fifteenth of its former value, at the end of 1985. France offered a handful of technical advisers, and the Guineans howled in protest. They wanted the hundreds of Frenchmen whom Houphouët-Boigny had replaced with Ivorians.

France's position seemed about to shift slightly in 1981. François Mitterrand at first paid less attention to Africa than did Giscard d'Estaing. He was not, for one thing, a big game hunter. Socialist ministers seemed less willing to be branded as neocolonialists. More importantly, France was running short of money. But by late 1985, the new president was known as Mitterrand *l'Africain*.

At the annual French-African summit, he told his colleagues, "The colonial era is over, and I will not bring it back even to help you out. You are countries, sovereign states, like France; we speak as equals." But, he added, France would be their *avocat*—their advocate and counsel—in dealing with Western creditors. "France is more sensitive to the needs of your continent," Mitterrand said. "She has no more merits than the others, simply a history, an experience." The summit, originally for former French colonies, was attended by most states on the continent.

Mitterrand's offer rattled the Treasury, caught by surprise. The president volunteered to sponsor a separate meeting on African debt, rather than folding the problem into a more general U.N. session. Treasury officials feared such a conference would endanger individual arrangements made by each country with the creditors' Club of Paris. But the Africans were happy.

Africans had begun to look elsewhere to plug ever more gaping holes in their budgets. Competitor nations faced the same economic pressures as France. Some probed deeply for markets in the *chasse gardée* and were prepared to offer aid to pay for their hunting licenses. French Africans, shopping for lower prices and better terms, sought to diversify.

By 1980, two-thirds of all science and technology doctoral candidates from the Ivory Coast were studying in the United States. In 1985, two Senegalese cabinet ministers had American M.B.A. degrees. The Ivory Coast sent home 959 French-subsidized *coopérants* —teachers, administrators, and technicians—leaving just over 2,000. The French community dropped toward 30,000, nearly half its peak level. In almost every former French colony, government contracts were awarded with increasing frequency to Britons, Belgians, Dutch, Americans, Canadians, Germans, Japanese, and Israelis, among others.

One morning in 1985, I flew from Paris to Libreville, Gabon, on what for twenty-five years was virtually a French domestic route. Only the few foreigners, non-French and non-Gabonese, need visas when they arrive. One chooses UTA, a private French airline, or Air Gabon, which relies on contracted Air France staff. Just after takeoff, two businessmen from the former French colonies of Senegal and Cameroon broke into an argument. In perfect English, they were debating the backcourt offense of the Washington Redskins.

BUT THE FRENCH windbreak survives nearly intact, and no nation, Western or Eastern, seems anxious—or able—to replace it.

The Bank of France guarantees convertibility of the CFA franc, the common currency, at a fixed rate with the French franc. The Africans are assured credits, simplified commerce, and easy travel abroad. For this privilege, African central banks keep two-thirds of their foreign exchange holdings under French control. France gives generously from a dozen pots: budgetary supports, trade subsidies, investment credits, development projects, arms. Africans come to Paris to sign the deals, and Frenchmen remain in Africa to oversee them.

French bankers settle deals over a glass of Pernod, without a lot of the annoying paperwork Americans require. Often businesses generously refund part of their profits back to the man who signed the contract.

Altogether, there are perhaps 300,000 Frenchmen in all of Africa, private citizens and people on official contracts. Airlines, factories, even government departments are run by the French on management contracts. French schools train officials, businessmen, and officers.

French military bases watch the continent. Paratroopers are stationed in Senegal, at the western bulge, in the Ivory Coast, in Gabon, and in the Central African Republic. The Foreign Legion is in Djibouti, on the Red Sea, and at Mayotte, an Indian Ocean island still flying the Tricolor. In 1985, 8,500 men were based in the region, not counting 1,278 French military advisers. Troops stormed down from Corsica twice to help Zaire, a former Belgian colony. And France intervened fifteen times in twenty-five years in its own former colonies.

A total of 1,909 African officers, long a constant number, trained in France during 1984. The published budget for French military cooperation with Africa was 805.9 million francs for 1985, up from 154 million in 1970.

The defense accords are mutual. Thomas Sankara of Burkina Faso made that point at a Paris press conference, and French reporters chortled. "There is not a Burkinabe who does not remember an uncle or a father who died so that France could be free," Sankara said, bringing an awkward silence to the room. "I would advise you to remember that."

Economic assistance comes from too many sources to count. Sometimes it involves elaborate aid programs, with feasibility studies and controllers' reports. Sometimes the Elysée simply writes a check to make up a budget deficit.

Signs of an Anglo-Saxon world muscling in are not yet alarming. There is a Super Chicken in Abidjan, near the Hilton where *USA Today* and *Playgirl* are displayed next to *Le Monde* and *Paris-Match*. But there are also Burger Kings on the Champs-Elysées and a Hilton in the shadow of the Eiffel Tower. To get from the Abidjan airport to the far side of town, you take boulevard Valéry Giscard d'Estaing across the Charles de Gaulle Bridge, on down boulevard Charles de Gaulle to boulevard François Mitterrand.

Dakar, Senegal, the grandfather of French African cities, retains its moldy old flavor.

Moscow has fallen flat in French Africa after pushing hard in

Guinea, Mali, and Madagascar. In Brazzaville, the Congo, or in Cotonou, Benin, the billboard slogans of nominally Marxist governments make no impact on the quantity of fresh oysters flown down regularly from Brittany. When a government's overriding ideology is to stay in power, it looks for convenience from its benefactor. The humorless Russians mix badly in Africa, and they try to take more than they give. France controls subtly; the Soviets prefer ironclad lines of power. Besides, as any African leader can tell you, Red Square is not the place Vendôme.

Tension crackles just under the surface. In the Central African Republic, whites live in villas and downtown Bangui apartments, clustering at night at the Rock Club and restaurants by the river. Kilometer 5 is the *quartier populaire,* a vast African slum. In 1986, a French Jaguar took off on a training flight from Bangui. Something went wrong, and the pilot ejected. The aircraft fell on an Islamic school in the heart of Kilometer 5; it killed 23 people, mainly boys, and injured another 30. Africans stoned whites and stormed through the city. Some of the 4,000 French residents huddled in the embassy. French authorities were shaken. The Jaguars at Bangui make up the strike force France relied upon to hold Libya at bay in Chad.

But after a bitter week, the crisis passed. Victims were flown to France for treatment and the school was rebuilt. But French airmen are now known in Kilometer 5 as *les jaguars.*

An extreme example of *trompe-l'oeil* is Gabon. That bite-sized enclave on the west coast of Central Africa, best known as the forgotten bit of jungle where Albert Schweitzer cured lepers, demonstrates what French diplomacy can accomplish with makeup and mirrors.

Two books are sold side by side in Libreville hotel lobbies. According to *L'Implantation Coloniale au Gabon,* by Nicolas Metegue N'nah, independence was "the fruit of more than 120 years of continuous struggle." But in *Le Colonisateur Colonisé,* the last French governor of Gabon, Louis Sanmarco, leaves a different impression.

Of the fourteen African governing councils offered a choice, only Gabon's chose to join France as a *département,* meaning statehood. Sanmarco wrote:

I considered that a triumph, the triumph of 130 years of French colonization which resulted in this request for integration, the posthumous triumph of sailors, foresters, settlers, administrators who, with all their faults, worked not all that badly in this country to make people love France to that degree. Why not say it?

He described how he flew to Paris to negotiate statehood.

I expected to be treated as a triumphant victor who had added another pearl to the crown. I was received like a dog in a bowling alley. The minister, Cornut-Gentile, was even rude: "Sanmarco, have you fallen on your head? . . . We don't have enough Antilles [small troublesome states]? Go on, independence like everyone else."

Failing all else, Gabonese leader Léon M'Ba designed a flag bearing a small Tricolor in the corner. It was rejected in Paris. Reluctantly, M'Ba took Gabon out of the nest to take its place with the others.

But France left the windbreak. In 1964, a popular political opponent led a successful coup against M'Ba. Within forty-eight hours, French troops rushed in from Dakar and Brazzaville to put him back in office. The rebels suffered twenty-seven dead and forty-four wounded. When M'Ba fell ill, French strategists lined up behind an up-and-coming former postal clerk named Albert-Bernard Bongo (later El Hadj Omar Bongo; the president converted to Islam when Gabon joined OPEC). Legitimized by a questionable election, Omar Bongo took over in 1967. He is still in power, protected from any eventuality by his presidential guard—which is commanded by Frenchmen.

At independence in 1960, there were 5,000 Frenchmen in Gabon. Today, there are 26,000. In a country with 750,000 inhabitants, the ratio of whites to Africans approaches that in Rhodesia before Zimbabwean independence. French teachers outnumber Gabonese two to one. Vital government documents can move from ministry to ministry without leaving French hands. French secretaries and unskilled workers advertise for work in the local classifieds.

I chatted one day in 1985 with a young Gabonese professional, waiting out the initial period of wariness until it seemed that we were telling each other what we really thought. "Don't you sometimes feel there are too many white faces around here?" I asked. "On the contrary," he said. "There are not enough." A minor diplomatic flap was raging at the time. France had announced that, in the interest of "Gabonization," it was reducing by twenty-eight the 630 teachers and advisers it partially funded. Hundreds of others, in different categories, would not be affected. Gabonese authorities complained that France was abandoning them.

The French-owned Mbolo Supermarket stocks fifteen brands of Camembert cheese along with eleven kinds of dog food. Libreville's water supply tastes like a swimming pool, but it is clean enough. Still, Gabon imports 6,000 tons of water a year from France, and fifteen tons of *foie gras,* along with almost every tomato, potato, onion, beefsteak, green bean, and kilo of rice, wheat, or corn consumed in Gabon. On Sunday afternoons, French bankers, civil servants, and businessmen wait in forty-five-minute traffic jams to have their boats pulled from the water at the marina. Generations ago, French missionaries clothed African maidens, but Libreville beaches are sprinkled with topless, sometimes bottomless French ladies.

The Scotch Club, across from the French consulate, might be any late-night boisterous *boîte* in St.-Tropez, jammed to paralysis with sun-tanned youths in windsurfer T-shirts and long-legged women with a day's wages invested in their hairdos. The only difference is that in a St.-Tropez club, there would be more blacks. At the Bataclan, half the place is black—the women. French marines, traveling salesmen, and bored husbands drop in regularly for a little paid temporary miscegenation.

In Libreville, you wake to a tinkling voice on the radio, a dead ringer for the uniformly sweet voices on Paris' Radio FIP. She reads the horoscope, the modern version of ghostly superstitions Gabonese brought from the forest, and plays Michel Sardou. You can hop in a Peugeot 205 (or a Honda, as in France) and drive down a road labeled with the same little red "N1" marker you will find in Réunion or Rouen. There is even a French-style *autoroute* to the port. For most of the way, it is a regular overcrowded African two-lane blacktop. You recognize it by the stylized blue and white sign depicting a freeway under an overpass.

At the post office, mailboxes say Gabon, France, and Foreign Countries. Sometimes the television anchorman slips and, after detailing President Mitterrand's movements, says, "And now for the international news." In Gabon, as in the Ivory Coast, newscasters use satellite relays of correspondents' reports from France's TF1 and Antenne 2, but only in the Ivory Coast do they make the cosmetic gesture of slicing off the signature at the end. In the evening, Libreville's *jeunesse dorée* gathers at Le Bowlingstore to watch American films dubbed in French. Or, at the Dragon d'Or Chinese restaurant and bar, they browse among the rack of Astérix comic books, reading about their ancestors, the Gauls.

A friend of mine asked a Gabonese woman in a shop if she could pay in French money. The shopkeeper was amazed at the question. "But of course we take francs, madame. This is France."

The big yellow Hertz sign was not French, but the woman at the counter was. Renting cars is just one of those businesses the French cannot get down, whatever the fancy franchise. It is not in the French commercial spirit to try harder for strangers. The woman was very pleasant and made reservations for me in Togo and the Ivory Coast. I asked for confirmations. "We don't give them." But I needed to know, I explained, so I could make other arrangements if necessary; I depended upon a car. "No rental agency gives confirmations," she explained. "But I rent cars all over the world and . . ." She was still very pleasant but firm as granite. "No, monsieur, car rental companies never give confirmations anywhere in the world." I swear to God.

(For balance, let me add the time I reserved an Avis car in Paris, got a computerized confirmation, and forgot to bring the slip when I went for the car. The woman stared at me as if I were an unprincipled liar trying to weasel away one of her cars. In the end, a friend had to waste ninety minutes bringing the slip to her from my home. When it appeared, the woman was furious at having been shown to be wrong; she made an insulting remark about me to another customer and literally flung the contract at me. I didn't bother with the manager. The time before they rented me a car with a bald short-distance emergency tire on it; I didn't discover it until I had driven on it 1,000 miles over freeways and winding mountain roads. His only response was a shrug and a look that said, with reason, alas: Idiot.)

THE FRENCH, with their own position consolidated, just laugh off Bongo's idiosyncrasies. While I was there, he fulminated against "foreigners": Lebanese businessmen who endangered some of his commercial operations. In a speech repeated half a dozen times on television, he urged police to raid their shops. And, he added, army patrols should take whatever liberties they wanted with prostitutes from neighboring countries. "After they have passed among seven or eight soldiers," he said, "they will learn."

For years, diplomats, academics, and journalists have attempted to work out whether France comes out ahead when the costs of its windbreak are compared to the various financial benefits. Few doubt that France does well for itself. In Gabon, that impression is unmistakable.

"Well," remarked a senior French official who asked not to be named, "our cooperation operates at a loss in some of our other former colonies. I don't see why we shouldn't make a profit in Gabon." He outlined France's view:

> It is only natural that Gabon will diversify its markets and interests as time goes on. As we say in France, you can't put all your eggs in one basket. The military base, that's something else, just an agreement. Like you Americans have in Cuba. But France is so established here that sometimes we ask ourselves if we're not here alone. It is not good to be so present. Certainly there will be fewer French in the future. But I think it is only natural that we do everything we can to protect our position.

I asked how long Frenchmen would continue to run Gabon.

"Well, our position here is not eternal, it must evolve," he said, adding with a hearty chuckle, "Look at it this way: they've resolved the problem of colonialism. Before whites made the blacks work for nothing. Now, they make the whites work for money."

A lot of money. Government people on contract make roughly

twice what they would earn in France. Private businessmen often do better. A carpetlayer from southern France can wing down to Libreville on a contract, charge heavily for materials he can get at a discount, and come out even farther ahead on his taxes. The bigger the company, the wider the possibilities.

Foreigners who have tried say that breaking into Gabon is like setting up a video games arcade on turf controlled by the New Jersey mob. One seasoned African businessman laid out the situation:

> The oil companies manage because they're big enough, and they don't have to bribe. But for most things, it's twenty years too late. If you're ready to pay 15 percent on the side, you might make a deal, but you risk buying the wrong guy. And you've got the whole system to fight. It doesn't matter if you offer something cheaper because it's in no one's interest to lower prices.

Bribery aside, outsiders face a finely woven curtain of supplier contracts, management agreements, distribution networks, bank credit, investment guarantees, and pricing agreements, all controlled by a small group of French businessmen with official support. Interlocking subsidiaries can disguise profits and assign losses to Gabonese government partners. What is legal is all but impenetrable. What is not is impossible to find.

Take chickens. The same French group imports cheap feed, raises chickens, and markets poultry and eggs. With powerful Gabonese partners to protect against imports and local competition, profits are substantial. Or roses. Four Libreville florists sell 1,000 roses a week, flown from Paris, at five dollars each. A local producer turned out hydroponic roses at far less cost, but no one would market them.

Or the water. Gabonese entrepreneurs persuaded a French bottler to join in producing mineral water. An American potential investor decided that even if the plant were located near Libreville or Port-Gentil, by far the dominant markets, the project would be risky. But the plant was to be 500 miles inland, as far into Gabon as possible without leaving the country. It was a two-day drive on a hard road from Libreville. It was also, coincidentally, near Bongo's home village. The investor calculated the transport to Libreville as three times more expensive than flying real Evian water from Paris. But the bank loan would be backed by official French guarantees. The Gabon government would protect the project. Management contracts and commissions meant that private French interests would make their money even if the plant ran at a loss.

In French Africa, the laws of economics are political.

Most of Gabon's oil is produced by Elf-Gabon, which provides a third of the total production of its French parent company, Elf-Aquitaine. Gabon owns only 25 percent of Elf-Gabon. Most such companies share production with local governments, absorbing the costs themselves. Elf shares whatever profits it declares. With special marketing arrangements, and operations between dollars and francs, the margin of maneuver is wide.

"The most incredible thing I've heard in this business," remarked a visiting American oilman, "is that in twenty years Elf-Gabon has never been audited."

But that is nothing unusual; it's the French system. My pal Stanley, a retired multinational president who controlled French companies, explained it this way: "French law requires a *commissaire aux comptes* to make sure accounting is done properly, but he only checks to see that the numbers are in the right columns. He has no responsibility to check against vouchers to make sure the numbers relate to reality."

And a senior French diplomat said, "You Americans, you audit everything. We only audit when something is wrong."

Gabon's uranium, estimated at 20 percent of the West's reserves, is a greater mystery. As in Niger, the French do the mining and keep the books. Since uranium is classified as a strategic material, very little is said about it.

President Bongo, whose personal fortune is deep in the substantial category, seems in no hurry for a public audit of anything in Gabon. With all opposition quashed, and faithful French commanders to calm troubled waters, he rules with leisurely grandeur. The daily paper, *Union,* each day tops the front page with news of his routine appointments. Just in time for the 1977 summit of the Organization of African Unity, he completed an $800 million presidential palace, complete with a marble elevator to lift his Bentley limousine up to his bedroom.

And the president can be generous.

"Once I lost my watch in Gabon, just some cheap watch I left somewhere," a friend in the Quai d'Orsay told me. "Bongo somehow heard about it and sent me a new one. It was worth $3,000. They were upset when I insisted on giving it back. They figure they can just buy people."

Bongo is not a man to appreciate criticism. One book not for sale in Libreville is Pierre Péan's *Affaires Africaines,* which came out in 1983.

Péan, a French journalist who had worked in Gabon's Finance Ministry, aimed a spotlight at the French businessmen, diplomats, mercenaries, and thugs who cohabit in the shadows of Africa. He profiled the "Gabonese clan," a small group of right-wing Frenchmen and Gabonese millionaires who manipulated French policy to their own benefit. He documented secret official payments and cover-ups and traced questionable contributions to French political parties. He revealed how French business interests, with Gabonese connivance, plundered the economy, and he described secret Masonic ceremonies linking Bongo and his Gabonese associates to French partners. Foccart was always in the shadows.

Especially interesting was Péan's cast of characters. After the failed putsch in Algeria, the French dynamited the 1st REP headquarters at Zeralda, but its dust settled all over Africa. Colonel Le Braz from the 1st REP set up Bongo's *Garde Présidentielle* and he recruited ex-legionnaires for its ranks. When he retired he was replaced by "LouLou" Martin, another Legion colonel who holds the rank of general in Bongo's army. Maurice Robert went from African head of SDECE to director of Elf-Gabon to ambassador of France. Maurice Delauney, an old colonial administrator who fought on behalf of Cameroon, took his turn as French ambassador. And then there was Bob Denard and his mercenary buddies.

Denard, a large, flamboyant man with short hair and a meaty jaw, "did" Indochina, went for training in the United States, and in 1952 moved back to Morocco where he was born (unless it was Caen, or near Bordeaux; his past is murky) in 1929. He worked for an American security company and fought with underground groups against the *bradeurs d'empire,* those who would give up the colonies. In 1954, he was linked to the plot to kill Mendès-France. After fourteen months in jail, he joined the police. Then he showed up in Katanga with, as Péan aptly phrases it, "unofficial but effective help from Paris"; we'll get to that later.

"Bob Denard thus 'would work' directly or indirectly during close to twenty years for the Elysée or SDECE without ever appearing officially on personnel roles of any administration," Péan wrote. (In fact, it is closer to thirty years. He is still active, under a different name, in the Comoros.) "A mercenary used for all the *'coups tordus'* (dirty tricks) of the Republic, he would serve as scapegoat, at the right moment, to distract the ire of the press and the opposition."

Péan picks up Denard in Gabon in September 1971, lying in wait for an opponent of Bongo, Germain M'Ba. It was his first job in Gabon after long adventures in the Congo. M'Ba was executed; Péan implicates Denard and then notes that French officials covered him. Later, Péan presents evidence of how Bongo hired Denard and other French adventurers to murder his wife's lovers. At times, Péan points out, French police did not investigate with all the energy that might be expected.

The book shows how several of Denard's ill-fated Bay of Piglets operations were mounted from Gabon, with French help. With help from the CIA, he raised a French mercenary force to operate in Angola. Under Soviet attack, they fled to Namibia three months before the end of their contract. Earlier, a French mercenary operation from Gabon, under Jean Kay, failed in Cabinda. Denard made another disastrous try at Cabinda. And then there was Denard's attack on Benin.

At 7 A.M., on January 16, 1977, an unmarked four-engined plane set down in Cotonou and disgorged about 100 men, mostly white. They grabbed the nearest vehicles, raced into town, and blasted away at the presidential palace. Within three hours, they were racing back to their plane. They escaped a few steps ahead of the Benin army but left behind two dead, some prisoners, and documents describing their purpose. Gilbert Bourgeaud—Bob Denard— had led a mercenary force recruited from Gabon. The aircraft was one of a small fleet used to help break the Western blockade against Rhodesia.

Denard did better in the Comoros, picturesque but dirt-poor little islands near Réunion. Mayotte insisted on remaining part of France, but the other three islands of the group chose independence. In 1975, Denard installed Ali Soilih in place of Ahmed Abdallah. Then, in 1978, he raided the little Indian Ocean island again and put Abdallah back in office. Both coups, wrote Péan, among others, were mounted from Gabon. The second time, Denard stayed as minister of defense. He left his official position to shift to business, drifting back and forth between the Comoros and South Africa. But his associate, Roger Ghis, known as "Commandant Charles," ran the presidential guard of mercenaries with far more power than the official Frenchmen advising the army. French business interests control the economy; many Comoreans keep French passports and commute to Marseilles. "The situation remains particularly troubled and scandalously anachronistic," observed the left-leaning magazine *Afrique-Asie.*

In Gabon, Bongo was outraged that François Mitterrand's government allowed Péan's book to appear. Was there not, he demanded, a French law banning insults to foreign heads of state? For a month and a half, he banned the use of the words "France" or "French" on official media, including the powerful radio station Africa No. 1, which transmits to seventeen million French-speaking Africans. During that time, terrorists bombed the French marines' camp in Beirut, killing fifty-eight, and Mitterrand flew to Lebanon. Africa No. 1 had to mention only the U.S. casualties suffered in a companion assault.

Bongo courted the U.S. ambassador, who carefully avoided offending the French by overresponding. He shopped for imports in other European markets. He did not dismiss the French officers in his presidential guard or send home French advisers.

Hands were wrung at the Quai d'Orsay. Whatever Gabon's value to France in francs and barrels of oil, it is a cornerstone of the empire. Transall aircraft stop for gas at Libreville on their way to rescue Mobutu or to change presidents of the Central African Republic. Jaguar fighters stand by ready for anything. The base provides rear support for operations in Chad. In the late 1960s, when France supported Biafra in a secession that would weaken English-speaking Nigeria, a mercenary air force flew from Gabon. Secret flights to Rhodesia were staged from Libreville. French intelligence loves the place.

Soon after the storm, Prime Minister Pierre Mauroy hurried to Gabon. Other French ministers followed. And then, France produced the *pièce de résistance*. Bongo was brought to Paris with a state welcome reserved for the queen of England and the president of the United States. His arrival was covered live on television. The Garde Républicaine trotted alongside his motorcade, sabers flashing and plumes fluttering. A diva trilled for him at the opera. Reporters followed his every move.

French police had banned a press conference by Bongo's opponents, saying it "might endanger public order and damage international relations." But Bongo skipped his own customary press conference because his hosts could not guarantee that Péan would not be there. France, after all, was a democracy.

That was enough. Bongo kept his four villas on the Côte d'Azur, and relations returned to normal. "It is as when there is a quarrel in a family," a senior Gabonese official told me a year later. "One gets mad, words are exchanged. And then it is over." What else would one expect in a country where the president comes from a town called Franceville?

No one in Gabon is betting that France's unchallenged influence will go on forever. There are rumblings of discontent among younger Gabonese, officials, and people in the street, which reflect feelings across French Africa. Two incidents made clear to me both the depth of these rumblings and the extent to which France is implanted. I'm making no bets in either direction.

At Mbolo Supermarket, where 15,000 items are displayed on shelves in what looks like a gigantic blue tin aircraft hangar, I tried to take pictures of Gabonese shoppers. A large woman caught me by the Camembert rack.

"Why did you take my picture?" she demanded.

"I was photographing cheeses, madame, and you happened to be in the picture." It was a dumb thing to say.

She leaped at me and swatted at the camera, trying to smash it. Batteries spilled out of the flash, clattering on the floor. She screamed at me, and I tried to calm her. With a deft twist, she wrapped the camera strap around my wrist, making a combination of handcuffs and dog leash. She marched toward the cops, dragging me along behind.

It was most undignified. I managed to dig my heels in by the canned corn.

She wanted the film. I could understand her position; I had been sneaky, and she didn't know who I was. But I had some good stuff on the roll and did not want to give it to her. The woman continued shrieking, and a small crowd gathered. I looked at the faces.

A handful of youths stared at me in clear hatred. All they knew was what was evident: the woman had a complaint, and I was white, probably French. One of them grabbed the camera and tried to break it open. I saw no way to save the film without involving the police. In fact, I doubted I could avoid the police, in any case. And I knew enough about Gabonese police not to relish the encounter. I opened the camera, handed over the film, and the matter was settled.

Given the woman's hysteria and the youths' anger, it was a little scary. But only a little. At the height of the fracas, a grizzled French paratrooper materialized beside me. He stayed long enough to ensure that the danger would pass. Then, without a word, he dissolved from view.

ON A FLIGHT to Paris, I sat next to a young Gabonese cabinet minister who, after a half-bottle of Bordeaux, let down his guard.

"You know, we are finally learning to deal with the French, to do these things for ourselves. Until now, we shopped for everything in Paris, even ideas. If the French didn't make something, we paid them to get it for us. They had a monopoly, no service, no choice. Now we go straight to where we can get the best equipment, the best deal. . . .

"Elf, for example. You know, American companies came along and found oil on concessions that Elf had looked at and said were no good. That made a real impact, up here," he said, tapping his head. "It opened our eyes. The president said those guys must be trying to hide something for later. When someone is your friend, and you trust him, and something like that happens, it has an effect. . . .

"The French are always talking about emotional ties. Well, it's emotional one way. From us. They play on our emotions to make money off of us. With a new generation, I don't think it will be that way."

The plane neared Charles de Gaulle airport, and I asked the minister where he stayed in Paris. He looked at me, surprised, as though I were a little slow.

"At my place," he answered. "In the sixth *arrondissement.*"

CHAPTER THIRTEEN

Africa II: Chasse Gardée

ON AN ARCTIC FRENCH afternoon in November 1985, I went to see the emperor. Bokassa I had called a press conference. Several beefy Frenchmen with short hair and lumpy jackets checked my credentials. Then I found a plush velvet chair among the tangle of television cables and waited for his majesty.

I noticed a framed gold medal stamped with the face of Charles de Gaulle. Bokassa had called him "Papa" (de Gaulle hated that) and he wept bitterly at the general's funeral. And there was a photograph of Bokassa inscribed, "To my dear relative and very good friend, Valéry Giscard d'Estaing." Apparently it had been returned to sender.

A darkwood desk sat raised on a low purple platform, under formal portraits of two of the only three French-speaking emperors since Charlemagne. There was Napoléon I, of course, chin firm, nose finely chiseled, and eyes fixed on some distant corner of the world he expected to conquer by dinnertime. And then, with a self-satisfied smirk that made Napoléon seem humble, there was Bokassa.

The second portrait was a photograph, taken in 1977 when Jean-Bedel Bokassa, French army sergeant turned president of the Central African Republic by coup d'état, was crowned emperor of the Central African Empire. The coronation cost somewhere between $25 million and $90 million, most of it in French foreign aid. It looked as though Bokassa's uniform cost most of it. He held a plumed and cockaded admiral's hat, and eight rows of colorful ribbons flashed on his breast. On the left side. The right side was occupied by a huge gold cross of the French Légion d'honneur. Sashes and swords led the eye to his boots: gleaming black, each with a sunburst of gold from ankle to toe.

With a flourish, Bokassa himself appeared, wearing much of the above.

The emperor sat down and read, in a monotone, an eight-page text. France deposed him in 1979, he said, and he was a political prisoner. The government seized all his identity papers, including his French passport. All he had left was his French military volunteer card issued by the Free French Forces in World War II; he had thoughtfully added a photocopy—recto, verso—to the press kit. Police followed him everywhere and obliged him to go home if he spent two nights away.

"Home" is an eighteen-room château dating from 1750 set back in a small park at Hardricourt, west of Paris. But, he said, it is all he has. Three châteaus and two houses were seized for taxes. His accounts are blocked. He lives on a monthly military pension of 5,998 francs but receives none of the social security or family allowances due him.

"Try to raise nine kids on that, plus the costs of the château," he said. Most of his other forty-four children were in Bangui with his seventeen wives, who have all left him. He wanted to be there, too, in the worst way.

He would just climb on a plane and fly to Bangui, he said, but that was impossible. The French had installed Colonel Frédéric Mansion as a "super chief of state" next to the president, General André Kolingba. In a garden stroll afterward, he told me, "President Mitterrand has ordered Mansion and the others to shoot me if I show up in *Centrafrique.*" He sent his twelve-year-old son, Jean-Bertrand, to Bangui but Mansion put him back on the plane to Paris.

Bokassa displayed one of the last ten copies of his book, *Ma Vérité.* French authorities had burned the rest. Valéry Giscard d'Estaing was not pleased with some of the crudely phrased—and emphatically denied—allegations: that the former French president had impregnated the Empress Catherine and arranged an abortion; that he demanded diamonds on each of his semiyearly visits to a

200,000-acre hunting reserve kept for him so he could pillage ivory; that he dallied with an ever-changing assortment of local women; and so on.

From his dais, Bokassa declaimed:

"This barbarous act, arrest, illegal detention, hostage-taking, and the seizure of goods and personal archives is an act of piracy in which my people did not take part at all."

France, he declared, violated all his internationally guaranteed human rights. Worst of all, Guy Penne, the Elysée Africa czar, would not return his phone calls.

The press conference ended on a touching note. Bokassa posed with his eight-month-old son, Jean-Bedel. Reporters nosed around the château; it was unheated and the family lived mostly in the kitchen, among an untidy clutter of pots and pans, laundry, and broken toys. On a large stove, gas burners were turned up full blast for warmth.

Bokassa complained about his gas and electricity bill; twice he threatened to demonstrate outside the Elysée palace with all nine kids, and the bill was mysteriously paid. After all, he said, Mitterrand had a *caisse noire,* a slush fund, for such things. Christmas, he said, would be brightened by gifts of food from his few faithful friends in France. Later three of Bokassa's children were picked up for shoplifting records and perfume. "It was sausage," he said. "They were hungry." The state put them in a home when he said he was too poor to bail them out.

"Sometimes God helps poor people," he said, and a thin film of tears formed in his eyes.

It was hard, somehow, to summon up a great deal of pity. This was not my first encounter with Bokassa. I recognized, for example, the heavy ebony cane with which he had laid open the forehead of my friend and colleague, Mike Goldsmith. In 1977, Bokassa's goons had seized Mike when he received a garbled message from Johannesburg; that "proved" he was a spy. He was brought to Bokassa who, without a word, knocked him unconscious, kicked him, stamped on his glasses, and imprisoned him for a month. For much of the time, he was handcuffed too tightly, with little food and no doctor for his festering wounds.

Giscard d'Estaing had put up with that sort of behavior; also with the emperor's arbitrary murders, apparent cannibalism, massive corruption, and flights of bizarre behavior. *Le Canard Enchaîné* and *Le Monde* disclosed that the president had accepted diamonds several times as gifts from Bokassa. However, Giscard d'Estaing contained the scandal in an accepted French manner: he refused to answer impertinent reporters and brought the judicial power of the state to bear on anyone who pushed too hard.

Bokassa was deposed only after he clubbed to death children whose parents protested against buying school uniforms from a factory he happened to own. Eyewitnesses testified later that nearly 200 youngsters were killed in a prison yard; Bokassa took part personally in the massacre, Central African Republic courts determined.

At first a French cabinet minister dismissed the massacre as "a pseudo-event." But it was too widely reported; there was no ignoring it.

Opération Barracuda was smooth and brutal. Bokassa's cousin, former Central African Republic president David Dacko, was awakened at his home in Paris and bundled onto a plane. Maurice Robert, Africa director for SDECE, came along for the ride. French troops, already based at Bangui and Bouar, flashed a little steel, just in case. No problem. Bokassa was in Libya at the time; he got the message. The deposed emperor headed for Paris but was refused permission to land at Orly. *"Bande de cons* (you pack of jerks)," he yelled into his pilot's microphone, "give me clearance, or I'll land on the *autoroute.*" He was diverted to the Evreux air base, where his plane was surrounded. Giscard d'Estaing called in a favor from Félix Houphouët-Boigny, and Bokassa accepted exile in the Ivory Coast. Two years later, Houphouët had had enough. You made him, he told the French; you take him. And they did.

GOLDSMITH AND I visited Bangui together, by coincidence, late in 1984. We drove to the villa Bokassa built for his Romanian wife at Kolongo, a little suburb on the river outside Bangui.

The original house was a weekend chalet in French colonial style, with high ceilings, a raised porch, and shutters. But behind it, in the huge jungled park, Bokassa wrought tacky splendor. A one-story mansion, looted and half demolished, rambles aimlessly in long corridors of cramped guest rooms and stingy bathrooms. The splintered wooden frame of Bokassa's massive revolving bed dominates a small bedroom. His secret bedroom, the one his wife didn't know about, is across the courtyard with a hidden entrance for girlfriends. The looters did not deface a portrait of the emperor, in a Napoleonic tunic, set into the wall over a side entryway.

In a center courtyard, Bokassa built a pavilion for private audiences, an island in the pool reached by a causeway in the manner of Akbar the Great at Fatipur Sikri, but somewhat less grand. There he received state guests, such as Giscard d'Estaing. And a few steps away is a large room which now bears an inscription scrawled in chalk on the wall: "Torture chamber and cold room where Bokassa kept human bodies."

Police found Bokassa's walk-in cold locker a few days after the power was cut. Goldsmith, there at the time, said the room reeked of the unmistakable smell of human flesh. A coroner identified the remains of a local professor who had disappeared, according to later testimony. He also found human joints trussed in string like standing rib roasts. At an official hearing, one of Bokassa's cooks swore he knew nothing about the freezer's contents or about any unusual bent to his former boss' dietary habits. A second cook, however, said he had prepared human flesh for Bokassa and, occasionally, for unwitting guests, including two high-level French visitors.

Bokassa added two other touches of his own: the crocodile pond and the lion cages.

An aging guard named Paul showed me around the place, recounting its lore without embroidery in the time-worn patter of a sexton pointing out old gravestones in a churchyard.

Here, Paul said, indicating a gazebo in a clearing, was where Bokassa held his trials until three or four in the morning. Alleged offenses were varied. In one case, three guards were suspected of sleeping with Bokassa's neglected Romanian wife. The guilty were fed to the lions or the crocodiles, depending on Bokassa's mood. One victim was the lionkeeper, accused of taking home to his family some meat meant for his charges. Bokassa, as befitted justice, threw him into the lion cage. He remained unharmed in the cage for twenty-four hours because the lions knew him. So Bokassa tossed him to the crocodiles, who didn't.

Paul yanked on a rusty lever to show how the cages worked. The lions were left unfed and cramped for days in an inner cage before anyone was offered to them. The handcuffed victim was placed in the outer cage, and the latch was pulled.

Bokassa vehemently denies the testimony of his former retainers. But not convincingly. French engineers drained the crocodile pond after Bokassa left the country. They found most of eight human skeletons, their bones marked deeply by crocodile teeth.

The ex-emperor was sentenced to death *in absentia* on Christmas Eve, 1980, on a series of charges including murder, embezzlement, and diamond fraud. Mainly, it was the massacre of children. Bokassa was outraged at the verdict. After all, he told interviewers, he loved children. Hadn't UNESCO's Director-General Amadou Mahtar M'Bow asked him to sponsor the Year of the Child in 1979?

Another charge was cannibalism, although the evidence was not ironclad. French officials who sought to disprove the accusations before Bokassa's downfall suddenly found it in their interest to reverse themselves, to justify the coup d'état. In a front-page comment, *Le Monde* editor Jacques Fauvet asked some pertinent questions.

Why did Giscard d'Estaing persist so long in intimate relations with a tyrant he denounced as "cruel and contemptible" immediately after deposing him? How did Bokassa serve France's African policy? And, as for the diamonds, what was gained by disguising or silencing the truth?

Giscard d'Estaing was voted out of office the next year, but not necessarily because of Bokassa.

For the French, Bokassa was one of the surprises of the system; they had tried to make the best of him. Officers who had known him were not impressed; one reported he was too dumb to do anything but carry the flag. His father had been caned to death by colonial administrators and, despite his twenty-three years in the French army, no one was sure about him. In the mid-1960s, French agents planned a coup against Dacko, who had grown too close to the Russians. As Dacko floundered in power, Bokassa moved in and eliminated the gendarme commander the French had tapped for the job.

After Bokassa, the French took no chances. The Colonel Mansion whom Bokassa mentioned was installed as aide to President André Kolingba, with ill-defined but overwhelming powers. In one case, a private French air charter company had negotiated a contract, and Mansion walked in as a cabinet minister was about to sign it. "Don't sign," the colonel said, according to a French source I trust. The minister looked helplessly at a cabinet colleague, who just shrugged. The minister laid down his pen.

"The Central African Republic is important to us, and that's why we keep a strong man there," a senior French official explained in 1984 to a new man in the Quai d'Orsay.

"You mean Kolingba?"

"No, of course not. Mansion."

OFTEN THE FRENCH system works well, as it was designed. As I drove out to see Bokassa, I noticed red, yellow, and green Senegalese flags lining the Champs-Elysées. President Abdou Diouf was in town. On a continent of catastrophes Diouf, like Senegal, is a symbol of French triumph. Calm and effective, thoughtful and humane, Diouf took over from Léopold Sédar Senghor. He was elected in voting that left little to chance, but you can't have everything in Africa. Senegal is a stable cornerstone of the continent, the first French foothold in Africa, and an intellectual base of *francophonie*. It is still emphatically oriented toward Paris. But it is no economic power. Diouf told Mitterrand he did not have the cash to pay government salaries until the end of the year. There was a little gentlemanly haggling, but he flew home with a check in his pocket.

At independence, a senior French civil servant named Jean Colin took up Senegalese citizenship and a place in the cabinet. For a quarter-century a loyal Senegalese official, he has drafted economic plans and government strategy. His relations with France are also excellent.

In places, the system works but French planners wring their hands in the background. The Ivory Coast is France's showcase in Africa, and the "Ivorian Miracle" is one of those standard phrases of modern Africa. Houphouët-Boigny, loyal to France since the first glimmers of self-rule, came back at each election with majorities approaching 99 percent, but perfect democracy was not the goal. Guided by French advisers, aided by French investment, he produced rich returns from coffee, cocoa, and palm oil in a climate of calm and stability. But in early 1986, the perennial president was deep into his eighties and showed no sign of passing on power. Anything could happen in the vacuum, French analysts knew, especially with a stagnant economy and crippling social problems.

Captain Sankara took power in Upper Volta and changed its name to Burkina Faso. He heaped scorn on the French legacy and struck up a friendship with Libya. But in early 1986, he made his ritual visit to Mitterrand.

And sometimes things go totally awry, but French flexibility finds a way to profit, anyway. In Zaire, for example. When Zaire (then the Congo) took independence from Belgium in 1960, everyone was ready for the spoils. The Russians backed Patrice Lumumba. The Americans were behind Joseph-Désiré Mobutu.[1] And the French gambled on Moise Tshombe. Almost immediately, Mobutu, among others, buried Lumumba. Mobutu was not yet in power, but Moscow was out of the game. Not, however, Paris.

Tshombe had seceded in Katanga (now Shaba), and his Belgian military advisor suggested he raise a mercenary army. So Tshombe hired Colonel Roger Trinquier, veteran of Indochina and Algeria, kindly made available to Tshombe by de Gaulle. With Trinquier came Major Roger Faulques, master interrogator of the 1st REP during the Battle of Algiers, and a score of French mercenaries who edged aside the Belgians. But Trinquier got mixed up in the Lumumba murder. France backed away from the international scandal; Trinquier resigned from the French army and retired with a payoff from Tshombe. Faulques, Denard, and others stayed, however, to fight a pitched battle with United Nations forces. Eventually beaten, Faulques moved on. Denard stayed around to dabble in Congo politics over the next seven years.

By 1964, the Congo was ablaze with rebel warfare. Mobutu, helped by the CIA, seized power and imposed peace. Tshombe, beaten in Katanga, prepared a comeback from Europe. SDECE and his mercenary pals stuck with him. But Tshombe was lured onto an airplane by a French bodyguard named François Bodenan, believed to be working for the CIA; he was hijacked to Algeria, where he died in captivity.

This is where I came in. My first job as a correspondent was to wait in Kinshasa for the Algerians to deliver Tshombe to Mobutu, as promised. Of course, they never did. The Americans, meanwhile, quietly helped Mobutu quell yet another uprising. He had liked the idea of mercenaries and brought in his own under Michael Hoare. "Mad Mike" (he is not so mad any more; I visited him again on a trip to South Africa in 1985) had no great love for French mercenaries. Hoare relied more on Britons, Belgians, Germans, and whites from southern Africa. He put down the rebels and left. Not long afterward, Mobutu's mercenaries rose against him.

Denard and a Belgian planter-mercenary named Jean "Black Jack" Schramme feared that Mobutu was about to disband his white mercenary army. They revolted in July 1967, in the eastern Congo. Denard neglected to warn thirty men under his command in Kinshasa; all were arrested and slaughtered. Only one, an Algerian, was able to talk his way out because he was not European. Denard was wounded and flown out to Rhodesia. Schramme captured Bukavu. In 1968, as Mobutu's troops pounded Bukavu in a final assault, Denard tried to rescue Schramme with a pincer movement from Angola. His men came on bicycles.

It was yet another Denard Bay of Piglets. After an initial success, the thinly armed mercenary column lost time arguing over objectives and making needless feints. Denard had expected Mobutu's troops to run, as usual. When the Congolese fought back, Denard's men fled, leaving some dead and captured behind.

Authorities were so anxious to gloat over Denard's defeat that they flew every foreign reporter in town to Katanga to have a look at the bodies. (Each correspondent was handed a thick envelope of cash to cover expenses; I'll never forget the look on the Information Ministry official's face when I handed mine back to him.) While the press corps was conveniently bottled up in Katanga, meanwhile, the International Committee of the Red Cross evacuated the mercenaries from Bukavu across the river to Rwanda.

A side bit of glory for France: a Corsican photographer from the

Associated Press Paris bureau, Spartaco Bodini, infiltrated the mercenaries' prison compound by looking like one of them. When a Belgian officer asked him to be on the lookout for a "fucking photographer who we're going to take care of," he infiltrated his way back out again.

By then, Mobutu had every reason to detest France. But the French conducted themselves with flair and conviction. Champagne glasses clinked undiminished at the ambassador's splendid residence overlooking the Congo River. And Paris got the message.

The next time Katangans attacked from Angola, Denard was gone and France was on Mobutu's side. In 1977 and 1978, France dispatched troops to protect Kolwezi in Shaba (Katanga) Province. By 1984, Mobutu had placed regular French officers in command of an elite paratroop unit. A small rebellion broke out in the east, and French-led troops quashed it in three days.

Mobutu was a member in good standing of the club of former French colonies; French aid flowed in accordingly. In my two years in Zaire, I saw clear evidence of arbitrary killings, torture, and unjust imprisonment. A mildly critical local editor, a man I liked a great deal, was thrown into jail after I left, and he died from the abuse. Estimates of Mobutu's personal requisition of state funds run to more than $4 billion; they are likely accurate. He regularly creams off profits from the few enterprises that make money for Zaire.

None of that deterred Jacques Chirac from declaring in Kinshasa in 1985 to a conference of forty French-speaking mayors from twenty-six countries:

[President Mobutu] is a respectable and profoundly Francophile man who is ulcerated by attacks of certain media. France has every interest in good relations with Zaire, and I don't understand the morbid taste of some to criticize our friends. The Mobutu myth has been exaggerated by certain media and it is particularly unjust. Zaire was an anarchic country which called for a particular charisma.

Seven months earlier, Mobutu sent the French into a mild panic. Mitterrand visited Zaire just before the French-African summit, and

Mobutu said he was too busy to go. In fact, he was angry that Mitterrand's wife had not come along. She was critical of Mobutu's human rights record, and he took her absence as a political gesture. Hasty negotiations increased French aid to Zaire, and Mobutu's agenda suddenly cleared.

DIPLOMACY IS the preferred French approach. *In extremis,* however, there is still the Foreign Legion. I knew about the Legion, like everyone else, from dim memories of *Beau Geste* remakes and a lot of dubious legend. It came to life for me in a cruddy little bar in Djibouti. (Honest.) It was steaming hot, and I ordered a Coke. Suddenly, a twenty-six-pound ham dropped out of the air and landed on my wrist. *"Unngh,"* came a noise like an ore truck climbing up a hill, "one does not drink Coca-Cola here." OK, I said, watching my fingers turn white from the grip on my wrist, I'll have what you're having.

He was actually a nice guy, I discovered, once I stopped trembling. He looked like a Mount Rushmore carving, but harder. He was short on hair and I.Q., but he must have been four feet across the shoulders. He had no neck; ropy muscles sloped outward from his ears.

"What do you think of those goddamned Commies about to take over in Paris?" he asked, offering me a broad hint about what I should think. It was 1981, just before presidential elections between Giscard d'Estaing and Mitterrand. "We are on red alert," he said. "Don't tell anyone. But if that Commie wins, *paf!* We're headed for Paris." I promised not to tell anyone.

A little later, I met two more legionnaires, or rather ex-legionnaires. They were Britons who had just deserted from Djibouti and had walked three days across the Somali desert. Both were medium-sized and intelligent, but each had burned and chiseled hardwood features. "Fuckin' hell, it was," said one. They described days that started before dawn and ended late at night, jogging with heavy loads of rocks, murderous discipline, crippling marches.

I decided to learn something about the Legion.

Louis-Philippe first commissioned *une Légion d'étrangers* in 1831 to do battle outside the kingdom. In Algeria, for example. An early general defined their mission: "You, legionnaires, are soldiers to die.

And I will send you to where death is." An endless list of names engraved at the Legion's memorial near Marseilles attests that his promise was kept.

Volunteers had to be between eighteen and forty years of age, foreigners, and holders of a good conduct certificate. These days, those conditions rarely apply.

The Foreign Legion numbers 8,500 men, of 105 nationalities; about half are French. Their peak strength was 50,000, during World War II, and they lost 10,483 men in Indochina. After 1962, Algeria took over their proud camp at Sidi-bel-Abbès. Now they are based in a drab little enclave in the industrial sector of Aubagne, near Marseilles, where legionnaires print Christmas cards and run addressograph machines. In Guiana, they build bridges and tear up local bars. In the South Seas, they guard nuclear test sites. In Mayotte and Djibouti and Bouar, they wait.

Sometimes the order comes. The 2me REP (the Second Foreign Paratroop Regiment) scrambled onto planes at their base in Corsica to beat back rebels for Mobutu. More often, they do push-ups and take showers.

"It is crazy, crazy," said a young German on the beach in Corsica, not yet through with his first year. "After two years in this outfit, you are out of your fucking mind. Nothing to do. It's not so bad in summer; you can look for girls. Otherwise, train, jump, work. It is fucked."

Like a lot of legionnaires, he had had a little police trouble at home. What? "Oh, I was in jail." Why? He smiled slowly and, as an answer, smacked his right fist into his left palm. Legion policy is not clear-cut on this score. Blood crimes are frowned upon, and an intelligence section tries to weed out the murderers and rapists. "But a few minor scrapes that prove a candidate is a man," an official spokesman, a colonel, told me, "well, what the hell . . ."

Calvi, Corsica, is thick with legionnaires. You can spot them in swimming suits: muscles hard and dark as jerked beef, ramrod posture, and chests shaped for displaying medals. In uniform, they stand out like flashing neon lights from lesser beings. You can slice cheese on the two creases down the backs of their shirts. Their white kepis, by decree and tradition, are spotless.

A woman I know fell in love with a legionnaire, a Frenchman, on one vacation in Calvi. She flew back later to see him but decided the relationship had no future. He liked to slug her and then lock himself in a room and play Nazi marches. Others, I have been told by women with experience, are real gentlemen.

Each year the Legion takes up to 1,800 new recruits, and 7,000 men apply, the colonel told me. They are asked their purpose for volunteering and given intelligence tests and a rigorous medical examination. Are they checked for AIDS? I asked. The colonel shot me a nasty look and replied that they were.

The deal is simple. They sign up for five years and put up with whatever the noncoms and officers decide to dish out. After that, they can reenlist; maybe 40 percent do. Pay is the same as in the regular army, but boot camp is twice as long, and discipline is a hell of a lot worse. In exchange, the Legion takes them under a new name and France smiles benevolently on their application for citizenship when it is all over. Legionnaires can rise to sergeant, but most of the officers are French army.

"Of course, the officers are French," replied a sergeant assigned to brief me on a visit to Aubagne. "That proves the men are fighting for a flag, not for money." Legionnaires sometimes call themselves mercenaries; that is not recommended, however, for a visitor who enjoys breathing.

Probably no organization reveres its relics like the Legion. There is, above all, Captain Danjou's hand. When Napoléon III seized Mexico, he forgot to send the Foreign Legion. Officers protested, and a contingent was sent west. A unit under Danjou, protecting a French convoy, was ambushed at Camarón, near Veracruz. For hours, sixty-five legionnaires held off 2,000 Mexicans. The last five legionnaires ran out of bullets; they charged with bayonets. Every year on April 30, the Legion eats *boudin* (blood sausage) and gets blind drunk to celebrate the victory. To exhibit blind bravery, in the Legion, is to *faire le Camerone.*

Danjou, who ordered the stiff resistance, had a wooden hand. His body disappeared in the battle. But some time later, someone retrieved the dark wood hand from the Mexicans. It is at the legion museum at Aubagne, right there with the tattered flags and dented medals. On Camerone Day, it is marched along at the Legion's ceremonial cadence of eighty-eight steps per minute.

———

THE LEGION IS the most colorful of French units in Africa, but it is not alone. At any one time, up to 9,000 men rotate among bases from Dakar to Libreville to Djibouti and points in between. And the Force d'Action Rapide sits in southern France. The navy plies African waters regularly, its ports of call serving as a barometer of French relations. In 1985, the *Jeanne d'Arc* called in Madagascar for the first time since the former colony moved away from France twelve years earlier. On the other hand, the vessel dropped New Zealand from its schedule.

Military accords keep African heads of state close to Paris. Few trust their own armies very far, and outsiders are risky. The Americans will seldom help a president in trouble. The Russians will, but then they tend to stay forever. France, however, is a handy neighborhood cop, asking nothing more than continued loyalty and privileged relations. That is why the abrupt end of *Opération Manta* in Chad was such a jolt to French-speaking Africa.

Chad has plagued France since Major Lamy was killed civilizing it. French troops spent three years in Chad getting independence going. Then they returned, off and on from 1968 to 1975, to suppress rebels and bandits in the north. For France, *le Tchad utile* (useful Chad) is the agricultural south along the Chari River up north to where the great desert starts. For Libya under Colonel Muammar Qaddafi, however, every sand dune and salt flat in Chad is useful.

Qaddafi, with ambitions and oil revenues too big for his under-populated Mediterranean state, seeks outlets wherever he can. Chad, his southern neighbor, is a logical backyard. Through Chad, Qaddafi increases contacts with French Africa and black Africa. Chad extends his border to the vast Sudan, where he sees Moslem brothers clamoring for his enlightened guidance, and to Nigeria, the giant of black Africa.

When French forces went back to Chad yet again in 1977 for a three-year campaign against rebels, Libya was deeply involved on the other side.

But France, in the meantime, cultivated privileged ties with Libya. True, Qaddafi is an exasperating megalomaniac who burned down the French embassy in 1980. True, he also invaded Chad in 1980 and attempted to absorb the fragile state into Libya before pulling back north. But he carries political and financial weight; he has a $13 billion arsenal and a country full of Eastern-bloc advisers; he controls oil; and he can provoke the Americans. The French prefer not to ignore people like that. Mitterrand, from 1981, sought a balance.

As "Colonel Spartacus" wrote in his controversial book, *Opération Manta,* "a suspicious boiling was heard in the Chad basket." In June 1982, Hissène Habré overthrew President Goukouni Oueddei in N'Djamena. Habré, a bitter enemy while a rebel, was an ally not only of France but also of the United States, Egypt, Sudan, and Zaire. The fortunes of politics. Goukouni moved north and linked up with Libya.

The Libyans had moved into the Aouzou strip, a disputed patch of desert between Libya and Chad that French and Italian colonizers never got straight. In mid-1983, Goukouni's forces, backed by Libya, rolled over the important town of Faya-Largeau, at the center of Chad, 480 miles north of the capital. France gave Habré arms and supplies (385 million francs' worth in 1983) but would not intervene. Goukouni moved south. Habré counterattacked; in July, against French advice, he recaptured Faya. Then Libya strafed and bombed government positions with Soviet-built MiGs. Mobutu had given Habré a few small fighters, but the distances were too great. He pleaded for French Jaguars.

Paris was pissed. If Habré had hung back, France might have negotiated something with Libya. Now there was a war on, and half the world screamed for the French to face their responsibilities. "The Americans," grumbled a senior French adviser to one of my colleagues, "want to defend Chad to the last Frenchman."

Mitterrand demurred. But French intelligence counted eight Libyan raids with MiGs—and with Mirages. France cut off arms sales to Libya in 1980, but not before delivering the last of thirty-two Mirage interceptors and Super Frelon helicopters. Qaddafi, meanwhile, denied any involvement and demanded that the United States withdraw its nonexistent forces. He warned that any "foreign intervention" in Chad would be an act of war against Libya.

Arms were not enough and troops would be too much, so France again called out the dogs of war. René du Lac, Bernard's old friend and colleague, was paid to recruit a small secret force—mainly

Frenchmen—to buck up Habré. They did not tip the balance but made an impact. In one skirmish they recovered ten machine guns from the Libyan-backed rebels; du Lac had sold them earlier to Qaddafi.

In Paris, mention was made of the Dey of Algiers' fly whisk. The French found themselves in yet another of those situations where the familiar terms "honor" and "responsibility" made collars itch. In postmortem debate, national assemblymen roasted the Socialists for not backing Habré with more vigor. Newly appointed Foreign Minister Roland Dumas reminded them of Major Pierre Galopin, "murdered in conditions you know by the one whose cause you today espouse." Galopin was executed in 1975 under the command of Habré while seeking to free two French hostages they held. Nonetheless, one deputy told Dumas, "It is shameful to be governed by such men [as you]. You are dishonored." Before the debate, human rights workers had shown that Habré was responsible for massacres of civilians in the south.

Meanwhile, back in Chad, France decided at the last minute against a plan to bomb Libyan aircraft in the poorly mapped Aouzou strip; what if they inadvertently hit Libyan territory? Goukouni's forces pushed east, backed by Libyan T54 and T55 tanks. Defense Minister Charles Hernu suggested that France ask the Americans to protect its Jaguars with F-15s from Sudan. No Americans, Mitterrand said.

There had already been several flaps with Washington. The Americans offered AWACS and waited for a French response. Senior U.S. and French diplomats told me later what had happened. The Americans needed an urgent reply so they could install a ground support force. It was late in Washington and after midnight in Paris. Finally, a top French aide told the Americans to go ahead; Mitterrand had approved. The next morning, Mitterrand was furious. He had not approved, and the operation was called off.

From the beginning, according to well-placed French sources, the Americans had pushed arming Habré as a means of striking hard at Qaddafi. The French argued that only Goukouni could persuade the Libyans to leave; if Habré hit too hard, Goukouni would be forced to rely even more heavily on Qaddafi.

Habré, embittered by the delay and battered by Goukouni,

snarled at the French. On August 9, he was told about *Opération Manta.* France was sending in *les paras.* Habré wanted planes, not troops, but he was in no position to argue. The next day, Faya fell again.

Opération Manta halted Libyan advances, but the price was staggering. The money was one thing; for a long time, it was estimated to cost up to $400,000 a day. But it also inspired fury among the officer corps and pointed out some severe weaknesses of the French military.

Despite their world-ringing field of action, French forces depend on an aging fleet of small Transall C-160s. Committed to buying French, they shun the workhorse U.S. C-130 Hercules used by NATO partners. For their dramatic assault on Kolwezi in 1978, the 2me REP was flown down in U.S. Air Force transports.

Forced to carry fuel, a Transall could carry only ten tons on the 3,000-mile trip from France to N'Djamena. Then Algeria forbade overflights; transports had to stop at Casablanca, Dakar, and Abidjan to refuel. The air force had bought some secondhand DC-8s from UTA, but passenger door configurations limited their use.

Communications were another problem. International telephone lines went through Libya and Algeria. All messages went by a rattling old teletype to Bangui for relay into the French military network. Flash messages could take more than ten minutes; routine traffic took days.

By August 23, the French had 1,525 men in Chad prepared to head north, to be followed by huge shipments of ammunition, videotapes for the officers' mess, and bottled Evian water. The number grew to 3,000 men and stayed near that level.

The adventure was not popular. In a poll by *Paris-Match,* 52 percent of the sampling thought France had special responsibilities in its old colonies; 32 percent did not. But 63 percent said that that did not justify risking French soldiers. Half opposed the war, and as many feared it could turn into a new Algeria or Indochina. And 46 percent, against 39 percent, felt France did not have the means to fight it.

As the war dragged on, N'Djamena was its old self. Alan Cowell of the *New York Times* went to dinner at a new restaurant on avenue Charles de Gaulle, and the waiter apologized, "I am sorry, sir, the

Beaujolais is finished, but there is Côtes du Rhône." There was also ice cream flown from Paris at $9 a quart, Charolais beef, and Pont l'Evêque cheese. In the crumpled, bullet-pocked ruins of their capital, some Chadians missed the people who had put in the electricity and telephones two decades before. One accountant told Cowell, "We were civilized by the French."

After fifteen months of a standoff, Mitterrand decided to declare a victory and leave. But he had some trouble pulling it off.

On November 11, French foreign minister Claude Cheysson sent this pleasant little telegram to his Libyan counterpart, Ali Triki, at the Organization of African Unity summit meeting:

> My dear Ali, your message of November 10 just reached me. It is that of a friend, and I am very touched. I, too, like the direct relationship between us. It has been effective; you recognize it, and it is clear. It is also pleasant. How many times and from how many cities of four continents have I heard your voice on the telephone: *"Alors, Claude, ça va?"* . . .
>
> We will have more frequent and imperious reasons to communicate in this way, but I hope that our ties will remain close. Because what you wanted—in a way that is too flattering to me —to take from our efforts, our policy, requires numerous exchanges of views between us; perhaps even joint actions. . . . Have I been indiscreet in writing you this way, in Addis? I did not want to wait for your return . . . to thank you for your message.[2]

That day, France and Libya announced a joint withdrawal from Chad. A statement said, "The evacuation operations of French forces in Chad and the Libyan units ended today, following the intervention of mixed teams of observers as foreseen under the agreement signed between the two continents."

"The purpose of the operation [Manta] was to make the foreigner leave," Cheysson said in a television interview. "He has left. Chad is once again in the hands of the Chadians." And he added one of those formulations that make other diplomats sit at French feet to learn wisdom: "If they stay, we will stay; if they go, we will go; if they come back, we will return."

At that point, Mitterrand flew to Cyprus to meet Qaddafi, against the advice of practically everyone. Mitterrand argues that it is best to reason with adversaries face to face. The French president, perspiring in a suit and tie, sought to persuade Qaddafi to move his troops out quickly. He threatened and pleaded. Qaddafi was relaxed, in his habitual mocking manner.

Three days later, the Americans muscled into the picture. A senior U.S. official briefed reporters on satellite intelligence: "We share our information with the French, and we both know that most of the Libyan troops with their equipment are still in Chad."

A Foreign Ministry spokesman said the government stuck by its statement and had nothing to add. Then Cheysson and, finally, Mitterrand had to admit that, yes, the Libyans were still there, but . . . A commentator on the state-owned TFI television newscast summed it up nicely. Of course the French knew the Libyans were still there, but that was supposed to be a secret; the Americans had no business embarrassing their allies that way.

Mitterrand had to suffer a gleeful round of editorials in European, American, and some French papers under headlines heavy with the word "humiliation." The problem was most serious in Africa, however.

When the 1983 French-African summit ended at Vittel, Mitterrand asked what other country could summon so many African nations to such a meeting. The strength of the community was that so many heads of state turned up. In 1984, attendance was lousy. Seyne Kountche of Niger went to Washington to see Reagan. Houphouët-Boigny did not feel like traveling. Other leaders had pressing business elsewhere. The message was clear: France had been made to look ridiculous, and Mitterrand had failed to protect the family.

Winding up the summit, however, Mitterrand was clear. France had respected its engagements. It would not be an all-purpose gendarme, fighting everyone's battle to the hilt. Mitterrand gambled that time would be on France's side. Qaddafi's oil revenues dropped from $22 billion to $9 billion in a year, diminishing his taste for foreign adventure. Goukouni lost power among the rebels; Habré bought off some of his own enemies. Africans grumbled some more and then dropped the subject. After all, what choice had they?

In 1985, in Paris, attendance improved. Sankara skipped the meeting, but he sent word through his embassy that he held "a great deal of friendship" for Mitterrand.

The Libyans, meanwhile, were still there. Mitterrand had vowed not to accept a de facto partition of Chad, but that was what developed. Qaddafi proposed a novel idea: a buffer force should occupy the disputed zone where France and Libyan troops once faced off. A buffer of Libyans, that is. War, he warned, was not a good idea. If France tangled with Libya in Chad, Libya would stir up trouble in New Caledonia and Guadeloupe and elsewhere overseas.

Early in 1986, Chad flared up again, just in time for elections. Goukouni pressed Hissène Habré's forces, attacking below the "red line" drawn at the 16th parallel. The French estimated rebel strength at 4,000, along with 4,500 Libyans, against 5,000 government troops. Qaddafi was calling Mitterrand's bluff.

On February 16, 11 French Jaguars peppered BAP-100 bombs on a concrete runway the Libyans had built at Ouadi Doum, in northern Chad, after the withdrawal accords. The dramatic gesture was costly; the French jets were refueled in midair and protected by Mirages. But the papers were full of praise. Mitterrand had saved French honor and reassured the Africans without another Manta. It was a blow that could not be returned. Some commentators recalled Margaret Thatcher's rewards from the Falklands War.

On February 17, a Libyan Tupolev 22 placed three bombs square onto the runway of N'Djamena airport and flew off unopposed. French Defense Minister Paul Quilès called it a "blind"—read, cowardly—attack from at least 10,000 feet, out of reach of French ground defenses. Reporters who saw it put the altitude closer to 300 feet.

Both runways were working again within days. The unending match game on again, tied, 1-1, in yet another quarter. France set up a logistics team of 500 men. Still plagued with transport limitations, the French swallowed pride and called on giant U.S. Air Force C-5 Galaxies. Qaddafi did not push the showdown, but France would have to stay on guard in Chad. Such are the burdens of power.

France managed to recoup some prestige in 1985 with a fresh attack against a favorite old target: South Africa. Violent repression and a state of emergency offered new grounds for condemning South Africa, and African governments appreciate outside attacks on Pretoria, toward which their own position is ambiguous. When I first arrived in Kinshasa in 1967, Mobutu excoriated white racism at a news conference, demanding a total boycott of South Africa. I glanced down to look at the refreshment he had offered: grape juice from the Cape. The Togolese joked about ships that made the world's fastest trip to Yokohama. They left Togo with phosphate for Japan and came back, days later, laden with South African goods. At the time of this writing, every country in black and Arab Africa is consuming South African goods, directly or via some ruse.

After South African police cracked down hard on black townships in 1985, Prime Minister Laurent Fabius led the European Economic Community to take measures against South Africa. However noble his intentions, the policy provoked a snort from the French in South Africa.

In Johannesburg, I met Jacques-Yves (this is not his real first name), a Frenchman working for the South African government. "It just means things will take a few days longer, and some middleman will make a little more money," he said. "If there is money to be made, no sanctions will work."

France embargoed arms sales in 1977. But in the four previous years, Paris sold $450 million of South Africa's total $622 million arms purchases, including 95 Mirage IIIs, 48 Mirage F-1s, 155 Aérospatiale helicopters, and at least four Daphne-class submarines.[3] South Africa still makes effective use of carefully preserved Mirages, kept aloft with black-market or homemade spare parts. They are so valuable the South Africans won't even fly them in bad weather.

Jacques-Yves was in Rhodesia when a white-minority government fought a bitter battle, theoretically isolated by outraged Western governments. "The Rhodesians were supposed to have only seven Alouette helicopters," he said, with a laugh. "I counted forty on one mission alone. The stuff would come in brand new, in crates, from Paris. De Gaulle just wanted to annoy the British. He sent huge amounts of supplies, munitions. You could see it stacked on the tarmac, in plain sight, imported through the oil people and others who had regular commercial dealings with Rhodesia."

That was when de Gaulle also helped Odumegwu Ojukwu maintain his secessionist state of Biafra against a heavy Nigerian on-slaught. Shadowy French pilots ran an air bridge between Rhodesia and Biafra via Libreville, Gabon. Weapons and supplies from Biafra also came down to the Ivory Coast. De Gaulle is reported to have said to Foccart, "These *braves gens,* we must do something for them." Coincidentally, he was helping to weaken a powerful English-speaking state in the center of French Africa. France did not recognize Biafra, but Gabon and the Ivory Coast did. French interests, meanwhile, had oil rights in part of the breakaway eastern region. Faulques turned up in Biafra to raise a mercenary army, but he did not last long. Ojukwu counted heavily on Rolf Steiner, a German former legionnaire who marched in Biafra under Legion colors with their motto dating back to Louis-Philippe: "Honor and Fidelity." In his memoirs, Steiner says that France supplied him until he refused to push its interests with Ojukwu.[4]

I was covering that story and, routinely, would trip over French blockade runners who regaled bar girls, colleagues, and occasional journalists with their exploits.

Ojukwu escaped by flying secretly to Libreville; then he settled into exile in Abidjan. (From where he made a great deal of money running taxis and trucks in Washington.)

When the war ended, Nigeria took its revenge on the French, but not for long. By the end of 1985, France was Nigeria's best customer and was just passing Britain as leading supplier. Nigeria was the number two oil supplier to France, and 130 French businesses were established there. Even during the war, SCOA and CFAO, French trading companies, thrived in Lagos. Peugeot sales in Nigeria helped the French automaker survive a tough period in France. In Kenya, another former British showcase, the Peugeot dealer is President Daniel arap Moi. Business is business.

Mitterrand's first African guest of 1986 made the usual speech: "We have a future without limits." Roland Dumas remarked, "When times are difficult, you know who your friends are." The visitor was Foreign Minister Bolaji Akinyemi of Nigeria.

Soon after the March 1986 elections, policy began to shift. Jacques Chirac, as prime minister, sent the French ambassador back to South Africa. He named as cooperation minister Michel Aurillac, a conservative who had kept close tabs with Maurice Robert, Foccart and former SDECE people. Bongo was in deep financial trouble because of plummeting oil revenues, but Aurillac assured him France was there.

Mitterrand continued his interest in Africa, but socialist ideology was in short supply. France, in any case, had been old-line Gaullist in Africa since Jean-Pierre Cot made a vain attempt to break the old patterns as cooperation minister during the early 1980s. "We tried to be even-handed and deal directly with human development," a close Cot aide told me at the time, "but we just could not do it."

WHEN JACQUES Foccart left the Elysée in 1974, seven pickup trucks carried off his secret files to three carefully prepared hiding places, according to Patrice Chairoff, who devoted a 42-page chapter to him in *B . . . Commes Barbouzes.* His only official function was director of a lobby group called the French Banana Committee. "Foccart awaits his moment," Chairoff wrote. He quoted a close aide of Foccart's:

> Giscard's victory is only a respite and the victory of the Union of the left [under Mitterrand] is inevitable. Backs to the wall, the government will face a situation [where] neither the police nor the army are sure, and they will have to repress, toughly and crisply, selectively but massively, and then, they will all come to eat out of our hands because only we can do that work, a job that once done will not keep us from sleeping.

After the March 1986 elections, Chirac made his first African trip as prime minister to the Ivory Coast. He emerged, grinning broadly, to embrace Houphouët-Boigny. Behind him was his new adviser on African affairs, grinning just as broadly. It was Foccart, seventy-three and full of spirit.

CHAPTER FOURTEEN

North Africa: Beurs *and* Beaufs

THE FORT IN *Beau Geste,* P. C. Wren's 1924 novelized paean to the French Foreign Legion, might be the 300-year-old Turkish outpost at Bou Saada. The Legion lived there, with their camels and kepis, on the edge of the Algerian Sahara. One night legionnaires painted three-foot-high white letters on an outside wall: *"Ici c'est la France à tout jamais."* This is France. Forever. In 1962, when the French slunk away from Bou Saada and the rest of Algeria, the letters were left in place as a symbol of victory. By now, wind and sand have rendered the words almost unreadable, and time has worn down the irony.

A quarter-century of love-hate relations between France and Algeria suggests that the legionnaires were somehow right, after all. France marked Algeria indelibly, but Algeria has made its mark on France. When the flag came down, a million European French—that is, whites—lived in Algeria. Now a million Algerians live in France.

Islam is the second religion of France; the 2,400,000 faithful include 800,000 Moslems of French nationality.

The accords that created *Algérie Algérienne* foresaw a symbiosis that each side needed. Despite the bitterness, Algeria wanted economic and technical help. And France wanted the *dialogue privilégié* it seeks in every region shaped by French civilization. Beyond that, the political geography that once made them so close suggested that they could each be dangerous enemies.

At first, there was free movement between the two countries.

Moslems who decided to try their luck in France were welcomed. Diehard *pieds-noirs* could take their time coming home. Moroccans and Tunisians had been granted easy access to France, and large numbers moved north with few problems.

In 1968, France and Algeria negotiated an accord: Algerians could work in France, but they needed papers. Still no problems. During the 1970s, France boomed; its crops needed picking; its assembly lines needed unskilled labor; its streets needed sweeping. Recruiting teams rounded up Algerians by the thousands. When the going was good, 700,000 workers, together with 300,000 family members, moved into France.

It was the European pattern. West Germany had its Turks; Belgium and Switzerland imported foreigners by the trainload. And France, after all, was the *terre d'asile,* land of asylum. France had 181,354 refugees in 1986, more than any country in Europe.

Immigrant workers were not exactly the same as political refugees, but the rhetoric was the same. France, the universal nation, was generous. I had seen it myself, from Latin America. Virtually every leftist revolution in South America—and a great deal of right-wing plotting—was rooted to some degree in Paris. Open French borders saved thousands of Latin American lives and nourished intellectuals crushed by censors. For centuries, France had sheltered refugees from European courts.

In 1985, the French government organized a festival of the "liberties and rights of man." Bishop Desmond Tutu, recently awarded the Nobel Peace Prize, flew up from South Africa. Lech Walesa, an earlier Nobel laureate, couldn't leave Poland. But he sent a message: "France is the natural place for such a debate."

The 1980s, however, had brought recession. Up to then, the self-enriching value of sheltering the homeless outweighed the impact on the economy or the society. And with any luck, internal strife in their home countries ended before refugees attracted the attention of neighborhood vigilantes and ended up as a sore point in *Le Figaro.* But by 1985, there were 2,400,000 French out of work, and few people missed a simple calculation: the immigrant work force totaled about 2,400,000.

Suddenly, few issues generated more heat than *les immigrés.* The Poles and Portuguese were not really at issue; *les immigrés* was mainly code for North Africans. And North Africans, numerous Moroccans and Tunisians notwithstanding, meant Algerians.

Racism is an unpopular word in France, but racists abound. No one knows how many blacks, browns, or yellows are in the civil service; personnel records don't record race. But people notice. Tennis star Yannick Noah, with an African father and a French mother, was "the Cameroonian" until he started winning big; then he was French. In a *Paris-Match* poll in late 1985, 71 percent of respondents thought the French were racist toward immigrants. A smaller percentage would call themselves racists.

There is, therefore, a subtle lexicon for making one's point. Used properly, it allows one to welcome outsiders who fortify France's reputation as a land of *liberté, égalité, fraternité,* but not those who carry a cost.

After a brief course in conversational racism, I went to Marseilles. It is France's second city, with a million inhabitants and the busiest harbor in the country. An old Phoenician trading port, Marseilles was already in need of urban renewal when the Romans appeared. How French can you get? Pastis, a stroll down the Canebière, the French Connection, *la Marseillaise.*

A French colleague had just come back. "It is incredible," he said unhappily. "You walk around downtown at night and all you see are Arabs and blacks and things like that."

At the old port, I worked my way through a bouillabaisse of five kinds of fish and lobster and then approached the owner. He had thirty years in the business, and he looked as if he had spent every day of all of them leaning on his zinc bar, drinking Ricard to his customers' health.

I began, "Marseilles has changed, hasn't it?"

That might have meant, of course, that the city had modernized; or that the Germans had leveled much of the old town; or that there were a lot of American tourists, like me. In code, however, that meant: "There are too damned many Algerians, right?"

He shook his head in profound grief. "Six million immigrants, *c'est trop.* France can't take that many. Two million, okay. But six million? It is ruining us. They are taking the jobs. They cost money, Social Security."

Numbers are a key to conversational racism. He was a sixmillioner, a hard case. Jean-Marie Le Pen, of the archly conservative National Front, uses that figure. You get it by adding up all the immigrants, all North Africans with French nationality, all dark-skinned people from the overseas departments and territories, and everyone just back from holiday having spent too much time on the beach.

Official government figures for 1985, based on residence permits, totaled 4,450,000 immigrants, including 860,000 Portuguese, 780,000 Algerians, 520,000 Moroccans, 425,000 Italians and 135,000 black Africans. INSEE, the national research institute, prefers 3,600,000 since some people with residence visas have gone home. There are perhaps another 500,000 clandestine immigrants (or half that or double that, depending on your politics) equivalent to the Mexican "undocumented aliens" in the United States. Because of strict limits imposed, the figure grew by less than 1 percent over that of 1984. More Algerians left than arrived because the government helped 20,000 workers (45,000 people, counting families) to go home.

MANY ALGERIANS IN France cannot return; their property was confiscated and they were sentenced to exile for fighting to help keep Algeria French. Among them are sons of men who died for France.

Harkis sometimes find themselves in pathetic circumstances. Captain Paul Barril recounts, in *Missions Très Spéciales,* how his elite gendarmes took all night to dislodge Ahmed Bouhzan from his house in a village in eastern France. He refused to pay his electric bill and then barricaded himself inside. "He was a former *harki* who wanted to settle the score," Barril wrote. "He had a very fine service record, with the French army. He was all alone in this village, without friends, without a companion, and he fell back on himself, on the battles he had fought on his native soil. I think he decided to die in a last barrage of honor. He wanted, like the Legion, to *faire Camerone.*" Bouhzan held out against tear gas and hails of bullets. At dawn, a sharpshooter finally dropped him.

BY MOST CALCULATIONS, immigrants make up just over 7 percent of the national population, less than in West Germany, Belgium, or Switzerland. Three-quarters of all immigrants have lived in France for ten years or more. Those who make a point of looking, however, can scare themselves to death.

In places, Marseilles might be Algiers. I leaped aside to avoid a Mercedes with Algerian plates near the Porte d'Aix and almost landed in a sidewalk souk of embroidered robes and veils. Old men bent over Korans in doorways once trod by bourgeois merchants rich from the colonial trade. On Fridays, the mosque overflows onto the street.

The heart of Marseilles is the Canebière, a Mediterranean Champs-Elysées, lined with trees and the signatures of the usual gang of Frenchmen: Daniel Hechter, Ted Lapidus, Christian Dior. The avenue was decorated for Christmas, and I saw a sidewalk Santa. He was a slim, short North African, awash in the billowing folds of a red suit. A white cotton beard hung unconvincingly under his own black mustache. Later, I saw a newspaper article headlined, "They have stolen the Canebière from us."

In the Marseilles district of Belsunce, a street market turns over $1.5 billion dollars a year in radio and electronic gadgetry, clothes and textiles and other items; 80 percent of the customers are Algerian tourists. They arrive on an average of 35,000 a week at the airport, and each spends an average of 10,000 francs. Belsunce is the Maghreb's biggest market, with many items found nowhere in North Africa.

In the March 1986 elections, Le Pen's National Front took 25 percent of the vote in Bouches-du-Rhône, which includes Marseilles.

And it is not only Marseilles. Or Lyon, or Paris.

The northern city of Roubaix, near the Belgian border, is crippled by unemployment. Some residents call their city Algiers, or the Medina; 20 percent of the population has a foreign nationality, and half of those are North African. In the 1985 local elections, the National Front polled 20.86 percent. And the trend was not encouraging. The first baby born in 1986 was named Kaci Khouidni.

One Sunday, I drove up to the main *place* at Savigny-les-Beaune, in Burgundy, as deep into *la France profonde* as you can get without drowning in pinot noir. The first person I saw was an Algerian, cheerfully hawking rugs and sheepskins loaded over his shoulder.

Some French rejoice at the new texture added to their culture. Damned few, however.

At Radio Gazelle, a Marseilles FM station run by immigrants for immigrants in a half-dozen languages, I talked about racism with Boualem. He is French, by law and by right. His father bled for France in World War II but preferred to take Algerian citizenship when offered the choice. Boualem was born in France, and his nationality is French. In practice, he is a *Beur.* The *Beurs* are children of North Africans who migrated to France in the 1960s and 1970s, a generation that is neither Arab nor French. The word is a short form of *Arabe,* spelled backward and jumbled in *verlen,* a popular street argot.

Their nemesis is the *Beauf,* short for *beau-frère* (brother-in-law), from a comic book satire of a vulgar, narrow-minded, and bigoted type of Frenchman. Time, it seems, is widening the circle of people the *Beurs* call *Beaufs.*

"Look," said Boualem. "Last night I left the radio, and there was a French woman closing her shop. She took one look at me and slammed down the grille, grabbed her keys, and huddled in fear over her purse. These people think automatically we are thieves and criminals. That is racism."

Ah, but crime statistics show that a lot of Algerians do steal, it is argued. But that would not be necessary if they could get jobs on an equal basis with white French, it is answered. The polemics are less important than the perceptions. A large percentage of the French feel that foreigners—essentially North Africans—are deforming their culture. And an equally large number of North Africans feel that the average French person makes their lives miserable.

Boualem is hopeful. "Every generation has its racism, and we are the latest to come. Last time it was the Italians. Next it will probably be the yellow man, the Asians."

Curiously, I had just found a report on immigration by the French Ministry of Social Affairs and National Solidarity. It included a speech by the minister, Georgina Dufoix. She began by citing a telegram to Paris from the little Crusader port of Aigues-mortes, down the road from Marseilles:

> Effervescence somewhat calmed by presence of troops. . . . Six dead and twenty-six injured, including four or five mortally. Investigation continues. It will be very difficult.

That was the result of race riots on August 17, 1893, against Italians brought to work in the salt marshes at wages French laborers would not accept. Three years later, the newspaper *La Patrie* observed of Italian immigrants:

> They arrive like locusts from Piedmonte, Lombardy and Venice, Romagna, Naples, even Sicily. They are dirty, sad, ragged; entire tribes migrate north, where the fields are not devastated, resting strangers to the people who receive them, working at reduced rates, alternately playing with the accordion and the knife.

From time to time, excess foreigners were packed off. In 1935, one million were sent home—largely Italians—and 8,405 foreigners were jailed for not having papers.

Madame Dufoix's position, the government's and the mainline opposition's, is that immigrants must be welcomed as part of the society. "My objective," she told the National Assembly, "is that by this policy for all people we have in our charge, more truth will surround that ideal which makes France at once more French and more universal: Men are born and die free and equal in right."

Mitterrand was clear at a news conference in late 1985: "Immigrants who have been given papers, who bring their work here, are at home in France. . . . Any other sentiment is racial hatred."

But who had scrawled on the side of the train station, *"Trop de bicots, je vote Le Pen"?* Why did Le Pen's National Front win 11 percent of the vote for European Parliament elections in 1984, more than the Communist Party, which had scored at least 20 percent in other elections? Why did a 1985 poll show that 40 percent of France agreed with Le Pen's call for a referendum on immigration? That is code for wanting fresh laws against foreigners.

He could hardly be more clear on his position. Early in the European Parliament election campaign, he said, "Tomorrow, if you don't stay on guard, they will install themselves at your place, eat your soup, and sleep with your wife, your daughter . . . or your son." His slogan is "The French First." Historian René Rémond describes Le Pen's vision as a poor man's Vichy.

Despite the *terre d'asile* mythology, individual French have never been wildly tolerant of outsiders. Xenophobia remains, normally, at a quiet chill, lurking behind the code words and subtle actions. At such times, it can be approached with humor.

My friend Annie's mother is from the Vendée, a region of people so old-line French that they were all but wiped out for supporting the Bourbons. Her father, from Pondicherry, has been a French civil servant all his life. Annie thinks *Vendéenne* and looks like an Arab princess. One of her great joys is to nod toward a passing Algerian and remark to anyone of the bourgeoisie within earshot, *"Tsk, on n'est plus chez soi,"* one is no longer at home here. "They see my face and don't know what to think," she laughs.

When her parents were married, racial mixes were a curiosity; Asians, Arabs, and Africans were exotic to some and easily isolated nuisances to others. They were hardly numerous enough to ruin a neighborhood. Mixed families could integrate well as long as they ignored the injustice and humiliation that inevitably intrudes. Her mother caused a major ripple bringing home an Indian to the Vendée, where even the cows bear uniform markings. But he was cultured, without complexes, and thoroughly housebroken, a product of French schools and colonial governments in Pondicherry and Indochina. He found tight jaws, but he loosened them by being French down to the finest Rabelasian touches. "No one could believe this dark-faced man sitting at the head of a table in La Coupole singing 'Le Curé Pinot.' "

He had to give up his appointment as station manager for Air France in Niamey, the capital of Niger. Form demanded a lighter shade of pale. But there were other jobs.

The exoticism changed with decolonization and the independence of Algeria. It is one thing to heed the satirical call of Americans who fought the civil rights battles of the 1960s: take an Indian to lunch. After all, if a French Indian makes you lunch in return, you will never eat better. It is another when six million people of the darker persuasion muscle into your parks and cafés, praying to Allah while waiting to move into your job or your bedroom.

Le Figaro magazine, almost a parody of itself as a house organ for the far right, published a dossier entitled, "Will France still be French in 2015?" Its cover showed Marianne, the symbol of France (the current model is Catherine Deneuve), swathed in an Arabic veil

affixed by a rosette of blue, white, and red. According to its demo-
graphic projections, in thirty years there would be 46,200,000 "real"
French and 7,900,000 ENE, that is, non-European foreigners: 90
percent Islamic.

Madame Dufoix called the article "reminiscent of the wildest
Nazi theories." She said the calculations assumed that immigrant
women's fertility rates would remain constant at 4.69 per thousand
and that French women's would continue to drop. The facts, she
said, were that French birth rates were stable and immigrant rates
were dropping steadily.

The *Beaufs,* however, seized the study as proof that France was
in for a permanent crime wave and an ever louder wail of the
Moslem call to prayer.

Seen from the other side, of course, the view is different. *Beurs*
are even less happy than white French that so many immigrants take
drugs and knock old ladies on the head to steal their purses. Ethnic
background, however, does not impart shared responsibility. Their
dues are paid in full. Whoever else forgets, they remember the
35,000 Moslems in French World War II cemeteries. For 150 years,
French authorities have told them they were part of France. The law
says that when someone is born in France, his passport is blue
whatever color his face may be.

It does not always work that way. "I will call up about an
advertised job, and things will be going fine on the telephone until
I give my name," Boualem said. "Then the guy suddenly remembers
the job is already filled." We were still at Radio Gazelle. A young
man from Martinique had come in and sat down. I asked him if it
was the same with black French. "Hah, are you kidding?" he replied.
"Black is black. I usually get farther than the Arabs; my name is not
Mohammed, it is Jean-Marc. That means I have to show up so they
see my face before they remember the job is filled."

Jane Kramer, in *The New Yorker,* observed that white Parisians
have seized upon *le black feeling:* African food, music and clothing.
But *le black feeling,* she noted does not extend to the subject of real
estate.

In a widening mood of frustration, conflict can take nasty turns.
French police have some blacks in their ranks, but not many; there
are few Moslems. Their methods are not known for inspiring love

among immigrant communities. On September 3, 1985, *La Marseillaise* reported that a man was shot dead by police in the ghetto of La Paternelle. "One body, two versions," it said. Police had chased some armed youths robbing a hi-fi delivery truck. They caught up with one. The police said the man pumped shotgun fire at them, and he was killed in a gunfight. Witnesses said the man tossed away his gun and yelled, "I give up," before two officers shot him at point-blank range. "Like a dog," said one. The victim, and the witnesses, were *immigrés;* that is, ethnic North Africans who may or may not have been French citizens. The incident sparked two hours of rock-throwing and tear gas assaults. A visit by the regional perfect and the Algerian consul calmed feelings.

But the tension is electric.

Three weeks later, Kader Gasmi, twenty-seven, complained to the court about what is known in France as a *passage à tabac.* He said police stopped him on a routine identity check and took him to the station to check on his car registration. During questioning, he said, a policeman suddenly said, "Hey, we've got one from La Paternelle." He testified:

> He insulted me in front of ten officers . . . taking me as responsible for the events. . . . He and some of his colleagues jumped on me, hitting me so hard I fell against the cabinet. I was dead of fear . . . I thought my last hour had come. Then they put handcuffs on me and locked me up. I shouted for them to tell my family and get a doctor. I had several broken teeth, a broken nose, general contusions, and a broken arm. I don't know how long it was before they decided to do something. They wrote a report that I refused to sign because they wouldn't let me read it.

Gasmi insisted that he had no police record, had done nothing wrong, and was nowhere near the La Paternelle rioting. But his affidavit said:

> Kicking me, they put me into a car and took me [to another jail]. I think it was 3 A.M. I yelled for a doctor. To get one, I had to sign their deposition without reading it. I suffered enor-

mously and was dead of fright. A doctor finally came and demanded I go to a hospital. . . . An intern examined me and made X-rays. Then I was taken back to jail where they only gave me aspirins. Only the next morning, I was taken again to the police station where one of the more generous policemen advised my family and my lawyer.

His doctor admitted him to the hospital where his injuries were confirmed. His lawyer brought suit and, at last check, the matter was under investigation. Often such investigations come down to conflicting testimony with no result.

At Radio Gazelle, Boualem had a newspaper clipping that began, "Once again, it has been shown that police are not safe entering . . ." and it described how four officers were injured by young toughs as they arrested a drug dealer. Boualem, who lives nearby, has a different account. He said the suspect had fled to a neighbor's apartment, and police kicked down the door in pursuit. The neighbor was a woman with a pregnant daughter and a ten-year-old son. Police slugged the woman, who happened to be in their way, according to Boualem. The daughter rushed to intervene and she, too, was beaten. The son, watching his mother and sister brutalized, hit one of the policemen with a rock.

Police deny the witnesses' account, and local newspapers lean toward official reports. But the Arab telephone works in Marseilles and Paris even more efficiently than it did in Algiers. True or not, residents believe the witnesses' version.

It is similar in Paris. Most incidents go unreported, but *Libération* pursued the case of Micheline Koubi, who left a Paris nightclub at 5 A.M. near where a man had been stabbed. Police grabbed her. "They threw me in the van. A peace officer called me dirty Jew, dirty Arab, whore. And he slapped me viciously four times." At the hospital, doctors ordered her to bed for ten days because of her injuries. Her father came to get her, bringing along his military honors from the war. "Get out of here, or we'll throw you down the hole," police told him. That was in the eleventh *arrondissement*.

Mrs. Koubi tried to file a complaint but police would not record it. When a reporter intervened, an officer told her, "Be nice. Don't complain right away. We have to find the man in question. This is the first time this has happened." In fact, *Libération* noted, police from the same station had beaten up an African cab driver and wouldn't register his complaint. Madame Koubi is French, but her skin is dark.

Each incident is one more shovelful of coal under a boiling pot in which little melting is going on. At times, the pot boils over.

One Sunday morning in 1985, an unemployed twenty-two-year-old walked into a café in the Brittany village of Chateaubriand and pumped his shotgun at a group of Turkish workers. Two died on the spot. The killer, Frédéric Boulay, told police, "I don't like foreigners." And he added, "Non-European foreigners." He was sentenced to life imprisonment. But twenty-two of the 300 Turkish families in Chateaubriand left France. "They went to find a little more security and respect in the country under . . . the bloodiest dictatorship in Europe," *Libération* wrote.

Later on, at Le Puy, Charles Mandon ignored the little sign in his building asking tenants to be quiet after 10 P.M. At 9:45 P.M., he and his son walked downstairs and emptied rifles into a roomful of noisy Moroccans. Two were killed and five were wounded. Eyewitness accounts vary on the details. A small march protesting racism broke up in disarray, harassed by townsfolk yelling, "France for the French."

Elsewhere in France, a café owner refused to serve Algerian youths. One of them shot him to death, and police had to rescue the Algerians to prevent a lynching.

Three young Frenchmen, turned down by the Foreign Legion, beat up an Algerian and threw him off a moving train. In Lyon, three punks offered a young Algerian a whiskey. When he did not chug it down, they stripped, burned and cut him. "The Arab's head bounced off the wall like a punching ball," one witness put it.

Obviously enough, among four million people, many of them destitute, there is crime and violence. In back streets of Paris, Africans and Arabs deal openly in drugs, with a system of lookouts to warn against police raids or suspicious strangers.

And there is abuse of official hospitality. One youth from Niger was caught collecting support checks as a political refugee from six regional social security offices.

Beurs and others formed SOS Racism, a nationwide group to

promote goodwill among immigrants and the French. The group was launched with a march of 300,000 people into the Place de la Concorde for a rock-against-racism concert. Everyone turned out on stage: the Djurdjura Sisters, Fine Young Cannibal, Carte de Séjour, Indochina.

A godfather of SOS Racism is Bernard-Henri Lévy, a young intellectual superstar, who told a reporter:

> In 1981, I published *l'Idéologie Française,* a book that was bludgeoned by critics, buried under insults, in which I said the French were profoundly racist, that our national fascism is only asleep and Petainism only interrupted. I was called paranoid, a *provocateur.* Alas, my book seems today to have been terribly prophetic.

Lévy said he and his friends were alarmed by the "banalization" of racism. "We saw the possibility of creating the first great youth movement since May 1968." Marek Halter, a prominent critic of anti-Semitism, joined the movement, calling it the new revolution. "Music," he said, "has replaced the guillotine."

SOS Racism's spokesman, Harlem Désir, lives in Chinatown near the porte d'Italie. He is the French equivalent of a South African colored: his mother is from Alsace and his father from Martinique.

The group sold two million badges showing an open hand, palm facing outward, with the slogan, *"Touche pas à mon pote"* (don't touch my pal). The *Beurs* had a rallying symbol, and the *Beaufs* had a new code word: *pote.* At five francs each, the badges paid for rallies and publicity. But the fad wore off, leaving SOS Racism in debt. Politics split the movement, and activists argued over what was racism.

Role models are giving some identity to the *"Beur* generation." Mehdi Charef, who arrived in France at age ten, wrote a best-seller at age thirty-one called *Le Thé au Harem d'Archimède.* That translates to *Tea in Archimedes' Harem.* But it also plays on words, as in Archimedes' Theorem. Radio *Beur,* covering the Paris area, has 400,000 listeners. It launched a voter registration campaign aimed at an estimated 1.5 million French of North African extraction. A few *Beur* politicians have won municipal posts; some ran for the National Assembly in 1986 despite some gratuitous beatings in the street.

TF1, one of three state-owned networks, broadcast in 1985 a dramatic program entitled "We Are All Immigrants." It noted that most French had roots that were other than Gallic or Frankish. At one point, a young Algerian mother recounted how her eighteen-year-old son was murdered in a racist assault. A majority of callers, however, complained that they felt they were no longer in France.

The president of the FAS (Fund for Social Action for Immigrants) argued that the amount of money spent helping immigrants was greater than the national budget of Mali. He neglected to mention that the funds were contributed by immigrants themselves.

In a curious switch, *Actuel* magazine ran a poll in 1985 asking immigrants what they thought of the French. North Africans found the French to be straightforward but racist; one out of two did not want his daughter to marry one. One in three North Africans would not come back; four out of five did not want French nationality. The French, North Africans said, were self-centered and ungenerous. A thirty-five-year-old woman remarked, "When my French neighbor receives her mother, the mother brings her own steak. If I did that, my mother would bury me alive."

Among North Africans, 76 percent have French friends; only 60 percent of blacks and 54 percent of Asians do. Among all immigrant groups, 38 percent felt France had too many immigrants.

"The spirit of tolerance," my journalist friend Claude puts it, "lives mainly in the Frenchman's image of himself. It is *de la littérature.*"

In Marseilles, conflict is plain between the official wish to do the right thing and a heavy racist public opinion. Perhaps 12 percent of the city's one million inhabitants are immigrants. Marseilles shares with the national government the costs of a *Maison de l'étranger,* an active and cheerful center to help immigrants handle their paperwork and fit into the community. Algerian film festivals alternate with original theater productions. Paintings and drawings hang on the walls. But in the excellent little library and documentation section, cuttings from the Marseilles press reek of hostility.

When will we stop excusing ourselves? [asks an unsigned letter to *Le Méridional*]. Have we forgotten we are at home in France and we are citizens of an independent and sovereign nation? Have we forgotten we have the right to accept or refuse to shelter whomever we want on our national soil? Must we fight to prove that we refuse the Arabization and the Islamization of our country, cradle of Christianity? When will we admit that in times of crisis, priority must be to aid our nationals and firmly ask those that have nothing to do here with us to return to their country which has such need of the "richness" they carry—which must be cruelly lacking in their country of origin?

Our pride to be French, European, and Western is degraded every day in the name of anti-French racism carried by a mass of useless people who pass their time with invectives, parades, festivities, and in vacation camps. *Messieurs les potes,* who forget the dignity of the French people, at least accept the facts: France has rejected you. If you have a little dignity, shut up, one has seen and heard enough of you. Forget us and go join your roots. What enrichment for those roots and what happiness for France!

Another said, "I would be very grateful if you could tell me how I might find the badge, 'Don't Touch My Pal.' But written in Arabic so that the poor people who do not understand the subtleties of our language might realize that reciprocity is equally valid."

Le Pen's partisans, meanwhile, came up with their own variation: "Don't Touch My People."

Despite official assurances, there is concern in government circles. Edouard Bonnefous, chairman of the Senate finance committee, noted in *Le Monde* that two million foreign workers came to France since the boom of the 1960s. They performed a service to France and were paid for it. Now, he said, the state should help unemployed foreigners go home. Under legislation he sponsored, immigrants leave France voluntarily with an indemnity averaging 100,000 francs to cover the expenses of establishing themselves at home. Tough new measures were imposed to prevent them coming back illegally. The families of legal immigrants are often turned back at the border.

Racial tension grates on relations between France and Algeria, strained at the best of times. The 1968 agreement gave Algerians a privileged status. But the new French law of July 17, 1984, which many Algerians fought to see passed, left them in the cold. It took eighteen months to bring Algerians under the new provisions.

The legislation is clever. When it was first passed, 2.5 million foreigners—not Algerians—received ten-year residence permits. They can stay, whether or not they have work. Newcomers are given temporary visas; if they lose their jobs, they are out. Algerians' permits were linked to employment. If they lost their livelihood, they fell into limbo. If they left France for six months, they started from zero. After Algerians were brought under the law, new permits for any foreigner were very hard to get.

Algerian authorities argue that immigration is a natural right because of French colonial policy. They would just as soon have their unemployed on French rolls rather than their own. Wage remittances are a welcome source of foreign exchange.

As the 1986 National Assembly elections approached, politicians spoke with conversational racism dictionaries at their elbows. Raymond Barre, like Mitterrand, was crystal clear in defending immigrants. Some others skirted the edges; everyone shunned Le Pen, but the anti-immigrant vote he attracted was tempting.

Catholic and Protestant hierarchies sat down with Freemasons, Jews, and orthodox churches, in a common stand against racism, saying that "discriminatory, extreme ideologies find each day a stronger hold in our country. . . . These attitudes generate incomprehension, hate, and too often murderous violence."

Pierre Simon, grand master of the Freemasons, said, "There are people less to the right than Le Pen who are beginning to turn their language a little in hopes of draining away votes."

Jacques Toubon, speaking for the neo-Gaullist Rally for the Republic (RPR), responded, "We refuse a chilly or mean France [frileuse ou méchante], but we want a French France." Didier Bariani, who wrote the UDF's report on racism, said that refusing to talk about immigration was substituting one intolerance for another. "There is no indecency in having a debate about the future of French society."

After the election, rhetoric hardened. Tough new security laws gave police wide powers to hold foreigners and, with few formalities, expel them. Complaints of brutality burgeoned. Freelance violence continued. In May, a "French Commando Against the Maghrebian (North African) Invasion" blew up a Turkish bath in Marseilles.

And the incidents continue. A Congolese official, Benjamin Tsila, on a study leave in Paris raced for his commuter train with no time to have his ticket punched. He asked the inspector to punch it. Instead the inspector tried to fine him. They argued as the train reached Tsila's stop. The inspector tried to hold him on board. The train started up again and Tsila fell to the track. He died waving his ticket to mortified witnesses.

André Santini, the new minister for repatriated citizens, estimated unemployment among 80,000 children of *harkis* at 85–95 percent. He offered incentives for employers to hire them, but it was not clear who would pay the cost. He also assured *pieds-noirs* they would finally be looked after adequately.

The program for "assisted return" continued, not to everyone's delight. In the town of Montbeliard, nearly 6,500 immigrants went home. Schools closed for lack of pupils, taxes plummeted, and merchants found themselves hurting badly. Only the Front National rejoiced. Mysterious tracts circulated reading: "Only one choice: the suitcase or the coffin."

At one point, Jack Lang, as minister of culture, said that forcing out immigrants would be bad for the reputation of France. At the level of individuals, France's reputation has already suffered. Subtracting the Portuguese concierges tucked away behind doors and the retired Americans lost in the bushes and Frenchified foreigners who pass unnoticed in the stuffiest of circles, France's immigrants amount to a paltry few percent. The *Beaufs* who abuse them in the name of national honor do far more to spoil the society than a few more spoonfuls of couscous in the French pot-au-feu. Tolerance, it seems to the outsider, is a vital element of the French mission to civilize.

THE IMMIGRANT issue is, in fact, only one hoop the French must keep aloft in their high-wire balancing act of a North African policy. Algeria and Morocco are mortal enemies with clashing ideologies. Tunisia's Westernized socialism with a firm hand can veer toward Morocco on the right or Algeria on the left. Libya, never French and hardly a historic *pote* of the French, is always ready to give the tightrope a yank when Paris least expects it. And France usually manages to keep a *dialogue privilégié* going with each of the four.

The French know that privileged friendship has more to do with privilege than friendship. A common language, and shared history that has not always been bitter, form a basis for negotiation. The rest is a matter of balancing mutual advantages.

France is Algeria's best customer and biggest supplier. Most of Algeria's other exports go to the EEC via Paris. France buys a third of its natural gas from Algeria at prices sometimes 25 percent above the open market. That deal alone, according to *Gaz de France,* cost the French balance of payments two billion unnecessary francs in 1985. There is other aid, either overt or hidden in a dozen separate state accounts. Paris, more than Washington or London, coexists with Algeria's East-bloc tendencies.

In exchange, the French profit. They build the Algiers subway and sell *L'Equipe,* a sports newspaper that is wildly popular in Algeria. They export wheat, Chanel, and wheel bearings. And France carries weight in a pivotal Arab state, a Third World leader. For a modern-day seat of empire, influence amounts to what possession used to be. The less defined the influence is, the less vulnerable it is to attack.

Giscard d'Estaing was the first French president to visit Algeria, in 1975, but he did little to move relations beyond a slightly chilly balance of mutual interest. Mitterrand pushed hard to warm them up. In 1981, he brought to Algeria twenty-eight crates of historical documents, from water surveys to family records. President Chadli Benjadid came to Paris in 1983 and laid a wreath on the tomb of France's unknown soldier at the Arc de Triomphe. After all, for all anyone knew, the hallowed remains might be those of an Algerian rifleman.

But there is also Morocco. The word friendship is a little more apt between France and Morocco. Less blood was spilled in colonial times. Moroccans integrated more easily into France. And King Hassan II is the sort of dictator that Western leaders like: committed to capitalist enterprise and political stability with a minimum of disruptive rhetoric. His territory covers the strategic shoulder of Africa, across from Spain and Gibraltar.

French *rapprochement* with Algeria spurred Hassan to widen his options. The Reagan Administration became interested. Republican strategists determined that Morocco was America's neighbor, a little water notwithstanding. With long runways and spacious harbors, Morocco was a perfect staging point between the United States and the Middle East. Rummaging around in history, Reagan's diplomats found all sorts of historic ties.

French teeth gnashed; this was not Gabon. France had paid heavily for decades to retain its friendship with Morocco. There was *l'affaire Ben Barka,* for example.

Mehdi Ben Barka, popular leader of the Moroccan opposition, was bundled into a French police car on October 29, 1965, on his way to lunch at the Brasserie Lipp in St. Germain-des-Pres. He was driven outside of Paris, executed, and buried. It was soon clear that thugs linked to Service 7 of SDECE had joined Moroccan agents in the kidnap and murder. French police covered up clues. Eighteen months later, de Gaulle declared, "This must finish. The real culprits must be found. Oufkir and Dlimi [Moroccan officials] must be convicted. The king [Hassan II], of course, is an accomplice, even the instigator, of the crime."[1]

De Gaulle dissolved Service 7 and placed SDECE under the control of the defense minister. But neither he nor any of his successors shed light on the French agents' involvement, or on who gave the orders. SDECE, later DGSE, remained under the defense minister's control for twenty years until unidentified agents were once again caught killing in the name of France, in New Zealand.

With Reagan courting Hassan II, the French shifted their balance slightly from Algeria. They continued to supply three times more military hardware to Morocco than did the United States. Mitterrand tacitly backed Hassan's claim to the Western Sahara, thus outraging Algeria, which supports the Polisario movement's push for that territory's independence.

In 1984, the tightrope twanged dangerously.

Mitterrand visited Hassan's summer palace at Ifrane. He was looking for help in ending the Chad war. Libya had just "merged" with Morocco, the seventh time Qaddafi had attempted to enlarge his stage with ill-fated unions. Before the merger collapsed, the French hoped to work a deal: Libya could stop supplying arms to the Polisario against Morocco in the Western Sahara; Morocco would help Libya—and France—find a face-saving way out of Chad.

The visit was supposed to be secret, but Hassan announced it. The Algerians reacted bitterly. By his presence, Mitterrand had blessed the merger, which was a threat to Algeria. A month later, Mitterrand flew to Algiers to cut his losses. The official daily, *El Moudjahid,* carried no comment, just photos of the two smiling chiefs of state and a caption: ". . . the exchange of views is the embodiment of the dialogue which Algeria and France wish to conduct, in serenity and confidence."

France's *beau geste* followed within days. Foreign Minister Claude Cheysson attended ceremonies for the thirtieth anniversary of the All Saints Day uprising that started the Algerian War. Opponents invoked the frightful word *forfaiture,* tantamount to treason among generals. "A shameful and scandalous blunder," said Michel Poniatowski. "This government has not even honor." Michel Noir, deputy from the Rhône, called it "a crime against the memory of French assassinated that day." *Le Recours,* which groups *pied-noir* organizations, denounced an "indecent affront to the honor and dignity of France." Edgar Faure, a major figure of the period, evoked the pain he felt that France might associate itself with an episode "marked by the massacre of a family of teachers."

Cheysson replied that deserting Algeria would be treason to those who fought so that France could remain a presence. After twenty years of independence, he said, "France no longer has the possibility of conducting itself differently from others."

Chadli called the storm an internal French matter. But it bore a cost. In the weekly *Jeune Afrique,* Abdelkader Chanderli observed, "The derision . . . and stupidity unfortunately tarnish the image of a people and a nation one might have thought could still teach the world elegance and generosity." He suggested that under this new code of honor of "infantile grudges and susceptibilities of badly raised children," Frenchmen had best avoid Waterloo Station or Trafalgar Square in London. "I fear the glorious past of France has left just about everywhere souvenirs that are best forgotten. . . . if there is a country rich in memories of defeats and humiliations inflicted on others, it is the Hexagon that no longer extends from Dunkirk to Tamanrasset. Britain never would have objected to its government taking part in celebrations of American independence. . . . the English have kept their sense of fair play, even when they draw first."

Clever, if a cheap shot. The Algerians had little claim to elegance and generosity after their fierce settling of scores in the 1960s. FLN leaders fought among themselves for supremacy and waged war on dissenting factions. At independence, with a nationalistic flourish, leaders tore down every trace of France, including road signs and traffic markers. It was chaos, since most literate adults read only French, not Arabic.

The French signs came back. Today, from a distance, Algerian towns seem transplanted from the Midi: neat lines of trees, a substantial *hôtel de ville* (town hall) on shaded central squares, rows of shuttered shops. But the time has been hard on Algeria, with a struggling economy and grave social problems.

In any case, the waters calmed. After Cheysson's trip, the president of Algeria's legislature said, "Bilateral cooperation is going well, and relations are very good." France sent down fifty-eight more crates of documents despite protesting *pieds-noirs*. "At least leave us the Algeria of old papers," said one. Another suggested that at least France should send back an immigrant with each box.

Then it started again. Prime Minister Fabius, in Morocco, said, "This is my first visit to a Maghreb country, and I wanted it to be Morocco." Before he could make it to Algiers, the state-run media dragged out the war and aimed it at France. On the fortieth anniversary of Sétif, Algerian television told in bitter detail how 40,000 Moslems were killed in repression. It showed a 1961 sequence filmed by an East German alleging that the French had tied 150 Moslem prisoners to stakes near its first nuclear test at Reggane to measure the effects of radiation on humans. The source was an unnamed German former legionnaire. Algérie Presse-Service, lauding the production, denounced "a crime against humanity, among so many others, of French colonialism."

France denied the "insulting and lying allegations" and said it "regrets anything that might damage the quality and future of

Franco-Algerian relations." Life-sized dummies were used, it said, not people. The statement ignored an APS remark that France ran Algeria like a concentration camp and practiced genocide.

Fabius reached Algiers in June and evoked "completely privileged relations." It was the thirtieth or the thirty-fifth time a senior official had flown down since 1981 to strike that note. Racism was a constant problem, but the list was long: not enough gas and oil purchases; not enough aid; not enough technology was being transferred; no help on the Western Sahara; overall, an apparent lean toward Morocco.

Fabius's visit was reported dryly and briefly, in contrast to the enthusiastic coverage of the Swedish leader Olof Palme. He, according to *Moudjahid,* knew how to reconcile his convictions and his actions and Sweden was "the only one of the small circle of the richest countries that was credible when it proclaimed its solidarity with the South."

The Algerians demurred on major contracts sought by France. In Paris, *Gaz de France* accountants grumbled privately about "horribly expensive and increasingly unrealistic" prices to Algeria. Holland and the Soviet Union were dropping their rates. But, they said, for Mitterrand the issue was taboo.

The FLN weekly *Révolution Africaine* published a fifteen-page report on torture that likened French generals to Nazi executioners. It was time, it said, "that France overcome its complex as a former colonial power and judge with serenity the truth about the colonialism imposed on the Algerian people." And, "Algerians should not be condemned to amnesia while France continues to cultivate ... the memory in its youth by the constant recollection of the facts of Nazi Germany and the war of 1939–1945."

The Algerians argued that those who demand punishment for Klaus Barbie should understand the bitterness felt toward French torturers. To make that point, *Révolution Africaine* compared the murder of Resistance leader Jean Moulin by Barbie's Gestapo agents in Lyon to that of Larbi Ben M'Hidi by the French.

The tone eased, and the rhetoric died away. Few French leaders expected it to be gone for good. To some extent, it was a useful political device. But more, it was a lingering pain, on both sides, that would not soon disappear.

Slowly, differences are being settled. Algerian authorities, for example, finally agreed to let children of divorced couples spend a few days' vacation with their mothers in France. That took a summer-long sit-in by French mothers at the embassy in Algiers and repeated visits by two French cabinet ministers.

After thirty years, the revolution is slipping into the past. An Algerian filmmaker reconstructing the war used a cast born mostly after independence. The old figures are coming home. Ben Bella, the first president and leader among the nine revolutionary fathers, was restored to honor after fourteen years of imprisonment and then exile. Belkacem Krim and Mohammed Khider were executed by FLN agents abroad in the 1970s, but their bodies were finally brought back. Algeria has more pressing economic problems that can no longer be blamed on the French: You cannot find orange juice in a country that was once France's orange grove.

Youngsters are still taught to remember grandfathers whom the French threw off cliffs and left to die—or those who were forced by the FLN to swallow their French military medals. But a senior Algerian leader summed up the feeling to a French reporter, late in 1985: "When we speak of foreigners, that might mean Germans, Americans, or Spaniards, but not the French. For us, they will never be foreigners like the others."

CHAPTER FIFTEEN

Middle East: Hall of Mirrors

A STRING OF crumbling French crusader forts rises from high ground across the Levant. They protect nothing and represent little power; but they are still there, after eight centuries. Like France. In North Africa, the French loom large, balanced precariously at center stage. But in the Middle East, they are nowhere and everywhere, moving within a hall of mirrors that only the architects of Versailles could have fashioned.

An Arab intellectual can argue that France has passed from the Middle Eastern theater. But he will likely adorn his discourse with the thoughts of Camus. No matter who is responsible for the morning's acrid odor in Beirut streets, it is the Lanvin sold from the back of decrepit Renault station wagons that masks it. The Arabic tongue is enriched regularly with new nouns: Exocet AM39, Mirage 2000, Super-Etendard, Super-Frelon. After the damage of classic power is done, it is often French engineers who clean it up.

King Hussein of Jordan was motivated by more than a shopping list when he said during a 1984 trip to Paris, "France has an important role to play in the Middle East in search for a solution to the problems of the region. I have said it often." That role is not clear, least of all to the French. But the Middle East is like that.

France is marked by its history in Lebanon and Syria. But apart from its weight in the power balance, it plays a vital role in the rush of modern events. Its diplomats and salesmen move easily in societies that baffle others. They understand the power of symbols, the subtle melting away and resurrection of alliances, the flexibility of the spoken word. When you do it with mirrors, you can apply Descartes with empirical pragmatism.

Some anti-Semitism aside, France is a home for Jews and a declared friend of Israel. The French never maintained a presence in the Gulf, and oil sheiks feel little cultural draw to Paris. But no matter. For Islamic politicians, businessmen, warlords, and terrorists who feel hemmed in by the stern lines of East and West, Paris is a secular Mecca. It is the capital of live and let live—or not.

Fanatical factions wage war on Paris streets. The Saudi embassy was seized in 1973, then the Iraqis'. Arabs fired fourteen bullets into a Palestinian envoy; another was killed later by a car bomb. A former Syrian prime minister was murdered in 1980. Someone had killed an Iraqi nuclear scientist earlier. A bomb demolished the rue Copernic synagogue in 1980, killing four.

Intelligence officers had reached informal understandings with some groups that they would not be harassed if they kept terror out of France. In the 1980s, however, there were too many amateurs, fanatics, and governments involved. Terrorists machine-gunned the lunchtime crowd at Goldenberg's delicatessen in 1983, and six people died. Beirut-based Armenians blew up the Turkish Airlines counter at Orly Airport, along with innocent victims. A blast shattered an anti-Syrian newspaper office on rue Marbeuf in 1984, killing one passerby and injuring a score of others. A gunman missed the U.S. chargé d'affaires in 1981, but another shot the U.S. military attaché; later an Israeli diplomat was killed. In 1984, Iranian terrorists killed an exiled general who had worked for the shah. Someone else shot the United Arab Emirates ambassador. There were scores of other incidents. Barriers in front of the American and Israeli embassies bristle with arms. Some plots are foiled in time. Others, undetected, are carried out by shadowy elements who benefit from the *force majeure* of greater policy goals.

Mostly, however, life is pleasant in Paris. Beyond the Eiffel Tower, along the river, is a cluster of high-rises the Parisians call Beirut-sur-Seine. Many of the apartments are owned by Lebanese who have gotten their money and themselves out of Lebanon. Uncounted thousands are French, whose Lebanese roots go back generations, and thousands more are fresh arrivals, floating between Paris and Beirut as combat rises and falls. A Paris radio station, la

Voix du Liban, keeps them informed. A large community of Syrians also lives in Paris.

"My Syrian in-laws just got their French nationality," my friend James told me. "They're going to vote for Le Pen. They figure there are too many immigrants in France. And they don't consider themselves Arabs, anyway. They're Phoenicians."

France, by tradition, is officially tolerant. In 1978, editors asked their Paris correspondents to check out some holy person named Khomeini who was trying to overthrow the shah of Iran with a Sony tape recorder. That seemed normal. Whoever ruled Iran traditionally had a holiday home in France, and Paris was the center for every faction seeking to take over his power. When Shah Mohammad Reza Pahlavi was temporarily forced out of Iran in 1953, he had to go to Rome. Mossadegh, the prime minister who seized power, had too many supporters in Paris.

Ayatollah Ruholla Khomeini turned out to be worth watching; we slower reporters caught up on the background. The shah had prevailed upon Iraq to expel the ayatollah. Neither Kuwait nor Syria would have him. He wanted to stay in Islamic territory, but Algeria turned him down. Sadegh Ghotbzadeh, living in Paris, brought him to France. It took Khomeini a few days to agree to take refuge in a country that had fathered the Crusades and, after all these years, still adored Christ. But, *après tout,* Iranians did not need visas for France.

Flora Lewis of the *New York Times* already knew about Khomeini. She happened to be calling at the Quai d'Orsay on the day he arrived in France, and she asked about him. "They did not know he was coming," she told me later. "I'm sure he just showed up." After three months, he would need a visa to stay. That would be no problem.

Khomeini settled comfortably into the village of Neauphle-le-Château, west of Paris; he pronounced it "Noffal." He had the plumbing ripped out to install Turkish toilets and bricked off the women's quarters. He was in the heart of a godless country, a long way from Qom and Mecca, but he had direct-dial telephones.[1]

The French let the ayatollah telephone his revolution to Iran; after all, what if he succeeded? Police made sure no one embarrassed France by hurting him. With a little help from the Quai d'Orsay,

the municipality granted drivers' licenses in twenty-four hours instead of the usual two months. The local post office supplied two
telex and six phone lines. Khomeini brought in fifty security guards.
His people were convinced that the CIA had rigged an ice cream
truck to eavesdrop on him; he decided not to ask the French to
intervene in case they might install their own microphones.

Theoretically, visitors and refugees are supposed to stay out of
politics. In four months in France, however, Khomeini gave 132
radio, television, and press interviews, and he made fifty declarations
for clandestine broadcast in Iran. He spoke directly to Iranians who
thronged the villa daily, by the end a total of 100,000.

In Tehran, meanwhile, the weakening shah swallowed increasing
quantities of pills washed down by mineral water from France.
President Valéry Giscard d'Estaing was so convinced the ayatollah
would triumph that he discreetly persuaded his allies not to overdo
their come-what-may support for the shah.

Khomeini did triumph, of course; he loaded his revolution
aboard a chartered Air France 747 and flew home with it from
Charles de Gaulle Airport.

The shah went to Egypt. An aide later said he was bitter that
France kept him out. "I don't think Charles de Gaulle would have
acted in that way," the shah was quoted as saying. "But him, he was
something else." Nonetheless, part of the imperial family settled in
France, where the shah owned chunks of Paris and the Riviera, with
other investments no tax authority could trace. Diehard royalists
filled French papers with advertisements denouncing the Islamic
revolution.

Steadily, the flotsam and jetsam of the Islamic revolution floated
back to Paris, which eventually became so full of anti-Khomeini
plotters that France earned the title of Satan, along with the United
States. A terrorist bombing killed eighteen in Tehran in 1984. With
a curious lapse of memory, Ali Akbar Hashemi Rafsanjani, speaker
of Iran's parliament, said, "We consider the French government a
party to this crime because of its treatment of criminals as political
refugees, providing them with all the facilities."

Then the Iraqis admitted hammering Iran with five Super-
Etendard jets, equipped with Exocet missiles, borrowed from the
French navy. Their new fleet of Mirages was still on the way.

Hundreds of thousands of Iranians mobbed the streets chanting, "Death to Mitterrand. Death to France."

Et alors? Not everyone in the Khomeini crowd would have forgotten "Noffal," and the wheel would turn. Bitterly opposed to the United States, Iran needed France. *Libération* published what it said were minutes of a secret meeting in Tehran to set up "independent brigades" to terrorize enemy nations: Gulf states and France. The Iranian embassy protested angrily, denouncing a plot to sour improving relations. Sure enough, the pendulum swung slowly back.

France sought to keep a relatively even keel with Iran to hedge bets. But Saddam Hussein of Iraq, Khomeini's major foe, was a friend of the French; they had built him a nuclear plant. So were the Israelis, who had bombed the plant, and a French engineer in the process. And also the Palestine Liberation Organization. Its Paris envoy played Christmas carols on his guitar on French television.

Among other modern monuments, Mitterrand put up the Institut du Monde Arabe, a block of glass and geometry at the end of boulevard St. Germain, towering over the Seine just across from the Ile St. Louis. A billboard at the site declares its purpose is to meld ancient civilizations, those of the Middle East with that of France.

It is a noble sentiment, but a tall order in today's climate. As I studied the half-finished project recently, my face—squinting in concentration—must have seemed disapproving. A car passed and its driver, an Arab, shouted to me: "Don't look like that. You are a racist."

FRANCE'S TRACK RECORD in the Middle East suggests little cause for Moslem warmth. With intermittent lapses, the French allied themselves with the Ottoman Turks. French engineers, military strategists, merchants, investors, and teachers went to Turkey. Ottoman legions fought the Austrians. Under the tacit Turkish accord, French missionaries settled among Maronite Christians in Lebanese mountain strongholds and beyond. In the nineteenth century, French and local Christian capital developed a rich silk-spinning industry, helped by a port at Beirut, roads, and a cog railway to Damascus, all built by the French. Beirut grew from a village of 8,000 in the 1820s to a city of 130,000 less than a century later.

Into the 1900s, France was on a full-blown mission to civilize the Levant.[2]

France joined Britain and Russia in the sneaky Sykes-Picot agreement of 1916, with secret terms that assured Russia southern sea passages and divided Arab territories between Britain and France. After World War I, Britain and France legitimatized their presence with League of Nations mandates. General Henri Gouraud planted the Tricolor and set up a government. He wrote shortly afterward:

> I might compare Syria to a little daughter born to France after the war. . . . Without doubt, it is in that sentiment of a mother of a family that Parliament has given me the necessary credit to pursue "the sacred mission of civilization."

Gouraud, devoutly Christian, made it clear that France was no newcomer to the region:

> Without going back to the Crusades, which have left magnificent castles so moving to contemplate for their splendor and force, our missionaries, sailors, engineers have, since long ago, brought their devotion and intelligence to these coasts. . . . There is not a foreign country in the world, except in the south of Belgium, where French is spoken as fluently as in Lebanon.[3]

The Hashemites, under King Faisal, claimed historic rights to Syria. But in 1920 Gouraud swept west from Beirut and ran Faisal out of Damascus. He broke up Greater Syria into autonomous states under French control, weakening Moslem nationalist factions. To Lebanon, he added Tripoli in the north, Sidon in the south, and the rich Beqaa Valley. Maronite Christians held political sway in a Lebanon the Syrians called artificial. Druzes and Sunni Moslems, among dozens of factions, were splintered and balanced precariously against each other.

One day, disenfranchised leaders warned, Lebanon would collapse, and bloody wars would redivide the turf.

Nearly sixty years before Gouraud, a French naval officer named de Chaille had warned, "[The Maronites] have no desire other than to be governed as in the past; they have ancient privileges which they owe to the protection of France and it is a concern of France only to preserve these for them." The Maronite patriarch, he said, "refuses to understand anything, appreciate anything, or even hear anything" about new trends or requirements of the time. But by 1914, the Maronites clung so fanatically to the French that they taught their children to recite *"Inna faransa immana hanuna."* Truly, France is our benevolent mother.

For the French, Maronite loyalty, even if from self-interest, was a sign that their civilizing mission produced a return. Also, the Maronites were a useful force to counter rebellious factions who wanted France to leave.

From the beginning, nationalists harassed the French. Senegalese troops battled insurgents. When dissidents captured Damascus, French forces shelled the city. George Seldes, an American correspondent for the *Chicago Tribune* who reached Damascus, reported the dead at 1,000, but French censors changed the figure to 500. Seldes wrote later that he was the only reporter in town. Because of heavy French censorship, he said, most people believed inflated Moslem accounts of up to 25,000 dead.

France's position, outlined in the *Revue des Deux Mondes* of December 1921, was "to maintain, to improve, the Ottoman Empire which was so favorable a means for expanding our influence." The mandate, it said, "responds marvelously to our past in the Orient, and to our idea for the future in that part of the world. Since the Crusades, our nation never sought a territorial domination in the Levant."

Seldes concluded,

And so France saved the Christian Lebanon and got no thanks. She built schools and roads. She found epidemics and conquered them. . . . Law and order were enforced. Billions of francs were spent. "Imperialism" was at work. What did France take out of Syria? Nothing. It is an almost barren land, spotted with beautiful oases . . . but no cotton plantations, no vast mineral wealth, no agriculture, no oil, no hope of oil. . . . Militarism, exploitation, imperialism? All I found was intense disgust with the mandate on the part of the French while the natives who cried for freedom and independence feared that the enemy religious cult would

fight them unless a foreign power spent its money there maintaining order.

Nonetheless, France stayed. In 1936, the Front Populaire government in Paris promised independence to Syria and to Lebanon, after
a three-year period. But in 1939, a new government knelt to military pressure and dropped the idea. France lost face, and the nationalists were furious.

With France crippled by the war, Syrian Moslems demanded a
final break. Neither Vichy nor de Gaulle found a solution. On May
8, 1945, insurgents began a wave of strikes, riots, and assaults on
French garrisons in four cities of Syria. Nationalists rejected a
proposed independence that maintained French air and naval bases,
schools, and control of the oil pipeline to Iraq.

Fighting was bitter, and French civilians were attacked. Nationalists boycotted French shops, banks, and schools. On May 28, the
French bombed a rebel-held sector of Damascus. Then the British
moved in.

Britain, still fighting Japan, feared that upheaval in the Middle
East could endanger their supply line. In any case, the entente
cordiale carried limited weight in the Middle East. London and
Paris were rivals in the region, and British troops forced the French
to withdraw.

Le Monde estimated the week's casualties at 400 Syrians killed,
100 missing, and 500 wounded. In ten days, the French lost eighty
to 100 killed and 200 to 300 wounded. Charles-André Julien, in
Foreign Affairs, estimated the losses at twenty-eight French and
twenty-five native troops killed; the Syrian-Lebanese dead were
about 600, with 300 wounded. In 1946, the *Revue Socialiste* carried
extracts of Julien's article, which the French government censored,
then released. In the original, it began:

> The functioning of the Syria-Lebanon mandate was perverted
> from the very outset. Neither the English, nor the French, nor
> the Syrians believed in the value of the obligations it entailed,
> and none of them played entirely fair. Varied shrewd dealings
> during the First World War left the Arabs defiant and embit-
> tered. . . . French statesmen played a deceptive game. . . . Badly

informed public opinion believed that France had acquired a new colony, and the high commissioners acted in that spirit. They made every effort to paralyze demands for nationhood instead of stimulating and at the same time canalizing them. The attitude of minor officials aggravated the situation still further. Unlike England, France had no corps of specialists in Eastern affairs. . . . She had recourse to a colonial personnel which imposed on the politically advanced Syrians an authoritative paternalism of a sort little likely to gain their support.

The French imposed forced labor, collective fines and imprisonment, and the belief that common faith assured Christian loyalty, Julien wrote.

In fact, even before World War I a French envoy reported back a common expression among Maronite leaders: any one of them would set the country ablaze to light his cigarette. Syria and Lebanon, each on their own, sought to build nations with little hope of communal generosity among religions and factions.

France moved up and down sharply on the Maronites' shifting popularity polls. Sunni Moslems distrusted the Christians and the French alike. They did not want a Christian government of any sort. Their interest was a greater Syria, not a greater Lebanon dominated by Western-oriented Christians. And beyond the Levant, France's standing was low among Moslem leaders.

Partly to spite the British, France helped to launch the new state of Israel. The *Exodus,* carrying Jewish refugees, sailed from Marseilles. Then the French invaded Suez. War and repression were vicious in Algeria. France armed Israel heavily in the early 1960s, providing the Mirage fighters that wreaked such havoc in the 1967 war.

De Gaulle stopped arms sales to Israel after 1967, just before he left office. He decried the Israelis for shooting first, condemned "expansionist ambitions," and made what Israelis called anti-Semitic remarks. All arms supplies were cut off, including spare parts. Israeli foreign minister Abba Eban charged that France's policy toward the Jewish state was "not one iota less hostile than the Soviet Union's."

Five missile-firing gunboats, ordered and paid for by Israel before the embargo, were blocked at Cherbourg. The Israelis howled in protest; Egypt was menacing their waters and the boats were vital to their survival. France held firm.

But before dawn on Christmas, 1969, the boats left port. Before President Georges Pompidou began bellowing orders down the phone line, they were in international waters. According to the French, they had been bought by respectable clients, for cash. A Norwegian gentleman negotiated the deal for the Starboat Company, Box 25078, Oslo. The company was, in fact, registered in Panama; Starboat, as in Star of David. Its principal shareholder was Israel, as might have been obvious. When *l'affaire* took on its capital *A,* which was immediately, the French asked the Norwegians about the company. Starboat? Never heard of it.

Military authorities in Cherbourg had refused to take responsibility for the boats—they were too hot to handle—so it was not clear who was supposed to approve their release. The boats were lined up ready to go for two days, but the local newspaper publisher said he suppressed the news at the shipbuilders' request. He explained, "We were guided by the sole concern of not harming the . . . most important local industry which employs more than 1,200 people." Two generals were fired, and France apologized.

L'Express wrote, "The Israelis have played well and ridiculed the French government."

Arab leaders, gnashing their teeth at photos of Moshe Dayan jumping for joy on the wharf as the boats chugged into Haifa, were not convinced. Nor were many French. The cover seemed too transparent to be innocent of connivance at some level, and public opinion seemed to like that idea. Commercially, trade with the Arab world amounted to a billion francs a year, 1.5 percent of France's total, the same level as with Sweden. And emotionally, the French leaned toward Israel. Jean Daniel wrote in *Le Nouvel Observateur,* "The embargo was decided against the French, and maintained against the will of the French despite promises made to the French; it is today violated by the French."

L'Express concluded its report: "In majority, [the French] prefer Israelis to Arabs, and the *Guignol* [a Punch-like fool] to the gendarme. Especially when the *Guignol* pays cash."

But France assured Gamal Abdel Nasser that he was "among their friends." Israel got the boats. Pompidou kept his job. A few days later, a ship arrived in Cherbourg to load 4,879,000 francs worth of arms bought by Iraq.

And just about then, France sold 110 Mirage fighters to the new leader of Libya, Colonel Muammar Qaddafi, giving firepower to his newly energized air force.

De Gaulle himself had been immensely popular among the Arabs: he had freed Algeria, bearded the Americans, kept Britain out of the Common Market, withdrawn his troops from NATO—and cut off Israel. But the popularity, historians generally agree, did not extend to France.

The early 1970s brought a clear shift. Britain announced in 1971 that it was pulling its armed forces back from east of the Suez. Then the Arabs discovered the power of their hold on the world oil flow. France, already stepping toward the Arabs' camps, quickened its pace, with a diminished chance that *Perfide Albion* would drop banana peels in their way. France moved quickly to fill a void left by Britain among its former colonies. Arab leaders were happy to find a European source of arms and diplomatic support, free of postcolonial complications.

It was a costly policy for the French image. In the euphoria of new Arab strength, Palestinian terrorists pressed their demand for attention. They succeeded at the 1972 Munich Olympics. Black September, linked to Al Fatah, broke into the Israeli compound. Terrorists killed a weightlifter and a trainer and seized nine hostages. After negotiations, German police stormed in; all the Israelis were killed. Three surviving Palestinians were jailed, but the Black September group hijacked a German airliner three weeks later and forced their release. Israel bombed camps in Lebanon and Syria and set about tracking down those responsible. One mastermind was identified as Abu Daoud.

In 1973, Black September raided a garden party at the Saudi embassy in Khartoum; they seized diplomats from the United States, Belgium, Saudi Arabia, and Jordan. Among their demands was the release of Abu Daoud, imprisoned in Jordan. All capitals refused. After killing two Americans and the Belgian chargé d'affaires, they reduced their ransom. But they still wanted Abu Daoud. Finally, they were overpowered. Six months later, Black September seized another Saudi embassy, in Paris. They demanded Abu Daoud, and Hussein freed him.

And then, in January 1977, the French consulate in Beirut gave a visa to a tall man with a distinctive mustache, an Iraqi passport, and a thick SDECE file; he was to attend the funeral of a PLO envoy murdered in Paris. It was Abu Daoud. He and a companion were met by French protocol, given a police guard, and received at the Quai d'Orsay by French officials anxious to play a role in Middle East peace talks. Then he was arrested.

The Direction de la Surveillance du Territoire picked him up at his hotel bar, either to embarrass the rival SDECE or through bad coordination. Interior Minister Michel Poniatowski approved the order. When the Foreign Ministry found out, a duty officer went white. "But why?" he demanded into the phone. "This is a diplomatic catastrophe." It was, of course. The West Germans asked for Abu Daoud; so did the Israelis. Giscard d'Estaing told Poniatowski, "You have made a horrendous gaffe. But the longer we hold this Abu Daoud, the harder it will be to free him."[4] Pressure would mount for his prosecution. Arabs would want him freed. The Palestinians might seize yet another embassy, a French embassy.

The only way out was the courts. The appropriate judge scheduled a hearing for a week later. Impossible, the Elysée objected. Abu Daoud was rushed into court. The German extradition request was rejected on a questionable technicality. The Israelis were turned down on an equally dubious 1927 law. Abu Daoud was freed the next day and put on a plane for Algiers.

Domestic reaction was bitter. In Le Nouvel Observateur, the eminent lawyer Jean-Denis Bredin demolished the legal arguments. He noted that judges were furious over the pressure applied to the courts, and he concluded: "Here is a sickening spectacle. A government weak and slippery at the same time! A judiciary without rigor! Ministers too well trained to lie! We are all deprived of justice and humiliated at being made so ridiculous."

But it was worse elsewhere. Ilana Romano, widow of an Israeli athlete killed in Munich, said, "France understands oil more than blood." Israeli foreign minister Ygal Allon added, "Before a minimum of courage and a maximum of weakness, France failed the test." The *New York Times* editorialized, "The decision leaves the sad but inescapable impression of a nation that shows itself willingly senseless, abject and even cowardly in the face of the blackmail of terror." The *Washington Post* said that France had "mortgaged its foreign policy for Arab oil and Arab markets. . . . What does it matter if the fruits of this boot-licking policy are nonexistent?"

And West Germany's *Bild Zeitung* echoed: "The France of grandeur lifted his arms before terrorism instead of against it. . . . France, weak, cowardly and humiliated, is on its knees."

CIVIL WAR, meantime, shattered much of the trappings of France in Lebanon. Luxury hotels along the Corniche were burned and mortared until they resembled blackened slabs of Gruyère cheese. The bankers and the blonde sunbathers hurried off, leaving Beirut to warring militias. But in some ways French political influence increased.

The Maronites, after pinning their hopes on the Americans and the Israelis, returned to the French. There is a cultural, spiritual and emotional holdover. But more, France defends the borders of greater Lebanon, and Christian leaders count on them to stand by their creation. Ghassan Tueni, publisher of *An Nahar* in Beirut and former Lebanese ambassador to the United Nations, outlined this for me in Paris.

> You will hear Maronites say, 'the Americans abandoned us,' as though the United States was some charity organization. Their only hope is France. There is a feeling that Europe is bound to play a greater role, especially France because of its ties with the Arabs. And France can talk to the Israelis with more freedom than the Americans can.

If Lebanon provided a French entry point to the Middle East, however, it offered little else but anguish. With an oil crisis crippling its economy, France needed more tangible benefits for its foreign policy.

Pursuing a reliable supplier of oil, France had settled on Iraq.

Their ties were historic; the French had kept nearly a quarter interest in the Iraq Petroleum Company when they relinquished to the British other claims on Iraq.

Jacques Chirac, prime minister under Giscard d'Estaing, visited Baghdad in 1974. He negotiated a major exchange of arms for oil under terms that were not made public. The deal has linked France and Iraq since then, but it has not always been smooth.

A year after Chirac's visit, three Arabs fired bazookas at an Israeli airliner, missed, and instead took over Orly Airport for seventeen hours. After wounding twenty people and holding, then releasing ten hostages, they flew to Baghdad. In 1978, an Arab commando seized the Iraqi embassy. The terrorists surrendered. But just as French police were putting them into a van, Iraqi guards blazed away at the prisoners from the embassy windows, killing a French police inspector.

Also, the Iraqis wanted a nuclear reactor.

The nuclear dilemma has been hard on France. De Gaulle built his own bomb after the Americans withheld vital technology in the 1950s. Later, scientists perfected small reactors for generating electric power. France spent heavily on research and development; it ended up with a valuable export commodity. But no French leader was anxious to destabilize the world by selling a nuclear bomb.

It was a perfect situation for anyone seeking to build his own Cartesian bridge to a lucrative sale. Those in the atom business know that almost any exported nuclear technology can move a dedicated bomb-maker closer to his goal; the principal safeguard, goodwill, can be ephemeral. But American, Canadian, and other European salesmen work hard to export peaceful nuclear technology to solid citizens in developing nations. There is a Non-Proliferation Treaty and a regulating body. But in practice, everyone draws his own line on what is too much and who is too risky. As one French exporter told a colleague, if you build a steel plant, who is to say someone won't make guns with it?

French diplomats, privately, had no illusions about Iraq. Saddam was a hard man with a grim record, and he was geographically suited to thump his sworn Zionist enemy. He knew Israel had plutonium, using a research reactor the French built at Dimona. (Israel also smuggled enriched uranium from a plant in Pennsylvania with the knowledge of two U.S. presidents, *Rolling Stone* reported in 1977; France has no monopoly on operating close to the line.) The Israelis had demonstrated often enough that their own security took precedence over virtually everything else. Baghdad was not your ideal site for Islam's first Bomb.

France agreed to build a nuclear reactor under carefully negotiated terms, and Frenchmen would remain nearby to supervise its development. At one extreme, some specialists opposed any such risk and left their jobs. At the other, some willfully skirted government safeguards in the belief that science is science and business is business; someone else would fill any void the French left, anyway. More did their jobs with reservations, following policy. And a few leaked secret documents to two journalists, Steve Weissman and Herbert Krosney, writing a book called *The Islamic Bomb.*

My own research was less thorough than theirs, but I cross-examined Krosney, a friend whom I know to be careful and honest. Unless otherwise noted, *The Islamic Bomb* is my source on French-Iraqi nuclear dealings.

In May 1981, the French were just finishing the Tammuz I reactor at the Nuclear Research Center outside Baghdad. Mitterrand, only days in office, had ordered an urgent, secret review of Giscard d'Estaing's safeguards. "Iraq had no legal obligation not to use the reactor to irradiate uranium," a French Foreign Ministry official told the authors later. "That was a loophole. We wanted to close it."

It was a touchy issue. French diplomats had worked to prevent danger, but some salesmen pushed for new contracts. By 1980, French imports from Iraq were 23.5 billion francs against exports, mainly arms, of 4.5 billion francs. Iraq was a secure source of 20 percent of France's oil. Frenchmen caught contravening official policy risked penalties. But matters of conscience—a different reading of Descartes—did not merit moral outrage.

By Friday, June 5, the report was lying on the foreign minister's desk, ready to be initialed and sent to the president. It was too late.

Early Sunday morning, on June 7, eight Israeli F-16s streaked toward Baghdad, each carrying two 2,000-pound MK-84 iron bombs. Six F-15s escorted them, ready to fight off any Jordanian or Iraqi planes they met on the way. The attack force flew tightly bunched to look like a commercial airliner on radar screens. The first bombs hit the lead and concrete reactor dome with delayed-action fuses. They penetrated before blasting jagged holes. Seconds later, another wave placed bombs precisely into the openings, destroying the reactor. The Israelis chose a Sunday when Frenchmen would be at home. But Damien Chaussepied, a twenty-five-year-old engineer, was at work. He died under the rubble.

Had Prime Minister Menachem Begin known of Mitterrand's report, he might have postponed the raid. Perhaps not. Some French diplomats suspected that Begin did not consult Paris in order to avoid a diplomatic entanglement. Yuval Ne'eman, an Israeli scientist and political leader, told Weissman and Krosney, "Why should we put our faith in [the French] even if they ask us to? Especially after they have been so careless in this entire matter." And an Israeli official, who insisted on anonymity, told the authors, "They're whores. Anything goes in their nuclear industry. Everybody knows it, even the Iraqis. That's why they went to the French to buy in the first place."

Mitterrand reacted sharply, but he condemned the raid, not Israel. He made it clear that the reactor would be replaced only with adequate safeguards. By 1984, to expedite the agreement, Iraq agreed to stringent conditions, including the use of low-grade uranium known as "caramel" to fuel the reactor. But, conveniently, Iraq's prolonged war with Iran allowed France to keep the issue in limbo.

In 1982, Mitterrand addressed the Knesset, the first French president to visit Israel. The Tammuz raid had delayed the trip once, and the Israelis had annexed the Golan Heights. But he arrived in March to declare himself a friend of Israel. Just to keep French credentials clear, Foreign Minister Claude Cheysson said earlier in Iraq that France supported a Palestinian state on the West Bank.

France darted among its mirrors but without much success. Le Monde headlined a dispatch from Beirut: "The waffling of French policy is seen by Arab leaders as a mixture of naïveté and duplicity."

MIDDLE EAST analysts are divided over what France really got out of its Middle East oil policy. Iraq fell behind on payments, and concessions were made. Forward commitments lost their allure when world oil prices fell. The balance grew steadily more precarious as Iraq continued its quagmire war with Iran. By late 1983, France began paying in blood.

At 5 A.M. on October 23, an explosion demolished the Drakkar building, barracks of France's contingent of the Multilateral Force in Lebanon. Fifty-eight French marines were killed. Back home, their countrymen watched horrified at newsfilm of marines struggling to free a man trapped under giant chunks of cement and steel. Only his hand protruded, and his friends squeezed it to comfort him, weeping in fury. A simultaneous blast at the U.S. barracks killed 241 U.S. marines.

Mitterrand flew to Beirut and climbed in a helicopter to visit survivors, grim in a bright orange life jacket.

French and U.S. officials blamed the attacks on pro-Iranian Shiite Moslem extremists. They planned a joint reprisal assault near Baalbek. Hours before, however, the Americans backed out. Washington was divided over the operation from the beginning. Then, when U.S. intelligence told the French the targeted terrorist camp had been hurriedly abandoned, France went ahead, anyway. Aircraft off the *Clémenceau* pounded an empty barracks and, because of a malfunction, also dropped bombs on a nearby mountainside. In Tehran, leaders of the revolution announced that thirty-four men were killed in air raids. But the successful attack was a separate operation by Israel. In France, there was some satisfaction of revenge. Among their allies and enemies, however, the French had appeared foolish, and the stakes of the conflict rose.

In Lebanon, the pro-Iranian Hezbollah party said Shiite sappers destroyed the French barracks because of continuing arms sales to Iraq. Hezbollah leaders warned more would follow.

The bombing and reprisal complicated yet further French relations with Syria. France has relied upon its dwindling capital of historic links with Syria in order to nudge Baathist leaders toward moderation. For Paris, Damascus represents yet another entry point to the Middle East. But, with alarming frequency, reality shattered the mirrors.

French ambassador Louis Delamare was assassinated in 1981 in the Syrian-controlled sector of Lebanon. French intelligence linked the killing directly to Syria, according to French reporters, and DGSE agents secretly bombed Baathist headquarters in Damascus, killing thirty-eight people. Later, Syria was held responsible—in internal reports—for the fatal bombing on rue Marbeuf in Paris. Some analysts saw Syria behind the Drakkar attack, as revenge for the Baathist headquarters explosion. But Mitterrand chose to keep talking with Syria, and President Hafez Assad was not taxed publicly for any of the actions.

And in late 1984, Mitterrand flew to Damascus, the first head of state in Syria since independence. The ceremony was moving, but Assad's message was brutal: your influence is nothing more than cultural; keep out of the way. Assad was after the old dream of a Greater Syria, and he had little need of France. He spoke directly to Washington and Moscow, the two capitals that directed heavy fire. Assad's French is excellent, but summits on *la francophonie* are not his style.

France kept up its diplomatic campaign in Syria, tailoring its Palestinian policy with Damascus firmly in mind. But in 1985, more mirrors were cracked. Islamic Jihad, linked to Hezbollah, kidnapped French diplomats Marcel Carton and Marcel Fontaine in Beirut, along with a thirty-eight-year-old French researcher, Michel Seurat. And then Jean-Paul Kauffmann, a respected magazine reporter, was added to the group. None would be released until France halted its aid to Iraq, their captors announced.

At the same time, Shiite snipers began picking off French officers and legionnaires of a lightly armed French observer force that was in Beirut at the request of Lebanese authorities.

France dispatched secret envoys to plead with Iranian leaders to find some face-preserving solution. Assad was also asked to help. Even if Syria might not be directly involved, French analysts reasoned, it could influence the captors in Lebanon. Before Christmas, hopes rose. The four Frenchmen were expected to be released along with American hostages from a TWA flight hijacked to Beirut. Details leaked out about a secret deal for France to contribute to Hezbollah and supply some arms to Iran. The arrangement, never made clear, collapsed. And then two months later, as French legislative elections approached, Islamic Jihad put the hostages at the center of the campaign.

The French sparked the crisis with a *bavure*—in the form of a quiet accord—that stunned public opinion. Two pro-Iran Iraqis were arrested in Paris and, screaming in protest, placed aboard a flight to Baghdad. Amnesty International released what it called an unconfirmed report that at least one of the men was executed in Iraq; some French papers reported that as fact.

In Paris, officials blamed the expulsion on a foul-up in communications between ministries. Law required a complex review before any expulsion except in urgent cases where a foreigner's presence endangered the security of the state. The law did not explain why a state that emphasizes its ability to defend its interests might be threatened by foreign prisoners. The procedure would be changed, but the damage was done.

Enraged, Islamic Jihad announced it had put to death Michel Seurat. The remaining three prisoners would be executed if France did not recover the Iraqis, alive. The captors also demanded that France free a five-man squad imprisoned for an attack on Shahpur Bakhtiar, former Iranian premier. And France would have to stop its support to Iraq.

Mitterrand persuaded Saddam Hussein to pardon the two men and let them fly back to France. Nothing was said on the other conditions. As the March 16 elections approached, Islamic Jihad played on frayed French nerves. An officer was shot to death in the courtyard of the French ambassador's residence in Beirut, the seventh observer force victim in a year. Photos were released to prove Seurat was dead. But they showed no wounds, leaving some doubt. And then a videotape followed: the hostages declared themselves to be innocent victims of French foreign policy.

The conservative daily, Le Figaro, editorialized: "It is all of France that has been murdered, humiliated, slapped, because its government, by its clumsiness, its timidity, its faults, its incapacity has allowed itself to be murdered, humiliated, slapped."

Seurat's Syrian-born wife, persuaded that she was a widow, electrified television viewers. "Hezbollah executed my husband, but he was murdered by [French Minister of the Interior] Pierre Joxe." She excoriated the government for insisting that it did not negotiate with terrorists while, in fact, it did. She said, for example, Paris had agreed not to pursue Abu Nidel's Palestinian fanatics if they did not operate in France. Eyes red and glittering with hostility, she concluded: "France is a doormat."

Fabius, however, was firm. "We will not cede to blackmail intended to divide our nation." Political ranks closed behind him. The hostages were not debated as an issue. French television showed bits of the videotape without the Islamic Jihad propaganda that narrated it. As expected, the conservatives won a legislative majority. But their majority was too slim to suggest that Islamic Jihad influenced the outcome.

Soon after elections, kidnappers seized a four-man television crew from the state-owned Antenne 2. Later, there was a ninth hostage: eighty-four-year-old Camille Sontag, a retired businessman about to return to France after forty-three years in Lebanon.

French arms continued to flow to Iraq. The decision was affirmed by the new prime minister, Jacques Chirac, who had forged the alliance with Baghdad a decade earlier. He would not have an easy time. Moments after Chirac was sworn in, a bomb shattered a shopping mall on the Champs-Elysées, killing two passersby and injuring another twenty-eight. It was only the latest in a series, set by Shiite fanatics protesting French Middle East policy.

Chirac pulled the French observer force out of Lebanon and pressed negotiations with Iran. Besides Iraq, there was a problem about a billion dollars paid out by the shah for a nuclear power project; Iran wanted it back. And there were the Iranian dissidents still operating from Paris.

In May, Ali Reza Moayeri, Iranian vice premier, emerged smiling from a meeting with Chirac. Discussions "were in a very friendly climate," he said, and he was delighted. Chirac added, "Iran is an old society, a civilization, a great culture. France is ready to normalize relations with that country."

Shortly thereafter, Massoud Rajavi, leader of the dissident People's Mujahedeen, left France. Officials said that was voluntary, but the pressure was thinly disguised. Abolhassan Bani Sadr, leader of a less virulent dissident faction, remarked, "The French attitude is not worthy of a democracy. At this rate, Iran will demand they dissolve the National Assembly. I condemn all regimes that use human beings as currency." But he stayed in France along with a range of anti-Khomeini Iranians.

French authorities said Rajavi abused his rules of asylum which forbid political activity. He went to Iraq from where Khomeini, ironically enough, came to France to mount political activity that overturned the Shah.

FRANCE HAS PAID heavily in the Middle East, but who hasn't? The Americans left Beirut first, with far greater losses. Paris cannot write economic plans, or change presidents, as it can in Africa. Its good offices cannot resolve conflict. But whose can? President Jimmy Carter's Camp David accords were a mixed blessing for the Middle East, relieving some pressures while increasing others. For the French, power is based on the assumption of a powerful stance: conviction and flair.

Before and after Mitterrand's meeting with Assad, Israeli prime minister Shimon Peres and King Hussein each have come to Paris to work on their relations.

France, as a cultural power, enjoys advantages denied to military powers. It can maintain a balance resting on illusion. In the Middle East, especially, it need only declare friendship; no one expects proof. France, Mitterrand maintains, is the only power that can talk to the Arabs and the Israelis with equal objectivity.

Against the fortunes of a chaotic world, Mitterrand explained to American viewers on "Face the Nation," France would fulfill any role it agreed to fulfill. Any retreat would, at the very least, be orderly. In the meantime, France acts the part. When the Multinational Force arrived to supervise evacuation of the Palestine Liberation Organization, the first troops ashore were the French Foreign Legion. Their colonel strode up to the Israeli officer there to greet them. "Shove off," he told the Israeli. "We don't need you to show us how to occupy a position."

Above all, France insists on its independence of action. Politically, it represents some form of middle ground. Few Arab leaders trust the Soviet Union, however valuable treaties of friendship might prove. The United States is too big to act as an honest broker. Britain, in a general way, is seen as being too close to the Americans.

"France can contribute to keeping the Middle East from being delivered to the superpowers," King Hussein remarked in 1985, a theme he repeats often. "We expect France to continue defending the positions she has taken up to now."

Payment is not always in full or on time, but honest brokering can be lucrative in the Middle East. If Iraq can't shop in Moscow and won't shop in London, there is Paris. Saudi princes may prefer Annabel's to Régine's, but Dom Pérignon goes down better than Guinness stout. If some arms deal is too delicate for anyone else to touch, there is always a chance a Starboat Company might find a way to handle it.

And none of that stops Shimon Peres from exulting in Paris about the "closeness of the very special Franco-Israeli relations." On his second trip to France in ten months, he said that if the Soviet Union allowed thousands of Jews to emigrate to Israel, as hoped, France would supply the aircraft. Laurent Fabius spoke of Israel, in ringing terms, not only as an ally but as a friend.

Up to a point, of course. The French were not pleased when Defense Minister Yitzhak Rabin called their soldiers "carrion." Or "bastards" or "manure," according to French dispatches. The word he used was *neveloth,* a biblical term for the slaughter of animals without proper purification. Whatever the translation, the Quai d'Orsay summoned Israel's ambassador to call it "rude, undignified and unjustified." To add to the injury, Rabin was referring to the 1,350-man French detachment to the U.N. forces in Lebanon (UNIFIL). In 1982, Israeli armored columns rolled over French (and other) positions en route to invade Lebanon, so infuriating one officer that he leaped on a tank and brandished his pistol.

When Israeli aircraft battered PLO offices in Tunisia in a reprisal raid during 1985, Mitterrand and the government objected in clear terms. Chirac, Gaullist mayor of Paris and presumed presidential candidate, sent his own telegram, condemning "a murderous military operation . . . an unqualifiable act." Not only were civilians killed in the raid, but also Tunisian civilians. Tunisia is in the family.

The magazine *France Pays Arabes,* published by the Franco-Arab Solidarity Association, carried all messages in full. In the same issue, it profiled Mohamed Sadiq el Mashat, Iraq's ambassador in France. He regretted that Britain and West Germany showed such little friendship when war broke out with Iran in 1980. Relations were very good with the Soviet Union and just warming with the United States. But, he concluded, "Our cooperation with France grows each year in all aspects; we are establishing *relations privilégiées.*"

French connections reach farther into the Gulf. Qatar, reared by the English, has 6,000 British residents and 500 French, but it is mysteriously Francophile. Paris built a large new embassy, with an active commercial section.

And there are the arms. France is the second largest supplier of arms to the Middle East, after the United States. In 1984, Saudi Arabia bought Crotale missiles and an antiaircraft system worth $3.4 billion. The United Arab Emirates ordered eighteen Mirage 2000s, for $530 million. The French also sold manufacturing technology. Egypt exports its own Mirage 2000s and Gazelle helicopters. Brazil is muscling into traditional French markets—Iraq, for example— with weapons of its own.

In the early 1980s, more than three-quarters of French arms sales went to the Middle East. Since 1984, French export strategists have worked hard to sell more weapons in their neighborhood. Atlantic Alliance armies tend to pay on time and stick more closely to agreements. And, unlike many Middle East states, they know who their potential enemy is.

FRENCH ENGINEERING salesmen are also reconsidering their enthusiasm for *gros coups* in Middle Eastern markets. In mid-1985, *Libération* sent a reporter to spend twenty-four hours with French companies building the Cairo subway. Société Générale d'Entreprise, a subsidiary of Saint-Gobain, and nineteen French and Egyptian companies won the contract for more than one billion francs in 1981. The French government financed the project at 3 percent annual interest, with a grace period of five years before payment was due.

The main line from Tahrir Square is charted along the eastern side of the Nile, on land settled within the last century. But local authorities, fearing archeological disaster, have commanded so many route changes and detours that engineers must use a computer to keep track of them. The project was running two years late and was projected to cost three times as much, the paper reported. The planned ten miles of diverted cables and canals reached sixty miles and was still growing.

Internal wars of authority blocked work, tied up equipment, and cost fortunes in fines and bribes, according to *Libération*. One example: For months engineers sought a way to avoid a thick tube of vital cables from the telephone exchange. Someone cut the tube by accident and found it empty.

"German, American or Japanese competitors point to the project —highly unjustly, by the way, but that is good old commercial war —to grab at our expense the rare metro contract now under negotiation, in Caracas, Algiers, Shanghai or Montreal," the paper said. To the point, it said, that one of the French company presidents called a news conference to criticize the project's management. "In brief," it said, "here are our Frenchmen on trial against themselves."

OVERALL, FRENCH POLICY is to keep talking and, if necessary, absorb the losses. The Gaullist view looks at history, not headlines. There are, of course, detractors. After the Beirut carnage, among a dozen pages of color photos in *Paris-Match*, Marc Ullman questioned whether "maintaining dialogue" should replace determining blame. He recalled that France took no action against Syrian terrorism and "safeguarded a special relationship" with Iran despite its taking of U.S. hostages. In the Middle East, he noted, the stronger party is considered right.

In the end, beyond the politics and the profits, there are the words. France knows their value. A lot fewer people speak French in the Middle East than the Alliance Française might think, but the total is no small number. On arriving in Beirut for the first time, I remarked on the perfect French of the office helper who had come to meet me. He was a little wounded. "But," he said, "do you think we are not civilized?"

CHAPTER SIXTEEN

Asia and the Pacific:
Kanaky and La Bombe

FRANCE NEEDS NO mirrors or high wires in the South Seas. It reaches island backwaters even the *Bounty* mutineers would not have wanted. From New Caledonia, 800 miles east of Australia, to the last flecks of Polynesia, approaching South America, there are two Pacifics: French and the rest. In bare feet or Guccis, the French live well, with social security, Gilbert Bécaud and all the refinements civilization has to offer. Lately, however, attention has settled on one word in particular: *la Bombe*.

Atmospheric nuclear tests were shifted from Algeria to French Polynesia in 1966. Neighbors complained, and testing was taken underground in 1975. From then until mid-1986, eighty-one devices were exploded. French scientists report no noticeable effects beyond a slight heave of the earth at detonation. But the fourteen-member Pacific Forum, from Australia to Nauru, complains bitterly.

For France, it is a simple case of *j'y suis, j'y reste.* National security is at stake. If France can stare down a Soviet premier, it will not bend to a king of Tonga. And the French like their Pacific role. Even in an age of supersonic Concordes, it takes cabinet ministers two days to get from Paris to Papeete; they fly over a lot of far-flung islands on which to stick a flag.

But even the French find it hard to ignore the furor over *la Bombe,* especially when it is aggravated by yet another word: Kanaky. That is what Melanesians want to call New Caledonia if they can wrest it away from France.

Kanaks are ethnic Melanesians; even the spelling of the word is charged with emotion. People who favor the status quo prefer Canaque. Kanak connotes a tilt toward independence. Most Melanesians use the *K,* and so will I, without taking sides.

The island had fallen on hard times when I first arrived in 1972. World nickel prices were down, and prices of everything else were rising fast. An executive of Société le Nickel told me about it at lunch. With the white Burgundy and *fruits de mer,* I heard about local wages getting out of hand. The cost of staples—silk ties and cheeses—was raised over the red Bordeaux and *côte de boeuf marchand de vin.* By the time we finished the *mousse au chocolat,* coffee, brandy, and Cuban cigars, I was all but reduced to tears. The man might have to sell his second cabin cruiser.

The Kanaks were divided. Many were bitter that *Caldoches,* the local version of *pieds-noirs,* had settled on their best land and bulldozed their traditions. Nationalist leaders considered themselves to be under colonial rule, with all its nameless and intangible humiliations. But others, no small number, saw themselves as French. At Le Nickel, Melanesian employees got an annual home-leave ticket to the *métropole,* just like the *z'oreilles.*

The *Caldoches* regarded themselves at home on *le Caillou,* the Pebble, where many traced their roots back three generations. Many have Melanesian blood from the prison colony days when Frenchwomen were few.

After 1981, Socialist authorities in Paris nudged the island toward autonomy. Nickel earnings were down, and subsidies from Paris approached a billion francs a year. A friendly split, before things got nasty, would allow close postindependence ties with France: military base agreements, mutual trade advantages, and protection for French citizens wishing to stay. The risk was small. If relations soured, there was always Wallis and Futuna nearby to complete the global strategic chain. The Socialists scheduled a referendum on self-determination for 1989.

But it was not that easy. People imported over the years had left patchwork demographics. By 1984, of the island's 145,368 inhabitants, only 61,870 were Melanesians, or 42.56 percent. There were 53,974 whites, 37.12 percent. Another 12,175 Wallisians and Futunans, and 5,570 Tahitians, mostly wanted jobs and peace under the

Tricolor. So did the 5,319 Indonesians, 5,249 Vietnamese and others, and 1,212 Vanuatuans.

Many Kanaks demanded that France stay. Others, knowing what had happened to the *harkis* after Algeria, held their peace but planned to vote to remain French.

In Territorial Assembly elections in July 1979, 40.23 percent of the vote went to the RPCR (Rassemblement pour la Calédonie dans la République), an affiliate of the Gaullist RPR. The Front Indépendantiste won 34.42 percent. A third party, with 18 percent, aligned itself with the RPCR. In 1982, prodded by the Socialists, the swing party shifted its support, and *indépendantistes* dominated the legislature.

By January 1983, hard-liners began pushing for faster change. Two gendarmes were killed in political violence. In 1984, the Socialist Kanak National Liberation Front (FLNKS) ordered an "active boycott" of the November 18 elections. Seventeen of its leaders flew off to Libya for a crash course in troublemaking. Graffiti warned of trouble: "Immigrants into the sea!" "Qaddafi!"

The RPCR won 70.87 percent of the vote. Dick Ukeiwé, a Kanak RPCR senator and leader of an absolute Assembly majority, declared victory. So did Jean-Marie Tjibaou, a burly former priest who headed FLNKS.

Only half the registered voters turned out. In one town, someone scrawled on a wall: "I will secretly kill any Kanak who goes to the polls." FLNKS teams firebombed voting booths and hijacked ballot boxes. Incidents were reported at one of every two polling places.

But a legislature was elected. *Le Monde* announced, *"Le Pire Evité."* The Worst Avoided. Not exactly.

The next day, the Kanaks resumed their old war with France. Militants stormed the gendarmerie at Thio, in the north, and seized guns. FLNKS militants besieged police in their barracks and *Caldoches* on their farms. They seized another village and mounted roadblocks elsewhere on the island. FLNKS avoided serious violence; it was testing its strength. The government elected to waffle.

Libération interviewed the subprefect of the Loyalty Islands, a hostage in his own office at Wé, Ukeiwé's hometown. The account was unsettling. *FLNKS vaincra*—FLNKS will win—was scrawled in black on the white prefecture door. The subprefect inside, Jean-Jacques Demar, was black, a French civil servant from Martinique, held powerless along with his white French assistant. They each went home at night guarded by young militants who favored Bob Marley T-shirts and red headscarves.

"I'm all right," said Demar. Mainly, he was bored. "I'd like to have V. S. Naipaul's *Crocodiles of Yamoussoukro* to read."

For six days, the prefecture Tricolor was not the familiar blue, white, red but rather the FLNKS' blue, red, green, with a yellow sun and a stylized totem pole.

The occupation of Thio dragged on, and Paris was getting edgy. Puma helicopters with reinforcements were met with shotgun fire. Police landed and squared off against Kanaks, weapons drawn. But then they lowered their guns and went to await developments with the local gendarme hostages.

Caldoches began oiling their shotguns, furious at official hesitation. They cleared some roadblocks and mounted their own. The mood grew uglier. And then blood started to flow.

First accounts were muddled. "They killed Eugène Guérin and cut up his wife." Newspapers reported the death, but police found Guérin alive, just badly beaten. Within twenty-four hours, however, a crowd of fifty Kanaks approached Emile Mazière's farm on the Col de Crève-Coeur. In a gunfight of confused origins, he was shot in the back, and he died in the ambulance. Six Kanaks were wounded.

Le Figaro, staunchly right wing, carried an enormous headline: "The Rifle Not the Suitcase." Every French person over thirty-five got the message. Here was the agonizing dilemma of Algeria, *le fusil ou la valise.* The paper pictured half-naked militants with wild hair at Thio, lounging against a military helicopter sprayed with graffiti like a New York subway car. Another photo showed a despondent old man named Rouillard, looking like Albert Schweitzer in a straw hat and white moustache, sitting at Kone airstrip with his wife, his dazed little terrier on a leash, and a pathetically small pile of belongings.

Thierry Desjardins, veteran *Figaro* correspondent not noted for affection toward *indépendantistes,* described an angry meeting of settlers forming a militia. They all knew Mazière, whose grandfather had pioneered the farm. He quoted one: "Tonight, I may kill a Canaque pal with whom I've lived forty-five years on this corner of the earth. Or maybe he will kill me."

A commentary entitled "The Old Dream of Decolonization" noted that de Gaulle got credit for giving away Africa and Algeria; the Socialists at least wanted to turn loose the few crumbs left. And an editorial concluded:

> The specter of a colonial war haunts the spirits of the left, although it amounts to reducing to impotence a handful of *excités* —a few hundred at first, then a few thousand—who abusively pretend to represent the Canaque people and who would have doubtlessly been brought to reason by gendarmes if these had not been condemned to kill time in playing *belote* [a card game].

But it was more than *Figaro*. Each night, the television brought angry and anguished scenes to French who were still trying to locate the island in their atlases. The opposition condemned what some called spineless and humiliating laxness. Newspapers picked up the theme. In Milan, *Corriere della Sera* evoked "Mitterrand's Algeria."

On December 1, Nouméa slammed down its iron shutters and declared itself "a dead city" to mourn the first victims. But thirteen remote farmhouses were burned, and many feared worse would come. Authorities held back. They argued that a few thousand gendarmes more would make little difference, and a harsh response would unleash massive retaliation. A special envoy flew out from Paris to make a report.

Paris suspected a Third World/Anglo-Saxon plot. The Quai d'Orsay had already protested after the Australian foreign minister denounced "one of the last vestiges of colonialism in the South Pacific." Reporting on the elections, *Le Monde* declared that the Kanaks were "encouraged in their separatism by the young independent states in the Pacific and by Australia which dreams of imposing its influence."

Thio remained two-thirds deserted, and Kanaks turned back a convoy with food and medicine. *Figaro* found the Douyéres, a couple in their eighties, poor and sick, held prisoner, robbed, and told they would be shot if they did not leave their land within fifteen days. They had spent fifty years in the simple wood farm-house they built themselves. "FLNKS is making it plain that no one, even among the poorest, is safe . . . from revolutionary law," the paper said.

Tjibaou set up a provisional government but told reporters, "We don't have the means to make war. It is not serious, it is a joke to talk of war against France." The roadblocks, he said, were "to protect our militants in the face of colonists who are very well armed." Not all his lieutenants agreed. Attacks continued on isolated farms. *Caldoches,* agitated, eyes red from sleepless nights, shot back.

Giscard d'Estaing, Raymond Barre, and five Gaullist former prime ministers issued a joint statement condemning Mitterrand for failing to deal with "an insurrectional situation" and debasing French credibility.

Mitterrand sent Edgard Pisani, a former minister and confidant of de Gaulle, to pick up the pieces. Pisani promised to restore order and consult all sides. Hours after his first televised speech, two more Kanaks were killed, bringing the death toll to at least five; a second *Caldoche* had been shot dead. Three police had been wounded, as well as six civilians, two beaten and left for dead.

And then, the next morning, news came of the massacre at Hienghene. A planter named Maurice Matride and his neighbors, fed up, laid a coconut tree across a road and stopped two pickups of Kanaks driving home from a nighttime meeting. They blinded the victims with a searchlight and opened fire. Ten were killed, including two of Tjibaou's brothers; a third brother was badly wounded. At first, police said the Kanaks were killed on their way to burn Matride's house. But Matride told gendarmes he had planned it: "We were harassed, threatened, and our nerves cracked."

The killers were *métis,* descendants of settlers who had married Kanaks. But in the racial structure of New Caledonia, they were considered Europeans. That was just one more complexity to baffle the French watching in alarm 12,000 miles away.

Raoul Lapetite and his six sons were among the confessed killers. *Libération* dug up the diary of F. Lapetite, his grandfather, who arrived with a wife and eleven children in March 1899, unable to make a living in France. In Nouméa, he wrote, they found lodging by "dispossessing tribes of spiders. (Our mission is doubtless to dispossess tribes.)" He was given farmland at Hienghene taken from Kanaks. The Kanaks built his home and asked for food. "Poor people, they were the ones who planted all this," he wrote. "We are beginning to get used to these savages who are like children." Lapetite lamented the Kanaks' heavy drinking and indolence. "As for civilization, the Kanaks have taken our vices, and that is all."

After the massacre, the mood darkened. More settlers fled the bush; others bought more bullets. As Kanaks mourned in Hienghene, 5,000 people gathered on a palm-fringed parking lot by the sea at Nouméa. Men in shorts with sunburned knees, women in summer dresses, Vietnamese, Tahitians, bellowed their support for a French Caledonia. They sang the "Marseillaise," adding volume to the part that goes, *"aux armes, citoyens."*

The Melanesians were split. At one rally, a hefty Kanak woman screamed at television cameras, "We are here to show everybody that we want to be French, under no matter who, all ethnic groups together." In the grainy monochrome newsreels from Algeria, Europeans and Moslems had melded together in the crowds. This time, in crystal-clear color, black and white hands rose together in a swirl of blue, white, and red.

Parallels with Algeria were hard to resist, despite the smaller scale and far greater distance from France. Like Algiers, Nouméa tried to live its normal life while rebellion crackled in the *bled.* French wives and Australian stewardesses tanned bare breasts by turquoise water. Kids revved their Hondas and ate elaborate ice cream *coupes* in noisy downtown cafés. The Brie and Brouilly came in as usual on the UTA run from Paris. But, fired by the odd bomb or phone calls from the bush, Nouméa, like Algiers, began to smoulder.

There were none of Massu's *paras,* but along with Pisani, Paris sent units of the hard-minded GIGN elite police. Transports ferried heavy equipment from Tahiti and France; order was to be reestablished.

When Algeria broke, however, the minister in charge had been François Mitterrand. This time Mitterrand was president, and he was not about to let history repeat itself.

When Giscard d'Estaing argued that New Caledonia be made a department, Fabius delivered his own version of the Maspétiol report. Of the 972 top-ranked civil servants, Fabius noted, six were

Melanesian; 900 European families owned more land than all the Kanaks combined. Melanesians had not been given the vote until 1956. The territory had to be offered self-determination. "You say self-determination," Giscard d'Estaing countered, "but the echo comes back independence."

Pisani freed seventeen Kanaks arrested for disrupting the November elections. Despite his brothers' deaths, Tjibaou lifted the roadblocks to await a political settlement. His minister of security, Eloi Machoro, held out at Thio, but later converted his barriers to checkpoints. But Tjibaou insisted to reporters: "Peace and security in Caledonia are called Kanak independence." In three months of existence, FLNKS had become the main arbiter of Kanak aspirations; its strategy was to keep up the pressure until France pulled out.

But a power struggle loomed within FLNKS. Machoro, who swaggered before the cameras in a fatigue cap and bare chest, predicted violence. Most French first saw him in a photo on November 18, demolishing a ballot box with an axe. FLNKS might send more militants to Libya or Cuba, he said, and establish relations with the Soviet Union and Vietnam, mainly, he told reporters, to piss off France.

On January 7, Pisani revealed his plan: a referendum in six months to ask 75,000 voters—Kanaks and anyone with more than three years' residence—what they thought of independence. If they voted yes, France would withdraw on January 1, 1986, but a treaty would cover military bases, aid, French rights, and internal security. Paris would stay in spirit, supported by more tangible evidence of friendship. He urged a yes vote for both France and independence. No one was happy. Tjibaou said a vote was beside the point: "We are the rightful owners of the country." Ukeiwé said, "We are French and we want to stay French. We cannot discuss independence."

In Tahiti, Gaston Flosse, political head of the French Polynesian Government Council, objected that "independence would be a catastrophe" for both New Caledonia and Polynesia.

Four days later, blood flowed again. A *Caldoche* farmer named Tual left his lunch table to find out why his dogs were barking. He took along his seventeen-year-old son, Yves, to investigate. Tual heard a noise and fired into the bushes. The bushes shot back, killing the boy.

Nouméa erupted. Crowds gathered at the iron gates of the High Commissioner's office, chanting, *"Pisani Assassin!"* *Caldoches* set alight the nearby home of Jean Guiart, an ethnologist who had spent forty years in New Caledonia and was widely believed to have inspired the FLNKS' radical tactics. The building was the island's oldest structure, an officers' mess built in 1854. Rioters hijacked the fire truck and turned hoses on gendarmes in battle gear who watched, immobile.

When crowds marched on the government headquarters, police charged. Gendarmes pumped 137 tear gas canisters and swung truncheons all night long to quell rioters. Sirens screamed. Dentists and shopkeepers shouted that they were ready to die for a French Caledonia. The elegant little tropical capital choked in smoke. Angry men ripped out parking meters and heaved paving stones at police. One youth shouted, "They're firing on us because we want to be French."

Later, Guiart shook his head. "I don't understand how they could have let this happen," he told *l'Agence France-Presse.* "These people try to destabilize the territory. It is not the Melanesians, who only respond to provocations of the over-armed right."

While Nouméa rioted, police combed tribal areas near Tual's farm at Bouloupari, sixty miles away, kicking open doors and interrogating Kanaks. Patrols moved north toward La Foa, Machoro's stronghold. *Libération* interviewed Victor Moindou, a FLNKS hard-liner, who said, "It had to happen. Tual occupied land stolen from the tribe, and he knew it. We've had ten dead, and there will be dead on their side." Tjibaou's moderation was his affair, Moindou said. FLNKS would decide its policy at a congress the next day.

But at dawn, the GIGN cornered Machoro, Marcel Nonnaro, and thirty-seven of their men on a ranch near Thio. What happened then is confused. Police first attributed all deaths to a heavy exchange of fire. Then officers said that Machoro would not surrender, and a sharpshooter with a precision scope had tried to drop him with a shoulder shot. FLNKS insisted that Machoro was coming out, his rifle trailing at his side. But the result was clear. A bullet had struck him full in the sternum, and he died shortly afterward.

Rumors reached Nouméa almost immediately, and new crowds formed outside the High Commissioner's office near the place des Cocotiers. At 10 A.M., the news was confirmed over a loudspeaker. Some roared approval, their fists thrust into the air; some did little dances of joy. Satellites relayed the scene to French television sets that evening. It might have been a film clip from the Forum in Algiers.

Tjibaou called it murder and accused Pisani of complicity. Gendarmes reenacted the episode for reporters to show how the tall grass had limited their options. But *Paris-Match* quoted an unnamed ranking officer: "Let's remove sentiment and be frank. We had to 'neutralize' him before the media made him a star . . . he wanted his war and he got it." Just eliminating Machoro would be suspect, he said, but in a large operation . . . "You know what I mean?"

In *Des Affaires Très Spéciales,* journalists Jacques-Marie Bourget and Yvan Stéfanovitch assert that Machoro was shot dead by a sharpshooter "on loan" to the gendarmes from a specialized paratroop unit, using a deadly 5.56 caliber cartridge. The paratrooper's presence was kept secret. The authors say that officials wanted Machoro dead, but they wanted the gendarmes to think the death was an accident.

Pisani declared a state of emergency and ordered a 7 P.M. curfew. FLNKS said that the "barbarous act" brought the situation back to zero and demanded "the pure and simple restoration of Kanak people's sovereignty over their country." That overworked formulation, "tense calm," was never more apt. The *paras* were called in to protect docks and airfields. Altogether, there were 6,000 police and troops on the island, one for every twenty-four civilians.

Mitterrand himself came out a week later, flying for fifty hours only to spend twelve hours on the ground. Pisani kept him indoors for security. But outside, a crowd of 35,000 people, some with their faces painted in blue, white, and red, clamored for the right to keep their flag. Mitterrand ordered negotiations but also announced that the island's military installations would be expanded.

He promised that Le Nickel would soon reopen its Thio mine.

Within days, seven giant ore trucks were burned, along with commercial fishing boats, apparently by *Caldoche* extremists. Kanaks accused them of trying to sabotage employment. But FLNKS hardliners destroyed 90 percent of the vehicles at Kouaoua, paralyzing the only nickel mine still in operation.

Tjibaou and Ukeiwé each went to Paris to lobby. So did François Neorere, local leader of Le Pen's *Front National,* who showed up in a blue, white, and red vest and said, "Sixty years of France in my heart, believe me, that leaves traces. My education with the Marist brothers gave me a love for French culture, for France, civilizing and generous."

Tjibaou said that he was a man of peace, representing peaceful people, but that "France is the *patrie* of the French; it is not the *patrie* of the Kanaks." On the way home, he stopped in Algeria to denounce French colonialism.

For the next months, Pisani kept on talking. But he insisted, "Change is unavoidable and irreversible." In April, Fabius altered the plan. The referendum was put off until after the March 1986 legislative elections. Voting would be held no later than December 31, 1987. Meanwhile, the island would elect four separate regional assemblies. Nouméa was expected to vote European; the rest, Kanak.

Tjibaou said the plan at least would allow the *indépendantistes* to prepare a more effective takeover later. With its militant wing crippled, FLNKS had little choice. Ukeiwé dismissed the plan as racist, but he had no choice, either.

Then FLNKS decided to take over education. "The school problem is tied to the colonial problem," said Yeiwene Yeiwene. "We have enough texts that talk of trains and snow and our ancestors the Gauls." Also, he said, Kanak children were not safe at school.

Sporadic clashes kept tension high. A Melanesian hacked to death Roland Lecomte on March 9, the twentieth death since November. Melanesians rose against police raids into villages. On April 8, a white teacher, Simone Heurteaux, was hit by a rock and killed as she drove along a mountain road. Nearly 3,000 teachers marched in the capital, demanding protection. Journalists had to rescue the resident correspondent of the *Melbourne Age,* whom *Caldoche* fanatics accused of leaning toward the *indépendantistes.* "Let her go get raped at Thio," shouted one.

On May 8, 200 Melanesians defied a ban on public gatherings and marched into downtown Nouméa. *"France dehors!"* a leader bellowed into a megaphone. Quickly, a crowd of 150 *Caldoches* formed around RCPR leader Jacques Lafleur. The two groups met head on, threw rocks, and fell into a pitched battle. Célestin Zongo, a nineteen-year-old Kanak, was shot dead; ninety-five people were injured, including thirty-eight policemen. Four days later, someone tossed a bomb into the only school on the island that trained Melanesians for a senior certificate. Seven people were hurt. Moments earlier, forty Melanesian children had passed by the spot.

Defense Minister Charles Hernu arrived on May 10 on a nuclear-powered submarine, only hours after France set off its biggest test ever of *la bombe* at Mururoa. He said he wanted "to show the world we are here." He also discussed plans to spend 300 million francs on military bases at Nouméa to increase troop strength by 50 percent to 4,500.

A Paris court convicted Tjibaou of threatening French territorial integrity; Ukeiwé brought the charge. He was given a year's suspended sentence. It was appealed.

In June, Pisani moved to Paris as minister for New Caledonia. Paris papers nicknamed his job Mission Impossible. Fernand Wibaux, the new high commissioner, told Kanaks, "Our objective is to prepare New Caledonia for the accession to independence. Independence is a right, I understand, and the Kanaks have a right to a legitimate existence. What I seek is the way to bring this about."

French authorities reformed land tenure; Kanaks were given back land which they could lease to *Caldoche* farmers. The *Caldoches* responded by twice burning down the land records office.

FLNKS put up new barricades at Thio to protest police methods; *Caldoches* bulldozed them. Both sides met to talk but ended up shouting insults. Incidents peppered the papers. Kanaks stoned the car of a twenty-two-year-old white public works employee; he fired at random and wounded an eight-year-old girl.

In Paris, opposition leaders lost a legal battle to block the elections, which were scheduled for September 29.

Le Pen landed on the island just in time for the September 24 anniversary of its occupation by France. He brought Algeria with him. Before an enormous crowd, he jabbed the air with his finger and bellowed, "In the streets of Algiers, on January 26, the same demonstration under the *drapeau tricolore* clashed with the machine guns of troops who fired for minutes. I hear it now, 'Hold your fire, lieutenant. Hold your fire.' Five minutes later, there were 100 bodies in the street. . . ." Then, slamming the podium with an open palm, he yelled: "And these people now don't have the right. . . ."

But Le Pen agreed to give way to Jacques Chirac, the opposition's main gun, to avoid splitting the pro-French vote. Chirac visited an RPCR Kanak stronghold, bringing as a gift a video recorder and films, including one called *The Moment to Kill.* His big moment was before a roiling, heaving, chanting crowd in Nouméa, at the place des Cocotiers.

Chirac shifted from somber to raucous to thundering. New Caledonia belonged to France, and he would block Socialist efforts to give it away. "By the preconceived engagement to move at any cost toward independence, spurning the most evident realities, the Socialists have a heavy responsibility before history, and they will have to face that." Building to a pitch, he belted out his conclusion over a sea of waving Tricolors and banners:

"When a people is on its feet, as you are; when a people resists, as you have done, its destiny faces no doubt. Tonight, I tell you . . . you can be confident. You are innumerable. You are strong and determined. You are France."

No one needed a translation: *Je vous ai compris.*

Voting went smoothly. The *indépendantistes* won majorities in three of the four regions, as expected. Eighty percent of all Kanaks showed they wanted independence. FLNKS-dominated regions controlled the mines and richest land. But anti-independence candidates got far more votes, 61.21 percent to their adversaries' 34.82 percent. They won a twelve-seat edge in the forty-six-seat Territory Congress elected as well as in the regional assemblies.

And each side dug in to wait for a new French National Assembly. A right-wing majority in Paris could reverse the Socialists' plans and forestall independence. But Tjibaou counted on his own new strength to make that impossible. He sought to prove that his people could govern responsibly and control their extremists. He banned alcohol for his leaders until independence; it was time to work, he said. Meantime, opposing forces would have to talk.

The situation was more tense than calm. White farmers, finding horses murdered and corn fields burned, took their revenge as they could. French gendarmes dotted the roads trying to keep order. A *Libération* reporter interviewed one at a checkpoint: "We can't watch everything; we don't stop the buses, it takes too long to check everyone. And we come from France and don't know the faces. Besides, even if we stop them . . . *bon, allez,* I've said enough. Move along."

Soon after Chirac's government took power, Thierry Desjardins was back. "The Tricolor Floats Over the FLNKS Stronghold," a *Figaro* headline screamed. Bernard Pons, the new conservative DOM-TOM minister, flew out to New Caledonia in April. In a forty-five-minute speech, he mentioned neither Kanaks nor Melanesians but railed against a "minority" that sought to impose its will. FLNKS called it a provocation; he replied, "You can't satisfy everyone."

Pisani's plan for independence-association was scrapped. Instead, Pons proposed a referendum on self-determination in 1987, with Kanaks and Caldoches voting. He undercut the four assemblies, giving budgetary power to a viceroy from Paris. And he reversed Kanak land tenure measures "so limited space could be put to best use." His goal was economic development, not institutional change. France would bring in about $55 million to prime the pump.

FLNKS militants loosened their ties to Libya. The spasm of violence had passed, but tension remained. Tjibaou worried over a French military build-up; he smelled Algeria. The Pons plan, he said, "only confirms what the Algerians have told me: 'Never trust the French, they are all liars.'"

He added: "To speak of marines and paratroopers, that is the permanent colonial mentality. France would always be the apostle of Good bringing light to the savages. Perhaps people will only move from this thinking when there are deaths, like in Algeria. It is a shame."

POLYNESIA watched New Caledonia closely. But a domino would have to fall hard to make waves 3,600 miles away in Tahiti. The societies and situations are different. There is ferment on Tahiti, the urban center of paradise. Seventeen separatists were arrested in late 1985 for skirmishing with police and burning a building. In-dependence-minded parties poll up to 15 percent in some elections. In 1986, Oscar Temanu's Tavini Huiraatira No Porinetia won two territorial legislature seats, the first for an independence party in twenty-eight years.

But Polynesians mostly shrug at the idea of driving out France. *Indépendantistes* are scattered among 166,800 inhabitants spread on 130 islands over 1.5 million square miles, an area larger than Western Europe. The islands' main resources are France itself and the CEP, the Centre d'Expérimentations du Pacifique. Paris spends fifty million dollars a year subsidizing the territory.

In places, Polynesia still qualifies as paradise. One morning I stood among the hibiscus in a Mooréa cove and watched an old four-master under full sail appear from the mists and tack in toward me over the reefs. It was Captain Bligh, back for more breadfruit. Actually, it was the Spanish navy on a training sail. But only a calendar could have identified the century.

But along with the lush splendor that captured Gauguin are beaches closed by pollution, parking meters, Big Burgers, video arcades and smog, club sandwiches and Club Meds. And on the palm-fanned atoll of Mururoa, paradise is lost completely.

MURUROA MEANS "place of the big secret." It houses 3,000 French specialists and legionnaires, all men but for a score of women. A plant desalts drinking water; just in case, the navy brings in 1,500 gallons of mineral water a day. Testing is done in holes bored underwater, down to 1,200 meters, in the basalt of a dead volcano. No one is ever blown up watching them, French officials like to say. But that is not the problem.

Visiting teams of scientists from New Zealand, Australia, and New Guinea found that humans were exposed to less radiation in Mururoa than in Paris. But they could not assure themselves about the eventual risk of leaks. They had to depend on French statistics, largely controlled by the military, to measure medical effects. Some areas were banned to them, and they were not allowed to witness an actual test.

A Greenpeace briefing paper noted that a bomb exploded in 1979 halfway down an 800-meter shaft, causing a local tidal wave. "Some observers" believe radioactive tritium contaminated the sea, Greenpeace said. In 1981, the *Guardian* quoted "authoritative reports" that radioactive material had been leaking for years through a crack fifteen to nineteen inches wide and a half-mile long. A storm in 1981 dispersed some plutonium into the lagoon, according to Greenpeace. And, the paper adds, scientists worry that each new blast weakens the basalt formations, increasing chances for some future catastrophe.

French specialists deny that any danger exists and discount the possibility of any leak before at least 500 years. Their safety record is impeccable, they argue.

Not everyone agrees. In 1961, the minister of overseas territories, Louis Tacquinet, promised that "no nuclear tests will ever be made by France in the Pacific Ocean." By 1963, the Foreign Legion began occupying the atoll. The Commissariat à l'Energie Atomique assured that "not a single particle of radioactive fallout will ever reach an inhabited island." Scientists promised that tests would take place only when the winds were blowing the other way. De Gaulle went to see the first atmospheric test in May 1966. He was late arriving, and the winds had changed. According to Greenpeace, he demanded that the test take place anyway; he was busy. As a result, a 120-kiloton blast dusted traces of fallout as far as Western Samoa, 1,800 miles downwind.

Nagging questions arise, such as the letter from Mayor Lucas Paeamara on Mangareva, a simple plea for someone to come look at the worrisome rates of cancer and infant deformities among his 582 people. Mangareva, 260 miles from Mururoa, is the closest inhabited atoll. It suffers from Ciguatera disease, traced to eating fish that feed on damaged coral. It causes unbearable itching. The people had to cut out fish, their staple. Paeamara blamed no one, but he hoped someone would come look. A planeload of French journalists came out from Tahiti six weeks later. They focused on the Ciguatera which, experts said, had nothing to do with *la Bombe*. One headline: "It itches but it doesn't glow."

Alan Rusbridger of the *Guardian* spoke to John Doom of the Polynesian Protestant Church who has been studying cancer problems. "We can only trust our own observations that more and more people are sick now—cancers, leukemias, all sorts. The problem is getting the proof."

Oscar Temara, mayor of the Papeete suburb of Faaa, said, "I have seen a lot of people dying of cancer in recent years. . . . But nobody can prove anything."

Among other things, Greenpeace was after proof. Each year, its tiny flotilla pushed the French limits, not only protesting nuclear tests but also bringing back water and mineral samples for analysis. Who knows, the French worry each year, what Greenpeace might find or concoct? France was shifting into a new nuclear generation. The M4 submarine missile needed a new 150-kiloton warhead. And there was the Hades missile. Besides, it was enough that other governments butted in. Greenpeace was a ragged band of *écolos* telling Paris to test its devices in Montpellier, not Mururoa. France is not anxious for advice on what it should do on French territory.

For twelve years, Greenpeace had come back each year. Once the French rammed them. Greenpeace chairman David McTaggart nearly lost an eye in a savage beating that embarrassed the government. Greenpeace was not just a pain in the ass; it was a threat to the *rayonnement* of France.

South Pacific support for Greenpeace seemed to grow each year, and trouble in Kanaky made matters worse. Mitterrand warned of "exterior appetites" and said, "France must preserve in this distant region . . . a position which it must not lose." To ensure that his subtlety was not lost on the Anglo-Saxons, he added, "If natives no longer pose a problem in Australia . . . it is because they have been killed off. That is not the way chosen by France."

On July 10, 1985, the tension exploded, literally. Two underwater charges tore a six-by-eight-foot gash in the hull of the *Rainbow Warrior* in Auckland harbor. The fourteen-man crew was making their last preparations before steaming toward Mururoa. At the first explosion, Fernando Pereira, chief engineer and photographer, raced below for his cameras. The second blast killed him. The 150-foot trawler sank like a stone.

Only by chance, five crew members decided at the last moment to sleep in town. The blasts destroyed their bunks. An hour before the attack, eight to ten people were meeting below decks in the fish hold.

"Who Is Making War on Greenpeace?" asked a large black *Libération* headline. New Zealand prime minister David Lange called the bombing "a major criminal act" with "political and terrorist implications. . . . Greenpeace has millions of friends and a few dozen enemies." He named no names.

France recorded its outrage. Environment minister Huguette Bouchardeau expressed sympathy for the crew. The French embassy in Wellington issued a condolence statement: "It would be terrible if a criminal act was at the origin of the double explosion and the death of a man." Charles Montan, political counselor, said, "France was absolutely not responsible. The French government does not act in this manner with opposing parties." France had not been concerned about the impending protest, he said, because Greenpeace had promised to respect international law.

A Greenpeace spokesman noted only that the sinking would save France a lot of trouble, since the fleet could not sail without the *Rainbow*. McTaggart said later that he did not immediately suspect the French: "I did not think they could be that stupid."

Within three days, police arrested a French couple with false Swiss passports on an extended honeymoon in the New Zealand winter. Allowed one call, they rang 846-8790 in Paris, a panic number of the Direction Générale de la Sécurité Extérieure. Police traced the number through Interpol, situated just outside Paris. Interpol went to the French police. Within five days of the explosion, the international police network implicated five French counterintelligence agents.[1] Police told the Interior Ministry, which, it is believed, told the Elysée. No one, of course, told reporters. New Zealand police continued searching out the missing pieces, and French authorities feigned ignorance.

Two weeks later, the French weekly *VSD* carried a full-page photo of the arrested woman: big round plastic glasses, Audrey Hepburn hair, towel clutched to her face with both hands. Its story began like the Gérard de Villiers thrillers sold by the stack in any French airport:

A fogless *quai* in the port of Auckland. With a cliff at the end of the jetty. Above, there are a few little houses and a large white building. A trawler the color of night, the *Rainbow Warrior* is attached to the dock like a goat to its stake. A solid boat, decorated with a white bird, that no longer smells of mackerel since the ecologists of Greenpeace decided to make it the flagship of their protest campaign. *Rainbow* is there when it is necessary to save whales, baby seals. . . .

A headline read: "Who is Sylvie-Claire Turenge, arrested after the attack of the ecologists' boat? Neither Swiss nor a teacher, as her passport says, but, according to the British, a French secret service officer with the rank of captain. . . ."

And at the top, in huge black letters, the label that would obsess the French press for the next two months: *l'affaire Greenpeace.*

L'Evénement du Jeudi broke the same story. It said officials feared that Greenpeace would spy on a secret airfield France built to back up the U.S. space shuttle program. *VSD* said that Greenpeace had special gear to measure the force of France's neutron bomb. Privately, experts laughed off both ideas. More likely, the French were just exasperated by the yearly hassle, especially since they were testing a new generation of warheads. The *Rainbow Warrior* might have put small boats ashore. France could have used more conventional—and honorable—means, some suggested. But McTaggart told *Le Monde,* "We were getting more dangerous. This year, we had a transmitter that could send satellite photos. Pictures of French sailors beating up on Greenpeace people could be very embarrassing."

The details were enticing. A mysterious yacht, *L'Ouvéa,* disappeared in the Pacific. The French doctor who chartered it had gone to ground in Dieppe. A pleasant-looking French woman ecologist, after cozying up to Greenpeace, had slipped off to Tel Aviv. An old deputy of Bob Denard's, a mercenary wholesaler named René Dulac, had recruited thugs for the mission. Someone left behind a Zodiac, a French-made rubber dinghy, and French diving gear. The accused couple was picked up when they returned a rented van they had used ostentatiously around the port.

It seemed more like the work of the Katzenjammer Kids under Inspector Clouseau than an operation worthy of France. All that was missing, one agent grumbled in Paris, was a beret, a *baguette,* and a bottle of Beaujolais.

Quickly, insiders with axes to grind helped reporters chop away the underbrush. Individuals followed their own scruples. If the original target was Greenpeace, some also took a whack at rival secret agents, the British, the Socialists, and Mitterrand himself.

The French press tried out investigative reporting with mixed results. Facts appeared, changed, receded, and surfaced again. *Le Canard Enchaîné* broke some new ground, as usual, but it revealed the Turenges' true identity incorrectly. *Le Point* suggested that the missing *Ouvéa* crew was hiding in the Gabonese presidential guard. *VSD,* boasting later about its scoop, quietly corrected Madame Turenge's name to Sophie and named her Françoise Prieur. Then she was Captain Dominique Prieur. A small slip. But *VSD* had also linked the operation squarely to senior Elysée aides, and the government filed suit. The magazine admitted casually that a source had mixed up a date—two key people had met after the operation and not before—but its story stood.

In the end, France admitted responsibility but gave no details. The arrested couple pleaded guilty to manslaughter, cheating the curious out of a trial. Newspapers accused Mitterrand of lying and covering up the facts. This was *Warrior* gate. Or Waterloogate. Or Watergaffe. Or Underwatergate. But the bang ended in a quiet whimper. The French, who never understood how the Americans could toss aside a perfectly good president over a minor scandal, took a different approach.

Watergate was abuse of internal espionage and a coverup; in the end, a president fell. *Warrior* gate was foreign espionage in a friendly nation, with an innocent victim and a sunken ship; in the end, reporters noted, French secret police were able to increase fivefold their wiretaps on political opponents and civil servants of questioned loyalty.

Some questions remained unanswered, such as who did it, and why? No one established what Mitterand knew, or when he learned it. When the trail grew close, people stopped asking questions. France appeared callous, bumbling, and deceitful. But the ship of state steamed on, the whole business amounting to a hard thump in the hull from floating debris. American columnist William Pfaff wrote:

> Nobody wanted it to become a French Watergate. The reason would seem to be a sense of national vulnerability, outweighing

partisan interest in the government's humiliation. The United States could go to the bitter end in the Watergate affair, driving Richard Nixon out of the White House, because Americans believe that the United States is invulnerable. No one considered the costs of pursuing an abstract justice to whatever end. This is a luxury which, it seems, the French collectively concluded they cannot afford.

Authorities searched the *Ouvéa* at Norfolk Island, but Australian law did not allow the crew to be held without charge until New Zealand detectives and police chemists could get there. The yacht headed for Noumea and disappeared forever. A ranking official in a past government remarked bitterly, at the end, "At first I thought the press had grown intoxicated by a Watergate role and would follow this to the end. But then I realized it was a *coup monté*— a setup—like everything else."

Le Monde split hairs. In Watergate, Nixon's goal was personal; in *l'affaire Greenpeace,* whatever French officials did, even if it was "stupid and criminal," was meant in the interest of the state. The entire episode, including that explanation, said a great deal about France.

Only after the story broke did Mitterrand order a rigorous investigation of the "criminal and absurd" incident. He asked Bernard Tricot, a trusted aide of de Gaulle, to issue a report. Tricot had a drawback: *tricoter* means "to knit" in French, and few commentators would resist the pun. The DGSE, nicknamed *la Piscine* after the public pool across from its imposing headquarters, was already the butt of ridicule.

Defense Minister Charles Hernu, responsible for the DGSE, told reporters, "I have a clear conscience. My position is clear: I want all the truth to be known."

Awaiting the official word, reporters dug hard. They retraced DGSE agents' steps. The Turenges reached Auckland on June 22 and went north. At the Beachcomber Hotel in Paihia, the honeymooners slept in separate beds and gave a Paris address. *L'Ouvéa,* meanwhile, pitched up there from New Caledonia, in difficult water and bad weather. The crew filled a page in the guest book of a local pizzeria. The captain, Raymond Velche, rented a Ford van and left a roll of

electric bomb wire inside. He bought a pair of New Balance running shoes which left incriminating tracks. Other purchases aroused
the suspicions of a local ship chandler. The Turenges were seen again
on July 10. Two hours before the blast, yacht club guards saw a
frogman ditch the Zodiac and climb into their camper.

Major Alain Mafart—Turenge—would complain later about
nosy islanders who spied on suspicious characters.

The couple would have gotten away in the end except that they
waited around a half hour for a small refund on their rented van.
Police found on them clumsily altered receipts—obviously for pad-
ding an expense account—which further weakened their flimsy
honeymoon cover.

The mysterious mole was unmasked. Frédérique Bonlieu—Lieutenant Christine Cabon—had infiltrated Greenpeace and staked out
the trails. Within a month, New Zealand police had 1,000 pieces of
evidence against the French agents.

Three New Zealand detectives came to Paris and got nowhere.
Opposition senator (and future interior minister) Charles Pasqua
complained, "This is shameful. How long will we tolerate this
unacceptable New Zealand interference on our territory?" Another
politician demanded an end to meddling into services meant to
assure the security and independence of France.

Greenpeace, meanwhile, said it was not giving up. The 200-foot
tug *Greenpeace* was diverted from Antarctica to Mururoa to join a
ketch, the *Vega,* and two other boats. Mitterrand ordered the navy
to keep them out of French waters, with force if necessary.

Libération put it, "The hour is grim in the gutters of the Republic: *petit pipi* threatens to become *grand caca."* Immediately afterward, the *caca* hit the *ventilateur.*

Tricot produced twenty-nine pages on August 26, after seventeen
days of investigation. He found that neither the government nor the
DGSE had given any order to sabotage the *Rainbow Warrior;* six
DGSE agents had gone to New Zealand only to spy on Greenpeace,
with the approval of the Elysée; no clues suggested who sank the
boat or why; he believed that all witnesses had told him the truth.
He said Mitterrand's military chief of staff, General Jean Saulnier,
had approved the expenses, estimated by other sources at about
$225,000. But the money was only for spying. The saboteurs, Tricot

said, might be "isolated men, moved mainly by political passion, or rather one might suspect others' secret services." In sum, France was blameless.

With a flourish of style, he added that the French agents did their assigned job well. "I believe to have understood, but this applies of course only to the bachelors, that our compatriots applied a sustained attention to the feminine sector of the population."

The *Libération* headline was "Tricot Washes Whiter." Editor Serge July suggested that Tricot might be the Lewis Carroll of French espionage. Alain Madelin of the UDF said, "Tricot takes the French for imbeciles." Prime Minister Lange observed that the report was too transparent to be called a whitewash. He said spying alone was a grave violation of international behavior. And he was angry that only Tricot was given access to three men wanted for murder in Auckland. The *New Zealand Herald* added that if splashed with all the perfume in Provence, the scandal would still smell like a skunk.

Tricot acknowledged in interviews that witnesses might have lied to him.

The next day, Fabius asked Hernu to correct "substantial failings" in the DGSE. He asked New Zealand to provide "proof" against the French agents. And he announced a tighter legislative control over French secret services, saying,

> The identification of the culprits remains to be established. We hope that New Zealand authorities reach the truth as quickly as possible. Our condemnation is not, as one has sometimes heard, against the poor execution of a dubious project; it is an absolute condemnation of a criminal act. The guilty, whoever they are, must answer for this crime.

Opposition response was muted. "My country, right or wrong," said Giscard d'Estaing. (*Le Monde* identified that as "a British formula whose author is a certain Steven Decatur, an American major who lived between 1779 and 1820." A *Monde* reader later recalled how the rest went: "Right or wrong, my country. If it is right, keep it right. If it is wrong, make it right.")

Greenpeace had a few questions. Why five combat divers for an information mission? Why did the agents leave before Greenpeace sailed and abandon their photos on the *Ouvéa?* Why did the *Ouvéa* leave on July 9, in terrible weather, through dangerous water, with reported structural damage?

Defense Ministry officials told selected journalists it was the British; DGSE agents had bought their Zodiac at Barnet Marine in London. French papers said the owner was a former British spy who warned his friends who, in turn, tipped the New Zealanders. The owner himself said he confirmed to police that a Frenchman bought the boat after officers traced it back to him from its markings. The Foreign Office was upset. And the *Daily Mail* dismissed the whole thing as "Bonapartist insolence."

The DGSE liked best the hypothesis of *Le Soir* in Brussels: Greenpeace did it themselves to make the French look bad.

A *Sofres* poll suggested that only a third of France was interested in *l'affaire Greenpeace.* But the press kept up the pressure. French correspondents covered the New Zealand courts. In France, a *juge d'instruction* builds a dossier against a suspect, combining the role of police, prosecutor, and judge. People stay locked up until this is ready, even if it takes years. The French had trouble with curious points of Anglo-Saxon law, notably that suspects answer only for what is proven against them in court, and are considered innocent until then. Or that courts, diplomacy, and executive decisions are kept separate.

And the press reported the color. Florence Décamp of *Libération,* who referred five times to the "deposition earing," ridiculed the New Zealanders' spelling of French dishes which continued to sell like hot croissants. She was also not fond of the frog legs wrapped in apricot with Camembert sauce. Another reporter was amazed that people bought newspapers by leaving money in an open box.

The papers noted international hostility and scorn. In West Germany, Greenpeace membership rocketed. "In no other country is the idea of *raison d'Etat* so widely held as in France," said Werner Holzer, editor of *Frankfurter Rundschau.* The French public, more revolted by the clumsiness of their spies than the act itself, banded together to cover an inexcusable act, he said, "as if France could never lose."

In Paris, a steady stream of leaks continued, but the Tricot report stayed afloat. Then Mitterrand seized the initiative. On September 12, he climbed onto a Concorde and flew to Mururoa. He established a center for advanced French studies in the Pacific, and he invited heads of government in the region to come watch the tests. Australian prime minister Bob Hawke replied that if Mitterrand was so interested in proving the tests' safety, he should "have those absolutely safe tests in metropolitan France."

Lange was also hostile. He said the sabotage was akin to an act of war. He called the Quai d'Orsay pompous for summoning his ambassador to demand fair treatment for the Turenges under international law. The French consulate had not even contacted the couple, Lange said.

Mitterrand asked Lange to cease his "unfounded accusations" against France. But no sooner had the president returned to Paris than *Le Monde* fired its broadside. It reported on September 18 that a third team, two French navy divers apart from the Turenges and the *Ouvéa* crew, had sunk the vessel. They had been trained at the secret base at Aspretto, in Corsica, where Mafart had been an instructor. Hernu, or his top aides, ordered the mission, or at least knew about it. *Le Monde* used the conditional tense so favored by French reporters: "might have sunk" or "should have sunk." That was good enough. *Le Canard Enchaîné* had already broken the "third team" story. Now it was confirmed by the archbishop of the French press.

Edwy Plenel revealed in *Le Monde* the Turenges' last mistake. They rang the DGSE, and New Zealand police listened in on an extension. When Interpol went to the French police to trace the number, Interior Minister Pierre Joxe was informed. And, *Le Monde* said, he told Mitterrand about July 18, a week after the explosion.

The weekly *L'Express* substantiated the account. It said that Mitterrand was advised of French involvement on July 17, and the president demanded the details. According to *L'Express,* senior military people, possibly Hernu, lied to him at least until August 7. General Saulnier had "signed the budget estimate" on the operation beforehand, *L'Express* said, adding that such expenditures would have to be approved by the defense minister as well as a ranking Elysée official.

Libération weighed in with another huge headline: *"Mensonges."*

Lies. Others followed. At a stormy cabinet session, Mitterrand demanded of Hernu, his friend for thirty years: *"Je veux savoir."* I want to know.

Among French officialdom, passing the franc was easy enough. The affair began with a memo from Admiral Henri Fages, commander at Mururoa. He said France had to *anticiper* Greenpeace. When the memo, moving from Hernu's office through channels, reached the DGSE high command, that word was underlined twice. That is one of those subtleties of French: *anticiper* can simply mean anticipate, as in "be prepared." Like the English equivalent, it can mean forestall. But it can also mean: prevent, at any cost.

On September 18, Hernu insisted that no one under his command had received orders to sabotage the *Rainbow Warrior.* He denounced "rumor, insinuation, and slander" and said, "I know that in this affair, in the shadows, there is malignancy, and that forces me to bring this to light." The next day, Mitterrand ordered Fabius to clean house. "This cannot last," he wrote. The day after that, Fabius asked Hernu for his resignation. The DGSE chief, Admiral Pierre Lacoste, refused to name the French agents sent to New Zealand; he was fired. And on Sunday, September 22, Fabius addressed the nation in a funereal monotone:

> The new Minister of Defense has informed me of the first conclusions of [his] investigation. . . . It was agents of the DGSE who sank this boat. They acted under orders. This truth was hidden from Counselor Tricot. . . . The [agents] evidently must be cleared of blame because it would be inacceptable to expose military people who must obey orders and who have sometimes in the past accomplished very dangerous missions for our country. *Mesdames et messieurs,* the truth of this affair is cruel but it is important that I am engaged in assuring that it is totally and clearly established.

Reaction was harsh. Lange called it a sordid act of state-backed terrorism. Pfaff wrote:

> What official with the slightest sense of political, or of human, realities could possibly have believed that to sink a Greenpeace

ship would deter the anti-nuclear movement? To sink the boat was to present . . . a gold-plated public relations gift. To do it in such a way that a man was killed was worse. To tell convoluted lies about it all was simply suicidal.

The loss of Hernu crippled Mitterrand, who had counted on his prestige with the right to help in the March legislative elections. For the president, it was also a tragic personal loss. His goodbye was touching, but it was unavoidable.

In a television interview, Fabius laid the blame squarely on Hernu and Lacoste. He—and certainly the president—was innocent. "My conviction is that the responsibility was at their level," he said. "In a democracy like ours, the responsibility rests at the political level, that is, the minister."

Fabius was roasted for kicking a fallen scapegoat. Why a minister and not the prime minister? some editorialists asked. One wondered about the value of the convictions of a prime minister in peril. Most agreed that Hernu simply wore the hat, as the French say. "Hernu Sacrificed," *Libération* put it in heavy type. What about Saulnier and the president's inner circle? With the government's credibility near zero, the truth was hard to find. Reporters learned that the new defense minister, Paul Quilès, found vital documents missing. Lacoste threatened to reveal embarrassing details if his former men were implicated, another report said.

"Democracy supposes transparency in public affairs, authority and responsibility," wrote Max Gallo, editor of *Le Matin* and Mitterrand's former spokesman. The right-wing *Le Figaro* and the radio station Europe 1 reported that Fabius had known the details since July 17. *Figaro* persisted: Mitterrand had to have known.

"This is not a government," fumed François Léotard, an opposition leader (and minister of culture in 1986), "this is the Raft of the Medusa." French political crises are at least elegant. He referred to the Géricault painting in the Louvre showing frantic shipwrecked passengers and crew members scrambling over the dead for a place on a life raft.

But the case was closed. "There are no government lies," an Elysée spokesman announced. Five military people were arrested for leaking secrets to the press. French officials told New Zealand they regretted that the sinking had damaged their relations, but they avoided a full apology. Nor did they promise to punish any agents. A month earlier, Fabius had promised legal action if it appeared that Frenchmen were involved.

Within a week, the new director of the DGSE, General René Imbot, announced that he had sawn off all rotten branches. A Foreign Legion veteran, sixty and hard-minded, he declared he had crushed a sinister plot to destroy French secret services. Now, he said, the DGSE was "bolted shut" and above reproach.

Among the tide of letters to *Le Monde* was one from Colonel Trinquier, the former legionnaire and Congo mercenary: "France is not America where the press can launch a new Watergate-type affair. The mass of French people, all political nuances combined, remains patriotic and knows by instinct where the real interests of our country lie."

Pfaff accurately gauged public reaction.

France is a cynical nation where international politics are concerned. The crime, in French eyes, is that those responsible have made France look ridiculous before the world. They have made France seem incompetent and mendacious; and this is unforgivable.

About then, Bernard Tapie was a guest on *"Sept sur Sept,"* a Sunday evening television program on which public figures comment on the news. Tapie, who made millions buying up failing companies and steamrolling them into the black, is one French ideal: an amateur boxer and singer with Rambo frown lines, a *bon vivant,* rich and pushy, brimming with style and conviction. He put it this way:

It is unimaginable, the disproportion between the event and the reaction that followed. . . . I am proud to be French, to belong among the five most powerful countries in the world, and I am ashamed to have a secret service incapable of carrying out this sort of operation. I always believe in results. If as one of the five most powerful nations, we haven't got people who can sink a boat without everyone knowing about it, we are really the bottom.

Then they tell me it might have been on purpose; that is even worse. . . . And I am ashamed at all these rats who come out of their holes to feed on this without giving a damn about its effect abroad. To show the government as liars, poltroons. Even if it is true, the honor of France is at stake. There must be a measure of *pudeur* [decency]. They don't have the right to make us look like a country governed by jerks simply because they might win three more percentage points.

But soon enough, Hernu emerged a hero. He received thunderous applause at the Socialist convention in Toulouse and headed the list of candidates for the Rhône district. Mitterrand received Mikhail Gorbachev in Paris before the Geneva summit, and appeared once again like a president of France.

Greenpeace went to Mururoa as promised; the French kept them clear of the tests, as threatened. The *Greenpeace,* stricken with a faulty generator, was repaired by two French technicians; the boat was banned from Tahiti. The navy boarded the *Vega* and turned it around, but no one was roughed up. The sailors promised to bring champagne the next time. On October 25, the French exploded yet another nuclear device. "The sovereignty of France is not open to discussion," Fabius said, no longer on the defensive. "The nuclear tests are necessary to us. We will conduct them as other countries do."

The thirty-eight-minute trial on November 4 brought one last flurry. Prosecutor David Morris could not prove that Mafart and Prieur placed explosives on the hull. Although Mitterrand and Fabius had each called the act "criminal" and promised that the guilty would pay, France would not deliver the four key suspects or answer vital questions. As a result, the murder charge was dropped to manslaughter. ("Man's laughter," *Le Monde* misspelled it inadvertently.) Both defendants pleaded guilty. The French claimed a victory.

Le Figaro reported snidely: "In English, one would call this brutally a deal. Almost a contract. In French, one would say a tacit accord, a compromise, a consensus." Conviction would be followed by expulsion within weeks, if not days, the paper said. France would quietly compensate New Zealand. "Looks like we'll be eating a lot more lamb chops," remarked one radio commentator.

Libération, in an editorial, was ironic:

> At the sunset of this serial, at times *rocambolesque,* sickening or sordid, one doesn't know whether to heave a sigh of relief—all's well that ends well—or be contented with writing off the list of fallen as settlement: a minister, a few officers. . . . In the end, a lot of people for a simple Portuguese photographer. But wasn't he the only sticking point in the whole affair?

The word was that France would help New Zealand sell dairy products and lamb in the European Economic Community. "Butter and *gigot* for spies," Michel Rocard, the Socialist leader, was quoted.

Lang was furious:

> They are not for sale. The question of a plea is a matter for the solicitor-general. The system of justice in this country is not a matter of convenience for the government. It is a system of justice. That is why they are not for sale. . . . This is a process of law, not for sordid haggling, selling of prisoners.

Chief Justice Sir Ronald Davison echoed his irritation: "People who come to this country and commit terrorist activities cannot expect to have a short holiday at the expense of our government and return home heroes."

Most French commentators snickered. When New Zealand asked for damages to cover the enormous cost of investigation and trial, French papers called it "ransom."

Prieur and Mafart were each sentenced to ten years in prison. Contrary to expectations in Paris, they were not home for Christmas.

By then, the world had lost interest. Many people never paid much attention, like the American schoolkid interviewed on French television who confused the *Rainbow Warrior* with the *Titanic.* French teachers abroad did not insist on two of the universal words their language has produced: *chauvinisme* and *sabotage.* The U.S.

government never did work up to a condemnation. Vice President George Bush, heading a study group on terrorism, would not comment. In the United Nations, U.S. ambassador Jeane Kirkpatrick said the act was obviously not terrorism since France clearly did not intend to "kill, maim, or torture" anyone.

Paris-Match offered yet another scoop in early 1986: the third team was deliberate disinformation; the *Ouvéa* crew sank the *Rainbow Warrior*. Yawn.

In New Zealand, people still walked around displaying the slogan "You Can't Sink a Rainbow." But in France, where *l'affaire Greenpeace* quietly died, the Cartesian method required more proof of that than a lapel button.

Two months after the Turenge trial, Fabius told correspondents that negotiations were frozen because New Zealand insisted on holding French citizens. I asked him if *l'affaire Greenpeace* would have an impact on the crucial March legislative elections. "No," he replied. "I don't think so." He was right.

But nagging concerns remained. State agents had threatened to reveal damning secrets if their colleagues were unmasked. Lacoste refused to give his ministers operational details, saying his "duty" prevented it. He said the order came from a "political authority," presumably a minister. No one was punished. Jean François-Poncet, foreign minister under Giscard d'Estaing, said, "No minister has the right to mislead the president." If *Le Monde* was correct that Hernu knew, "This is not a matter for resignation, but a case of treason."

Other secret excesses were scrutinized at least in half light. Magazines reported that Yves Bonnet had been forced to resign as head of the DST because he resisted political pressure to increase wiretapping and smear writers who annoyed authorities. For a while, the ugly DGSE building evoked tourist curiosity.

The key questions remained unanswered. Who gave the order? Who knew? André Fontaine, editor of *Le Monde,* worried that no one had the courage to take responsibility. "Too many people who might have been responsible acted like the schoolchild caught in the act who points to his friend and says, 'It wasn't me, it was him.' " A government in such a situation cannot exercise serious controls; he called it terrifying to hear a president say he learned of his agents' excesses from the newspapers. That, Fontaine said, could undermine confidence between the army and the state, or shatter the national consensus over nuclear dissuasion.

At one point, Lange touched a raw nerve: "If there is one little thing ticking away for France in the issue, it is the corruption of civilized standards."

Other condemnations stung as much from their source as their content. *South* magazine, favored in the Third World circles France likes to frequent, rubbed salt in the wound. And one editorial observed: "This betrays a degree of paranoia, ruthlessness and cynicism which is staggering. It splashes blood on innocent hands. It ranks as one of the most execrable of dirty tricks in recent times." That was the *Cape Times* of Cape Town, a paper more accustomed to attacking the South African government which Fabius had just denounced for state terrorism.

In a major French poll, half the respondents said that a country like France had no right to use such means. Sociologist Alain Touraine noted that the French were prone to shrug off *l'affaire Greenpeace* for reasons of state. It touched their ultimate umbrella, the independent nuclear force that assures their international political role. But, he said:

> It should have made us realize the profound degradation of our political life, which is dominated by a little *raison d'Etat* and a lot of social vacuum. Isn't it high time to renew the life and the dialogue of society and its actors to put the state and its perverse reason under examination?"

But at the height of the New Caledonia crisis, Jacques Chaban-Delmas, a Gaullist and former prime minister, a Resistance hero and stalwart of the political landscape, put the nuclear question in its French perspective:

> If France disappears in New Caledonia, Polynesia (and the test sites) will be next. . . . Your children will be poor little nonentities after the year 2000, because if France ceases to be a nuclear power, it ceases being any sort of power at all.

The whole business almost started again at Queen's Wharf in Auckland just before New Year's Eve, 1985. Customs inspectors found 5,500 rounds of ammunition and disassembled machine pistols hidden near the engines of the French freighter *Ile de Lumière*. Mercenaries were preparing to blast the Turenges out of prison, one New Zealand paper guessed. A judge thought differently. He fined the ship's cook, who admitted to having bought the munitions in Australia; he said he had planned to sell them to the highest bidder in New Caledonia. His captain laughed that off. The cook, settled in New Caledonia after a brief stretch in Chad, was an ardent anti-*indépendantiste,* he said. He was helping to stock the loyalist arms chest.

With some rue, the French recognized the 1,500-ton vessel. A few years earlier, the *Ile de Lumière* had been chartered by A Boat for Vietnam, a committee composed of Jean-Paul Sartre, Yves Montand, and Simone Signoret, among others. It was a hospital ship for the Vietnamese boat people.

The incident quickly faded, but not without some grumbling in Paris. A television commentator observed that inspectors only found the ammunition because of an extrathorough search; New Zealand was picking on France.

TO AN OUTSIDER in France, the aftermath of the *Rainbow Warrior* was nearly as astounding as the event itself. Mitterrand drew a clear line in a foreign policy statement: "No one can argue that France should diminish its surveillance of the atolls and renounce its tests on the strength of an act that does not morally engage our country."

New Zealand, somehow, had become the bad guy, and France was quietly boycotting its meat, fish and fruit until it released the two French citizens it was holding. Import licenses were refused without explanation; cargo was turned away as incorrectly labeled. Complaints to the French foreign and agriculture ministries brought no reply.

French television reported, briefly and offhandedly, that New Zealand courts issued arrest warrants for the *Ouvéa* crew.

"The French have a curious way of looking at things," Lange told

Le Monde in a discreetly placed interview. "We appreciate France's diversity, its sophistication, its qualities and its culture, but perhaps we are wrong."

He called it extraordinary that New Zealanders had been painted as abnormal Anglo-Saxon monsters. He said:

> This has became a matter of national pride, a political symbol, much more than a military imperative. France wants simply to buy back two prisoners who have pleaded guilty to murder. The sabotage can be easily presented as an act of international terrorism perpetrated with the support of a state, for political purposes. What New Zealanders have the most trouble understanding is that the French government, which at first denied any involvement and then condemned the act, promising to do all possible to punish the guilty, suddenly decided to turn around and change the status of the guilty to that of good, loyal soldiers following orders. I don't doubt they were, but for us, they are criminals.

He hoped, despite it all, "to maintain civilized relations between two countries."

The new government in Paris discreetly sought to freeze New Zealand butter and meat sales to the EEC. Negotiations broke down. New Zealand wanted reparations and France wanted back "the hostages." In May, authorities indemnified Pereira's family but not Greenpeace. Edouard Leclerc, the supermarket magnate, pushed a boycott of New Zealand products under the slogan, "Let's not be sheep." He decried "odious blackmail." (His gasoline-mogul brother, Michel, who had whipped up fury against Middle Eastern Arabs over oil prices, was otherwise occupied, sentenced to prison for fraud and abuse of confidence.)

With stone walls in France, New Zealand did not pursue investigations. Police and legal costs had already run deep into the millions. Lange acknowledged that many millions more in export earnings were at risk, but that was a price small nations had to pay for their sovereignty and dignity.

He told a BBC phone-in program in April, "We have no prisoners for sale, thank you very much." That, for most French commentators, meant the price was not yet high enough.

Hernu won his National Assembly seat easily and discussed the possibility of running for president in 1988. Just before the vote, he lunched with correspondents and shrugged off the affair. Why did France do it? The Pacific nations were ganging up on France. Wasn't it a little extreme? Every government defends its interests. How many take their quarrels to the *place publique?* That one stopped him. He smiled engagingly and replied: "Good question." Then he added: *"Oouuf,* whether this damaged France's image in the world, I'm not sure."

Later, I went to a demonstration demanding the release of French hostages in Lebanon. A speaker had said: "No cause is worth the taking of innocent lives." I mentioned this to a table of writers and intellectuals at a Paris dinner party that evening, and I brought up the *Rainbow Warrior.* "How can you make a comparison?" demanded one man, to general agreement. "France had no intention of killing anyone. That silly fool ran back for his cameras. He should have fled after the first warning blast." Here was the ultimate in French wrongfooting. Fernando Pereira had killed himself.

LOST BETWEEN Kanaky and *la Bombe* was a quiet mouse roar from independent Vanuatu, until 1980 called the New Hebrides. France and Britain ran it jointly by what they called a condominium; islanders called it the pandemonium. There were three governments: French, British, and local. Prisoners could pick their jails. British jails were nicer, but the French served wine. Britain seized the higher ground for the governor's residence. The French governor ran up a higher flagpole so the Tricolor could be the same height as the Union Jack.

At independence, a Presbyterian preacher named Walter Lini was elected prime minister. But in the northern island of Espíritu Santo, French planters and merchants backed Jimmy Stevens. He was defeated and jailed; 1,000 French were expelled from the island.

In 1983, after England fought its Falklands War, Vanuatu clashed with France over two tiny uninhabited islets off New Caledonia. It sent its entire navy: one yacht. Crisis was averted.

France and Britain struggle quietly here for influence. French aid, at nine million dollars a year, is slightly higher. Half the 3,000 whites in the capital of Port Vila are French, and the Alliance

Française works overtime to teach the language. Australians threaten
to tip the balance. But neither side makes waves. A "green letter"
from the government can expel a foreigner overnight.

GLOBAL strategists say that the Pacific is especially important to
France because of lost ground in Asia. Paris once dominated the
South China Sea, and its political influence bore heavily northward
to China and eastward to Japan. But French economic roots were
never deep in most of Asia.

Sudest-asie magazine quoted a French industrialist: "Our trade
with Asia is derisory. Our products are too expensive, our protec-
tionism is outrageous, and our industries are incapable of competition." The remark was made just after 1900.

By the time France was ejected from Indochina, its *rayonnement*
was a weak glow. "France is a ghost in this region," observed a
senior Singaporean official. France competes hard in Southeast Asia
but lags behind most industrial nations. In 1983, 12,100 French lived
in the region, the lowest number for any area of comparable size.

But French cultural residue is thick and rich. Marguerite Duras
writes with passion of her youth in Indochina. Edouard Axelrad
writes of the war. Sections of Left Bank Paris, redolent of *citronelle*
and *nuoc mam,* might be Cholon or Vientiane. Despite the long
American war, most Vietnamese, Cambodians, and Laotians see the
West through optics ground in France. When Truong Nhu Tang
went to Albania for the Viet Cong, he spoke in French.

Prince Sihanouk, deposed as ruler of Cambodia but figurehead
of an exile coalition government, remains close to France. He speaks
to Mitterrand often in his high-pitched and eloquent French. When
peace meetings collapsed, they were usually to have been held in
Paris. And when Sihanouk took diplomats inside the Cambodian
border in early 1985 to fete his coalition, the toasts were drunk in
champagne. Just before this, Foreign Minister Hun Sen of the Viet-
nam-dominated Cambodian government, on a "private" visit to
Paris, had described ties with France: "We have a proverb in Cambodia: if you cannot build a concrete bridge, you can always throw
across the river a bamboo walkway."

Vietnam bases few political decisions on sentiment. But in January 1985, Hanoi made a simple, cold gesture to France. Five Viet-

namese were condemned to death, accused of spying for China, Thailand, and the West. One was Mai Van Hanh, a retired Royal Air Maroc captain who took French citizenship after leaving Vietnam. Another was Tran Van Ba, who claimed to be French but had no proof from Paris. Fabius appealed for clemency for all. Mai Van Hanh and another man received life imprisonment; the other three were executed on schedule.

In China, France presses a slight advantage. The old French Club in Shanghai was torn down to make room for a Japanese hotel. But French telephones, textiles, Peugeots, profiteroles, engineering projects, and armaments move steadily into the Middle Kingdom. Thirty thousand French tourists a year visit China. Pierre Cardin led the way, but Yves Saint-Laurent dazzled the Chinese with a retrospective of his designs. "I think we have a mutual interest in simplicity," he said, adding that without Chinese silk, he likely would not be in business.

Ten leading Chinese cadres came to France to study public administration in 1985. "The French are teaching us method," one said. In Peking that year, Foreign Minister Roland Dumas happily heard the Chinese tell him France's world role was steadily growing. Five months later, he was even happier. The state enterprise Framatome had finally nailed down a contract to build an elaborate nuclear power plant near Canton.

To the east, France has joined the pack seeking a foothold in Japan. But the balance tilts in the other direction. At one point, so many Japanese video recorders flooded France that officials made importers clear them at the obscure customs post in Poitiers, where paperwork moved at a snail's pace.

To the west, in India, France pulled out all stops, evoking its old grandeur. Pondicherry was handed back in 1954. But Raymond Magry, in his seventies, still welcomes guests on the airy veranda of his Grand Hôtel d'Europe. He reminisced in 1985. "Imagine, when the French ships came in, the parties and grand balls, women in long dresses and generous décolletés, men in evening dress or braided uniform. . . . Right here, you had to see how everything shown like a thousand diamonds."

France suffered in India for selling nuclear technology to Pakistan, but not seriously. In January 1985, Indian papers splashed news about a spy ring that trafficked in documents wholesale, to the West and East. Ten Indian officials were involved, and three Frenchmen were implicated. A French military attaché was suddenly yanked back to Paris; it was for consultations, officials explained. Press reports said he was expelled. Two mysterious French businessmen fled the country. In India, that sort of affair could go either way. A billion dollars in arms deals, among other things, hung in the balance.

"They treated the French with velvet gloves; it was amazing how the Indians hushed it up and smoothed it over," a correspondent friend in Delhi told me later. "The newspapers talked about France, but not Rajiv Gandhi. In Parliament, it was always 'the foreign this' and 'the foreign that' with no names. If it had been the British or the Americans, it would have gone a lot differently."

Six months later, Gandhi ascended the Eiffel Tower with Mitterrand to inaugurate the Year of India in France. India, an emerging power and a Third World champion, was an attractive friend for France. And for India, tiptoeing twixt East and West, France was a natural ally.

"Your passion for liberty and reason, your contribution to the arts and good taste, the work of your thinkers, scientists and technologists cannot be easily matched or surpassed by any other nation," Gandhi said. Pondicherry had sheltered Indian freedom fighters, he recalled. And he noted:

> Victor Hugo, who died 100 years ago, has said, "I represent a party which does not yet exist: the party of revolution, civilization. This party will make the twentieth century." Perhaps not without significance, my party, the Indian National Congress, was born the year Hugo died.

On live television, elephants lumbered by the Trocadero. Dancers swayed to sitars. Ladies in saris dumped rose petals and a flask of Ganges water in the Seine. The water was brown. But the Indians signed a contract for French engineers to build twenty-seven purification plants along the Ganges for five billion francs. They also bought telephones, helicopters, and Airbuses.

The euphoria even survived *l'affaire Munna*.

Mohammed Munshi had come to Paris from Jaipur with Munna, the eight-year-old bear he had raised since it was two days old. Mitterrand welcomed Munna with an official pat on the head. When Gandhi left, bear and handler stayed to open an Indian restaurant on a barge in the shadow of the Eiffel Tower.

But the "Victor Hugo Brigade" did not like the ring in the bear's nose or the small cage in which he lived. One night a commando of French animal lovers chloroformed a watchman and bearnapped Munna. Two weeks later, police found the bear in a zoo. He was nearly dead, depressed without his master and disoriented without his ring. Reunited, Mohammed and Munna went home. Franco-Indian friendship lived on.

CHAPTER SEVENTEEN

Canada: A Few Acres of Snow

THE COLORS OF France snap in the North Atlantic winds over Place Charles de Gaulle, St. Pierre, just about where Cartier planted his flag in 1535. From the rocky little islands of St. Pierre and Miquelon, tucked away off the Newfoundland coast, France built the empire that spanned the St. Lawrence River and snaked down the Mississippi to New Orleans. Except for the nine times English gunboats seized the place—and the four times England deported all the residents and burned St. Pierre to the ground—the islands have been France's anchor in North America. Now they are all it has left.

For more than two centuries, France in North America has amounted to 60,000 raw and rocky acres, peopled by 6,100 descendants of cod fishermen from Brittany, Normandy, and the Basque country. Cartier today is just another name on the duty-free watches. St. Pierre and Miquelon is the oldest and smallest bit of overseas France. And it exhibits all the problems of keeping a sailing ship empire in a satellite age.

A Paris-appointed *préfet* represents France, and islanders elect assemblymen and senators. Two councils, with divided authority, make local decisions. Just like the Haute-Savoie, French officials like to say. That is not exactly true.

The blizzardy day I arrived, in 1985, a mob of fish packers seized the *préfet* by the armpits, frog-marched him along the frozen quai to his official launch, and ran him out of town. Gendarmes sat peaceably at headquarters, not even directing traffic around the tumult. The issue at hand was who got to unload a new factory trawler when it put into port six times a year. But no one missed the wider significance.

France has worried over its American holdings for nearly five centuries. Even after Napoléon sold off Louisiana, passionate voices rose in favor of a North Atlantic base. For strategic purposes, for trade, and for *rayonnement,* they argued, France belonged in North America. For 180 years, the last little French toehold has played a role surpassing its size.

ONLY THE MORE serious geography students have ever heard of the islands. A St. Pierrais in Paris was stung when a postal clerk asked a fortune to mail a package home. In St. Pierre, a *département,* domestic rates applied. But the clerk thought St. Pierre was in Greenland. I spent thirty-five minutes on the phone in New York trying to determine the direct-dialing code. Operators could not find St. Pierre. "Canada?" repeated one when I explained it was a French territory located within Canada. "What province?" Finally, a supervisor came on and announced, "It is a new country in Europe."

Getting there was harder still. Flights go from Halifax and St. John's, Newfoundland. In the summer, they are daily. But there is the fog; an overnight trip can take a week. In winter, flights are three times a week unless there is (and there usually is) too much icy wind. Ferries run sporadically from Newfoundland, but the port is a five-hour drive from the nearest airfield. Paris is never closer than two days away.

The town of St. Pierre is a tight cluster of shingled and wood-slat buildings, painted in yellows, reds, mauves, greens, blues, cheerful even under muddy ice. The old stone structures might be on the French north coast but for the lack of hedges, trees, or flowers. Merchants don't bother with the charming little signs of most French villages; everyone knows where he is. The Biarritz, a raucous, high-tech disco, is an unmarked little gray house. A shingle hangs outside Le Caveau, a Basque-flavored restaurant in a converted bank vault and rum-runner's warehouse, but winds tend to blow it down.

On narrow streets heading uphill, rough-hewn walls and foundations suggest permanence. But gales and fire prevent buildings from lasting long enough to age gracefully. St. Pierre's landmark is the dockside post office; with parrot's-beak gables and weathered old sidings, it is like nothing North American. The islands' features are bare rock, sandy beaches, and a few wind-ravaged trees.

Peugeots and Renaults crowd the few roads, but St. Pierre claims the world's oldest Ford agency, with uninterrupted sales and service since 1919. A hardware store is emblazoned "Affiliated with Handy Andy," pronounced Andy Andy. Cajun plink-plank flavors the music at the AIDs Bar in the Hôtel Ile de France, owned by an Algerian. In the Bar Le Relais, Eric Clapton is Living on Tulsa Time, and Freddy Fender sings in Spanish. Canadian quarters work interchangeably with francs in the video games. Snack bars sell "oignons rings."

Still, a quick sniff tells you it's France: warm croissants, Pernod, *sauce Béarnaise,* Joy. As everywhere else in France, the menus make the best of local specialties. Cod guts are *fraises de morue.*

On my flight in, among the bearded faces and battered parkas, I saw an impeccably shaved caricature of old France: gleaming gold-rim spectacles, burgundy silk tie, midnight-blue suit with a blue Legion of Merit ribbon in the lapel. Another was a butcher from La Rochelle, on his own mission to civilize. He was on loan to local butchers to teach them how to cut meat. "They do it like the Americans," he explained in a solemn tone, reflecting pity and disbelief. "With a saw."

The Catholic church, with its little stone steeple, dominates St. Pierre. Its influence is declining, residents say. But at the Biarritz, in full 2 A.M. liquefied debauchery, the disc jockey stopped to announce that a small cross had been found. The young woman most likely to win a wet T-shirt contest, with the widest wanton leer in the place, raced to reclaim it.

Downtown, a *pétanque* pitch sits just behind the Basque *fronton* court where players with little baskets slam handballs at unbelievable speed.

Above all, St. Pierre and Miquelon acts French.

I had a morning appointment with Gérard Lefèvre, the *préfet.* On the way, I stopped to see the head of Interpêche, the fish plant around which the islands turn. He was worried about a docker's strike, which paralyzed his exports. The dockers were fighting with his packers. Each claimed the right to unload the *Bretagne,* a newly commissioned factory ship on which the island depended. Interpêche was in danger of going under, he said. Without it, the only employer would be the government.

Then an aide rushed in and murmured something in his ear.

"You must excuse me," the director said. "All my workers have just left the plant to expel the prefect."

French overstatement, I thought. But just in case, I hurried over to the *Préfecture.*

Had the people who stormed the Bastille smelled like fish, what I found might have been a rerun in miniature of 1789. No one seemed about to lose his head, but there was the unmistakable scent of French revolution.

Crowds roiled outside the little wooden building. An angry few with a grievance were diluted by the curious, enjoying a break from life on an island where nothing ever happens. Inside, the rabble ruled. Men in parkas streaked with fish slime jammed the narrow hallway. Some joked and laughed; others spewed curses and smacked knuckles into calloused palms. In the dead of the North Atlantic winter, a *complexe d'Astérix.*

In the prefect's office, workers sprawled on upholstered chairs and on the floor. A loutish youth in a filthy knitted green wool hat thumbed through a coffee-table book. They tracked fish scales and muddy snow across the green carpet, pacing back and forth to the windows to shout to others below on the street.

Lefèvre, in a dark gray suit and bordeaux tie, sat stiffly behind his desk under a somber portrait of François Mitterrand. He affected interest in a sheaf of papers on the desk. From time to time, he gazed at nothing in particular, light glinting off his metal-rim glasses.

A hall door opened and a voice said, "Monsieur Rosenblum?"

An aide pulled me inside and closed the door. It, uh, did not seem, er, as if the *préfet* could keep his appointment. The aide was polite and controlled, but his fingertips fluttered like aspen leaves.

"I'm certain you won't think badly of St. Pierre because of this," he said. "It has its good side." He then outlined a few of them. But people grow excitable over small things, he explained. After all, unloading the *Bretagne* amounted to only twenty hours of work for twelve men, six times a year. Why all the fuss? "You see how they are here," he said. "Small things become important."

It was, of course, impossible that they would expel the prefect. It would blow over; they were just worked up. After all, he is the representative of France. He was trying to reach a compromise solution and all would end happily.

I asked why the gendarmes did not simply clear the building. No one was armed with so much as a codfish, and only a few dozen workers formed the kernel of protesters.

"Oh, no," he said. "Our twenty-five to thirty gendarmes are not the force necessary to hold back a civil outbreak of 100 people. What can we do?"

He shook my hand and urged, "I would advise you to treat this as an anecdote, not an event. It really doesn't mean anything."

In fact, it meant a great deal. Lefèvre was not only the personification of France, he was also the director of 1,000 civil servants on the islands—half the work force. (In Miquelon, the number of government workers per inhabitant is as high as fifty times that of French villages.) He also controlled French subsidies in a state where imports exceed exports by four to one. By one set of figures, France spends $4,200 a year per inhabitant.

I asked how much of the national budget was spent each year on St. Pierre and Miquelon. His answer was one I had heard often in Paris and around the empire: "We don't know, there are too many factors involved." Surely, I said, such calculations were made. "I suppose one could amuse oneself by doing that," he replied. "But we don't."

In the hallway, I asked for an explanation from an apparent leader, a tall young man, tough-looking in a stained green field jacket. He said it was plain that the fish packers were in the right. An earlier decree had spelled that out. But, he said, Lefèvre had been waiting for months to make a clear statement.

"He has to decide, and if he does not, he's gone on the plane to Halifax," the man told me. "*C'est tout.*"

Nothing changed for three hours. Then word came that the Halifax flight had been canceled because of bad weather.

"What now?" I asked the head fish packer.

"The runway is closed, not the sea. We'll use a boat. Or he can swim. We'll take him to the wharf in a wheel chair. But he's gone."

He was enjoying his role as spokesman until I asked his name. "We've seen too much crap in the papers for us to give any names," he said. This was a routine I had heard often enough in Paris but never in a town visited by reporters once a decade. I got his name from someone else, for the form, and then figured what the hell.

True to their word, at 2 P.M. the workers scooped Lefèvre out of his chair, pausing only long enough to let him put on a fur coat against the freezing wind. They hustled him down 300 yards of waterfront, across Place Charles de Gaulle, to the little ferry dock. For half an hour they stood guard as the launch, Petit Miquelon, idled in place. Finally, the boat cast off and putted ignominiously out of the harbor.

The préfet did not make the two-hour crossing to Canada as ordered. Instead, he made for the less populated island of Miquelon, to the north. He broadcast a victory statement, but his day was lost. Senator Marc Plantegenest, president of the elected General Council, took over negotiations. When the workers tried to push a point, he retorted, "I am not a préfet that runs for the plane every time I get a fright."

After much banging of tables and upturning of noses, the fishery workers scored their points. A commission from Paris reached a compromise that recognized the dockers' monopoly on cargo but let the fish plant crews load the containers on board. Lefèvre was summoned to Paris "for consultations." A few days later, he appeared on a list of prefects being reassigned "on a routine basis." No new post was immediately available.

The workers were delighted at imposing jungle rule on the island. Just in case, they took their precautions. They roughed up the cameraman of the government's television station and threatened to attack the newsroom if he did not relinquish his film. The threat proved empty but also needless; the camera was jarred and blocked constantly, and the footage was blurred. A gorilla in a mustache smacked me for taking pictures, and his buddies announced they would toss me into the thirty-three-degree water if I continued.

Later, the spokesman and his pals turned out to be fairly nice guys with selective memories for the facts of the preceding day. They explained their caution. In an earlier disturbance, the government used television film to identify workers who vandalized state property. "Now," announced one of the leaders, indignant, "they face prosecution." Did it occur to them that constitutional republics tended to impose accountability for public disorders? Or that marching down the street in broad daylight, shoving along a kidnapped French *préfet,* would not go unnoticed even if they decided to censor the press? It had, but they did not give a damn. The constitution is a point of principle and, as such, easily elbowed aside when self-interests intervene. It was only logical.

For islanders whose livelihoods depend on Interpeche, any solution that calmed tempers was a happy one. But reflections were bitter.

"There goes order, there goes the Republic," muttered a professional man at the edge of the crowd. "Any jerk can do anything he wants and no one will do anything about it."

A self-employed gentleman who spoke a lot of sense during my visit put it like this:

> The state is afraid to do anything, just like it was in New Caledonia. All it would take would be a few cans of tear gas, and everyone would go home, and there would be some respect for France. Instead, we have this. You watch, someone is going to get pushed in the harbor and frozen, or hit in the head by accident, and we will have violence. Now, with the Change, the local politicians will be able to do anything they want.

The Change was a step away from France—not far—engineered by local politicians and backed by an unofficial poll of voters who seemed to have little idea of what it meant. In early 1985, St. Pierre and Miquelon became a "territorial collective" rather than an overseas department. As a result, it was no longer part of the European Economic Community, and it could deal more freely in the dollar zone surrounding it. But some business leaders, Chamber of Commerce president Louis Hardy for one, saw little practical advantage. The main effect was reducing the power of *les mayous.*

Mayou, a corruption of an old word for carpetbagger, is the equivalent of *z'oreille* in a territory with only people of European stock. The *préfet,* for example, is one. There is no racial connotation.

But a *mayou* is an outsider in a society that would just as soon have its subsidies transferred by mail and not delivered in person.

The Change is a technical one, Georges Lemoine, minister of the overseas departments and territories, explained to me in Paris. "In St. Pierre and Miquelon, we have 6,000 fellow citizens who wish to live under the French flag. We will accommodate them. The cost is irrelevant."

But the new status places more decisions in the hands of the General Council. A lot of St. Pierrais are happier that way.

"We are a peaceful little community, with our own way of life," said Joseph Lehuenen, local historian and museum curator, whose gray lapels are festooned with the red ribbon of the Légion d'honneur. No propagandist, Lehuenen can recount from his prodigious memory every black day of the islands' past.

"They call the coast off Miquelon and Langlade the graveyard of the Atlantic," he said with some pride. Until politely sidetracked, he had launched on a recap of each of the 675 shipwrecks in local waters since 1790.

I asked him about murders. He leaped to a pile of dog-eared notebooks and recited from one marked "1982": ". . . a forty-one-year-old Basque descendant, Edouard Etchéverria, was found dead, stabbed by twelve knife wounds. . . ." If you don't count the 1929 shooting of a Norwegian sailor by an American rum runner, it was the only killing of this century. In the 1800s, there were only three, including one St. Pierre has not forgotten.

In 1848, Joseph Néhel stabbed a man in a bar. French law prescribed the guillotine, so one was brought up from Martinique. The only executioner to be found was a local drunk, who panicked at the last moment. He finally released the blade, but in the meantime, Néhel's struggling had twisted the frame, and the blade stuck. Horrified authorities finished the job with a butcher knife.

Lehuenen brightened when the subject shifted to the islands' heyday, from 1919 to 1933, the period of American Prohibition. Rum runners in eighty fast craft sneaked up to 300,000 cases of booze a month into the United States, from black French Caribbean rum to Scotland's finest whiskeys. There were reverses, such as when the U.S. Coast Guard blasted the *I'm Alone* out of the water. A Frenchman on board froze before he could be rescued, and an international incident lingered for six years. But St. Pierre's fortunes of today were made by converting fish freezers, basements, and bank vaults into liquor warehouses.

The traffic started when Bill McCoy, the original "Real McCoy," selected St. Pierre as a jump-off point for his quality contraband. Al Capone spent a night at the Hotel Robert and left his straw boater as a souvenir. Local archives contain a complaint from an American bootlegger:

> Queer, you people down there, a French colony, don't keep a decent brandy. You can buy it all right, but I am damned if one can get a decent drink of brandy in St. Pierre. Brandy is one thing that can't be imitated. Any amateur can tell a good drink of brandy from that rotgut they sell down there. I am afraid you fellows want to make too much money. A puncheon of alcohol and you're all set! Color, and flavor.

With the slightest encouragement, Lehuenen produces his treasure: a mantel clock engraved with the signature of Charles de Gaulle. He was mayor when de Gaulle sanctified the islands by a visit in 1967. That, he pronounces, was the greatest day of St. Pierre and Miquelon history.

De Gaulle—and what he stood for—has loomed large in the islands' lore since Christmas Eve, 1941, when France invaded the French colony. It was over this invasion of St. Pierre and Miquelon that de Gaulle first incurred the wrath of Franklin D. Roosevelt and his secretary of state, Cordell Hull, which colored American attitudes toward him, and his toward America, for decades.

After Germany occupied France, the islands' governor declared his loyalty to the Vichy government, but few St. Pierrais were happy about it. Many had volunteered to fight the war, enthusiastic even after they were billeted with black troops from the French Caribbean by officers who knew little of the islands' ethnology.

De Gaulle sought to rally the islands. He argued that radio transmitters off Newfoundland could aid Nazi ships in the North Atlantic. But Roosevelt trod a careful line during the war's early years, and he insisted on de Gaulle's assurances that he would do nothing to provoke the Vichy government.

On the day de Gaulle promised U.S. envoys he would take no action, he secretly ordered an assault. The submarine *Surcouf* and three corvettes, lying off Halifax, took the islands without a fight. Hull railed in public against the "so-called" Free French Movement. Words like "duplicity" peppered his private documents.

De Gaulle's 1967 visit shone warmth on a population which, however much it refers to "the French" as if France were a foreign country, clings tightly to the emotional and financial comfort of the motherland.

And de Gaulle, more than anyone before or since, bridged the gulf between the last bit of France and the vast territory that Louis XV abandoned. But on that North American trip, he tightened jaws across English-speaking Canada. From a balcony of the Montreal Hôtel de Ville, facing the column commemorating Lord Nelson, he bellowed, *"Vive le Québec Libre."*

A generation of French and Canadians have debated his meaning. De Gaulle made no move to reclaim Quebec after two centuries nor to incite a war of independence. His cry was rhetorical and symbolic, but in France those are no small adjectives. Spoken at the height of a quiet revolution among Quebecois, his words pounded themselves into history.

Feelings have since calmed. But France and Canada, under elaborate wraps of courtesy and gentle diplomacy, are at war. France claims a 200-mile territorial limit around its islands which, in places, are fifteen miles from Newfoundland. The practical issue is codfish. But surveys suggest that offshore oil lies within the disputed boundaries, as well as extractable minerals. A popular theme in St. Pierre is the Falklands War between Argentina and Britain.

"Canada is not Argentina and will not invade," observed Louis Hardy of the Chamber of Commerce. "But they have other ways of pressuring us. We are a foreign power in their midst." A local official put it, "Oh, we irritate them, all right. We are, as we say in France, a thorn in their foot."

Senior officials of France and Canada were about to take their dispute to a third party in 1986. "We have no designs on St. Pierre and Miquelon, which have been French for a long time," a Canadian negotiator told me. "But a 200-mile limit is a little excessive when it reaches into Canada, and there are problems with fishing rights. Let us just say the French make life interesting."

At times, there is more hostility between St. Pierre and Paris over Canada than between Paris and Ottawa. In early 1985, the Socialist deputy from St. Pierre, Albert Pen, suggested to an aide of Fabius that France send warships. Later, he wrote a blistering letter to the prime minister:

> Negotiations after negotiations, and the Canadian position hardens ceaselessly, while our economy declines inexorably: 26 percent growth in unemployment in a year. You refuse to take into account our budgetary difficulties, sheltering behind a decentralization that could not be applied here. . . . What good is a new statute recognizing we are neither the Côtes-du-Nord nor the Seine-Maritime? . . . Must we wait, arms crossed, for Paris to finally agree with Ottawa behind our backs? I fear . . . it would be better for us, St. Pierre and Miquelon, to deal with Canada ourselves. . . . *Outre-mer,* apparently, fidelity does not pay.

FROM THE CANADIAN side, the picture is different. In the Maritimes, few Canadians are sure where the islands are, let alone worry about them. Ottawa holds all the cards on any procedural question. And in Quebec, where the roots are French, Quebecois see themselves as no more tied to France than the St. Pierrais see themselves as French-Canadians.

People on both sides insist that only language links the French and French-Canadians. For the rest, ties are historical and sentimental. And even to say common tongue is pushing it slightly.

The French like to point out that their language is free of the awkward corruptions of Quebec. If, for example, the Quebecois insist on saying *magasiner* for "to go shopping," the St. Pierrais prefer the pure Parisian usage: *faire le shopping*. In Quebec, a weekend is a *fin de semaine*. In St. Pierre, as everywhere else in France, it is *un weekend*.

More important than vocabulary, though, is accent. Quebecois tend to sling around their syllables like bundles of beaver pelts or sawn logs. They waste little effort routing vowels through tortuous nasal passages. Rather than savoring consonants and releasing them gently, they hammer them out, adding a brief drawl for good measure. It is cold in Quebec, and the language that developed reflects the life of those who spoke it. It is hard and practical as a double-bitted axe.

The French could not imagine Canada's weather. Rabalais, depicting the winter, reported that it was so cold, sailors' words froze in mid-air. In springtime, crews on passing ships could hear the conversations of the previous winter. Some French of the time weren't sure he was exaggerating.

The extreme is a colorful argot called *joalle,* or horse; that's how *cheval* comes out at forty below. But higher Quebecois is pleasant and pure, tinged with *z* sounds where the French would put a *d.*

"The French always compare, and say, 'Well, in France, we do it this way,'" said my friend Hélène in Montreal, whose French sounds like tinkling bells. "They go on until you say, 'Well, fuck, go back to France. We don't need you.'"

But she loves France, from where her grandparents migrated. "I am French-Canadian but when I go back, I am from Normandy," Hélène said, pronouncing it "Normanzie."

Quebecois is rich in references to the church, and only the reckless risk offending the faith. Few curses are worse than *tabernac,* taking tabernacle in vain. "Catholicism," says Hélène, educated by the good sisters, "has the same hold here as voodoo in Haiti."

Hélène remembers that ten years ago, working for Bell Laboratories in Montreal, she was forbidden to speak French with friends in the cafeteria. Law 101 of 1975 changed all that. Now Bell Laboratories, and everyone else, has to use French for all signs, public notices, and official communications.

In Montreal, Law 101 seems a bit forced. On television, "Three's Company" becomes "Vivre à Trois," with clumsy dubbing that misses the word play. Kentucky Fried Chicken is somehow not *poulet frite.* The city feels French, with its wrought-iron exterior staircases. And its churches; Mark Twain once observed that you couldn't point a canoe in Montreal without running its bow through a church window. But it is also heavily Victorian and modern American. After a decade of Law 101, some English merchants had enough and reverted to their old signs, and the law was in court.

In the narrow, winding eighteenth-century streets of Quebec City, however, French is the natural language. And in the backwoods and on farms, the question does not arise. Few rural people can stumble through the most rudimentary English.

"People around here know they trace back to France, a long time ago, but they never think about it," remarked Pierre, a graphic artist I met in the upcountry village of St. François de la Rivière du Sud. "They don't think of it as the language of France. They speak their language."

In sophisticated circles, France is a constant. "Intellectuals who want to increase their cultural impact have to pass via Paris, like it or not," observed Sylvie Maes, a French psychologist married to a Dutch-Canadian in Montreal. "At the same time, they want to be on their own." Young professionals avidly watch rebroadcasts of France's beloved "Apostrophes," a weekly clash of authors' wits. Families on remote farms tap heavy boots along with Michel Drucker's Saturday night special, "Champs-Elysées." *Paris-Match* sells out quickly. A quarter-million French-Canadians a year vacation in France for holidays, admitting to a certain pleasure at being referred to as *nos cousins*.

France is a cultural ally to people in an ostensibly bilingual nation who, from time to time, still hear "Speak white!" when they travel out of Quebec.

A French diplomat with ample Canadian experience said:

> There is a deep love-hate relationship, no question about it. After the Plains of Abraham, French officials went home. All that were left were the priests. Many were bitter at separations between the French church and state, and they projected a certain image of France. A lot of French-Canadians have not gotten over how Louis XV abandoned them. They have had a different development, obviously, and their way of life is completely different from that in France.
>
> But there is an attraction to France, a fascination with it, and the young French working here push this to the hilt. It's a huge team effort to sell France, to rekindle feelings of attachment. Not political, but cultural and emotional.
>
> I don't think the Quebecois think of themselves as French in

any way. But I'll tell you one thing: when someone is invited to the consul general's residence—even for the most boring of ceremonial events—he comes.

The lingering Quebecois dream of independence from Canada seems to be over. In 1984, René Lévesque ended a sixteen-year battle to separate Quebec from Canada. The mood shifted; members of his Parti Québecois, like those in the opposition, were more worried about jobs and salaries. But the idea of a Quebec linked culturally to France remains entrenched, nurtured by vigorous official campaigns.

In 1965, a poll showed few French even knew where Quebec was; many placed it in South America. At the time, a cultural accord appropriated the equivalent of $2 million for exchanges and education on both sides of the Atlantic. Twenty years later, resources were eight times greater.

Eighty thousand French live in Quebec, and most have taken out dual citizenship. A thousand French students study in Canada. Under an exchange program 600 professionals from France and another 600 from Quebec work on technical assistance contracts.

But a reverse spin works against Franco-Quebecois cooperation. In 1984, the Quebec government bought 9,000 computers designed in France and built locally. That touched off a storm between those who decried a sentimental purchase, without regard to quality, and others who denounced a prejudice against French technology. As a result, officials in Paris complained, Quebec shunned France's best technology. The Renault Alliance caught hold, according to the French, because it was made in the United States.

Nonetheless, Canadian politicians ignore the French factor at their peril. John Crosby of Newfoundland blew his chances some years back when someone asked him how he would speak with French Canadians. He said he would do what he did when speaking with the Chinese ambassador: use an interpreter.

For decades, Canadian prime ministers were hostile to any direct cultural link between French-speakers and Paris. Brian Mulroney changed the pattern, clearing the way for the 1986 *francophonie* summit. He came to Paris with Quebec premier Robert Bourassa, who promptly invited everyone to Quebec for the next summit.

Prime Minister Richard Hatfield of New Brunswick also led a delegation because of all the Acadians in his province. He could speak no French, however, and he had no interpreter.

In fact, Canada is moving in on the mission to civilize. "There they were, selling like crazy and pushing their own cultural leadership among Third World delegations," a Canadian journalist told me. "On one hand it was shocking, and on the other, funny as hell."

Mulroney noted in his address, "It makes us a unique country, to be nourished by two cultures which are among the richest in modern civilization. . . . For us, *la francophonie* is more than being pro-French and defending linguistic purity . . . it is fundamentally for us the sharing of our existence and of our possibilities for growth."

In 1986, Canada put $280,000 in trust so that the Académie Française could each year honor someone for contributing to "the *rayonnement* of universal *francophonie.*" The grant was announced with an almost comical fanfare in simultaneous news conferences linked by a scratchy telephone line. "It is marvelous that by modern technology we are speaking across the ocean," Maurice Druon of the Academy told Canadian culture minister Benoît Bouchard, "and our language is French."

But the lines may never be clear. When Prime Minister Pierre Mauroy visited Canada in 1983, protocol demanded a long goodby. He left Quebec with a ceremonial send-off, officially ending his state visit. But before returning to Paris, he stopped in Ottawa to leave Canada.

CHAPTER EIGHTEEN

United States: Les Amerloques

CANADIANS MAY BE mixed in their feelings for France, but Americans career wildly twixt phobia and philia. Almost anyone who has stopped briefly in Paris can wrap up the French in a few stereotypes. Those who have not usually harbor ironbound prejudices anyway, for or against. And any American who knows the French well tends to love them and hate them with equal passion.

In France, where Americans—*les Amerloques,* in slang—are seen in the same extremes, such ambivalence seems only natural.

French-American relations have varied sharply at every level since before the United States was a country. How you see them depends on where you pick up the thread. History is the worst place to start.

French teeth gnash at Americans' somewhat selective view of the past, which tends to date Creation from somewhere in the eighteenth century. By then, the French had shaped modern philosophy and perfected 340 different ways to make cheese.

If it weren't for us, Americans constantly remind the French, you would all be speaking German. If it weren't for the French in the 1780s, of course, Americans would be paying a stamp tax to Queen Elizabeth II. Families who suffered German occupation in the 1940s, or who were bled white between 1914 and 1918, do not feel that the United States breezed in and won either war alone.

The two societies are hardly strangers.

American pioneers moving west were not grateful to the French
for inciting the Indians to massacre them in their sleep. Back in 1727,
a merchant named David Coxe warned:

> The French, who all the world acknowledge to be an enterpriz-
> ing, great and politick Nation, are so sensible of the Advantages
> of Foreign Colonies, both in reference to Empire and Trade, that
> they use all manner of Artifices to lull their neighbors A Sleep,
> with fine Speeches and plausible Pretenses, whilst they cunningly
> endeavor to compass their Designs by degrees, tho' at the hazard
> of encroaching on their Friends and Allies, and depriving them
> of their Territories and Dominions in time of Profound Peace,
> and contrary to the most Solemn Treaties.[1]

But then there was Walt Whitman: "Again thy star, O France, fair,
lustrous star, in heavenly peace, clearer, more bright than ever, shall
beam immortal."

Only a few hundred Americans a year visited France in the mid
1800s, but travel writers loved the place. "We shall always remember something of pleasant France and something also of Paris, although it flashed upon us as a splendid meteor, and was gone again,"
Mark Twain wrote in *Innocents Abroad*. One detail: "In Marseilles
they make half the fancy toilet soap we consume in America, but
the Marseillaises have only a vague, theoretical idea of its use, which
they have obtained from books of travel." But at Versailles, Twain
waxed lyrical over the people who showed the world the way.

In his last years, de Gaulle noted that France's independence
might displease "a state which might believe that because of its
power it is invested with a supreme and universal responsibility."
He added, "The reappearance of a nation whose hands are free,
which we have again become, obviously modifies world politics
which, since Yalta, seemed to be confined to two partners only."
American statesmen were repeatedly tempted to remind him how
France managed to reappear with untied hands.

Across an ideological gulf, Reagan and Mitterrand forged some
of the closest U.S.–French links ever. The French president repeats
de Gaulle's message, that world peace and justice depend on more
than two poles. But he is nicer about it. The practical politics change

by the month. To look at French-American relations, it is safer to start in the warmth of the rhetoric. And the symbols.

As the Paris metro rattles over the Bir-Hakeim Bridge from the fifteenth *arrondissement* to Passy, a glance to the left reveals the Statue of Liberty: torch, spiky crown and all, a hallucinatory flash of the view from the Staten Island ferry. The original stone lady on the Seine, rarely seen by visitors, is the symbolic godmother of the United States.

France gave the United States a larger version in 1886, a century after French troops helped the Continental Army throw off British rule. Most people had forgotten where it came from until 1986 when the combined hoopla of two nations reminded them. From July 4 to Bastille Day, Americans heard of little else.

At the time of the gift, France was launched full tilt on Jules Ferry's mission to civilize. What greater source of pride than a strong nation that took root thanks to gentle guidance from Paris and the force of French arms? The name of the hour was the same one evoked generations later by Americans storming the beaches of France in peril: Marie-Joseph-Paul-Yves-Roch-Gilbert du Motier, marquis de Lafayette.

Today, forty-two American cities and towns bear the name Lafayette. Some have all but forgotten the "Hero of Two Worlds," the French statesman who served as a major general under George Washington. But Lafayette, Louisiana, is a living temple to the glory of things French. Sort of.

A sign at the airport proclaims Lafayette as the heart of Acadiana, a land of spiritual borders that is home to the descendants of French settlers who were deported from eastern Canada by the British: the Cajuns.

The first families lived isolated in Acadia, in what is now Nova Scotia, from 1604. Then Britain moved in. Acadians would not swear to fight their French kinsmen in Quebec, so in 1755 they were dispatched into diaspora. A few thousand reached New Orleans, but the citified French there regarded them as trash. The Spanish, having just taken over Louisiana, had enough problems. The Cajuns and their ancient Norman ways were shuffled off to the swamps.

The Cajuns became Americans in 1803, like everyone else in Louisiana. To reach America, they only had to cross the Atchafalaya

Basin, so dense with cypress and mangrove it took a week to canoe twenty miles.

Around Lafayette today, the potbellies and pickups, and the polyestered lawyers cruising the Hilton bar, do not suggest anything Louis XV left behind. I-10 slices over the bayous. *Cou rouge* (as in redneck) oilmen swarm overhead in helicopters. Cajuns and outsiders each imbue the other with their strongest traits. But it is soon clear to the visitor that more than the 'Chafalaya has held off 180 years of American colonization.

I had a telephone number. Mike Doucet—Beausoleil, as he appears on records and at Carnegie Hall—responded in good cheer, gamely receiving yet another Anglo probing the Cajun craze. When I got to his house, he brightened. *"Ah, mais tu parles français?"* Then I blew it by differentiating Cajun from "pure French." He heaved a sigh, and I realized language was no simple matter in Louisiana.

Doucet is a master fiddler, but in the bayou country, musician is not a category. Music is not for making money; it is for two-stepping and the *fais do-do* (meaning "Go to sleep," as in "Get the rug rats to bed so we can party.") In real life, Doucet is a writer, historian, and teacher.

He and his wife, Sharon, live on the last two acres of what was his family's 900-acre soybean farm. The handsome, ramshackle wood house, built in 1820, is a French-American history lesson in itself: Canadian lines, a Haitian-style porch, tucked back in the Spanish moss of southwestern Louisiana.

Doucet, too, is ramshackle and handsome, bearlike, with deep laugh wrinkles and a prematurely graying beard. In English or French, he speaks with a soft how's-your-granddaddy? drawl that conveys the warmth that permeates Cajun territory.

After a bit, the Doucets paid the supreme, if not rare, Cajun compliment: they invited me out for mudbugs. At Alligator Cove, in front of a baking pan piled fourteen inches high with crawfish steamed in cayenne pepper, Mike talked about Acadiana.

"The culture here is Creole, homegrown. It's not so much France. The language is basically the seventeenth-century French the people spoke when they left. That's pure. But it has been a long time. When the Acadians were booted out by the English, France didn't come to their aid. There's no great love for the French. Still . . ." He tore the heads off a few more crawfish and warmed to the subject.

"I went to France in 1974 for a few weeks and stayed six months. I love it there, and I go back all the time. And the French are fascinated by our culture, our music. It is a mix, French, people from Haiti, other blacks."

Was it true, as some argued, that migration from Haiti had completed France's crescent through America, from the mouth of the St. Lawrence to the South American coast?

He shrugged and laughed.

"You know, when the British conquered, they made everyone bow to the crown. The Spanish, they killed everyone. With the French, they made love to everybody. You can't say, hey, that's it, anymore." He meant that by now the blood lines are hard to trace, and cultures are melding.

Doucet worries that the French flavor may die out if children stop speaking the language. But like many Cajuns, he is skeptical of an officially backed program that brought teachers from Europe.

"They'd be talking about the Eiffel Tower to kids who'd never seen anything higher than a grain elevator," he said. "Parisian French is not what the kids hear outside."

The teachers, 300 at first and fewer now, were brought in by the Council for the Development of French in Louisiana (CODOFIL). It is state-funded but more an extension of the personality of James (Jimmie) Domengeaux, an oilman and former congressman who organized it.

Tireless, and not one to avoid publicity, he insists that French French must be the lingua franca for a Cajun cultural revival. CODOFIL's little building in Lafayette is a shrine to the cause.

In 1975, Domengeaux had stricken from the books a 1921 law forbidding children to speak French in school. Cajuns recall having to kneel on corn kernels, their noses pressed to a small circle on a blackboard, as punishment for confusing "thank you" with *"merci."*

More recently, the state legislature agreed to provide French instruction in any school where 25 percent of the parents wanted it. Lack of funds, however, has left that as mainly a good intention. CODOFIL has a long way to go. French visitors note that Domengeaux himself does not read French, and his wife does not speak it.

Many Cajuns speak French without any help from Baton Rouge, or Paris. Russel Dupuis, who describes himself as a Cajun-American Indian born on the 'Chafalaya River, wrote to the *Acadia Times:* "What we do not need, and never did, is Gallic imperialistic meddling. We know and understand ourselves. . . . Imperialism is like a parent who never willingly gives up, even when the child is mature. We want out from your microscope, stop riding our tail-gates!!"

Perhaps 800,000 Louisianans understand some form of French, but the range is wide: Creole French from New Orleans, stilted and rare; *français nègre,* a pidgin French evolved by the freed slaves and upper-class whites left too long with their nannies; and Cajun, a blend of early Renaissance French laced with Southern street jive.

And there is the real thing. The week I was in Lafayette, so was Eugène Ionesco, presenting a play. Which one? *Parlons Français.*

One morning, I drove south, pursuing research as a flimsy excuse to kill time before the next meal. At St. Martinville, I visited Father Jean-Marie Jammes and ran smack into the language question again.

The French Foreign Ministry had sent Père Jammes to Louisiana as one of three "animators" to promote French culture. He was a priest, but he also had a doctorate in sociology from the University of Chicago. The program was abandoned, but he changed bosses and stayed. He was assigned to the parish of St. Martinville, once known as *le Petit Paris* for its splendid (and long since forgotten) opera and its coterie of aristocrats who hid there from the guillotine.

"Cajun is not Creole, it is a pure form of French, with some different nuances," Père Jammes assured me. "French people can understand it easily." To prove it, he showed me a Cajun-English dictionary compiled recently by a Lafayette-born priest named Jules Daigle.

Cajun is French, but the nuances are not always subtle. For the verb "to tape record" the French say *enregistrer sur un magnétophone.* Father Daigle's dictionary has it as *recorder sur un tape recorder.*

The dictionary was a smash success, and orders came from across the world. One customer was the Académie Française.

Père Jammes also showed me an article he had published, self-explanatory from the title: "How and Why We Can and Must Save French in Acadiana." He is optimistic.

"It is hard to speak French when the television is blaring English," he said. "You switch to English yourself without realizing it. But people realize the advantages of French, and no one is humiliated for speaking it. Now the American government is protecting minorities, and languages—it is a better time."

On a drive down to New Iberia, I asked Father Jammes if the church played as big a role in preserving Acadiana's French character as it did in Quebec. "Yes, definitely," he said. In case of confusion, he added, "Very definitely." Any doubt was dispelled two minutes later.

We pulled up to a gigantic red brick hangar of a store emblazoned "Rosary House, Wholesale Only," over a five-foot white plaster statue of the Virgin Mary. That, like the two sprawling warehouses behind it and the tin barn across the street, was jammed with every manner of plastic Jesus, kitsch Lord's Prayer lamp, stained glass panel and hymnal.

"People still go to mass here," Père Jammes said. "Every Sunday morning, my church is filled to overflowing."

Heading out of town, I stopped at the *Teche News,* a weekly that happened to be celebrating its hundredth year. The editor and publisher, Henri Bienvenu, breathed gentle Southern charm.

"The language was in terrible danger of fading away," he said. "CODOFIL has given a tremendous impetus. I'm forty, and a lot of people my age were not taught French at home."

Since Cajuns spoke French, he explained, descendants of the aristocracy learned English as their badge of having been civilized. As in New Orleans, French blood and family background were important, not so much the language.

It was lunchtime, and I raced for the nearest thing Acadiana has to the Golden Buddha: Mulate's in Breaux Bridge. At night, its low ceiling bows upward from the raucous chank-a-chank music and the stomping swamp boots. A 1948 "Roy Acuff for Governor" poster peels off one wall near a tattered crawfish net. At midday, there is food: stuffed mushrooms and crab; crawfish *étouffée,* smothered in a brown butter and pepper sauce; gumbo; red beans and rice; Jolie

Blonde beer (which says, "Bottled by Pearl Brewery, San Antonio, Texas" in small print). It is, as the French say, to die.

"Mulate's represents what Cajun culture is all about," said the owner, Kerry Boutte, stating a simple fact. "Cajun has become a catchword for whatever some entrepreneur wants to turn out. It has high visibility. We've been real careful to keep this place Cajun. Cooking is something we don't ever want to lose."

Again, language came up. "Well, I don't feel any particular affinity to the French, or animosity," Boutte put it. "But, you know, CODOFIL, they brought out people from France to teach. It's different here. We're self-conscious when French come and demand that we say something. They ridicule us. If they ask, I say, 'Oh, on parle un peu.' Our French is different, you know. If I want to say I'm going back home, I might say, 'je vais back à la maison.'

"We don't want to talk like the French. We like our language. It's fun."

In Baton Rouge, I stopped to see the governor's brother and omnipresent adviser, Marion Edwards. A successful but lavish gubernatorial campaign had left the governor $4 million in the hole. His brother had saved the day with a novel idea: a trip to France.

He signed up 618 people for a week's trip in a chartered jumbo. Shepherded by the governor, the tour got into the locked back rooms of Versailles, penetrated the circles of power, and ate from star-speckled menus. Each person paid $10,000, and the profit was substantial.

"It was the biggest calculated risk of my life," Edwards said, "but we had a massive turnout. It was because of a feeling people here have toward France. The trip had to be what it was."

Governor Edwards was received into an elite fraternity of wine-tasting chevaliers. He seized the ceremonial silver cup and, with a loud whoop, chugalugged its contents. Officials smiled politely at his near-misses with the language. At Versailles, he noted the French had opened for the group parts of the palace rarely shown to visitors. He observed: "My brother must have taken care of someone."

Despite his name, Edwards is from near Lafayette. He believes ties with France are strengthening.

With jet travel, he said, people can see France for themselves. It is no longer an abstraction, kept alive by tradition and folklore. The Cajuns, he maintains, are rooted deeply in modern France.

"It is the way of living," he said. "They live like we live, a *joie de vivre*—you know what that means?—pleasure-seeking . . . more prone to accept life as it is rather than moaning about what it should be."

I tried hard to liken the French *joie de vivre* to the Cajuns'. Somehow, I couldn't picture any Frenchman I knew yelping, *"Eeee-hee-heee,* this'll knock your dick in the dirt." But he seemed convinced.

AFTER CAJUN country, New Orleans seems like a Walt Disney mock-up: Frenchland. The roots are plainly there, but they have grown into something totally different. Most of the French Quarter is, in fact, Spanish. What is French is so aggressively and self-consciously so, the visitor is left wondering, so what? At the old quayside market coffee house, a pompous inscription announces that real French people actually drank coffee on that very spot. The menu includes T-shirts and souvenir mugs.

On the place d'Armes, a painter displayed a portrait of Catherine Deneuve with the added note: "French film actress, internationally known beauty."

Fine restaurants are packed with, naturally enough, American tourists. If New Orleans evokes Paris, it is the Paris of early August when every French person who is not bedridden is somewhere else.

In the sumptuous manors and polished manners of blooded Creole families, the old reality is still strong. The New Orleans Historic Archives documents every brioche ever baked in Louisiana. But a friendly French official gave me a candid view:

"Here, they are trying to keep alive a souvenir. Perhaps 600 French citizens are registered in Louisiana, mostly older people. Unfortunately, it is romanticism not rooted in fact: no French companies, no new blood, no way to keep alive the promise."

The French, he said, were in California and Texas, Florida and Georgia, making money like crazy. From New Orleans, I flew to Miami and saw what he meant even before I got my bags back.

A snotty little white poodle pranced through the Miami airport attached to a blonde lady who could only be described as chic:

sunglasses pushed up onto perfectly shaped hair; a kilo of makeup blended to near invisibility; Parisian sun frock molding very pleasant angles. Her reedy voice spilled across the teeming arrival hall: *"Mais, quel bordel, tu sais. . . ."* Her name was Florence; she was French. Her husband was a perfume executive, and they had been in Florida four years.

"You know, when Mitterrand was elected, the words 'socialist' and 'communist' scared a lot of French people," she explained. "Now we are settled here, and I like it very much. Our economic center is here. But our social life is in Paris."

The 1981 elections sent waves of French—and French money—into the United States, just as aristocracy fled the guillotine two centuries earlier. Most felt right at home.

The French have seasoned the American melting pot from the beginning. Pierre-Charles l'Enfant, the town planner, is why Washington, D.C., is at once so esthetically pleasing and such a nightmare for Nigerian cabdrivers new to the job. Charles Prud'homme, a French-Canadian, was one of the first to find nuggets at the start of California's gold rush. Lazare Frères founded San Francisco's first bank so miners could deposit their earnings. And Jack—as in Jean-Louis—Kerouac eventually wrote about what all that gold did to California's soul.

The historic trivia starts with the word America. French maps first used it, taking the name from cartographer Amerigo Vespucci. Those who prefer the present need only look around. At least 200,000 French live in the United States, and another million visit each year.

Recently I took a back road through the Navajo reservation in northern Arizona. Too long on the road, I wanted to curl up quietly for a while under the big toe of Americana. At a tumbledown trading post, strange tongues reverberated from the saguaro-rib rafters: a family of French tourists were remarking on the fried bread.

IN ATLANTA, the French built the subway. The Bank Indosuez and Crédit Lyonnais are thriving there. American chefs dip at the knee before La Française in Chicago. With 100,000 French

between them, Los Angeles and San Francisco feel as French, in
places, as Paris feels American. Large French communities stand out
in Houston and Detroit.

But New York? Stand in the heart of midtown at, say, 52nd
Street and Fifth Avenue. Cartier, on one corner, faces Piaget across
the street. The third corner bears the blue, white, red stripes of Air
France. The set is not complete. The fourth corner is Japan Air Lines,
right next to La Grenouille.

Just before I first went overseas in 1967, I worked at 50 Rockefel-
ler Plaza and bought my last batch of boxy Oxford-cloth button-
down shirts downstairs at an all-American clothing store named
Kent. Now the new tenant has put up the same sign displayed below
my apartment on the Ile St. Louis: Société Générale. In case anyone
misses the point, there are also the words "A French Bank."

And the old French presence is modernizing.

The Librairie Française is still there, as it was during World War
II when it was a haven for French publishers evading Vichy's
censorship. A poster downstairs bears a tribute from writer Jacques
Maritain: "Upon the free soil of the United States, works of French
expression could continue to appear, attempting to give a voice to
the thoughts of a fettered France." Upstairs, it stocks *Ouest-France*
and *Nice-Matin* from the provinces, *Votre Bébé,* Tin Tin, and French
bubblegum. When French football teams play in the Coupe de
l'Europe, crowds clog the promenade watching the shop window's
video monitor. The store is authentically Parisian, down to the sign
reading "Positively no refunds."

French products are passing from sophisticated luxuries to basic
staples. Never mind the Perrier, which is as American as Michelin
tires. Orangina and Bonne Maman jams reach neighborhood gro-
ceries.

If you scratch the surface, you still find the French, the best and
the worst. In the Manhattan TWA office one morning, a ragged-
looking young American came in and asked a woman at the counter
to do something with his People Express ticket. I'd noticed her
already: tight frown wrinkles, thick makeup, pulled-back blonde
hair. French. Taped to her computer was a postcard from a nudist
camp in southern France, along with a small Tricolor. She pierced

the traveler with a withering stare and let him know that her airline, TWA, did not deal at that class level. As he walked out, crushed, she muttered, "Incredible."

After an initial assault on American cultural imperialism, Mitterrand's minister of culture, Jack Lang, shifted toward energetic proselytizing. He came to New York with a French film festival and paid homage to Hollywood.

Americans dive vicariously with Cousteau. They love it when, in a Charles Boyer accent, he threatens to sink the *Calypso* rather than sell it for commercial exploitation. Reagan gave him a Presidential Medal of Freedom, the closest thing he could produce to the Légion d'honneur; it outranks the medal Lang gave Jerry Lewis.

Cousin, Cousine plays on and on at the cinemas. At American universities, comp. lit. majors follow Jacques Derrida in trival pursuit of Heidegger and Hegel. Not much is new, but there is Marguerite Duras. And there is always Proust—or Albert Whatshisname?

A sizable fringe loves France. And there are the France freaks who show off commendable French, lingering on the flashier dipthongs, until they give themselves away with an Elmer Fudd *r*.

The movement, however, is westward. Hemingway's generation was lost in Paris, but the feast has moved back home. Among French artists, writers, and artisans, the pull of New York, and the United States behind it, has been overwhelming.

"But there is a very good reason," said Martine Vermeulen, a potter who crossed the Atlantic in 1961 and stayed. "In France, the mentality is restricted, blocked, everything is impossible. In France, they close the door in your face and walk away. Here, there is always a possibility. If someone can't help you, he will help you find someone who can."

In the 1950s and 1960s, when Germans leaned toward America, French people like Martine were rare. "The snobs in France loved America but didn't want to admit it, for all their arrogance," she said. "Now all that is gone."

For years now, her atelier and gallery on Bond Street have served the purpose of a colonial cathedral.

"Aha," she said with a bright laugh, when I mentioned the proposed name of this book, "but I have been on a mission to civilize for twenty-four years. That is what we French can do. And I have civilized a lot of Americans, taught them of the beauty of breakfast in bed, to celebrate every day, the pretty little things that make a meal a festival. . . ."

Her floor is set in subtle blue tiles like a carpet. A stylized clay cow's skull perches over a mantel. Her shelves are stocked with delicate but earthy platters and pots, cups and urns. She does a brisk business among French tourists who can no longer find her sort of skills at home.

"It is not that the French are taking over but that the Americans are progressing, becoming sophisticated," Martine said. "When I arrived, they didn't know cappucino from croissants. Terribly backward. Now, the fascination of Americans for all that is French, it is phenomenal. It is passionate. It adds something to their existence, a charm, a joy."

Martine sent me to her friend Alain Delouette, proprietor of La Rousse restaurant on 42nd. He immediately picked up the theme.

"In the last years, such a big change. . . . When I came, Americans knew Brie. Camembert, maybe. Now, you find a gourmet shop on every block. One hundred in New York. And customers who are expert at what they see. Cheese, wines. And restaurants. . . . Before, you served *coq au vin, cuisses de grenouille, escargots, canard à l'orange.* That was it. Not any more. You try to get by with that stuff now, and you're out of business in a week. My croissant supplier makes 15,000 a day and can't keep up. . . ."

French analysts pick to death the new American fascination. Explanations involve Springsteen's Levi's and Reagan's slim grasp of economics. I, for one, am confused. I asked a French friend just back from America. She sounded like a recent escapee from a Manchurian mindwash.

"My God, how can I find words? The energy, the power, the imagination. . . . I went to the Jefferson Memorial at night. I could feel him talking to me. I was so overcome with what I heard, felt, experienced, it took me a week after returning just to absorb it all."

However emotional the draw, it is heavily economic. The art market in New York is well heeled. Jobs pay well, and businesses have flourished. For French industry and exporters, the United States is a huge market they are only beginning to penetrate.

France is second in the world in commercial aircraft production; first in trains; third in rocketry; fourth in automobiles. The French excel in medicine and biosciences. And few Americans know it.

"It is not merely ignorance but rather a psychological refusal to see France as an advanced industrial nation and a leader in technology," said Edith Cresson, then cabinet minister charged with pushing foreign trade and modernizing French industries. "Americans need the image of a France of perfumes and fine food and vacations. They won't believe anything else."

I spoke to Madame Cresson in Washington at the modernistic little city of an embassy France just built in Georgetown. She had come on a trade mission, along with 150 potential investors who were meeting with French businesspeople who had already made it in America. French investment in the United States, at about $6.3 billion, was less than Taiwan's or South Korea's. "We are far behind," she said, "the fourth exporter in the world but the ninth to the United States. It will not be easy."

She did her best. Her voice, in slightly accented English, wafted from radios across the country: "We love the United States, and we think it is a wonderful market."

Later, I met a French textile executive, a veteran of the U.S. market, and told him about the embassy extravaganza. He chuckled. "They think you come here on an official mission, shake hands, and then go home and make money. Hah. The Americans don't buy that way, or do business that way. They want service, action, and they won't stick with you if you don't deliver." Time, he allowed, will tell.

Regularly, one side or the other manages to stir up the basic peace. When a Long Island judge banned the Concorde from Kennedy Airport, Giscard d'Estaing fumed at Jimmy Carter. He would not believe an American president could not deliver an appellate decision. Negotiations over oil supplies, interest rates, currency exchange, and trade balances are seldom pleasant.

In 1985, Reagan's ambassador, Evan G. Galbraith, was quoted in an interview as saying that the French Communist Party was "sort of outside the law" and should not be allowed in the government. The Foreign Ministry protested, calling that meddling in French politics.

What really galls the French, however, is how American leaders look at world power. A senior French official remarked to me, "Do they take us seriously? No, I don't think so. We serve a certain purpose for them, of course, but the Reagan Administration, like others before it, feels they are the cornerstone of Free World security, and the allies should follow along with whatever they feel is right."

I tried this out on an official friend, a ranking State Department man who follows European affairs. "It's true, most Administration people regard France—all allies, to some extent, but mainly France —as a pain in the ass to be placated and kept informed but not essentially a major element in the world power balance. That's a mistake, but it's not new."

A main obstacle lingers from the past. "De Gaulle's understanding of world politics violated fundamentally what George Kennan identified a generation ago as the 'legalistic-moralistic' approach to foreign affairs," wrote Robert O. Paxton in the *New York Review of Books*. Americans see themselves as a chosen people, freed of Europe's corruption, and they see allies as "an army of the righteous in which one enlists once and for all, as in an act of personal salvation." De Gaulle, in contrast, "was in recent European history the boldest and most unsentimental practitioner of traditional national-interest diplomacy. Americans could tolerate a backslider, but not an unblushing apostate." Paxton noted:

> What touched Americans most was that de Gaulle doubted their good intentions. Taking it as normal that all states seek their own interests, de Gaulle saw and proclaimed American self-interest where Americans wanted to see their own idealism and generosity. This was more than a disagreement; it was a moral affront.

Reagan discovered this when he sought to enlist the newly elected Mitterrand in holy war against the Evil Empire; he tried to block the Trans-Siberian gas pipeline via Germany to France. But Paris, and Bonn, saw that as neither effective nor in their own interest.

When the French refused overflight permission and obliged U.S. aircraft to add 2,600 miles to their assault on Libya in April 1986,

Reagan was acid. "I see no justification for this," he said. Across the country, people fumed. One veteran noted that he was happy France allowed Americans landing rights on the beaches in 1944. Families cancelled their welcome for French foreign exchange students. Johnny Carson flung a pie at an actor made up as a Frenchman. But soon afterward, Reagan and Mitterrand embraced. Such disputes were in the nature of things, the French president said. And Reagan produced a hoary, "Let today be the first day of the rest of our lives."

Unruly or not, France has its weight. American strategist planners do not overlook France's nuclear force. France motivates the European Space Agency, which competes with Americans to deposit sophisticated gadgetry into orbit. To Reagan's suggestion that allies subcontract components of his Strategic Defense Initiative, Mitterrand replied, *merde,* with only slightly less tact than de Gaulle might have used. France sought to line up European partners behind Eureka, their own high-technology program with Star Wars potentialities.

Some Americans attribute such duplication to French cantankerousness and an unrealistic, wasteful pride. In France, the optics are different. The French have seen a great deal since Vercingétorix. If a finger is to rest on the button, they want it to be a Gallic finger.

And, stepping back from Doomsday, other questions arise. Is France prepared to lose more scientists to Silicon Valley? Can France, with crippling unemployment, happily sell bloated goose liver and Chanel Number Five to a superpower growing steadily richer and more powerful?

The Gaullist, neo-Gaullist, and proto-Gaullist response is clear enough.

Arriving at the White House in 1984, Mitterrand evoked the warm ties of "brothers in arms who together have shed their blood from Yorktown to Beirut." And he added:

> Because France is strong, independent, and confident in itself, true to its great past . . . and sure of its citizens, my country, within its means, can and wants to engage in discussions with all parties on all subjects.

Later in his visit, he let Americans know why he thought so:

> France is a much older nation and to us the United States
> appears still quite young. . . . I believe that our civilization carries
> a message that is not for us alone, that it can be understood and
> accepted by the greater part of humanity.

But in the realm of symbols, national interests slip away conveniently in the name of historic friendship. And as traffic increases
across cultural bridges, France and the United States seem to be
moving closer together.

In late 1984, a team of ten fine metalworkers came over to fix
the Statue of Liberty's makeup. They were funded privately and
officially from both sides of the Atlantic. The men, from Reims in
the heart of Champagne country, were chosen as among the best
iron craftsmen in the world. They brought two tons of hand tools,
including 100 hammers they made themselves.

They tried to make friends with their neighbors late one night
by rapping on the window with a bottle of wine. Police responded.
Their work was delayed because Iron Workers Local 455 protested
the hiring of foreigners. Jean-Michel Grés, one of the group, told
a *New York Times* interviewer how they spent their time: "We
watch the baseball, and they are with the clubs and the running. And
there is American football and they jump on top of each other and
then get off, time after time."

But, they concluded, the Atlantic was not all that wide. Said one,
speaking of his American colleagues: "We are not so different. Some
of them are so big and have tattoos. But they love the statue just
as we do. I saw one of them kissing her."

CHAPTER NINETEEN

Caribbean and Latin America: La Question

NOT LONG AFTER sending the Statue of Liberty to the United States, the French dispatched another shipment across the Atlantic. A Jewish artillery captain named Alfred Dreyfus was exiled to a rock called Ile du Diable, Devil's Island, off the South American coast. He fashioned a stone bench during his imprisonment, and he sat pondering the vagaries of French character. Today, you can do the same. Around the old bench, it is peaceful and absolutely quiet. Except for the moment, every few weeks or so, when an Ariane rocket streaks off the launchpad nearby.

Until World War II, French Guiana was an impenetrable jungle peopled by primitive Indians. It was a dumping ground for prisoners, men like Papillon, who stood little chance of escape against the sharks, mosquitoes, and smashing surf. It is still an impenetrable jungle, but it is France. The Indians, still primitive, are French citizens. And instead of society's dregs, France ships out the finest scientists and engineers it can get to sign a contract for the space center at Kourou.

French Guiana—*Guyane*—was the only French property in South America, which Spain and Portugal divided up while François I was otherwise occupied. Now it is the only piece of the continent to fly a European flag.

IN CONTRAST, Guadeloupe and Martinique are the sort of islands that send travel writers to the thesaurus. They are run-of-the-mill paradise: fine sand and lush flowers, turquoise waters, lavender mountains, reggae and rum punch. That is the physical part. In every other aspect, there is no mistaking them.

A gigantic building dominates the four-lane boulevard into Pointe-à-Pitre, the commercial center of Guadeloupe. Eleven stories high, it covers an entire block, modern, businesslike, and forbidding. It dwarfs the nearby post office and all else around it.

It is the Social Security building.

"Ah, that," laughed a French official when I asked him about it. "That and the church are the two most visited buildings in the islands."

And more than the church, that building symbolizes why the *indépendantistes* face a long uphill struggle. When unemployment in the *métropole* hovers near 10 percent in France, it is above 30 percent in Guadeloupe. Separatists blame that on Paris. But Guadeloupe produces almost nothing, and what jobs there are come largely from the government. Souvenir T-shirts are made in China; shells are packaged in the Philippines.

"In my heart, I am an *indépendantiste,*" remarked a woman who lives well on her salary. "Probably 40 percent of the people are. But when it comes to reality, we have no choice."

Guadeloupeans live well; only Martiniquais and Puerto Ricans earn more per capita in the Caribbean. When they fall sick, when they lose a breadwinner, when they retire, when they get the sack, they have a friend in the Social Security building. French authorities stretch the limits to include common-law couples because so many children are born out of wedlock.

The giant building is a safety net against the sort of misery suffered in Haiti and other parts of the Caribbean. The airport is another.

Why are Antillean mothers all misshapen? runs a popular riddle, posed with bitter amusement. Because every kid is born with a suitcase in his hand. An estimated 180,000 Guadeloupeans and Martiniquais, a quarter of the islands' population, live in France.

But hard times are squeezing shut the safety valves. Fewer jobs are to be found in Paris, and illegal immigrants from Haiti and Dominica are swelling the jobless ranks in Guadeloupe. Pressure is increasing to limit social benefits everywhere in France.

Guadeloupe, for years billed as a model island paradise, is now, stretching no figure of speech, a tropical time bomb.

Being French, Guadeloupeans have a higher threshold of misery than their Caribbean neighbors. The elevated standard of living is a mixed blessing.

There is a private car for every three people, a higher ratio than in metropolitan France, let alone Haiti and Dominica. The capital's narrow streets are choked solid all day long; overpowering fumes and drivers' curses cloud over the picturesque island balconies.

An overlay of *France moderne* leaves Pointe-à-Pitre halfway between what it once was and Marseilles. A gleaming branch of Société Générale fronts the old open market. The old row houses, with battered shutters and fancy ironwork, stand out like bad teeth among the white and glass of modern structures. A cloverleaf traffic exchange, past computer shops and an overcrowded yacht harbor, feeds into a tin-roofed slum.

In Guadeloupe, as in other DOM-TOMS, official wages carry a 40 percent premium, largely to offset inflation caused by the extra 40 percent. The minimum wage of 3,200 francs a month is six times Haiti's.

"Such a gulf separates those who have and those who don't that there is bitterness, tension, and unhappiness," remarked a tourism executive whose job is to say the opposite. "It is not that people are really poor here. It is the frustration of knowing what everyone can do that you can't afford."

Prospects worsen by the year. Field hands cost too much; farmers make little money from sugar or coffee. About 50,000 acres, a third of all arable land, lie unused. The government spent 90 million francs in 1984 to produce 500,000 tons of sugar and save 600 jobs; beet sugar imported from France would cost one-third of that. "This," one official put it, "is *grand luxe* sugar." Industry is incidental: the odd window shutter factory or cannery.

The state was investing nearly a billion francs a year in Guadeloupe's economy by 1985. In 1981, it was half that. In Martinique, state expenditures account for 80 percent of the gross domestic product.

American economists estimate that for every government franc spent in Guadeloupe, Martinique, and Guiana, 95 centimes are spent on goods and services from the *métropole*. Private French studies suggest that the figures more than balance out.

But that perpetuates a closed circuit, economically and politically unsound. For growth, there is only tourism. And that promises no solution. The French faith in the North American market rests heavily on self-delusion. Guadeloupe is pleasant enough, but it is no rare jewel. The mark of development intrudes on its charm. Pointe-à-Pitre's urban sprawl is ugly.

"Exquisite, no?" asked a friend, pointing out a concrete barracks behind a chain-link fence. "That's a new resort . . . beautiful." It was yet another palm and schlock hotel in the Bas-du-Fort zone outside the capital.

In one of them, the French manager extolled the island in American-accented English. "Once more people in the United States discover the fabulous scenery and the warmth of our people, they will come down in great numbers."

Talking to Americans who had discovered Guadeloupe and Martinique injects some doubt.

"God, they are so *awful*," fumed a New York legal secretary, putting in her two weeks in the sun at a French chain hotel. "They're rude, they ignore you, they cheat you, and they charge you a fortune." Elsewhere, a Canadian woman, herself a hotelier, was less complimentary.

The hotels exemplify the extremes of the Antilles. At the Auberge de la Vieille Tour near Pointe-à-Pitre, one clerk, exuding warmth and gaiety, battled for me against the archaic telephone system. The next snarled like a prison guard with a toothache, refusing to undertake the gargantuan task of changing twenty dollars. It was a common pattern, in hotels and elsewhere.

Normally in France, the desire to please weakens the farther one gets from the cash drawer. Small hotelkeepers tend to like customers, not only for the money but also for the testimony to their *accueil*, their welcome. At medium-sized places, employees risk trouble if they sneer at guests when the boss is around. In the big hotels, however, staffs are motivated only by a theoretical principle that customers should get what they pay for. That does not count for much.

In the French corporate mentality, it is natural to exchange francs at seven to the dollar when the banks give eight. Or to triple the telephone rate—even with direct dialing—as a service charge.

But in the Antilles, a wild card is thrown into the standard French games: social, often racial tension. A ripple of hostility can overwhelm feeble feelings that the customer might be right. Yet the reverse applies. Traditional island warmth can add unexpected humor and joy to simple commercial exchanges.

The result is like traveling in the Soviet Union. You are at the mercy of human nature. If you fall upon someone who is susceptible to your particular charm, you hit the jackpot. If not, may the Lord have mercy on your soul.

Unlike in the Soviet Union, what you get, with or without a smile, is likely to look good, feel nice, or taste fabulous. This is not only France; it is the islands.

One of my happiest moments ever was at Madame Basile's, a little clapboard house on the north coast. My friend René took me there, after a long ride through the pitch-dark canefields. Madame Basile belongs up there with Escoffier. She piles the plate with *poisson court-bouillon, blaff,* and *boudin.* Mounds of beans, rice, and fried bananas flank the plate. I slowed down to catch my breath, and she rushed over. "What's wrong? You're not hungry? It's not cooked right?" Before I could answer, she was howling abuse at the kitchen. Only the modest bill reminded me I was not an invited guest at her home.

But coming and going, I found the other extreme.

I flew into Guadeloupe after two months in Canada, the United States, and Haiti; instantly, I was back in France. At the Vieille Tour, a handsome woman with blonde hair and blue eyelids sat at the lobby tourism desk, beaming warmly at something. My glance crossed hers and I smiled back. The thermostat dropped forty degrees. Eyes narrowed to a blank stare. Mouth snapped to a tight straight line. As in the *métropole,* French outposts are not the place for mindless North American Have-a-Nice-Dayism.

On the way out, at the airport newsstand, I brought some magazines to the woman at the counter and waited for her to finish picking at a fingernail. She scowled briefly, totaled the bill, and mumbled, "Twenty-three francs, sixty." She snatched my fifty-franc note and, without bothering to look up, dropped the change in my direction. The coins missed my outstretched fingers. Not even the spectacle of a sweating, swearing tourist pawing among the bags of mints and heaps of *Le Matin* for his twenty-six francs brought a smile to her lips.

Guadeloupe feels tense. It is hard to pin down, but it is obvious. I went with a friend to the home of Marie-Christine, a government employee of some standing. She had the sort of working person's living room you might find in the fifteenth *arrondissement:* glass-fronted buffet with knickknacks, vacation snapshots, a few books, and a lace doily. She poured a *ponch,* prunes steeped in rum, powerful enough to run a tractor. On French TV, we watched Stacy Keach, in a white linen painter's smock, playing *pétanque* in a Provençal village.

I asked Marie-Christine if she felt she was in the same country as that game of *pétanque.* "Not really," she said. "You know, a country is an organic unit where people feel a certain common tie. This is artificial."

Outside her building, someone had scrawled, *"Mort à la Tornade Blanche."* The White Tornado was an elite unit of head-knockers flown from Paris to investigate persistent bombings.

The island's peculiar overlay of self-satisfaction forms a strong defense against terrorists seeking to destabilize the islands. "Look," a local journalist told me, driving along a ramshackle row of wooden slums fronting on an open ditch, "this is a far better standard of living compared to the English." At the hospital: "Look, the most modern in the Caribbean." At a second yacht harbor: "There is nothing like that in the English islands."

I remarked to him each time we passed some hostile graffiti, which was often. He admonished me not to make too much of it. "You should not exaggerate. We have a capitalist mentality in a country that produces nothing. But everything is fine here. There is some ferment, but, after all, this is France, and people like it that way. Those against it are a very small minority."

I said goodnight and suggested calling him later at the office. "I'm working at home these days. The paper was burned down." By whom? "Probably by the *indépendantistes.*"

The *préfet,* Maurice Saborin, was clear about what he was up against. For one thing, each year more youths seem attracted to extreme positions.

"My greatest worry is over the young people, half desperate, coming out of school well educated onto the job market," he told me. "It is a very serious problem, let's be honest about it."

Saborin was a textbook prefect, charming and crisp, with gold-rimmed spectacles and a nicely cut suit. He had been unplugged from his last job, a department in the *métropole,* and would be connected to another. He called himself an administrator, with no function as a political analyst, and then set about disproving that with an astute reading of the complex situation.

He stressed Mitterrand's policy, that of most governments since Guadeloupe and Martinique became departments in 1946. If a majority of voters want independence, appropriate negotiations will take place. If not, legality and security must prevail.

That last part, the prefect acknowledged, was no small job.

An outlawed fringe has exploded hundreds of bombs since 1981 when the Socialist government promised to increase local leaders' power. Four extremists were blown up by their own bomb in 1984. But another four bystanders died in the violence, including an elderly American tourist.

"The independence movement exploits race to the hilt," Saborin said. "Every conflict ends with a call for whites to go. . . . And among the whites, there is racism against the Antilleans [blacks]. The situation here is capable of growing violent very fast."

Qaddafi, he added, meddled in Guadeloupe the way he did in New Caledonia. "I have new evidence that Libyan involvement goes much farther than simple contacts." Two Libyan delegations visited the island, and Guadeloupeans went to Libya. Outside funds supported two radio stations and a newspaper. "It is not cheap to run media like that, without a scrap of advertising."

Saborin said he was determined to prevent terrorism from causing panic. Someone had tried to kill him the year before. But he shops for his own tomatoes, unguarded in the market. His office in Basse-Terre, a rambling old island mansion set back in a park of palms, is hardly protected. I drove in with a casual wave to a bored gendarme. Another officer cheerfully conducted me to the prefect's office without asking who I was or what was in the odd-shaped black bag I was carrying.

At the airport, security guards often wave passengers through without a glance, not even turning on the X-ray machine.

But terrorism is never far away. An Association of Small and Medium-Sized Industries meeting opened with a minute of silence for bombing victims. "You have to understand, this place is small and everyone knows the victims," said the manager of a large hotel. "One bomb here is equal to 1,000 bombs in New York."

In any case, terrorism is not the major problem.

Independence candidates poll only a few percentage points in elections, but their weight is felt throughout Guadeloupe. I drove half an hour down the road to see Claude Makouke, a physician and leader of the Union Populaire pour la Libération de Guadeloupe. Elections proved nothing, he said; the French manipulated them at will. Terrorism was deplorable, he added, but what did the French expect from frustrated people?

"We feel the people are entitled to use every means available to convince the colonialists to leave," he said.

Makouke's UPLG had just organized what they called an assembly of the last French colonies. Delegates took part from every DOM and TOM except St. Pierre and Miquelon. The French Polynesians sent a message of solidarity but did not attend. The meeting's slogan in Creole: *On Sel Chimen, Lendependans.* In French, that would read: *Un seul chemin, l'indépendance.* A single road, independence.

"As the French government proclaims internationally the rights of peoples to choose for themselves, the political reality in Guadeloupe is the opposite," Makouke told delegates. "Reactionary forces are more and more aggressive. . . . France is the occupying colonial power. Relations are those of domination, subjugation, colonial ties. They are intolerable, and they should be completely destroyed."

François Yves, of the Martinique Conseil National des Comités Populaires, stretched for color:

The French colonists are like professional gamblers on Mississippi River boats. They invite you to play and insist you use their marked cards. They are flanked by servants who reveal your hand

and, at last resort, by murderers to slit your throat on the way out in case, by some chance, you win. French democracy is a ruse. The cards are stacked.

The Kanaks pronounced their own struggle a guaranteed success and exhorted others to follow.

Some French snickered that a simultaneous Jehovah's Witnesses rally outdrew the *indépendantistes* by a wide margin. Desjardins, in *Le Figaro,* hooted, "Flop. There is no other word."

But Saborin was not among those laughing. "Sooner or later," he said, "something is going to break loose. It would be a serious mistake to underestimate the *indépendantistes.*"

Three months later, Pointe-à-Pitre was cut off behind barricades of burning cars, felled trees, and ripped out toilets. Screaming youths with Molotov cocktails faced off against riot gendarmes flown from Paris in Boeing 747s. The riots were caused by a freshly arrived white math teacher who kicked a rowdy black student in the buttocks. Slave owners did that, and Antilleans don't like it. Georges Faisans, a burly *indépendantiste,* whacked the teacher in the leg with a machete. Faisans, jailed for three years, went on a hunger strike. After two months, violence exploded.

At the same time, Luc Reinette, serving twenty-three years for terrorism, escaped from prison. He hid out in the hills, like runaway *marrons* of the last century. From hiding, he announced that French officials had secretly discussed independence with him in 1983. Paris denied it, but Reinette's followers believed him.

Frustrated youths joined the riots, spurred on by veteran militants. If Faisans was not freed, they warned, blood would flow. Reinette's banned Caribbean Revolutionary Alliance, after a year of silence, warned it would terminate "the insupportable arrogance of French bandits who conduct themselves like masters in our country." It threatened to punish not only the teacher but also a dentist accused of anesthetizing and raping a fourteen-year-old girl.

Paris moved quickly to reach some solution. An appellate court reviewed Faisans's case and then released him. A cry of *"Yo lege!"* —"They let him go!"—rippled around Pointe-à-Pitre. Barricades were lifted. After the triumphant chanting and fist-waving subsided, *indépendantiste* Amédée Etilce told reporters that the outburst gave

Guadeloupeans a new dignity: "This was a turning point; things will never again be as they were before."

Maybe. There are others who recall that the islands, though left-leaning, voted three to one for Giscard d'Estaing over Mitterrand in 1981. The false rumor went round that Mitterrand was soft on independence.

THE FALLOUT was not violent in Martinique, a short hop south, beyond Dominica. On Martinique, the social temperature is lower, and the small independence movement is split. Still, *l'affaire Faisans* made an impact among youths and the jobless whose patience is wearing thin.

Aimé Césaire, deputy from Martinique, mayor of Fort-de-France and poet of negritude, argues for autonomy. Strong links to France are vital, he maintains, but the island must take its own decisions and shape its own economy and society.

Mitterrand said decentralization had brought that about. In a visit in 1985, he made the same point on both islands. "From now on," he told one crowd, "you can be Guadeloupean, pride yourself as Guadeloupean, conduct yourself as Guadeloupean while being proud and happy to call yourself French, citizens of the French Republic."

Such a dichotomy is hard to put into practice. In Martinique, for example, a colleague of mine called on a local tourism official who insisted on his spiritual independence from France. Just then he answered his phone. The man stood up, brought his heels together, and for the next five minutes repeated, *"Oui, Monsieur le Préfet."*

And in Paris, a nurse from the islands grumbled to me, "They colonized us and told us we're all the same, but in truth you're only French on your identity card." She was bitter because her brother studied until 3 A.M. for months to be a police inspector in spite of a racist superior. Eventually, her brother cracked under the constant riding, and he slugged the officer. Now he is trying to be a gym teacher.

Others are, as the president says, proud and happy to be French. And it is clear that they are. Martinique is France down to the statue of its most famous daughter, Napoléon's Joséphine. She is in the vast waterfront park, right hand clutching a rose to her bosom, left lying atop a relief of the emperor's face. The inland sugar mill at which she was born is in ruins. In a small museum there, her white stockings, with a little red embroidered *J*, and her crown are on display along with chains her family used on the slaves.

Martinique's sugar industry is also in ruins. Wages and costs are too high, so two-thirds of local consumption is of beet sugar from France. And the whole economy is like that. At the *Préfecture,* a thoughtful young official told me:

> We could cut away Martinique with little loss. It has no strategic importance any more. We certainly make no money from it. But France does not exist but for its culture and history. There is a certain naïveté, a certain feeling that we can bring something of importance to people. Our presence in the Antilles is an expression of that. We are here for affection. How could a German, say, understand that sort of thing?

GUIANA, WITH ONLY 80,000 inhabitants, is mostly jungled hinterland sheltering endangered tribes of Indians. French officials restrict visitors and settlers. But the pull is strong for Indians who want to work in Cayenne, the louvered and leafy colonial-style capital. Guiana is the most backward part of France. But at Kourou, the combined French space research center and European Space Agency launch site is the twenty-first century.

The contrast is stark. Kourou, fifty miles west of Cayenne, is a shabby little fishing town across from the abandoned prison islands. Its barroom tables dip at the center from ham fists banging on them for attention; a Foreign Legion detachment lives nearby in concrete apartments left vacant by a first space project that went bust. Kourou reeks of boredom, and tension can hang as heavily as the humid air. The place exploded briefly in 1985 when someone killed a legionnaire.

The victims' friends had no idea who did it, so they systematically smashed whatever they found: car windshields, bar tables, whorehouse doors, windows, and the heads of unfortunate passersby. Townsfolk, fed up, got out their own bats and shotguns. By midnight, two platoons of gendarmes were racing down from Cayenne. Final result: one dead, nineteen injured.

A Socialist politician blamed the extreme right for pushing tension. The Legion colonel said his men acted on their own; they did not need prodding by politicians. "One should not hide the fact that conflicts between legionnaires on the town and civilians have been numerous, but up to now they were settled among individuals and the Legion's own service of control."

Some called it a small race riot. Others said it was simply what happens when you put 600 combat-trained men in a small town where local women are guarded at musket point by their families and the white women are married to computer programmers.

The rocket people live in freshly built suburban clusters which crowd the town. They are linked to the capital by a mirror-smooth, extra-wide section of highway.

"We call that the *Route des Blancs*—the White Man's Road— because they would have never built anything so nice just for us," an engineer-turned-*indépendantiste* named Michel Kapel told me. "It is there so that the Ariane rockets don't get jolted on the truck ride from the port at Cayenne to the base."

Kapel heads a party called PANGA. The acronym means "Attention" in local dialect. I noted that it was also an African word for machete. "All the better," he grinned. Kapel wore a giant straw hat with frayed edges, huge comic sunglasses, a yoked Levi vest with no shirt, and ragged pants; he smoked a fat cigar and carried a guitar. After a few minutes' conversation, it was clear he was no clown.

Before leaving Paris, I had asked Georges Lemoine, minister for the DOM-TOM, about the new independence movement there. He shrugged and replied, "How many are there? What do they amount to? Not much."

Kapel agreed that the numbers were small. "That is not the point. The world does not like colonies any more, and France gets away with it because people don't notice," he said. "How much money and prestige do they get from Kourou? For Ariane, they need peace. We will not give them peace. The Europeans will force them to end their antiquated domination."

Did he mean violence, I asked? Kapel hedged a little. Destabilization was a better word, he said. "If they fight us, we'll fight back."

There is clearly discontent. A wide fringe complains that France has done little to develop the long-forgotten enclave while impos-

ing policies against the people's will. But the *préfet,* Bernard Cour-
tois, was probably right. Few of the malcontents would reject
massive French support to a virtually nonexistent economy. And a
great deal of people in Guiana are happy to be French.

Indépendantistes seize an argument heard elsewhere in the DOM-
TOM: France tries to weaken local societies by moving in other
ethnic minorities and by assimilating local people into the French
mainstream. PANGA objects to the absorption of Laotians while
long-time residents from Haiti, Brazil, and Surinam are expelled.
"We are becoming a minority," Kapel said.

Cayenne is like no place else. Over the Place des Amandiers drifts
the clack of mah-jongg tiles as Chinese merchants win and lose large
chunks of the town's retail trade. Sun-browned Frenchmen organize
commerce and banking at café tables by a park of giant palm trees.
On the waterfront and downtown, the old buildings stand in rows:
handsome white columns among rusted tin roofs; collapsing carved
wood balconies and wrought iron scrollwork. "They will tear down
this town and put up a concrete monstrosity, in this land of beautiful
wood," remarked my friend Edmond. "Look around, it is ghastly."
But there is still plenty left.

I am a connoisseur of such raunchy backwaters as those found in
Manila, Panama City, and Lagos. In Cayenne, I found the Versailles
of raunchiness: Chicago. It is a modest-sized two-story bar in a small
slum just over the stinking canal at the edge of Cayenne. The top
floor is routine raunch. A loud band pumps thunderbolts of reggae
into a sweating, slithering human mass generally enjoying itself.
Downstairs is a simple bar; no hookers, armed bandits, or legionnaires. But there is a way people watch you, through eyes narrowed
with suspicion and rum. I could imagine some Hollywood casting
director gleefully scooping up each patron with a butterfly net.
Halfway through one beer, I realized why Edmond, built like a
truck, had been reluctant to come.

By the old power plant, Brazilians squatted in wood-scrap slums
as bad as anything in a Rio *favela.* It was not what France considered
to be housing.

IN EARLY 1985, France inaugurated in Guiana three 500-
kilowatt transmitters, using eleven antennas, capable of carrying the

faintest nasal vowel to the ends of Patagonia and, of course, north-ward as well. They doubled the potential audience of Radio France Internationale. Communications Minister Georges Fillioud explained, "Neither a tool of propaganda nor an instrument of domination, international broadcasting is a privileged means for France to send to foreign nations a sign of recognition but also an appeal: an appeal for exchange, for a dialogue of cultures."

Beyond radio waves, bank loans, and trade missions, France ventures only spasmodically into the rest of Latin America. Old ties remain with Brazil and Mexico. Venezuelans, Argentines, and Peruvians look to Paris for culture and luxury. Most of the region finds France useful as a non-*Yanqui* Western power. But France has higher priorities.

In 1981, Central America was a major interest for the newly elected Socialist-Communist coalition. It was a painless place to differ from the Washington view that every conflict was part of a grand East-West struggle. Mitterrand's wife, Danielle, was captivated by the region. Régis Debray, a leftist intellectual who hobnobbed with Che Guevara in Bolivia, was brought into the Elysée as a counselor. France joined Mexico to lead efforts toward negotiation with El Salvador's dissidents. France sold low-grade military gear to Nicaragua.

Mitterrand reminded Reagan that anti-Communist forces are not necessarily pro-democratic. He reinforced his credentials by embargoing arms to Chile. But the position was not so painless. The Reagan Administration had enough trouble accepting that a government with Communists in the cabinet was a reliable partner. Otherwise, there was little advantage to an energetic Central American role, and French attention flagged.

In 1985, a visit to France by Argentine president Raul Alfonsin emphasized that Latin America is not so far away. He evoked his country's old fascination with France; some French have even forgiven Ambassador Gainza Paz, of years past, who brought his own cattle to Paris to assure himself of decent beef. And Alfonsin made a beeline for Toulouse, birthplace of Carlos Gardel, the tango king.

FRENCH TRACES are strong on an island that has been out of the empire for 180 years: Haiti. Until Indochina and Algeria, no other colony had managed to throw off France in war. And, some Haitians grumble, they are still paying.

Few countries suffer as much misery per square mile. World Bank figures put per capita income at $200 a year, but most Haitians earn nearly nothing. Of eight million inhabitants, perhaps 60,000 have three-dollar-a-day factory jobs making the major leagues' baseballs or assembling electronic parts. Many farmers, with badly eroded land, cannot afford to grow even basic food crops for their families.

When France settled in two centuries ago, this was the richest agricultural colony in the Americas. Turmoil, greed, and neglect are destroying the land. Of eighteen healthy watersheds, twelve are left. A U.S. government study estimated that only one will remain by the year 2006. Once-thick forests are now deserts where peasants scavenge the last stumps and bushes to sell as fuel. Farmers work slopes so steep that some literally must lash their ankles to stakes to keep from falling out of their cornfields.

A small elite controls the best land and creams off the economy. Their mark is a command of French civilization: culture, language, and manners, kept fresh with regular pilgrimages to Paris.

Some argue that that is changing. "We look to New York now and idiomatic English is valued above elegant French," said a jour-nalist-politician whose English is as idiomatic as his French is elegant. "They might talk about Paris, fashions and all, but France is finished. With all the movement, the immigration, it is New York."

He said the French no longer seemed interested in Haitians (they need visas now to visit France) and, in fact, never mixed much with Haitians from the earliest days.

"*Merde,*" said a Port-au-Prince businessman, with *café-au-lait* skin and *salon* manners buffed to a sheen, an expert in art, music, and noble thoughts. "The truly educated and sophisticated Haitians look more than ever toward Paris. This is a bastion of Frenchness in America. Pure, from the eighteenth century. When a Haitian goes to France, he has the feeling of already having been there. For convenience and business, okay, the U.S. Ah, but France . . ."

Whatever Haitians' feelings toward France, it is clear that, for better or worse, they are out of the empire. A writer named Serge recalled, "I studied in France, and I went there to be a Frenchman.

All Paris would throw open wide their arms to welcome me and, man, I was ready. It did not work quite that way."

Haitians deal calmly in black and white, and racism goes down badly. Serge said that when he applied for a job as a clerk, a Frenchman asked all candidates to line up, French on the right and foreigners on the left.

"I was Haitian, so I went left," Serge said. "But this Martiniquais went to the right. The white guy yelled, 'I said, French to the right, foreigners to the left.' This went on, the guy yelling each time louder, until the Martiniquais said, 'Look, I'm French, from the Antilles.' At which point the man bellowed straight into his face: 'I said, French to the right, foreigners to the left.'"

France is represented from a grand mansion set back in the trees, now as seedy as imposing. Inside, a senior diplomat was cautious. Yes, there were historic ties, and there was the language. France helped all Third World nations. There might be more aid, after increased U.S. assistance, but certainly no struggle to retain influence. Would any of France's constantly traveling leaders be in soon? Well, the minister for cooperation came in 1980. "But," he concluded, "Haiti is very small and far away and people are very busy."

But that was before February 1986 when Haiti rose against Baby Doc. Duvalier, in official French circles, was suddenly a dirty word. The young dictator decided to bolt while he could, and the Americans offered him a ride to anywhere but the United States. Late at night in Paris, U.S. authorities persuaded the French to take temporary charge of the French-speaking pariah. With extreme reluctance they agreed on a week. But frantic phone calls produced no takers for Baby Doc. In Gabon, Omar Bongo replied, "My country is not a garbage can." Only Liberia gave a qualified yes, but Duvalier wasn't interested. On French radio, he said: "France is the only country where I feel comfortable. When I decided to come here, I had not the slightest doubt I would be welcomed." His wife, Michèle, added: "France is the country that most suits us. Its culture, its hospitality." Its boutiques. She had been welcomed often in the past, bringing planeloads of friends and fortunes in overweight on shopping sprees.

Fabius wanted the deposed dictator out of France. Mitterrand waffled. "Our constitution says we must accept anyone who serves liberty, but I am not sure this person best defends human rights," he said. But he added, "He is not such a burden. One must not exaggerate." Shortly afterward, the United States took in Ferdinand Marcos, and French officials simmered; many felt they had been had.

The Duvaliers remained cloistered in a three-star converted abbey at Talloires, on the lovely Lake Annecy, while their lawyers sued French authorities to let them stay. It was embarrassing timing. At the Francophone summit in Paris, speakers harped on the theme of French liberty and *largesse.* Duvalier argued he was under virtual house arrest, with a room bill alone of 120,000 francs a day. In occasional interviews, he repeated the magic words: "We have always looked to France as *terre d'asile,* of refuge." He was certain France would not betray its humanitarian mission. Finally, the French forced Duvalier out of the Alps. He went, instead, to the Riviera. He was allowed to move to a small estate north of Nice, with four acres of grounds, a pool and tennis courts. But, the French added, he was restricted to the Côte d'Azur *département* of Alpes-Maritimes.

Not everyone was happy to see Duvalier deposed. Jean Dutourd, tongue half in cheek, warned that his disappearance might mean the end of French as Haiti's language. *Le Canard Enchaîné* retorted that he should declare Duvalier's victims as *"morts pour la France."* They died for France.

A few thousand French live in Haiti, priests and nuns included. But the little port of Jacmel, linked to the capital by a French-built mountain road, has the unmistakable stamp of a French island colony. The words *Liberté, Egalité, Fraternité* are emblazoned across the town hall. Houses in faded pastels, streaked with mossy slime and chipped with age, rest on fancy iron pillars shipped out as ballast. Cobblestone courtyards and dripping fountains are hidden behind louvered windows. Worn stairs lead to balconies and tiered walkways. Inside, Louis XV buffets and massive provincial tables hold dusty bottles of Bordeaux and pastis.

But a glance at the dates suggests that Jacmel remains French-style by choice. Hurricanes and fires have ravaged the town regularly. Almost nothing, save the ornate iron columns, antedates the bitter revolution.

A Port-au-Prince physician-historian explained his perspective of both sides:

> Haitians don't like the French; they like the French language. It is that simple. Like in Canada, the Quebecois only wave the French flag when they want to make a point against the English-speakers. It sets them apart. And the French, they don't like to lose. Look at Napoléon III. His was a great epoch: France exported and produced creative works. But he lost and was forgotten. It is the same here. In Haiti, France lost.

The first omens were not good. At independence, Haitians made a new flag by ripping the white from the center of the tricolor. Every leader since has viewed France with mixed feelings. Intensely anti-Communist, President-for-life (it did not work out that way) Jean-Claude Duvalier was correct but cautious when Mitterrand took office. But Duvalier's extravagant wife, Michèle, took planeloads of friends to shop in Paris. And he spent heavily to seek a favorable press in France.

Haiti has gone through a lot of tyrants since Napoléon, but French remains a court language that sets presidents comfortably above the masses. When Duvalier addressed the nation, he might as well be speaking Korean for many who understand only Creole. But the words were less important than the message. Which is, he was not asking that they vote for him.

The feeling for Haiti comes on the horse trail, a sort of *équiphérique,* to the Citadelle. The road passes the crumbling remains of King Christophe's stone palace, inspired by Versailles and only slightly less grand. The difference, of course, is that Versailles still functions. Christophe named it Sans Souci, but it is hard to imagine him without cares, considering his situation at the time. He must have had a few *soucis,* because he designed one of the most heavily fortified, trickily engineered, painstakingly built—and totally useless—forts in history.

We rode up Joseph-and-Mary style behind our handlers, who trotted along reciting fragments of history. The Citadelle was 21,000 lives in the making. Forced laborers, just freed from French slavery, died of exhaustion; others fell from the cliff face. Christophe heaved people over the edge for minor breaches of code. The mortality rate has since dropped, but our horses were better shod than most Haitians. Our guide climbed the sharp rocks on a few scraps of leather held in place with string.

The Citadelle's stone ramparts form a flat parade ground, with five sharp turns and no railings despite a sheer drop to the rocks far below. Christophe impressed visitors occasionally by neglecting to give the order to turn right. In such instances, troops loyally marched over the edge. The fort was built like a gigantic stone battleship sitting 1,000 yards up on a mountaintop and was just as practical. Fifteen miles from Cap Haitien, the cannon bristling from its walls could not heft an iron ball to the harbor and offered little defense against attack from the sea. Invaders could isolate the fortified peak, and rule the rest of Haiti until only skeletons remained in the Citadelle. I asked our guide about this. "Ah, no. It was very good protection. Christophe had a French architect design it." That might have been the answer. Or Christophe knew something I don't.

It didn't matter. The king died of a stroke before the fort was finished, and the French never came back. Napoléon no longer needed Haiti to protect Louisiana, and he was busy elsewhere. The Citadelle remains an American version of the pyramids, except that the people who built it were newly free.

"Haiti never fully developed into a state; it is a sort of proto-state," remarked an American anthropologist friend who spent years there. "It has the trappings but no inner reality. What was the model at the time? Napoléon. Despotic personal rule. This is France's main legacy, and it has not changed since."

I MADE ONE other stop in the Caribbean. St. Barthélemy, a dependency of Guadeloupe an hour's flight north, is a perfect French creation. The airport snack bar is St. Tropez macho. Local heroes, their chest hair just out of curlers, dazzle lady tourists with early-Belmondo gestures. The tiny Swedish-built port of Gustavia feels Scandinavian in its primness, but its shop windows are France. Its disco, Le Must, is Paris *yé-yé* where only the transients go. *Les gens cool* are at Le Sélect, as they would be in Montparnasse. There are, of course, differences.

In Montparnasse, stuffy waiters in black and white float among the tables, which they flick with a rag at the drop of an ash. The St. Barth version is raucous and raw. Its barman is classic island flotsam: barefoot in torn shorts and T-shirt, an army hat over hair that shoots out in all directions. He runs back and forth, cheerful and rapid, slopping rum into plastic cups and snapping fresh Bankie Banx tapes into the stereo. The Swedish owner has sprinkled memorabilia of Scandinavian royalty among hard-rock posters, scrimshaw, moth-chewed books, and bits of ships that passed in the night. Reggae music pounds, and laughter is loud. A sign outside pushes the bar's famed cheeseburger: "Over 56,000 sold." But in its way, Le Sélect is just like its namesake. A basic clientele lounges around battered tables, inside and out, scrutinizing everyone who comes into view. One is ostentatiously graded and, like it or not, handed a report card.

At Le Tamarin, toward the beach, a hybrid macaw in brilliant reds and blues sits in a giant spreading tree screeching, "Fuck off." The place is run by friendly Parisian dropouts who do an unbeliev-able red snapper in *beurre blanc*. Paradise might be sipping chilled Muscadet next to an explosion of hibiscus and bougainvillea, in reds, pinks, and purples, stirred by soft, spicy breezes. Minimokes rattle past full of French tourists paying no heed whatever to the sign reading, "Nudism is prohibited in St. Barthélemy."

I met a hospitable French couple; both had grown up on the tiny island. They were furious at developers from the *métropole*. "They bring in every nail, even their own laborers, and take back all the profits," the husband said. "And they are putting up all sorts of garbage, driving up prices, and ruining the island. Even the Ameri-cans are leaving."

That night, I went to the Licorne. People crowded a dance floor open to a light, flower-scented wind. Like everywhere in the Carib-bean, carnival music thumped, beer flowed, and people "jumped up." But no one laughed or grinned as they do everywhere else. The few blacks seemed self-conscious. The whites had that Castel's mask of contrived boredom. In the islands, strangers dance and mingle with some abandon. But at the Licorne, an outsider asking a stranger to dance risks the reception Jack the Ripper might expect when offering to show his knife collection.

St. Barth is the islands, but it is France.

CHAPTER TWENTY

Europe: In the New Old World

FRANÇOIS MITTERRAND did not make it to the 1985 superpower summit between Ronald Reagan and Mikhail Gorbachev. But France did. At one point, a Soviet official briefing reporters reached into his pocket, pulled out a slip of paper, and read off a snatch of Voltaire: "I have never had but one prayer: O God, make my enemies ridiculous."

The pen is not mightier than the Bomb, but you can get a lot more daily use out of it. With a *force de frappe* that is now structured to project nuclear warheads beyond the borders of West Germany, the credibility of France is based on more than ink. But the French know that megatons are no real measure of power.

Once Reagan or Gorbachev throws his nuclear weight, it is too late to matter. Until he does, what really matters is how he holds his fork. And who invented forks? (The Italians, in fact, but who does everyone *think* invented the fork?)

In the view of some, France's role has changed only a little since Charlemagne defined it a millenium ago. Accidents of history have left France a medium-sized nation; fifty-five million people cannot dominate the world, even if they are French. But they can still guide it. If some less enlightened peoples choose not to follow *la bonne voie,* that does not reflect on those patiently holding aloft the light.

Most French would agree that their light has dimmed. But most would also add that it should beam brightly again, and that it can.

The British once ruled a quarter of humanity. With its navy

under full sail, Britannia unsettled the most powerful of French statesmen. But the British folded up the Union Jack and went home, content to look inward and steadily decline. England has sixteen islands strewn about the globe, and 85 percent of all international telephone conversations are conducted in English. *Et alors?* Who knows that? Germany rose and fell once too often. Now, troubled by an internal political division and a present tainted by the past, Germans focus their attention on living well. Italy dropped out of the empire business with the demise of *il Duce.* The rest of Europe, as de Gaulle once put it, *c'est la verdure.* It is garnish. The superpowers, musclebound, parvenus, obsessed with balance, somehow escape the equation.

That leaves the people who brought you Voltaire. And a rabies cure, and the Cuisinart.

This analysis buckles under the weight of numbers. France's economy is only the fifth largest in the world. West Germans earn more per capita, with lower unemployment and less inflation. The Japanese, dismissed by de Gaulle as "transistor salesmen," steamroll French markets, abroad and in France. Even Britain outsells the French.

But numbers, like megatons, are not the measure. France simply steps to its rightful place at the head of the line. Cool hauteur rises above others' niggling complaints. A bad patch followed the leftists' victory in 1981. As usual, however, France confounded lesser civilizations. As Washington worried over Reds in the cabinet, a new senior minister close to Mitterrand told me, "Americans just don't understand. Only we Socialists can finish off the Communists."

France cleaned up the economic mess made during the first few years of dabbling on the left. The Communists dropped out, and the next Socialist prime minister was a young technocrat whose hobby was show jumping. Inflation was curbed, and unemployment stabilized near 10 percent. The franc had slipped perilously but caught itself. Debt was controlled and the balance of payments remained on keel. Nationalized companies had to show a profit or perish. The fields and farms, France's source of recovery since medieval wars, produced rich export crops. The largest source of foreign exchange came from tourists, attracted as beetles to a flame by *la lumière du monde.*

And, in 1986, France voted right. Mitterrand stayed, but Gaullists ran the government.

De Gaulle saw France as a drawbridge from West to East, anchored on one side but capable of spanning chasms that NATO military partners could not. He recognized Peking in the 1960s, when American maps showed China as a little island off the coast of a massive blank spot. In Peking, I asked a senior French diplomat whether Paris reaped rewards for that foresight. "Not really," he said. "But we enjoy a certain privileged political dialogue. The Chinese tend to see us as a locomotive for the European Economic Community. In a sense, we lead the way."

The French like this idea of being Europe's driving force. It was Jean Monnet who laid the tracks for the Common Market, and de Gaulle who continually derailed it. Three presidents since de Gaulle have wrestled with his devils, seeking a balance between towering French nationalism and a desire for France to forge European unity.

If France is not, in fact, the leader of Europe, the community turns on the short axis between Paris and Bonn. When Reagan first sketched his Star Wars fantasy, Mitterrand refused to sign on as a subcontractor. Instead, he tried to rally Europe behind an idea called Eureka to tackle every problem from space research to AIDS. If Eureka research shaped technology for a Strategic Defense Initiative, its architects said, all the better.

Airbus Industrie, a European venture with its plant at Toulouse, is 35 percent French. In early 1985, Airbus was pressing Boeing, aiming for a third of the $150 billion airlines were expected to spend by the turn of the century.

Ariane and the European Space Agency compete for an expected $52 billion in business by the year 2000. The program is as much a source of pride as income. It is a European consortium, but most Frenchmen regard it as their own. The agency's Paris headquarters approved a game called Spacego, in eight languages, in which players race for riches in space aboard European and U.S. rockets. When a Challenger spacecraft exploded in 1986, killing seven Americans, French newscasters were quick to point out the competitive implications.

French-only projects brighten the aura of European technology. Dassault alone makes twenty-one different models of aircraft, with sales of 15.6 billion francs in 1984. The Mirage 2000 stresses the metal of any MiG on the market. The Train à Grande Vitesse and subway systems are seldom absent from speeches on modern France.

For the first time in 2,000 years, French defense strategy no longer envisions Teutonic hordes swarming over the Rhine. The threat has shifted one border eastward. If the French have no illusions about civilizing Germany, they can at least help protect it. French and other Western strategists fear that an ill-defended West Germany might be tempted to shift toward neutrality. That could mean a separate peace with the Soviet Union, which it cannot discourage militarily.

A U.S. umbrella covers Germany, but the eternal question persists: will Washington sacrifice Hamburg to spare Detroit?

France developed a 47,000-man Force de Réaction Rapide, prepared to strike at any edge of the empire. Its range is limited by too few short-range Transalls. The main purpose is as backup support for Germany, where 50,000 French troops are still based along with U.S. and British forces. A new generation of Hades missiles, with a 200-mile range, will be able to reach East Germany in the 1990s —until a Soviet SDI renders them useless. France developed the neutron weapon the United States turned down.

West Germany, anxious to be more than an expendable doormat for any potential European ground conflict, develops weapons jointly with France. And the French sell them in places Germans fear to tread.

German chancellors and French presidents have been close since de Gaulle and Konrad Adenauer. Giscard d'Estaing and Helmut Schmidt were friends and mutual admirers. Mitterrand and Helmut Kohl installed a hot line between them. But relations with Washington always intercede. Bonn agreed to take part in Reagan's SDI, causing a ripple with the French.

But the Atlantic Alliance works like that. It is a tug of war with the European end of the rope unraveled into disparate handfuls. France merely has to grab hold of a sizable strand, and keep it taut. No one forgets that a half-dozen French nuclear submarines cruise at the will of Paris, permanent wild cards in the delicate balance.

Europe often prefers Gaullist national-interest politics to the moralistic-legalistic sort Kennan defined. Reagan's personal war with Qaddafi demonstrated that. West Germany, Italy, and Britain, like France, deplored Libyan-backed terrorism, but few saw that as a reason to dent their own economies. Each found it easy enough to cite some example of American hypocrisy to justify a policy of business-as-usual.

For all its reputation as a stubborn maverick, France is a solid anchor of NATO. In early 1986, journalist Thierry Wolton revealed that in 1981 Mitterrand delivered to Reagan intelligence from a French mole in the KGB who was known to only five Frenchmen. The agent, "Farewell," delivered to France 4,000 documents in eighteen months and made possible the expulsion of forty-seven Soviet agents in 1983. It was among the most valuable acts of espionage since the war.[1]

European pacifists protested the deployment of Pershing and cruise missiles. Not, however, in France. It helped that no missiles were placed in France, but the French have remained convinced, since de Gaulle, that their lives depend on a nuclear shield which they themselves wield. Beneath *l'affaire Greenpeace* lies a bedrock principle: France is prepared to take extreme measures to defend its nuclear capacity.

Though committed to the West, France treasures its role as a moderating influence between the blocs. Before the summit, Gorbachev spent three days in Paris. It was the seventeenth Franco-Soviet summit since de Gaulle took power.

On French television, Gorbachev said cooperation would deepen in trade, research, space exploration, and cultural projects. It was standard boilerplate, but it had a new ring. The Russians had received fifty French industrialists in Moscow. Crédit Lyonnais, established at St. Petersburg in 1878, was the first Western bank in Moscow, in 1972. It financed much of the pipeline from Siberia to Europe which Reagan tried hard to block.

Mitterrand had explained in Washington that continental neighbors had to talk without hostility. "We have had friendly relations with [the Russians] for several centuries." Not quite, but it was close enough for diplomacy. He skipped Reagan's presummit briefing in New York for Atlantic allies. The short notice smacked of a summons, the French said.

Mitterrand declined to negotiate separately on the *force de frappe,* but Gorbachev's presence in Paris amounted to something similar. Meanwhile, Raisa Gorbachev watched six models show forty-three creations at Yves Saint-Laurent and left with a sizable flask of Opium under her arm.

French police banned demonstrations. Warm speeches did not recall Mitterrand's visit to Gorbachev's predecessor. He had Russians choking on their vodka, discarding the *pro forma* toast to say what he thought about their treatment of Andrei Sakharov.

Two weeks after the summit, Mitterrand's guest was Wojciech Jaruzelski, and much of France was up in arms. No other Western leader would receive the Polish general. France, home to Polish exiles for centuries, had stood firmly behind Solidarity. *France-Soir,* the right-wing daily, screamed, "Visit of Shame." Fabius told the National Assembly he was "personally troubled" by the visit. Polish television showed seventeen minutes of Jaruzelski in Paris: meeting Mitterrand, laying a wreath to Polish war victims, cruising the Seine in a *bateau-mouche.* Somehow, the cameras missed the bitter demonstrations that paralyzed Paris traffic.

Mitterrand explained that a president of France maintains relations among states. Not agreeing with a head of state is no reason not to see him. The issue was touchy, he acknowledged. But, he told reporters, "History will prove me right." History, of course, seldom delivers clear verdicts, as the French understand well. In any case, it did not count as a state visit. Mitterrand marked that point as only a French leader could: Jaruzelski did not enter the Elysée by the main door from the courtyard. He was led through the garden to a side entrance, for tradesmen and dictators.

A FEW DAYS after Soviet planes shot down Korean Air Lines flight 007, I was off to Moscow. Western airlines boycotted the Soviet Union, and governments denied Aeroflot landing rights. Air France, however, had a flight. I rose before dawn to miss the morning traffic. We were kept standing by for hours, and the flight was finally called at lunchtime. Passengers filed on board, each lost in thoughts of a last good Air France meal before the boiled cabbage and rubber chicken of Moscow. "We regret to announce," interrupted a voice reflecting little regret, "that no food or beverages will be served on this flight." Why? I asked the purser. He gave me that gentle smile one gives the slow. *"Mais,* we have to make our protest."

I looked around. Not a Russian in sight. The Kremlin would doubtless tremble in shame on learning that France's state-owned airline expressed disapproval by starving its full-fare passengers en route to Moscow.

THE WEIGHT OF France in the New Old World is less Napoléon than it is Hans Christian Andersen. Today's emperors are short on clothes. In such a situation, they are not in a position to brag too loudly about their tailors. A corps of polished diplomats and politicians manage to clad France in remarkable finery. But Cartesian flexibility, clumsily applied, can expose France to ridicule. In the case of UNESCO, for example.

In the mid-1970s, French editors joined Western colleagues in warning of a threat to reporting. Third World leaders had seized upon Soviet efforts to equip governments with the moral right to ban, expel, censor, or arrest foreign correspondents. Their reason was noble: to improve the often inadequate and inaccurate picture portrayed of their countries. But for many, the purpose was different. For them, objective reporting meant relaying only information they generated themselves.

UNESCO director-general Amadou Mahtar M'Bow liked the idea. Authoritarians outnumbered democrats, and the issue was popular among the Afro-Arab nations that supported him. Soon correspondents felt the results. In Africa and Asia, I was denied visas, or permits for internal travel, by officials who cited UNESCO codes. Many governments, counseled by UNESCO experts, drafted policies that put stumbling blocks between correspondents and reality.

Western diplomats at first made things worse. Rather than refuse any compromise on the principle of press freedom, they negotiated wording. The result was a grab bag of statements condemning censorship while laying out ways to implement it. But by 1983, American editors got through to Reagan. Washington gave notice it would leave UNESCO unless it respected access to information and also trimmed its waste. A General Accounting Office survey found financial scandal, and press controls remained an issue. The

United States withdrew at the end of 1984, depriving UNESCO of
25 percent of its budget.

The next year, Britain gave notice. British journalists and officials
had been the first, and the most eloquent, to denounce threats to
reporting. The Thatcher government, giving up on reform, said it
would spend its UNESCO budget directly in developing countries.

The French were furious. UNESCO was a perfect vehicle for the
Socialist government's Third World campaigns: painless, well-
funded, and far-reaching. Even better, its massive headquarters was
in Paris, a source of pride and income for France.

At the 1985 General Conference in Sofia, the French ambassador
to UNESCO was Gisèle Halimi, a lawyer with neither journalistic
nor diplomatic background. By custom, geopolitical caucuses select
representatives to the Drafting and Negotiation Committee. Western delegates wanted a solid front, argued by cool and seasoned
voices. They had five seats and six candidates. Madame Halimi lost.
She then took her candidacy to the full membership. Third World
delegates, delighted to have a sympathetic spirit in the Western
camp, voted her in. "I won by plebiscite," she proclaimed.

According to Western delegates, she then got onto the Executive
Board by rallying Africans to vote against the Icelandic envoy
tapped to head the Finance and Administration Committee. A Sudanese was elected instead. Africans then supported her for another job.
With the Icelandic candidate out, the West had a vacant seat to fill.
The Executive Board ended up with fourteen African members:
eleven French-speaking states, Ethiopia, and two others. M'Bow is
from Senegal.

The British, disgusted by the conference, confirmed their decision
to withdraw. French commentators called that slavish obedience to
Washington, ignoring Britain's record of criticism. Singapore went,
too. That was painted as Commonwealth solidarity although Sin-
gaporeans had planned to leave even before the Americans. They
waited to avoid any connection with Reagan's decision.

I went to see Madame Halimi in Paris for her version of Sofia
and a briefing on France's position on UNESCO. I asked why she
had called Britain's decision political if London was to apply the
same money to cultural projects. She advised me to ask Mrs.

Thatcher. I pursued the question, and she said, "Nothing that occurred at Sofia justified Britain's decision." Halfway through the
next question, she broke in.

"You're writing a book for whom? What title? When is it
coming out?"

I told her the name of the American publisher and said that a
French translation was under negotiation.

"Aha. So you don't even have a publisher," she said. Before I
finished the next sentence, she cut in: "I don't have time to help you
write a book. I have written books. When I write a book, I go to
the documentation."

We are, therefore, left with the documentation.

Le Monde, under the headline, "Relations between France and its
Western partners are degraded yet further," reported that Madame
Halimi had weakened the Western negotiating team by going to the
full membership. "The composition of the group was thus determined, by the French move, by members not a part of it," the article
said. "Other Western representatives took it very badly that their
colleague imposed herself, with support from the outside, in an
instance where her partners did not want her seated. And some note
that is hardly the sort of gesture to convince those who were
considering leaving to stay in the organization."

She replied to *Le Monde:*

"France, because of the energetic role it plays within UNESCO,
deserved quite naturally to be part of the group. This is the first time
it has been excluded by its partners."

Agence France-Presse quoted a senior official of an unnamed
"powerful East bloc" country as saying that the French ambassador
had provoked a Western consensus against herself. He was a senior
Soviet delegate, in fact, who was steering East bloc support away
from involvement in press controls and from M'Bow's controversial
leadership. His remark, carried by AFP, was: "She does not understand. She knows very well what she wants. But she does not know
what the others do not want."

I reminded Madame Halimi that French editors had pioneered the
debate, and I gave some examples of how UNESCO actions ham-
pered reporting. She cut me off. "I studied the dossiers. There is not

one word, not one sentence in UNESCO documents that endangers freedom of the press."

Just to be sure, I repeated, "You are saying the French position is that UNESCO does not represent any threat to freedom of the press?"

"No. It does not."

BUT THAT IS also one of the strengths of France. It is a serious country, rich in substance and potential, which need not always be taken seriously. A traveler in the Old World finds that no European can mention the French without leaking at least some judgment: an arching of the eyebrows, a licking of the lips, an energetic rubbing of the stomach, or a sharp kick toward an imaginary seat of the pants.

In each country the judgments, if extreme, are never unanimous. Italians tend to like the French, or at least admire them. Except for those who loathe them. A friend of mine in Rome mentioned to Italian friends that he had sublet his apartment to a French couple. "What?" they sputtered. "Are you crazy?" Their prejudice was that French tenants were overbearing, hard on the furniture, and likely to pay with a bad check. Germans must like the French; enough of them come to visit. And so on.

French views toward other Europeans are less violent and less diverse. I met a very pleasant French multinational executive based in Rome who summed up his thoughts on Italians and the rest: "Rather agreeable but, ah, somewhat primitive."

The French and Spanish work hard on friendly relations against all odds. After the European Community extended territorial waters to 200 miles, France claimed much of the Bay of Biscay. Madrid, hoping to enter the Common Market, did not object, but Basque fishermen did. When a French patrol boat fired on Spanish trawlers 140 miles off La Rochelle, wounding at least six fishermen, a storm broke. In one Basque village, crowds screamed, "France, assassin!" In Madrid, people threw eggs and excrement at the French embassy. Near the border, Spaniards burned French trucks, a tactic used earlier by French protesting Spanish vegetables and fruits coming across the Pyrenees. "It's just a fishing incident," a French Foreign

Ministry official remarked in March 1984. "It's unfortunate but we tried to warn them and intercept the boat peacefully." *Cambio 16* editorialized: "Geography condemned Japan to have earthquakes and the Caribbean to endure hurricanes. Our curse has been to be the neighbor of France."

But in 1985, King Juan Carlos visited Mitterrand, who promised harsh treatment for Basque terrorists who seek refuge among French Basques. France had already begun deporting suspected Euskadi terrorists, triggering a tide of Basque vandalism against French interests in Spain. France is Spain's best customer and, like it or not, geographic buffer to the rest of Europe. Just before Christmas, 1985, a new crisis opened painful wounds: France, not Spain, won the contract for Europe's first Disneyland.

For sheer terror and amusement, nothing approaches the mutual regard of the British and the French. Once in a while a commentator remarks, "Relations are more friendly between Britain and France after . . ." Friendly has nothing to do with it. Hot and cold blasts across the Channel (or the Manche; the French have their own word for it) antedate William the Conqueror. French infants are taught *"Perfide Albion"* right after *"Maman"* and *"Ce n'est pas ma faute."* A British child learns only later that a frog is also a small green amphibian.

Horace Walpole, in the eighteenth century, decried France's "insolent and unfounded airs of superiority." More recently, Barbara Cartland, romance novelist in her eighties, said that France was the only place where you could make love in the afternoon without people pounding on your door to ask if you were ill. François Mauriac wrote in 1937: "I do not understand and I do not like the English except when they are dead."[2]

The British middle classes are perhaps unreasonably hard on the French. After French farmers hijacked cheap British lamb (after Britain banned cheap French turkeys), the *Sun* in London ran a contest for the best "Froggie jokes." Some entries:

"First man: 'I managed to get an English dictionary for my French wife.' " Second man: 'That's a good swap.' "

"Why do surgeons hate operating on the French? They only have two moving parts—their mouths and their bottoms—and they're both interchangeable." Or:

"How did France, humiliated in World War II and without a single bomb dropped on Paris, finish up as a great power in Europe?"

"Dunno—I give up."

"So did the French."

But the French take their revenge on *les rosbifs,* often with less humor. My friend Claude, a journalist, found himself in a Normandy bar on his way home from an extended visit to England some years ago. He had adopted London local color: a derby, umbrella, even spats. He ordered *Viandox,* a beef bouillon the French put in white wine. Next to him, a grizzled old Frenchman decided to perform for his neighbors. *"Bah,* he should be drinking tea, this stupid Englishman." Encouraged by the general laughter, and the certainty that a stupid Englishman could not understand French, he rambled on, "What's he coming here for, to bother us, this English jerk . . . why can't he stay home where he belongs, polluting France with his fucking—" About then, Claude turned and broke in. *"Vous voulez fermer votre claque-merde?"* (Would you mind closing your shit-trap?) Remorseful silence prevailed.

There is a certain English implantation past Calais. The French have taken over the word "snob," not necessarily the attitude, but certainly the word, along with fashionably soiled Burberry's trench-coats and Range Rovers *(les Rahnges).* France knows comedian Benny Hill. But *pub* is a French word all on its own, meaning advertising (as in *publicité*). The real penetration is in the other direction.

A whole fringe of society waits breathlessly at Dover for the *nouveau Beaujolais.* Diners seek out French names on restaurants to escape roast beef and two vegs. Britons may call that rich dark wine claret, but any Frenchman can recognize it as Bordeaux. England has produced a playwright or two, I suppose, but anyone can pronounce Marlowe. The points are awarded for what happens at the roof of the mouth at the end of Molière.

In the 1960s, cross-cultural invasion kept an even balance. The English called their contraceptives French letters; in France, they were *capotes anglaises.* But in the 1970s, French travelers found a great deal of France in England.

And now the 1980s have produced the ultimate outrage. In Sloane

Square, right next to the tube stop, in the very *quartier général* of the Sloane Rangers, there is L'Oriel. It is a French brasserie-café, complete with waiters who deftly sprinkle scorn on the clientele in Charles Boyer accents. There is only one concession to England: the rolls are hard as rocks.

THE SUBSTANCE of Anglo-French relations is deep and wide. France and Britain built the Concorde together and defended their technological masterpiece against the derision of accountants. Their trade has grown sixfold in the last decade, and cross-Channel traffic is heavy enough to justify the 200-year-old dream of a fixed link between them. Both sides have agreed on plans for a railroad joining Britain to the continent. Nonetheless there were members of parliament who objected, as Lord Palmerston did in the last century, to spending money to shorten a distance that was already too short.

Mitterrand visited the queen in 1984 amid the pomp and grandeur only two historic seats of empire could produce. His message was that Europe must push the superpowers toward direct comprehensive arms control talks. He addressed Parliament, protected by Guardsmen in bearskin helmets. On the walls of the Royal Gallery where he spoke were two forty-five-foot-long frescoes. One depicted Waterloo; the other, Trafalgar.

Queen Elizabeth, in diamonds, fed the French president good English beef and scampi with lobster sauce in a grand ballroom under six huge crystal chandeliers. "Ours is the history of unity and diversity, cooperation and rivalry, friendship and disdain, war and peace," she said. "Let us never forget how much we share—a commitment to peace, freedom, and democracy, a stubborn spirit of independence. . . . We have outgrown conflict and disdain."

One British writer recalled an earlier sovereign, King Edward VII, escorted by cuirassiers through Paris in 1903 to formalize the Entente Cordiale. People jeered and shouted, *"Vivent les Boers."* The king remarked, "The French don't seem to like us very much." And an aide replied, "Why should they?"

After World War I, Lord Curzon, then foreign secretary, came to Paris to remonstrate with Prime Minister Raymond Poincaré. The French had pulled troops back from Chanak, leaving a small

British unit alone against Ataturk's raging-mad nationalists. At the Hôtel Matignon, Poincaré lost control and raved for fifteen minutes. Curzon had to be helped into the next room. He collapsed on a sofa, hands shaking violently, and told his ambassador, "Charley, I can't bear that horrid little man. I can't bear him. I can't bear him." Then he wept.[3]

Some years later, Sir Anthony Eden had French hands trembling when he backed down at Suez, with French forces out front.

Competition remains fierce, if sometimes friendly. The British entered the Common Market after de Gaulle died; then they elected Margaret Thatcher, who badgered her partners for a better deal. The *Times* of London observed that many French see Mrs. Thatcher the way the British regarded de Gaulle: a tiresome person to deal with but one whom they wished their own leaders resembled more.

When the Pentagon decided to make its largest ever purchase abroad, a battlefield communications system, the Americans leaned toward France's $4.3 billion offer, the RITA. Mrs. Thatcher, pushing Britain's Ptarmigan, appealed to Reagan to consider who was the more faithful ally. But the Ptarmigan cost $7.1 billion and was not yet in use. RITA won, and a French commentator remarked that that was to be expected "even though some people will stop at nothing."

Even the pomp and grandeur of Mitterrand's visit to the queen ended in a quarrel. French security agents, apparently to prove the British fallible, buried explosives in the French ambassador's garden. English dogs sniffed out the explosives immediately, and English members of Parliament demanded to know what was going on. Mrs. Thatcher's observations were sharp; twelve days earlier she had nearly been blown up by an Irish terrorists' bomb. The French, in heated self-justification, implied that British colleagues set them up. The Britons asked to be tested, according to the French.

That blew over quickly. But the episode of the Exocet had all the makings of a modern-day Fashoda incident.

For people who tuned in late, the Falklands War seemed like a sudden flurry over a needless piece of real estate, seized upon by generals in need of diverting a disgruntled populace. The last part is correct; certainly not the first. From the first grade, Argentine children learn, *"Las Malvinas son nuestras."* At the same time, the

1,800 Kelpers who populate those wind-blown rocky islands center their lives around two pillars: sheep and Queen Elizabeth. I visited the Falklands in 1975 and left amazed. An hour in the pub offers evidence enough, but I scoured Port Stanley and did not find a single resident who wanted to shift allegiance to Buenos Aires. Margaret Thatcher, rooted firmly in empirical principles, could not have avoided war.

The risk was enormous for Britain. Had the Argentines sunk an aircraft carrier, as they repeatedly claimed they had, they might have won. London would have staggered under the loss of life, of military advantage, and of image. The key to the war was air-to-sea missiles. When the war began, Argentina had a fleet of French Super Etendard aircraft and five Exocet AM39 (air-sea) missiles. They had not, however, worked out how to attach, arm, and fire them.

On May 4, 1982, an Exocet sank the destroyer H.M.S. *Sheffield*, with a loss of twenty seamen. At Aérospatiale, which makes the missile, there was some jubilation on the assembly line. Nothing ghoulish over the victims; it was simply pride in a technological job well done. In Paris, meanwhile, British diplomats worked furiously to dissuade France from allowing more Exocets to fall into Argentine hands. The French stopped sales to Argentina but approved a shipment to Peru, and the British learned of the deal only at the last minute. "These days we cannot afford to maintain spies among our allies," a senior British officer remarked to me with a very thin smile. "Only our enemies." At a 4 A.M. meeting with senior French officials, British attachés and the ambassador made a last-ditch attempt to stop the Exocets, already loaded for export. The French argued that Peru had promised not to reexport the missiles. Finally, Thatcher telephoned Mitterrand, and the Exocets were not sent.

Published reports in Paris and London said that French technicians who had not been officially sanctioned had helped the Argentines arm the missiles. In London, I called on a man in a position to know, who asked not to be named. Did French experts arm the Exocets and then, at an official level, assist Britain in working out a defense against them? "Yes," he said. "That seems to be the case." As a strategy, it was only partially successful. When an Exocet was aimed at the British convoy, seamen confused its guidance mechanism (designed, ironically, in Britain) by firing off projectiles of aluminum strips. The Exocet missed its targeted warship. Instead, it sunk the *Atlantic Conveyer,* a cargo ship in the fleet.

Immediately after a ceasefire was signed, but while Britain still had 4,000 troops on the Falklands and feared a revenge strike, France resumed the shipments. In one month, five Exocet air-to-sea missiles were dispatched along with nine Super Etendard aircraft and a another shipload of munitions. Mrs. Thatcher acknowledged that France had contracts to fill but confessed to being extremely ir- ritated. British sailors from the *Hermes* fought a few pitched battles on French docks. And members of Parliament branded the move "near treason" and demanded economic vengeance.

Exocets reached such stardom that their black market price rose to a million dollars, five times their shelf price. But there weren't many around; the Argentines could not find any more.

Two years later, Aérospatiale took out a full-page ad in the *Economist* in London. It was not to apologize but rather to counter damaging claims that an Exocet failed to explode when it hit the tanker *Alexander the Great* in the Gulf War. It boasted: "Exocet is and remains the leader in its category . . . that's why it upsets people so much!" Aerospatiale condemned slander in Britain which claimed that the *Sheffield*'s Exocet had not exploded. As evidence, it quoted published remarks by Captain Salt, the ship's commander.

Aérospatiale noted that an ignorant public does not realize the Exocet's mission is to disable a ship, not necessarily to sink it.

These at times rather unspectacular results have therefore made the non-explosion hypothesis more easy to swallow. But in real- ity the high number of broadcasted results point to the contrary: from the beginning of the Iran-Iraq conflict up to 10th July last [1984], 112 ships were hit by Exocets (60 confirmed, 52 proba- ble). Out of 103 cases that were analyzed, 57 ships either sank, ran aground or were towed home for scrapping; damage to the other 46 was variable. Out of such a large number . . . only one case of non-explosion was recorded.

As the ad noted, "The Falklands conflict suddenly brought Exocet into unexpected limelight . . . some advertisements for detection systems even refer to the missile using 'Exocet' as a common noun."

Aérospatiale had, it said, 2,000 units ordered, with Exocets in service in twenty-seven countries.

At the height of the missiles' stardom, I went to the ancient little city where they are made: Bourges, the perfect picture of bourgeois France. It was once a stronghold of Vercingétorix; now it is one of the handsomest cities of *la France profonde*. The tourist office boasts of its cheese and Sancerre, of Jacques Coeur, the merchant who enriched King Charles VII, and, above all, of its stunning cathedral with foundations dating back to the Romans. But not of the Exocet. Inhabitants have been wrestling with their consciences ever since Napoléon III moved his cannonworks here a century ago. The fabled French 75s were made in Bourges.

The Aérospatiale public relations man said he could tell me nothing without Defense Ministry clearance, not even his own name. The missile is made at a government-owned plant on rich farmland at the edge of town, masked by trees and guarded by ill-tempered dogs. At a nearby café, a retired hardhat named Arthur told me, "The Argentina junta is terrible, like Hitler. But this is commerce." Deputy Mayor Marguerite Renaudat, a Communist with blued hair and a motherly manner, said, "This is not a simple problem for Bourges, with our old vocation of arms manufacturing. We are for armaments and peace." But at the Chamber of Commerce and Industry, Secretary General Henri Cotte was blunt: "If the unfortunate conflict between Britain and Argentina has allowed the world to discover French arms, I can only rejoice and hope that our business doubles."

In the cathedral, an elderly souvenir seller had never heard the word Exocet (which means, incidentally, flying fish in French). "Exocet? Exocet?" she repeated. Then, glancing down at postcards of Bourges' favorite king, she brightened. "Ah! You mean, Charles *Sept.*"

ARMS SALES offer France a political advantage, but they are also lucrative. After food, armaments are France's biggest selling item, 60 billion francs in 1984. The Socialists announced on taking office in 1981 that they would scrutinize all customers and add an element of "morality" to their arms exports. Only Chile was crossed off the list. Selected gear went to Nicaragua, instead. Once arms go to Belgium or Switzerland, the trail evaporates, and energy to pursue their eventual destinations flags. The system offers ample rationalization for those whose consciences need it.

In late 1985, when Reagan was freezing Qaddafi's assets and ordering all Americans out of Libya, the state-owned French television reported that France had acted secretly as broker to help Libya buy hand-me-down Argentine gunboats.

Looking ahead, the analysts disagree on France's role in the New Old World. Paris has long since lost its role as capital of the universe, but France is no toothless power. The answer, of course, depends on the shape of the world around France.

If the arms race moves into orbit, the French nuclear force could face obsolescence. France's conventional power is questionable. A senior general was censured in 1985 for saying that the French arsenal was inadequate and out-of-date. But that was hardly news. When the rapid-action force prepared to march for the first time on Bastille Day, *Le Canard Enchaîné* noted that the army had requested 154 Transalls, fifty-six for the FAR alone; but there were only sixty-five altogether. The paper recalled Operation Manta in Chad, when it took three months to transport 3,300 men, 12,000 tons of freight, thirty helicopters and 700 vehicles; there were 150 round-trips by DC8s; constant flights by thirty-six requisitioned jumbo jets from UTA; and eighty round-trips by Transalls, which can cover 2,400 miles carrying four tons of cargo. "But, for the moment," *le Canard* said, "at least the Rapid Action Force knows how to march."

But money is pumped regularly into the nuclear program. New technology is pursued, as in biomedical research and the other sciences, with *rayonnement* firmly in mind.

And there are still the intangibles. France adds up to more than the sum of its parts. You can still feel the slight electric charge at diplomatic gatherings when the French ambassador walks into a room. He represents not only the Fifth Republic but also Voltaire.

The Cold War thawed to détente, but that, too, is going. New balances and approaches are forming, and they are not clear. "I'm looking for a new word for 'détente,'" Flora Lewis told me at the end of 1985. She will most likely find one. And my bet is that, like détente—and *rapprochement* and *fin du monde*—it will be a French word.

CHAPTER TWENTY-ONE

A Modern Mission

BACK BEFORE HE hired I. M. Pei, a Chinese-American, to
create a reflecting glass pyramid at the entrance to the Louvre,
French culture minister Jack Lang enlivened one of those deadly
United Nations conferences in Acapulco. He denounced ". . . this
financial and cultural imperialism that no longer, or rarely, grabs
territory but grabs consciousness, ways of thinking, ways of living."

He meant the United States. The French, in the midst of discover-
ing America the way the Lost Generation found France a half-
century before, did not think much of the speech. Judging from his
actions in the following years, neither did Lang. But Lang meant
what he was trying to say in 1982.

In a world of satellites, transistors, cheap flights, and easy borders,
Western nations can do little more than add flavor to an amorphous
Atlantic omniculture. In most places, that is a side issue. Not in
France. Culture is what makes a nation of fifty-five million sit at
the most privileged of tables. Every French person knows that a
counter-clockwise twist of the rheostat portends ignominious decline. France might—*que Dieu la protège*—go the way of Britain.

Culture is the Maginot Line. Properly defended, it allows France
to radiate civilization, according to its historic mission. But the
Anglo-Saxons loom. On top of films, music, and advertising, foreign television is ever more pervasive. There is a nightmarish specter
of reality; only a state of mind protects Paris from becoming a
suburb of Dallas.

It seems that *rayonnement* might be a diminished priority behind the more pressing pursuits of economic growth and political solidity. Times are hard in Western Europe. Among *les grass roots,* the concern is jobs, not glory. The alarmists wonder whether French democracy will survive its second century, until 1989.

But the radiance of French culture is not a luxury, it is a fundamental point of departure. Without it, *ça, alors* . . .

Each country has its comparative strengths and weaknesses. Sustained competition in unfamiliar markets is not France's forte. The French, by and large, are lousy salesmen; few believe the customer is right. French bureaucracy is hard on international business. But France has two advantages. One is that its products are generally good. The other, far more important, is the heat emitted by a handsome business card that radiates France.

"All forays out of the Hexagon have ended unhappily," Fernand Braudel observed in 1985, "but there is one permanent triumph of French life that is a cultural triumph, a *rayonnement* of civilization. The identity of France is this *rayonnement,* more or less brilliant, more or less justified."

But French grandeur today, he added, rests on past glory. The menace is that the *rayonnement* may grow steadily less brilliant and, therefore, be increasingly less justified. No one forgets de Gaulle: "France cannot be France without grandeur."

THE WEEKLY *Le Point,* in a cover story entitled, "How to Resist the American Cultural Invasion," noted that European culture ministers met at Delphi in mid-1985 to reflect on the transitory nature of *gloria.* Had they switched on the television that day, they could have seen Montpellier by satellite, where 30,000 electrified youths in jeans and UCLA T-shirts, crushing Coke cans with their cowboy boots, were singing along with Bruce Springsteen and the E Street Band, "Born in the USA."

FUTURE FRENCH grandeur will be built largely at home. France is out of the colonization business. Political chaos may force a Sixth Republic, but not a Third Empire; not even the fanatic Bonapartists in Corsica expect a Napoléon IV. De Gaulle defined France's world role, but events beyond French control shape the script. Still, if no longer producer or director, France remains a principal actor. It can at least upstage the cast and bring down the house.

France's modern empire is figurative but substantial, particularly among the vast populations who live toward the bottom of the page in World Bank reports. To developing peoples, America exports red sorghum and money. The Soviets offer ideology and used MiG fighters. But France sends foreign aid shipments of civilization.

As the Algerian War was ending, with French Africa independent, de Gaulle dispelled any nagging fears: "We have always had a humane mission and we have it still; policy must adapt itself to our genius." And: "France comes from the depth of ages . . . the centuries call her. But she remains herself throughout time."

Twenty-five years later, Mitterrand's message was fraught with unsettling defensiveness. English pressed in from all sides. French was nearly absent in the Far East. Even French diplomats sometimes forgot to speak their own language at international meetings.

In defense of Culture, France relies most heavily on the language. French is a fine tongue, and its keepers tremble at the advance of *franglais,* or its insidious offshoot, *framéricain.* But, offensive as it is, English is hardly a threat to the culture. The French do not "borrow" words any more than Napoléon borrowed the obelisk at Luxor. They bring them home, implant them in a figurative place de la Concorde, and drive past them every morning with a self-satisfied smirk of possession.

The French use some English for concepts not readily found in their own language, such as *fair play* and *gentleman.* Other words just muscle their way in. It is perfectly proper French to say, *"Un gentleman en bluejeans et blazer lit un best-seller sur le ferryboat."* But mostly, by the time an alien word earns its *carte de séjour,* the French have colonized it.

In French, *un look,* pronounced "luke," means the image conveyed by careful primping, facial expression, and clothing, as in *un look cool*. The Académie Française accepted *blue jeans* long after French designers created a whole new *look* from the Levi's we wore as kids. Not many American *drugstores* have full-blown restaurants, electronics supermarkets, and movie theaters.

Take *le fast food.* Immediately, the French played on the words: It is, for some, *fast fou.* In French, *fou* means crazy, or soaring far beyond what is seemly. (Or, with real *esprit,* it is *faste fou:* a *faste* is an ostentatious banquet.) They began their own chains and added *herbes provençales* and *gruyère* to the recipes. And application made the concept exclusively French. When the first McDonald's opened just off the Champs-Elysées in 1976, an elegant gentleman ordered: *"Un Beeg Mac, s'il vous plaît. Pas trop cuit."* Not too well done.

Faceless staffs, not having to answer to customers, dealt with unfamiliar pressure by throwing raw patties onto buns. The French lined up at counters according to custom, side by side and shoving, all clamoring for attention. In *The New Yorker,* Calvin Trillin devised the Prix du Hamburger and explored fast food in Paris. He wrote:

> I couldn't imagine that any fast-food outfit could afford to rent a store on the Champs-Elysées wide enough to accommodate more than one or two French lines. Also, it occurred to me that a customer who finally reached the head of a line at a French Burger King might ask for a couple of Whopper burgers, an order of fries, and a chocolate milkshake only to have the counterperson poise a scratchy quill pen over some exceedingly long forms, look up sourly, and say, "Granmuzzer's maiden name?"

Gretchen and I stopped at a service area on the *autoroute* south. *Un fast-food* featuring hamburgers had opened next to *le self,* the traditional self-service cafeteria. Gretchen, reared in Idaho, is of the "catsup" persuasion. She asked for some. *La countergirl* gave her a quizzical look. Finally, Gretchen explained in flawless French that catsup was a sort of tomato sauce applied to *hamburgers* and *hotdogs* and she was certain some could be found behind the counter in foil packets. *"Ahh,"* the young woman said, fixing Gretchen with that piercing stare the French reserve for foreigners who defile their language, "you mean *ketchup."*

Poisoning the language is one thing. But some fear that fast food might do worse. What if, as a result of this trend, the French lost their regard for decent food? What if Hell had ski lifts? The best French chefs still chart their lives by Michelin stars. Most give no more thought to the Big Mac than a ballet dancer would to a jogger. Not long ago, I had a chicken salad at Alain Chapel's near Lyon.

Actually, it was "a salad of *roquette* lettuce, rare mountain greens, and slivers of young Guinea fowl from Bresse with garlic-rubbed crusts in nut oil."

There is fear that foreign hordes might crowd out the French at decent tables. In 1986, the more famous restaurants were filling up months in advance, and cash deposits were required with reservations. Some restaurateurs devised the perfect Parisian solution. They fixed a 40 percent quota on bookings from people with funny accents and non-French names. "As far as filling our *salles* with Americans, we would do better to build annexes under a sign of Uncle Sam," said Claude Terrail of the Tour d'Argent. But he is not unreasonable. Downstairs and across the street from his restaurant, he sells *foie gras de canard frais* and four kinds of honey for American rejects to leave conspicuously around their kitchens. You can even buy a Tour d'Argent ashtray to make it look as if you ate there. In fact, Terrail told one food writer, he put the shop in a vacant location so no trashy *couscous* joint could lower the tone of the street corner.

Other restaurateurs, like Paul Bocuse, reach out to the masses but defend the sanctity of their dining rooms. The balance is delicate, however. Roger Viard, or rather Monsieur Roger, retired in 1985 after forty-seven years at Maxim's, twenty-five of them as head maître d'hôtel. And that's not all. At his last New Year's Eve party, there were more Lebanese and American tourists than *tout-Parisiens*. Rather than the traditional black and white party favors, there were false noses and gaudy hats. Viard told Hebe Dorsey (who is a sort of Eiffel Tower among society scribes), "It is not Maxim's that has changed. It is the world that has changed."

France is keeping pace. Maxim's is now owned by Pierre Cardin, who has placed so many *PC* monograms on bizarre articles in remote places that the initials might as well stand for *Père Civilisateur*.

Electronics help pigs sniff out truffles. Banners exclaiming *"Le Beaujolais nouveau est arrivé"* outshadowed in Kinshasa streets the signs welcoming Mitterrand on a visit to Zaire. And now there is kosher Beaujolais.

Inroads penetrate, however. A classy little *épicerie* on the Ile Saint Louis sells Fauchon's products but also Old Paso chili con carne and two strengths of enchilada sauce. And American chocolate chip cookies. "We make them here, but they are not French copies," the shopkeeper told me. "They are the real thing." She added, "We even have pumpkin pie, *pour le Sanksgiving.*" Papa Maya, a Paris Mexican restaurant with roots in San Antonio, advertises, "The Eiffel Tower now has Taco Power."

Lang worried that French restaurants might slip to the function of those elsewhere in the world: just serving food. In France, he was dead right to insist, food is a pillar of culture. And not only its preparation and presentation. The great Carême codified cuisine in twelve fat volumes, and there were things even he didn't know. That French chefs travel worries no one; Escoffier spent most of his career on a civilizing mission to London. But, just to make sure the pillar is not eroded, Lang organized a school for advanced French cuisine.

Not to worry. You can still get one of the world's finer meals at a Paris train station. At Le Train Bleu in the Gare de Lyon, under baroque gilt-scrolled ceilings, with pastels of cherubs and landscapes and Sarah Bernhardt, you can eat *foie gras* and watch your train load for Milan. On the same plush banquettes, colonels and colonial officers put away their last decent *gigots* before traveling down to Marseilles to board their ships and go off to settle the world.

USING FOREIGN words is hardly new. Lyautey, nearly a century ago, argued that French policy should be, "*Le right man for the right place.*" Nor is it only one way. I've never heard anyone say, *un je ne sais quoi* in Paris. In New York, it is as common as *gwon, get outta heah.* Or, *déjà vu,* pronounced, dayja voo. The *Washington Post* observed in an editorial that languages are like little kids, seizing words that delight them with no thought to origin; banning a word's use merely adds to its flavor. As Truman Capote's Holly Golightly might remark over a *croissants* and *café au lait* breakfast at Tiffany's, "quelle ridicule."

Words go back and forth, like people. Les Ateliers Gaget, for example, built the Statue of Liberty in Paris and then flooded the world with small reproductions of Mlle. Liberté. "Chewing their words like gum," as a Parisian journalist observed, Americans produced the words, *gadget*.

The French love the word *gadget,* and they love gadgets even more. One of Mitterrand's creations in Paris is La Villette, a half-billion-dollar erector set cradling a giant silver golf ball, on the site of an abandoned slaughterhouse. Two and a half times the size of the Centre Pompidou, it is a playland showcase of science, technology and industry. La Villette is to cost $80 million a year to operate as a reminder to the world that France entered the twenty-first century ahead of schedule. And it was opened, on the night Halley's Comet passed, with nineteenth-century French flair. Amid the electronic gadgetry, cellists in tails and the Radio France choir performed Berlioz.

La Villette symbolizes the French concern for its image as a modern innovator—and exporter. France has not registered a year-end trade surplus since 1978. Japan puts twice as many students through the higher levels of education, with emphasis on industrial training. That is no small worry. In a major policy statement, Mitterrand said: "One wins Austerlitz when one takes away a position in electronics or biology. One loses Waterloo when one abandons automobiles or machine tools. These are the real modern battlefields."

This is a principal reason for defending the language. The French devised the word *logiciel* for software and set about writing sophisticated programs in their own language. "Must we translate into English the orders we give our machines?" the president asked.

The Académie Française rails at *le marketing* when *commercialisation* is perfectly adequate. A special commission has actually made it a crime (punished by a fine, not a jail term) for some use of foreign terms in advertising and business when French ones will do. When French words are not available, they are invented. Thus, the English "fuel" is, in French, *fioul.* "Cash flow" becomes *MBA* for *marge brute d'autofinancement.* And, to match the acronym for a type of bond called CATS, the French came up with *fonds d'Etat libres d'intérêts nominaux.* That is, FELIN.

A group known as AGULF took forty-four companies to court in 1985 for violating the 1975 law. TWA, for example, was fined $500 for issuing boarding passes in English at Charles de Gaulle Airport. To protest foreign words in commercials, Lang wrote to the head of the broadcasting authority, in English: "Should we fail to take steps promptly, we will most certainly lose our identity as a nation—give up our very soul."

But the use of Americanisms in business reflects a penetration much greater than linguistic. Whatever the French call it, they are thinking hard about old ways of producing, advertising, and placing goods in the market. A growing number of French executives leave Harvard Business School with a perfect command of American, from computer jargon to corporate sleaze.

"Supermarket" was quickly consumed and digested; the French broadened the concept to the *hypermarché*. French entrepreneurs run Bigg's in Cincinnati, four times the size of most supermarkets, perhaps in revenge for "Dynasty."

Not long ago, Americans had to come up with "smart card" to match the *carte à mémoire*. Once the French decided against turning up their noses at credit cards, they invented one with a microprocessor stamped onto it for fast authorizations and automatic banking. Credit cards are now so common that drivers can pay twenty-cent freeway tolls with any of a handful. This is France, of course. Small-merchant associations howled that banks took too much of a commission. "When we explain to Parisians how much that little insect of a card costs us, they understand very well and take out their checkbook," a hotelier in the south told a *Libération* reporter. But banks ordered twelve million smart cards to be ready by 1988.

Some worry about a brain drain or, more properly, a *fuite des cerveaux*. The French are attracted not only by American concepts, but by America itself. When Mitterrand visited Silicon Valley in 1984, Steve Jobs was brutally frank about the French lag in computer technology. Not long before Jobs got the delete key at Apple, a new, flashy young executive showed up at the company's headquarters: Jean-Pierre Gassée, "the Frenchy," who had directed Apple-France. But brain drain is not terminal. It takes less time to fly home to Paris from the North Carolina Research Triangle than it does to drive from St. Tropez back to avenue Foch. And well-paid French engineers and executives can take only so many hush puppies.

The most serious concern is over television, films, and advertising. And with reason. At 8:30 A.M., there is "Peyton Place," with a very young Mia Farrow. At midday, there is "Starsky et Hutch."

And then "Dynasty" and "Columbo" and the never-ending saga about guess which ranch. One French carmaker sells its latest model on TV, with dramatically done special effects, by driving it into Grace Jones's mouth. On Antenne 2, programming ends with "Les Vidéo Clips." French teenagers who forgot that their uncles died in Indochina thrill to *Rambo.* Fans watching Clint Eastwood point a pistol at someone pondering whether to attack do not need the subtitle: *"Faites mon jour."*

French television bought "Miami Vice," an event worth three full pages in *Libération.* "Intense, man," the paper observed.

On television, France rang in 1986 with, yet again, Springsteen and "Born in the USA." Chauvinists could have changed channels —to a Fred Astaire retrospective, followed by *Three Little Words* in the original English.

France produced a home-grown "Dallas" called "Châteauvallon." It was a national event. For all the critics' wisecracks, it was an engaging program. The opening aerial shot showed, rather than "Souzfork," the stately Berg manor on the Loire. The Bergs had grown rich and powerful from their provincial newspaper. Florence Berg, a chic Paris lawyer who received clients in a pink satin jogging suit, inherited the paper. But the actress, Chantal Nobel, was injured in an accident after the first season. The producers decided not to write her out of the script; instead, they canceled the show.

Mickey Mouse is no longer just a frequent visitor to France; he has been granted permanent residence. Europe's first Disneyland, on 4,500 acres outside Paris, is to receive ten million people a year. It immediately produced a labor squabble worthy of Scrooge McDuck. Developers wanted flexibility to hire and fire according to seasonal demand. French unions called that "a massacre of workers' rights." Authorities were bitter at guarantees developers wanted on paper. "We're not a banana republic," remarked a senior French official. Some French wondered why France was not exploiting Astérix instead of an imported rodent.

The nation's main event is still a bicycle race, up the Alps, along the Riviera, and through the Normandy hedgerows: *le Tour de France.* Its official drink is no longer Perrier, however; it is Coca-Cola. A boastful commentary in the *Wall Street Journal* made too much of that. One French racer remarked, "So? I don't like Coke, and I am not going to pedal any faster to the finish to drink one."

All is not lost. There are still Frenchmen who hear "Rambo" as Rimbaud, the eccentric French poet who assaulted Africa, not Vietnam. An American journalist honeymooning in the Champagne region asked at dinner for Perrier. "Tout de suite, madame," replied the waiter, and he popped the cork from a bottle of Laurent Perrier. It was a $50 drink of water, with no water.

But Americans are coming in from all sides, poking into France's most treasured institutions—and the French psyche.

La Comédie-Française, founded in 1680, offered three one-act farces by Feydeau in 1985. The director, Stuart Seide, was born in Brooklyn. He spent fifteen years in Paris and caught on fast to France; Lang granted him a subsidy. Seide chose to put on Feydeau. He told Mary Blume, in the *International Herald Tribune* Weekend section:

> The plays are very funny but very cruel. People talk about Jewish humor, gallows—in Feydeau someone says, "Your mother is dead" and it's a laugh a minute from that moment on. The production is funny but it isn't gay. French audiences, especially at the Comédie-Française, are very reverential—a lot of them see that Feydeau is cruel, but they don't want to believe it.
>
> What you have in Feydeau is people making totally rational self-justifications in total bad faith. The characters justify themselves with a certain logic and then contradict themselves with equal logic. Everyone talks very fast and no one listens. I guess I've gotten pretty good at that, too.

Americans are affecting French journalism. Christine Ockrent, broadcast superstar, did her boot camp at CBS. Serge July, editor of *Libération,* ordered his reporters to "Saxonize": to dig deeper and write harder. Let loose in France, *Saxonisation* could be poisonous to the beloved rhetoric. A prized skill is the ability to speak eloquently and at length on a subject about which the speaker knows nothing. Gaps in knowledge are spanned with the conditional tense or, *in extremis,* a wild stab in the dark.

The Univeristy of Nantes accepted a thesis in 1986 from a sixty-six-year-old student who "demonstrated" that Nazi gas chambers did not exist.

Masters of French rhetoric seize on an impression and then wing it. Sometimes they miss the mark. Alphonse de Chateaubriant, winner of the Prix Goncourt and the French Academy's grand prize, wrote in 1939: "The physiognomic analysis of Hitler's face reveals . . . his immense kindness. Look at him, in the midst of children . . . he is immensely kind, I repeat it."

French scientists, among the world's most accomplished, often rail at the rhetoric. Claude Lévi-Strauss oversees in France a sociological database produced at Yale University. It contains millions of references with line-by-line indexes of works on every people of the world. Twenty copies exist, eighteen in the United States, one in Japan, and one in France. No U.S. agency makes a move overseas without first consulting the file, Lévi-Strauss said. In twenty years, he added, not one French public official has ever consulted it.

Levi-Strauss, for many young Frenchmen, is more familiar as the name of a San Francisco pants maker.

Some political veterans, such as Michel Debré, warn of total eclipse if France does not beam more brightly. They want more emphasis on cultural heritage. Jacques Séguela, media master and image-maker, fears the past is fading away. He told a reporter, "My son does not know Molière, but he knows J. R."

But even Molière has a shelf life. He is immortal but as much universal as he is French. Cultures are not defended, they are nourished. Shakespeare did not save the English.

In 1944, Georges Duhamel produced a slim volume entitled *Civilisation Française* in which, ignoring the moment's humiliation, he catalogued the countless glories of France. He wrote:

> The traveler who goes from nation to nation encounters everywhere people to learn French, to speak French and to find pleasure in it. France does little, in sum, for such a grand result and what one ordinarily calls propaganda—frightful word—figures little in the cordial favor. If foreign peoples love to learn French, to speak it, to write it, it is that our beautiful language is the key to a great civilization.

Today's mission is to remind the world of that fading reality.

French radiance depends heavily on its source of light, *la ville lumière,* the capital of the world. Only the king of France or the president of the Republic can mess around with Paris. Henri IV, four Louises and a pair of Bonapartes committed grandeur to space and stone. And each modern overlay has a name. The ugly high-rise at Montparnasse: Pompidou. The preserved old roads along the quais: Giscard d'Estaing. Mitterrand himself chose Pei for the Louvre. He also guided plans for an opera at the Bastille and four other major new landmarks.

De Gaulle inadvertently let Paris slip badly. André Malraux, his culture minister, looked after grandeur in a manner rarely seen since Sully and Colbert. Malraux's lofty gaze saw monuments and *maisons de culture.* Meantime, venal and clumsy developers ate away the edges of Paris. More recently, the scourge has struck les Halles, what Zola called the belly of Paris.

I first saw Paris the night they shut down les Halles, in 1968. Almost forever, greengrocers had bought produce there at dawn from wholesalers who rumbled in all night from the farms. Hectic trading was done under elegant iron and glass umbrellas, the Pavillons Baltard. Near Saint Eustache church, a row of brasseries served steaming thick onion soup, paved with melted Gruyère and bread. Workers stopped off at the bars for *un petit coup* against the cold, or for the hell of it. Hookers faced the morning with oysters and absinthe.

But the trucks choked Paris streets. The noise was deafening. The rats had their own *force de frappe.* In the student revolt of May 1968, so many demonstrators hid in its warren of alleys that it became the Casbah of Paris. Les Halles was coming down.

On the last night, young crowds snake-danced through the streets. A pick-up orchestra climbed onto a stone fountain and played "Those Were the Days" with trumpets and tubas, encouraged by a barrage of wine bottles pitched to them at each pause. I was with a friend, and we wanted onion soup at Le Pied-de-Cochon. Do not miss it, we had been told. The place was jammed. Waiters spun among small tables set in a barnlike room. A kindly maître d'hôtel built us a rickety table by the cash register. This was the promised Paris.

In its place, de Gaulle wanted Versailles splendor. Pompidou wanted downtown Chicago. Giscard d'Estaing and Jacques Chirac, prime minister and later mayor of Paris, did not know what they wanted. In compromise, les Halles was a twenty-six-acre hole in the ground. Costly studies were made and filed away. The building dragged on for years.

Today, les Halles is a stark multistory underground shopping mall, sinisterly modern and reeking of hamburger grease, where you can get your body sequined or your wallet lifted. The Pavillons Baltard were trucked off and junked, replaced by featureless plastic and concrete. "A monster," concluded art critic Pierre Cabanne of *Le Matin*. "It is one of the most distressing architectural white elephants ever imagined. The heart of Paris has been forever disfigured and plundered." *Ah, oui.*

Outside Paris, some châteaux and churches edge toward collapse. The skills to repair them are disappearing as fast as the old fortunes necessary to pay for them. The French tax is based on visible signs of wealth. A fat Austrian bank account is less splendid but far easier to keep. The old towns of worn stone and hardy geraniums are increasingly blemished with garish *grande surface* discount stores and sore-thumb housing projects. Parts of modern France bear as much resemblance to classic proportion and style as Athens sprawl does to Ancient Greece.

But there is plenty left of Paris and France. On that first night in Paris, we walked from les Halles to the Ile Saint Louis. Now, from any of the little stone bridges on the Seine, the gentle orange lights still sparkle. The view has not changed much since Sully stood admiring his handiwork more than three centuries ago. You can exit almost any *autoroute* and follow the cobblestones to a France of slow-turning cheeses and wild raspberries.

Some people fear it is the French themselves who are disappearing. They argue that the French no longer live up to France. Young people, traveling and looking outward for nourishment, no longer take the time to worry about curdling sauces. The great figures are dying off, taking their age with them. Polls track a steady decline in values, traditions, and old skills. Pure French people, this argument goes, are destined to live on artificially protected ground, on a sort of postindustrial Indian reservation.

Merde.

It is true, as Steven Spielberg lamented on an Academy Awards night, the coming year would not produce a new Truffaut film. But every Wednesday, *Pariscope* lists the 300 movies shown each week in town. Bardot retired long ago to save baby seals, but a dozen talented young actresses raise box office receipts.

Simone de Beauvoir and Jean Genêt, the grand rebels, died within a day of one another in 1986. But each left a lot behind.

Sartre is no more dead than Marx is, or God. He was fresh in the news in 1986 because of a biography by Annie Cohen-Solal; every second reviewer confessed a desire to nibble the author's neck. *Magazine Littéraire* carried a recent who's who of sixty-three philosophers worthy of argument. The flashy ones are as famous as rock stars. Bernard-Henri Lévi marches against racism. Derrida and his gang of deconstructionists pick apart whatever Descartes left intact.

Even if most French had never heard of him, Claude Simon won the 1985 Nobel Prize for literature; unlike Sartre in 1964, he accepted it. A far better known French author writes Proust-sized novels on a subject long thought pornographic: money. Paul-Loup Sulitzer scorns a hypocritical *bourgeoisie* that uses words like *parvenu* to put down people who make their own fortunes.

Sulitzer is popular in America, where a lot of French artists are now found. Pierre Boulez was music director of the New York Philharmonic until 1977 and he teamed up in concert with Frank Zappa.

That hardly suggests, as some argue, a decline of French culture. The new nature of borders obliterates the old guidelines. It is harder today to base cultural superiority on illusion. But it is easier to exhibit talent (or genius, when it appears) to a lot of people at once.

And the point is not which individuals one can cite. A society's level of *civilisation* is determined not by its summits but by its base camps. It is not easy to measure.

NO ONE TAKES more polls than the French. Since poll-takers cannot correct for the vast number of French who slam doors in their faces, the results are often dubious. But I found at least one useful poll in 1985. *Le Chasseur Français* found that 84 percent of respondents thought contact with nature is essential; 45 percent had left, or were about to leave, the cities to live closer to nature. But only 0.5 percent could identify the leaves of an oak, elm, beech, or birch.

And a Sofres sampling suggested that 82 percent of the French believe their politicians lie to them. In spite of that, 55 percent think politics an honorable profession.

French self-delusion mingles with a devaluation of labels. Politics do not follow a linear concept between right and left. France has red millionaires and downtrodden Fascists. The radicals, *les radicaux,* are moderate.

Alain Duhamel noted, "It is a comic misunderstanding, an ironic mistake of history: the English, Spaniards, Belgians, Dutch, and Scandinavians believe they live in monarchies; the French think they are in a Republic. In reality, the reverse is true." Mitterrand himself remarked that the president of France has too much power. A hostile National Assembly could temper that. But Duhamel is right: France elects a king.

Chirac provoked crisis in 1986, immediately after moving in as prime minister. His constitutional powers rivaled those of the president. He decided to attend the industrialized powers' summit in Tokyo, with Mitterrand. For starters, where would he sit? Anywhere, his aide remarked dryly, but under the table. Unwittingly, he made the pecking order clearer than he would have wished. Mitterrand took the Concorde. Chirac bought a ticket on Air France.

Cohabitation was thus defined. One could cohabit government offices but not a throne.

The French are basically conservative, fond of strong leaders and the status quo, until they decide to change both. A century and a half after the July Revolution, royalists can choose between two branches of pretenders in the wings. The comte de Paris, the uncrowned Henri VI, traces himself back 1,000 years to Hugues Capet.

When Socialists and Communists took power in 1981, Baron Guy de Rothschild checked out of France with a bitter note of goodby. Patriarch of the French Rothschilds, society leader and lover of horses, he was the most famous of financial refugees fleeing the left. His family bank nationalized, he moved to New York. He wrote to *Le Monde:* "A Jew under Pétain, a pariah under Mitterrand

—for me, it is enough. To rebuild on ruins twice in a lifetime is too much."

Rothschild blamed Socialist excesses and other such spasmodic fits on French attitudes toward money. The French, he told an interviewer, love money more than any other people. "They are different from the Americans, who are obsessed with making money. The jealousies, the pettiness of the French are very specific regarding money." His book, *The Whims of Fortune,* began: "[The French] cling to a pathological distinction between their own possessions, which are sacred, and anonymous riches labeled 'finance,' which are suspect."

In 1985, at seventy-six, the baron decided to come home. The government had realized that soaking the rich was not such a great idea; politics had shifted to the right. But mostly he returned because France was still France.

Just before the 1986 elections, I met another former bank director who had been nationalized out of a job. He was not bitter. "The Socialists were needed to unite the country in 1981, and now they are not," he said with a shrug. "That is French politics."

IT COMES DOWN to personal judgment. Like any reporter's, my address book bulges with the names of experts: the historians, the savants of *Sciences-Po,* the French who live the lives I observe as an outsider. My shelves buckle under reports, figures, assessments, and cuttings squirreled away over a decade. I've pondered at length how to track the French mission to civilize with fairness and balance. It was Sempé, who captures France with a few flicks of a brush, who reassured me: "If you drew, you would see this. Someone always says, 'You forgot a young person, or a trade unionist, or a woman . . .' Never mind all that. Go for the feeling."

Sempé asked if I didn't find the French to be pretentious. That was what got to him.

As Descartes would say, yes and no. Sempé is not pretentious, for example. Pretense suggests assuming airs that are not backed by substance. France exudes substance. You cannot fool even some of the people some of the time for five centuries. The French spirit is rich in broad qualities and examples of individual greatness.

But, of course, the French are pretentious. That is their greatest quality, their most exasperating drawback, and their source of price-less natural wealth. Who else could have assumed the posture of universal greatness from the immortal achievements of a few? Who else could have shaped a civilization on refinement and *politesse* and then set off in gunboats to share it with the world?

There is a better term than pretentious. Naturally, it is French, and it defies translation. It is *quant-à-soi*, meaning self-esteem, a sort of confident aloof pride that is shaped and transmitted by a society. When one has it, one can *rayonner*.

Possessed of *quant-à-soi*, a Frenchman can take a position and answer to no one for it. Certainly not to a foreigner. To avoid *malheur*, he might have to keep that position secret. He might have to follow someone else's orders, perhaps under humiliating circum-stances. But he can hold his position and dismiss any contradiction with self-delusion. Defeat and humiliation pass. What matters is conviction, and flair.

In the French *quant-à-soi*, grandeur began at Biberacte, where Vercingétorix assembled the Gauls to defy the universe. Mitterrand, like any French president, is at his best on the ancient sites, claiming his spiritual heritage. Little, in fact, links the smooth intellectual Socialist president to the howling mad Celt with dirty long blond braids. But that is not the point.

A French leader establishes a link with the spirits. Thus il-luminated, it does not matter if the sky falls on his head. The Sun King built Versailles in perfect symmetry so light would radiate from his navel as he slept on his back. De Gaulle communed with the Gallic forest. Others choose more modest symbolism. But their role is the same. *Civiliser*, according to Larousse, means first "to bring out of a primitive state" and then "to polish the mores."

Simple facts do not bear out this leading role. "France is the fifth-ranking power," a friend on the *Wall Street Journal* pro-nounced the other day, whipping out World Bank figures to prove it. Of course, he is right.

Braudel himself agreed, right up to his death. For him, the seats of world commercial power were, in turn, Venice, Amsterdam, London, and New York. France succeeded only by being close to the center. The French blew their one chance to be great, he said, in Canada and Louisiana. Since 1763, it was all downhill. France might have built Europe after the war, Braudel said, but its *quant-à-soi* got in the way. "The sad thing," he told one interviewer, "is that France loses too often."

This proves nothing. Ah, goes the logical reply, but Braudel was the greatest historian of his age. And he was French. Eminent historians simply add richness to the debate. And bean-counting foreigners do not matter. France is great because it is great. An outsider who does not see that is disqualified from judgment because of an obvious failing: he is not French.

That France loses often is easily rectified. A young American I know remarked recently to his nine-year-old French pal that France had not won a war in 100 years. You're crazy, the kid replied. We won both world wars. No one had taught him that Germans had occupied France or that allies helped in the fight.

Traditionally, French reporters have helped along this self-delusion. Sanche de Gramont recalls describing in 1961, in the New York *Herald Tribune*, atrocities committed by French paratroopers on Tunisian civilians. He wrote:

> Michel Debré, then Premier, asked his press secretary whether I was a French national. On being told that I was, he said: "Tell that fellow that he is a very poor advocate of France." I wondered about the fragility of a regime that could only tolerate advocates. The border between criticism and lack of patriotism is blurred. It is considered disloyal to bare French failings to the outside world.

French reporters are starting to poke holes in the self-delusion. Pooled television coverage and computerized news agencies leave them no choice. When Marchand's Tricolor toppled into the Nile mud a century ago, snickers were limited to the immediate vicinity. The BBC would have loved footage on it.

And French governments find that impressing the benighted is no longer a small chore. The cost of trade beads escalates when rivals are handing out pieces of the moon. France's focus on specific high technology has made an impact. Still, it is not easy.

One year, France waited in vain for Mitterrand's New Year message, live from his country home near Bordeaux. The crane that was supposed to lift the antenna was off pruning trees. A year later, during a televised interview, he declared with finality that only state control could ensure technical excellence of television. Suddenly, his face froze in grotesque contortion. The picture flickered, the sound wavered, and transmission ceased for several minutes.

Giscard d'Estaing had his sniffer airplane. France put a substantial sum into a mysterious Belgian bank account for an Italian's dubious invention to find oil from the air. The government enjoined an official investigator to hush it up. Money down the hole is one thing. But *le look* of France?!

These are not sidelights but symbols in a nation whose grandeur is symbolic. Gaullism works for France; but it requires a de Gaulle. The French survived defeat, occupation, and eclipse. Ridicule would be a catastrophe of a different magnitude.

BEFORE FINISHING this study, I took a last plunge into *la France profonde*. First, I saw Jean-Claude and Hélène, both in advertising, world travelers, and the best of modern France. In their old mill house near Vézelay, I watched Hélène's father, Roger, pan-broil a beef rib in shallots. This does not mean putting on a funny apron and flinging a steak on the charcoal. Roger's recipe begins with spending forty-five minutes with the butcher discussing the relative merits of pieces of meat. He uses a splash of vinegar to *déglacer,* gauges the heat like a nuclear physicist, and produces a steak you could fight a war over.

I asked Jean-Claude if his son would be able to produce such a dish at Roger's age. "Look," he said, "Lorenzo will go see how Americans do things, and travel. He's growing up in a more open world. But he is learning where he comes from—and his grandfather's recipes. What I hope is he will have both roots and wings."

We went off to inspect the Burgundy wine country. At Clos de Vougeot, a vineyard so hallowed that French army units salute when marching past, my heart sank. The château's ancient stones had been sandblasted to a sheen. Heavy oaken doors were coated in something like congealed model airplane glue. A sign in four languages commanded: "No tipping." Cheap wrought iron blocked the entrance to a massive vault illuminated by stained plastic windows. A scratchy tape narrated the past. The grand entryway was domi-

nated by a souvenir counter selling pencils stamped with the vineyard's name at three for ten francs. There was an outrageously priced
stamped leather map of the wine country, which would make a
Taiwan kitsch king blush in shame. The winery probably still had
its heady aroma, but I could smell only exhaust from the tour buses.

We stopped at Savigny-les-Beaune, built around a château decorated in a relief of *rocaille* studded in handsome patterns on a
perfectly proportioned facade. A sign announced the château's new
purpose: a motorcycle museum. Even in 1986 France, it was hard
to imagine a fourteenth-century Harley-Davidson. The village
square was deserted except for an ambulant salesman: an Algerian
lugging a pile of rugs and sheepskins.

But we drove among darkening grapes to Romanée Conti, the
world's most expensive rural real estate, just an unassuming little
vineyard marked by a 150-year-old Calvary. And thoughts turned
to Lunch. An American will buy a house with less time and thought
than a Frenchman spends on determining where to eat lunch. Beaune
was out: too many tourists. One place was investigated and rejected.
Too full? No, too empty. I bordered on despair, sliding deep into
crankiness. My friends found the perfect spot. Of course. And then
we visited the *caves* of Louis Latour.

Not a symbol was out of place in the village of Carton. The
stooped old lady was there with her *filet* shopping bag of onions
and macaroni; the men in blue overalls, faces black with grease, bent
into the guts of a Citroën 2CV; Jean Gabin, in a frayed flannel suit,
ambled down the cobblestones by the old church, *Le Petit Parisien*
under his arm. We found only winemakers at the winery. Some
flashy technology sped up the process, but the old presses were still
there. When biological profusion clogs the old oak vats, an old-
timer takes off his boots and climbs in to degunk them. Our host
was a young Englishman who used to make dandelion wine; he
cared about wine and was studying at the source.

We bumped among dim underground vaults of stacked bottles
to a spiral stone stairway leading into blackness. The bottom level
was a set for Dracula meets Joan of Arc. Walls oozed green and
purple slime. Spooky long beards of mold hung from the prone
bottles and scarred wooden racks. Spiderwebs blocked the narrow
passages. And we sat down among bottles that were lying there

when Americans were fighting over slavery, to sip wine in the deepest innards of France.

Later, I went skiing at Val d'Isère. At a bar called Bananas, Ginny the Australian bartender was warm and efficient. After four seasons at the Val, she had trouble counting to twelve in French. "I panic when a French person comes in," she said, with a laugh. It was not serious; the few French who did come usually spoke English. The best hotel is the Squaw Valley, with the manager's Ford Bronco out front and a giant tin sign advertising Indian Motor Oil nailed to the wall. It houses Val d'Isère's finest restaurant, the White Ocean, which serves flapjacks.

They are not exactly flapjacks. They are *crêpes au saumon Vonnassien,* potato pancakes of fresh salmon, red salmon caviar, and a sauce of ethereal lightness. Didier, the young chef, worked with Georges Blanc, who created the dish.

In Paris, I took a long cab ride and talked to the driver. His taxi was a Soviet-built Lada, rare in France, and I remarked on it. He was defensive. "Yeah, the car is Russian, the driver is French. It's a solid car, good economy." His friends gave him a hard time, he explained. Why a Commie car when there were Peugeots, Citroëns, and Renaults in the world? I asked if the French were like that. His monologue lasted from the Pont-Marie to the place des Ternes, twenty-three minutes.

They are so narrow-minded and small, I tell you. . . . Last night, I had an Algerian in the cab who came for medical treatment. He had no hotel, and it was late. He went into five places. At every hotel, the same story: "Sorry, we are full." So I said, "Let me try; you stay in the car." At the first hotel, I explained I had a fare who needed a room. "But of course." They look at the Americans and say, "Oh, look what those bastards do to their blacks" and never see their own hypocrisy. . . . You're writing a book on the French? You'd better make it a long one.

Then I asked about him. He did volunteer church work to help the distraught. His son fought racism. In a self-effacing way, he conveyed the opposite of every trait he had decried in the French. But he was French, too.

On television, not long after, I watched the Saturday-night shouting match, "Droit de Réponse." For ninety minutes each week, a dozen notables of the present and past ignore one another to shout their own opinions above the general din. The subject that night was the children of Vichy. American historian Robert Paxton mentioned that Pétain led the only energetically collaborationist government in Europe, and he deported Jews even before Hitler asked. A voice, loud and hectoring, cut him off: "I don't butt into his affairs to tell him about the Indians in America." A minister in the Vichy cabinet tried to show how Pétain had protected the Jews. Marie-Claire Mendès-France observed that sending 79,000 Jews to their deaths was not very effective protection.

This was France: forty-five years later, some French were deluding themselves about brutal blackness in their past. And other French were rubbing their noses in it, making sure the record was clear. It seemed to me a better use of the airwaves than tracing the imaginary banalities of some Texas grease magnates.

I took a last flip through the clippings. Dreyfus was back in the news. The government commissioned Tim, a well-loved Jewish sculptor, to do the wronged officer in bronze. All was forgiven. L'Ecole Militaire, however, did not want the statue in its courtyard. All was not forgotten.

In a quick round of French roulette, I chose three last sources. There was Jacqui, a reformed bum at 37: "This country is finished, done. It can't compete. All over the world, people laugh at us. If you fall on your face here, you'll never get up. Look at the government: it's like the Shah of Iran ruling with the Ayatollah Khomeini."

There was an unnamed cab driver. My car had broken down in the middle of traffic; I approached him for help and, as soon as he saw I might mean bother, he sped away, spraying me with gravel. But then there was Madame Tourdes, the garage lady whose lunch got cold as she helped me out of the mess. She is one of those people who motivate outsiders to like the French as much as France. And she is not worried about the future of either.

Finally, I called on *la Vieille Dame du Quai Conti*, which is the Académie Française. I went to a news conference marking its 350th anniversary.

It was here that Cardinal Richelieu struck the match to light the world's path. And ever since, from plush grey and green armchairs under a soaring dome, an ever-replenished body of forty *Immortels* have tended the flame. The writer Michel Mohrt was brought into the circle in 1986, and Jean d'Ormesson welcomed him. Their speeches covered four full pages in *Le Monde*. D'Ormesson declaimed:

> "What purpose the Academy?" is one of those recurrent questions posed by imbeciles when they exhaust the charms of the weather. . . . What purpose? *Mais,* none, like all delicious and somewhat great things. What purposes cats, the Temple of Abu Simbel, the islands of the Italian lakes, the flamingos of the Camargue, military parades and the strutting of animals who wish to dazzle their conquests, the very old oaks of our fields, our memories of happiness? What purpose rites and ceremonies? To the eyes of a world dominated by money, by power in all of its aspects, by collective movements, fleeting and blind, what purpose the Academy? None. None at all. Its purpose is to be *beau*.

Maurice Druon, secretary in perpetuity, entered the room with two other members. We all rose. They sat before a huge Aubusson tapestry: Ceres, goddess of grain, clutching a sheaf of wheat in a chariot drawn by golden lions. Druon embodies French civilization. A dark suit with pinstripes and rich silk tie, mannerly tufts of grey-white hair emitting intellectual energy, charm and *politesse* edged with the subtle hint of potential arrogance. That he used teams of helpers to write often inane historical novels was totally beside the point.

He selected each syllable with infinite care, placing it ahead of him just so and then sinking into it as if it were a velvet cushion. In subtle patterns, he repeated key phrases, his voice booming and then dropping to a barely audible rasp. L'Académie was finishing the ninth edition of its dictionary. It would have 45,000 words. The eighth, published in 1935, had 35,000 words. French is evolving, he said, in its role of providing the means to precisely and clearly define the arts and sciences.

We had a light snack, the usual. Bits of fine marinated salmon on toast, *jambon d'Auvergne*, hazelnut mousse. Druon captivated a small group. He paused to unscrew the metal cap of a fat Havana and lit it with elaborate care. Waving the cigar, he pronounced:

"What is tradition, after all, but progress that has succeeded."[1]

I asked Druon about the phrase *mission civilisatrice*. "But of course it is in use," he said. "I use it myself." And its origin? "I don't know; I really cannot say," he replied. Then he reflected a moment, lifted his chin slightly and added, "It just naturally comes to mind."

WHEN SCHOOL started again in the fall of 1985, 12,300,000 children went back to a new curriculum. An experiment in *éveil* (awakening) to encourage individual expression was junked in favor of basic values: discipline, rigor, effort. Basic subjects were back: French, math, science and technology, history and geography. An emphasis on moral development was added. "Civic education," the government said of the new course, "develops honesty, courage, refusal of racism, love for the Republic."

This was Jules Ferry. The study of colonies was replaced by computer science, but the foundations were the same. In second grade, pupils contemplate a verse from Louis Aragon: "I found my lady by the water, my lady is France and I am her Lancelot." And they sing the "Marseillaise," complete with the impure blood spilled from enemies to drench French furrows. The message is more subtle, but the mission is the same.

Every culture keeps handy a few brief snatches of enduring popular wisdom. America is too young to have proved the value of any truly transcendental saying. But the French have one, nicked and worn from overuse, but apt on a minefield in ancient Gaul, at the court of the Sun King, in a Gabon supermarket, or in the little French village of St.-Paul lost out in the Indian Ocean: *Plus ça change, plus c'est la même chose.* The more things change, the more they remain unchanged.

It is likely there will always be an England. It is certain there will always be a France.

Notes

Chapter One

1. *Nouveau Dictionnaire Etymologique et Historique* (Paris: Larousse).
2. This translated extract is from Sanche de Gramont's *The French* (New York: Putnam, 1969), an amusing but hard-eyed look at France by a correspondent of French and American origin.
3. Emil Schreyger, *l'Office du Niger au Mali* (Weisbaden: Steiner, 1984).

Chapter Two

1. The contrast with Britain was marked. Associated Press correspondent Michael Goldsmith, a Briton, was arrested in the Central African Republic in 1977, as described in Chapter 13. Asked to help, the British government replied, "When a British subject finds himself in difficulty in an area where we have no representation, he must look out for himself." Goldsmith was freed in thirty days after intervention by African heads of state.
2. Jacques-Marie Bourget and Yvan Stefanovitch, *Des Affaires Très Spéciales* (Paris: Plon, 1986).

Chapter Seven

1. This quotation is from Jean Meyer, *La France Moderne* (Paris: Fayard, 1985), who has mixed his own paraphrase with direct citations from Machiavelli's *De Natura Gallorum*.
2. W. H. Lewis covers Challes's voyage in *The Splendid Century*

(New York: Morrow, 1978); Challes tells it himself in *Voyages aux Indes* (Paris: Plon, 1933).

3. Sanche de Gramont relayed this fragment of Racine in *The French*. I presume the translation is his.

4. Meyer, *La France Moderne*.

Chapter Eight

1. Slavery figures are disputed; these are Philip D. Curtin's estimates, cited by Pierre Pluchon, *Histoire des Antilles et de la Guyane* (Toulouse: Privat, 1982).

2. These figure are cited in the massive *Histoire des Colonies Françaises* by Gabriel Hanotaux and Alfred Martineau (Paris: Plon, 1929). Abbé Reynal confirms them in his work, cited in the text.

3. W. C. Stinchcombe, *The American Revolution and the French Alliance* (Syracuse, N.Y.: Syracuse University, 1969). Similar figures and deployments are found in *The War of American Independence: Military Attitudes, Policies and Practices, 1763–1789* (Urbana, Ill.: University of Indiana, 1971) and in Jean-Baptiste Duroselle, *France and the United States* (Chicago: University of Chicago Press, 1976). France's costs were believed to be two million dollars per year for 5,000 ground troops, as well as naval costs. It was never clear what was grant and what was loan. Beaumarchais sought repayment after the war. U.S. authorities finally settled with his descendants for 800,000 francs in 1835.

Chapter Nine

1. Marvin Zahniser, *Uncertain Friendship* (New York: John Wiley, 1975).

2. Henriette Celarié, *La Prise d'Alger* (Paris: Hachette, 1929).

3. Edward Behr, *The Algerian Problem* (London: Hodder and Stoughton, 1961). Behr, an old Algerian hand, dug out Saint-Arnaud's letters.

Chapter Ten

1. Once again, this is Sanche de Gramont, *The French*.

2. Paul Johnson, *A History of the Modern World* (London: Weidenfeld and Nicolson, 1983).

3. Nicole Priollaud, *La France Colonisatrice* (Paris: Liana Levi, 1983). A fascinating collection of thoughts on French colonization.

Chapter Eleven

1. Johnson, *History of the Modern World.*
2. Jean Lacouture, *De Gaulle*, Vol. 1, *Le Rebelle* (Paris: Seuil, 1984).
3. Michael R. Marrus and Robert O. Paxton, *Vichy France and the Jews* (New York: Basic Books, 1981).
4. Johnson, *History of the Modern World.*
5. Alistair Horne, *A Savage War of Peace* (London: Macmillan, 1977). I am especially indebted to this carefully researched account. The Algeria section is drawn from a number of published works, news dispatches, and personal interviews, but I found Horne, and the following cited work of Edward Behr, to be particularly useful.
6. Behr, *Algerian Problem.*
7. Horne, *Savage War of Peace.*
8. Behr, *Algerian Problem,* quoting from Jules Ferry's *Le Gouvernement de l'Algérie.*
9. Horne, *Savage War of Peace,* among others.
10. Horne, *Savage War of Peace.*
11. This is essentially Horne's account *(Savage War of Peace),* which is corroborated by others.
12. A former senior aide of Delouvrier's told me this; he asked to remain anonymous.
13. Michel Lévine, *Les Ratonnades d'Octobre* (Paris: Ramsey, 1985).
14. Again, Horne's careful research turned up this quotation from Flanner.
15. Horne, *Savage War of Peace;* also Johnson, *History of the Modern World.*
16. French military statistics are difficult to pin down. Defense Minister Charles Hernu reported the figure of 21,600 to the Senate on Jan. 20, 1982. Other figures are from Horne, *Savage War of Peace.* For Indochina, an Army spokesman gave me these figures in June 1985: 36,480 French dead; 21,000 missing; 72,200 wounded.

Chapter Twelve

1. Pascal Chaigneau, *La Politique militaire de la France en Afrique* (Paris: Centre des Hautes Etudes sur l'Afrique et l'Asie Modernes, 1984).
2. Roger Faligot and Pascal Krop, *La Piscine* (Paris: Seuil, 1985).
3. Faligot and Krop, *La Piscine*.

Chapter Thirteen

1. The Americans outdid the French in meddling in the Congo. A month after Lumumba was elected prime minister of the Congo, the CIA decided to kill him. An agent brought a specialized poison to Léopoldville, but the job was botched. Events then took care of themselves. A U.S. Senate commission determined that Allen Dulles gave the order and might have had reason to believe President Eisenhower wished him to take such a drastic step; Eisenhower's role was not established. The commission decided that it was in the long-term U.S. interest to admit the facts in the hope that other nations would respect a will to expiate wrongdoing.
2. *Le Monde* carried the leaked text on December 5, 1984.
3. F. Roy Willis, *The French Paradox* (Stanford, Cal.: Hoover Institution, 1982). Willis cites the U.S. Arms Control and Disarmament Agency.
4. Rolf Steiner, *The Last Adventurer* (Boston: Little, Brown, 1978).

Chapter Fourteen

1. *Libération,* citing *Cahier du Témoignage chrétien,* no. 54, February, 1973.

Chapter Fifteen

1. These details are included in Amir Taheri, *Khomeiny* (Paris: Balland, 1985). Taheri is a journalist in exile who knows his Iran.
2. Jonathan Randal covers this material in *Going All the Way* (New York: Viking, 1983), and he kindly discussed his current research on France in the Levant in personal interviews.
3. Gen. Henri Gouraud, "La France en Syrie," *La Revue de France,* April 1922.
4. *Le Nouvel Observateur,* January 17, 1977.

Chapter Sixteen

1. This information came from an Interpol source who cannot be named; later, official French sources substantiated it.

Chapter Eighteen

1. Max Savelle, *The Origins of American Diplomacy: The International History of Angloamerica, 1492–1763* (New York: Macmillan, 1967).
2. Zahniser, *Uncertain Friendship.*

Chapter Twenty

1. Thierry Wolton, *Le KGB en France* (Paris: Grasset, 1986).
2. Johnson, *History of the Modern World.*
3. Johnson, *History of the Modern World.*

Chapter Twenty-one

1. This was a direct quote from Druon's own acceptance speech to the Académie in 1967. In welcoming him, Sanche de Gramont notes, Louis Pasteur Vallery-Radot could not resist quoting some of the inanities in his books, such as: "Like nearly all those destined to the follies of passion, Mary had one eye slightly smaller than the other."

Bibliography

Ardagh, John. *France in the 1980s.* London: Secker and Warburg, 1982.

Atlas Colonial Français. Paris: L'Illustration, 1929.

Balandier, Georges. *Au Temps des Colonies.* Paris: Seuil, 1984.

Baldwin, Marshall. *History of the Crusades.* Vol. 1. Madison: Univ. of Wisconsin, 1969.

Bare, Jean-François. *Le Malentendu Pacifique.* Paris: Hachette, 1985.

Barril, Paul. *Missions Très Spéciales.* Paris: Presses de la Cité, 1954.

Barzini, Luigi. *The Europeans.* New York: Simon and Schuster, 1983.

Behr, Edward. *The Algerian Problem.* London: Hodder and Stoughton, 1961.

Benoit, Pierre. *Océanie Française.* Paris: Alpina, 1933.

Bergot, Erwan. *Gendarmes au Combat.* Paris: Presses de la Cité, 1985.

Blet, Henri. *Histoire de la Colonisation Française.* Paris: Arthaud, 1946.

Bodard, Lucien. *The Quicksand War.* Boston: Little, Brown, 1967.

Bordonove, Georges. *Les Templiers.* Paris: Fayard, 1977.

Bourget, Jacques-Marie, and Yvan Stefanovitch. *Des Affaires Très Spéciales.* Paris: Plon, 1986.

Braudel, Fernand. *La Méditerranée et le Monde Méditerranéen à l'Epoque de Philippe II.* Paris: Armand Colin, 1949.

———. *La Méditerranée.* Paris: Arts et Metiers Graphiques, 1977.

———. *L'Identité de le France.* Paris: Arthaud, 1986.

Brunschwig, Henri. *Noirs et Blancs dans l'Afrique noire Française.* Flammarion, Paris, 1983.

Burin des Roziers, Etienne. *Retour aux Sources.* Paris: Plon, 1986.

Caesar, Julius. *Conquest of Gaul.* Harmondsworth, England: Penguin, 1951.

Caron, François. *La France des Patriotes.* Vol. 5, *Histoire de France.* Paris: Fayard, 1985.

Casanova, Jacques-Donat. *America's French Heritage.* Paris: Documentation Française, 1976.

Celarié, Henriette. *La Prise d'Alger.* Paris: Hachette, 1929.

Cerny, Philip C. *The Politics of Grandeur.* Cambridge: University Press, 1980.

Chaigneau, Pascal. *La Politique militaire de la France en Afrique.* Paris: Centre des Hautes Etudes sur l'Afrique et l'Asie Modernes, 1984.

Chairoff, Patrice. *B . . . Comme Barbouzes.* Paris: Moreau, 1975.

Challes, Robert. *Voyages aux Indes.* Paris: Plon, 1933.

Chamberlain, M. E. *Decolonization.* Oxford: Basil Blackwell, 1985.

Cohen-Solal, Annie. *Sartre.* Paris: Gallimard, 1985.

Cook, Don. *Charles de Gaulle.* New York: Putnam, 1983.

Crété, Liliane. *La Vie Quotidienne en Louisiane.* Paris: Hachette, 1978.

Darcy, Jean. *Cent Années de Rivalité Coloniale.* Paris: Perrin, 1904.

De Beauvoir, Simone. *Force of Circumstance.* Harmondsworth, England: Penguin, 1968.

De Berthier de Sauvigny, G. *La France et les Français vu par les voyageurs américains.* Paris: Flammarion, 1985.

De Gaulle, Charles. *War Memoirs.* New York: Simon and Schuster, 1967.

De Gramont, Sanche. *The French.* New York: Putnam, 1969.

De Grèce, Michel. *La Nuit du Sérail.* Paris: Orban, 1982.

Delale, Alain, and Gilles Ragache. *La France de 68.* Paris: Seuil, 1978.

Delpey, Roger. *Affaires Centrafricaines.* Paris: Grancher, 1985.

De Pourtalès, Guy. *Nous à qui rien n'appartient.* Paris: Flammarion, 1931.

Des Champs, Hubert. *Les Pirates à Madagascar.* Paris: Berger-Levrault, 1972.

Desjardins, Thierry. *Nouvelle Calédonie.* Paris: Plon, 1985.

Dorgelès, Roland. *Sous le Casque Blanc.* Paris: Editions des France, 1941.

Douville, Raymond. *La Vie Quotidienne en Nouvelle France.* Paris: Hachette, 1964.

Duhamel, Alain. *Le Complexe d'Astérix.* Paris: Gallimard, 1985.

Duhamel, Georges. *Civilisation Française.* Paris: Hachette, 1944.

Dumont, René. *L'Afrique noire est mal Partie.* Paris: Seuil, 1962.

Duroselle, Jean-Baptiste. *In Search of France.* Cambridge: Harvard University Press, 1963.

————. *France and the United States.* Chicago: University of Chicago Press, 1976.

Dutourd, Jean. *La Gauche la plus bête du Monde.* Paris: Flammarion, 1985.

————. *Les Taxis de la Marne.* Paris: Gallimard, 1956.

Duval, Paul-Marie. *La Vie Quotidienne en Gaule.* Paris: Hachette, 1952.

Dyson, John and Joseph Fitchett. *Sink the Rainbow.* London: Gollancz, 1986.

Emmanuelli, René. *La Vie de Pascal Paoli.* Calvi, Corsica: Accadèmia d'i Vagabondi, 1976.

Espaces. *L'Identité Française.* Paris: Tierce, 1985.

Faligot, Roger, and Pascal Krop. *Services secrets en Afrique.* Paris: Le Sycomore, 1982.

————. *La Piscine.* Paris: Seuil, 1985.

Favier, Jean. *Le Temps des Principautés.* Vol. 2, *Histoire de France.* Paris: Fayard, 1984.

Flachère, R. P. A. *Sous la Menace des Idoles.* Paris: Plon, 1938.

Garnier, Francis. *Voyage d'exploration en Indochine.* Paris: La Découverte, 1985.

Gide, André. *Voyages au Congo.* Paris: Gallimard, 1927.

Girardet, Raoul. *L'Idée coloniale en France, 1871–1962.* Paris: La Table Ronde, 1972.

Goldschmidt, Arthur, Jr. *A Concise History of the Middle East.* Boulder: Westview Press, 1979.

Gregorj, Ghajcumu. *Chroniques irrespectueuses sur l'Histoires des Corses.* Calvi, Corsica: Accadèmia d'i Vagabondi, 1982.

Grimal, Henri. *La Décolonisation.* Paris: Colin, 1965.

Grosser, Alfred. *Affaires Extérieures.* Paris: Flammarion, 1985.

Grousset, René. *L'Épopée des Croisades.* Paris: Plon, 1939.

Guillebaud, J. C. *Les Confettis de l'Empire.* Paris: Seuil, 1976.

Hamdani, Amar. *La Vérité sur l'Expédition d'Alger.* Paris: Balland, 1985.

Hanley, D. L., A. P. Kerr, and N. H. Waites. *Contemporary France.* London: Routledge and Kegan Paul, 1984.

Hanotaux, Gabriel, and Alfred Martineau. *Histoire des Colonies Françaises.* Paris: Plon, 1929.

————. *La France en 1614.* Paris: Nelson, 1914.

Harmand, Jacques. *Vercingétorix.* Paris: Fayard, 1984.

Heinrich, Pierre. *La Louisiane.* New York: Burt Franklin, 1908.

Hill, John Hugh. *Raymond IV, Count of Toulouse.* Syracuse, N.Y.: Syracuse University, 1962.

Hoffmann, Stanley, *Decline or Renewal? France since the 1930s.* New York: Viking Press, 1974.

Hoffman, Stanley, and others. *In Search of France.* Cambridge: Harvard University Press, 1963.

Horne, Alistair. *A Savage War of Peace.* London: Macmillan, 1977.

————. *The French Army and Politics.* London: Macmillan, 1984.

L'Immigration Maghrébine en France. Paris: Les Temps Modernes, 1984.

Jacquier, Henri. *Piraterie dans le Pacifique.* Paris: Latines, 1973.

Jenkins, E. H. *A History of the French Navy.* London: MacDonald and Jane's, 1973.

Johnson, Paul. *A History of the Modern World.* London: Weidenfeld and Nicolson, 1983.

Jullian, Camille. *Vercingétorix.* Paris: Tallandier, 1977.

July, Serge. *Les Années Mitterrand.* Paris: Grasset, 1986.

Kahler, Miles. *Decolonization in Britain and France.* Princeton, N.J.: Princeton University Press, 1984.

Kennan, George F., *The Fateful Alliance.* New York: Pantheon, 1984.

Kennedy, Ludovic. *A Book of Sea Journeys.* London: Collins, 1981.

Kingsley, Mary H. *Travels in West Africa.* London: Macmillan and Co., 1897.

Klarsfeld, Serge. *Vichy-Auschwitz.* Vol. 1. Paris: Fayard, 1983.

————. *Vichy-Auschwitz.* Vol. 2. Paris: Fayard, 1985.

Knibiehler, Yvonne, and Regine Goutalier. *La Femme au Temps des Colonies*. Paris: Stock, 1985.

Lacouture, Jean. *De Gaulle*. Vol. 1, *Le Rebelle*. Paris: Seuil, 1984.

――――. *De Gaulle*. Vol. 2, *Le Politique*. Paris: Seuil, 1985.

Lacouture, Jean, and Simonne Lacouture. *Vietnam*. Paris: Seuil, 1976.

Lamb, David. *The Africans*. New York: Random House, 1982.

Langlais, Pierre. *Dien Bien Phu*. Paris: Editions France-Empire, 1963.

Lapping, Brian. *End of Empire*. London: Granada, 1985.

Lauga, Henri. *De la Banquise à la Jungle*. Paris: Plon, 1952.

Leblond, Marius. *Les Grandes Heures des Iles et des Mers Françaises*. Paris: Colbert, 1943.

Ledwidge, Bernard. *De Gaulle et les Américains*. Paris: Flammarion, 1984.

Le Gall, Joel. *Alésia*. Paris: Fayard, 1963.

Lemoine, Maurice. *Le Mal Antillais*. Paris: L'Harmattan, 1982.

Les Expéditions Françaises au Tonkin par un Missionaire. Société de Saint-Augustin. Lille: Desclee, de Brouwer et Cie., no date.

Lestocquoy, Jean. *Histoire du Patriotisme en France*. Paris: Albin Michel, 1968.

Lévine, Michel. *Les Ratonnades d'Octobre*. Paris: Ramsey, 1985.

Lewis, W. H. *The Splendid Century*. New York: Morrow, 1978.

Loubat, Bernard. *L'Orge de Berengo*. Paris: Lefeuvre, 1981.

Lot, Ferdinand. *La Gaule*. Paris: Fayard, 1967.

Luethy, Hebert. *France against Herself*. New York: Meridian, 1957.

Lyautey, Hubert. *Lettres du Tonkin et de Madagascar*. Paris: Armand Colin, 1921.

Lyautey, Pierre. *L'Empire Colonial Français*. Paris: Editions de France, 1931.

MacShane, Denis. *François Mitterrand*. London: Quartet, 1982.

Mangin, Charles. *Lettres du Soudan*. Paris: Portiques, 1930.

Marcilly, Jean. *Le Pen sans Bandeau*. Paris: Grancher, 1984.

Mariotti, André. *Journal de Campagne en Corse an 1731*. Calvi, Corsica: Casalonga, 1982.

Marrus, Michael R., and Robert O. Paxton. *Vichy France and the Jews*. New York: Basic Books, 1981.

Marseille, Jacques. *Empire Colonial et Capitalisme Français.* Paris: Albin Michel, 1984.

Maurois, André. *A History of France.* New York: Farrar, Straus and Cudahy, 1948.

McDermott, John F. *Frenchmen and French Ways in the Mississippi Valley.* Urbana, Ill.: University of Illinois, 1969.

Mercier, André François. *Faut-il Abandonner l'Indochine?* Paris: Editions France-Empire, 1954.

Mermet, Gerard. *Francoscopie.* Paris: Larousse, 1985.

Meyer, Charles. *La Vie Quotidienne des Français en Indochine.* Paris: Hachette, 1985.

Meyer, Jean. *La France moderne.* Vol. 3, *Histoire de France.* Paris: Fayard, 1985.

Michel, Henri. *Histoire de la Résistance.* Paris: Presses Universitaires de France, 1950.

Mitterrand, François. *Réflexions sur la Politique Extérieure de la France.* Paris: Fayard, 1986.

Mockler, Anthony. *The New Mercenaries.* London: Sidgwick and Jackson, 1985.

Montagnon, Pierre. *La Conquête de l'Algérie.* Paris: Pygmalion, 1986.

Murray, Simon. *Légionnaire.* London: Sidgwick and Jackson, 1978.

Myrdal, Gunnar. *Asian Drama.* London: Allen Lane, 1968.

Parkinson, Wenda. *This Gilded African: Toussaint L'Ouverture.* London: Quartet, 1980.

Parkman, Francis. *The Parkman Reader.* Edited by Samuel Eliot. Boston: Morison, Little, Brown, 1955.

———. *France and England in North America.* Vol. 2. New York: Library of America, 1983.

Paris, Paulin. *Guillaume de Tyr.* Paris: Firmin-Didot, 1879.

Péan, Pierre. *Bokassa Ier.* Paris: Alain Moreau, 1977.

———. *Affaires Africaines.* Paris: Fayard, 1983.

Pernoud, Régine. *Les Hommes de la Croisade.* Paris: Tallandier, 1982.

Peyrefitte, Alain. *Le Mal Français.* Paris: Plon, 1976.

Pierre, Andrew. *The Global Politics of Arms Sales.* Princeton, N.J.: Princeton University Press, 1982.

Pluchon, Pierre. *Histoire des Antilles et de la Guyane.* Toulouse: Privat, 1982.

Priollaud, Nicole. *La France Colonisatrice*. Paris: Liana Levi, 1983.

Proust, Louis. *Visions d'Afrique*. Paris: Aristide Quillet, 1925.

Randal, Jonathan. *Going All the Way*. New York: Viking, 1983.

Raynal, Abbé Guillaume. *Histoire philosophique et politique des Deux Indes*. Paris: François Maspero, 1981.

Rocolle, Pierre. *Pourquoi Dien Bien Phu?* Paris: Flammarion, 1968.

Rodman, Selden. *Haiti*. Greenwich, Conn.: Devin-Adair, 1984.

Rousset, Paul. *Les Origines et les Caractères de la Première Croisade*. Geneva: University of Geneva, 1945.

Runciman, Steven. *A History of the Crusades*. 3 vols. Cambridge, England: University Press, 1951.

Saint-Hamont, Daniel. *Histoires Algériennes*. Paris: Robert Laffont, 1979.

Sanmarco, Louis. *Le Colonisateur colonisé*. Paris: ABC, 1983.

Sassier, Philippe. *Les Français à la Corbeille*. Paris: Robert Laffont, 1985.

Schlarman, J. R. *From Quebec to New Orleans*. Belleville, Ill.: Buechler, 1929.

Schreyger, Emil. *L'Office du Niger au Mali*. Weisbaden: Steiner, 1984.

Seldes, George. *You Can't Print That*. Garden City, N.Y.: Doubleday, 1929.

Servan-Schreiber, Jean-Jacques. *Lieutenant in Algeria*. New York: Knopf, 1957.

Smith, William H. C. *Napoléon III*. Paris: 1982.

Sofres, *Opinion publique 1985*. Paris: Gallimard, 1985.

Spartacus, Colonel. *Opération Manta*. Paris: Plon, 1985.

Stacey, C. P. *Québec 1759*. Toronto: Macmillan, 1959.

Stasi, Bernard. *L'Immigration, une Chance pour la France*. Paris: Robert Laffont, 1984.

Steiner, Rolf. *The Last Adventurer*. Boston: Little, Brown, 1978.

Stinchcombe, W. C. *The American Revolution and the French Alliance*. Syracuse, N.Y.: Syracuse University, 1969.

Strachey, John. *The End of Empire*. London: Gollancz, 1959.

Sunday Times, The. *Rainbow Warrior*. London: Arrow, 1986.

Taboulet, Georges. *La Geste Française en Indochine*. Vols. I and II. Paris: Adrien-Maisonneuve, 1955.

Taheri, Amir. *Khomeiny*. Paris: Balland, 1985.

Tallant, Robert. *Voodoo in New Orleans*. Gretna, La.: Pelican, 1974.

Tharaud, Jérôme, and Jean Tharaud. *Alerte en Syrie*. Paris: Plon, 1937.

Tillion, Germaine. *Algérie en 1957*. Paris: Minuit, 1957.

Tilly, Charles. *The Contentious French*. Cambridge: Belknap, 1986.

Trial, Georges. *Okoume*. Paris: Je Sers, 1939.

Tulard, Jean. *Les Révolutions*. Vol. 4, *Histoire de France*. Paris: Fayard, 1985.

Van Loon, H. W. *The Story of Mankind*. New York: Washington Square Press, 1939.

Versini, Xavier. *La Vie Quotidienne en Corse au Temps de Mérimée*. Paris: Hachette, 1979.

Vie, Jean-Emile. *Faut-il abandonner les D.O.M.?* Paris: Economica, 1978.

Villère, Sidney Louis. *Jacques Philippe Villère*. New Orleans, La.: Historic Collection, 1981.

Weissman, Steve, and Herbert Krosney. *The Islamic Bomb*. New York: Times Books, 1981.

Werner, Karl F. *Les Origines*. Vol. 1, *Histoire de France*. Fayard, Paris, 1984.

Weygand, Général. *L'Arc de Triomphe de Paris*. Paris: Flammarion, 1960.

Willis, F. Roy. *The French Paradox*. Stanford, Cal.: Hoover Institution, 1982.

Wolton, Thierry. *Le KGB en France*. Paris: Grasset, 1986.

Yost, David S. *France's Deterrent Posture and Security in Europe*. London: Adelphi Papers, International Institute for Strategic Studies, 1984.

Zahniser, Marvin. *Uncertain Friendship*. New York: John Wiley, 1975.

Zeldin, Theodore. *France 1848–1945: Anxiety and Hypocrisy*. Oxford: Oxford University Press, 1981.

———. *The French*. New York: Pantheon, 1983.

Zumthor, Paul. *Guillaume le Conquérant*. Paris: Hachette, 1978.

Index

El centinela

El centinela

Robert Crais

Traducción de Ana Herrera

Rocaeditorial

Título original: *The Sentry*

© 2011 by Robert Crais

Primera edición: noviembre de 2012

© de la traducción: Ana Herrera
© del diseño de la cubierta: Mario Arturo

© de esta edición: Roca Editorial de Libros, S. L.
Av. Marquès de l'Argentera, 17, pral.
08003 Barcelona
info@rocaeditorial.com
www.rocaeditorial.com

Impreso por Liberdúplex, S.L.U.
Crta. BV-2249, km 7,4, Pol. Ind. Torrentfondo
Sant Llorenç d'Hortons (Barcelona)

ISBN: 978-84-9918-521-7
Depósito legal: B-22.645-2012
Código IBIC: FF

Para Clay Fourrier. Desde River Road
a lo más alto del letrero de Hollywood,
mi compañero de vuelo en busca de los sueños.
Con cariño, admiración y unas cuantas
febriles gotas de sudor.

Nueva Orleans

2005

*L*unes, 4.28 de la madrugada. La estrecha habitación del Barrio Francés estaba llena de humo de velas baratas que olían a miel. Daniel miró a través de los postigos rotos y el cristal tembloroso hacia la parte alta del callejón, y vio una estrecha rendija de la plaza Jackson entre cortinas de una lluvia torrencial que daba vueltas sobre Nueva Orleans como una bandada de murciélagos locos en la tormenta. Daniel nunca había visto caer la lluvia hacia arriba.

Le encantaban esos condenados huracanes. Volvió a cerrar los postigos y abrió la ventana. La lluvia le dio de lleno. Sabía a sal y olía a peces muertos y a algas. El viento de nivel cinco clavaba sus garras en Nueva Orleans a más de ciento sesenta kilómetros por hora, pero allí, en aquel callejón, en un apartamento barato de una sola habitación encima de un local donde vendían los típicos bocadillos *po'boys* criollos, el viento no era más fuerte que una brisa arrogante.

Se había ido la luz de aquella parte del barrio hacía casi una hora; de ahí las velas que Daniel había encontrado en el despacho del gerente. Luces de emergencia que funcionaban a pilas iluminaban algunos edificios cercanos, otorgando un resplandor azulado a las paredes temblorosas. Casi todos los ocupantes de dichos edificios se habían ido; no todo el mundo, pero sí la mayoría. Los más tozudos, los indefensos y los idiotas se habían quedado.

Como Tolley, el amigo de Daniel.

Tolley se había quedado.

Era un idiota.

Y ahora allí estaban, en un edificio vacío, rodeado por edificios vacíos, en medio de una tormenta escandalosa que había obligado a huir de la ciudad a más de un millón de personas, y a Daniel le parecía genial. Todo aquel ruido, todo aquel vacío, nadie que oyese gritar a Tolley.

Daniel se apartó de la ventana arqueando las cejas.

—¿Hueles eso? Así es como huelen los zombis que han vuelto de la muerte con una vida antinatural. ¿Te gustaría ver a un zombi?

Tolley ya no estaba para respuestas, la verdad, atado a la cama con diez metros de cuerda de nailon. La cabeza le colgaba a un lado, hinchada y rota, aunque todavía respiraba. De vez en cuando daba una sacudida y temblaba. Daniel no permitió que la falta de respuesta de Tolley le detuviera.

Saltó a la cama. Cleo y Tobey se apartaron de su camino, le dejaron pasar.

Daniel tenía un paquete de jeringuillas en su mochila, junto con algunos *poppers*, metanfetamina y otros productos farmacéuticos selectos. Sacó todo el equipo, le metió un chute a Tolley con un poco de cristal y esperó a que le hiciera efecto. Fuera, algo explotó con un «pof» ahogado, cuyo sonido no se acabó de llevar el viento. Probablemente un transformador de la luz entregando su alma, o quizás una pared que se había caído.

Los ojos de Tolley parpadearon, súbitamente frenéticos, y luego se concentraron en un punto. Intentó soltarse al ver a Daniel, pero, en realidad, ¿adónde iba a ir?

Daniel dijo muy serio:

—Te he preguntado si has visto a algún zombi. Aquí hay, lo sé de buena tinta.

Tolley negó con la cabeza, cosa que jodió un poco a Daniel. De camino a Nueva Orleans, seis días antes, donde había sido enviado para encontrar a Tolley basándose en una pista absolutamente exacta, Daniel decidió que esa era su única oportunidad de ver a un auténtico zombi. No podía soportar a los zombis, encontraba ofensiva su existencia. Los muertos deben estar muertos, y no levantarse y volver a andar por ahí, arrastrando los pies, vomitivos, flojos. Los vampiros tampoco le gustaban, pero los zombis le ponían frenético. Daniel sabía por una fuente fiable que en Nueva Orleans había unos cuantos zombis, y quizás un par de vampiros también.

—No seas así, Tolliver. Se supone que en Nueva Orleans hay zombis, ¿no? Con todo ese vudú y esas mierdas que tenéis aquí de los zombis de Haití... Tienes que haber visto algo.

Los ojos de Tolley brillaban por la droga. Uno de ellos, el izquierdo, era una bola de un rojo brillante, con las venas estalladas.

Daniel se limpió la lluvia de la cara. Estaba cansado.

—¿Dónde está?

—Juro que no lo sé.

—¿La has matado? ¿Eso es lo que intentabas decirme?

—¡No!

—¿Te dijo ella adónde iban?

—No sé nada de...

Daniel lanzó su puño hacia el pecho de Tolley y recogió el Asp. El Asp era una varilla de acero telescópica de unos sesenta centímetros de larga. Daniel la dejó caer con fuerza sobre el pecho de Tolley, los muslos y las pantorrillas, golpeándole con furia. Tolley chilló y se retorció en sus ligaduras, pero no quedaba nadie que pudiera oírle. Daniel siguió con su castigo durante largo rato, luego arrojó a un lado el Asp y volvió a la ventana. Tobey y Cleo se apartaron de su camino.

—Quiero ver a un maldito zombi. Un zombi, un vampiro, algo que haga que valga la pena este puto viaje.

La lluvia caía con fuerza, caliente y salada como la sangre. A Daniel no le importaba. Allí estaba, había recorrido todo aquel camino, y ni un solo zombi a la vista. Todo lo que valía la pena se lo estaba perdiendo. Una vida de lamentables decepciones.

Miró a Tobey y Cleo. Resultaban difíciles de distinguir con aquella luz parpadeante, emborronados, pero lo lograba.

—Apuesto a que podría matar a un zombi, uno contra uno; en serio, me gustaría probarlo. ¿Creéis que podría matar a un zombi?

Ni Tobey ni Cleo respondieron.

—Que no lo digo en broma, podría cargarme a un zombi. A un vampiro también, pero aquí estamos, perdiendo el tiempo con esta mierda. Preferiría estar cazando zombis. —Señaló hacia Tolley—. Eh, chico. —Volvió a la cama y lo despertó de

11

nuevo—. ¿Crees que me podría cargar a un zombi, eh, uno contra uno?

El ojo rojo daba vueltas y la sangre chorreaba de la boca deshecha. A Tolley se le escapó un susurro blando, de modo que Daniel se acercó más. Parecía que aquel cabrón estaba largando por fin.

—¿Qué dices?

La boca de Tolley se movió, intentando hablar.

Daniel sonrió, animándole.

—¿Oyes ese viento? Si yo fuera un murciélago, habría extendido las alas y habría salido volando de esta cabronada de sitio con toda mi alma. ¿Adónde han ido, chico? Yo sé que ella te lo dijo. Dime adónde fueron, para que pueda irme de aquí. Dímelo, sencillamente. Casi estamos ya. Échame una mano y me largo de aquí.

Los labios de Tolley se movieron, y Daniel supo que estaba a punto de cantar, pero el poco aire que le quedaba se escapó.

—¿Has dicho al oeste? ¿Iban hacia el oeste? ¿Hacia Texas? Tolley estaba muerto.

Daniel se quedó un momento mirando el cuerpo y luego sacó la pistola y le metió cinco balas en el pecho a Tolliver James. Fueron unas horribles explosiones que cualquiera que se hubiese podido quedar por allí habría oído, aun con aquel viento de león. A Daniel le importaba un pimiento. Si alguien venía corriendo le pegaría un tiro también, pero no vino nadie… ni la policía, ni los vecinos; ni un alma. Todo aquel que tuviera dos dedos de frente estaba agachado y acurrucado, intentando sobrevivir.

Daniel cargó la pistola, la volvió a guardar y luego sacó el teléfono por satélite. Las antenas de móvil no funcionaban en toda la ciudad, pero el teléfono por satélite iba de maravilla. Comprobó la hora, dio al botón de conexión y esperó a que hubiese línea. Siempre llevaba unos segundos.

Entre tanto se enderezó, se estiró un poco y recuperó sus modales habituales.

Cuando se realizó la conexión, Daniel informó:

—Tolliver James está muerto. No ha proporcionado nada útil.

Escuchó un momento antes de responder.

—No, señor, han desaparecido. Eso sí puedo confirmarlo. James era una buena pista, pero no creo que ella le dijese nada.

Escuchó de nuevo, en esta ocasión un buen rato.

—No, señor, eso no es cierto del todo. Hay tres o cuatro personas aquí con las que me gustaría hablar, pero la tormenta ha convertido este lugar en un desastre. Casi con toda seguridad habrán sido evacuados. No lo sé. Déjeme un tiempo para localizarlos.

Más conversación al otro lado, pero luego terminaron.

—Sí, señor, comprendo. Usted hace lo suyo, yo lo mío. No le decepcionaré.

Una última palabra del jefe.

—Sí, señor. Gracias. Le mantendré informado.

Daniel cerró el teléfono y lo dejó a un lado.

—Gilipollas.

Volvió a la ventana y dejó que la lluvia lo empapara. Todo estaba húmedo ya: la camisa, los pantalones, los zapatos, el pelo, todo, hasta los huesos. Se agachó para ver mejor la plaza. Un barril de petróleo de doscientos litros iba dando tumbos por la entrada del callejón, de acera a acera, seguido por una bicicleta, arrastrada de lado, y luego un trozo desgarrado de contrachapado que iba aleteando y planeando como una carta arrojada a la basura.

Daniel gritó al viento todo lo fuerte que pudo:

—¡Vamos, venid a por mí, putos zombis! ¡Mostrad vuestros auténticos y antinaturales colores!

Daniel echó atrás la cabeza y aulló. Luego ladró como un perro, y aulló de nuevo antes de volverse hacia la habitación a recoger su equipo. Tobey y Cleo habían desaparecido.

Tolliver había escondido ocho mil dólares bajo el colchón, todavía envasados al vacío, que Daniel encontró cuando registró la habitación al principio. Probablemente fueron un regalo de la chica. Daniel se metió el dinero en su mochila, lo comprobó todo para asegurarse de que Tolliver no tenía pulso y fue al pequeño baño donde había dejado a la amiguita de Tolliver después de estrangularla, bien limpia y metidita en la bañera. Un hilillo negro de hormigas ya la habían encontrado, y no había pasado ni un día siquiera.

13

Cleo dijo:

—Vete ya, Daniel. No lo jodas más.

Tobey dijo:

—¿Ir adónde, con una tormenta como esta? Parece más lógico quedarse.

Daniel decidió que Tobey tenía razón. Era el más listo y normalmente tenía razón, aunque Daniel no siempre podía verlo.

—Vale, supongo que tendré que esperar a que acabe lo peor.

Tobey dijo:

—Espera.

Cleo dijo:

—Espera, espera.

Como ecos que se desvanecían.

Daniel volvió a la ventana. Se inclinó hacia fuera entre la lluvia de nuevo, vigilando la boca del callejón por si pasaba algún zombi.

—Vamos, malditos, quiero ver aunque solo sea a uno. Un asqueroso zombi, es todo lo que pido.

Si aparecía un zombi, Daniel pensaba saltar de la ventana, ir tras él y hacer pedazos su carne putrefacta y antinatural con los dientes. Después de todo era un hombre lobo, y por eso era tan buen cazador y asesino. Los hombres lobo no le temen a nada.

Echó atrás la cabeza y aulló igual que el viento, y luego apagó las velas y se quedó allí sentado con los cadáveres, esperando a que pasara la tormenta.

Cuando acabase, Daniel encontraría su rastro, los perseguiría y no pararía hasta que fuesen suyos. No importaba lo mucho que le costara o lo lejos que se fueran. Por eso los hombres del sur le usaban para esos trabajos y le pagaban tan bien.

Los hombres lobo siempre cogen a su presa.

Los Ángeles

Hoy

*E*l viento no le despertó. Fue el sueño. Oyó el viento
intenso antes de abrir los ojos, pero fue el sueño lo que le
despertó aquella mañana cuando todavía estaba oscuro. El
gato era su testigo. Agazapado a los pies de la cama, con las
orejas gachas, un gruñido bajo en el pecho, un gato negro y
desgreñado le miraba cuando Elvis Cole abrió los ojos. El
rostro guerrero del animal estaba furioso, y en aquel
momento Cole supo que ambos habían compartido la pesadilla.

Se despertó en la cama de su buhardilla bañado por la luz
azul de la luna, sintiendo que su casa temblaba cuando el
viento intentaba tirarlo de su posición encaramada allá arriba, en las colinas de Hollywood. Un extraño fenómeno
atmosférico en la región central formaba unos vientos de
cincuenta a setenta nudos desde el mar que llevaban días
azotando Los Ángeles.

Cole se incorporó, ahora ya despierto y queriendo des-
prenderse del sueño, una pesadilla horrible que le había
dejado inquieto y deprimido. Las orejas del gato seguían
bajas. Sacó la mano, pero el animal saltó de la cama como un
charco de tinta negra y Cole dijo:

—Yo también.

Miró la hora por costumbre: las tres y doce minutos de
la mañana. Buscó por la mesilla para ver si tenía la pistola
(por costumbre, también) pero se detuvo al momento al
darse cuenta de lo que estaba haciendo.

—Venga, hombre, ¿para qué?

La pistola estaba allí, como siempre. A veces la necesitaba, pero la mayoría de las veces no. Viviendo solo, con la única compañía de un gato enfadado, no parecía que hubiese motivo para llevársela. Ahora, a la tres y doce minutos, en medio de una noche agitada por el viento, le recordaba lo que había perdido.

Cole se dio cuenta de que estaba temblando y salió de la cama. El sueño le había asustado. El destello en la boca del cañón, tan brillante que chispeaba en sus ojos; el olor a carbón de la pólvora sin humo; una niebla resplandeciente y roja que le moteaba la piel; unas gafas de sol rotas que saltaban por el aire... imágenes tan vívidas que le despertaron de repente.

Temblaba mientras su cuerpo iba eliminando el miedo.

La parte de atrás de la casa de Cole era un ventanal de cristal en forma de triángulo que le ofrecía la vista del cañón que había detrás de su casa y una imagen como un rombo polvoriento de la ciudad que quedaba detrás. En aquel momento el cañón se veía azul a la luz intensa de la luna. Las casas dormidas de abajo estaban rodeadas por árboles azules y grises que se agitaban y bailoteaban con aquel viento de San Vito. Cole se preguntó si alguien de allá abajo se habría despertado igual que él, y si alguien habría sufrido una pesadilla similar: ver que asesinaban a tiros a su mejor amigo en la oscuridad.

La violencia formaba parte de él. Elvis Cole no la quería, ni la buscaba, ni disfrutaba de ella, pero quizás eso era lo que se decía a sí mismo en momentos como aquel. Su estilo de vida le había costado la mujer que amaba y el niñito al que había llegado a querer también, y le había dejado solo en aquella casa sin otra compañía que un gato furibundo y una pistola que no necesitaba guardar.

Y allí estaba aquel sueño que le había dejado la carne de gallina, tan real que parecía una premonición. Miró el teléfono y se dijo: «No, es una tontería, es una estupidez; son las tres de la mañana».

Pero hizo la llamada.

Un solo timbrazo y respondieron. Eran las tres de la mañana.

—Pike.

—Eh, tío. —Cole no sabía qué más decir, sintiéndose muy idiota—. ¿Estás bien?

Pike dijo:

—Bien. ¿Y tú?

—Sí. Lo siento, tío; es tarde.

—¿Pasa algo?

—No, nada, solo un mal presentimiento, nada más.

Se quedaron los dos en silencio. Cole lo encontraba algo violento, pero fue Pike quien habló primero.

—Si me necesitas, voy.

—Es el viento… Este viento está loco.

—Ajá.

—Cuídate.

Le dijo a Pike que le volvería a llamar pronto, y colgó el teléfono.

Cole no sintió alivio alguno después de la llamada. Tendría que haber sido así, pero no lo fue. El sueño tendría que haberse desvanecido, pero no. Hablar con Pike lo hacía mucho más real aún.

«Si me necesitas, voy.»

¿Cuántas veces se había puesto en peligro Joe Pike para salvarle? Habían luchado en el bando de los buenos los dos juntos, y ganado, y a veces perdido. Habían disparado a gente que hizo daño, o que estaba haciendo daño, y les habían disparado a ellos también, y Joe Pike le había salvado la vida a Cole más de cien veces, como un arcángel bajado del cielo.

Sin embargo, ahí estaba el sueño, y no acababa de desvanecerse…

Chispazos en la boca de un cañón en una habitación sombría. La sombra de una mujer en la pared. Unas gafas de sol dando vueltas por el aire. Joe Pike que caía entre una horrible niebla roja.

Cole bajó al piso de abajo en la casa oscura y salió al porche. Hojas y otros restos le golpearon el rostro como arena en una playa barrida por el viento. Las luces de las casas de abajo brillaban como estrellas caídas.

En los momentos peores, en noches como aquella, era

17

cuando Elvis Cole pensaba en la mujer y el niño, y se decía a sí mismo que la violencia de su vida se lo había arrebatado todo, pero él sabía que no era cierto. Aunque se sentía a veces muy solo, todavía tenía más cosas que perder.

Podía perder a su mejor amigo.

O a sí mismo.

PRIMERA PARTE

El pescadero

1

Seis minutos antes de ver a los dos hombres, Joe Pike se detuvo en una gasolinera Mobil para hinchar una rueda. Notó que iban a cometer un delito en cuanto los vio. Estaba en Venice, California, a las 10.35, un día cálido y soleado, no lejos del mar. Había comprobado la presión de los neumáticos antes de dirigirse al gimnasio, y resultaba que a la rueda delantera derecha le faltaba un kilo trescientos. Si no hubiese necesitado hinchar el neumático no habría visto a los dos hombres ni se habría visto implicado, pero el caso es que la rueda estaba baja de presión. Y se paró a hincharla.

Pike añadió el kilo trescientos y luego rellenó el depósito de gasolina. Mientras la bomba iba funcionando inspeccionó su Jeep Cherokee rojo buscando abolladuras, arañazos, asfalto de la carretera, y luego comprobó el nivel de todos los fluidos.

El líquido de frenos: bien.

La dirección asistida: bien.

La transmisión: bien.

El anticongelante: bien.

El todoterreno, aunque no era un vehículo nuevo, estaba inmaculado. Pike lo mantenía meticulosamente. Cuidarse a sí mismo y cuidar su equipo era algo que le habían inculcado cuando tenía diecisiete años, siendo joven marine, unos hombres a los que respetaba, y la lección le había servido muy bien en sus diversas ocupaciones.

Mientras Pike cerraba el capó, tres mujeres pasaron en bicicleta por el lado contrario de la calle, moviendo sus bonitas piernas y con sus esbeltas espaldas arqueadas sobre los manillares. Pike las vio pasar, y las mujeres se fijaron en dos hombres que venían caminando en dirección contraria (parpadeo) que a Pike le parecieron problemáticos; dos tipos de veintitantos años, con el cuello lleno de tatuajes de bandas, caminando de esa forma que Pike, durante su época de oficial de policía, llamaba «andares disimulados». Los pandilleros eran comunes en Venice, pero esos dos no iban relajados, como un par de indigentes sin nada en la cabeza; se balanceaban con fría arrogancia, de lado a lado, demostrando que estaban muy tensos. El que iba junto a la acera miraba los coches aparcados, cosa que, según sabía Pike, sugería que buscaban algo que robar.

Este había pasado tres años como patrullero de la policía de Los Ángeles, donde aprendió a conocer bastante bien a la gente. Luego cambió de ocupación y empezó a trabajar en entornos de conflictos graves y muy peligrosos en todo el mundo; allí aprendió a conocer mucho mejor las claves sutiles del lenguaje y la expresión corporal. Su vida dependía de ello.

Entonces Pike sintió una punzada de curiosidad. Si los chicos hubieran seguido andando se habría olvidado, pero se detuvieron junto a una tienda de ropa de mujer de segunda mano justo en la acera de enfrente. Pike ya no era oficial de policía. No patrullaba por las calles buscando criminales; tenía otras cosas que hacer, pero todo en la postura y la expresión de aquellos dos disparó una alerta roja en su cerebro. La tienda de ropa femenina era un lugar ideal para robar un bolso.

Acabó de llenar su depósito, pero no entró en el vehículo. Un BMW estacionó en la gasolinera justo detrás de su Jeep. La conductora esperó un momento, pero luego tocó el claxon y le interpeló desde su coche.

—¿Va a salir?

Pike estaba concentrado en los dos hombres, guiñando los ojos debido a la luz matutina, aunque llevaba gafas de sol. La conductora volvió a tocar la bocina.

—¿Sale o qué? Necesito gasolina.

Pike seguía atento a los dos hombres.

—Capullo.

La mujer retrocedió y se fue a otro surtidor.

Pike vio que los dos hombres mantenían una breve conversación y luego pasaban junto a la tienda de ropa y se dirigían a un local donde vendían bocadillos. Un letrero pintado a mano en el escaparate decía: WILSON: COMIDA PARA LLEVAR - PO'BOYS Y SÁNDWICHES.

Los dos hombres fueron a entrar, pero inmediatamente retrocedieron. Salió una mujer de mediana edad con una bolsa blanca y un bolso muy grande. Cuando salió, uno de los hombres volvió rápidamente a la calle y el otro se llevó la mano a los ojos, intentando ocultarse, sin duda alguna. Los gestos eran tan reveladores que las comisuras de los labios de Pike se levantaron un poco, todo lo que se podían aproximar a una sonrisa.

Cuando la mujer se fue, los dos hombres entraron en la tienda de bocadillos.

Pike sabía que probablemente se trataba de dos tipos que querían dar una sorpresa a un amigo, o quizá comprar un sándwich, pero quería ver cómo acababa el asunto.

Cruzó la calle entre los coches que pasaban. La tienda de bocadillos era pequeña, con dos mesas diminutas delante, ante el escaparate, y un pequeño mostrador en la parte de atrás donde se pedía la comida. Un menú escrito con tiza y un póster de la Superbowl de los New Orleans Saints adornaban la pared detrás del mostrador, junto con una puerta que probablemente conducía a una despensa o almacén.

Los acontecimientos se desarrollaban muy deprisa en el interior. Cuando Pike llegó a la puerta, los dos hombres tenían a un hombre algo mayor en el suelo, y le daban puñetazos en la cabeza el uno y patadas en la espalda el otro. El hombre se había encogido formando una bola, intentando protegerse.

Los dos atacantes dudaron cuando Pike abrió la puerta, y cogieron aire como ballenas que salen a la superficie. Vio que llevaban las manos vacías, aunque podía haber alguien más detrás del mostrador o en la despensa. Entonces el tipo de los puñetazos volvió a la carga, y el que daba patadas se volvió hacia Pike con la cara congestionada y amenazadora. Pike pensó en los documentales de animales, cuando los gorilas de espalda plateada se hinchan para parecer más feroces.

—¿Quieres tú también, cabrón? Largo de aquí —dijo el tipo.

23

Pero Pike no se fue. Entró y cerró la puerta.

Vio una vacilación de sorpresa en los ojos del que daba patadas, y el de los puñetazos volvió a dudar. Creían que iba a salir corriendo —eran uno contra dos—, pero Pike no huyó.

La víctima (el hombre que estaba en el suelo) seguía acurrucado formando una pelota, y murmuró:

—Estoy bien. Dios mío...

Mientras, el de las patadas se hinchó para hacerse más grande. Levantó los puños y cargó contra Pike: un matón callejero hundido en su propia violencia intentando ahuyentarle. Pike se movió rápidamente hacia delante, y el sorprendido matón se paró en seco, desprevenido ante el ataque del desconocido. Luego Pike se agachó y aceleró, con tanta suavidad como el agua que fluye sobre las rocas. Atrapó el brazo del hombre, lo dobló hacia atrás y lo obligó a bajar al suelo con fuerza, rompiéndole el radio y dislocándole el cúbito. Le golpeó una sola vez en la nuez con el canto de la mano —el agua se arremolinó ahora sobre las rocas—, mientras se levantaba para dar un puñetazo en la cara al otro. Pero este ya había visto suficiente. Retrocedió pasando junto al mostrador, rebotó en la pared de atrás y enseguida salió corriendo por la puerta trasera.

El hombre de las patadas puso los ojos como un gato que se ha tragado una bola de pelo al intentar respirar y chillar al mismo tiempo. Pike bajó una rodilla a tierra, observando la puerta de atrás mientras lo registraba en busca de algún arma. Encontró una nueve milímetros y lo dejó abatido para cerciorarse de que no había nadie detrás del mostrador ni en el cuarto de atrás. Después volvió al matón, que estaba acurrucado, y le quitó el cinturón para atarle las muñecas. El tipo chilló cuando Pike le retorció el brazo roto hacia la espalda, e intentó levantarse, pero Pike apretó su cara contra el suelo y dijo:

—Ya basta.

Había neutralizado al asaltante y asegurado la situación en menos de seis segundos.

El hombre mayor había intentado sentarse mientras Pike trabajaba. Este le preguntó:

—¿Está bien?

—Bien, sí, sí.

24

Pero no lo parecía. La sangre velaba su rostro y salpicaba el suelo. El hombre vio las manchas rojas, se tocó la cara y examinó sus dedos rojos.

—Mierda. Estoy sangrando…

Levantó una rodilla, pero se torció hacia un lado y acabó cayendo de culo. Pike cogió su teléfono y marcó el número de emergencias.

—Quédese quieto. Voy a llamar a una ambulancia.

El hombre miró a Pike guiñando los ojos, y este comprendió que tenía problemas para enfocar.

—¿Es usted policía? —preguntó la víctima.

—No.

—No necesito ambulancia. Cuando recupere el aliento, estaré bien.

El matón retorció la cabeza para mirar a Pike.

—¿No es policía y me ha roto el brazo? Cabrón, será mejor que me suelte…

Pike le sujetó con una rodilla, haciendo que el otro diese un respingo.

Cuando la telefonista de emergencias estuvo en línea, Pike le describió la situación y la herida de la víctima; le dijo que tenía a un sospechoso detenido y le pidió que enviase a la policía.

El hombre hizo un débil intento de levantarse otra vez.

—Es igual, joder. Deje que se vaya ese gilipollas.

Pike había visto todos los tipos de heridas violentas que podía sufrir un ser humano, así que las conocía bien. Las producidas en el cuero cabelludo provocan muchísima sangre, pero normalmente no son graves, si bien un fuerte golpe había estado a punto de partirle la frente al hombre.

—Quédese sentado. Tiene usted una conmoción.

—A la mierda. Estoy bien.

El hombre se fue incorporando, se puso en pie y luego se desmayó y cayó al suelo.

Pike quiso ir a atenderle, pero el matón estaba intentando levantarse.

—Será mejor que me sueltes, tío. Si no te arrepentirás.

Pike metió el dedo pulgar en una zona del cuello de aquel hombre, donde la raíz del nervio C3 emergía de la tercera vértebra, y la aplastó hasta el hueso. Eso hizo que su hombro y su pecho se entumecieran de repente con un agudo latigazo de dolor. Se le cerró el diafragma y su respiración se detuvo; el nervio C3 es el que controla el diafragma.

—Si te levantas lo vuelvo a hacer. Y te dolerá más.

Pike aflojó la presión, sabiendo que el hombro y el brazo de aquel hombre le arderían como si los hubiesen incendiado con napalm.

—¿De acuerdo?

El hombre lanzó un gruñido, abriendo mucho los ojos hacia Pike, como un chihuahua que contemplase a un pitbull.

—Ajá.

Pike enderezó al hombre mayor para que pudiera respirar con más facilidad, y luego comprobó su pulso. Era fuerte, pero las pupilas tenían distintos tamaños, cosa que indicaba una conmoción. Apretó un puñado de servilletas de papel sobre la herida del tipo para detener la hemorragia.

El matón dijo:

—¿Quién cojones eres tú, tío?

—No vuelvas a hablar.

Si Pike no se hubiese parado a hinchar su neumático no habría visto a los hombres que cruzaban la calle. No habría conocido a la mujer a la que estaba a punto de conocer. Nada de lo que estaba a punto de pasar hubiese pasado. Pero Pike se había detenido. Y lo peor estaba todavía por llegar.

La ambulancia vino seis minutos más tarde.

$\mathcal{L}$as sanitarias eran dos mujeres recias, de cuarenta y tantos años. Se pusieron unos guantes de látex cuando vieron la sangre y comenzaron a trabajar con la víctima mientras Pike las ponía al corriente.

El agresor, de cara al suelo, con la rodilla de Pike en su espalda, dijo:

—Este tío me ha roto el brazo. Me ha atacado. Necesito algo para el dolor.

La que dirigía el equipo miró a Pike. Se llamaba Stiles.

—¿Es este el hombre que ha hecho esto?

—Él y un amigo.

—¿Tiene el brazo roto de verdad?

—Ajá.

Le dijo a Pike que dejara que el tipo se incorporase, y luego hizo una seña a su compañera.

—Ocúpate del guapito ese. Yo me quedo con este.

Stiles consiguió despertar a la víctima, cuya habla era turbia y confusa, aunque se fue centrando conforme ella le tomaba el pulso y la presión sanguínea. Se identificó como Wilson Smith, venido de Nueva Orleans después de la tormenta. Pike encontró interesante que no se refiriera al huracán Katrina por su nombre; lo llamó «la tormenta». También notó que no tenía lo que Pike habría llamado acento sureño. Parecía más bien de Nueva York.

Cuando Stiles le pasó la luz de una linterna por los ojos, Smith intentó apartarla.

—Estoy bien.

—No, señor, no está usted bien. Tiene una herida en el cuero cabelludo y está conmocionado. Creo que necesitará al menos diez o doce puntos. Nos lo vamos a llevar.

—Estoy bien.

Smith intentó apartarla otra vez, pero se puso a vomitar de repente. Después se tranquilizó y cerró los ojos. Pike miró cómo trabajaban las sanitarias mientras esperaba a los policías. Ya estaba metido en aquel lío, de modo que tenía que quedarse. No podía hacer otra cosa.

Los primeros policías aparecieron al cabo de unos minutos. La que estaba a cargo era una mujer latina de mediana edad, con los ojos muy serenos y galones, que se presentó como oficial Hydeck. Probablemente el nombre anglosajón le venía de matrimonio. Su compañero era un recluta grandote y de aspecto duro llamado Paul McIntosh, que se quedó de pie con los pulgares metidos en su cinturón de la marca Sam Browne como si quisiera que ocurriera algo más.

Hydeck habló tranquilamente con Stiles unos minutos, preguntó a víctima y sospechoso qué tal se encontraban y luego se volvió a Pike.

—¿Es usted quien ha llamado?

—Sí, señora.

La telefonista del servicio de emergencias ya les habría proporcionado la información que les dio Pike.

—Ajá. ¿Y cuál es su nombre?

—Pike.

El matón, al que estaban acomodando un cabestrillo hinchable, dijo:

—Este tío me ha roto el brazo, ¿sabe? Tienen que arrestarle. Quiero presentar cargos.

Hydeck le pidió su identificación. Pike le tendió su carné de conducir, que McIntosh copió en un formulario junto con su número de teléfono. El sospechoso no llevaba, cosa que a Pike no le sorprendió: el noventa y cinco por ciento de las personas a las que había arrestado siendo policía no tenían carné de conducir válido. El tipo se identificó como Reuben Mendoza, y aseguró que nunca le habían arrestado.

McIntosh se acercó a él, imponente.

—¿Estás en una banda?

—No, hermano, estoy limpio.

McIntosh señaló las iniciales que llevaba en el cuello: VT. Pike, las sanitarias y los policías sabían que significaba Venice Trece, una banda latina.

—¿Por qué llevas entonces el tatu de Venice Trece?

—Son mis iniciales.

Hydeck dijo:

—¿Cómo sacas VT de Reuben Mendoza?

—Así es como se dice en europeo.

Pike les contó lo que sabía con frases cortas y claras, como se le había enseñado cuando era policía patrullero, y entregó a Hydeck la pistola que le había quitado a Mendoza.

—Tenía esto en el bolsillo.

Mendoza dijo:

—No es mía, tío; no me cargues eso. No había visto nunca esa pistola.

—¿Estaba golpeando al señor Smith con ella?

—No que yo viera. La llevaba en el bolsillo.

Mendoza insistió:

—Te voy a demandar, tío; por haberme atacado. Me ha hecho algo en el cuello, como el señor Spock. Me ha hecho mucho daño.

McIntosh le dijo que se callara, y luego se volvió otra vez hacia Pike.

—¿Y el que huyó? ¿Llevaba arma?

—Si la tenía no la vi. Cuando entré, el señor Smith estaba ya en el suelo. El otro hombre le estaba dando puñetazos en la cabeza y este le daba patadas. Cuando lo cogí, su compañero salió corriendo por atrás. No vi ningún arma.

McIntosh sonrió a Mendoza.

—Tu colega te ha dado la espalda, hermano. Se ha ido derechito por la puerta.

Hydeck le pasó el arma a McIntosh, le dijo que la guardara segura en el vehículo y llamó a una segunda ambulancia. La víctima y el sospechoso no podían ser transportados en el mismo vehículo.

Otro coche de patrulla y la segunda ambulancia llegaron unos minutos después. Los policías recién llegados sacaron a Mendoza, mientras Stiles y su compañera metían la camilla.

29

Hydeck interrogó a Smith mientras las sanitarias trabajaban con él. Le dijo que los dos hombres pidieron un bocadillo, pero que él quería cerrar para ir al banco y les dijo que se fueran. Se negaron, y así empezó la pelea.

Hydeck parecía desconfiar.

—¿Así que no intentaron robarle ni nada por el estilo? ¿Se metió usted en una pelea solo porque ellos querían un bocata y usted quería cerrar?

—Quizá les dije algo. Se me fue de las manos.

Las sanitarias le estaban metiendo en la camilla cuando Pike la vio entrar por la puerta de atrás. Ella no vio las ambulancias y los vehículos de policía que estaban delante, y los uniformes que atestaban el pequeño espacio la detuvieron en seco, como si se hubiese golpeado contra una pared invisible. Pike vio que sus ojos saltaron de las sanitarias a la camilla y a la policía (pam, pam, pam) absorbiendo toda la escena hasta que (pam) los ojos de ella se clavaron en él, y ahí se quedaron. Lo miró como si no hubiese visto nunca nada igual. Pike supuso que tendría treinta y pocos años. Su piel era olivácea y llevaba una rayita pintada en torno a los ojos; eran bonitos, y la rayita los mejoraba. Vestía un vestido de lino sin mangas, sandalias planas y el pelo negro y corto. El vestido estaba arrugado. A Pike le gustaban los ojos bonitos.

Entonces Hydeck y McIntosh se volvieron, y los ojos de ella se apartaron de él y fueron hacia los agentes.

—¿Puedo ayudarle? —preguntó Hydeck.

—¿Qué ha ocurrido? Wilson, ¿estás bien? Wilson es mi tío.

Smith miró más allá de las sanitarias.

—Es Dru, mi sobrina.

Su nombre era Dru Rayne, y fue de Smith a la policía mientras le contaban lo que había ocurrido.

—¿Y te han atacado aquí, en la tienda? ¿Te han agredido?

—Me las estaba apañando bien solo, pero este hombre se metió.

Dru Rayne examinó a Pike de nuevo, y esta vez pronunció dos palabras como si los policías, las sanitarias y su tío fuesen ciegos o no estuvieran allí, creando un momento entre los dos que no incluía a nadie más.

—Muchas gracias.

Pike inclinó la cabeza una vez.

—¿Se pondrá bien?

—Le tendremos en observación. Con heridas en la cabeza como esta, se los quedan toda la noche.

—No me pienso quedar. Cuando me den los puntos me voy.

Dru Rayne se trasladó a la camilla y miró a su tío.

—Wilson, por favor, no seas así.

Hydeck le dio su tarjeta a la señora Rayne y le informó de que sus detectives probablemente querrían interrogar a su tío en el hospital. Las sanitarias acabaron de sujetarlo con las correas y Pike vio que su sobrina las seguía. No volvió la mirada hacia él al irse.

Hydeck esperó hasta que se fueron y luego se volvió hacia Pike. Todavía tenía su carné de conducir.

—¿Cree usted que lo que ocurrió aquí fue una discusión por un bocadillo?

Pike negó con la cabeza y Hydeck echó un vistazo de nuevo a su carné.

31

—Me suena. ¿Le conozco?

—No.

—Sus tatuajes me dicen algo...

Pike llevaba una flecha de un rojo intenso tatuada en el exterior de cada uno de sus músculos deltoides. Eran visibles porque llevaba una sudadera gris con las mangas cortadas. Unas gafas de sol de dotación estatal negras y brillantes como el caparazón de un escarabajo ocultaban sus ojos, pero las flechas marcaban sus brazos como anuncios de neón. Señalaban hacia arriba. Pike medía metro ochenta y cinco, pesaba un poco más de noventa kilos y sus brazos eran muy musculosos. Llevaba el pelo corto, al dos; la piel muy bronceada, y tenía los nudillos ásperos y llenos de cicatrices.

Hydeck acarició el borde de su carné.

—La mayoría de la gente sale corriendo si ve una paliza como esa. Pero viéndole, supongo que sabe cuidarse. ¿A qué se dedica, señor Pike?

—Negocios.

—Claro.

Pike esperaba que ella le preguntara qué tipo de negocios, pero le devolvió su carné. Si notó el bulto de una de las dos pistolas que él llevaba escondidas, lo ignoró.

—Supongo que el señor Smith ha tenido mucha suerte de que usted pasara por aquí. —Le entregó una tarjeta de visita—. El detective le llamará, pero aquí tiene mi tarjeta. Si se acuerda de algo mientras tanto, llámeme.

Pike cogió la tarjeta y Hydeck se fue con McIntosh en su coche patrulla. Dru Rayne estaba con su tío mientras las sanitarias abrían su vehículo. Le tomaba la mano mientras hablaba con él, y parecía muy concentrada. Luego se alejó un poco y las sanitarias deslizaron la camilla en la ambulancia. Hydeck y McIntosh subieron al coche patrulla, encendieron las luces y detuvieron el tráfico para que saliera la ambulancia. Las sanitarias se dirigieron hacia el hospital y los policías se volvieron en la dirección opuesta para atender otra llamada.

Dru Rayne miró la ambulancia. Lo hizo hasta que desapareció, y luego corrió de vuelta a la tienda. A Pike no le gustó esa forma de correr. Parecía que lo hacía para ponerse a cubierto.

—¿Por qué miente? —preguntó Pike.

Ella se sobresaltó y dio un respingo.

—Me ha asustado.

Él asintió, y luego pensó que a lo mejor debía disculparse.

—Lo siento.

Ella le dirigió otra sonrisa de agradecimiento y pasó detrás del mostrador.

—Soy yo. Estoy un poco nerviosa, supongo. Tengo que ir al hospital.

—¿Por qué miente su tío?

—¿Qué le parece? Tiene miedo de que vuelvan.

—¿Ya han estado aquí antes?

Ella apagó las freidoras y puso las tapas en los contenedores metálicos de condimentos, hablando mientras trabajaba. Wilson parecía neoyorquino por su acento, pero el de ella era mucho más suave, quizá porque era una mujer.

—Viven aquí, igual que nosotros, de modo que tenemos que pensar en esas cosas. La gente así siempre vuelve.

—Si cree eso, debería decírselo a la policía. Hydeck parece muy competente.

Ella inclinó la cabeza.

—Creí que usted era de la policía.

—No.

—Parece un policía, o algo así.

—Solo pasaba por aquí.

Ella volvió a sonreír y le ofreció la mano a través del mostrador.

—Dru Rayne. Puede llamarme Dru.

—Joe Pike.

—Es muy amable lo que ha hecho, ayudar de esa manera, señor Pike. Gracias.

Se estrecharon la mano, y luego Dru Rayne volvió a su trabajo, hablando por encima del hombro.

—Bueno, no querría parecer maleducada, pero tengo que cerrar todo esto para poder ir al hospital…

Pike asintió, pensando que no había motivo alguno por el que no pudiera irse, pero no lo hacía. Le miró la mano: no llevaba anillo de casada.

—¿Quiere que la lleve?

—No, es igual. Pero gracias por ofrecerse.

Pike pensaba en algo más que decir.

—Hable con la policía.

—Ya nos arreglaremos. Usted no conoce a mi tío; probablemente les esté insultando.

Le dedicó una cálida sonrisa, pero Pike sabía que ella no iba a decirle a la policía más que su tío.

Dru fue apilando los contenedores de metal y metió toda la pila en la habitación de atrás. Cuando desapareció, Pike escribió su nombre y su número de móvil en una libretita para pedidos que encontró junto a la caja registradora. Escribió su número personal, no el de negocios, el que había dado a la policía.

—Le dejo mi número. Si me necesita, llámeme.

Ella todavía estaba atrás.

—Vale. Muchas gracias de nuevo.

Pike volvió a su Jeep, pero no se alejó de allí. Encontró el callejón de servicio que corría por detrás del local de Wilson y esperó en el extremo más alejado. Unos minutos más tarde salió Dru Rayne, cerró la puerta y corrió a meterse en un

Tercel plateado. Era un modelo antiguo, con la pintura del parachoques trasero rozada, y necesitaba limpieza. Pensó que parecía preocupada.

Se quedó sentado en el Jeep un rato, luego salió y recorrió toda la manzana, primero por el callejón y luego por la acera. Se fijó en las personas que iban por las aceras y en las tiendas, y en los tejados de los edificios que lo rodeaban. Examinó a la gente que iba al volante de los coches que pasaban, pensando en lo que ella había dicho: «Siempre vuelven».

Pike estaba al otro lado de la gasolinera cuando un Monte Carlo color granate fue pasando lentamente con las ventanillas bajadas. Dos jóvenes iban en el asiento delantero y un tercero detrás, los tres con tatuajes de bandas y cara de expresidiarios. Miraron a Pike al pasar, de modo que él les devolvió la mirada.

El hombre que iba en el asiento de atrás imitó una pistola con la mano, apuntó y apretó el gatillo.

Pike les vio irse, pensando cómo había corrido Dru Rayne para ponerse a cubierto.

«Siempre vuelven.»

«No —pensó Pike—. No si te tienen miedo.»

*E*n otras circunstancias, la oficial Hydeck habría informado a su comandante de guardia de que la víctima y el sospechoso se dirigían hacia el hospital. Su comandante de guardia habría facilitado esa información al oficial de guardia de la oficina de detectives, que a su vez habría despachado a unos detectives al hospital, donde estos habrían hablado con Smith y Mendoza, y probablemente también con las sanitarias. Si Mendoza hubiese identificado a su cómplice, el caso habría estado resuelto. Si Mendoza se hubiese negado a cooperar, los detectives habrían llamado a Pike para una entrevista. Le habrían dicho que se acercarían a su hogar, o al lugar donde trabajase, o habrían concertado una cita en un sitio que a todos les resultase agradable, todo muy discreto y amistoso. Así habría funcionado si Pike hubiese sido una persona cualquiera, pero este sabía que para él las cosas irían de otra manera. Alguien reconocería su nombre, y lo que harían los investigadores y cómo enfocarían aquel caso sería diferente.

Tenía razón.

Ocho horas y veintisiete minutos después de que Pike viese el Monte Carlo granate, volvió a casa y se encontró con dos detectives en el aparcamiento. Vivía en un complejo residencial cerrado en Culver City, no lejos del lugar del ataque. Los edificios estaban agrupados en manzanas de cuatro unidades, y diseñados de tal manera que cada dos o tres manzanas compartían aparcamiento. Para abrir la puerta y entrar al complejo se requería una tarjeta magnética, pero allí estaban, un hombre y una mujer detectives, esperándole en un predecible Crown Victoria color marrón.

Salieron del coche cuando Pike aparcó, y le esperaban con sus insignias cuando salió del Jeep. El hombre tenía unos cincuenta años, con el rostro grueso, el pelo rojo ya escaso y una americana informal de verano; la mujer era unos quince años más joven, con el pelo negro intenso, los ojos negros y un traje pantalón azul marino que le colgaba un poco, como si hubiese perdido peso recientemente. Su arma abultaba la chaqueta por la cintura, y se quedó de pie con la mano cerca por si tenía que sacarla, nerviosa. Pike se preguntó qué habría oído contar de él que la había asustado tanto.

El detective de mayor edad dio un codazo a la mujer, como si señalara una jaula del zoo.

—Joe Pike.

Luego le habló a Pike más alto, como si este fuese un animal que no se hubiese dado cuenta del codazo.

—Cuando me dijeron que eras tú pensé: «Bueno, si este tío no me pega un tiro, me arreglará la jornada».

36

Lo dijo de tal manera que Pike se sintió impelido a examinarle más de cerca. Le parecía familiar, pero no le reconocía. El hombre comprendió la confusión y levantó más su insignia para que la viera.

—¿Qué, Pike, no te acuerdas de mí? Jerry Button, de Rampart. Ahora estoy en Pacific Station. Esta es la detective Futardo. Estamos en lo de la agresión a Smith, así que no nos dispares, ¿vale? No nos pegues un tiro.

Cuando mencionó Rampart se acordó de todo, pero aquel Jerry Button no se parecía en nada al joven y despierto oficial que Pike recordaba. Este pesaba trece o catorce kilos más, tenía la piel llena de manchas y los ojos hinchados. Aquel Jerry Button había pasado por la academia un par de años antes que Pike, y era oficial de patrulla ejecutivo en la división de Rampart cuando Pike era un simple recluta. Se llevaban bien, pero no eran amigos. Button le dio la espalda cuando Pike dimitió, como la mayoría de sus colegas. No les culpaba.

Examinó sus tarjetas de identificación a una distancia de más de un coche. Futardo era una D-1, lo que significaba que era nueva en la división de detectives y recién salida de la patrulla. Button era ahora D-3, un grado superior que normalmente ostentaban los supervisores. Era demasiada caballería para un simple atraco.

Pike preguntó:

—¿Qué tal está el señor Smith?

Button le ignoró mientras guardaba su insignia.

—¿Llevas armas?

—Dos. Tengo permiso.

Button dio un codazo a Futardo de nuevo.

—Ya te lo he dicho: siempre va armado.

La cara de Futardo era un búnker pequeño y oscuro.

—¿Comprobamos los permisos?

—No. No puedes ir dejando caer por ahí tantos muertos como este tío sin tener los papeles en orden. Los tienes en regla, ¿verdad, Pike? Siempre se te ha dado bien.

Miró a Button hasta que este finalmente se echó a reír, y levantó las manos.

—Era broma… Vamos dentro, cuéntame lo que ha pasado.

—Aquí fuera estamos bien.

—Vamos, hombre, entremos. Dentro estaremos mejor.

—Si hubieses tenido la cortesía de llamar, podrías entrar. Como no ha habido llamada, nos quedamos fuera. Las groserías, mejor fuera.

Button se puso serio.

—¿Vas a cooperar o no?

—Pregunta lo que quieras.

—¿Aquí, en el aparcamiento?

—Aquí.

Button y Futardo sacaron un bloc cada uno.

—Vale, pues aquí entonces. Ya sabes lo que necesitamos: dinos lo que pasó.

Pike relató la secuencia de acontecimientos igual que se los había descrito a Hydeck, incluyendo la descripción del segundo asaltante y la llegada y acciones de la ambulancia y la policía. Futardo escribía rápido para seguirle, pero Button parecía aburrido, como si ya hubiese oído todo aquello antes y no le preocupase demasiado si era de una manera u otra.

—Según la oficial Hydeck, sacaste una pistola de nueve milímetros y le dijiste que se la quitaste a Mendoza. ¿Es correcto?

—Sí.

—Mendoza dice que tú se la pusiste.

—¿Y qué dice el señor Smith?

—Que no vio ningún arma. ¿Está mintiendo?

Pike recordó el momento en que registró a Mendoza.

—No. Estaba boca abajo cuando yo cogí el arma. Si no vio la pistola antes de que yo llegase, tampoco la vería después. Estaba en el bolsillo de Mendoza.

Button miró a Futardo.

—Bien, veamos las fotos.

La agente sacó de la chaqueta un sobre marrón, y de este extrajo varias fotos.

—Nos gustaría que echase un vistazo a algunas fotos policiales. Cada hoja…

Button la interrumpió.

—Ya sabe lo que son. Era uno de los nuestros, no lo olvides.

Cada hoja contenía seis fotos en color de hombres adultos entre los veinte y los treinta años, todos ellos aproximadamente de la misma altura y peso. Como cada hoja tenía seis fotos las llamaban «six-packs». Pike habría jurado, por los tatuajes que llevaban, que la mayoría de ellos eran o habían sido miembros de la banda de Mendoza.

Identificó al compañero de Mendoza en la segunda hoja, en la parte de en medio de la hilera inferior.

—Es este.

Futardo inclinó la cabeza para ver.

—Bien. Alberto Gomer.

Button silenció a su compañera con una mirada que la hizo palidecer. Había cometido un error de principiante: identificar a un sospechoso por el nombre ante un testigo, y Button más tarde le echaría una bronca por ello. Ella se humedeció los labios nerviosamente antes de continuar.

—¿Firmará una declaración jurada y testificará a tal efecto bajo juramento ante un tribunal?

—Sí.

Futardo se sacó un bolígrafo de la chaqueta, le tendió el papel y el bolígrafo. Le temblaban las manos.

—Rodee la imagen que está identificando como la del

hombre al que vio atacar al señor Wilson Smith en esta fecha, y firme.

Hizo lo que le decían y firmó. Button no era mal tipo cuando Pike lo conoció, pero se había vuelto amargado y desagradable. Pensaba que seguramente sería un gilipollas como compañero de trabajo.

—¿Lo reconoció también el señor Smith?

Button bufó.

—Ninguna de estas personas le pareció familiar al señor Smith. Es curioso, ¿verdad? El señor Smith no es lo que podríamos llamar un testigo útil.

Futardo se suavizó por primera vez mientras retiraba las fotos.

—Tiene miedo.

Button volvió a bufar y le dio pie a su compañera.

—¿Quiere preguntar algo más, detective?

Futardo acabó lo que estaba escribiendo y miró a Pike de nuevo.

—Volvamos al momento en el que vio por primera vez a Mendoza y a su amigo. ¿Qué estaba usted haciendo?

—Poniendo gasolina.

—Ajá. Y ¿qué hacía en Venice?

—Eso, poner gasolina.

—¿Así que estaba allí por casualidad?

—¿Tendría que haber estado en otro sitio?

—¿Conocía usted al señor Mendoza antes de esta mañana?

Futardo le observaba de cerca, y Pike se dio cuenta de que Button también. Como si los dos hubiesen estado intentando llegar a ese punto desde el principio y se propusieran examinar su reacción. Tendrían que haber preguntado por Wilson Smith y Reuben Mendoza, pero le estaban preguntando a Pike por Pike.

—¿Adónde queréis ir a parar con esto?

—Adonde sea. De todas las personas de Los Ángeles, eras tú precisamente el que estaba ahí arreándole a ese cerdo.

—Preguntadle al señor Smith.

—Te lo estoy preguntando a ti. Tú eres el que hace interesante este asunto.

—Esto no va conmigo.

—Esto va con lo que yo digo que vaya.

Pike asintió, y comprendió entonces por qué un D-3 estaba llevando una simple investigación de un atraco. Su voz sonó tan tranquila como una hoja flotando en un estanque cuando dijo:

—Hemos terminado.

—Habremos terminado cuando yo lo diga.

Futardo parecía asustada, y de repente interrumpió para distender la situación.

—A continuación mecanografiaremos su declaración, y le convocaremos para volver a reunirnos y que la firme. Debe usted firmarla.

Button la hizo callar.

—Ya lo sabe. Vete al coche. Yo iré dentro de un minuto.

Futardo cogió la libreta y las fotos y se fue, muy aliviada.

La voz de Pike siguió sonando muy tranquila:

—¿Qué le has contado de mí para que esté tan asustada?

—La verdad.

—No has venido aquí por la acusación contra Mendoza.

—Tenemos cien atracos cada día. Un asalto de mierda más no es nada.

—¿Qué te ha pasado? Tú antes eras mejor…

Button vio a Futardo entrar en el coche y luego examinó un momento la cara de Pike, como si intentase pensar una respuesta.

—Soy oficial de policía. Creo en la ley, y he dedicado mi vida a defenderla, pero para ti, Pike, la ley no es nada. Esos jóvenes policías hablan de ti como si fueras una especie de pistolero de leyenda, pero yo sé que eres un mierda. No me gustó lo que ocurrió cuando eras oficial, ni cómo saliste de aquello, metiendo en la mierda a mucha gente hasta que te echaron del departamento. Eres peligroso, Pike. Hay algo malo en ti, y tarde o temprano te eliminaremos.

Button se fue a su coche y le habló por encima del hombro.

—Gracias por tu cooperación. Estaremos en contacto.

En cualquier otro caso, Button y Futardo intentarían averiguar qué ocurrió realmente en la tienda de Wilson Smith y se asegurarían de que Mendoza y su cómplice no pudieran hacer daño de nuevo a la víctima y a su sobrina. Así funcionaría si Pike fuese otro cualquiera, pero sabía que con él las cosas serían de una manera muy distinta. A Button no le importaba el atraco, ni si Wilson Smith volvía a sufrir otro ataque u otro robo. Lo que quería Button era machacar a Pike, y eso significaba que Wilson y su sobrina estaban solos.

Pike se alegraba de haber dado su número a Dru Rayne.

41

*N*o esperaba que le llamase tan pronto.

Veintidós minutos después de las ocho de la mañana siguiente, Pike iba en su coche a la armería cuando sonó su teléfono. No reconoció el número entrante, pero de todos modos respondió.

—Pike.

—Han vuelto. Me dijo usted que le llamase, pero no sabía si debía hacerlo o no...

Era Dru Rayne.

Pike echó un vistazo al reloj para ver la hora, y luego dio la vuelta hacia la tienda de bocadillos, pensando que podía alcanzarla en menos de seis minutos.

—¿Están en la tienda ahora? —Oyó voces tras ella y pisó a fondo el acelerador—. ¿Señorita Rayne? ¿Está bien?

—Han roto el escaparate y... sí, sí, estoy bien. Supongo que fue anoche. Ay, Dios mío, lo siento mucho, no tendría que haberle llamado. Wilson es... Lo siento, tengo que dejarle.

Pike soltó el acelerador, pero siguió dirigiéndose a la tienda, y una vez más aparcó junto a la gasolinera al otro lado de la calle. Dejó su Jeep y se fue a la acera para obtener una mejor visión. El escaparate delantero de la tienda había desaparecido casi por completo, y la puerta principal estaba abierta del todo, sujeta con un cubo de basura. Un joven con un palo rompía tranquilamente lo que quedaba del cristal, quitándolo del marco. Cerca se encontraba una mujer que llevaba un vestido color turquesa señalando hacia los trozos de cristal que quedaban, como si le fuera indicando cuál romper a continuación.

Unas sombras se movían en el interior, pero Pike no sabía si Dru Rayne era una de ellas.

Examinó la zona circundante, pero no vio a nadie que le pareciera sospechoso. Mendoza todavía estaría en la cárcel esperando la comparecencia ante el juez; probablemente los que estaban detrás de aquello eran los amigos de la banda de Gomer o Mendoza, que se vengaban por su arresto.

Pike fue andando por la acera para ver mejor los edificios de los alrededores. Nadie atrajo su atención, pero su alarma interna sonó repentinamente al notar el peso de unos ojos que le contemplaban. Conocía a jóvenes soldados recién llegados del desierto que llamaban a eso «sentido arácnido», como en las películas de Spiderman. Decían que si uno pasa en el desierto el tiempo suficiente desarrolla un sexto sentido, como si te picasen hormigas enfurecidas cuando estás en el punto de mira. Pike había recorrido selvas, desiertos y todo lo que un hombre puede recorrer durante la mayor parte de su vida, y ahora notaba ese escozor. Dio entonces una vuelta completa de trescientos sesenta grados, poco a poco, observando los escaparates de las tiendas, los tejados y los coches que pasaban, pero no vio nada. La sensación fue menguando como la marea que retrocede, hasta que desapareció.

El hombre de la gasolinera salió de su oficina cuando Pike volvió a su Jeep. Parecía preocupado.

—No lo dejará aquí, ¿verdad? Dejó usted inutilizado el surtidor de gasolina más de una hora ayer.

—No, hoy no.

El hombre pareció aliviado.

Pike se subió en el coche y se fue al callejón que había detrás de la tienda de Wilson; aparcó junto al Tercel y entró en el local.

Wilson y Dru estaban en la habitación delantera, junto con un joven y la mujer del vestido turquesa. Las mesas que normalmente estaban situadas junto al escaparate se encontraban apartadas a un lado. Dru estaba junto a ellas, hablando por teléfono mientras Wilson barría trozos de cristal hacia un cartón que el chico usaba como recogedor. Wilson había sido fiel a la palabra que dio a las sanitarias de que no iba a quedarse en el hospital. Una venda amarilla y cuadrada le cubría la mitad de la frente.

43

La mujer del vestido suplicaba a Wilson.

—¿Quieres hacer el favor de escuchar a Dru? No deberías hacer esto. Se te caerá el cerebro.

—Mejor. Así acabará mi sufrimiento.

Pike vio que los vándalos habían hecho algo más que romper el escaparate. Una enorme salpicadura de pintura verde llenaba el suelo, y otro borrón verde formaba un extraño arcoíris en la pared que había detrás del mostrador.

Dru fue la primera que vio a Pike. La sonrisa bailó en sus ojos, y luego levantó un dedo para indicarle que tenía que acabar la llamada. A continuación lo vio Wilson, y empujó furiosamente para colocar los cristales en el cartón.

—Mire todo esto. ¿Lo ve? Le dije que echase a ese desgraciado, sin más, pero no… Ahora esos gilipollas quieren vengarse de mí.

La mujer del vestido turquesa se dirigió al chico que sujetaba el cartón.

—Ethan, cuidado con ese cristal. Cuidado, no te cortes.

Dru acabó la llamada enseguida y se acercó, haciendo un gesto con el teléfono.

—Eran los cristaleros. Dicen que vendrán en cuanto puedan.

Wilson barrió con más fuerza.

—¿Y lo harán gratis?

Pike estaba concentrado en Dru. Se había puesto unos pantalones cortos y una camiseta desgastada, en sus prisas por llegar a la tienda, y tenía el pelo alborotado y los pies manchados de verde. Pike pensó que sus bonitos ojos parecían preocupados aquella mañana, pero no podía dejar de mirarla… como si fuese un libro que él quisiera leer.

—¿Está bien?

Aquella sonrisa de nuevo, rápida y tranquilizadora… Dru se acercó un paso más.

—Sí, estoy bien. Gracias por venir. No quería hacerle perder el tiempo…

—Tendría que haber llamado a la policía.

Dru miró a la mujer del vestido turquesa.

—Ya han estado aquí. Betsy ha visto los cristales rotos cuando ha llegado esta mañana y ha llamado a la policía incluso antes de llamarnos a nosotros.

La mujer se presentó.

—Betsy Harmon, de la tienda de al lado. Fue increíble cómo salvó usted a Wilson.

—Nadie me salvó. Yo lo tenía todo controlado —dijo el aludido.

Betsy levantó las cejas.

—Tú alégrate de que salvara tu culo canijo y dame las gracias por haber llamado a la policía esta mañana. Necesitarás el informe para el seguro.

Wilson lanzó un bufido mientras ayudaba a Ethan a tirar a la basura los cristales rotos que llevaba en el cartón.

—No tenemos seguro, señora mía. Pagamos según vamos haciendo, pasito a pasito. El dinero no crece en los árboles. —Le guiñó un ojo a Pike—. ¿Sabe cuánto me costará lo de emergencias?

Wilson respiraba fuerte. Pike pensó que quizás había dejado el hospital contra el consejo del médico, pero allí estaba, arreglando su tienda. Le gustó eso, y supo que él seguramente habría hecho lo mismo. Se volvió hacia Dru.

—¿Falta algo?

—No, la policía ya nos ha hecho mirar. Solo han roto el escaparate y tirado la pintura. No creo ni que hayan entrado.

—Eran los mismos policías de ayer; la chavalita mexicana, ¿cómo se llama? —dijo Wilson.

Dru frunció el ceño.

—A la oficial Hydeck probablemente no le guste que la llamen mexicana. Ni chavalita.

—Se supone que lo se dirá a los detectives, aunque la verdad, no creo que sirva para nada. Yo le he dicho: «¿Sabe qué?, mejor hágame un favor y no se lo diga. Tendría que haber visto a esos idiotas que vinieron al hospital». —Wilson dejó de barrer y miró a Pike—. ¿Por qué me preguntaron tantas cosas sobre usted? Estaban más interesados en usted que en mí. Así no encontrarán nunca al idiota que hizo esto.

Dru levantó los ojos hacia Pike.

—Ha tenido que hacerlo el hombre al que arrestaron, ¿no? Ese tipo y su amigo.

Pike explicó que Mendoza todavía estaba en custodia, lo cual dejó a Wilson muy disgustado.

45

—No importa si fue él, si fueron sus amigos o sus malditos parientes. Espere y verá. Cuando salga, vendrá aquí y lo romperá otra vez él mismo.

Wilson levantó la escoba y continuó barriendo, pero dudó como si hubiese perdido el hilo de sus pensamientos. Luego se dio la vuelta lentamente y se tambaleó. Dru chilló:

—¡Wilson!

Ethan fue el primero que llegó y lo cogió, tambaleándose bajo el peso muerto del hombre, mientras Pike lo agarró por los brazos. Wilson se agarró a una mesa para apoyarse y se sentó en un taburete.

—Estoy bien. Dejad que me siente…

Dru estaba pálida.

—Vamos, tranquilízate. Respira. Cálmate un poco, te voy a llevar a casa.

Él le apartó las manos, pero Pike le cogió las muñecas y se metió entre ellos. Wilson intentó apartarlo pero no pudo. Pike le habló con voz suave:

—Se va a hacer daño. ¿No lo ve?

El hombre levantó la vista y lo fulminó con la mirada, pero Pike no se apartó ni lo soltó: lo sujetó hasta que se relajó. Finalmente lo soltó, y Wilson apartó los ojos.

—Ya vienen los cristaleros. Tenemos que limpiar todo esto. En cuanto se arregle todo este follón me voy a casa, pero dejadme descansar un rato, por favor.

Pike miró a Dru y luego les dejó algo de espacio.

Salió por la puerta principal y se quedó de pie en la acera. Pensó en la policía. Hydeck era una buena oficial, pero aquel no era el crimen del siglo. Button y Futardo debieron de emitir la orden sobre Alberto Gomer el día anterior; quizá visitaron su última dirección conocida, o quizá no, pero si Gomer no abrió la puerta no debieron de perder demasiado tiempo con un caso de atraco. Quizá le hubiesen pasado el tema a patrulleros como Hydeck y McIntosh. El retrato de Gomer se habría distribuido al repartir el trabajo junto con fotos y órdenes de detención de violadores, asesinos, pedófilos y otros criminales peligrosos que se creía que podían estar en la zona. Hydeck y McIntosh probablemente habían dejado caer unas palabras entre las bandas de Venice que conocían, preguntando por actos de vandalismo y diciéndoles que era mejor que no volviera a ocurrir, pero la investigación no habría ido más lejos. Estaban demasiado ocupados persiguiendo a violadores y asesinos.

Pike examinó los edificios, coches y tejados de nuevo. Esperaba notar la sensación de que le observaban, pero no sentía nada, así que volvió adentro. Miró a Wilson primero y luego a Dru.

—Esto no volverá a ocurrir.

Wilson puso mala cara.

—¿Es usted un adivino? ¿Cómo sabe que no volverá a ocurrir?

—Porque hablaré con ellos.

Wilson se echó atrás en el taburete como si Pike no fuese más listo que los gilipollas que fueron a verle al hospital.

—¿Sabe qué? Déjelo ya, ¿vale? La cosa ya está hecha, y no sabemos quién ha sido, así que no lo empeore. —Hizo una seña hacia Betsy—. Entre tú y este, al final vais a conseguir que me asesinen.

—No seas idiota —contestó Betsy.

Dru se quedó mirando preocupada a su tío, luego se alejó y se dirigió al almacén. Pike la siguió y la encontró llorando. Cerró los ojos con fuerza y luego los abrió, pero las lágrimas no desaparecieron.

—Es un hombre imposible. Ha resultado muy difícil intentar salir adelante en este sitio, y ahora encima tenemos a esa gente. —Cerró los ojos de nuevo y levantó una mano, como deteniéndose a sí misma—. Lo siento.

Pike le tocó el brazo. Le dio un sencillo toque y luego bajó la mano.

—No pasa nada.

—Llevo años diciéndome eso a mí misma.

—Esta vez es diferente.

Pike volvió a su Jeep y una vez más miró la hora. Gomer estaba desaparecido, pero Pike sabía dónde encontrar a Mendoza. Seguramente lo habrían llevado a la comisaría de policía de Pacific Community, esperando su acusación formal después de darle el alta del hospital. La oficina del fiscal del distrito tenía cuarenta y ocho horas para formular una acusación contra él a partir del momento de su arresto, pero Pike

47

sabía que probablemente lo habrían puesto el primero de la lista a causa de su herida. Eso significaba que era posible que aquel mismo día, en algún momento, formularan la acusación. Si había algún tipo de fianza, lo soltarían.

Pike llamó a su armería. Tenía cinco empleados, dos a tiempo completo y tres que habían sido agentes de policía. Un hombre llamado Ronnie dirigía la tienda, y llevaba mucho tiempo con Pike.

—¿Te las podrás arreglar sin mí esta mañana?

—Sí. ¿Por qué?

—Ha surgido algo. Voy a estar ocupado un tiempo.

—Tómate el tiempo que necesites. Haz lo que te parezca.

—¿Puedo pedirle a Liz que me haga un favor?

—Si está disponible… ¿Qué necesitas?

La hija menor de Ronnie era fiscal antibandas de la oficina del fiscal de Compton. Pike le explicó lo de Reuben Mendoza, que esperaba en la comisaría de Pacific para su aparición ante el tribunal.

—Probablemente presenten una acusación formal hoy, pero quizá se lo queden hasta mañana. ¿Puede averiguármelo?

—¿Dónde puedo encontrarte?

—En el móvil.

—Te llamo enseguida.

Ronnie lo llamó ocho minutos más tarde.

—Es hoy, lo han llevado esta mañana. Será en el juzgado del aeropuerto, en Hawthorne. ¿Necesitas alguna ayuda?

—No, estoy bien.

Pike cerró su teléfono y se fue a cazar a Reuben Mendoza.

*E*l juzgado del aeropuerto era uno de los cuarenta y ocho tribunales superiores que se extendían por las mil hectáreas del
condado de Los Ángeles. Se encontraba en el rincón sudoeste
del enlace entre la autopista Century y la de San Diego, a
menos de un tiro de piedra del aeropuerto de Los Ángeles, y
parecía una polilla verde gigante con las alas de cristal, luchando por elevarse en el aire.

Pike dejó la autopista 405, entró en La Ciénaga de camino
al tribunal y encontró un lugar para aparcar con una visión
fácil y cómoda de la entrada posterior. El público podía entrar
en el edificio por las dos entradas, la principal y la trasera, pero
Pike sabía por experiencia que los acusados que pagaban fianza eran liberados siempre por la puerta de atrás. Sabía también
que el tribunal de comparecencia no tenía un calendario a raja-
tabla para ver a los acusados. En aquel mismo momento
Mendoza estaría en una celda de detención con otros muchos;
su orden de aparición ante el juez cambiaría según los horarios
de abogados públicos y privados, reuniones entre abogados y
clientes, peticiones y alegatos. Pike no tenía ningún problema
por esperar, y podía hacerlo el día entero, si era necesario, pero
sospechaba que el personal del tribunal se compadecería del
brazo roto de Mendoza.

Pike se acomodó. Tomó aliento, lo exhaló desde lo más
profundo de los pulmones y volvió a repetir esa respiración
honda. Sintió que su cuerpo se relajaba y que su corazón iba
más lento. Contempló la puerta y suspiró, sin pensar en
nada. Podía quedarse así sentado durante días, y lo había

hecho en lugares mucho menos cómodos que un vehículo limpio y seco a la sombra de una polilla gigante. Encontraba una gran paz en la espera, y la facilitaba mucho el no pensar en nada.

A las 11.07 el Monte Carlo de color granate entró en el aparcamiento. La comisura de la boca de Pike se movió un poco. El vehículo indicaba que Mendoza había pagado su fianza y llamado a sus amigos para que vinieran a buscarlo, y ahora lo estaban sacando.

Pike examinó al conductor, único ocupante del coche. Esperaba que fuese Gomer, pero no: era un joven latino con una bandana atada a la cabeza y un bigotito fino. No aparcó en el lugar designado, sino que se situó en el bordillo, junto a la puerta. Otra buena señal.

Noventa segundos más tarde Reuben Mendoza salió de la polilla con una sonrisa en la cara y un yeso que le cubría el antebrazo, desde la mano derecha hasta justo por debajo del codo. No usaba cabestrillo. Mendoza señaló a su amigo con las dos manos, hizo un exagerado movimiento de hombro para exhibir su yeso, enseñó al tribunal el dedo corazón de cada una de sus manos y se subió al coche.

Pike los siguió hasta la 405, dejando que el Monte Carlo se situara cinco o seis coches por delante entre el tráfico ligero de última hora de la mañana. No parecían tener prisa, de modo que Pike tampoco se apresuró. El Monte Carlo entró en la autopista de Marina, luego subió por Lincoln Boulevard y se dirigió a una zona comercial de baja categoría junto a Venice Boulevard. Varias manzanas más allá fue aparcado ante un taller llamado Our Way Body Mods. Una verja de hierro de dos metros de alto protegía el solar, con unas puertas dobles en la entrada de la calle principal y la secundaria. Estas estaban abiertas. Un edificio de servicios, con dos zonas de reparación al aire libre, se encontraba detrás de un pequeño aparcamiento donde los vehículos estropeados esperaban que los arreglasen y los coches recién reparados o *tuneados* esperaban que los recogiesen. La mayor parte de los vehículos eran coches de fantasía, vehículos de importación japoneses que llevaban unos alerones muy sofisticados y motores potenciados con óxido nitroso, clásicos americanos como Bel Air o Impalas cortados para que quedaran más bajos y pintados con unos colores tan vivos como si fueran caramelos.

Cuando el Monte Carlo aparcó, varios hombres salieron de las zonas de reparación para saludar a Mendoza. Pike contó hasta nueve cabezas, excluyendo a Mendoza y su chófer. Negocios como Our Way Body Mods a menudo eran propiedad de bandas familiares de distintas generaciones. Se llevaban como negocios legales o semilegales, pero su objetivo fundamental era que los miembros de la banda pudieran asegurar que tenían empleo cuando hacían apelaciones a jueces y funcionarios de libertad condicional. Tales negocios también servían como clubes, puntos de entrega y de evasión de impuestos y para blanquear ingresos ilegales de la banda.

Mientras los hombres se apiñaban en torno a Mendoza, Pike observó sus caras. La mayoría llevaban historiados tatuajes de la banda y la cabeza afeitada, moda que había reemplazado al pelo engominado hacia atrás como marca de estilo entre «colegas». Pike sabía que no todos aquellos hombres eran de la banda. La mayoría sí, pero un par probablemente solo eran aspirantes, y quizá dos o tres más fueran solo amigos. Tres de ellos mostraban la grasa y la suciedad propias del trabajo, pero la mayoría simplemente pasaban por allí. Vio al hombre que le había apuntado con la mano desde el asiento trasero del Monte Carlo, pero Gomer no se encontraba allí. El tipo abrazó a Mendoza y lo levantó del suelo, y, cuando otros hicieron la broma de intentar coger el yeso de Mendoza, los apartó juguetonamente. Protegía a su amigo. Cualquiera de aquellos hombres podría haber atacado la tienda de Wilson, pero Pike no tenía manera de averiguarlo, aunque pensaba que conocía a alguien que podía ayudarle mucho con aquel problema.

51

Pike buscó en la agenda de su móvil hasta que encontró el número y marcó. Le respondió una chica muy animada.

—Ojos de Ángel. ¿En qué puedo ayudarle?

—¿Está Artie?

—Sí. ¿Quién le llama?

—Dile que Joe Pike va para allá.

Pike se dirigió a una casita pequeña estucada en un barrio residencial al este de Abbot Kinney Boulevard. Conocido por la gente que vivía allí como la Ciudad Fantasma, las calles estaban llenas de casitas modestas, originalmente construidas en los años treinta para trabajadores afroamericanos. Algunas de las zonas de la Ciudad Fantasma se habían aburguesado lentamente, pero no todas, dejando un triste recuerdo de días pasados y sueños no realizados. Pero los hombres como el padre Arturo Alvarez intentaban cambiar aquello.

El padre Art no era sacerdote, aunque las mujeres y niños que estaban a su cargo le llamaban padre y lo trataban con todo el amor y respeto de un ministro de Dios. Artie Álvarez era un asesino. Mató a su primera y única víctima cuando tenía solo once años. Era un chico de trece años de Shoreline Crip llamado Lucious T. Jefferson, cuyo único pecado fue pasar pedaleando con una bicicleta azul Schwinn por delante de la casa de Artie. Este era brutalmente sincero al explicar cómo y por qué había matado a aquel chico, una historia que contaba a menudo ante alumnos de escuelas elementales, líderes ciudadanos y grupos de empresarios en toda la Zona Sur. Hablaba a los chicos porque esperaba cambiar su vida a mejor. Y también hablaba a los líderes ciudadanos y a los empresarios para recoger dinero para sufragar sus programas.

El calor era inmisericorde aquella tarde de agosto, el día que Artie cometió homicidio. Él, sus dos hermanos menores y su hermana, que aún era un bebé, se encontraban en las escaleras delante de casa, esperando que su madre volviese de su trabajo como gobernanta en Cheviot Hills. Su padre no estaba, lo que quiere decir que se encontraba pasando una temporada en la prisión de Soledad. Artie recuerda que él y sus hermanos se inventaban mentiras sobre su padre cuando estaban aburridos, y se entretenían fingiendo que era un forajido importantísimo en lugar de un vulgar borracho con un ligero retraso mental por inhalar demasiado disolvente y cola. Artie y sus hermanos habían llegado a un paréntesis de calma en sus historias cuando pasó Lucious Jefferson pedaleando. La hermanita pequeña, Tina, estaba encima de las rodillas de Artie cuando este vio a Jefferson con su bicicleta azul tan bonita. El chico ni siquiera los miró. Pasó pedaleando, despacio, y por pura rabia, por la rabia que albergaba en su corazón, Artie exclamó:

—¡Fuera de nuestra calle, asqueroso negro de Crip!

Jefferson, que hasta aquel momento no había prestado atención alguna a los cuatro niños que estaban en los escalones, hizo una seña de una banda y gritó a su vez:

—¡Frijolero de mierda! ¡Que te den por culo!

Tal y como contaba Arturo la historia, le entró una rabia tan brutal que se quedó solo en el mundo. Sus dos hermanos y su hermana desaparecieron. Todo pensamiento hacia su madre, que estaba a punto de volver a casa, desapareció, y la razón tal y como la conocen los hombres civilizados dejó de existir. No tiene recuerdo alguno de que empujase a su hermana, que estaba sobre su rodilla, ni de los chillidos que esta dio cuando se hizo una brecha tan grande con el escalón que tuvieron que ponerle ocho puntos de sutura en la cabeza.

Artie entró corriendo en casa, cogió el rifle del calibre 22 de su padre de debajo de la cama, miró frenéticamente a ver si estaba cargado y luego salió en tromba de la casa. Cogió a Lucious Jefferson una manzana y media más allá, mientras este esperaba para cruzar una calle con mucho tráfico, y allí apoyó el cañón del rifle en su espalda y apretó el gatillo. Lo mató. Lo asesinó. Le metió una bala del 187.

Lucious Jefferson ni siquiera vio venir a Artie. Estaba mirando el tráfico, esperando un hueco en el río incesante de coches, cuando su asesino corrió tras él y le disparó entre las vértebras torácicas T5 y T6, destruyéndole la espina dorsal y enviándole un fragmento de hueso a la arteria pulmonar desde la protuberancia transversal de la T6. Artie diría más tarde que en aquel momento el mundo real y la realidad de lo que había hecho se estrellaron contra su ser como una ola inusitada, despertándole y sacándole del lugar ciego de su rabia y aplastándole con el horror de lo que había hecho. Lucious cayó hacia adelante en su bici, se derrumbó y aterrizó de espaldas en el suelo. Tenía los ojos abiertos como platos, tan abiertos que parecían globos que sobresalían de la cara. Artie vio el terror y el dolor en los ojos del chico moribundo, un dolor horrible fluyendo de ellos como un espíritu que abandonaba su cuerpo y flotaba hacia él, cambiando para siempre su vida.

Después de aquel hecho terrible, Artie Alvarez pasó tres años en una institución especial para chicos, donde se mostró

53

reservado, se sometió a una terapia regular y recibió la visita de los ojos de Lucious Jefferson cada noche en sueños. La arrogancia de su juventud fue reemplazada por la culpa y una vergüenza indecible. Al final obtuvo el título de bachillerato y la licenciatura en psicología en Northridge, estado de California, y se convirtió en asesor de grupos juveniles, organizaciones sin ánimo de lucro y programas de prestaciones sociales de toda la ciudad, con el objetivo de acabar con la violencia mediante la educación. Creó Ojos de Ángel como programa benéfico para niños en peligro, y trabajó con bandas por toda la ciudad. Lo de «en peligro» significaba en peligro de unirse a una banda, en peligro de volver a las drogas, en peligro de convertirse en prostituta, en peligro de caer en la delincuencia. El mensaje de Ojos de Ángel era sencillo: «Actúa como si alguien te estuviera vigilando». Ese era el lema de la organización: «Alguien te vigila». Su público pensaba que era una referencia a Dios, hasta que Artie explicó que no había pasado ni una sola noche sin ver los ojos torturados de Lucious Jefferson en sus sueños. Lucious Jefferson vigilaba.

El cuartel general de Ojos de Ángel ocupaba una casita estucada en una calle residencial. Cuando apareció Pike, la casa estaba rodeada por una docena de niños mayorcitos y adolescentes de ambos sexos, junto con dos consejeros de veintitantos años. La mayoría de los jóvenes eran latinos, pero también había entre ellos afroamericanos, anglosajones y asiáticos. Armados con pinceles y rodillos, estaban pintando la casa de un bonito color beis bajo la dirección de Artie.

Cuando este vio a Pike fue a abrir la cancela. Llevaba pantalones cortos, sandalias y una camiseta con el logo de Ojos de Ángel.

—Marisol me ha dicho que ibas a venir. Me alegro de verte, amigo.

—¿Tienes un minuto?

—Espera... —Llamó a su ejército de pintores—. Señoras y señores, aquí tenéis a mi amigo el señor Joe Pike. Por favor, dadle la bienvenida.

Los chicos respondieron.

—Hola, señor Pike. Bienvenido a Ojos de Ángel.

Artie sonrió y Pike asintió.

—¿Cuántos tienes?

—Veintitrés hoy. Otros veinte en el centro del sur de Los Ángeles. Y dieciocho en Van Nuys.

Aunque Artie empleaba a consejeros que vivían en las diversas casas, a sus chicos no se les permitía residir en ellas, excepto breves estancias si corrían riesgo de sufrir abusos físicos en casa o de ser atacados por las bandas del vecindario. Aquellos lugares existían para que ellos tuviesen un lugar adonde ir, consejeros con los que hablar, tutores que les ayudasen con sus estudios y un refugio pacífico de las aguas tormentosas de sus vidas. Artie Alvarez no cobraba nada por esos servicios, y cubría sus costes recogiendo fondos y donaciones. Aunque el recinto estaba limpio y ordenado e iban a pintar la casa, Pike notó que en el tejado faltaban tejas, que había mosquiteras de las ventanas rotas y otras señales de que la organización andaba escasa de fondos. Cuando Pike lo mencionó, Artie se encogió de hombros.

—Es la economía. El estado está arruinado. La gente rica no se siente tan rica como antes, de modo que da menos. —Sonrió a los chicos como si admirase el valor que demostraban para querer cambiar—. Nos las arreglaremos. Ahora vamos, hablemos de lo que quieras.

55

Pike siguió a Artie hacia la casa. El salón estaba amueblado como una oficina y sala de espera con dos escritorios, dos sofás y dos sillas. Una joven latina muy guapa, probablemente Marisol, se encontraba en el escritorio delantero, hablando por teléfono mientras escribía en un ordenador. Al pasar, Artie dijo:

—Joe, Marisol. Marisol, Joe.

La chica levantó una mano como saludo sin interrumpir su conversación. Intentaba convencer a un restaurante local de que donase la comida que les sobraba a un refugio para niños maltratados. Pike notó que una perla de sudor resbalaba por un lado de su cara, y ella se la limpió. No había aire acondicionado en aquella casa.

Artie le condujo a lo que en tiempos fue el dormitorio principal, pero ahora servía como su oficina. Todas las ventanas estaban abiertas y un par de ventiladores movían el aire, pero aun así hacía calor. Las frescas brisas del océano raramente se aventuraban tan lejos del mar.

Artie se dejó caer en una silla de segunda mano frente a un antiguo pupitre de profesor.

—Siéntate. ¿Qué puedo hacer por ti?

—La Venice Trece.

—Sí. Durante años tuvieron el Oeste. ¿De qué camarilla estamos hablando?

—Malevos Pacíficos.

—Los gánsteres del Pacífico. Están en el extremo del bulevar, justo al lado del agua.

—Quiero hablar con el jefe.

Cada camarilla tenía su propio líder, conocido como el jefe. Artie elevó las cejas y se echó atrás.

—¿Quieres decir hablar en plan charlar o como alguien que no volverá a decir una palabra nunca más?

—En plan charla. Si quisiera lo otro no te habría metido a ti.

Pike explicó la situación de Mendoza y Gomer, y los actos vandálicos que habían tenido lugar. Comprendía bien a los pandilleros por su época de policía. Podía matarlos, pero no hacer que le escucharan. Solo su jefe tenía ese poder. Si su líder les decía que dejaran a Smith en paz, lo harían. Una petición muy razonable, hecha con un espíritu de cooperación.

—Mmm… Así que quieres hacer una petición personal —dijo Artie.

Pike asintió, y Arturo se volvió a echar hacia atrás.

—Pues no veo por qué no. Tienen un chico nuevo, Miguel Azzara, que llaman Mikie. Te sorprenderá.

Pike asintió de nuevo. Mikie.

—¿Tienes alguna relación allí?

—Hablo con toda esa gente. La V-Trece, las bandas de Culver City y Santa Mónica, los Shoreline Crips. No les gusto a todos, pero saben que intento hacer las cosas bien, y tienen hermanos y hermanas pequeños. —Dio unos golpecitos en el escritorio, pensativo, mientras examinaba a Pike—. ¿Quieres que sepa con quién está tratando?

—Lo que creas que será mejor.

—No responde a las amenazas.

—Esto no es una amenaza.

Artie pensó un momento y luego se encogió de hombros.

—Puedo ponerme en contacto, pedirle un favor personal. Es un tío listo; no es lo que cabría esperar.

—Bien.

Art se rio al coger el teléfono.

—Dame un momento, ¿vale? Veré lo que puedo hacer.

Pike captó la indirecta y salió, dejando a Art para que hablase en privado. Unos minutos más tarde este salió con una respuesta: Miguel Azzara accedía a reunirse con Pike a las tres en punto, aquella misma tarde.

$\mathcal{M}$ikie Azzara se reunió con Pike en una cafetería en Abbot Kinney Boulevard, no lejos de los canales de Venice. El cielo de la tarde allí, cerca de la playa, estaba claro y azul, y la temperatura era de veintitantos grados. Pike se sorprendió cuando Artie le dijo dónde quería reunirse Azzara. Abbot Kinney era una zona de restaurantes de categoría, tiendas de diseño, galerías de arte y bares, y allí, sentado en la terraza de la cafetería, se encontraba rodeado por atractivas mujeres ricas que pegaban perfectamente con el entorno. La mayoría estaban bronceadas, tenían entre veinte y cuarenta años y parecían además muy en forma. Casi todas llevaban ligeros vestidos veraniegos o pantalones cortos y sandalias, y ninguna de ellas fumaba. No era un lugar que soliera frecuentar un veterano de la V13.

Pike llegó temprano y se sentó fuera, tal y como habían acordado, y se tomó un café solo. El café estaba flojo, pero no le importó.

A las tres y cinco, un Prius negro se paró junto a la acera, al otro lado de la calle. Un hombre cercano a la treintena salió de él, echó un vistazo al tráfico que venía y luego atravesó hacia la cafetería. Llevaba un abrigo ligero de Hugo Boss, informal, encima de una camisa de AC/DC, vaqueros a medida y sandalias. Era esbelto, iba bien afeitado y resultaba lo bastante guapo como para ser modelo de *Esquire*. Las mujeres sentadas alrededor de Pike lo observaron cuando se acercaba.

El hombre miró a la multitud al acercarse a la acera, según vio Pike, y llegó hasta la mesa. Sonrió y ofreció su mano, enseñando unos dientes perfectos y unos hoyuelos.

—¿Señor Pike? Michael Azzara. El padre Art me dijo que le reconocería sin problemas. ¿Puedo sentarme?

Pike asintió, observando que el otro se había presentado como Michael, y no Mikie ni Miguel. Iba arreglado y limpio, y con un aspecto tan distinto de los perros callejeros veteranos del taller de chapa y pintura como el Prius de un Bel Air del 56 rojo intenso. Miguel Azzara parecía un universitario de la USC, aunque más robusto, como si en el instituto se hubiese dedicado a la lucha.

Azzara se sentó, cruzó las manos y miró a Pike con inocente curiosidad.

—Adoro al padre Art. Hace mucho por nuestra comunidad.

Pike asintió y esperó a que Azzara continuase.

—¿En qué puedo ayudarle?

Ahora, sentado, Pike notó que la piel en un lado del cuello de Azzara estaba moteada con débiles imperfecciones. Debió de tatuarse a los catorce o quince años, pero en algún momento entre aquella época y la actual se había sometido al láser. Pequeñas cicatrices marcaban los nudillos de su mano izquierda y dividían la línea de su ceja izquierda. Quizá no siempre tuvo un aspecto tan distinto de los hombres del taller de chapa. Levantó la taza.

—¿Quiere tomar algo?

—No, gracias. ¿Qué es lo que desea?

—¿Habla por los Malevos?

Azzara comprobó primero si las mujeres que estaban cerca les oían. Una mujer de treinta y muchos le miró y sonrió. Azzara le devolvió la sonrisa, como una estrella de cine.

—¿Qué tal?

Ella se sonrojó y se volvió otra vez hacia sus amigas, fingiendo que no babeaba. Azzara se volvió de nuevo hacia Pike.

—Por eso estoy aquí, sí. ¿Qué desea?

Era la tercera vez que se lo preguntaba.

—Reuben Mendoza y Alberto Gomer.

—Esos chicos son idiotas. Mendoza acaba de ser arrestado.

—¿Y sabe por qué?

—Sé que he tenido que pagar su fianza. ¿Se trata de eso?

—Yo soy el hombre que lo detuvo. ¿Supone eso algún problema entre nosotros?

59

Azzara pareció sorprendido.

—Depende de lo que quiera. Si quiere dinero por algún motivo, por ejemplo un soborno por negarse a testificar... Entonces, sí, sí que puede haber algún problema.

—Nada de eso.

—Ya me imaginaba que no. No si el padre Art responde por usted.

Pike expuso los hechos exactamente tal y como lo había hecho a Hydeck, Button y Artie Alvarez. Le contó a Azzara que Wilson Smith era un amigo y que a primera hora de la mañana alguien había asaltado su tienda.

Azzara escuchó con el ceño fruncido, pensativo, asintiendo ocasionalmente como suele hacer la gente, y no habló hasta que Pike hubo terminado.

—Ajá. Bien. Ya lo comprendo. Esa gente son amigos suyos. No quiere que los fastidien.

—Eso es.

—Hecho.

Pike esperó, pensando que habría algo más, pero no fue así. Al cabo de unos momentos, Azzara se dio cuenta de que Pike no pensaba decir nada más, de modo que se explicó para llenar el silencio.

—Ese asunto es calderilla, una tontería. Lo único que hace es atraer a la poli y cabrear a las unidades de los antibandas. ¿Para qué? ¿Para que un idiota como Mendoza pueda comerse un bocadillo gratis, o timarle a un tío veinte pavos? ¿Vale la pena tanto problema por veinte dólares, que yo tenga que estar aquí sentado con usted? Por favor...

—La Trece dejará en paz la tienda del señor Smith. No habrá más vandalismo. Ni problemas.

Azzara se movió, irritado por tener que ocuparse de un asunto tan insignificante como aquel.

—Ya está hecho. ¡Por favor, esa tontería de la pintura! Pero ¿estamos en el colegio todavía? Mire, no sé si fue Gomer o quién fue; es la primera vez que oigo hablar de todo esto, pero lo averiguaré y se acabará. No quiero que esos *vatos* vayan por ahí haciendo cosas así. Esta es la lección del asunto: usted y yo sentados ahora, perdiendo el tiempo. Es absurdo.

—Gracias —dijo Pike.

Azzara miró la hora, suspiró y examinó a Pike un momento. Pike se preguntó por qué aún no se había ido. Ya habían terminado: Miguel Azzara ya podía dejarle. Pero el joven se inclinó hacia delante y bajó la voz.

—El padre me ha explicado que usted era un hombre peligroso. Pero yo le he dicho: «Art, ¿estás loco? ¿Ese tío quiere enfrentarse a mí?».

Pike meneó la cabeza.

—No quiero enfrentarme a usted.

Azzara levantó la mano.

—Ya me lo ha dicho Art. Ha especificado que usted no representa ninguna amenaza, y que así se lo manifestó para asegurarse de que yo lo supiera. Eso me parece muy bien. Estos temas del respeto son importantes. —Pike sabía que iba a decir algo más, así que esperó—. Me ha dicho que hay cosas de usted que debería saber, y me las ha contado. No sé si se lo está inventando todo, pero me ha explicado unas cosas muy extrañas. Como no sabía si me quería asustar o qué, le he dicho que parase. —Levantó ambas manos gesticulando mucho, reviviendo la conversación con Art—. Yo le he dicho: «¿Qué me estás contando, Art, que ese hombre quiere ir a la guerra contra mí? ¿Que si no le doy lo que quiere vendrá a por mí, a por los míos, toda la Trece?» —Pike esperó—. Art ha contestado que no, que no era nada por el estilo; sencillamente se sentía obligado a explicármelo, ya que nos estaba reuniendo a los dos; pero me ha asegurado que todo esto no partía de usted. Él quería que yo supiera con quién estaba tratando. ¿Puede imaginarse?

Azzara hizo una pausa esperando la respuesta, pero Pike no respondió.

—Usted no habla mucho.

—¿Qué quiere que diga?

—No tiene que decir nada. Pero si hay algo que yo debo saber, entonces hay cosas que usted tiene que saber también. —Azzara se inclinó hacia delante y miró a Pike—. Parece usted peligroso. Parece todo lo que me dijo Art, pero parecer es distinto a ser. Yo también sé lo que parezco.

—¿Hay algún problema?

—Quiero que las cosas queden bien claras entre nosotros.

Entiendo que usted no me está amenazando. Viene a mí como un hombre, pidiéndome que ayude a sus amigos.

—Sí.

—No hago esto porque crea que hay ninguna amenaza implicada.

—Lo comprendo.

—¿Conoce usted La Eme?

—Claro.

—Entonces entenderá por qué no tengo miedo.

La Eme era la mafia mexicana, tan abundante en número de miembros que controlaba todo el comercio de droga en el sudoeste de Estados Unidos y prácticamente poseían todas las prisiones de California y Arizona. Era un ejército criminal dentro de las fronteras de Estados Unidos.

—Comprendo.

Azzara mostró los hoyuelos y se puso de pie.

—De hombre a hombre me lo pide. Y de hombre a hombre yo le respondo. Está hecho. Diga a sus amigos que se tranquilicen. Hablaré con mis colegas y esas cosas no volverán a ocurrir.

Pike miró al otro lado de la calle.

—¿Le gusta el Prius?

—Me encanta. Es importante ser responsable con el medio ambiente. ¿Qué conduce usted?

—Un Jeep.

—Pásese al verde, señor Pike. El planeta necesita amor.

Azzara enseñó los hoyuelos otra vez, le ofreció la mano y se dirigió hacia su coche.

Una llamada. Sencillo. Hecho.

Tendría que haber acabado todo ahí, pero no fue así.

Cuando Pike volvió a la tienda de bocadillos, el aire estaba caliente por la brisa sedosa que soplaba hacia el interior. Los cristaleros habían acabado ya su trabajo, y ya estaba instalado el nuevo escaparate. En la puerta se veía un letrero que decía CERRADO, pero Pike vio que alguien se movía en el interior.

Fue por la puerta trasera. En la puerta había un enorme ventilador enchufado. Dru estaba de rodillas junto al mostrador, frotando el suelo con algo que parecía una toalla grande. Las dos mesas pequeñas se encontraban pegadas a la pared de atrás, y las sillas vueltas del revés y colocadas encima, con las patas sobresaliendo como si fuesen cornamentas. En todo el local olía fuertemente a trementina. Probablemente llevaba toda la mañana limpiando el suelo, y ahora intentaba quitar la trementina.

Pike la contempló. Estaba de espaldas a él, con el culo en pompa, apretando la toalla con ambas manos. Iba descalza, aunque el suelo había quedado cubierto aquella misma mañana de añicos de cristal. Vio cómo se movía su espalda mientras restregaba el suelo con la toalla, subiendo y bajando hasta apoyar los talones. Estaba muy bronceada: hasta las plantas de los pies las tenía bronceadas.

Pike pasó alrededor del ventilador y dio unos golpecitos en la pared, «toc toc».

Dru miró despreocupadamente por encima de su hombro y siguió frotando. Sonrió como si ya le esperase y le gustara que él hubiera vuelto.

—Eh. ¿Qué tal queda esto?

—Mucho mejor.

—La pared está bien, pero el suelo se ha estropeado. ¿Ve cómo se ha metido la pintura en las juntas? Esos desgraciados lo han estropeado.

Pike vio que tenía razón. La pintura se había introducido en las ranuras entre las baldosas de linóleo amarmolado y se quedaría allí hasta que cambiasen el suelo.

—No volverán —dijo.

Dru hizo una pausa y luego se puso en pie, quitándose un mechón de pelo de la cara. Levantó las cejas y Pike vio humor en sus ojos, como si ella ya supiera cómo iba a acabar aquella historia y quisiera burlarse de él.

—¿Y cómo lo sabe?

—Esa gente está en una banda que tiene un líder, como cualquier organización. He hablado con la persona ante la cual responden.

Lo examinó un momento y luego puso una voz más profunda, intentando imitar a Marlon Brando.

—¿Le ha hecho una oferta que no ha podido rechazar?

Pike no sabía muy bien qué decir, de modo que pasó junto a ella para mirar el escaparate nuevo. La calle parecía normal.

—¿Ha conseguido que su tío se fuera a casa?

—No sabe estar en la cama. Se marea cuando se pone de pie, pero no me quiere escuchar. Es así.

Pike miró las mesas, que esperaban volver a su sitio.

—¿Le ayudo con las mesas?

—No, es igual. Ya me encargo.

Asintió. Había hecho todo lo que había podido, le había dicho que no tendría más problemas y ahora no se podía hacer otra cosa que esperar que Azzara cumpliera su palabra. Ya habían acabado pero, como el día anterior, él no quería irse.

—Ha hecho un buen trabajo.

—No ganaremos ningún premio de belleza.

Pike pasó junto a ella hacia el mostrador y vio que su número de teléfono estaba pinchado en el tablero de los pedidos.

—Vale. Si necesita cualquier cosa, llámeme.

—Ring, ring. —Él se volvió y la vio sonriendo—. Era yo, que le llamaba. —Dejó caer la toalla en el cubo y se miró a sí misma—. Estoy mojada, hambrienta y huelo a trementina.

Quiero una cerveza. ¿Qué tal si nos tomamos una? Hay un sitio pequeñito aquí cerca que está muy bien, el Sidewalk Café. ¿Qué le parece? Yo invito.

—Bien.

El Sidewalk era todo lo que no era el diminuto local de comida para llevar de Wilson, con una barra grande, asientos dentro y fuera y una situación espectacular en Ocean Front Walk. La zona exterior ya estaba llena de clientes habituales que habían venido a disfrutar del anochecer, pero la camarera reconoció a Dru y los acompañó sonriendo a una mesa. Corredores, patinadores, turistas y gente de la playa iban pasando por la acera entre el café y una hilera de vendedores y artistas callejeros. Detrás había un parque con el césped muy bien recortado, unas palmeras ondulantes y una enorme extensión de arena. Justo delante de su mesa un par de artistas callejeros pintados de color plata fingían ser hombres mecánicos, bloqueándose y moviéndose espasmódicamente al unísono. Un maletín abierto a sus pies tenía un letrero de cartón: SE ACEPTAN APORTACIONES.

Dru ya sabía lo que quería y desdeñó el menú.

—Yo tomaré una hamburguesa y un Blue Moon. Tienen unas hamburguesas estupendas aquí, muy gruesas y jugosas. ¿Quieres una?

—No como carne.

La camarera esbozó una sonrisa chispeante.

—Yo tampoco. Los nachos vegetarianos son la bomba, y me encanta la ensalada Corita.

—Una cerveza me irá bien. Corona.

Mientras se iba la camarera, Dru se echó atrás en su silla y sonrió.

—Tío. Tienes pinta de carnívoro total.

Pike observó a los vendedores de fuera y a la gente que pasaba. Miró hacia la playa y la gente que estaba detrás de las palmeras. Era la costumbre. También miró a Dru Rayne. La cara redonda, uno de los dientes delanteros superpuesto con el otro, una cicatriz en el puente de la nariz que hacía juego con las arruguitas que empezaban a cortar las comisuras de sus labios. Ya no era ninguna niña, estaba al principio de la treintena. Apenas a tres metros de distancia pasaban chicas pati-

65

nando en bikini, modelos de ropa de baño con cuerpos bien trabajados y bomboncitos playeros recién salidos del sol, pero Dru Rayne le atraía como un imán.

Ella le tocó el brazo.

—Gracias. Por ayudar a Wilson y por todo lo demás. De verdad, gracias. —Pike asintió. Como no ofrecía conversación, ella rellenó el hueco—. Tengo curiosidad... ¿qué haces? Quiero decir que a qué te dedicas.

—Negocios.

Dru se echó a reír; levantó una mano, como si se disculpase, y se tapó la boca con la mano libre.

—Lo siento. Reírse ahora está mal. No debería reírme.

A Pike le gustaba su risa. Era fuerte y confiada, como si estuviera totalmente a sus anchas. Le gustaba la familiaridad que ella mostraba: él había pasado la mayor parte de su vida buscando y manteniendo el control.

Los ojos de Dru mostraron timidez, como si se le hubiese ocurrido algo y estuviese a punto de decirlo.

—¿Puedo preguntarte una cosa?

Pike asintió sin dejar de mirarla.

—¿Recuerdas que Wilson dijo que los detectives que vinieron al hospital preguntaron por ti?

Pike miró a lo lejos, al agua, porque sabía adónde iba a conducir aquello. Ella le tocó el brazo de nuevo y la volvió a mirar.

—Nos dijeron que antes eras oficial de policía, pero que lo dejaste porque eras peligroso. Ese detective al que vimos, el barrigudo...

—Button.

—Dijo que no se podía contar el número de personas a las que habías matado. Que te gustaba tanto matar gente que lo dejaste para dedicarte a ser mercenario, y que no debíamos ni acercarnos a ti.

Al oír lo que ella decía Pike recordó su conversación con Miguel Azzara, con la diferencia de que esta charla hacía que se sintiera expuesto de una forma que no le gustaba. Pike había matado hombres, sí. Se había puesto en situaciones en las que la muerte era inevitable, pero sabía que la mayoría de la gente no entendería ni sus motivos ni sus razones. Raramente hablaba de esas cosas.

—¿Es verdad? —preguntó Dru.

—Antes era policía, y fui militar profesional contratado después de dejarlo. Lo de los muertos es lo que quiere creer la gente como Button.

Ella asintió, y él se preguntó qué estaría pensando.

—¿Eres peligroso?

—Eso cree Mendoza.

Dru sonrió de nuevo.

—¿Es una broma? Has hecho una broma...

Pike analizó una vez más el entorno. No se proponía hacer ninguna broma, pero si ella quería reírse le parecía bien.

—¿Te molestó que Button dijese eso?

—No. Me gusta estar contigo. Me siento a salvo. ¿Es raro acaso?

Cambió de tema cuando llegó la hamburguesa.

—¿Y tú? ¿Volverás a Nueva Orleans?

Dru miró el océano un momento. Parecía pensativa. Se comió un trozo de la hamburguesa y bebió un poco de cerveza.

—Prefiero esto. He viajado mucho después del huracán, pero en ninguna parte estoy como aquí. Estuve en Jackson, luego en Little Rock con mi hermana y su marido. Mi madre se fue a Atlanta. Todo el mundo anda por ahí... Wilson estuvo un tiempo en Houston, luego en Dallas; después volvió a Nueva Orleans, pero no sé; era demasiado duro...

Calló y se encogió de hombros.

—¿Volviste?

—Un tiempo, pero no quedaba nadie por quien volver. No tenía novio, y mi familia estaba desperdigada. No tengo ninguna propiedad, así que me fui de nuevo y pasé un tiempo con mi madre y luego con mi hermana. Más tarde Wilson vino aquí y le gustó, así que pensé que podía probar yo también. Me gusta esto. Quiero quedarme.

A Pike le gustaba ver cómo se reflejaban los pensamientos en su rostro cuando hablaba.

Los hombres robot quedaron empatados. El más menudo recogió sus ganancias, cerró el maletín y se puso al lado del más grande, ambos adoptando la misma pose exagerada. Se alejaron al unísono con sus articulaciones tiesas. Nadie les vio marchar, excepto quizá Dru. Pike no podía asegurar si ella miraba a los robots o algo que estaba tras ellos… tal vez el sol que iba bajando.

—Es bonito esto —dijo ella. —Se desperezó y estiró las manos hacia el cielo, sonriendo de nuevo—. Me encanta el aire. Todo el mundo se burla de la contaminación, pero casi todo el tiempo está claro. ¿No te gusta? ¿No te gusta este aire fabuloso del mar?

—Sí.

Y entonces Pike vio a un hombre justo ante la tienda de surf, unas puertas más allá del restaurante. En la entrada había una estatua de tamaño natural de un surfista con cabeza de tiburón, y el hombre estaba detrás de ella. Se movió cuando Pike se dio la vuelta. Fue un movimiento pequeño, como una boya balanceándose en una ola, justo lo suficiente para desaparecer detrás de la tabla de surf del tiburón.

El tipo era delgado, oscuro, y probablemente latino, aunque Pike no pudo verlo lo suficientemente bien dado el mal ángulo. Tras aquella rápida ojeada, calculó que el hombre tenía poco más de cuarenta años, la cabeza afeitada y los brazos peludos.

Dru sonreía perezosamente.

—Es bonito estar aquí, así.

—Sí —contestó él.

Ella no veía los ojos de Pike detrás de las gafas oscuras, y no sabía que estaba vigilando al hombre. Este saltó de detrás de la estatua y se unió a un grupo de turistas que pasaban. Llevaba una camisa desabrochada color naranja pálido, de manga corta, encima de una camiseta blanca, vaqueros oscuros y gafas de sol. La camisa y la cabeza calva le sonaban, y Pike se dio cuenta de que el hombre les había adelantado antes. No le había visto volver, cosa que despertó sus sospechas porque tenía una gran conciencia de la situación, lo que suponía que notaba todo lo que se encontraba en su entorno. En el mundo de Pike, las cosas que no notas pueden hacerte daño, y así suele ser.

Mientras el hombre se iba acercando, Pike vio que llevaba un tatuaje en un lado del cuello que podía significar que estaba afiliado a alguna banda, pero no lo veía con la claridad suficiente para asegurarlo. Se preguntó si lo que pasaba era que Azzara le había mentido y los amigos de Mendoza seguían empeñados en su juego, o si bien Azzara no había tenido tiempo de retirar a los sabuesos.

El hombre dejó el grupo de gente y ocupó una posición detrás de un vendedor callejero que ofrecía sombreros y camisetas. Ahora estaba usando un teléfono móvil, y Pike se preguntó si estaría hablando o solo fingiendo.

—Mejor nos vamos —le dijo a Dru.

La cara de ella mostró una decepción exagerada.

—Uf. Qué cita más corta.

—¿Ha sido una cita?

—Podría ser.

Dru intentó pagar, pero Pike dejó el dinero en efectivo y le dijo que no hacía falta esperar el cambio. Cuando volvió a mirar de nuevo, el hombre de la camisa naranja había desaparecido. Intentó localizar al hombre, y ella se dio cuenta y se volvió a mirar.

—¿Qué estás buscando? —le preguntó.

Pike se colocó delante de ella, esperando que el hombre no hubiera visto el gesto.

—No mires.

Dru dio un paso hacia un lado, intentando ver…

—¿Es uno de esos tíos?

Pike volvió a colocarse delante.

—No te preocupes.

Estaba asustada, y ahora Pike se sentía irritado consigo mismo. Le cogió la mano. Era suave, pero firme.

—No pasa nada. Vamos. Te acompaño a casa.

Pike le apretó la mano una sola vez y luego la soltó, pero notó la tensión de ella mientras caminaban de vuelta a la tienda. Le tocó la espalda para detenerla dos veces, fingiendo mirar los escaparates para poder comprobar si les seguía alguien, pero el hombre de la camisa naranja había desaparecido, y no había nadie más.

Cuando llegaron a la esquina Pike hizo otra pausa. Comprobó los coches, las aceras, los tejados, las tiendas cercanas y la gasolinera que quedaba al otro lado de la calle. La tienda de bocadillos de Wilson estaba tranquila y sin perturbaciones, pero Dru caminaba como si se pudiera romper. Su confianza y soltura habían desaparecido, y Pike notó una sensación de fracaso. Había perdido el control del momento, y eso no le gustaba nada.

—¿Pasa algo? —preguntó ella.

—No. Demasiadas precauciones.

Dru negó con la cabeza.

—No pareces de los que toman demasiadas precauciones.

La siguió hasta el coche, el Tercel plateado aparcado justo delante de la tienda de bocadillos.

—¿Quieres que entre contigo?

—He hecho todo lo que podía en este sitio, créeme. Tengo que ir a ver a Wilson —explicó la mujer.

Pike asintió y se encararon el uno al otro, aunque ninguno de los dos hizo movimiento alguno para irse.

—Escucha. Gracias. De verdad. Ya sé que lo digo mucho, pero gracias.

—¿Puedo volver a verte?

La sonrisa de ella volvió.

—Una cita —añadió él.

Dru sonrió más ampliamente aún, pero la sonrisa se desvaneció entre lo que a Pike le pareció una oleada de incertidumbre.

—¿Qué pasa? —preguntó.

Ella sacó una billetera fina de su bolsillo, buscó entre las tarjetas y le enseñó la foto de una niña pequeña que llevaba un vestido cursi y estaba sentada en un sofá verde.

—Es Amy. Mi hermana la está cuidando hasta que sepamos si puedo establecerme aquí o no.

—Es guapa.

—Es el amor de mi vida. Tiene tres años.

Dru observó la foto un momento y se volvió a guardar la billetera en el bolsillo. Miró a Pike y apartó la vista, encogiéndose de hombros.

—No sé… Supongo que quería que lo supieras.

Él asintió, notando el temor de Dru de que él no quisiera implicarse con una mujer que tenía una hija. Le volvió a preguntar:

—¿Quieres salir conmigo o no?

La sonrisa volvió. Sacó el móvil y le pidió su número. Pike se lo dio y vio que ella le mandaba un SMS.

—Es mi número. Llámame. Me gustaría mucho salir contigo en una cita de verdad.

Guardó el teléfono y luego se puso de puntillas y le dio un beso en la mejilla. Pike le pasó la mano por la espalda cuando el cuerpo de ella se acercó al suyo. Estaba conmovido: le había entregado un pedacito secreto de sí misma contándole lo de la niña, y ahora, cuando retrocedió, se sintió obligado a hacer lo mismo.

—Lo que dijo Button… Ese no sabe nada de mí.

Se quedó callado, pensando cómo explicar mejor la vida que había llevado y las decisiones que había tomado, como rescatar a la familia de un hombre de negocios de un narcoterrorista nicaragüense o detener a unos bandidos que saqueaban granjas y pueblos en África Central. Había elegido aquellos trabajos como contratado militar con mucho cuidado, y hablar de ellos ahora parecería pretencioso e interesado. Así que finalmente desistió.

—Intentaba ayudar a la gente. Se me da bien.

No se le ocurría otra cosa que decir. Al final lo dejó, sintiéndose algo violento por haber sacado el tema.

Entonces Dru le puso la mano en el pecho, y a él le pareció que le tocaba el corazón.

—Estoy segura de que es así. —Se subió a su coche. Levantó la vista y lo miró—. ¿Nunca te quitas esas gafas de sol?

Pike se quitó las gafas. La luz hizo que guiñase los ojos, pero hizo un esfuerzo para que ella los viese.

Ella lo miró un momento.

—Bien. Muy bien. —Puso en marcha el coche y le dirigió una sonrisa de despedida—. Si vas a ser peligroso, igual podrías ser peligroso también para mí.

La vio alejarse y examinó todo el callejón. Nada.

Se puso las gafas, fue andando alrededor del final del edificio y volvió a su Jeep. Al llegar a la portezuela vio lo que parecía un folleto metido bajo el limpiaparabrisas, pero cuando estuvo más cerca vio que no era un folleto sino un papel doblado. Examinó todo el entorno de nuevo, y su radar interior le avisó del peso de unos ojos.

71

Cogió el papel y lo desdobló.

MALIBU VERDE
CUATRO PLAZAS POR DELANTE

Vio el Malibu verde aparcado cuatro plazas más allá justo cuando el hombre de la camisa naranja salía de la tienda de ropa de segunda mano. Este señaló con un pulgar el Malibu: Jerry Button salió por la puerta del pasajero, y un segundo hombre salió de la puerta del conductor. Era todo ángulos rectos y bordes, como un espejo que se hubiese roto y hubiesen vuelto a pegar con cinta adhesiva. Parecía impaciente, y examinó a Pike con ojos pensativos mientras se acercaba.

Button dijo:

—Este es Joe Pike. Pike, este es Jack Straw. Del FBI.

El aludido dijo:

—Me estás jodiendo, hermano. Esto tiene que acabar.

*E*l hombre de la camisa naranja se alejó cuando Button y Straw salieron del coche. No volvió a mirarlos ni a ellos ni a Pike.

—Demos una vuelta. Mejor si no nos ven —dijo Button.

El Malibu era de alquiler, completamente nuevo, pero olía a tabaco. Pike se sentó detrás, Straw al volante y Button en el asiento de al lado. Este se retorcía para ver a Pike mientras iban cogiendo la curva. Daba la impresión de que esperaba no volver a ver nunca más a Pike, pero allí estaba, y eso le irritaba.

—Este asunto entre tú y yo tenemos que olvidarlo ahora, ¿vale? El agente especial Straw es de la oficina de Houston Field. Resulta que tiene una investigación en marcha, y nosotros nos hemos metido por medio gracias a ti.

Pike miró hacia el retrovisor y encontró la mirada de Straw contemplándole.

—El hombre de la camisa naranja.

—Le voy a contar algunas cosas que preferiría no tener que contarle, pero no puedo divulgar dónde tengo a mi gente colocada. ¿Entiende por qué?

—Ya lo veremos.

—De acuerdo. Espere un momento, que me acerco a la acera y paro. Será más fácil hablar.

Straw recorrió tres cortas manzanas hacia el interior y aparcó detrás de una hilera de tiendas de ropa playera de categoría. En el momento en que se detuvieron bajó la ventanilla y encendió un Marlboro. Pike y Button bajaron también las ventanillas.

Straw se volvió hacia Pike y le enseñó sus credenciales: «Agente especial R. Jack Straw, Federal Bureau of Investigation».

—¿De acuerdo?

Pike asintió, preguntándose de qué iba todo aquello. Straw guardó su insignia y lo miró a través del humo.

—¿Qué piensa usted de Mikie Azzara?

Pike se sorprendió, aunque no demostró expresión alguna. Straw analizó su silencio y sonrió.

—No es el típico mafioso mexicano asqueroso y con los brazos tatuados de arriba abajo, ¿verdad? Es de la nueva generación, estamos encima de él... —Straw miró el reloj—. Y por eso sabemos que se ha reunido con él hace dos horas en el Starbucks de Abbot Kinney, después de lo cual ha ido a visitar a la señorita Rayne, y han ido al Sidewalk Café. Hacen una pizza muy buena. Mi plato favorito de todos los que he tomado allí.

Straw sacó la cabeza para echar un poco más de humo hacia fuera por la ventanilla, y luego miró a Button.

—Mi nuevo amigo, el detective Button, aquí presente, cree que esta conversación es un error.

El aludido miró por la ventanilla hacia fuera.

—Eso es. Lo va a lamentar.

—No lo creo, pero de todos modos necesito su ayuda, señor Pike, de modo que aquí estamos. ¿Le ha contado la señorita Rayne lo que está pasando?

—¿Qué tendría que haberme contado?

—Los dos «carnales» a los que sacudió, Mendoza y Gomer, no era la primera vez que habían ido a ver a su tío, y no le dieron una paliza solo por un bocadillo... Le estaban dando un aviso.

Button asintió.

—Es lo que comentamos tú y yo, Pike. Smith mintió. Esos tíos le estaban extorsionando.

Straw dio unas caladas más al cigarrillo. Parecía que estaba en forma, pero Pike pensó que probablemente no era capaz de correr más de cinco o seis metros.

—Mikie está metido en un asunto de protección: o pagas o su hombre te da una patada en el culo, te rompe el escaparate, te roba el camión o lo que sea. Es una cosa callejera, de pequeña escala, uno solo de los nuevos asuntillos que lleva ahora. Un nuevo enfoque. Estos tipos van improvisando a medida que hacen las cosas.

Button se removió en su asiento, mirando a Pike pero hablando con Straw.

—La chica quizá no lo sepa. Smith probablemente no quiere que ella se preocupe. Estaría jodido si ella le abandonase.

—¿Y qué tiene que ver todo esto conmigo? —preguntó Pike.

Straw dio otra calada.

—Acaba de asustar a Mikie, y eso es malo. Estamos controlando su negocio.

Pike inclinó la cabeza.

—¿El FBI metido en un chanchullo de protección de barrio?

Straw sonrió de nuevo.

—Me importa una mierda todo esto, pero los nuevos jefes, como Azzara, no se limitan a traficar con caballo como sus papás. La Eme está entrando en la edad moderna, señor Pike. Prueban nuevos modelos de negocio, y esto de la extorsión no es más que una muestra. También están desarrollando vínculos internacionales con diversos cárteles, y eso me interesa mucho. De ahí mi operación y esta conversación.

Pike miró a Button.

—¿No lo sabías?

—No hasta esta mañana.

Straw se acabó el cigarrillo y lo tiró por encima de su hombro.

—Con mis disculpas al detective Button, no teníamos fuerzas en el terreno hace dos semanas. Cuando supimos cuál era el nuevo negocio de Mikie, decidimos que ese era nuestro camino hacia la nueva cadena alimenticia de La Eme. Y todo va pasando muy deprisa.

Pike dijo:

—A través de una extorsión de barrio.

Straw se encogió de hombros.

—Está al nivel de la calle, podemos llegar y es fácil. Fácil significa rápido. Están apareciendo chicos nuevos como Azzara en los territorios de La Eme desde Brownsville a Phoenix y

75

San Diego, y ni siquiera sabemos quiénes son. Si entramos en el territorio de Mikie podremos averiguarlo, que era lo que estábamos haciendo hasta que usted se metió en medio. —Se movió de nuevo, como disculpándose—. Hermano, escuche; usted ha actuado bien. Si yo hubiera visto a esos payasos pateando a un pobre hombre habría intervenido también. Eso me parece muy bien. Pero ahora ya ha terminado todo, y necesito que las cosas vuelvan adonde estaban.

—¿Y eso qué quiere decir? —preguntó Pike.

Button se movió, furioso.

—Quiere que te metas en tus putos asuntos. ¿Es que no lo entiendes?

Straw levantó una mano, indicándole a Button que se tranquilizase.

—Le pido que se lo tome con calma. Apártese de Smith y deje que vuelva a sus cosas. No se convierta en su guardián personal. Deje que Azzara también vuelva a lo suyo.

Pike vio lo que quería Straw, y no le gustó ni pizca.

—Si Azzara vuelve a lo suyo eso significa que volverá a presionar a Smith y que Mendoza y Gomer serán libres de atacarle otra vez.

—Necesito a los hombres de poca monta para poder ir a por los grandes. Por ello, tengo que dejar que los pequeños salgan por ahí y cometan delitos para poder apretarles. Si lo hago bien, puedo usarlos como informantes.

Button asintió, todavía frunciendo el ceño hacia Pike.

—Smith no es el único tío al que están intentando exprimir estos cerdos, Pike. No está solo. Straw y su gente vigilan cinco o seis tiendas…

Pike se inclinó hacia Straw.

—Usted estaba vigilando este lugar y dejó que le causaran una conmoción cerebral. También permitió que tiraran un ladrillo al escaparate.

Straw dirigió a Button una mirada tan dura que podía haberle golpeado y sacado del coche.

—Nosotros no «dejamos» que ocurriera nada. Simplemente sucedió, pero ahora lo cubriremos todo mejor.

—No dejaré a esa gente colgada.

—No será así. Yo los cubriré.

—Dice que los tenía cubiertos cuando la conmoción cerebral.

—Pues lo haremos mejor.

Straw abrió su portezuela de pronto.

—Pike, salga un momento. Discúlpenos, detective.

Pike salió, dejando solo a Button. Straw dio la vuelta al coche y se reunió con Pike en la acera. Tenía los labios muy tensos, pero encendió otro cigarrillo y al hacerlo pareció relajarse. Abanicó el humo.

—La hemos cagado, ¿de acuerdo? Todavía no sabemos cómo hacen las cosas esos tipos, pero estamos aprendiendo. Apártese, eso es lo único que le pido.

Pike examinó al hombre. Straw tenía los ojos serios, pero también parecía nervioso. Como si hubiera apostado muy fuerte por algo y pudiera perderlo todo.

—Si se lo digo a Wilson y Dru, está perdido —le dijo.

—No lo hará.

—No tiene ni idea de lo que voy a hacer.

—Quizá. Pero he averiguado unas cuantas cosas. Trabajó usted para empresas de seguridad privada de primera fila. Incluso hizo algún trabajito para el Gobierno, de vez en cuando, aunque se supone que nadie lo sabe. Las personas que no saben cerrar el pico no tienen esas credenciales.

Straw miró a Pike frunciendo el ceño. Su sonrisa había desaparecido.

—Es sorprendente lo que puede averiguar un tipo como yo, ¿verdad? —Pike no respondió, de modo que Straw se volvió a encoger de hombros—. Escuche, ¿quiere que esa gente esté a salvo? Yo también, hermano, y le garantizo que a mi manera es mejor. Wilson Smith pudo acabar con esos tipos ya cuando estaba en urgencias, pero no lo hizo. Tiene miedo. Solo es un pobre hombre que quiere hacer bocadillos. Si me deja que consiga lo que quiero de Azzara, podré ayudarle de verdad.

A Pike no le gustaba nada de todo aquello, ni le gustaba Straw, ni el Malibu que apestaba a tabaco.

—¿Cuánto tiempo?

—Dos o tres semanas. Quizá menos.

Observó ambos lados de la calle, preguntándose si el hombre de la camisa naranja les estaría vigilando.

77

—Piénselo. Mientras tanto, no les diga nada ni a Smith ni a su sobrina. Tienen que actuar con naturalidad. Si les dice que les están vigilando, ya sabe lo que ocurrirá. Podría irme directamente a Texas —añadió Straw.

—El hombre de la camisa naranja es bueno —comentó Pike.

Straw lo miró de soslayo, entre el humo.

—¿Qué hombre de la camisa naranja? —Volvió a su coche—. Venga. Le llevaré al sitio de donde venimos.

—No hace falta.

Pike se fue andando.

9

Aquella misma noche, justo después de las diez, el aire era frío mientras Pike iba corriendo a su casa a través de Santa Monica, llevando una mochila de dieciocho kilos de peso. Pike era corredor. Hacía carreras desde niño, todos los días. A veces incluso dos veces al día, una por la mañana y otra por la noche, y tres o cuatro veces por semana llevaba una mochila cargada con cuatro sacos de harina de cuatro kilos y medio cada uno. Ni remotamente llegaba a los cuarenta kilos de peso que cargaba cuando era joven marine de las Fuerzas de Reconocimiento, pero le daba marcha al corazón.

Aquella noche subió los escalones de Fourth Street: ciento ochenta y nueve peldaños de cemento que subían por el abrupto acantilado desde el fondo de Santa Monica Canyon hasta San Vicente Boulevard. Ciento ochenta y nueve escalones era la altura de un edificio de nueve pisos, y Pike los recorrió veinte veces, subiéndolos de dos en dos. Prefería correr por la noche.

Durante el día, aquella escalera estaba repleta de fanáticos del *fitness* duro, así como de maratonianos, instructores de aerobic y gente corriente un tanto patosa que quería ponerse en forma. Pero por la noche, en la oscuridad, cuando era más peligroso, la escalera estaba desierta y Pike podía correr a tope. Le gustaba estar a solas con su esfuerzo y sus pensamientos.

Después, tras acabar con la escalera y volviendo a casa a la carrera, Pike eligió una ruta que pasaba por el local de Wilson. Era temprano todavía, y la gente estaba fuera de casa, pero la tiendecita estaba desierta. Pike se preguntó si el hombre de la camisa naranja estaría observando, pero la verdad era que no le importaba. Había decidido no contarles a Wilson y Dru que el FBI estaba vigilando su tienda, pero su silencio era lo máximo que pensaba conceder. Si Mikie hacía honor a su palabra, el tema estaba cerrado. Si no era así, la lealtad de Pike estaba con las víctimas, no con el caso que Straw pudiese o no montar. No pensaba apartarse. Sus flechas señalaban siempre hacia delante, nunca hacia atrás.

Cuando llegó a casa hizo unos estiramientos en el aparcamiento para irse enfriando y luego se quitó la sudadera, desactivó las alarmas y entró. Su piso era austero y funcional, con pocos elementos decorativos. El comedor estaba aparte, con la cocina; había un sofá, sillas y una mesa en el salón, y un televisor de pantalla plana para ver los deportes y las noticias. Una fuente de piedra negra de meditación burbujeaba en un rincón. Pike encontraba paz en su sonido natural, como si estuviera solo en el bosque.

Se quedó un momento de pie escuchando, no el agua, sino más allá… comprobando con toda seguridad que estaba solo. Lo hacía cada vez que llegaba a casa. La costumbre.

Se bebió medio litro de agua mineral y dejó la botella junto a otras que esperaban para ser recicladas. El piso estaba quieto y vacío, pero unas veces parecía más vacío que otras. Pensó en Dru Rayne y en la niña de la foto, y en por qué Dru había sentido la necesidad de enseñársela. Le gustó que le mostrase la foto; le parecía que eso hablaba bien de ella, y sugería que pensaba en él para algo más que una cerveza en la playa.

Cenó un poco de polenta, judías negras y brócoli con trocitos de pimiento picante que había sobrado. Comió de pie en la cocina.

No había tenido ninguna relación seria desde hacía mucho tiempo. Citas sí, y sexo también, y disfrutaba de una amistad íntima con varias mujeres, pero nada que se pudiera llamar una relación romántica. Quizá por el mismo motivo no tenía animales de compañía; a menudo desaparecía largos periodos de tiempo, y se iba sin avisar.

Pike se acabó la cena, bebió un poco más de agua y se quitó la ropa que aún llevaba. Echó una alfombrilla de espuma en el salón y procedió a hacer una serie de *asanas* de yoga. Después de una vida entera entrenándose en ejercicios de fuerza y artes marciales, podía apoyar el pecho en los muslos y la cara en las rodillas; y era capaz de estirar las piernas con una separación de ciento ochenta grados, y hacerse uno con el suelo.

Iba trabajando despacio, permitiendo que su cuerpo se fundiera con cada postura. Los únicos sonidos de su vida eran el agua borboteante, su corazón y el roce de su piel en la toalla. Al cabo de un rato adoptó la postura de resolución y meditó. Su cuerpo se calmó, su respiración se hizo más lenta y lo único que atendió entonces fue el sonido singular de su corazón. Cuarenta y dos latidos por minuto, muy lentos, como un trueno vivo en su pecho.

Meditó durante quince minutos exactos. No comprobó el reloj, pero llevaba casi toda la vida meditando: cuando pasaban quince minutos su conciencia volvía flotando a la superficie, y estaba de vuelta.

Inhalar. Exhalar.

A las once y cuarto de aquella noche subió sus cosas al dormitorio. La casa estaba ordenada y pulcra. Tenía el equipo limpio y preparado. Se duchó, se secó y se puso unos calzoncillos blancos. Bajó a buscar otra botella de agua y observó su teléfono móvil en el mostrador de la cocina: la pantalla mostraba una llamada perdida. Era el número de Dru. Había llamado mientras él estaba en la ducha, pero no había dejado mensaje.

La telefoneó y salió el buzón de voz: «Hola, soy Dru. Ya sabes qué hacer, así que hazlo». Sonó el pitido de los mensajes.

—Soy Joe.

Todavía estaba pensando qué más decir cuando la llamada se cortó. Volvió a marcar y esta vez acabó el mensaje.

—Llámame cuando quieras. No importa si es tarde.

Se llevó el teléfono arriba, apagó las luces y se metió en la cama. El colchón era duro. Las sábanas estaban tan lisas y tensas como la piel de un tambor. Escuchó el sonido del agua, que borboteaba suavemente en el piso de abajo, en su casa vacía. Se preguntó cómo sería tener los sonidos de otra persona allí.

Pike esperaba que ella le devolviera la llamada, pero el teléfono siguió silencioso.

81

SEGUNDA PARTE

Princesa de los ángeles

10

*H*ydeck llamó a las 10.08, identificándose como si no se hubieran conocido.

—Soy la oficial Hydeck, del departamento de Policía de Los Ángeles. Siento molestarle, pero ¿sabe usted cómo localizar a la señorita Rayne?

La falta de expresión profesional de su voz le dijo a Pike que algo iba mal.

—¿Por qué?

Hydeck dudó tanto rato que Pike oyó las llamadas por radio, de fondo.

—Alguien ha entrado en su tienda otra vez. Tengo un teléfono del señor Smith, pero no responde. He pensado que a lo mejor usted tenía el número de su sobrina.

Pike se preguntó por qué pensaba que él podía tener el número de Dru, pero descartó esa idea rápidamente. Estaba recordando a Miguel Azzara en la cafetería. Sonriendo. «Está hecho.»

—¿Está allí ahora?

—Sí, Pike; estoy aquí ahora mismo, intentando que vengan ellos también. Este lugar está hecho un desastre. ¿Tiene el número o no?

—Sí, espere.

Le dio el número de móvil de Dru, colgó y lo marcó de inmediato él mismo. Como la noche anterior, su llamada fue al buzón de voz. Dejó otro mensaje y decidió ver los daños por sí mismo. Casi con toda seguridad fue Gomer el que rompió el escaparate la primera noche, pero probablemente Mendoza quiso vengarse por su cuenta en cuanto lo soltaron. Después de verlo, Pike esperaba poder hacer que Azzara obligase a Gomer y a Mendoza a limpiarlo.

Cuando llegó esperaba encontrar roto el nuevo escaparate; no obstante, la tienda de Wilson parecía en perfecto estado. El escaparate nuevo estaba brillante e intacto, y la señal de CERRADO todavía se encontraba en la puerta. Un coche patrulla de la policía estaba aparcado delante, pero Pike no vio a Hydeck y McIntosh, de modo que dio la vuelta a la esquina, hasta el callejón de servicio. Los encontró apiñados en la puerta trasera, junto con Betsy Harmon y su hijo Ethan. Los cuatro se volvieron al verlo, y Hydeck fue a recibirle.

—¿Los han encontrado? —preguntó Pike, refiriéndose a Wilson y Dru.

—Hemos dejado más mensajes. Esa pobre gente se llevará un buen sofocón cuando vea cómo está esto. Esos cabrones realmente lo han hecho bien. —McIntosh intentó hacer una broma—. Pero la buena noticia es que podemos añadir a las acusaciones allanamiento de morada y eliminación ilegal de partes de animales.

—Deberías ver lo que han hecho. Es asqueroso —apuntó Betsy Harmon.

Ese día llevaba un vestido de un amarillo limón. Se quedó de pie, con los brazos cruzados, tensa y rígida.

Pike vio que la puerta de seguridad de metal estaba doblada por la parte de la cerradura, donde habían metido la palanca. La jamba de encima presentaba una muesca donde se había torcido el marco. Tuvo que ser un hombre fuerte o haber más de un hombre trabajando duro para poder doblar así el metal.

—La señora Harmon ha llamado al ver la puerta.

—No, he llamado cuando he visto lo de dentro. Qué degenerados. ¿Qué tipo de personas pueden hacer eso?

McIntosh abrió mucho los ojos mirando a Pike.

—Es muy desagradable, tío. Compruébalo tú mismo.

Pike pasó junto a los policías y abrió la puerta.

El olor húmedo de la sangre y la carne cruda le envolvió. Se desplazó por la despensa, pero se detuvo junto al mostrador en cuanto entró en el comedor. Un montón de moscas verdes habían acudido atraídas por el hedor, y zumbaban pasando lentamente por encima de su cabeza. El mostrador estaba rojo, con un charco viscoso de sangre seca que marcaba huellas de un carmesí oscuro hasta el suelo. Largos y gruesos trozos de lo que probablemente era hígado de buey, riñones e intestinos flotaban en la sangre como islas azules. Más piezas envolvían la caja registradora y la zona de preparación, y lo que parecía ser un enorme corazón de buey estaba clavado al cartel de Nueva Orleans. De las luces del techo colgaban tres cabezas de cabra despellejadas, con los ojos sin párpados, turbios y abultados. Había moscas verdes alimentándose de esos ojos.

Detrás de él, McIntosh susurró:

—¿Y si estos restos fueran de personas?

—No, no lo son.

—Ya sé que son cabezas de animales, pero la sangre podría ser humana. Los órganos podrían ser de personas.

—No lo son. La gente descuartizada huele distinto.

McIntosh observó a Pike y pareció preguntarse cómo podría saber aquello, y luego señaló a la pared, detrás del mostrador.

—Mire esto. Sus chicos han dejado un mensaje.

Dos palabras escritas con sangre en la pared, encima del mostrador de preparación: ESTOY AQUÍ.

«Estoy», no «estamos». En singular. Pike se preguntó qué significaría.

Hydeck entró junto a ellos.

—Vamos, tenemos que irnos. Ya tengo algunas fotos para el informe. Lo único que estamos consiguiendo es que entren más moscas.

—¿Ha llamado a Button? —preguntó Pike.

La irritación de Hydeck se convirtió en enfado.

—Sí, Pike; le he llamado. Estoy esperando que me diga algo. Ahora mismo estoy más interesada en que vengan los propietarios para que limpien y arreglen este sitio.

Pike pasó alrededor de las cabezas de cabra hacia la puerta delantera. Examinó la gasolinera y los edificios de enfrente y se preguntó si la gente de Straw habría visto algo, y si se habrían quedado allí parados viendo cómo pasaba todo.

—Vamos, Pike. En serio. No debería estar aquí —dijo Hydeck.

Pike salió con ellos. Betsy Harmon todavía tenía los brazos cruzados.

—¿Vendrá el CSI por aquí?

—Eso es en la tele. Los nuestros se llaman SID —contestó McIntosh.

Hydeck cerró la puerta. Con el marco doblado resultaba difícil, de modo que McIntosh se apoyó para ayudarle. Aun así, no se cerraba del todo.

—Esos trozos de carne, señora Harmon. La gente que hizo esto probablemente robó un mercado latino, donde venden carne de cabra. ¿A qué hora suele venir por aquí el señor Smith?

—Wilson llega siempre a las nueve, todos los días excepto el domingo. Si espera al proveedor viene más temprano, pero uno de ellos ya debería estar aquí. Siempre están a esta hora.

Pike miró el reloj y vio que eran casi las diez y media. Hydeck hizo lo propio, y frunció el ceño con impaciencia.

—Quizá no vengan hoy, como él está conmocionado... De todos modos debería estar en la cama.

Betsy Harmon se puso más tensa aún.

—En la cama no significa tener el teléfono desconectado. Alguien tiene que limpiar toda esta porquería.

—Ya le hemos enviado mensajes. No podemos hacer nada más.

—¿Y si no los miran? Esta porquería se va a pudrir y mis clientes lo olerán. Se ve desde la calle.

El teléfono móvil de Hydeck se puso a zumbar en ese momento. La agente miró el número entrante y se apartó para atender la llamada.

—¿Son ellos? —preguntó Pike.

—Es Button. A ver qué quiere.

Mientras Hydeck se alejaba, Betsy Harmon se volvió hacia Pike.

—No pueden dejar todo esto así, sin más, ¿verdad? ¿No deberían hacer algo?

Pike no sabía qué decir. No le gustaba nada que Dru y su tío no respondieran el teléfono. La sangre, las cabezas y el mensaje en la pared parecían algo más que un simple acto de vandalismo. Había una oscuridad en lo que se había hecho allí, como cuando aparece una sombra de repente en mar abierto.

Hydeck miraba hacia ellos mientras hablaba con Button, y Pike vio que algo iba mal por la postura que había adoptado. Su agitación fue creciendo a medida que avanzaba la conversación. Dejó el teléfono y volvió.

—El señor Smith y la señorita Rayne no vendrán hoy. Se van a Oregón.

Betsy Harmon retrocedió como si le hubiesen dado una patada.

—¿A Oregón? ¿Quién dice que se van a Oregón?

—El señor Smith. Al parecer ha venido antes y ha decidido que ya tenía bastante. Ha llamado al detective Button esta mañana.

—¿Y lo va a dejar todo así?

—No lo sé.·

—Pero ¿quién va a limpiar toda esta porquería?

—Lo siento, pero no sé nada más. Estoy segura de que se harán cargo de todo esto antes de irse.

Pike, sorprendido, se preguntó por qué no le habría llamado Dru.

—¿Han sido amenazados?

—Pike, mire en el interior y abra los ojos. Yo diría que eso es una amenaza. El tipo está asustado, y quiere salir de la ciudad hasta que esos idiotas se olviden. Dice que no piensa cooperar con ninguna investigación más. No sé nada más y, francamente, si a él le importa un pito, a mí también. —Miró a McIntosh—. Hemos acabado aquí. Vámonos.

—¿Va a venir Button? —inquirió Pike.

—Ya podemos esperar sentados. Estaba bastante cabreado.

La cara de Betsy Harmon estaba tensa por la ansiedad.

—Pero Wilson no responde al teléfono. ¿Y si lo deja todo tal como está?

—Si hay riesgo para la salud, el señor Smith será citado. Si no se hace cargo, le sugiero que llame al propietario o a la agencia inmobiliaria.

—¿Y ya está? ¿No van a hacer nada más?

—Es lo único que podemos hacer. Lo siento.

Pike vio cómo Hydeck y McIntosh volvían a su coche

89

patrulla, y luego sacó el teléfono y probó a llamar otra vez a Dru. Salió el buzón de voz, pero aquella vez no dejó ningún mensaje.

Junto a él, Betsy Harmon dijo:

—No me creo que se vayan así. Simplemente no me lo creo.

Pike tampoco se lo creía. Pensaba que cualquiera que pusiera cabezas de cabra y sangre en la tienda de un hombre quizá no se contentara con el vandalismo. Se guardó el móvil.

—¿Sabe dónde viven?

Betsy Harmon se animó por primera vez aquella mañana.

—Sí, claro. Están a unas pocas manzanas de aquí.

Alguna vez había ayudado a Wilson y Dru a llevarse a casa alimentos perecederos cuando se les estropeaba la nevera de la tienda. No recordaba la dirección exacta de la calle, pero le dio indicaciones a Pike y le describió la casa, en los canales de Venice. También le dio el número de móvil que tenía de Wilson Smith.

Cuando Pike volvió a su Jeep, Betsy Harmon lo llamó.

—Les vi.

Pike volvió la vista y la vio sonreír.

—A usted y Dru. Les vi besarse ayer. Ella parecía muy contenta.

Pike asintió una sola vez, un gesto tan nimio que ella quizá ni lo vio siquiera, y luego se subió al Jeep. Dru tendría que haberle llamado. No comprendía por qué no lo había hecho.

11

*L*os canales de Venice fueron el sueño de un hombre llamado Abbot Kinney, un millonario de la industria del tabaco procedente del este que urbanizó aquella zona como lugar de
vacaciones junto a la playa. En un principio los canales se exca-
varon para drenar una tierra pantanosa, pero Kinney pensó
que una Venecia podía ser igual de buena que otra y decidió
recrear la Venecia de Italia, con góndolas y todo. Se crearon
veinticinco kilómetros de canales, pero a lo largo del tiempo
muchos fueron rellenados o acortados. Los seis que quedaban
formaban un cuadrado perfecto, con cuatro canales corriendo
uno junto al otro y el quinto y el sexto situados en cada extremo, cortando la tierra en tres islas rectangulares idénticas. Lo
que empezó como un parque de entretenimiento se convirtió
en casitas para escapadas de fin de semana, y luego, en los años
cincuenta y sesenta, en decadentes bungalós ocupados por *hip-
pies*, gente de la playa y artistas. Pero la proximidad con la
playa y el valor creciente de las propiedades inmobiliarias
acabó por revalorizar la zona, y los destartalados bungalós fueron reemplazados por casas caras.

Pike siguió las indicaciones de Betsy Harmon hasta llegar
a la cuadrícula de angostos callejones que comunicaban los
canales. Cruzó un puente arqueado mucho más estrecho aún,
luego dio la vuelta por un callejón con casas apiñadas. Según
Betsy Harmon, Wilson y Dru vivían en la tercera casa desde
el extremo por el lado izquierdo, una casa de secuoya escondida tras una verja cubierta de hiedra. La encontró fácilmente y aparcó.

Los terrenos que se encontraban a lo largo de los canales eran pequeños, de modo que las casas tenían dos o tres pisos, y estaban construidas unas junto a las otras dando a la calle, con los patios delanteros frente a los canales y los garajes alineados en los callejones. Se había dispuesto una plaza de garaje al lado de la casa de Wilson, junto a una puerta de madera, pero la entrada estaba oculta por la verja. El garaje estaba vacío. Pike se sorprendió al ver la casa. Era de las caras.

Se dirigió hacia la puerta, pero la encontró cerrada. Llamó al timbre: sonaron unas campanas dentro de la casa, pero nadie respondió. Al apretarlo notó que un joven delgado, con el pelo negro y desgreñado, le contemplaba desde una ventana del segundo piso, en la casa de al lado. El observador se apartó cuando Pike lo vio.

Como seguía sin obtener respuesta, Pike se dirigió al garaje y dio unos golpes en la pared. Si Wilson y Dru se iban, uno de ellos quizás estuviese dentro haciendo las maletas mientras el otro compraba algunos artículos necesarios de última hora. De ahí que no estuviese el coche.

Tocó en la pared tres veces, no obtuvo respuesta y ya iba a golpear de nuevo cuando apareció una mujer en la puerta de la casa de al lado y lo llamó.

—¡Perdone!

Tenía cuarenta y tantos años, la piel curtida, llevaba unos vaqueros muy ceñidos y una camiseta también apretada que le marcaba mucho los pechos. Eran grandes, y ella quería que se viesen.

—¿Quiere echar abajo la casa? Le he oído llamar.

—¿Vive aquí Wilson Smith?

—Pues no, la verdad. Está cuidando la casa. El propietario está en Londres. Va mucho por allí. —La mujer frotó el pulgar y el índice entre sí—. Ha hecho mucho dinero con la tele.

Esto explicaba por qué podían vivir en aquella casa tan cara. Estaban guardándola.

—¿Pero viven aquí Wilson y Dru ahora?

—Así es. ¿Qué pasa?

—Ha habido algunos daños en su negocio. Tengo que hablar con ellos.

La mujer salió al callejón hasta que vio el garaje vacío.

—Bueno, el coche no está aquí, así que no sé qué decirle. Se lo contaré, si les veo.

El chico delgado salió a la puerta. De cerca parecía un adolescente. Se estaba comiendo un plátano y guiñaba los ojos como si le diera el sol. Pike comprendió que eran madre e hijo.

—¿Qué pasa?

—Está buscando a los Wilson.

Volvió a entrar en la casa.

—Me voy a echar un rato.

—¿Y qué tal si buscaras trabajo? —Mostró su disgusto con gestos teatrales mientras su hijo se iba arrastrando los pies—. Tres años en Berkeley y lo único que hace es echarse... Es culpa mía, supongo. No tenía a ningún hombre que le diera ejemplo.

Sus ojos se posaron en Pike demasiado rato; luego suspiró, como si se diera cuenta de que la idea que tenía tampoco era buena.

—Cosas de las madres solteras... —Le tendió la mano—. Me llamo Lily Palmer. ¿Y usted?

—Pike.

—Bueno, Pike, ¿quiere que les dé algún mensaje cuando les vea?

—Dígales que me llamen. Ya tienen el número.

Pike volvió a su Jeep, pero no puso en marcha el motor. Dru y Wilson quizá se irían, pero Pike tenía la sensación de que todavía no les había dado tiempo. Tendrían que arreglar algunas cosas, hacer el equipaje y todo lo que hace la gente cuando se prepara para salir de viaje. Se dijo que seguramente estarían haciendo todas esas cosas y por ese motivo no estaban en casa, de modo que decidió esperar.

Unos minutos más tarde volvió a llamar a Dru, y luego al número que le dio Betsy Harmon para Wilson. Ambas llamadas saltaron de inmediato a los buzones de voz, igual que tantas veces antes, lo que quería decir que sus teléfonos estaban apagados o los estaban usando. A Pike no le gustó nada todo aquello. Las probabilidades de que ambos estuviesen hablando por teléfono a la vez eran muy escasas, y nadie apaga el teléfono cuando se dispone a hacer un viaje.

Se bajó del Jeep y volvió a la puerta. Se aseguró de que el

hijo de Lily no miraba y saltó por encima de la cancela, introduciéndose en un patio pequeño. La puerta delantera estaba cerrada, y no mostraba señal alguna de que la entrada se hubiese forzado.

Pike se dirigió hacia la parte lateral de la casa, mirando cada ventana mientras iba pasando y buscando señales de manipulación. La primera estancia parecía un dormitorio para invitados, y la siguiente era la cocina. El dormitorio parecía intacto, pero la visión de Pike era limitada. Vio platos sucios, tres botellas de cerveza vacías y una tabla de cortar encima del mostrador de la cocina. Se dijo que los platos indicaban que Wilson y Dru pensaban volver a casa, pero las cabezas de cabra y las moscas le incordiaban sin parar, como el humo de la batalla.

Después de comprobar la última ventana del extremo más alejado de la casa, siguió hacia al patio trasero. Era pequeño, con una verja de madera baja que bordeaba la acera que corría a lo largo del canal. Una puerta con cerrojo conducía a la acera, y un kayak de fibra de vidrio azul estaba colgado en un pequeño muelle de madera, al otro lado de la cancela. Pike examinó las casas a ambos lados de la orilla. A pesar de las verjas y puertas, entrar en aquellas fincas desde el agua habría sido muy fácil.

Comprobó su reloj. Habían pasado cuarenta y cinco minutos desde que decidió esperar, pero ahora el tiempo que pasaba no parecía destinado a la espera. Más bien parecía que estaba dejando que se le escapase algo precioso.

Pike intentaba decidir qué hacer cuando vio al hijo de Lily Palmer. El chico había vuelto a su ventana del segundo piso, que le ofrecía la vista del patio trasero de los Wilson. Aquella vez no se ocultó. Sonrió con complicidad antes de volverse, y Pike se preguntó cuánto tiempo pasaría en la ventana.

Volvió a dirigirse hacia delante por un lado de la casa, salió y llamó a la puerta de Lily. Los ojos de ella se iluminaron al verle, y le dedicó una sonrisa complacida.

—Ah. Hola. Pensaba que se había ido.

—No. He estado mirando la casa de al lado. No le he contado toda la verdad. Wilson ha tenido problemas con mala gente. Me preocupaba que le hubiesen seguido a casa. ¿Ha visto u oído algo sospechoso?

La agradable sonrisa de ella se convirtió en una mueca de preocupación.

—No, creo que no. ¿Algo como qué?

—Voces, gritos. Coches desconocidos.

Ella frunció más aún el ceño, y luego gritó hacia la casa:

—¡Jared! ¡Jared, ven aquí!

El joven apareció unos segundos más tarde, sin camisa y todo embadurnado de crema solar. Su pecho delgado parecía el de un pajarito.

—Iba a salir.

—Este caballero quiere saber si has visto u oído algo sospechoso ahí.

—¿En la casa de al lado?

—Sí, en la de los vecinos. ¿Qué te pasa?

Jared se frotó sus costillas de parajito y asintió, mirando a Pike.

—Este estaba en el patio de atrás ahora mismo. Eso es bastante sospechoso.

—Ya sé que estaba en el patio de atrás. Me lo acaba de decir. Por favor, ¿quieres responder a este señor?

Jared se apartó el pelo de la cara e hizo el mismo gesto de desdén que había hecho en la ventana.

—Estaba mirando por la ventana. Probablemente intentaba verle las tetas a Dru.

Pike dio un paso hacia él, y Jared cruzó los brazos rápidamente.

—Tío, que era broma…

—Por favor, ¿quieres portarte como si fueras un hombre? Wilson y Dru tienen problemas. Intenta ayudar —dijo la madre.

—No he visto nada sospechoso. Lo siento. No he visto nada.

Pike echó una mirada hacia la ventana de Jared.

—Tienes buena vista desde tu ventana, pero ¿no miras a ninguna parte desde ella?

Jared se sonrojó.

—¿Qué quiere que mire, las paredes? Tío, en los canales de Venice todos los días son iguales… sol, agua.

—¿Cuándo los viste por última vez?

95

—¿A Wilson o a Dru?

—A cualquiera de los dos.

—Pues anoche, supongo. Me imagino que sería Dru. Entró cuando yo volvía de dar un paseo y la saludé. Ya sabe: le dije «eh, qué tal» y ella lo mismo.

Pike se acercó más y Jared se puso más tenso.

—¿A qué hora?

—A las seis, más o menos.

A Pike le pareció que cuadraba. Ella regresó directamente a casa después de dejarlo a él en la tienda.

—¿Y esta mañana?

—Esta mañana no he visto a ninguno de los dos. —Jared hizo una seña hacia el garaje—. Pero sí he visto el coche. He salido a pillar un batido de chocolate y lo he visto.

—¿Cuándo?

—Pues no sé, tío; temprano.

Su madre le ayudó a responder.

—Estaba empezando la segunda hora del programa *Today* cuando se ha ido, así que supongo que era más tarde de las ocho. Ha vuelto durante la segunda media hora, así que serían las nueve menos cuarto.

Pike intentaba ajustar el margen.

—¿Estaba allí el coche cuando has vuelto?

—Sí. Seguro.

—¿Y lo has visto salir?

—No. Lo he visto cuando he vuelto con el batido, pero no podría asegurar cuándo ha salido.

—¿Cuántos coches tienen?

—Uno.

—Solo tienen un coche —confirmó Lily.

—El Tercel plateado.

—Exacto.

Jared veía todos los días el Tercel plateado. Lo que una persona ve todos los días se convierte en invisible, pero lo que no es habitual sobresale. Había hecho esas mismas preguntas u otras muy similares mil veces, cuando era policía.

—Olvida el Tercel. Cuando has vuelto a casa con el batido, ¿has visto a alguien a quien no reconocieras? ¿Quizás un coche que no te resultase familiar?

Jared negó con la cabeza.

—No he visto a nadie así. Sí había un par de señoras con sus perros andando por ahí, y unos jardineros trabajando en la casa de los vecinos.

Pike dudó.

—¿En la de Wilson?

—Sí. Un par de tíos latinos.

Casi todas las casas de los canales empleaban a jardineros profesionales, y seguro que la mayoría eran latinos.

—¿Sabes que eran jardineros porque los habías visto antes, o supones que eran jardineros porque eran latinos?

Jared se puso muy rojo, como si le hubiesen acusado de ser racista.

—¡Tío! Han aparecido esos tipos, con ropa de trabajo; no iban vestidos precisamente para salir, han entrado por la puerta del jardín… ¿Quién iba a ser si no?

—¿Llevaban sopladores de hojas, cariño? ¿Una segadora? —preguntó Lily Palmer.

—Tampoco me he fijado tanto. No les he prestado atención.

Pike se tocó un lado del cuello.

—¿Tatus?

Jared apretó los labios como si rebuscara en su memoria, y luego de repente se animó.

—Sí, creo que sí; uno de los tíos sí; de eso me acuerdo, pero lo llevaba en el brazo.

Pike se quedó muy quieto, solamente se oía el suave susurro de su aliento y el lento y pesado latido de su corazón.

—¿Qué brazo?

Jared se tocó el antebrazo derecho.

—Este. Era uno de esos tatuajes que llegan hasta la muñeca desde el pulgar.

Mendoza llevaba exactamente ese mismo tatuaje cuando lo soltaron en el Tribunal del Aeropuerto.

—¿Y el coche todavía seguía ahí, cuando les has visto?

—Sí. Ahí estaba.

—Y después había desaparecido.

—Sí. Desaparecido.

Pike se volvió hacia la casa de Smith. Su corazón, con su

97

lento latir, se aceleró, hasta que empezó a golpearle en el pecho como los truenos en el horizonte. Había visto el exterior de la casa, pero muy poco del interior. Una pesadilla peor que las cabezas de cabra podía estar esperándole dentro.

Lily Palmer le tocó el bazo.

—¿Son las personas de las que hablaba?

Pike asintió, mirando todavía hacia la casa.

—¿Deberíamos llamar a la policía? —preguntó la mujer.

Él negó con la cabeza.

—Yo me encargaré. —Y dijo algo a Lily para ayudarla a calmar sus preocupaciones—: Cuando vea a Wilson o a Dru pídales que me llamen. Ya tienen mi número.

—Por supuesto. En cuanto los vea.

Pike volvió a su Jeep y retrocedió por la estrecha callecita. Dio la vuelta a la esquina, e inmediatamente frenó y aparcó.

Retrocedió al trote, echó un vistazo de nuevo a ver si alguien miraba y pasó por encima de una verja en un lado de la casa de los Wilson, lejos de los Palmer. Habiendo visto la propiedad ya una vez, sabía adónde quería ir y llevaba las cosas que necesitaba para entrar.

En aquel lado de la casa encontró una ventana que se usaba como ventilación para un lavadero. Se puso unos guantes de látex y se dispuso a trabajar. No había intentado forzarla antes, pero entonces hizo palanca con una barra pequeña y se introdujo por la abertura.

Una vez en el interior Pike se puso un par de fundas de papel encima de las zapatillas deportivas y se desplazó con rapidez por toda la casa. Su única misión era buscar cuerpos. No se entretuvo con nada más, porque no había nada tan importante.

Se deslizó por el lavadero hasta un vestíbulo, luego pasó junto a la cocina, el salón y un dormitorio pequeño con un baño adjunto. No tocó ni examinó nada, aunque miró todos los suelos rápidamente en busca de sangre. No encontró gotas ni salpicaduras obvias, ni señales de lucha violenta, y tampoco cuerpos.

Subió las escaleras de tres en tres hasta el segundo piso, y pasó por un despacho grande, un enorme dormitorio principal y el baño principal con tanta suavidad como si fuera líquido.

Recorrió toda la casa en menos de sesenta segundos, y no dejó de moverse ni un momento hasta que comprobó que no había ningún cadáver. Wilson y Dru no habían muerto allí. Sus cuerpos no le esperaban allí dentro.

Pike salió del dormitorio principal e hizo una pausa por primera vez en el rellano del segundo piso. Solo entonces, por primera vez, el mundo exterior lentamente penetró en él. Notó que se tambaleaba, solo un poco, como si hubiese habido un pequeño temblor de tierra. Un helicóptero pasó cerca. Captó olor a lilas, y supo que era el aroma de Dru.

Abandonó la casa por donde había entrado y se desplazó rápidamente de vuelta a su Jeep. Veía a Reuben Mendoza y las cabezas en la tienda de Wilson Smith. Veía a dos hombres abriendo la cancela de Wilson, uno con el brazo enyesado. Veía a Miguel Azzara con su sonrisa resplandeciente de modelo, diciendo que aquello no volvería a ocurrir nunca.

Hola, Reuben.

Hola, Miguel.

«Estoy aquí.»

99

*P*ike pasó junto al taller Our Way Body Mods, giró en la manzana siguiente y luego rodeó la manzana y aparcó en una zona de carga, al otro lado de la calle. Su situación en la esquina de una calle ajetreada hacía fácil el reconocimiento.

Quería a Gomer o Mendoza, pero no estaban por allí, ni tampoco Michael Azzara con su resplandeciente Prius nuevo. No obstante, el Monte Carlo color granate se encontraba aparcado junto a la acera, en el exterior de la verja.

Examinó a las personas que había por allí y su situación, la posición de los vehículos en el aparcamiento y todo lo que rodeaba el edificio. Algo en la tienda le preocupaba.

Pike contó un hombre en la zona de reparaciones y dos en el aparcamiento, junto a un SS396 dorado de 1969. El hombre del taller estaba colocando un guardabarros a un coche, pero se le daba mal. Ninguno de aquellos tipos le resultaba familiar, pero los que se encontraban junto al 396 llamaron la atención de Pike. Uno era bastante joven y llevaba ropa de trabajo manchada de grasa, y le enseñaba al otro algo bajo el capó. Este último llevaba botas de vaquero de piel de lagarto, un sombrero de *cowboy* Stetson blanco inmaculado y una camisa de vaquero rosa y blanca con una chaqueta deportiva de ante encima. Un cinturón con una enorme hebilla de latón sujetaba unos pantalones tejanos con raya bien planchada. Unos minutos después, el vaquero ya había visto lo que tenía que ver. Se dirigió hacia la zona de reparaciones y dijo algo al hombre del parachoques. Entonces apareció un tipo al que Pike reconoció del Monte Carlo: era el que le había señalado con la mano en forma de pistola, el que había levantado a Mendoza del suelo para darle la bienvenida a casa. Los dos hombres se estrecharon la mano y entonces el vaquero salió por la puerta principal hacia un Buick anónimo y se alejó.

Cuando lo vio irse, Pike comprendió lo que le incomodaba. El día anterior había una docena de hombres trabajando, y el taller estaba muy ajetreado. Aquel día en cambio solo quedaban tres tíos, y el taller de chapa estaba desierto. Todo aquello le pareció muy curioso, pero también haría su trabajo más fácil.

Dio de nuevo la vuelta a la manzana, y en aquella ocasión aparcó en una calle residencial detrás del taller. Se quitó la sudadera y se abrochó un chaleco antibalas ligero. Apretó bien las tiras de velcro, se volvió a poner la sudadera encima y se colocó correctamente la pistolera. Cuando estuvo ya preparado, salió del Jeep y se acercó al taller desde detrás.

El hombre del Monte Carlo había desaparecido, pero Pike vio al tipo del jardín ayudando a su compañero con el parachoques en el puesto más alejado. No se ocupó de ellos: quería al amigo de Mendoza.

Se detuvo en el primer puesto y vio al hombre del Monte Carlo en un despacho en la parte de atrás del edificio. Estaba ante un televisor, de espaldas a la puerta. Los Dodgers jugaban aquel día. Pike comprobó que los otros dos hombres seguían ocupados con el parachoques, y luego se dirigió hacia el despacho tan silencioso como un pez deslizándose por el agua.

En la tele, Vin Scully retransmitía el partido y los Dodgers iban ganando por 2 a 0 en la primera entrada, con dos carreras de David Snell. El hombre que miraba agitó el puño y gritó para sí.

—¡Eso, muy bien! ¡Enséñales a esos cabrones cómo se hace!

Pike pasó un brazo por el cuello del hombre, levantó sus pies del suelo y le cerró la arteria carótida, lo que hizo que no le llegara sangre al cerebro. El tipo luchó con fuerza unos segundos, pero quedó inerte al perder la conciencia. Pike le sujetó hasta que se quedó flácido, y luego lo bajó al suelo y le ató las muñecas detrás de la espalda con unas esposas de plástico. Había entrado así en casas docenas de veces, en distintas partes del mundo, normalmente en habitaciones llenas

101

de gas lacrimógeno donde enemigos hostiles y armados se escondían detrás de unos rehenes, desesperados por matarle. Sus movimientos eran expertos y eficientes.

Fuera, en la zona de reparaciones más alejada, los dos hombres todavía estaban atareados con el parachoques cuando Pike dejó el despacho. Estaban colocándolo en su sitio del lado del conductor: un hombre atornillándolo por delante y el otro por detrás. Pike se colocó en su ángulo de visión ciego y sacó su 357 al acercarse. Detrás de él, Vin Scully llenaba el silencio diciendo que Snell, de los Kansas City Royals, había sido una excelente adquisición.

Pike dio al primer hombre con la pistola encima de la oreja derecha, luego se dio la vuelta encarándose al segundo y accionó con el pulgar el percutor para que el tipo le oyese amartillar la pistola. Este se lo quedó mirando, con la boca abierta, sin emitir sonido alguno. Pike dirigió el cañón hacia el suelo.

—Abajo. Las manos detrás de la cabeza.

Obedeció de inmediato.

Pike ató a ambos hombres de pies y manos, luego susurró al que todavía estaba despierto:

—¿El tipo del despacho cómo se llama?

—Hector Perra.

—Cierra los ojos. Si haces un solo ruido, te mato.

Cerró los ojos.

Hector ya estaba en pie cuando Pike volvió al despacho. Iba dando vueltas, como un perro que persigue su propio rabo, intentando verse las muñecas. Luego vio a Pike, bajó la cabeza y cargó contra él.

Pike le dirigió con la cabeza por delante hasta el marco de la puerta, le incorporó de una sacudida y le dio con el reverso del puño en el puente de la nariz. Los ojos de Hector se nublaron, pero lo mantuvo bien sujeto.

—Mírame. Concéntrate.

Su mirada se aclaró. Pike formó una pistola con la mano, con el pulgar y el índice, y lo señaló.

—¿Te acuerdas?

Lo golpeó de nuevo, moviéndose tan rápido que Hector no lo vio venir. La cabeza dio una sacudida hacia atrás, pero Pike no le había golpeado fuerte. Lo quería despierto.

—¿Dónde están?

—¿De qué coño hablas?

—La gente de la tienda de bocadillos.

—No lo sé, tío. ¿De qué me estás hablando?

Pike observó los ojos oscuros. Estaban furibundos y llenos de miedo, pero también confusos. El padre Art había dicho que los Malevos tenían más de sesenta miembros conocidos extendidos por toda Venice. No todos ellos estaban relacionados con todos los delitos cometidos; es posible que ni siquiera supieran lo que hacían otros miembros. Pike supuso que Hector le estaba diciendo la verdad.

—¿Dónde está Mendoza?

—¿Y cómo cojones quieres que lo sepa yo? Por ahí, haciendo sus cosas.

—¿Le has visto esta mañana?

—No estamos casados, tío. Yo hago mi vida.

Pike le golpeó de nuevo, con más fuerza que antes, y luego lo sacudió para aclararle la cabeza.

—¿Cuándo fue la última vez que lo viste?

—Ayer. Después de que le soltaran.

—¿Dónde?

Quería ver si Hector le estaba diciendo la verdad.

—Aquí, tío. Los colegas le pagaron la fianza, pasó un poco el rato y luego se largó. Ya sabes cómo van esas cosas.

—¿Adónde fue cuando salió de aquí?

—A casa de su antigua novia, supongo. No sé. Íbamos a vernos luego, pero no apareció.

—¿Iba Gomer con él?

—No sé.

Pike registró a Hector en busca de armas, pero solo encontró unas llaves, un móvil y una cartera. Levantó las llaves.

—¿Son las del Monte Carlo?

Hector asintió y Pike señaló hacia la puerta.

—Vamos. Fuera.

—¿Te llevas mi coche?

—Te llevo a ti.

103

*P*ike empujó a Hector hacia el asiento del pasajero, se puso tras del volante y salieron disparados. Hector se encogió apartándose de Pike como un globo que se deshincha, cerrando y abriendo los ojos como el obturador de una cámara de fotos.

—¿Adónde me llevas? ¿Adónde vamos, tío?

Pike no respondió. Siguió conduciendo cinco manzanas más hacia el barrio residencial, para poner más distancia entre sí mismo y el taller de chapa antes de aparcar. Hector se encogió aún más, apretándose contra la puerta.

Pike rebuscó en la cartera de Hector. Encontró treinta y dos dólares, fotos de personas que probablemente eran familiares, algunos vales de descuento y dos permisos de conducir de California. Ambos tenían la foto de Hector pero con nombres, direcciones y fechas de nacimiento diferentes. Uno lo identificaba como Hector Francis Perra, con dirección en Ghost Town, y el otro como Juan Rico, con dirección en Van Nuys. Pike lo volvió a meter todo en la cartera y lo miró.

—Mendoza.

—No sé dónde está, ya te lo he dicho. ¿Cómo cojones quieres que lo sepa?

Pike sacó el Python y le apretó el muslo.

—Enséñame dónde vive.

Lo dirigió a un bungaló pequeño, de techo plano, situado en el borde de Ghost Town, cerca de Inglewood. El revestimiento exterior de estuco estaba estropeado por un escape de agua, pero el jardincito se encontraba sorprendentemente limpio. Dos palmeras fibrosas arrojaban unas sombras como pintadas con rotulador en un Honda Maxima que se encontraba aparcado en la entrada. Pike pasó por delante y aparcó en la manzana siguiente, que tenía vistas hacia la casa.

—¿Es ese su coche? —preguntó.

—El de su novia. La casa es de ella. Viven juntos.

—¿Y cómo se llama?

—Carla Fuentes.

—¿Tienen hijos?

—No, pero la zorra esa lo está intentando. Le dije a él que tuviera cuidado.

En la casa no había señal alguna de vida, pero ocurría lo mismo con la mayoría de las casas de los alrededores. Una mujer mayor iba podando unos polvorientos rosales en un jardín que estaba calle abajo, y un perro mestizo que probablemente se había escapado a base de excavar husmeó un letrero de la calle y luego salió corriendo. Pike habría preferido vigilar la casa hasta que Mendoza saliese o volviese a ella, pero le pareció que no tenía tiempo. Su naturaleza le llevaba a tomar la iniciativa, y eso significaba dar un paso adelante.

Se guardó la pistola en la funda, quitó las llaves del contacto y buscó bajo el salpicadero, en la base de la dirección. Desconectó los cables que controlaban los intermitentes de giro y el claxon, y salió del coche. Cuando tiró de Hector, que estaba en el asiento de al lado, este pareció esperanzado.

—¿Me dejas irme?

—No.

Pike cortó las esposas de plástico que unían las muñecas de Hector, pero inmediatamente le ató la muñeca derecha a la parte superior del volante y la izquierda a la inferior. Tensó bien las esposas.

—Joder, tío, que me corta…

Pike cerró la puerta.

—Si gritas no te gustará nada cómo acaba esto.

Fue directamente a la casa de Mendoza, atravesó la entrada y aceleró el paso. El acceso llevaba a un garaje separado de un solo coche, pero Pike corrió hacia la parte lateral de la casa. Iba agachado, levantándose solo lo suficiente para mirar por todas las ventanas mientras daba la vuelta a la casa. Pasó junto a una puerta trasera sin mosquitera y atravesó un patio pequeño. Las

105

dos ventanas siguientes estaban bloqueadas por las persianas echadas, pero vio un baño y un dormitorio en el lado opuesto de la casa. Ambos estaban vacíos, pero el váter permitía otear un ángulo del salón. Distinguió un televisor puesto, pero no a la persona que lo veía. Había al menos tres habitaciones que Pike no conseguía ver. Mendoza y Gomer podían estar en cualquiera de ellas, pero él no lo sabría hasta que no entrase en la casa.

Todavía estaba observando el salón cuando pasó una mujer joven con un bulto grande por delante del baño. Era Carla, la novia de Mendoza. Entró en el salón y luego desapareció dirigiéndose hacia la cocina.

Pike corrió al patio de atrás y llegó a la esquina de la casa cuando ella abría la puerta con el pie. Carla Fuentes salió con el bulto hacia el garaje. Llevaba una camiseta fina demasiado estrecha para sus redondeces, unos pantalones cortos de un morado intenso, e iba descalza. Abrió con el codo una puerta en un lado del garaje y entró. Llevaba la colada.

Pike esperó contando hasta cinco por ver si alguien la seguía, y luego cruzó el jardín a toda prisa. Se metió tras ella, que estaba introduciendo unas sábanas en una lavadora de carga superior. No se dio cuenta de que había alguien hasta que él la rodeó con sus brazos, tapándole la boca con una mano y sujetándole los brazos con la otra. Su cuerpo se puso tenso, con una sacudida de miedo. Era fuerte. Arqueó la espalda intentando soltarse, pataleó y le dio a Pike en las piernas. Este la apretó más aún, sujetándola, y le dijo con voz calmada:

—Estás a salvo. Quiero a Mendoza. —Ella intentó morderle—. ¿Está dentro?

Al final Carla dejó de luchar, pero su cuerpo estaba rígido. Pike le quitó la mano de la boca, pero estaba dispuesto a volver a taparla si chillaba. No lo hizo.

—Hijo de puta... ¿Quién coño eres tú?

—¿Está dentro Mendoza?

—¡Suéltame, cabrón! ¿Eres policía? ¿Quién eres?

—Sí, soy policía. ¿Está dentro Mendoza?

—No hay nadie aquí. No sé dónde está ese desgraciado.

—Vamos a ver.

Fue con ella hasta la casa, manteniéndola delante mientras sacaba el arma. Dejó que abriese la puerta, pero escuchó atentamente antes de que entrasen. La cocina olía a bacon y a marihuana. Oyó el televisor encendido, pero no había voces ni movimiento. Le susurró al oído:

—Despacio.

Mientras entraban la chica gritó de repente:

—¡Lucy, estoy en casaaaa…!

Pike la agarró con fuerza, pero ella soltó una risotada.

—Tío, que no está aquí. Tranquilo.

La llevó primero al salón. En la mesita de centro había una pipa de cristal grande para hachís frente al televisor, como si lo estuviese viendo. La empujó a través del salón y fueron al vestíbulo, y luego por el resto de la casa. Miró en los armarios, la bañera, debajo de las camas… No la soltó hasta que volvieron a la cocina, donde apartó una silla de la mesa y le dijo que se sentara.

—Que te den por culo, cabrón. No pienso sentarme en mi propia casa…

—Siéntate o te siento yo.

Pike vio un hematoma que empezaba a desvanecerse en la mejilla izquierda de Carla Fuentes cuando ella lo miró, clavándole los ojos en sus tatuajes, como si estuviera viendo algo familiar. Se sentó.

—Tú no eres poli. Tú eres el tío que le rompió el brazo.

—¿Dónde está?

—Si lo encuentras me lo dices. Y espero que le des una patada en el culo también.

Pike dio la vuelta a la cocina, buscando algo que le diera influencia sobre la chica o le ayudase a encontrar a Mendoza.

—Si sabes lo mío, señal de que le has visto.

—Y una mierda. Señal de que me llamó cuando le detuvieron. Dijo que vendría a casa anoche, pero el muy cabronazo no apareció. Qué vida más perra llevo.

Pike encontró un móvil color rosa en el mostrador, junto a un paquete de cigarrillos. Lo encendió y empezó a comprobar la guía.

—¿Estaba aquí esta mañana?

—¿No me escuchas? ¡No me ha llamado! Que se joda él y te jodes tú también. He tenido que hipotecar esta casa para pagarle la fianza. Si ese cerdo se escapa, yo pierdo mi casa.

107

Pike la miró sorprendido. Azzara le había dicho que él cubrió la fianza de Mendoza, pero ahora la novia le estaba diciendo algo distinto. Creyó a la chica. Tenía los ojos rojos y la comisura de los labios tensa. La fianza de Mendoza por su agresión no tenía que haber sido de más de cincuenta mil dólares, probablemente menos. El fiador la iba a despellejar.

Pike volvió al teléfono y encontró en la lista un número de marcación rápida que decía «Reuben». Memorizó el número y le devolvió a ella el teléfono.

—Llámale. Veremos dónde está.

—No contesta. Llevo todo el día llamándole.

Pike comprobó la lista de llamadas y vio que le decía la verdad. Había marcado el número de Mendoza catorce veces consecutivas y él marcó aquel número de nuevo. El teléfono de Mendoza saltó de inmediato al buzón de voz, de modo que Pike colgó.

—¿Te dijo lo que estaba haciendo cuando le rompí el brazo?

—Dice que peleando. Que te va a dar una buena paliza si te pilla.

—¿Me está buscando?

—Sí, eso dice, pero al verte ahora creo que mentía descaradamente.

Pike se preguntó si aquello significaba que el acoso a Wilson en realidad no iría dirigido a él. Haría daño a Wilson y Dru para cogerle. Dejó el teléfono con los cigarrillos y luego se quedó de pie ante ella.

—¿Por eso no volvió a casa anoche, porque me estaba buscando?

—Eso lo dijo solo para chulearse. Dijo que tenía negocios.

—¿Qué tipo de negocios?

—Tenía que ir a ayudar a unos amigos. Es lo que suele decir cuando va con la Trece.

—¿Asuntos de la banda?

—Eso es lo que significa ayudar a unos amigos. Me llamó desde la cárcel, tío, con la poli allí mismo, así que uno no puede decir lo que quiere decir. Dijo que tenía que ayudar a unos amigos, y que volvería a casa, pero no lo hizo, y no me llamó tampoco, y ahora tú te metes aquí. He tenido que hipotecar mi casa por ese puto desgraciado, y ahora parece que se ha saltado la fianza y se ha largado.

Pike creía que ella sabría algo más, pero no lo suficiente para ayudarle a encontrar a Mendoza.

—¿Dónde para él cuando no está aquí contigo?

—Esta es su casa. Le dejé que se viniera a vivir aquí. Nos vamos a casar.

—¿Qué coche lleva?

—Un El Camino del ochenta y seis. Marrón. Como una mierda.

—¿Y dónde guarda los papeles? El registro del coche, las facturas, esas cosas.

La siguió hasta el dormitorio, donde la chica sacó una caja de zapatos del cajón superior de un armario desgastado y lleno de arañazos. Contenía unas cuantas fotos familiares, información de su nacimiento y diversos documentos y recibos. Encontró la factura de venta y registro del El Camino, junto con los números de matrícula y de chasis. No perdió tiempo copiando los números. Se metió la caja debajo del brazo.

—Pero, tío, ¿qué estás haciendo? ¡Esas son sus cosas!

Vio un bolso azul grande que estaba en el tocador. Lo abrió y encontró la cartera de Carla.

—No tengo dinero ahí —dijo ella.

No buscaba dinero. Al ver las fotos familiares de Mendoza tuvo una idea. En la cartera ella llevaba una funda para fotos, y la primera de ellas era de Mendoza, sonriendo tanto que parecía una calabaza. Pike cogió la foto y volvió a dejar el bolso en el tocador.

—Eres un puto ladrón. Voy a llamar a la poli.

Pike creyó que ya no podía conseguir nada más y salió de la habitación. Carla Fuentes fue tras él, tirándole del brazo ansiosamente.

—Quiero hacerte una pregunta. Si se salta la fianza, ¿de verdad que me quitarán mi casa?

—Sí.

—Pero no es culpa mía si él huye.

—Tú firmaste la fianza.

—Espera un momento… Espera, espera, a ver. Si le matan,

¿pierdo la casa de todos modos? Si está muerto no pueden echarme la culpa, ¿verdad? ¿Me quitarán igual la casa?

Pike se detuvo al llegar a la puerta.

—No. Perderás las tasas de la fianza y la solicitud, pero el tribunal devolverá la fianza al fiador.

—¿Y eso qué quiere decir?

—Que no perderás la casa.

Ella se lo pensó un poco y el terror abandonó sus ojos, en parte.

—¿Qué harás cuando le encuentres?

—¿Qué te gustaría que hiciera?

—Romperle el otro puto brazo. Rompérselo bien, y luego darle una buena paliza y matarlo.

Pike salió al sol y se dirigió hacia el Monte Carlo.

14

*P*ike se subió al Monte Carlo, pero aquella vez en el asiento del pasajero, dejando a Hector atado al volante. Una vez más, este se acurrucó para alejarse de Pike todo lo posible.

—Mírame las manos, tío. ¡Míralas! ¡Se me están poniendo azules!

Pike hojeó los documentos que tenía en la caja, a ver lo que eran.

—¿Quieres soltarme ya? Suéltame, tío; esto es un secuestro. Es un delito federal.

—Cállate la boca.

Hector se calló, gruñendo entre dientes.

Pike encontró recibos de dinero e instrucciones para tres teléfonos desechables que Mendoza había comprado en Best Buy. Se preguntó si su amigo Elvis Cole podría usar aquella información para localizar a Mendoza o identificar a quién estaba llamando. Cole era investigador privado, y tenía relaciones con la mayoría de los proveedores de servicios de telefonía móvil. Quizá también pudiese encontrar a Alberto Gomer.

Pike examinó la foto de Reuben Mendoza y luego la metió en la caja. Estaba dando forma a un plan para sacar de su escondite a Mendoza, y aquella foto le iría muy bien.

—Quédate quieto —le dijo a Hector.

Este abrió mucho los ojos cuando Pike sacó su cuchillo, le cortó las esposas y lo dejó libre.

—Lárgate.

—¿Cómo que me largue? Este es mi coche.

—Fuera.

111

—Pero, tío, ¿te llevas mi coche?

—No te lo repetiré.

Hector abrió la puerta y salió, enfurruñado. Cerró mientras Pike se ponía tras del volante.

—Esto no está bien, robarme el coche... ¿Te llevas mi cartera también? ¿Y el teléfono?

Pike se fue hasta donde tenía el Jeep. Dejó la cartera de Hector en el Monte Carlo, pero añadió su teléfono a la caja que contenía los objetos personales de Mendoza. No se entretuvo en examinar esas cosas porque quería seguir presionando.

Fue directamente a casa de Lily Palmer, aparcó en el garaje de Wilson y llamó al timbre. Ella respondió al segundo timbrazo.

—Ya sabía que volvería. ¿Encontró al final a Wilson y a Dru?

—No, todavía no. ¿Está en casa Jared?

Ella suspiró.

—Siempre está.

Lo llamó en voz alta, y el ruido de las chanclas de Jared anunció su llegada. Se acababa de embadurnar de crema solar y llevaba una botella de cerveza en la mano. Frunció el ceño cuando vio a Pike y se quitó los auriculares del iPod.

—Tío, ya se lo he contado todo. No sé nada más.

—El hombre con el yeso... —Le enseñó la foto de Reuben Mendoza—. ¿Era este?

Jared miró la foto y esbozó una sonrisa de sorpresa que le hizo parecer orgulloso de sí mismo.

—¡Tío! ¡Es él! ¡El hombre del yeso!

—¿Estás seguro?

—A tope.

Jared sonreía y siguió vomitando recuerdos.

—El tío llevaba unos pantalones anchos color caqui, una camisa de cuadros grises abierta, muy grande, y una camiseta blanca debajo. Y era calvo.

Pike había visto a los testigos soltar una avalancha similar de recuerdos cuando era policía. Si a un testigo se le da un apoyo visual, un recuerdo que antes era vago a menudo se concentra. Los psicólogos llaman a estos recuerdos «desencadenantes», y la cascada de remembranzas resultantes son «cadenas de memoria».

—¿Recuerdas algo del segundo hombre?

Jared pensó un momento, pero su boca se entreabrió por el esfuerzo frustrado.

—No, no mucho. Estaba delante, ya casi pasando por la puerta. El hombre del yeso iba detrás. Recuerdo que tenía el pelo negro y llevaba gafas de sol. Sí, creo que llevaba gafas...
—Finalmente se quedó sin gas—. Lo siento, tío. No me acuerdo de nada más.

Ahora Pike podía relacionar a Mendoza con el lugar de los hechos mediante una identificación con foto. El segundo hombre era Gomer casi con toda seguridad, pero con Mendoza bastaba.

Volvió a su Jeep para decidir cuál sería su siguiente movimiento, pero sabía que al final tendría que volver a Button: era la última persona que había tenido contacto con Smith. Pike quería saber exactamente qué dijo Smith, cómo lo dijo y cuándo. Esas cosas podían resultar cruciales, y también podían hacer que Button volviese al juego. La policía aumentaría la presión sobre Mendoza, pero había que calcular muy bien el momento de su entrada: en cuanto se introdujese de nuevo, bloquearían los movimientos de Pike y frenarían su impulso. Tenía que cubrir los preliminares antes de que ellos entrasen, y mantener la delantera.

Pike cogió el teléfono de Hector de la caja, pasó unos segundos examinándolo y luego recorrió la guía de nombres. Encontró el número de Mendoza como R MENDOZA, pero no había nada con GOMER o ALBERTO. Ninguna entrada tampoco por AZZARA, pero sí por MIGUEL. Apretó el botón, oyó dos timbrazos y le respondió Mikie Azzara.

—No me molestes con gilipolleces del taller.

Respondía así porque el identificador de llamadas le decía que era Hector.

—Estoy aquí —dijo Pike.

Mikie dudó.

—¿Quién es?

—Uno de sus chicos lo escribió en la pared.

Azzara dudó de nuevo, pero esta vez reconoció la voz.

—¿Cómo tiene este teléfono?

—Quiero a Mendoza y a Gomer.

Azzara bajó la voz, como si estuviera en un lugar donde no quisiera que alguien le oyese.

—¿De qué me está hablando?

—Mendoza estuvo en casa de Wilson y Dru esta mañana. Y ahora han desaparecido.

Azzara se aclaró la garganta. Pike oyó algo de fondo, pero no pudo distinguir lo que era. Luego Mikie intentó tranquilizarle, y Pike se preguntó por qué.

—Escuche, no sé nada de esto, pero lo averiguaré. Se lo prometo… No tiene que preocuparse. Estoy seguro de que esa gente está bien.

—Es usted un mentiroso, Miguel. Me dijo que pagó la fianza de Mendoza, pero no lo hizo. ¿En qué más me mintió?

—¿Quiere escucharme? Ahora mismo estoy ocupado, pero le ayudaré, hombre. Tranquilícese. Deme unas horas y…

—El tiempo se ha terminado.

Azzara se quedó callado. Pasaron unos segundos antes de que volviese a hablar. Luego su voz fue más suave, pero no tranquilizadora.

—Está cometiendo un error. Piensa que está hablando con algún guapito mexicano, pero está hablando con La Eme. Somos doscientos mil. Debería esperar, como le digo. No le conviene entrar en guerra con nosotros.

Pike esperó, dejando que la presión de su silencio fuera aumentando. Cuando Azzara por fin habló de nuevo, su voz mostró una tensión que Pike encontró curiosa.

—¿Ha quedado claro? ¿Lo entiende? —Pike no dijo nada—. Le pregunto si lo entiende…

—No, es usted quien no lo entiende.

—¿El qué?

—Que eso es lo que yo hago, la guerra.

Pike colgó, y luego llamó a un amigo llamado Elvis Cole.

15

*L*os investigadores con experiencia se referían al lugar donde se había producido un secuestro como «zona cero». Era la intersección donde los caminos de la víctima y el perpetrador convergían y se unían en uno solo. Era una zona de emboscada, de una violencia furiosa y abrupta, o bien una amenaza discreta, donde dos vías se convertían en una sola, pero no se formaban en el vacío. El mundo físico quedaba alterado: un pez ondulaba el agua; un ave que pasaba arrojaba una sombra. Pike sabía eso mucho mejor que la mayoría porque había pasado gran parte de su vida intentando moverse sin ser visto u oído, o bien dejando algún rastro que los demás pudieran seguir. Era difícil. Jared Palmer había visto a Reuben Mendoza. Esa era la primera ondulación, pero Pike sabía que habría otras. El problema era el tiempo: estaba formando una ola con mucha presión y cabalgándola como un surfista que sale disparado por ese túnel verde. Pero volver a casa de Smith para seguir la pista podía costar horas y disminuir la presión. La ola podía derrumbarse. Necesitaba mantenerla, y creía que a nadie se le daba mejor encontrar y recuperar a personas perdidas como a su colega Elvis Cole.

Este era un investigador privado con licencia a quien Pike conocía de la época en que todavía llevaba placa. No parecía que hicieran precisamente muy buena pareja, ya que Pike era muy silencioso y reservado, y Cole en cambio era una de esas personas que piensan que son muy chistosas. No obstante, se parecían más de lo que la gente se imaginaba. Cole era un simple aprendiz en aquella época, y trabajaba para un detective angelino de la vieja escuela llamado George Feider, con el fin de acumular las tres mil horas de experiencia que el estado requería para poder darle la licencia.

Cuando consiguió las tres mil horas, Feider ya pensaba en retirarse y Cole quiso comprarle la agencia. Pike había dejado la policía por aquel entonces, y estaba ganando bastante dinero con contratos militares y de seguridad privada. Compraron la agencia los dos juntos, aunque Pike siempre permaneció en la sombra. Lo prefería así: que nadie le oyera ni le viera.

Mientras esperaba que llegase Cole Pike llamó a Hydeck y Betsy Harmon, esperando equivocarse sobre la desaparición y que Wilson o Dru hubiesen devuelto las llamadas o finalmente hubiesen aparecido en su cocina. Pero no fue así, y Betsy Harmon se quejó una vez más de que nadie había limpiado el estropicio.

Veinticinco minutos después de que Pike llamase a Elvis Cole, este entró en el Jeep procedente de un bar de Abbot Kinney, a unas pocas manzanas de los canales. Había venido rápido. Si llevaba algo entre manos cuando lo llamó Pike, no lo mencionó.

—¿Qué ocurre? —preguntó.

Pike empezó con el arresto de Mendoza dos días antes, y le esbozó la secuencia de acontecimientos, incluyendo la búsqueda de Mendoza y su llamada a Miguel Azzara. Cuando terminó, Cole examinó la foto de Mendoza y levantó la vista.

—Así que no crees que se fueran a Oregón.

—No. Si no hubiesen visto a Mendoza en su casa. A lo mejor sí, pero eso cambia el asunto por completo.

—¿Qué crees entonces, que les siguió a casa para amenazarles y que la cosa acabó en secuestro? ¿Que obligó a Smith a hacer la llamada?

Pike asintió, pero no quiso poner en palabras sus miedos más oscuros: que el secuestro se hubiese convertido en una carnicería.

—¿Has intentado volver a llamarles?

—Cada vez que lo hago sale el buzón de voz. No devuelven las llamadas.

Cole asintió con el rostro inexpresivo, como si estuviese examinando todos los ángulos del asunto.

—Eso es lo que ocurriría si les hubiesen quitado los teléfonos.

—Sí.

Cole echó una mirada alrededor.

—Olvidemos a Mendoza por un momento… Quizás estaban tan asustados que se imaginaron las malas noticias y apagaron los móviles.

—Wilson quizá, pero no Dru. Dru llamaría si pudiera.

—¿Sí?

Pike se dio cuenta de que Cole le miraba.

—La conozco.

—Ah.

Pensó que quizá tendría que haberlo expresado de otra manera.

—Nos tomamos una cerveza.

—Ya.

—Quedamos para salir. Ella me lo pidió.

—Ya veo.

Cole le pidó los números de móvil y dijo que intentaría preguntar por su actividad en el proveedor de servicios de telefonía. Pike se le recitó, y luego le entregó la caja de zapatos de Mendoza y el teléfono de Hector. Cole hurgó en el contenido.

—De acuerdo, con esto puedo empezar. ¿Qué pasa con la policía? ¿Lo están tratando como un secuestro?

—No saben nada de Mendoza.

Cole levantó la vista desde la caja.

—¿Por qué no?

—Quería que tú vieras la casa primero. Aportas una mirada nueva, eres más rápido y verás cosas que ellos se están perdiendo.

Cole intentó adoptar un aire modesto.

—Ni que decir tiene.

—Pero no tendrás mucho tiempo. En cuanto estés allí, yo me iré a ver a Button. Seguro que va a casa de Smith, así que nosotros tenemos que ir primero.

Cole echó una mirada de nuevo a la foto de Mendoza, y se la devolvió a Pike.

—Vamos, tenemos mucho trabajo.

Pike iba delante y Cole lo siguió en su propio coche. Como

las calles eran estrechas y el aparcamiento difícil, dejaron los vehículos en Venice Boulevard y se acercaron a casa de Smith a pie. Pike no quería tener otra conversación con los Palmer, de modo que se detuvo muy lejos de su vista y señaló la casa de Smith. Ya había hablado de Jared a su compañero. Cuando este vio la casa, echó una mirada a Pike.

—¿Un tío que se gana la vida con un puesto de comida para llevar tiene una casa así?

—No es suya, la están cuidando. Es de un guionista de televisión retirado.

—¿Has estado dentro?

—Solo para buscar cuerpos. Entré por la ventanita de un lado, en el lavadero, para no alterar la escena.

Explicó que no había encontrado señales de entrada forzada en el exterior de la casa, y nada de sangre ni señales de lucha ni en el aparcamiento ni en el jardín delantero. Quería que Cole se concentrase en el interior porque tendrían un tiempo limitado en cuanto él fuese a la policía.

—Cuando acabe con Button te llamo, te esperaré en casa de la novia. Los he metido en el juego a ella y a Azzara para hacer algo de presión sobre Mendoza. Cuando Button entre en escena la presión aumentará mucho más, y quizá Mendoza se quiera ir a casa.

Agobiar al enemigo era una táctica que Pike usaba en combate. Si se crea suficiente estrés en el objetivo, acaba por coger pánico y huir. Casi siempre vuelven a casa.

—Suena bien. Yo veré lo que averiguo sobre Mendoza y Gomer, y te relevo esta noche —apuntó Cole.

Ya habían terminado, y Pike sabía que debía irse, pero se quedó mirando la casa. Se imaginó a Dru y Wilson dentro después de volver de su tienda. Vio a Mendoza y al segundo hombre moviéndose hacia la puerta, e intentó quitarse de la cabeza lo que se imaginó a continuación.

Se dio cuenta de que Cole le había dicho algo, pero no lo oyó. Su compañero lo miraba con una expresión curiosa, y cuando volvió a hablar su voz era amable.

—¿Estás bien?

—Le dije que me ocuparía. Que no les volverían a molestar.

La repentina simpatía en los ojos de Cole hizo que Pike se sintiera algo violento. Apartó la vista.

—Eh... —dijo Elvis Cole. Pike lo miró—. ¿No soy el mejor detective del mundo? Yo me hago cargo, Joseph. La encontraremos.

Se alejó antes de que Pike pudiera responder.

Pike miró un momento a su amigo y luego se dirigió hacia su Jeep. El tiempo pasaba, y era enemigo suyo.

Se fue a toda velocidad a la comisaría de policía de Pacific Community.

16

*L*a comisaría era un edificio moderno y bajo, de ladrillo, rodeado por un muro y unos esbeltos pinos en Culver Boulevard, a un kilómetro y medio de la casa de Pike. Un asta con la bandera americana se erguía orgullosamente ante ella, al otro lado de un tablero que anunciaba un fiador. Las casitas de clase media que se alineaban en el bulevar eran limpias y atractivas. Esos barrios, como la propia comisaría, hacían que resultase difícil de creer que a menudo las guerras entre bandas rivales llenaban la calle de sangre a solo unos minutos de distancia.

Pike aparcó junto a la bandera a las 15.07. La guardia cambiaría a las 16.00, de modo que cualquier detective que no estuviera en el tribunal o sobre el terreno se encontraría dentro acabando su jornada. Necesitaba saber si Button era uno de ellos.

Llamó a Información de la comisaría para averiguar el número del detective, y luego marcó ese número.

—Pacific. Detective Harrison al habla.

—Soy Dale King, de administración. ¿Está ahí todavía Button?

Llamaba al nuevo edificio administrativo, que había reemplazado al centro Parker.

—Sí, no cuelgue, voy a buscarle —contestó Harrison.

Pike esperó hasta que la detective lo puso en espera, y entonces colgó. Creyendo que Button se negaría a verle, fue caminando en torno a la comisaría por el aparcamiento civil, y luego saltó un muro bajo y se dirigió a la estructura de aparcamiento de dos pisos donde guardaban sus coches los oficiales. No le gustaba perder el tiempo, pero no tuvo que esperar mucho.

Catorce minutos más tarde Button salió de la parte trasera de la comisaría con otros detectives y oficiales de uniforme de camino a sus coches. Llevaba un maletín, la chaqueta y la corbata en el otro brazo, y vestía una camisa azul claro con manchas de sudor en las axilas. Portaba también un pequeño revólver sujeto al cinturón.

Pike estaba detrás de una columna cuando pasó Button, dirigiéndose a su furgoneta Toyota color marrón claro. Se cambió la chaqueta del brazo derecho al izquierdo, y estaba buscando las llaves cuando Pike apareció ante él, saliendo de detrás de la columna.

—Button...

Este dio un salto a un lado. Buscó su pistola, dejando caer el maletín y las llaves que acababa de sacar de la chaqueta. Pike levantó ambas manos con calma, mostrando las palmas.

—No pasa nada.

Si Button se sintió violento por su reacción, no lo demostró. Recogió el maletín y las llaves y siguió andando hacia su furgoneta.

—Esta es una zona de aparcamiento para la policía. Vete de aquí.

—Los han raptado.

—¿De qué coño estás hablando?

—Wilson Smith y Dru Rayne. Han desaparecido.

Button abrió la puerta del coche y arrojó la chaqueta y el maletín dentro.

—Se han ido a Oregón, tío. Y otra cosa: Straw está que echa humo. No me importa demasiado, porque es un federal chulo y creído; probablemente te odia más que yo.

—Reuben Mendoza y otro hombre que quizá fuese Gomer han estado en casa de Wilson y Dru a las 8.45 esta mañana. ¿A qué hora ha llamado Smith?

Button ya tenía una pierna metida en la furgoneta, pero salió de nuevo, mirando a Pike con los ojos entrecerrados.

—¿Cómo sabes que me ha llamado?

—Por Hydeck. Estaba en la tienda de Smith cuando hablaste con ella. De ahí fui a la casa de ellos.

—¿De verdad?

—Tienen una cancela delante que hay que atravesar para llegar a la vivienda. El chico de la puerta de al lado ha visto a Mendoza y a otro tío entrando por esa cancela a las 8.45. Se llama Jared Palmer. Habla con él.

Pike vio la tensión en la cara de Button mientras este comparaba el odio que sentía por Pike con lo que estaba oyendo, como si tuviese que trepar una pared antes de poder seguir adelante. Finalmente se alejó un poco, dejando abierta la puerta del Toyota.

—¿Cómo sabe el chico que era Mendoza?

—No lo sabe. Le he enseñado esto. —Sacó la foto. Button le echó una mirada pero no la tocó.

—De uno a diez, ¿en qué medida está seguro?

—Un diez.

—¿Está seguro de la hora?

—La madre ha relacionado los hechos con el programa *Today*. Jared salió a buscar un batido de chocolate un poco después de las ocho y volvió pocos minutos después de la pausa de la media hora. Eso sitúa a Mendoza allí al menos a las ocho cuarenta y cinco. ¿Cuándo has sabido algo de Smith?

Button miró de nuevo la foto y esta vez dedicó un rato a examinar cuidadosamente a Mendoza.

—¿Y el segundo hombre? ¿Era Gomer?

—No tenía una foto de Gomer. ¿A qué hora has hablado con Smith?

—Sobre las nueve, justamente aquí mismo, quizás un poco más tarde —contestó Button. Frunció el ceño pensando en todo aquello y lo que podía significar si era cierto, pero aun así no quería aceptarlo. Meneó la cabeza—. No, no es posible. No dijo nada de eso.

—Quizá Mendoza le estaba apuntando con una pistola a la cabeza.

—No, imposible. El chico está equivocado.

—Ha visto el yeso, y eso no se lo he dicho yo, Button. Me ha dicho que el hombre iba enyesado. Lo ha visto entrar por la cancela a las 8.45.

Button miró de nuevo la foto, como si todavía no consiguiera verla con claridad.

—He hablado con él. Estaba bien.

—No si Mendoza estaba allí.

Button enrojeció y sus ojos se encogieron como si fueran dos bolitas oscuras.

—¿Me estás diciendo que he pasado algo por alto?

—¿Lo has hecho?

La academia enseñaba a los oficiales que la gente que afirma cosas bajo coacción ofrece señales reveladoras. Son deliberadamente lacónicos y dubitativos porque tienen miedo de decir algo erróneo. La estructura de sus frases a menudo es confusa o repetitiva por el mismo motivo, y su voz suele temblar o romperse debido a la contracción del esófago, causada por la adrenalina que fluye por su organismo.

—Te digo que estaba bien. No parecía un tipo que tiene una pistola en la cabeza. Ni siquiera ahora, recordándolo, me parece que hubiese ninguna de las señales.

—Entonces olvidemos las señales. ¿Qué ha dicho?

—Que la gente como nosotros (y eso nos incluiría a mí y a ti, Pike, a quien ha mencionado específicamente) no hacíamos más que empeorar las cosas, costarle una fortuna, y que les iban a matar por nuestra culpa. ¿Quieres más? Me ha dicho también que me metiera a Mendoza y todo el resto de Los Ángeles por el culo.

Button iba gritando cada vez más, de modo que tres oficiales que pasaron se quedaron mirando. Esperó hasta que se hubieron ido para seguir hablando, pero sus ojos seguían furiosos.

—Pero ¿a ti que coño te importa, de todos modos? No es asunto tuyo.

—Como dijo Smith, quizá lo haya empeorado.

Button apartó la vista como si se sintiera incómodo de repente.

—¿Por qué crees que han desaparecido?

—Eres la última persona con la que han contactado. Mucha gente les ha intentado llamar, pero no responden y no han devuelto las llamadas.

—Eso no significa nada. Puede haber cien motivos diferentes para eso.

—Por ejemplo que Mendoza pasó por su puerta.

123

Button se quedó de nuevo mirando el suelo, y luego suspiró.

—El tío estaba enfadado, ¿vale? Pero sonaba natural; solo enfadado y desahogándose. Me ha dicho lo que le han hecho en la tienda, lo de las cabezas y todo eso, y que se iban a Dodge unas semanas para dejar que las cosas se enfriasen.

—Oregón.

—Han dicho que tenían amigos allí. Y ya está. Aunque aceptase que Mendoza estaba en su puerta, nada de lo que ha dicho el tío llama la atención. No intentaba transmitir ningún mensaje oculto. No había ninguna súplica sutil de ayuda. No lo veo.

Pike se creyó la afirmación de Button sin dudar, aunque su descripción de la llamada no cuadraba con la presencia de Mendoza. Pike había esperado alguna insinuación o pista de lo que había ocurrido y de dónde podían estar.

—Entonces, ¿qué hacía Mendoza en su casa? —dijo.

Button suspiró, y Pike supo que se estaba preguntando exactamente lo mismo.

—¿Cómo se llama el chico?

—Jared Palmer. Vive en una casa blanca moderna, al lado de la de Smith.

Button se sacó un bloc y bolígrafo de su bolsillo y lo apuntó.

—Bien. Llevaré la ficha con las fotos de Gomer. —Se metió de nuevo el bloc en el bolsillo, pero no parecía demasiado contento—. ¿Te ha dicho lo del yeso él solo? ¿No le has dicho nada tú primero?

Pike negó con la cabeza, y Button frunció el ceño.

—Putos gilipollas. Mendoza se enfrenta a una acusación por agresión que sabe que el fiscal agravará a lesiones, y no es capaz de dejar las cosas…

Pike sabía a qué se refería Button, pero no dijo nada porque sus pensamientos eran demasiado oscuros. Las cárceles estaban llenas de asesinos convictos a los que habían servido un muslito de pollo cuando querían un cuarto, o que creían que les faltaban al respeto cuando una mujer no les hablaba en un autobús, o que estaban convencidos de que un camarero les ignoraba. Cuando un hombre se sentía frustrado o furioso, cualquier razón bastaba.

Button empezó a alejarse pero luego volvió. Pike vio que todavía tenía la foto de Mendoza. Se la tendió, pero, cuando fue a cogerla, Button no la soltó.

—Supongo que no recuerdas las normas, ya que devolviste la placa. Si tenemos que acusar a ese idiota has eliminado al chico, Jared, como testigo. Al haberle enseñado una foto como esta, su abogado alegará que tú convenciste al chico de que el hombre al que vio era Mendoza, aunque hubiese visto a otro. Y el juez lo aceptará.

Button soltó la foto y volvió a su furgoneta.

Pike sabía que tenía razón, pero el caso no le importaba nada. Lo que le importaba era Dru Rayne.

Estaba a mitad de camino hacia su Jeep cuando llamó Elvis Cole.

17

Elvis Cole

De pie en el callejón entre los canales, cuando Joe Pike lo dejó para ir a hablar con Button, Cole ya sabía que Pike pensaba en lo peor y que estaba en plan Terminator. Pike se había concentrado en un objetivo y seguiría adelante como una máquina, sin descanso. Cuando Cole era Ranger llamaban a esa actitud «compromiso con la misión», y el de Pike con la suya era excepcional. Pero Cole no estaba convencido de que hubiese pasado lo peor. Quería entrar en la casa sin ideas preconcebidas e interpretar los hechos tal y como apareciesen. Como decía Joe, quería verlo con una mirada nueva.

Se desplazó hasta la puerta delantera de Smith como si fuera un residente más que ha salido a dar un paseo. Pike le había advertido del problema con Jared, y le había explicado que era mucho más seguro saltar la valla por el lado opuesto al garaje, pero él quería ver la cancela que había usado Mendoza. La ventana de Jared estaba despejada, de modo que examinó la manija. Se cerraba con una cerradura sencilla, con llave, desgastada y rozada por el tiempo. Apretando un timbre en el poste se hacía saber a los de la casa que estabas allí. Probablemente habría otro botón en el interior que abriría la puerta. Una placa de metal cubría el hueco entre esta y el poste, donde el cerrojo encajaba. La placa estaba diseñada para evitar que alguien corriese el cerrojo, pero Cole sabía que era fácil de abrir. No veía cortes ni arañazos recientes en el metal que lo rodeaba, pero también sabía que era fácil no dejar marcas.

Comprobó que ni Jared ni otras personas estuvieran mirando y saltó por encima.

La puerta principal era de madera, normal y corriente, teñida de oscuro para que hiciera juego con el resto de la casa. Encima del picaporte se encontraba una cerradura Master incrustada en el marco. Cole sacó unos guantes de látex, eligió una ganzúa y un tensor de su equipo de ganzúas y empezó a trabajar. Dos minutos para la cerradura, uno para el picaporte. Entrenamiento cortesía del Ejército de Estados Unidos.

Abrió la puerta lentamente y entró en un pequeño vestíbulo embaldosado. La casa estaba fría. Olía a grasa, a marisco y a un aroma floral que no sabía identificar. Cole escuchó unos segundos, luego anunció con firmeza:

—Departamento de policía. Aquí el detective Banning, de la policía de Los Ángeles. ¿Hay alguien en casa?

Dejó pasar diez segundos más o menos y luego cerró la puerta y pasó el cerrojo. Entrar era lo más comprometido. Cole había dado con pitbulls, sonámbulos, tres hombres desnudos practicando yoga, siete niños abandonados de menos de cuatro años y una vez dos adictos a la meta adrenalínicos con escopetas del calibre 12 esperando a su camello. Aquel no fue uno de sus mejores días.

Sin moverse, examinó el suelo y las paredes del vestíbulo. No vio sangre, ni marcas de rozaduras intensas, ni casquillos, ni muebles tirados o fuera de su sitio, ni prueba alguna de lucha.

Su plan de ataque era investigar en el segundo piso primero, por si aparecía la policía, de modo que se dirigió a las escaleras, comprobando cada paso mientras iba subiendo. Pasó rápidamente por el rellano y luego fue al despacho. Pike ya le había explicado la distribución.

El despacho estaba muy bien amueblado, y estaba claro que pertenecía a alguien que había disfrutado de una carrera llena de éxitos en la televisión. Llenaban las paredes certificados de reconocimiento de series policiales que ya no estaban en antena, la mayoría de las cuales Cole reconoció por los actores. Todos aquellos documentos ostentaban el mismo nombre. Producido por Steve Brown. Escrito por Steve Brown. Dirigido por Steve Brown.

Aunque Cole no reconocía aquel nombre, le gustaban los programas.

127

—Buen trabajo, Steve. Bien hecho.

Aunque la habitación estaba bien amueblada, notó que había huecos vacíos en las paredes, donde faltaban algunos cuadros, y en los estantes, de donde se habían quitado también libros. No había tampoco ordenador, ni máquina de escribir ni ningún otro equipo de oficina presente, excepto un teléfono. Probablemente eran cosas que Brown había guardado mientras estaba fuera. No tenía sentido tentar a los huéspedes.

Descolgó el teléfono, pero no había línea. Posiblemente había dado de baja el servicio.

Aunque era improbable una entrada forzada en el segundo piso, Cole comprobó las ventanas y las puertas que conducían afuera, a la terraza. Las encontró todas intactas y se dirigió al dormitorio principal.

Era grande, desordenado y decepcionante. Cole había esperado averiguar si Smith se había ido voluntariamente al ver si estaban o no su ropa y sus objetos de aseo, pero era obvio que el propietario había dejado un guardarropa muy bien provisto. El enorme vestidor y el baño estaban repletos de ropa y objetos de tocador, muchos más de los que se habría traído un ocupante temporal. Cole no podía saber qué era lo que pertenecía a Brown y si había algo de Smith o faltaba alguna de sus cosas. Incluso había piezas de ropa de mujer, pero podían pertenecer perfectamente a una novia de Brown, tanto como a Dru Rayne.

Encontró un solo artículo que sabía que pertenecía a Smith: un archivador de metal abollado que se encontraba en el suelo, junto a la cama. Contenía recibos, facturas y estados de cuentas pertenecientes a la tienda de bocadillos, un recibo rosa por un Tercel del 2002, pólizas de seguros y otros documentos triviales de la vida cotidiana. Nada que no se pudiera dejar para pasar fuera un par de semanas, y nada que nadie considerase digno de ser robado.

Tras acabar con el segundo piso, Cole bajó las escaleras. Empezó en el lavadero, vio las marcas de Pike en la ventana y rápidamente se dirigió al dormitorio de abajo. Wilson se había instalado arriba, en el dormitorio principal; su sobrina abajo. A diferencia del dormitorio principal, este tenía la cama hecha y la habitación estaba limpia, arreglada y ordenada. Nadie

128

había tocado las ventanas. Cole encontró unas cuantas blusas, vestidos y pantalones vaqueros de mujer en el armario. No era mucha ropa, pero no podía saber si era todo lo que tenía la mujer o si se había llevado unas cuantas cosas para hacer un viaje.

Luego fue a la cocina, que se abría hacia una habitación grande con una cristalera que ofrecía una agradable vista del canal. Otro teléfono digital sin línea se encontraba en el mostrador, junto a un fregadero lleno de platos. Eso le molestaba. Era como las cabezas de cabra y la sangre: nadie podía irse dejando un desorden como aquel, pero Button aseguraba que eso era exactamente lo que había hecho Wilson. A Cole le daba mala espina todo aquello, pero en sí mismo no probaba nada. Quizá que Smith era un vago.

En el frigorífico había varios folletos de menús para llevar sujetos con imanes. Cole lo abrió y lo encontró lleno de leche, cerveza, refrescos y lo que parecían ser ostras fritas y gambas en unos contenedores de cartón blancos y grasientos. ¿Dos personas que se dedican a la restauración dejarían en el frigorífico una comida que sabían que se estropearía?

Cuando cerró la nevera vio una nota escrita a mano y sujeta a la puerta. No la había visto antes porque estaba medio oculta entre los menús.

EN CASO DE EMERGENCIA LLAMAR AL 911.
PROBLEMAS DE FONTANERÍA,
LLAMAR A NICKY TATE – 323-555-8402
SI ME NECESITÁIS MIENTRAS ESTOY EN LONDRES:
STEVE – 310-555-3691

En Londres eran ocho horas más. Era tarde, pero Steve Brown quizás estuviese levantado. Si Smith se preocupó de llamar a Button, quizá llamase también a su anfitrión. Cole marcó el número.

El teléfono de Brown sonó seis veces antes de que saltara el buzón de voz.

—Señor Brown, me llamo Elvis Cole. Estoy en Los Ángeles. Por favor, ¿podría llamarme con relación a Wilson Smith y Dru Rayne?

Cole dejó su número, colgó y luego fue a la ventana que estaba encima del fregadero. Era lo último que iba a comprobar antes de irse. No había encontrado ninguna prueba consistente de secuestro pero tampoco de un viaje, y ya estaba pensando a cuál de sus contactos de la policía de Los Ángeles llamar por el asunto de Mendoza y Gomer. La casa había sido una decepción, y ya tenía la cabeza puesta en otra cosa.

Examinó los cierres de la ventana y del marco interior, y entonces fue cuando vio un solo corte profundo en la parte exterior del marco: una muesca delgada y brillante que resplandecía en el metal, junto al cerrojo, mucho más brillante que el metal que la rodeaba. Cole tocó la manija y la ventana se abrió sin esfuerzo alguno. En cuanto la hubo abierto vio un hueco profundo en el marco. Cerró la ventana. La miró unos segundos y luego llamó a Joe Pike.

—¿Habías mirado la ventana de la cocina?

—Sí. Todas las ventanas.

—La de encima del fregadero.

—¿Has encontrado algo?

—Alguien la ha forzado. Lo estoy mirando. Hay una rascadura en el marco, al parecer donde resbaló el destornillador, y está doblado por el cerrojo. ¿Todo esto no estaba así esta mañana?

—No.

—El cerrojo está roto. La ventana se abre tranquilamente.

—Esta mañana no era así.

—Eso significa que ha ocurrido tres o cuatro horas después de que Jared viese a Mendoza.

—¿Has encontrado algo en la casa?

—Nada. No hay señales de que se los llevaran. Ni tampoco de que se fueran de viaje. Nada.

—Entiendo.

—Yo no.

—Ya lo entenderás más tarde. Acabo de dejar a Button. No tengo tiempo.

Cole dejó el teléfono y miró la ventana. Quizá no encontrase pruebas de delito alguno porque alguien ya las había encontrado. Quizás antes hubo muchas señales de lucha y alguien se había ocupado de limpiar la escena del crimen.

Volvió a la entrada principal, y estaba a punto de salir cuando vio un estante vacío de libros. Steve Brown mostraba una gran prudencia a la hora de almacenar sus artículos más valiosos. Quizá sus libros y su ordenador no fueran las únicas cosas que decidió ocultar.

Pasó los dedos por la parte superior de la librería y encontró una llave bastante desgastada. La probó en la puerta delantera, y vio que encajaba perfectamente en la cerradura. Brown había guardado dentro la llave de repuesto mientras se iba, en lugar de dejarla fuera, donde podía encontrarla algún ladrón. Un hábil movimiento de alguien que conocía todos los trucos, porque había escrito muchas series de policías.

Cole salió. Cerró con la llave y luego la escondió debajo de la verja. Abrió la cancela delantera, se aseguró de que nadie miraba, se quitó los guantes de látex y salió. Cogió aire una sola vez, profundamente, lo soltó y dejó que la tensión se fuera con él. Lo había mirado todo con una mirada nueva, y ahora era diferente, y quizá lo que temía Pike fuese verdad.

Cruzó el callejón para tener una visión mejor de la casa de Smith y miró a ambos extremos del callejón. Estaba lleno de casas pegadas unas con otras, y solo había una vía para que entraran o salieran los coches. Una persona podía entrar o salir por los puentes para peatones, pero para los coches solo había una manera. Era un lugar pésimo para cometer algún delito, pues ese tipo de lugares eran estupendos para los testigos.

Un hombre flaco, con el pelo negro y desgreñado, se asomó a la ventana superior de la casa Palmer. Debía de ser Jared. Se quedó mirando a Cole con el ceño fruncido y este le devolvió la mirada, pensando que si había un Jared quizás hubiese más.

Cole había decidido llamar a todas las puertas cuando un sedán Crown Victoria enfiló el callejón, dirigiéndose hacia él. Un hombre lo conducía y una mujer iba en el asiento del pasajero. Supo que ambos eran policías, y se preguntó si el hombre sería Button.

El enorme sedán de Detroit era tan ancho que llenaba toda la calle. Cole se hizo a un lado para dejarles pasar y les dirigió un alegre saludo con la mano.

—Bonito día, ¿verdad? Un tiempo estupendo para pasear.

El hombre lo miró como si fuese basura.

131

—Fantástico si uno no tiene que trabajar para vivir.

La mujer parecía violenta.

Cole siguió su camino. Tras él, el Crown Vic se detuvo frente a la casa de los Palmer y de él se bajaron el hombre y la mujer.

Fue andando por el centro de la calle, buscando casas que tuvieran grandes ventanas o terrazas con una vista clara de la calle, pero encontró algo mejor: una casa moderna, color verde oscuro; estaba justo enfrente, a dos puertas de distancia de la de los Smith. Tenía unas líneas elegantes, el tejado plano y una puerta grande de acero. Había una cámara de seguridad que parecía una burbuja negra sujeta a un muro junto a la puerta.

Cole comprobó lo que estaban haciendo los policías y vio que la puerta delantera de los Palmer estaba ahora abierta. Jared y su madre estaban en la calle con los policías.

Se acercó más aún a la cámara. Como estaba enfocada hacia la puerta, probablemente no tenía una visión completa de la calle, pero quizá bastase para que se viera un poco un coche que pasaba.

132

Notó ese sutil cosquilleo eléctrico que siempre venía cuando sabía que estaba de caza. Muchos sistemas de seguridad estaban conectados a una grabadora de vídeo; algunos solo grababan cuando se apretaba el timbre, pero otros lo hacían continuamente en un disco reutilizable. La cámara quizá no le diera nada, pero también podía dárselo todo.

Echó una última mirada hacia la casa de los Palmer. La puerta estaba cerrada, y ahora los dos policías estaban dentro, hablando con Jared.

Dio la vuelta a la esquina y entonces, como Joe Pike, echó a correr.

18

La oscuridad se abatió sobre Joe Pike como una ominosa nube negra. No sabía dónde estaba, ni cuándo, ni cómo se había dejado atrapar en aquella cosa horrible. Solo sabía que la sombra gigante lo sofocaba con una oscuridad de la que no podía escapar. La sombra cayó sobre él con la delicada suavidad de la niebla, pero al mismo tiempo le aplastó con el espantoso peso del cemento, un pozo de negrura creciente que llenaría pronto su boca, su nariz, sus oídos. Pike luchó desesperadamente por librarse, pero no podía mover brazos ni piernas. Se esforzó por librarse gruñendo, siseando, escupiendo, y las lágrimas salieron volando mientras movía la cabeza de lado a lado. No sabía qué era aquello, aquella sombra. No comprendía cómo podía sujetarle, por qué no podía escapar. Salía de la oscuridad, como siempre, y un día le mataría... como temía que le hubiese matado antes

*P*ike se despertó con las sábanas húmedas enrolladas en torno a las piernas. Estaba alerta y despierto, pero no tenía recuerdo alguno de su pesadilla. Nunca las recordaba. A veces, en los primeros momentos de conciencia, veía oscuras formas, una sombra sobre otra, pero nada más. Nada nuevo; no perdía el tiempo preocupándose por aquellas cosas. Había sufrido terrores nocturnos desde que era niño.

Miró su reloj. Las manecillas luminosas le dijeron que eran las 3.17. Cole le había relevado hacía noventa minutos, y ahora se encontraría sentado ante la casa de Carla Fuentes, esperando a Mendoza. Pike se había ido a casa a descansar un poco, pero su sueño había terminado por aquella noche.

Se deshizo de las sábanas y saltó de la cama. Vio su móvil en la mesita de noche y pensó en Dru. Comprobó el teléfono, pero no había mensajes ni llamadas perdidas.

Se puso unos pantalones cortos de atletismo color azul claro y la misma sudadera del día anterior, y se llevó los zapatos escaleras abajo, antes de ponérselos. No encendió la luz. No lo necesitaba, veía bastante bien en la oscuridad.

Abajo se bebió media botella de agua, se puso las zapatillas y se ató una riñonera de nailon. En ella llevaba el móvil, las llaves, el carné de conducir y una pistola de bolsillo Beretta del calibre 25.

Desactivó la alarma, la programó para que se volviera a conectar al cabo de sesenta segundos y salió.

Se quedó muy quieto, mirando a su alrededor, y luego se estiró y empezó a correr. Pike casi siempre corría por las mismas cuatro o cinco rutas, dirigiéndose hacia arriba, a Ocean Boulevard, a través de Santa Mónica, a los cañones, o en torno a las colinas Baldwin, o La Cienaga, más allá de los pozos de petróleo. Aquella noche corrió hacia el oeste, hacia Washington Boulevard, recto hacia el mar, luego hacia el norte hasta la punta de los canales de Venice y por un puente peatonal. Se detuvo en la parte superior del puente para mirar hacia abajo, al canal.

Un perro ladró hacia el interior, en algún lugar de Ghost Town, y Pike oyó vehículos en el cercano Pacific Boulevard, pero allí las casas dormían. El olor del mar era fuerte. El canal más grande, Grand Canal, corría hacia el océano a través de Marina del Rey, y llenaba de vida los cinco cauces interiores. En las aguas poco hondas nadaban los pececillos, y las plantas acuáticas crecían en ondeantes matojos.

Pike había elegido aquel puente porque desde allí se veía la casa de Dru. Muchas de las casas tenían luces exteriores de seguridad que ahora se reflejaban en el agua, pero la distancia y la niebla de la costa hacía que resultase difícil distinguir la de ella. Vio primero la de Lily Palmer, blanca y moderna, y luego la roja de secuoya de Dru, más lejos. Como muchas de las otras viviendas, estaba salpicada por las luces de los focos exteriores, probablemente accionados por un temporizador. Luego observó que en el dormitorio del piso de arriba había luz. Buscó sombras en ella, pero nada se movía.

Pike bajó del puente y se dirigió por estrechos callejones hacia la casa de Dru. Nada se movía, no había nadie, no ladraba ningún perro. «Esta gente debería tener perro...», pensó.

Las farolas y luces de seguridad ardían con intensidad en aquella estrecha calle, dando a la neblina un resplandor de un azul amoratado. Pike se detuvo junto a la casa de Dru. Unas pocas ventanas estaban iluminadas débilmente de color ocre en las casas que le rodeaban, pero la mayoría permanecían oscuras y todo estaba muy tranquilo. Nadie estaba despierto. Hasta la ventana de Jared estaba a oscuras.

Pike sacó su móvil de la riñonera y apretó el botón de marcado rápido para llamar a Elvis Cole. Este respondió al segundo timbrazo, en voz baja pero completamente alerta.

—¿Qué ocurre?

135

Pike habló susurrando.

—¿Te dejaste una luz encendida en el dormitorio de arriba de casa de Dru?

—¿Una luz?

—Estoy junto a la casa. Hay luz en el dormitorio de arriba.

—Estuve allí, pero no recuerdo encender la luz, ni tampoco haberla apagado. No sé.

—Mmm.

—¿Crees que hay alguien dentro?

—Me choca lo de la luz…

—¿Vas a entrar?

—Sí.

—La llave de repuesto que encontré está detrás de la verja, junto al poste de la entrada. No el que está cerca de la casa, sino el otro.

—Y tú, ¿qué tal?

—Luces apagadas, se acabó lo que se daba. La chica está en coma.

—Vale.

—Oye, llámame cuando te vayas de allí, ¿de acuerdo? Si no llamas tendré que ir a salvarte, y perderé a Mendoza.

Pike guardó el teléfono. Aspiró con fuerza el aire de la calle y el aroma del mar, escuchando, pero solo se oía el ruido ambiental normal. Entró en las sombras junto a la cancela, y luego saltó por encima y se dejó caer silenciosamente en el jardín. Hizo una pausa para escuchar y luego buscó la llave.

Le costó casi un minuto meterla en la cerradura, otro minuto dar la vuelta al picaporte y dos minutos enteros abrir la puerta. El vestíbulo estaba oscuro, solo lo iluminaba un leve resplandor que escapaba de arriba. Pike aguzó el oído para captar cualquier sonido de la casa, pero no oyó nada. Solo entonces cerró la puerta.

Se desplazó por la casa sin encender las luces, evitando las ventanas también. Las grandes dejaban entrar la luz suficiente para ver que no se había movido nada. Todo estaba tal y como él lo recordaba y como lo había descrito Cole.

Llegó a la habitación de arriba, pero no entró. Estaba encendida la lamparita de la mesilla de noche. Pike rememoró su rápido viaje por la casa aquella misma mañana, pero no

136

recordaba la lamparita. Era pequeña. Durante el día, su luz podría haber quedado ahogada por el sol, cosa que explicaría por qué ni él ni Cole la recordaban. Pero a Pike no le gustaba no saber las cosas, y la lámpara era un enigma.

Retrocedió, salió, cerró la puerta y dejó la llave junto a la verja. Se quedó de pie en el jardín un momento más, escuchando, y luego se deslizó entre las sombras a lo largo de la casa de Dru, hasta llegar al borde del canal.

Se preguntó dónde estarían Dru y Wilson, si estarían bien. Quería creer que sí, pero sabía que era improbable. Oyó de nuevo un ladrido distante y se dijo si no sería un león marino al otro lado de las esclusas.

Examinó las casas que había al otro lado del canal y el puente más lejano, donde había estado un rato antes. Sintió como si unos pies hechos de agujas subieran por su espalda junto con las palabras de la tienda de Wilson: «Estoy aquí».

Retrocedió entre las sombras. Acalló su aliento y silenció su cuerpo, dispuesto a escuchar. Buscó reflejos y movimientos en la otra orilla. El agua ondeaba. Las luces rebotaban en su superficie de obsidiana. Pike se preguntó si los predadores nadarían hasta allí, tan hacia el interior. Se preguntó si se esconderían bajo la superficie.

137

Daniel

*D*aniel lo vio cruzar el puente, un hombre alto que aparecía de repente en medio de la noche, con las gafas de sol bien colocadas ante los ojos. «A esta gente de Los Ángeles, ¿qué coño les pasa? Probablemente lleve crema de protección solar, también.»

Cleo susurró:

—Chist. Te oirá pensar.

Tobey dijo:

—Chist. Oirá tu cerebro.

Daniel dijo:

—Por favor, callaos. Disfrutad del agua. ¿No está buena el agua?

—Fría.

—Fría.

Daniel estaba sumergido hasta la nariz en el agua poco honda, escondido bajo un muelle de madera al otro lado del canal. Daniel, Cleo y Tobey, vigilando.

El tipo alto se fue del puente, susurró en la calle, pasó a través de una columna de luz azul, con los músculos duros. «¿Qué es eso que lleva en los brazos? Guiña los ojos. Concéntrate. Mira. Esas flechas grandes y rojas que lleva en los brazos, brillando como ascuas a la luz de un azul amoratado.» Daniel pensó que eran muy chulas.

—Te oirá.

—Chist. Te oirá, oirá, oirá.

El eco murió en el silencio mientras el tío alto desaparecía. Cuando el hombre se fue, Daniel fue avanzando por el

138

fondo fangoso, desplazándose hacia aguas más profundas mientras arrastraba con él su carga, tan despacio que el agua ni siquiera se movía, disfrutando del beso de los peces diminutos en su piel. Dirigiéndose hacia el puente.

Al cabo de un rato se deslizó por debajo del arco, luego giró hacia la casa, manteniendo su carga bien cerca mientras flotaba en las sombras. Llevaba desde el mediodía observando la casa, y su vigilancia había tenido éxito en dos ocasiones. Otros parecían vigilar la casa también, y ahora sabía que le buscaban a él. Se tomó eso como una excelente señal, y prueba de que estaba cerca.

—¿Lo notáis, chicos? Ya estamos cerca. Tan cerca que lo puedo tocar.

—Tócalo, tócalo.

—Tan cerca que casi lo puedo saborear, saborear.

—Aspira y huele, huele.

—Abre la boca y come, come.

Daniel susurró con ligereza:

—Por favor callaos.

—Callaos.

—Os.

Al final se callaron, y Daniel quedó muy complacido. Cómo le cansaban a veces esos dos.

Daniel osciló en la oscuridad, esperando sin tener realmente la sensación de que el tiempo pasaba, cuando un parpadeo negro se movió al final de la valla, captando su atención. Otro parpadeo, y lo negro se convirtió en sombra al borde del agua. Un destello de luz relampagueó encima de la sombra, brilló una vez más, y luego el brillo y la sombra desaparecieron. Daniel pensó en todo aquello y decidió que el brillo era la luz de una casa al otro lado del canal que se reflejaba en las gafas del tío alto. Tenía que ser aquello. El tío alto se había ido a su casa.

Daniel esperó en la sombra a que reapareciera, preguntándose quién sería aquel hombre y por qué estaría allí. Y acabó por sonreír, porque la verdad era siempre la misma: estaba allí por el mismo motivo que todos los demás. Valdría la pena hacer una llamada a sus amigos, cosa que haría a la mañana siguiente.

Daniel esperó otros veinte minutos más solo para asegurarse, pero la sombra y su brillo no volvieron. Como todos los buenos cazadores, tenía paciencia, pero al cabo de un rato decidió que ya era seguro moverse.

Susurró, con la suavidad de un beso:

—Encantado de conocerte.

Llevaba más de una hora sujetando el cuerpo, pero entonces lo soltó. El cuerpo se dio la vuelta, una mano se levantó como para decirle adiós y luego se hundió bajo la negra superficie.

Daniel esperó, vigilante, y se preguntó quién vendría a continuación.

TERCERA PARTE

El señor de la guerra y el trueno

21

$\mathcal{A}$ las siete y cuatro minutos de la mañana siguiente, Pike recibió la llamada que lo cambió todo. Un minuto antes, a las siete y tres, estaba mirando la casa de Carla Fuentes desde un arbusto de camelias en el jardín trasero, y el cielo lechoso prometía un día de niebla aun entre las hojas.

Había relevado a Cole a las cuatro de la mañana, aparcando a una manzana y media de distancia de la casa de Carla, en un profundo charco de sombras bajo un sicomoro. Se agachó tras el volante, a salvo mientras todo el barrio dormía todavía, pero sabía que la gente se empezaría a mover en cuanto amaneciese. Un hombre sentado en un vehículo aparcado llamaría rápidamente la atención, de modo que Pike encontró un nuevo sitio detrás del arbusto de camelias antes de que la parte oriental del cielo se iluminase. No veía la zona delantera de la casa, pero sí tenía una visión perfecta de la puerta de atrás, de la mayor parte del camino de entrada y del interior de la cocina, a través de las ventanas.

Se encendió una luz en el dormitorio principal a las seis y diez. Unos minutos más tarde se encendió también la de la cocina, y Carla Fuentes entró en ella. Estaba sola y llevaba una camiseta blanca. Pasó varios minutos ante el mostrador haciendo algo que Pike no pudo ver, y luego volvió al dormitorio. Pike supuso que había preparado una cafetera. Esto se confirmó varios minutos más tarde cuando ella volvió a la cocina, se sirvió una taza y se la llevó al salón. Pike pensó que probablemente estaba viendo la tele.

La vio dos veces más antes de las siete y tres minutos.

Durante ese rato salió el sol, los pinzones empezaron a cantar entre los arbustos y un sinsonte ocupó un lugar ruidoso encima del garaje. Pike pensó qué haría si Carla se iba de casa o si aparecía Mendoza, pero a las siete y tres no había hecho todavía ningún movimiento para salir y Mendoza no había llegado aún.

A las siete y cuatro minutos Pike recibió la llamada.

Su teléfono emitió un suave zumbido al vibrar. Lo llevaba en el muslo, donde lo había colocado para poder cogerlo haciendo el mínimo de movimientos, envuelto en una tela fina para ahogar el sonido. Le sorprendió que la identificación de llamada indicase CIUDAD DE LOS ÁNGELES. Eso significaba que la llamada se había originado en un teléfono propiedad del municipio. Pike no sabía si contestar o no, pero al final decidió coger la llamada.

Pike.

—Contestas rápido para ser tan temprano.

Era Button, que parecía tranquilo y cómplice.

—¿Has comprobado a Mendoza?

—Sí. Creo que tenías razón en lo que decías. ¿Le has encontrado?

—No.

—Puedo ayudarte en eso. Tengo aquí algo que quiero que veas. Ven a echar un vistazo.

La voz de Button sonaba tan inexpresiva que Pike sabía que no era una petición amistosa, y algo en la naturaleza de la elección de palabras y la hora temprana de la llamada le azotó como un viento del desierto.

—¿Se trata de Wilson y Dru?

—Si quieres te mando un coche.

—¿Los has encontrado?

—Estoy en Washington Boulevard, donde cruza el canal. No tiene pérdida.

—Dime si son ellos, Button.

Button colgó sin responder y el viento del desierto sopló en el pecho de Pike como el acero helado. Salió del arbusto, se deslizó por encima de la verja al jardín vecino y luego corrió hacia su Jeep. Estaba a menos de diez minutos de la posición de Button, y fue informando a Cole mientras conducía.

—¿Quieres que vuelva a lo de Mendoza? —preguntó Cole.

—No, espera. Si es Wilson o Dru, la policía aparecerá en su casa en cuanto despejen la escena del crimen. Si hay algo más en su calle, tenemos que encontrarlo ahora mismo.

—Ya, Joe, pero, escucha... —La voz de Cole se suavizó—. No pierdas la esperanza, ¿vale?

Pike interrumpió la llamada en silencio. Momentos después quedaba atrapado en un atasco, a tres manzanas del canal, y supo que se dirigía hacia la escena de un crimen importante. Un oficial uniformado desviaba el tráfico hacia el oeste obligando a todo el mundo a girar.

Cuando Pike se identificó, el policía le dirigió hacia un aparcamiento detrás de un restaurante tailandés. Varios coches de policía se encontraban a ambos lados del canal, y dos más bloqueaban el puente de Washington Boulevard. Un furgón del médico forense estaba en el extremo más alejado del canal. Mientras Pike aparcaba, vio que el nivel del agua estaba bajo. Los canales de Venice no fluían libremente hacia el mar: una o dos veces a la semana se abrían unas esclusas construidas en el puente, permitiendo que los canales se drenasen con la marea baja y se volviesen a llenar de agua limpia cuando subía la marea. Ahora era baja y el agua había retrocedido, revelando un muro bajo de losas de cemento gris que cimentaban las orillas y la suave pendiente del fondo.

Mientras aparcaba, Pike vio a Futardo. Estaba con un pequeño grupo de detectives y policías de uniforme al borde del canal, mirando algo en el agua. Button se había quedado en el otro extremo del puente con Straw. El hombre de la camisa naranja se encontraba con ellos, pero ahora iba de azul. Fue el primero que vio a Pike, luego Button y Straw se volvieron también. Button atravesó el puente hacia Futardo e hizo señas a Pike de que se uniera a ellos.

Pike notó que el corazón se le aceleraba al acercarse. Dos hombres con botas de pescador andaban por el agua, mientras otros dos tipos con botas hasta las rodillas extendían una lámina de plástico azul en el fondo fangoso. Los cuatro llevaban largos guantes de goma que les llegaban hasta los hombros. Una camilla esperaba solemne, cerca.

El rostro de Button carecía de expresión cuando Pike se

acercó, pero una profunda arruga surcaba la frente de Futardo. Pike se preguntó qué estaría pensando. Button ya se había quitado la chaqueta, anticipándose al calor que venía, y llevaba las manos en los bolsillos. No las sacó para saludarle. Por el contrario, hizo un gesto hacia el canal.

—Ahí lo tienes.

Pike miró y en aquel momento se dio cuenta de que todas sus suposiciones eran erróneas.

22

El cuerpo de Reuben Mendoza estaba de lado en la ligera depresión llena de agua que quedaba en el canal. El brazo enyesado se extendía hacia la orilla, como si hubiese intentado salir por sí mismo al morir, pero Pike sabía que no era el caso. Mendoza tenía el cuello cortado tan profundamente que se veía el hueso, y la palidez de un gris azulado de su carne indicaba que se había desangrado mucho antes de acabar empujado hacia la orilla. Llevaba unos pantalones holgados cortos de color caqui, una camisa de cuadros de manga larga tan grande que le envolvía como un chal y unos Keds, la misma ropa que había descrito Jared. Carla Fuentes podría conservar su casa.

Button chasqueó la lengua.

—A mí me parece que tu chico, Mendoza, no ha secuestrado a nadie.

Futardo se acercó más aún, contemplándole como los polis miran a un sospechoso.

—¿Reconoce usted a este hombre?

Pike asintió.

—¿Cuándo lo vio por última vez?

Pike miró a Futardo y vio que Button sonreía.

—Aquí la detective Futardo quiere abrir un expediente de homicidio. Cree que tú estás implicado.

Futardo se puso muy roja y sus delgados labios se pusieron más tirantes mientras Button seguía, aleccionándola.

—Este no es su estilo. Pike, aquí presente, le habría metido cuatro tiros a quemarropa, o le habría dado una paliza de

147

muerte, pero no lo habría hecho así. Eh, Eddie... —Un hombre con botas de pescador levantó la vista—. Dale la vuelta y ábrele la camisa, por favor. Queremos ver la herida.

La mayor parte del cuerpo seguía aún en el agua. Le dieron la vuelta de cara a Button, y luego retiraron la camisa de cuadros. Estaba desabrochada, tal y como había descrito Jared, pero la camiseta que llevaba debajo estaba desgarrada desde la parte superior izquierda del pecho hasta abajo, hasta los pantalones. Limpias de sangre por la inmersión en el canal, las costillas, como si fueran las estacas de una valla, sobresalían del pecho, y los órganos internos colgaban como globos azules del abdomen.

—Lo han destripado. Primero lo han matado cortándole el cuello, y luego lo han destripado, pensando que el cuerpo se hundiría.

Pike vio al equipo maniobrar el cadáver, y luego levantó la vista hacia el canal. Grand Canal era el más largo de los seis, dejando que los cinco cauces más pequeños respirasen hacia el mar a través de las esclusas construidas en el puente. Pike se preguntó cuánto le habría costado al cuerpo ir bajando desde los canales superiores, a medida que el agua se drenaba.

—¿Cuánto tiempo lleva en el agua?

—Gracias, Eddie. Ya está bien.

El equipo de recuperación volvió a su trabajo mientras Button respondía la pregunta de Pike.

—Como el agua está fría, el lapso es muy amplio: más de seis horas y menos de veinticuatro. Ya lo afinarán un poco más cuando lo pongan en la mesa, pero por ahora es lo mejor que nos ha podido decir el forense en la investigación preliminar.

—Podría haber ocurrido más tarde. Se los llevó primero, y luego alguien lo mató.

—Lo que tú digas, Pike. Y quizás una cosa no tenga nada que ver con la otra; yo no pondría la mano en el fuego.

—¿Habéis encontrado a Gomer?

—¿Crees que le ha matado Gomer?

—¿Lo ha identificado Jared como el hombre que iba con Mendoza?

—No le vio muy bien, pero yo dudo de que fuese Gomer. Ese es demasiado delgado para hacer algo así. Para matar a alguien como han matado a este hombre hay que ser un peso pesado.

Pike supuso que Button ya tenía varios candidatos para el asesinato, y él probablemente estaba en un lugar destacado en la lista, a pesar del comentario que Button le había hecho a Futardo.

Esta se volvió a acercar a él.

—Los detectives de homicidios quieren hablar con usted. ¿Quiere contestar algunas preguntas, o prefiere llamar a su abogado?

—Ahora me va bien.

Button sonrió otra vez.

—Si yo estuviera en tu lugar buscaría un abogado.

—No, estoy bien.

Pike no iba a decirles nada que Button no supiese ya. Si les contaba algo más, cambiarían su situación de persona implicada a sospechoso.

Button miró a Futardo.

—Diles que pueden hablar con él cuando acabe yo. Ve con ellos para que Pike y yo podamos charlar un momento. —La vio alejarse y luego se dirigió a Pike—. Déjame que te pregunte una cosa, entre tú y yo, y no me importa lo que te digan los de homicidios: ¿Sabes dónde están Smith y su sobrina?

—No.

—¿Crees que fue Smith quien hizo esto?

A Pike se le había ocurrido, pero dudó antes de responder.

—Para abrir las costillas de esa manera tienes que ser fuerte y saber muy bien lo que estás haciendo. No creo que tenga ni la habilidad ni la fuerza necesarias.

Button gruñó.

—A lo mejor no, pero los cocineros saben usar muy bien los cuchillos. Mendoza y Gomer fueron a amenazar al hombre como lo hicieron en su tienda, solo que esta vez se llevaron una buena sorpresa…

—Aun así, son dos contra uno.

—Gomer es de los que salen corriendo. Ya salió huyendo

149

cuando apareciste tú, y esta vez ha salido por patas al ver aparecer el cuchillo. Y entonces la cosa ha quedado uno a uno, con la chica ayudando a su tío. Una vez abatido, les entra el pánico y deciden librarse del cuerpo. Entonces Smith me llama diciendo no sé qué chorrada de Oregón, para ganar tiempo y poder huir.

—No tenían que huir. Si ocurrió así, le habrían matado en defensa propia.

Button gruñó otra vez.

—La gente se vuelve loca cuando mata a alguien, Pike. Por eso se dice que «se les sube la sangre a la cabeza».

Pike se preguntó por qué Button le estaría contando su teoría, como si estuvieran juntos en aquello, hasta que se dio cuenta de cuál era su auténtico objetivo: estaba intentando averiguar si Pike estaba implicado en el crimen o en el posterior encubrimiento con Wilson y Dru.

Pike se encogió de hombros, dejando que Button pensara lo que quisiera, y entonces reapareció Futardo. Parecía alterada.

150

—Jefe, tiene que ver esto. Es importante.

Button le dijo que no se fuera y fue a ver lo que quería la detective.

Los hombres de las botas de pescador tenían ya colocado el cuerpo en la lámina de plástico. Trabajando al unísono, levantaron el cadáver, pero no tenían buen equilibrio en el barro. Uno de los hombres resbaló, y el cuerpo cayó al suelo.

Pike sacó su teléfono. Le iba a hacer saber a Cole lo que estaba ocurriendo cuando vio que Straw se acercaba. El hombre de azul seguía en el puente.

Straw no se apresuró. Iba caminando despacio, como un hombre que piensa en lo que va a decir. Cuando llegó le hizo una seña a Pike.

—Ayer a esta misma hora se me puso dura pensando en ti. Hoy, no tanto.

Straw hizo una pausa. Pike sabía que ahora se suponía que debía preguntarle a Straw por qué no se le ponía dura ya, pero no lo preguntó. No le importaba. Finalmente, Straw señaló hacia la gente de homicidios. Los detectives hablaban como si estuvieran muy emocionados por algo, y dos de ellos

estaban al teléfono. Uno fue trotando hasta un coche patrulla que esperaba, y saltó al asiento de atrás cuando ya se
ponía en marcha.

—Nuestros amigos los detectives están divididos, la
mitad cree que lo hiciste tú y la otra mitad que fue Smith.
Incluso han hecho apuestas.

—¿Y qué apuestas tú?

—Yo creo que ni Smith ni tú tenéis nada que ver con
esto. Sobre las cabezas de la tienda de Smith, tampoco creo
que esos pandilleros tengan nada que ver. Aquí está pasando
algo más complicado.

Pike observó a Straw un momento y pensó que probablemente tenía razón. La operación de extorsión de Straw había
concluido, o sea que ahora estaba en busca de algo que la sus-
tituyera.

—¿Como qué?

—Ni idea.

—¿No estaban tus chicos vigilando la tienda?

Straw mostró su primera señal de irritación.

—Nosotros estábamos vigilando toda la calle, Pike.
Estábamos en la parte delantera de la tienda. Quienquiera
que armase ese follón entró por la parte de atrás y salió sin
ser visto. Pero ya lo sabes: estabas allí a la mañana siguiente.

—Qué lástima que no vieseis nada que nos pueda ayudar.

Straw apretó la mandíbula y examinó el terreno durante
unos segundos antes de levantar la vista.

—¿Tienes alguna idea de dónde está esa gente?

Pike señaló hacia el cuerpo de Mendoza.

—Pensaba que él los tenía.

—Si era así, entonces ahora los tiene otra persona.

—¿Quién?

—Quien sea. Veo a Smith y su sobrina metidos en algo
infinitamente peor que una extorsión. —Tendió una tarjeta a
Pike—. Si te enteras de algo o necesitas ayuda, házmelo
saber. Me gustaría mucho encontrar a esa gente antes de que
quien le hizo eso a Mendoza los encuentre.

Button y Futardo volvieron de su grupo. Pike pensó que
venían para llevarle con los polis de homicidios, pero Button
tenía noticias que le hicieron sonreír.

151

—Alberto Gomer ya no está desaparecido. Un vagabundo le encontró hace una hora en un coche aparcado en el extremo norte del canal con el cuello cortado de oreja a oreja. Con eso tu hombre, Smith, lleva ya dos en su cuenta.

Futardo hizo un gesto hacia los detectives de homicidios.

—Les gustaría hablar con usted ahora. ¿Está preparado?

23

Elvis Cole

Cuando Pike llamó a Cole aquella mañana para hablarle de la llamada de Button, Cole notó la tensión en la voz de su amigo. Pike era un hombre que no dejaba entrever nada, y que proyectaba un desprendimiento estilo zen que Elvis a veces encontraba divertido, y también admiraba. A menudo se preguntaba cuánto le costaba semejante calma a su amigo, y si Pike no tenía otra opción que pagar ese precio.

153

Cole había saltado de la cama y estaba fuera de casa dieciséis minutos después de que Pike colgase. ¿Quién necesita desodorante cuando eres el «mejor detective del mundo»? ¿Quién necesita cepillarse los dientes cuando estás luchando por exonerar de toda culpa a un amigo?

El tráfico matutino que bajaba desde el cañón hacia el oeste por Hollywood era asqueroso. Cole iba pegado a los parachoques de camiones de la basura, autobuses y gente que se dirigía al trabajo, todos ellos embotellados en calles reventadas por proyectos de construcción y mantenimiento muy mal planeados.

Todavía estaba a tres kilómetros de la carretera cuando sonó su teléfono. Pensó que podía ser Pike, pero no reconoció el número.

—Elvis Cole.

—Soy Steve Brown, de Londres, me había llamado usted.

Brown hablaba con firmeza, como si estuviera acostumbrado a reunirse con la gente y a conseguir que se hicieran las cosas. Cole calculó rápidamente: las ocho horas de diferencia suponían que en Londres eran las cinco de la tarde.

—Gracias por llamarme, señor Brown. Intento localizar a

Wilson Smith y Dru Rayne. Esperaba que quizás usted supiera cómo contactar con ellos.

—¿Y por qué iba yo a saberlo?

Cole pensó que era una respuesta extraña, considerando que esa gente vivía en la casa de aquel hombre.

—Creo que están alojados en su casa, cuidándola.

—¿Y por qué cree usted semejante cosa?

Ahora Brown parecía suspicaz, cosa que quizá fuese normal tras recibir una llamada de un desconocido que se encontraba a diez mil kilómetros de distancia.

—Su vecina, Lily Palmer, me dijo que le cuidaban la casa y me sugirió que le llamase.

—Ah, bien. ¿Y de qué se trata?

Cole esperaba que Brown le preguntase cosas y decidió limitar sus respuestas.

—La tienda de Wilson ha sufrido algunos daños. Intento encontrarle para decirle lo que ha ocurrido, pero parece que él y Dru llevan unos cuantos días fuera. Esperaba que usted quizá supiera cómo localizarles.

—Ah… —Brown se quedó callado.

—¿Señor Brown?

—Déjeme que le haga una pregunta. ¿Está viviendo esa gente en mi casa, Dru y ese hombre?

Brown empezaba a parecer algo furioso y Cole no sabía adónde podía ir a parar aquella conversación.

—¿Están ahí sin su consentimiento?

—Le dije a Dru que podía alojarse en la casa. Eso es todo. No conozco a ningún Wilson Smith. Nunca he oído hablar de él, y me cabrea bastante que haya metido a un tío en mi casa.

—Es su tío.

—Me importa una mierda si es su hermano gemelo, aunque tengo mis dudas. No era ese el trato. Yo no quería que entrase nadie más en la casa y ella me dijo que así sería. Y por eso se la dejé.

Cole notó un ligero escalofrío, y la conversación le fue gustando cada vez menos. Creía que era Smith el que se alojaba en la casa y que había invitado a Dru a vivir con él cuando ella llegó a Los Ángeles para ayudarle con su trabajo. Ahora todo eso se le venía abajo.

—Dru trabaja para él. El señor Wilson tiene un restaurante junto al paseo marítimo.

—Quizá, pero ella no trabajaba para nadie cuando le di las llaves. Vivía de una pensión alimenticia. No me habló nunca de ningún tío y, desde luego, tampoco me dijo que ese hombre se iba a trasladar allí.

Cole se humedeció los labios, remiso a hacer la pregunta que tenía que hacerle a continuación.

—¿Por qué dejó que se instalara Dru?

—Me la estaba tirando, ¿por qué si no? Ella quería salir del vertedero donde vivía y yo me venía para acá, de manera que era un buen trato para los dos. Me parecía una buena chica. Me ahorró el rollo de buscar a alguien para que cuidara la casa.

Cole se sentía hundido.

—Bien. Muchas gracias por llamarme, de verdad.

—Espere. ¿Cuánto tiempo se va a quedar Dru?

—No lo sé.

—La llamé cuando recibí su mensaje, pero no me ha devuelto la llamada.

—No podemos localizarlos a ninguno de los dos.

—Pero ¿de qué estamos hablando? ¿De unos días? ¿Un par de semanas? ¿Ha abandonado la casa?

—No lo sé.

—Maldita sea, ¿me está diciendo que ahora mismo mi casa está vacía? ¿Es eso cierto? ¿Se ha ido y nadie me cuida la casa?

—Así es, señor. Ahora mismo no hay nadie.

—Qué hija de puta. Qué cabrona.

Brown colgó, lanzando tacos, y se oyó el pitido de la línea.

Cole siguió conduciendo, tan confuso que no veía nada, y se dio cuenta de que no había hecho una pregunta obvia. Abrió la lista de llamadas entrantes y volvió a llamar a Brown.

—Soy yo otra vez, lo siento. ¿Ha hablado con Dru desde que está fuera?

—Joder, claro que sí. La llamo cada dos semanas más o menos, para asegurarme de que todo va bien y de que la casa está a salvo.

—¿Y ella nunca le ha mencionado al señor Smith?

—Esta es la primera vez que oigo hablar de él, y no me gusta nada. Si ese tío lleva todo este tiempo viviendo allí y

155

ella no me lo ha dicho es que me ha mentido, y no me gusta nada la gente mentirosa. Si la encuentra, dígale que será mejor que me llame, y para ayer. Quiero que esa hija de puta salga de mi casa.

Cole acabó la llamada sintiéndose mucho peor que antes. La imagen que ahora tenía de Dru Rayne era muy distinta a la mujer que le había descrito Joe. Tenía muchas preguntas más, pero se esforzó por centrarse en el hecho de que ella estaba desaparecida. Tenía que sonsacar información a los vecinos de Wilson Smith antes de que la policía cerrase aquella mina.

Llegó a los canales unos minutos más tarde y una vez más entró en la calle. Mendoza y su compañero habían pasado por esas mismas viviendas al ir y venir de la casa de Smith, que fue cuando Jared los vio, y ahora Cole quería comprobar si alguien más les había visto, pero primero se dedicó a las casas que tenían cámaras de seguridad.

Casi por costumbre examinó la ventana de Jared mientras iba recorriendo la calle, pero el chico no estaba. Sorprendente.

El día anterior Cole observó tres casas con cámara. Nadie respondió en la primera casa, de modo que introdujo una tarjeta de visita bajo la puerta con una nota pidiendo que le llamasen. Una mujer de mediana edad contestó en la segunda casa, y preguntó si él estaba con los policías que hablaron con ella el día anterior. Eso le indicó a Cole que Button y su compañera habían hecho la ronda después de hablar con Jared. Cole le dijo que sí, que iba con ellos, y dejó caer el nombre de Button para remachar la mentira. Preguntó si Button había pedido sus grabaciones de seguridad, pero no había sido así, y tampoco habría importado que lo hubiese hecho, porque las cámaras que tenía ella mostraban imágenes a tiempo real; no estaban conectadas a ninguna grabadora. La primera casa tenía posibilidades, pero la segunda era un fracaso.

En la tercera Cole tuvo más suerte. El ama de llaves le dijo que no sabía gran cosa del sistema de seguridad, pero que creía que las cámaras sí grababan. Explicó que su patrón estaba en el trabajo, pero que seguramente estaría encantado de hablar con Cole, ya que mostró mucho interés cuando le contó que la policía la había interrogado el día anterior. Cole dejó otra tarjeta y reconsideró su plan.

Sabiendo que Button había hecho las rondas despúes de hablar con Jared, Cole decidió que no tenía sentido cubrir otra vez el mismo terreno. La lista de testigos disponibles se limitaba a Jared.

Volvió a casa de Smith y encontró a Jared otra vez en su ventana, con su pelo negro y desgreñado, sin camisa y con unos auriculares en los oídos. Le estaba mirando.

Cole hizo un gesto de saludo y Jared se lo devolvió. Le hizo señas a Jared de que bajase y el chico se apartó de la ventana. Se abrió la puerta de la casa y salió.

—Eh, tío, ¿qué tal? ¿Eres de la policía o vas con el tipo alto?

—Con el tipo alto.

—Es un tío legal. Me cae bien. Ya le conté lo que sabía de esos pandilleros que vi. A él y a la policía. Estuvieron aquí ayer.

Jared había tenido mucha actividad los últimos dos días. Estaba muy a gusto.

—No estoy aquí por los pandilleros. Esperaba que me pudieses decir cuánto tiempo llevaba viviendo Dru en la puerta de al lado.

157

—Tío, es que se me da muy mal eso del tiempo…

Cole esperó, dejando que el silencio obligara a Jared a buscar una respuesta. Finalmente el chico se encogió de hombros.

—Pues unos tres meses. Steve se volvió a Londres hace tres meses. Ese tío sí que tiene pasta. Siempre está en Europa.

—¿Y ella se vino a vivir aquí el día que él se fue?

—La cosa fue así: Steve la trajo aquí, se la presentó a mi madre, «esta es la persona que me guardará la casa»… Ese rollo.

—¿Y cuándo vino su tío?

Jared miró al otro lado de la calle y esbozó una tímida sonrisa. Cole se preguntó a qué vendría la duda y la sonrisita.

—Al día siguiente —respondió.

Jared volvió a mirar al otro lado de la calle y Cole tuvo la sensación de que quería contarle algo con tanta desesperación que ni siquiera podía mantener el contacto ocular.

—¿Qué pasa? —preguntó Elvis.

—Yo veo cosas. Dru tiene un buen cuerpo, y lo enseña mucho. Si estoy tanto en esa ventana es por algo…

—Dime por qué, Jared.

—No creo que el tío Wilson sea el tío Wilson. No actúan como si fueran parientes, no sé si captas lo que quiero decir.

Cole miró largo rato a Jared. Sentía frío por dentro, pero tenía la boca seca y notaba que el sol de la mañana le calentaba la piel. Un nudo de rabia iba formándose en su pecho, como un fuego al rojo.

—No digas chorradas. No me cuentes esas cosas si son imaginaciones tuyas.

—Tío, tengo una vista estupenda de su jardín. Veo sus ventanas, y no suelen cerrar las persianas. Los he visto follando. Creo que a ella le gusta que los mire.

El frío aumentó tanto que Cole se sintió entumecido. Miró la casa de Steve Brown y se preguntó quiénes serían aquellas personas, y si todo lo que le había contado la mujer a Pike serían mentiras.

Miró a Jared, pero no sabía qué decirle. Lo único que pudo hacer fue afirmar con la cabeza.

No intentó ocultar lo que iba a hacer a continuación. Jared quizá hubiese vuelto a su casa, pero Cole ni se dio cuenta porque no le importaba.

Encontró la llave en su sitio junto al poste de la puerta, la abrió y entró en la casa. Sabía lo que quería, y para qué.

Se puso los guantes de látex en cuanto entró en la cocina. Durante su búsqueda anterior había visto bolsas de papel de comestibles dobladas y metidas en el hueco entre el frigorífico y el mostrador. Sacó unas cuantas bolsas, abrió una y la puso sobre la encimera. Eligió tres vasitos de cristal de los platos que estaban en el fregadero, los puso en bolsas separadas y colocó estas cuidadosamente dentro de la que tenía abierta. Recogió dos latas de Coca-Cola Light vacías y una botella de agua del salón y las embolsó de la misma manera. Luego subió al dormitorio principal a buscar el archivador de metal que contenía los documentos de Wilson. Lo llevó todo abajo, a la cocina.

Cole se detuvo en las escaleras que bajaban hacia el dormitorio de invitados cuando ya salía. Allí había unas cuantas cosas de Dru, pero se preguntó si realmente ella habría usado aquella habitación o si sería algo de cara a la galería. En el tocador había una barra gastada de desodorante antitranspirante Dry Idea. Lo añadió a la bolsa, la cerró y cerró también la cancela al salir.

Volvió a su coche, pero no puso en marcha el motor. Llamó a un amigo llamado John Chen, criminalista en el departamento de investigación científica de la policía de Los Ángeles.

—¿John? Necesito comprobar algunas huellas. Y lo necesito rápido.

—Tío, estoy descargándome unas cosas en Hawaiian Gardens. Pasaré aquí toda la noche.

—Necesito esto, John. Es para Joe.

Chen dudó, y eso le indicó a Cole que iba a aceptar.

—Vale. Vale, claro.

—Te puedo enviar las muestras. ¿Dónde estás de Hawaiian Gardens?

—Uf, no, hermano, aquí hay demasiados testigos. Reúnete conmigo en el centro dentro de un ahora. O digamos una hora y diez. Junto a los tribunales.

Cole cerró el teléfono y se dirigió al centro de Los Ángeles.

159

24

Elvis Cole

*A*l ser empleado del departamento de policía de Los Ángeles, John Chen, como los oficiales jurados, tenía prohibido realizar trabajo no autorizado, usar los recursos de la ciudad para obtener provecho personal o ayudar a investigadores privados civiles fuera de las normas. Eran normas buenas y válidas para preservar la integridad de las pruebas policiales, establecer un código de conducta profesional y dificultar la corrupción de los empleados.

John Chen era un corrupto.

Paranoico con baja autoestima, Chen vivía para los titulares, y esa era normalmente su baza. A menudo Cole le daba información y le permitía hacer grandes avances en casos que de otro modo no habría conseguido jamás. Dichos avances conducían a un perfil mediático que pocos criminalistas poseían. Habían citado a Chen más de una docena de veces en el *Los Angeles Times*, le habían entrevistado varias cadenas de televisión locales y le habían contratado como asesor técnico en películas basadas en dos de sus casos. Chen, cuya obsesión en la vida giraba en torno a las mujeres y el dinero, en aquel momento conducía un Porsche Boxster. Las mujeres, hasta el momento, se le escapaban.

Cole fue por la autopista I-10 y recorrió los veinticuatro kilómetros que transcurrían por la cuenca de Los Ángeles. Se acercaba ya a la zona de Mid-City y estaba a menos de la mitad del camino cuando sonó su teléfono y vio que era Pike. Se había estado planteando qué contarle, pero ahora la llamada forzaba las cosas. Si Wilson y Dru estaban vivos todavía, no le diría nada hasta que supiera algo más.

—¿Eran ellos?

—Mendoza y Gomer. Están muertos.

Cole notó un sobresalto de sorpresa. Mendoza y Gomer eran los depredadores. No tenían que morir. Si los depredadores estaban muertos, ¿dónde estaban las víctimas?

—¿Qué hay de Wilson y Dru?

—Nada. Mendoza estaba en el canal junto a Washington. Gomer, en un coche por el extremo norte. Si la policía ha encontrado algo en el coche de Gomer no me lo han dicho.

Pike describió rápidamente cómo los habían matado, cosa que dejó a Cole aún más inquieto.

—¿Cuándo ha ocurrido?

—Ya te lo contaré más tarde. Me están interrogando.

—¿Eres sospechoso?

—No será problema. Están poniendo las bases.

—Hay un tercer elemento en juego, Joe: la persona que abrió la ventana de la cocina.

—Ya lo sé. Lo he estado pensando.

161

Pike colgó y Cole siguió conduciendo, dejando que el flujo del tráfico le llevara a unos pensamientos cada vez más tétricos.

Cuando el departamento de policía de Los Ángeles cambió su cuartel general del destartalado y medio derrrumbado Parker Center al nuevo edificio de administración policial, a dos manzanas de distancia, se olvidaron de llevarse con ellos a la División de Investigación Científica. Bueno, no fue exactamente así, pero a los criminalistas les gustaba hacer aquella broma. La realidad era que, hasta que se encontrase una ubicación más adecuada, la DIC seguiría siendo el último reducto anclado en el pasado del departamento de policía de Los Ángeles.

Cole no fue hasta la antigua ubicación del Parker Center. Esperó a Chen junto al edificio del tribunal criminal, a seis manzanas de a distancia; llegó temprano y tuvo que esperar veinte minutos más a que llegase John.

Chen se introdujo en el asiento del pasajero del coche de Cole tan rápido como si cayese del propio cielo. Llevaba unas gafas de sol enormes, una gorra de los Dodgers muy metida tapándole la cara y una cazadora con el cuello vuelto hacia arriba, aunque aquel día acabarían por rozar los treinta y dos grados. La cabeza, redonda como un pomelo, la llevaba pegada a los hombros, como una tortuga en su concha. Ocultándose.

—No creo que me haya visto nadie, pero mejor salimos. Puede que me hayan seguido.

La típica paranoia de Chen.

Cole salió y se unió al tráfico, decidido a que aquel paseo fuese breve. Las noticias de Mendoza y Gomer le habían dejado con una preocupación mucho mayor aún por Smith y Dru Rayne.

Cole buscó en el asiento de atrás las bolsas y las puso en el regazo de Chen. No había mucho espacio. Este era alto, delgado, y parecía una mantis religiosa doblada en el asiento del pasajero.

—Es frágil, o sea que ve con cuidado.

—¿Qué hay dentro?

162

—Vasos, un par de latas de refresco… Cosas así. También hay una caja de metal que te daré cuando salgas del coche.

Chen se quitó las gafas de sol y se puso las normales. Los cristales parecían cortados de culos de botella de Coca-Cola. Miró en el interior de las bolsas.

—Mierda, hay muchas cosas. Tengo un montón de casos, y tan atrasados que hasta el atraso está atrasado.

—Ya sé que es mucho, pero no te rompas demasiado la cabeza. Las huellas pueden pertenecer a dos individuos, un hombre y una mujer, que viven en la residencia. Las huellas de la mujer tienen que estar en la barra desodorante; las del hombre probablemente estén en el archivador. Haz primero el desodorante y luego el archivador. Si sacas algo en limpio, igual no tienes que hacer nada más.

Chen no parecía contento, de todos modos.

—No digo que no pueda hacerlo. Simplemente estaba pensando cómo arreglarlo. Tendré que meter estas cosas en el plan de vuelo, y eso puede costar algunos días.

La unidad de huellas latentes estaba dotada de personal las veinticuatro horas del día los siete días de la semana. La acumulación de huellas esperando para ser analizadas era tan grande que la unidad empleaba casi ochenta especialistas constantemente para aguantar la marea. Con tantos casos retrasados para ser analizados, se mantenía una lista de espera por orden de llegada para reservar el equipo que se necesitaba para aquel trabajo. Esa lista se llamaba «plan de vuelo».

—Es demasiado tiempo. Lo necesito ya —dijo Cole.

Chen lo miró con acritud, pero pensativo.

—¿Para Joe? —Cole asintió—. ¿Qué pasa?

—Espero que tú me lo puedas decir. Si esa gente está fichada, Joe necesita saber por qué. Y yo también tengo que saberlo.

Chen se agitó, intentando ponerse más cómodo, o quizá por el nerviosismo. Era tan alto que las rodillas le sobresalían por encima del salpicadero y su cabeza tocaba el techo. Miró de nuevo en la bolsa, y luego a Cole, con unos enormes ojos de búho.

—¿Sabes quién soy?

La pregunta le cogió por sorpresa, pero Cole tuvo la sensación de que Chen no hablaba de él, sino que hablaba para sí mismo. Cole movió la cabeza.

—Seguro que sí, tío. Mírame: soy el tío al que los abogados defensores presentan como el bicho raro y torpe para que los jurados se rían. Oigo a los polis hacer comentarios socarrones cuando aparezco en la escena del crimen. Cada vez que me miro en un espejo, sé por qué se ríen las chicas.

—John, no tienes que…

Chen levantó un dedo y lo acalló.

—Cuando os conocí a vosotros dos Joe me aterrorizaba. Representa todo lo que me da un miedo horrible. Cuando aparece, nadie tiene huevos de hacer un chistecito o reírse. Ahí está, un puto monstruo de la calle, pero, de todas las personas con las que me relaciono, él es quien me trata con más respeto. —Levantó la bolsa—. Así que encontraré la forma de hacer esto. Para. Voy a empezar ya.

—Te llevo hasta allí.

—No, prefiero ir andando. Así tengo tiempo para pensar.

Cole paró el coche y Chen salió con la bolsa.

163

—John.

—¿Qué?

—Coge la caja.

Chen cogió la bolsa que llevaba dentro el archivador.

—Si hablas con Joe, no menciones esto.

Chen miró a Cole mucho rato, y luego de repente se alejó.

25

Elvis Cole

Cuando Cole llegó a su despacho se puso de inmediato a trabajar. La noche antes había pedido a una amiga de homicidios de la comisaría de Hollywood unos documentos sobre Mendoza y Gomer. Los habría usado para identificar a socios conocidos y parientes, pero ya no eran necesarios. La llamó para cancelar la petición, pero ella ya tenía la información impresa y le habría molestado correr aquel riesgo para nada. Entonces extendió el contenido del archivador de Wilson Smith en el escritorio. Con Mendoza y Gomer desaparecidos, Cole se centró en Wilson y Dru.

165

Rápidamente vio que la mayoría de los documentos estaban relacionados con el negocio de Smith, y los expedientes individuales contenían facturas, recibos, garantías de aparatos y contratos de arrendamiento. Smith compraba marisco fresco a un proveedor de San Pedro, pan para los bocadillos a una panadería en Boyle Heights, y había firmado un acuerdo de alquiler de un año con Lodester Properties por el local que ahora albergaba su cocina. Cole comprobó todos los recibos y facturas buscando una dirección anterior, pero todo se había enviado a la tienda de Smith. Cole hizo una lista de nombres y números de los diversos membretes por si tenía que llamarles, y dejó a un lado el expediente.

A continuación abordó el expediente del dinero. Había dos carpetas, una para cheques y otra para ahorros, con ambas cuentas en la sucursal de Venice del Golden State Bank & Trust. Los extractos bancarios se remontaban a ocho meses, lo que mostraba que ambas cuentas se abrieron el mismo día. La cuenta de ahorros se abrió con un depósito de 9 600 dólares, 2 000 de los cuales se usaron para abrir la cuenta de cheques. Dos semanas después de abrir la cuenta de ahorros se depositaron 6 500 dólares más. El primer extracto fue enviado a Smith a un apartado de correos en Venice, pero los siete siguientes, incluyendo el más reciente, a Takeout Foods, en Wilson. Cole copió la dirección del apartado de correos y luego examinó los extractos. Depósitos, retiradas de fondos y actividad de cheques, todo parecía razonable, y la mayoría de las retiradas se habían hecho para pagar el alquiler, los aparatos y los suministros. Los cheques cancelados estaban en el expediente. Smith, obviamente, era un hombre que no creía en la banca online. Tampoco en las tarjetas de crédito.

El archivador metálico de Wilson Smith no contenía nada que tuviese una fecha anterior a las cuentas que se abrieron ocho meses antes, nada de naturaleza personal y nada que uniese a Wilson Smith con Luisiana o con ningún otro lugar. Era como si aquel hombre hubiese nacido hacía ocho meses, con un depósito de 9 600 dólares.

Nada en el archivador nombraba ni estaba relacionado de ninguna manera con Dru Rayne. Era como si ella no existiese.

Entre los gastos se encontraba una factura mensual de teléfono. Pike le había dado a Cole los números de móvil de Wilson y Dru, pero este número era distinto. Cole lo marcó y respondió un mensaje grabado informándole de que Takeout Foods de Wilson estaba cerrado actualmente, pero que abría durante el siguiente horario. La voz era de mujer, y Cole pensó que debía de ser Dru. Tenía una bonita voz.

Cole colgó y se quedó mirando al infinito. Se dijo a sí mismo que estaban cuidando una casa, es decir, un alojamiento temporal, de modo que la mayoría de sus posesiones probablemente estarían almacenadas o guardadas en el garaje de algún amigo, pero sabía que todo eso era falso ya mientras lo estaba pensando.

Todo lo referente a Dru Rayne y Wilson Smith era raro.

Se echó atrás y se quedó mirando las puertas-ventana. Estas se abrían a un balcón pequeño, y veinte kilómetros más allá, al mar. Se podía ver el agua si el día era claro, pero aquel día un muro de niebla oscurecía su visión. Se sentía deprimido, y se preguntó qué tal le iría a Pike con la policía. No le gustaba saber cosas de Dru Rayne que Pike no sabía. No le gustaba la expresión que vio en la cara de Pike cuando se echó a la espalda la culpa de los problemas que pudiera tener aquella mujer. Había visto aquella misma expresión en el espejo demasiadas veces.

Marcó el número de la tienda de bocadillos para oír la voz de ella. Agradable, amistosa, con un timbre medio y un ligero toque de acento sureño. Una voz familiar que le producía un dolor en el pecho. Cole amó en tiempos a una mujer de Luisiana. Se involucraron tanto que Lucy y su hijo de ocho años se fueron a vivir con él. Fue un riesgo que corrieron todos y que no funcionó, de modo que Lucy y su hijo se volvieron a Luisiana. Eso decía ella, no Cole. Él habría seguido.

Cuando Cole se dio cuenta de que estaba pensando más en Lucy Chenier que en Dru Rayne, miró la hora. En Luisiana iban dos horas por delante. En aquel momento Lucy estaría en el despacho o en el tribunal. Trabajaba como abogada en una prestigiosa firma de Baton Rouge, y a Cole se le ocurrió que quizá le pudiera ayudar. También se le ocurrió que sencillamente era una excusa para oír su voz.

Una voz profesional respondió cuando él llamó.

—Oficina de la señora Chenier.

—¿Sabes quién soy?

La voz profesional de Loretta Bean se derritió, llena de calidez y suavidad sureña. Era la secretaria de Lucy.

—Eres un perro. No llamas nunca, y echo de menos tus piropos.

—Estaba perdiendo la cabeza por ti, Loretta. Tuve que dejar de llamar para no ponerme en evidencia.

—Qué cosas más terribles dices; claro que te pones en evidencia, pero aun así a mí me encanta… ¿Quieres a la señora Chenier?

—De muchas más formas de las que tú te imaginas.

—¡Ay, bicho malo! Espera y te pongo con ella.

Puso a Cole en espera y se quedó escuchando aquella música enlatada: Harry Connick junior al piano. Estuvo tanto rato en espera que Harry dio paso a Branford Marsalis antes de que se pusiera ella.

—Eh, hola. Siento haberte hecho esperar tanto. Estaba con un cliente.

Al oír su voz el calor se extendió por todo el cuerpo de Cole, a pesar del pequeño pinchazo de incomodidad que sentía en aquellos tiempos cuando la llamaba. Intentaba no hacerlo tan a menudo como antes, pero más por ella que por él mismo. No quería agobiarla, y tampoco quería que se cohibiese cuando él la llamaba.

—No te preocupes. Facturo por horas.

Ella se rio.

—Entonces me alegro de ayudarte. Aquí en Rotolo, Fourrier, Day y Chenier queremos que ganes muchísimo dinero.

—¿Tienes unos minutos? Puedo llamarte más tarde, si no es buen momento.

Las bromas en la voz de ella quedaron reemplazadas al momento por un cálido tono de contralto que siempre le hacía sentir que ellos dos estaban solos en una remota cabaña de montaña.

—Claro, cariño. Espera…

Le dijo a Loretta que no le pasara a nadie y volvió a su conversación.

—¿Va todo bien?

—Busco el historial de una mujer llamada Dru Rayne, y de un hombre llamado Wilson Smith. Ambos dicen que proceden de Nueva Orleans.

—Uf. ¿Y por qué me llama la atención ese «dicen»?

—Joe está relacionado con esa mujer, y no estoy convencido de que ella haya sido sincera con él respecto a sus circunstancias o incluso su identidad.

—¿Cuando dices «relacionado» quieres decir como novio y novia…?

Cole describió cómo Pike salvó a Wilson Smith de la paliza, y después conoció a Dru Rayne. Se saltó lo de las bandas latinas, secuestros y cadáveres con cortes tan profundos que casi separaban la cabeza del cuerpo. La violencia con la que él tropezaba como parte de su trabajo fue lo que, en parte, lo apartó de Lucy.

Cuando acabó, ella se puso en plan abogada profesional.

—Bien; en primer lugar, ¿hay algún posible delito aquí? ¿Joe les ha dado dinero?

Cole dudó, dándose cuenta de que tenía que describir aspectos de la situación que había esperado evitar.

—No, no es nada de eso. Han desaparecido. Quizá tengan problemas, así que estamos intentando encontrarlos.

Lucy se quedó callada un momento y Cole esperó no tener que decirle que Pike estaba siendo interrogado por el asesinato de dos miembros de bandas de Venice.

—Cuando dices que han desaparecido, ¿te refieres a una desaparición voluntaria o forzada?

—Podría ser cualquiera de las dos cosas.

—Maldita sea, Elvis; deberías hablar con la policía, no conmigo.

—La policía está haciendo su trabajo y nosotros el nuestro.

—¿Por qué no me sorprende eso?

—Ahora lo que me preocupa es Joe. Está muy implicado, y yo solo intento asegurarme de que sea por el motivo correcto. También intento averiguar en qué tipo de problemas anda metida esa gente.

—Espera… Ya le llamaré yo. No me pases más llamadas, Loretta; ya he salido de mi despacho… Vale, cariño, ya estoy aquí otra vez. Dime qué puedo hacer.

Cole sonrió. Le encantó cómo lo había dicho, sin dudar: «Dime qué puedo hacer».

—Si pudiese localizar a alguien que les conociese, quizá tendría una idea mejor de lo que está pasando. El problema es encontrar algo. Lo único que tengo son sus nombres. No hay direcciones anteriores, ni números de la seguridad social, ni última dirección conocida, nada. Ni siquiera tengo una foto de esa gente.

—Ya lo entiendo. Estoy pensando… —Se quedó callada y Cole la dejó pensar—. ¿Se fueron después del huracán?

—Eso es lo que dijeron. No sé si es verdad o no.

—¿Y él tenía un restaurante en Nueva Orleans?

—O lo tenía o trabajaba en él, no sé. Y ni siquiera sé si eso es verdad. Es cocinero.

—Vale, supongamos que es verdad; ¿sabes cómo se llamaba el local?

—Lo siento, Luce.

Ella se quedó callada otra vez.

—El huracán fue hace años. Había páginas web y servicios para que los refugiados volviesen a ponerse en contacto con su familia perdida, pero no sé si todavía existen todas esas cosas. ¿Conociste a Terry cuando estuviste aquí?

Terry Babinette era el investigador que solía usar el bufete de Lucy, un detective retirado de la policía de Baton Rouge.

—Le estreché la mano.

—Déjame que hable con él a ver si se le ocurre alguna idea.

—Sería estupendo, Lucille. Muchas gracias.

—No estás demasiado convencido, ¿no?

Cole no lo entendía.

—¿De qué?

—Antes me has dicho que no estabas convencido de que fueran sinceros con Joe. ¿Por qué no lo estás?

Cole puso un pie en el canto de su escritorio, notando de nuevo esa sensación negativa, ese temor instalado en lo más profundo de su ser de perder algo precioso.

—Tengo motivos para creer que su relación no es tal y como ellos la han descrito.

—¿La de Joe y Dru?

—La de Dru y su tío.

Elvis describió su conversación con Steve Brown, y luego repitió lo que le había contado Jared Palmer. Lucy exclamó con énfasis:

—Ay, Dios mío…

—Sí…

—¿Y te crees lo que dice el chico?

—Ha dado en el clavo con todo lo demás. Y Brown estaba furioso. Smith estaba viviendo allí sin que él lo supiera, y hablaba con la mujer cada dos semanas. Así que ella es una mentirosa. Le dijo a Joe que era ella la que se había ido a vivir con Wilson, y no al revés, de modo que es una mentirosa por partida doble. Puede mentir sobre su relación también.

—¿Y qué piensa Joe?

Cole dudó, porque todo aquello le reconcomía desde que habló con Jared.

—Joe no lo sabe. No se lo he dicho.

—Pero hombre, es muy fuerte…

—Me gustaría tener algo más que la palabra de Jared antes de decírselo.

Ninguno de los dos dijo nada durante un buen rato.

—Te echo de menos, Luce.

—Ya lo sé, cariño. Yo también… ¿Qué vas a hacer?

—Hablar contigo. Supongo que por eso te he llamado.

Ella suspiró. Un largo y lento suspiro al teléfono que él quiso sentir sobre su piel.

—¿Crees a ese chico?

—Sí. No puedo probarlo. No tengo nada salvo su palabra, pero, después de lo que dijo Brown, le creo. Creo que está diciendo la verdad.

—Díselo. —Cole asintió para sí, pero no encontró nada que decir—. Cuanto más tiempo esperes, peor será. Lo entiendes, ¿verdad?

—Sí.

—Joe ha nacido para salvar a las personas. Así es como él se ve, y así es interiormente. Está intentando salvarla, o sea que lo que siente por ella se irá haciendo más profundo.

—Ya lo sé.

—Yo sé que lo sabes. Tú también eres así. Por eso os encontrasteis el uno al otro, y por eso estáis unidos como siameses. Por eso hacéis lo que hacéis.

Cole se frotó el ojo izquierdo. Notaba la garganta obstruida.

—¿Y por eso te perdí?

—No me perdiste, cariño. Aquí estamos. Si él quiere salvarla, bien, pero se merece saber a quién está salvando.

—Es duro ser buen amigo…

—Si fuese fácil, cualquiera podría serlo.

—Me gustan las mujeres listas.

—A las mujeres listas les gustas tú.

—Será mejor que te deje.

—Llámame más tarde.

Cole colgó el teléfono. Aún era temprano, pero tenía muchas cosas que hacer, y Lucy le había dado una buena idea. Examinó la lista de proveedores de alimentos con los que había tratado Smith. Todos eran personas relacionadas con el nego-

171

cio de la alimentación y la restauración, que probablemente se intercambiaban informaciones sobre cocineros, cocina y restaurantes buenos y malos en los que habían trabajado. Era posible que Smith hubiese hablado de un restaurante de Nueva Orleans donde hubiese trabajado, o quizás de un chef, y que una de las personas de la lista se acordase. Tener un lugar por donde empezar haría mucho más fácil el trabajo de Lucy.

Cole abrió una botella de agua, cogió el teléfono y empezó a trabajar.

26

Elvis Cole

Cole todavía estaba en el despacho cuando Pike lo llamó y le dijo que se iba a acercar para contarle lo de los cuerpos. Cole sugirió que se reuniesen en su casa, diciendo que prepararía la cena mientras hablaban y que podían tomarse unas cervezas. No mencionó a Dru ni a Wilson, ni la horrible sensación que le producían las malas noticias que estaba a punto de comunicar a su amigo.

La moribunda luz del sol se iba fundiendo en una neblina color magenta cuando Cole subía por la colina hacia su casa. El tráfico en Laurel Canyon era brutal, de modo que tomó un atajo por el vecindario, serpenteando entre los árboles y las casitas con sus verjas de Outpost Drive a Mulholland. Cole conducía un Stingray Convertible amarillo de 1966 que le gustaba mucho. Corría estupendamente y era divertido conducirlo, pero no lo lavaba a menudo, de modo que estaba sucio. Pike lavaba su Jeep todos los días. Su inmaculada piel roja estaba tan brillante y pulida que Cole decía en broma que probablemente la suciedad resbalaba y se la llevaba el viento. Pensando en el reluciente Jeep de Pike, Cole se sintió triste. Habría sido un agradable paseo a casa cualquier otra noche, el Stingray con la capota bajada y el fresco aire del cañón perfumado de eucalipto e hinojo silvestre. Cualquier otra noche habría sido perfecto.

Su casa era de madera de secuoya, con tejado a dos aguas, en una calle pequeña en Woodrow Wilson Drive, en la parte superior de un cañón. La casita, que hubo que reformar, tenía dos dormitorios y dos baños, y Cole la compró un año que

173

andaba bien de dinero, antes de que los precios se disparasen. Si hubiese querido comprarla después no habría podido. No había jardín digno de ese nombre, ya que estaba colgada en lo alto de una pendiente, pero tenía una terraza que recorría la parte trasera de la casa y desde la cual había una vista magnífica del cañón y la ciudad.

Cole aparcó en el garaje y se dirigió a la cocina. Un gato negro se encontraba aposentado en el mostrador. Miró su cuenco al entrar Cole y emitió un suave maullido.

—Sí, ya. Vamos a arreglar lo tuyo lo primero.

Le puso comida fresca y agua, y luego sacó una cerveza Negro Modelo. El gato levantó la vista desde la comida.

—*Miau...*

—Vale, pero no demasiada.

Cole le puso un poco de cerveza en un platito.

El gato venía con la casa, y formaba parte de la vida de Cole desde hacía más tiempo que ningún ser vivo excepto Joe Pike. Era un animal de malos instintos, dado a atacar a la gente, Cole no sabía por qué. Una vez un hombre que reparaba el aire acondicionado y la calefacción estaba trabajando en la caldera en el armario de la entrada. El operario estaba arrodillado ante la puerta, de espaldas a la entrada, cuando el gato se le subió a la espalda y le mordió en el cuello cuatro veces. El seguro de Cole se hizo cargo de la reclamación, pero tuvo que hacer un trabajo especial sin contabilizar para su agente de seguros para poder obtener una nueva póliza.

—Va a ser una noche dura, amigo.

El gato saltó de su mano con sorprendente suavidad y volvió a comer.

La casa estaba caliente, ya que llevaba todo el día cerrada, de modo que Cole abrió las grandes puertas que daban a la terraza. Sacó un pequeño filete de falda del congelador para que se fuera descongelando, abrió una lata grande de alubias, las enjuagó y las reservó para que se fueran secando. Por aquel entonces ya se había acabado la primera Modelo, de modo que abrió una segunda y se la fue bebiendo mientras cortaba calabacines, berenjenas japonesas y dos tomates grandes para asarlos. Lo bueno que tenía cocinar era que te olvidabas de todo. Cortar y sazonar hacía que fuera más fácil no pensar. La Modelo también contribuía en gran medida a ello.

Cuando las verduras estuvieron preparadas Cole subió escaleras arriba, se puso una camiseta y volvió a la terraza para encender la Weber. El cielo era como una maravillosa sangría por aquel entonces, y le inspiró para tomarse otra cerveza.

Cuando entró de vuelta en casa, Joe Pike estaba ya en la cocina. Sin anunciarse, silencioso como un fantasma. El gato estaba metido entre sus tobillos, ronroneando. Pike era la única persona, además de Cole, a la que podía soportar aquel gato.

Elvis señaló con la botella hacia las verduras.

—Ensalada de alubias con verduras asadas. Quizás un poco de cuscús. Para mí, carne asada. ¿Te parece bien?

—Bien.

Claro.

Observemos cómo el amigo leal prepara el tema para la velada festiva.

—Voy a por una cerveza. Coge una tú, y me pones al corriente mientras preparo el carbón.

Pike sacó una cerveza del frigorífico. Cole cogió una tercera y lo siguió fuera. El gato fue tras ellos. Le gustaba examinar el promontorio en busca de ratones y ardillas de tierra.

Cole movió los carbones, cosa completamente innecesaria. Observemos la técnica inmaculada con la que el «mejor amigo del mundo» pospone con evasivas el momento de la verdad.

—Tú primero, luego sigo yo. ¿Qué les ha ocurrido a Mendoza y Gomer?

Pike le contó lo que sabía de Mendoza primero, y luego pasó a Gomer. Al principio Cole solo fingió escuchar, pero el aspecto visual de aquellos crímenes le atrajo. El cuerpo de Gomer se encontró detrás del volante de un coche aparcado junto al extremo norte del Grand Canal. La sangre que había en el vehículo sugería que fue asesinado allí mismo. El primer corte probablemente era una puñalada hacia abajo, en el lado izquierdo del cuello, que rebanó la arteria carótida, el esófago, gran parte de la musculatura circundante hasta el hueso —que resultaba visible—, y la parte superior del tórax. El segundo corte iba desde la oreja derecha atravesando la garganta hasta la base de la oreja izquierda, exponiendo también el hueso.

Pike dijo:

—No saben el momento de la muerte de Mendoza con certeza, pero Gomer probablemente murió entre las once de la noche y la una de la madrugada. Cuando la policía me ha dejado, he comprobado el lugar donde le han encontrado: tenía una vista frontal de la casa de Wilson. Probablemente Mendoza iba sentado en el otro lado.

Cuando Cole se dio cuenta de lo que estaba diciendo Pike levantó la mano.

—Espera un momento. ¿Me estás diciendo que esos dos tíos estaban vigilando la casa?

—Sí.

—Pero eso no tiene sentido… Si han cogido a Wilson y a Dru esta mañana, ¿por qué volver a la casa? ¿Qué era lo que querían?

—Quizás a alguien de quien les hablaron Wilson y Dru, pero es solo una suposición. Tal vez fue el hombre que les mató. La luz que he visto en el dormitorio del piso de arriba cuando te he llamado esta mañana probablemente era del asesino, el mismo hombre que entró por la ventana de la cocina.

A Cole no le gustaba nada todo aquello, ni lo que podía significar.

—Mendoza y Gomer han vuelto a buscar a ese hombre, pero el otro ya estaba allí. ¿Les ha visto primero y les ha hecho salir?

Pike inclinó la cabeza hacia el otro lado, y el ocaso color anaranjado se reflejó en sus gafas de sol.

—Sí. Creo que todavía estaba vigilando la casa cuando yo he pasado por allí esta mañana. Lo he notado.

Cole hurgó en los carbones y miró las pavesas que se arremolinaban al calor. Todo había cambiado en el espacio de un día. La extorsión de barrio se había convertido en una falsedad. El vandalismo y el asalto eran un truco de prestidigitación para ocultar algo mucho peor, y ahora Cole sabía que los magos eran unos mentirosos. Nada de todo aquello era real, y probablemente nunca lo había sido.

La voz de Pike surgió de las ascuas.

—Ahora tú.

Cole miró a su amigo.

—He hablado con Steve Brown, el propietario de la casa de Smith, y también con Jared. Tengo que contarte algunas cosas, y no te van a gustar. No creo que Dru haya sido sincera contigo.

Cole hizo una pausa para ver la reacción de Pike, pero fue la propia de un maniquí de unos grandes almacenes. El gato se apartó del borde de la terraza, pasó entre las piernas de Pike otra vez y luego se sentó, con los ojos entrecerrados, vigilante.

Cole dejó su botella en la barandilla.

—Brown no conoce a Wilson Smith ni ha oído hablar nunca de él. Dejó que Dru usara su casa porque tenían una historia. Se suponía que ella tenía que estar allí sola, y Brown se ha puesto furioso cuando ha averiguado que alguien estaba viviendo con ella. No sabía nada de ningún tío, ni de que Dru trabajase en el restaurante de Wilson ni nada por el estilo. Creía que vivía de una pensión. Hasta que hemos hablado esta mañana, esperaba reemprender su relación con ella cuando volviese.

Pike se quedó inmóvil, en el borde de la terraza. A Cole le habría gustado poder ver detrás de las gafas oscuras, pero esa imagen le estaba vedada.

—Después de hablar con Brown he ido a ver a Jared. Me ha explicado cosas que desmienten todo lo que te contó esa mujer sobre sí misma. No es bueno, Joe. Es muy malo, la verdad.

—¿Qué?

El gato se acurrucó a los pies de Pike. Su rabo se agitaba y retorcía mientras Cole contaba lo que le había dicho Jared. Hizo un resumen, pero no le ahorró nada.

—Si quieres hablar con él otra vez, iré contigo, pero creo que Jared está diciendo la verdad. Cuando le he dejado, he cogido algunas cosas de la casa que tenían las huellas de Wilson y Dru y se las he llevado a John Chen. No sé si esa gente está fichada, pero podría ser, y las huellas igual nos ayudan a averiguar quiénes son. También he hablado con

Lucy. Hasta que sepamos algo de Chen, lo único que he podido darle son sus nombres, pero su investigador está intentando ver si puede encontrarlos en Nueva Orleans. Y eso es todo. Eso es lo que he hecho.

Pike pareció tambalearse ligeramente, como si le empujara la brisa, pero el aire estaba quieto.

—Lo siento, tío. Si quieres que deje lo de Chen y Lucy, dímelo.

Pike se volvió hacia el cañón y puso las manos en la barandilla. Cole se preguntó si necesitaba agarrarse para dejar de tambalearse.

—No. Que sigan.

—Está bien. ¿Quieres otra cerveza?

Pike negó con la cabeza.

—¿Qué quieres que haga? —preguntó Elvis.

—¿Sobre qué?

—Estamos metidos en esto porque quieres ayudar a esa mujer. Y me parece muy bien, pero ahora quizás hayan cambiado las cosas…

—Ella sigue necesitando ayuda.

—Vale. Si es lo que quieres…

—Sí, es lo que quiero.

El gato agitaba el rabo a una velocidad frenética, y sus ojos eran dos ranuras peligrosas.

—Lo siento, tío —dijo Cole.

Su teléfono sonó. Cole no pensaba contestar, pero quiso darle algo de tiempo a Pike. Cubrió la parrilla y entró a buscar el móvil. Cogió el receptor un segundo antes de que saltara el contestador y habló por encima de la grabación.

—Eh, estoy aquí. No cuelgue… Voy a parar esto.

—¿Señor Cole?

Cole no reconoció la voz de aquel hombre.

—Sí, soy yo. ¿Quién es?

—Me llamo Charles Laine. Usted estuvo hoy en mi casa, en el canal. Habló con mi ama de llaves de mi sistema de vigilancia.

Cole miró hacia el exterior para ver dónde estaba Pike, pero este había abandonado la barandilla.

—Sí señor. Gracias por llamarme.

—No, tranquilo. ¿Es por la investigación policial? La policía vino ayer.

—Sí, señor, es lo mismo, pero yo no soy policía. Soy investigador privado con licencia, trabajando en un caso privado.

—Ya lo sé. Tengo su tarjeta. Irma dice que usted me preguntó si grabamos lo que recoge la cámara.

Cole miró al otro lado de la terraza, pero tampoco veía allí a Pike.

—Sí, señor. Estamos intentando identificar a dos hombres que quizá pasaran por su casa ayer por la mañana.

—Tal vez pueda ayudarle. El sistema que tengo sí que graba, pero no estoy seguro de que se vea el trozo de calle suficiente. Se ve una parte, sí, pero la cámara está enfocada para grabar a la gente que se acerca a mi puerta.

—Ya entiendo. ¿Podría echarle un vistazo a lo que tenga?

—Claro. Intentaré hacer una copia esta noche. Nunca lo he hecho antes, pero tengo un librito de instrucciones por alguna parte... Si funciona, se la daré mañana. Si no, igual tiene que venir usted aquí.

—Eso sería estupendo, señor Laine. Muchísimas gracias.

Cuando Cole colgó al final, salió a la terraza. Quería compartir la única buena noticia que había tenido aquel día, pero cuando salió, Joe Pike se había ido.

—¿Joe?

El gato tampoco estaba.

—¿Joseph?

El cañón se tragó su voz.

Cole volvió a la barandilla. Mucho más abajo, las primeras luces parpadeantes titilaban en la sombra. La oscuridad se iba acumulando en los oscuros tajos como una niebla morada, e iría trepando a medida que moría el sol hasta que acabara consumiéndolo. Pero ahora no, todavía no.

—No va a pasar nada, colega. Solo duele durante un tiempo...

Su voz era un susurro destinado solo a sí mismo.

Luego el gato gruñó, en algún lugar a su derecha y por debajo, en el promontorio. Empezó muy bajo pero fue aumentando de volumen, como un terrible grito de guerra, hasta que llenó todo el cañón con un angustioso gemido, como si estuviera sufriendo. Cole pensó que era el gato. Estaba bastante seguro de que era el gato.

Se inclinó por encima de la barandilla, intentando ver. Se estiró todo lo que pudo, intentó encontrar al gato escuchando su maullido, pero no vio nada. El animal estaba allí, pero tan bien escondido que no era capaz de encontrarlo.

A veces quieres ayudarles pero no puedes.

27

*E*l aire parecía muy limpio cuando refrescó, por la noche. Pike abrió la ventanilla del Jeep, dejando que el aire le refrescase la piel. Los faros que venían en sentido contrario, las luces de los frenos y los letreros de neón formaban arcos derretidos en el brillante capó. Al acercarse al mar las farolas reflejaron sus halos en la niebla, cada uno más brillante que el anterior. Pike volvió hacia los canales.

Gomer había sido asesinado en un solar vacío en el extremo más occidental del Grand Canal, donde se había derruido recientemente una casa. Pike había visitado aquel lugar por la mañana, cuando lo soltó la policía, pero a Gomer lo habían matado de noche y quería ver aquel lugar en la oscuridad, tal y como él y su asesino lo habrían visto. No tenía otro lugar adonde ir.

Aparcó en la calle y fue andando junto a un tráiler abandonado, por un terreno vacío, hasta el canal. Antes la zona estaba llena de policías, pero ya había quedado desierta. No mucho después de que se iniciase el proyecto se prepararon unos nuevos cimientos y llevaron un tráiler para que lo ocupase el capataz de la obra, pero en algún momento de esa secuencia de acontecimientos se acabó el dinero y la obra se abandonó. Gomer se dirigió allí y aparcó frente al canal.

La casa de Smith estaba a varias casas de distancia por la derecha de Pike, en la orilla opuesta, no muy lejos de la boca de un canal adyacente. Aquella situación ofrecía una buena perspectiva del jardín trasero de Smith, la mitad de las ventanas de la planta baja y todo el segundo piso, pero Pike pensó que Gomer era un idiota por haber aparcado allí, donde era plenamente visible. Vio a algunas familias en las casas del otro lado del canal, y a gente que cruzaba el puente que cubría el canal adyacente, y supo que cualquiera de ellos podía verle a él, igual que podían haber hecho con Gomer. Una de las personas que vio a Gomer aquella noche lo dejó empapado en sangre.

Pike examinó las casas y las sombras que había más allá del puente peatonal y el juego de luces que incidía en el agua. Le pareció que comprendía todo lo que había ocurrido hasta que Mendoza y Gomer volvieron a los canales para ser asesinados. No entendía por qué habían vuelto, por qué les habían matado, ni quién lo había hecho, y ahora aquel asunto de Dru y Wilson hizo que se examinara de nuevo a sí mismo y a ellos, y todo lo que creía que era cierto. Quizás eso fuese bueno. Creía que la respuesta a todo ello se encontraba en aquel lugar, de modo que debía reconocer las señales. Si las encontraba sería capaz de recrear los acontecimientos y sabría lo que había ocurrido. Era como leer las palabras en un libro. Leer cada palabra y añadirla a las demás para construir una frase, y luego unir las frases y conocer la historia. Su tarea era encontrar las palabras suficientes.

182

Pike sacó su móvil y llamó a John Chen, que respondió con su típico susurro paranoico.

—¿Sí? ¿Quién es?

—Pike. Han embolsado dos cuerpos esta mañana en los canales de Venice. ¿Qué sabes de ellos?

Chen no respondió.

—¿John?

—Lo siento. Pensaba que me estabas preguntando por otra cosa.

—Sus nombres eran Mendoza y Gomer.

—Es cosa de Sandy Lancaster. Yo no me ocupo de ese caso. Pero ella está aquí, en el cubículo de al lado. ¿Qué necesitas?

Pike le preguntó si alguno de los dos mostraba signos de heridas defensivas o marcas de ligaduras, y si la policía había localizado el lugar del asesinato de Mendoza. Chen le dijo que no colgara, y Pike oyó murmullos mientras aquel hablaba con la criminalista del cubículo de al lado. Unos momentos después Chen había vuelto al teléfono.

—No, tío. Nada de heridas defensivas, y negativo también en lo de las ligaduras. Esos tipos no lo vieron venir, si eso es lo que querías saber.

—¿Y de Mendoza?

—No pueden confirmar nada hasta que tengan el resultado de los análisis de sangre. Dice que han encontrado una salpicadura bastante grande en uno de los puentes peatonales que hay por allí. No sé cuál.

—Vale, John. Ya me lo imagino.

Pike contempló el puente peatonal que unía el extremo norte de la calle de Smith. Habría otro puente seguramente en el extremo sur. Gomer vigilaba el lado norte, así que Mendoza vigilaría el extremo sur. Cada hecho era una palabra que construía la historia.

Pike se dispuso a despedirse, pero sus ojos se fijaron de nuevo en la casa de Dru.

—¿Has encontrado alguna huella en las cosas que te ha dado Elvis?

La voz de Chen sonaba suspicaz.

—¿Qué cosas?

—Las cosas que te ha dado Elvis hoy.

—No le he visto hoy.

—Acabo de estar con él, John. Me lo ha contado.

Chen dudó mucho más que antes.

—No estás mal, ¿verdad? Me dijo que no te lo dijera…

—Estoy bien. ¿Has sacado algo?

—No he tenido tiempo ni de ir a mear. Lo siento, tío; me pondré antes de acabar el turno. Te lo prometo.

—Vale, está bien. Solo preguntaba.

—Ya sé que es importante, como es tu novia y todo eso…

Pike sintió haber sacado el tema.

—No es mi novia.

—Todas las mujeres son un asco, tío. Nadie lo sabe mejor que yo. Ni siquiera puedo conseguir a una zorra que me rompa el corazón.

Pike cerró el teléfono y luego se concentró en Mendoza y Gomer, y se los imaginó vigilando la casa de Wilson. Se le

183

ocurrió que quizás Azzara los hubiera hecho matar. Tal vez averiguó que habían asesinado a Wilson y Dru y se puso furioso porque lo hicieron en contra de sus órdenes. Quizá les ordenó que fuesen al canal con cualquier excusa y envió a alguien a matarlos. Pike estaba pensando en aquella posibilidad cuando recordó la luz del piso de arriba y la ventana forzada. Una gente enviada a asesinar a Mendoza y Gomer no habría tenido motivo alguno para entrar en la casa. La ventana la había forzado otra persona, y Pike sospechaba ahora que había sido precisamente el asesino.

Pike volvió a recrear la imagen de Gomer y Mendoza vigilando la casa. El asesino era bueno. Ninguno de los dos hombres se había resistido ni había intentado defenderse. Los había cogido totalmente por sorpresa, y los había matado con gran limpieza y eficiencia a una velocidad abrumadora. Eso sugería a un profesional, o a alguien con un entrenamiento profesional. Si el asesino había forzado la ventana, probablemente ya estaba en el lugar cuando ellos llegaron, cosa que significaba que no había venido a por Mendoza y Gomer... sino a por Wilson y Dru.

Pike notaba que las piezas iban encajando. Las palabras empezaban a relatar una historia.

El asesino había llegado temprano a la casa, como ponía de manifiesto el momento de su entrada; no había encontrado lo que venía buscando y se disponía a esperar. Eso significaba que de alguna manera estaba conectado con Wilson y Dru. Pike había supuesto que Mendoza y Gomer secuestraron a Wilson y Dru, pero quizá su primer intento fracasó, de modo que volvieron a ver si tenían otra oportunidad. El asesino probablemente les vio tomar posiciones, y o bien sabía que esperaban a Wilson, o concluyó que así era al ver sus actos. Quizá los vigiló durante horas. Luego los mató, y probablemente siguió esperando a Wilson y Dru.

Cada nueva idea era una palabra, y cuanto más experimentaba Pike con ellas más le gustaba la historia. Las señales estaban ahí: lo único que tenía que hacer era leerlas correctamente y en el orden adecuado. Todavía quedaban huecos, preguntas, pero la veía desarrollarse ante él y le gustaba la sensación que producía.

«Estoy aquí.»

Un nuevo jugador había entrado en escena, pero quizá llevase en el juego mucho más tiempo de lo que nadie pensaba.

Pike se apartó del agua y recorrió en coche las escasas manzanas que le separaban del local de Wilson Smith.

185

28

*P*ike aparcó frente al local de Wilson. Un bar y una cafetería que había en la manzana siguiente todavía estaban abiertos, y también la gasolinera Mobil y la tienda de tatuajes, enfrente. Esperó a que pasara una pareja y luego se dirigió hacia el escaparate nuevo con su linterna y alumbró el interior. Las cabezas y vísceras de animal habían desaparecido, y el interior estaba limpio. Quizás el ayuntamiento hubiese enviado un equipo de limpieza, o a lo mejor Betsy Harmon y su hijo lo habían limpiado ellos mismos. No importaba ya, ni a Pike ni a nadie.

La luz iluminó la pared donde se había escrito el mensaje con sangre.

«Estoy aquí.»

Pike y la policía suponían que Mendoza y Gomer habían irrumpido en la tienda, igual que suponían que habían cometido el secuestro, pero la naturaleza del mensaje siempre había incomodado a Pike, y ahora se daba cuenta de por qué. «Estoy aquí» era un anuncio, y parecía un extraño mensaje para que lo dejaran Gomer o Mendoza, pero quizá no fuese tan extraño para el hombre que los había matado, si ese hombre iba en busca de Wilson y Dru.

Estoy aquí. Yo. En singular.

He llegado.

Temedme.

Pike pensó que ese hombre nuevo era el que había colgado las cabezas y echado la sangre, y lo había hecho para anunciar su llegada.

La historia ahora estaba clara.

No había escrito «he vuelto», porque no era que hubiese estado allí, se hubiese ido y luego hubiera vuelto al mismo lugar. «Estoy aquí» implicaba que había empezado su búsqueda en otro lugar pero acababa de llegar a este, cosa que sugería que había pasado un cierto tiempo. Les había estado buscando, y ahora les había encontrado y quería que ellos lo supieran, lo cual significaba que le conocían, o sabían que existía. Pike sospechaba de estas últimas conclusiones porque iban en contra de sus instintos. No se advierte al objetivo de que acabas de llegar. Wilson había visto el mensaje, lo había comprendido y había desaparecido de inmediato. Ahora Pike creía que la intención de huir de Wilson no tenía nada que ver con Mendoza y Gomer, y sí mucho que ver con la llegada del otro hombre, el nuevo.

Apagó su luz, se apartó de la ventana y observó las tiendas que estaban al otro lado de la calle, mientras pensaba en aquella contradicción. Wilson vio el mensaje, le entró el pánico y salió huyendo. Quizá fuera ese el asunto: quizás el hombre les advirtió porque quería que huyesen, como un cazador que levanta a las piezas de sus escondites. Probablemente estaba observando el local de Wilson cuando este llegó por la mañana. Probablemente lo siguió de vuelta a casa, pero Mendoza y Gomer interrumpieron su juego.

Pike volvió a su Jeep en busca del número de teléfono de Jack Straw. Este respondió al tercer timbrazo. Parecía relajado y algo perezoso, como un DJ en una emisora de *jazz* de FM.

—¿Tenías a alguien vigilando el local de Smith, estos últimos días? —preguntó Pike.

—Sí. A ratos. ¿Por qué?

—Quizá viesen al hombre que mató a Mendoza y a Gomer.

—Espera.

Pike oyó unos sonidos como si Straw estuviese tapando el teléfono con la mano. Continuaron casi un minuto antes de que volviera a ponerse al aparato.

—Mira al otro lado de la calle.

Pike miró y comprendió que le estaban observando. Straw volvió a hablar enseguida.

187

—¿Ves la sala de tatuajes?

—Sí.

—¿Y el despacho que está encima?

Se veían unas ventanas negras con un rótulo de SE ALQUI-LA pegado con cinta adhesiva al cristal. Claro.

—Entra en el local de tatuajes y ve por la parte de atrás. Verás una escalera. Si el hombre del mostrador te dice algo, dile que estás con la banda.

Pike cruzó entre los coches y fue al local de tatuajes. Un hombre calvo, con tatuajes en el cuero cabelludo y las mejillas y un enorme aro de metal atravesándole la nariz estaba leyendo una novela de James Ellroy detrás del mostrador. Levantó la vista cuando entró Pike, pero volvió a su lectura cuando este señaló hacia el techo.

Pike pasó junto a unas paredes forradas con miles de dibujos de tatuajes, atravesó una estrecha puerta trasera y subió un tramo de escaleras metálicas. Straw esperaba en la parte superior, vestido con unos vaqueros y una camiseta ancha con el cuello en pico que necesitaba un lavado. Acompañó a Pike hasta una diminuta oficina con dos habitaciones, sin mueble alguno. La única luz procedía de una lámpara encendida en la habitación trasera. La delantera, que daba a la calle, recibía un poco de luz a través de la puerta entornada, pero las ventanas que daban a la calle estaban cubiertas con tela negra salpicada de recortes rectangulares para poder ver el exterior. El hombre de la camisa naranja estaba sentado en el suelo con las piernas cruzadas y la espalda apoyada en la pared. Miró a Pike con indiferencia y no hizo movimiento alguno para ofrecerle la mano.

Era un escondite desnudo que olía a pizza, a cigarrillos y a cuerpos. Unas maletas apiladas con ropa arrugada se encontraban en las esquinas, junto a unos colchones hinchables con sacos de dormir encima. En una bolsa de basura se acumulaban latas de refrescos vacías y vasos de Starbucks. El equipo de Straw había venido muy ligero: no planeaban quedarse tanto tiempo como se habían quedado al final.

Straw sonrió e hizo un gesto hacia la habitación.

—Te diría que cogieras una silla, pero no tenemos.

—Mendoza y Gomer no destrozaron el local de Smith. El

hombre que los mató fue el que lo hizo, y tus chicos a lo mejor lo vieron.

Straw y el hombre de naranja se miraron un momento, y luego el segundo se inclinó hacia delante, interesado.

—¿Qué aspecto tiene?

Su voz era más aguda de lo que Pike esperaba y con un toque liviano, como si acabara de superar un resfriado.

—¿Cómo te llamas?

Straw respondió por él.

—Es Kenny. No hace falta el apellido.

Kenny contempló a Pike con ojos penetrantes.

—¿Puedes describirlo?

—No lo he visto.

Kenny sonrió mientras se apoyaba en la pared, desaparecido su interés.

—Ah.

—Quería saber cuándo entraba y salía la gente, cuándo estaba vacía la tienda, qué tipo de alarmas podía haber. Eso significa que estuvo aquí.

—¿Ah, sí? ¿Y cómo sabes tú lo que quería?

Pike miró a Kenny y luego a Straw.

—Porque es lo que yo mismo querría. Está cazando a Wilson y Dru. Llenó el local de sangre para hacerlos salir, y probablemente siguió a Wilson de vuelta a su casa, pero Mendoza y Gomer se metieron por medio. Esto no va de un par de pandilleros que amedrentan a un cocinero. Esto es más gordo.

Straw y Kenny se volvieron a mirar otra vez, como si estuvieran manteniendo una conversación silenciosa, y luego Straw se encogió de hombros, mirando a Pike.

—No lo entiendo. ¿Por qué todo ese follón con la sangre y las cabezas si quería matarlos? ¿Por qué no matarlos sin más?

—No lo sé. Quizá para ver adónde iban.

Kenny sonrió, abriendo mucho los ojos como si Pike fuese un idiota.

—A lo mejor está loco. Si es que existe, claro.

Straw frunció el ceño mirando a Kenny, y pensando un momento.

—Vale. Te escucho. ¿Qué es lo que sabes?

189

Pike fue explicándoles todo su razonamiento sobre el mensaje dejado en el local de Wilson y las conclusiones que extrajo por la forma en que habían sido asesinados Gomer y Mendoza. Si Straw se preguntó cómo sabía tanto Pike de sus cuerpos, no lo dijo.

—Muy bien, no digo que me crea todo eso, pero, si tienes razón, y nosotros vimos al tío, ¿cómo podríamos saberlo?

Kenny murmuró para sí.

—Llevaba una camiseta en la que ponía ASESINO. ¿No te acuerdas? —Se rio para sí, pero Pike estaba concentrado en Straw.

—Tendríais que haberle visto más de una vez. Después de que pasara tres o cuatro veces os disteis cuenta de que seguía por allí. A la quinta quizás os preguntasteis quién era y por qué tenía tanto interés en el local de Smith.

Kenny miró a Straw.

—No recuerdo a nadie así. ¿Y tú?

—Solo a la gente que trabaja en las tiendas de alrededor, pero ya preguntaré a los chicos. Quizás alguno de ellos viese algo.

Kenny cruzó los brazos y cerró los ojos.

—Claro. Pregúntales.

Debajo de las ventanas tenían una cámara con teleobjetivo y un telescopio con visión nocturna en unas fundas. Una cámara de vídeo, unida por un cable a un ordenador portátil situado cerca, formaba también parte del montaje. Pike había visto ese equipo al entrar y lo señaló.

—¿Y vuestro vídeo?

Straw movió con la cabeza, y se desplazó para enseñárselo a Pike.

—Hemos ido siguiendo a los chicos de Azzara. Lo hemos puesto en marcha solo cuando hemos visto a uno de sus pandilleros. Es lo único que tenemos.

Pike miró los pequeños rectángulos recortados en la tela, iluminados por las farolas de abajo. Se preguntó cuántas horas habrían pasado viendo el mundo a través de aquellas estrechas ventanas.

—Comprobad el vídeo. Nunca se sabe.

Kenny murmuró de nuevo, sin abrir los ojos.

190

—Es verdad. Nunca se sabe.

Straw le dijo a Pike que lo llamaría si alguno de los suyos había visto algo, y luego lo acompañó a la salida, como si Pike les hubiese entretenido ya el tiempo suficiente. Kenny no abrió los ojos.

Cuando salió, Pike se dirigió a los canales de nuevo. Era tarde ya, pero no tan tarde como cuando fue asesinado Gomer.

No volvió a la obra. Aparcó en Venice Boulevard, junto a la casa de Smith, y luego se acercó a pie a la casa de Steve Brown. Pike pensaba en ella como la casa de Dru, y era la única vivienda oscura en la calle corta y estrecha. Jared tenía la luz encendida, pero no estaba. Probablemente se encontraba en el piso de abajo con su madre, adormilado delante de la pantalla.

Pike usó la llave escondida para abrir la cancela; luego pasó junto a la casa, fue hacia la verja y se dirigió al borde del canal. El agua desprendía un intenso olor. Rápidamente vio el lugar de la obra donde Gomer había sido asesinado. No intentaba ocultarse, quería que le viesen.

Pike se preguntó si el asesino usaba equipo de visión nocturna. Él tenía ese equipo, pero había decidido no usarlo. Si el asesino estaba allí, Pike quería que sintiera que tenía ventaja. Comprobó los cortes y sombras a lo largo de las orillas y entre las casas donde se podía ocultar un observador, y esperó que el hombre estuviese mirando. Su presencia podía significar que todavía no había encontrado a Dru y Wilson, y que quizás estuviesen vivos aún. Si el asesino estaba mirando, quizá sintiera curiosidad, se preguntase por qué Pike estaba en su jardín y decidiese echar un vistazo más de cerca. Tal vez decidiese matarle, cosa que sería aún mejor. Tendría que acercarse lo suficiente para usar su cuchillo, y a Pike se le daba bien el cuerpo a cuerpo. Quería saber qué sabía el otro.

La luz bailoteaba encima del agua. El ruido del tráfico de las calles adyacentes era intenso, y también la música y las voces que resonaban por todo el canal, pero todos esos sonidos vivos se desvanecerían a medida que la noche se fuese haciendo más profunda.

Pike esperaba solo en la oscuridad, preguntándose dónde estarían Dru y Wilson, cómo les habría conocido el hombre del cuchillo y si estarían vivos o muertos. Se preguntó de dónde vendrían, por qué estarían allí y por qué había tenido que hinchar su neumático aquella mañana en aquella gasolinera en particular y a aquella hora en concreto.

Nada de todo eso importaba en realidad, allí, en la oscuridad. Él le había dicho a ella que se ocuparía de todo. Le había dicho que no les volverían a molestar.

Pike susurró:

—Estoy aquí.

No importaba nada quién o qué era ella. Si le necesitaba, él acudiría.

Pike susurró de nuevo.

CUARTA PARTE

El príncipe de la soledad

29

*P*ike cambió de situación varias veces durante la noche, desplazándose de casa de Dru a otros lugares donde tenía visión de zonas en las cuales podía esconderse alguien que estuviese vigilando. No encontró a nadie y, a medida que el cielo se fue iluminando por oriente, se fue convenciendo de que el asesino ya no vigilaba la casa de Dru, lo que significaba que tenía lo que quería, o había seguido la pista de Wilson y Dru a otro lugar. Cualquiera de las dos posibilidades era mala, y dejaba a Pike hambriento de un nuevo rastro.

A las nueve y veinte de la mañana Pike cruzaba el puente de la avenida Dell cuando lo llamó Elvis Cole.

—Laine ha cumplido. Ha enviado un disco por mensajero.

Charles Laine. El vecino de Dru que tenía un sistema de vigilancia.

—¿Y sale algo?

—Acaba de llegar, pero necesito que vengas a verlo. Yo no he visto nunca a esa gente, no sé cómo son.

Pike observó la casa de Dru al otro lado del agua sin ningún entusiasmo. Cole tenía razón, pero Mendoza y Gomer estaban muertos, de modo que, aunque tuvieran la suerte de ver de reojo el secuestro, irse de allí para ver una grabación de un valor cuestionable le parecía ahora una pérdida de tiempo. Entonces se le ocurrió otra posibilidad que hizo que se interesase mucho más.

—¿Cuántas horas de grabación tenemos?

—Siete días desde el momento en que grabó el disco, que fue anoche. ¿Por qué?

Pike le contó a Cole su conversación con Straw y le explicó que creía en la profesionalidad del asesino. Probablemente había registrado la casa de Dru, igual que el local de comida para llevar, y quizás era la persona que había forzado la ventana de la cocina. Eso significaba que era posible que el asesino se hubiese desplazado por delante de la cámara.

—Bien, pues ven aquí y veamos si se puede usar para algo este material. Laine me ha dicho que veremos un trozo de calle, pero no sabremos lo que significa eso hasta que no lo comprobamos. Igual no vemos más que sombras.

El viaje a través de la ciudad duraba cuarenta minutos, pero Pike aparcó pronto junto a la casa de Cole y apareció en su cocina.

Se sirvió una taza de café solo, cogió un *bagel* con pasas de los que tenía Cole y siguió a su amigo hasta un escritorio en el salón. Sacaron unas sillas de la mesa del comedor y Cole se sentó frente a su Mac. Introdujo el disco y el dispositivo empezó a girar con un suave zumbido. Ninguno de los dos habló mientras esperaban, como si la expectación envolviese en silencio a los dos hombres.

Unos momentos después apareció un programa de reproducción de discos mostrando cuatro capturas de pantalla. Eran de cada una de las cuatro cámaras que monitorizaban el hogar de Laine, una a cada lado de su casa, otra detrás y la cámara de la puerta delantera. Pike vio que Cole se relajaba cuando aparecieron las imágenes.

—Ahí lo tenemos. Las cámaras graban simultáneamente en diferentes pistas. Laine ha dicho que podemos ver cada una separadamente, y desplazarnos adelante y atrás como si fuera un DVD.

Cole hizo clic en la imagen inicial, que se expandió y llenó toda la pantalla. La imagen era deslavazada y fantasmal, en gris y negro, con un código temporal en la parte inferior que indicaba que la imagen se había grabado a las 23.13 y 42 segundos de la noche anterior. Cole echó un vistazo.

—No está mal. Podemos ver un trocito de calle ahí al fondo, y está bastante claro.

A Pike no le parecía tan bien. La cámara estaba paralela a la calle, centrándose en los visitantes, que se encontraban en un pequeño hueco frente a la puerta delantera de Laine, de modo que su campo de visión era muy limitado. El tercio derecho de la pantalla era la puerta de acero. El tercio central era la pared del hueco, que quedaba justo enfrente de la cámara, donde los visitantes podían permanecer cuando apretaban el timbre. El último tercio de la pantalla mostraba una estrecha rendija de calle en la visión periférica de la cámara, al fondo. Si tenían que ver algo útil sería en aquella estrecha rendija.

—Muy turbio. Es difícil ver algo más allá de la pared —dijo Pike.

—Míralo por el lado positivo. Lo grabaron hacia las once y cuarto de la noche pasada con luz infrarroja. El fondo se iluminará durante el día. —Cole cruzó los brazos y volvió a mirar—. ¿Quieres buscar al asesino?

—Sí.

—Bien, pues piensa en esto: siete días significa que tenemos aquí ciento sesenta y ocho horas. Si lo pasamos a velocidad rápida, va ocho veces más deprisa, de modo que nos costará veinticuatro horas ver lo que hay, si volvemos al principio. ¿De verdad quieres pasarte todo ese tiempo buscando a un tipo al que no reconoceremos?

Pike pensó que podía limitar el tiempo.

—Podemos hilar más fino. El día que desaparecieron yo fui a su casa alrededor de las diez, y tú hacia la una. Quienquiera que forzase la ventana lo tuvo que hacer durante esas tres horas. Tres horas no es tanto.

Cole asintió, pero fue un asentimiento lento, y Pike supo que estaba pensando. Eso era bueno, porque siempre se le ocurrían buenas ideas.

—Mira, será mejor que empecemos esa misma mañana temprano. Si tienes razón con lo de que el asesino fue a registrar su casa, quizá pasara un par de veces antes de entrar. También es posible que siguiera a Wilson a casa desde el local, o sea que podemos cogerle siguiéndole, ¿no?

Pike asintió. Buenas ideas.

—Y también, si conseguimos ver algún momento del secuestro, sabremos qué tipo de vehículos estuvieron implicados, y podremos hacernos una idea de la situación en la que se encontraban Dru y Wilson cuando los cogieron. Eso podría ayudarnos a encontrarlos aunque Mendoza y Gomer hayan muerto.

—Empieza cuando quieras.

Pike quería hacerlo de inmediato.

Con el botón de retroceso, Cole fue saltando hacia atrás por el disco, de hora en hora, hasta la mañana del secuestro. Cuando las imágenes estáticas iban retrocediendo en el tiempo de la noche al día, Pike se sintió aliviado al ver que ganaban mucho en claridad, profundidad y color.

Cuando el contador temporal marcaba las 5.13 y 42 segundos de la mañana del secuestro, Cole dio al botón de reproducir y aumentó la velocidad. Aunque a primera hora de la mañana no había demasiada luz, las imágenes a tiempo real iban haciéndose cada vez más nítidas. El paisaje seguía inmóvil, pero la luz ambiental cambiaba y los colores se hacían más intensos a medida que avanzaba el contador temporal.

Vieron la primera señal de vida a las 5.36. Una figura pasó rápidamente por el extremo más alejado de la izquierda de la pantalla, y se desvaneció antes de que Cole pudiera darle al botón de pausa.

—Un corredor —dijo este.

Invirtió la grabación y la reprodujo a tiempo real. Una mujer corriendo apareció por el extremo izquierdo de la pantalla, de espaldas a la cámara. Como esta estaba paralela a la calle, parecía como si viniese desde detrás del lado izquierdo de la cámara por un camino ligeramente desviado de izquierda a derecha, y solo fue visible unos pocos segundos.

A las 5.54 apareció un segundo corredor, esta vez un joven con rastas en el pelo que corría hacia ellos por un camino junto a la cámara. Cole congeló la imagen para examinarlo.

—¿Puedes imprimir esta foto? —dijo Pike.

—Claro. ¿Crees que será él?

—Ya lo veremos.

Pike no tenía ninguna intuición sobre aquel hombre, en ningún sentido. Simplemente quería todas las fotos de todos los hombres que pudieran ser y que pasaron junto a la casa.

No se vio a nadie más hasta las 6.22 de la mañana, cuando pasó el Tercel plateado a gran velocidad.

—Son ellos —dijo Pike.

Cole hizo retroceder la grabación y la pasó hacia delante otra vez, fotograma a fotograma, hasta que tuvieron la mejor imagen posible del conductor. La imagen congelada era bastante granulosa, pero estaba claro que se trataba del rostro y los rasgos de Wilson Smith. Iba solo en el coche.

—Wilson. Ahí iba camino del local.

Cole imprimió la imagen y luego siguieron viendo la grabación a velocidad rápida.

La actividad en el callejón fue aumentando a medida que avanzaba la mañana. Detenían la imagen cada vez que pasaba una figura, y luego rebobinaban y la veían a tiempo real. El Tercel plateado reapareció a las 6.55, saliendo por la esquina izquierda de la pantalla cuando Wilson volvió a casa. El ángulo hacía imposible ver a Wilson tras el volante, pero no parecía que hubiese nadie más en el coche.

Entre las siete y las ocho de la mañana pararon la imagen dieciocho veces e imprimieron siete imágenes, pero ninguna de las veintidós personas que vieron parecía ser otra cosa que gente corriente que había salido a dar una vuelta o a correr. Pasaron dos coches por el campo de visión, a medida que los residentes iban abandonando sus hogares entre las 7.20 y las 7.45. Ninguno de ellos era el Tercel plateado, pero Pike y Cole se sintieron animados en ambos casos porque los conductores que salían eran claramente visibles.

Pike observó con la sorda esperanza de que Cole tuviese razón, de que pudiesen verlos partir antes de que llegase Mendoza, pero Jared pasó junto a la pared a las 8.07. Se fue haciendo más grande rápidamente hasta que desapareció por un lado de la cámara, dirigiéndose hacia su batido de chocolate.

—Vale. En algún momento a partir de ahora y antes de que vuelva Jared es cuando llegan Mendoza y Gomer —dijo.

Cole asintió sin apartar la vista de la pantalla.

Pasaron andando dos mujeres con perros pequeños, y luego otro hombre corriendo. A las 8.42 pasó otra figura rápidamente de izquierda a derecha, y Cole detuvo la imagen.

—Es Jared. Ya vuelve.

El chico llevaba una bolsa del supermercado. El batido.

Cole miró a Pike y luego meneó la cabeza.

199

—A tiempo real, Mendoza y Gomer están en la casa en ese momento. Es cuando los vio Jared.

—Usaron el puente peatonal.

—Sí. Y si tu asesino usó el puente y se quedó al final de la calle, no le veremos tampoco.

—Vuelve a pasarlo.

Cole dejó que la imagen pasara a tiempo real, y a las 8.53 apareció el Tercel. Pike se inclinó hacia delante cuando lo vio, mientras Cole paraba la imagen, la hacía retroceder y avanzaba de fotograma en fotograma. A medida que lo hacía, Pike vio que había tres personas en el coche. Wilson conducía, Dru iba en el asiento del pasajero, y otra figura iba detrás. Eso confirmaba que los malos habían usado el puente peatonal para entrar y obligar a las víctimas a salir. Era un buen plan, considerando que la calle era estrecha y sin salida, con tantos posibles testigos.

—Mendoza va detrás, pero solo veo a tres personas —dijo.

—Quizá lo dejaron junto al puente, por donde vino. ¿Es Dru la que va delante?

—Sí.

Cole imprimió la foto y luego hizo adelantar las imágenes.

Seis fotogramas más tarde, el ángulo había cambiado lo suficiente para revelar que en el vehículo iban cuatro personas.

—Ahí lo tenemos —dijo Cole.

El segundo hombre iba sentado detrás de Wilson, aunque todavía era difícil de distinguir. Cole avanzó la imagen dos fotogramas más, y la cara del segundo hombre emergió desde detrás de la cabeza de Wilson.

Pike examinó la cara borrosa, y luego se acercó más a la pantalla.

—Pasa uno más.

Cole adelantó la imagen.

—Uno más.

Pike notó un brote de sorpresa, luego la sorpresa se fundió en la calma que sentía cuando fijaba el punto de mira en un objetivo. Cole lo contemplaba cuando Pike levantó la vista.

—¿Qué pasa?

—Que ese no es Gomer. Es Miguel Azzara.

—Pensaba que no sabía nada de esto.

—Mintió.

Cole lanzó una mirada a Azzara.

—Dos personas han muerto, dos más han desaparecido y aquí el jefe aparece en un secuestro. Esto es más importante que un par de pandilleros cabreados porque los han arrestado. ¿Crees que estos tíos averiguaron lo de la investigación de Straw?

—No lo sé.

—Quizás a Azzara le preocupara que Wilson pudiera hacerle daño. Tal vez a Mendoza y Gomer los mataron porque pensaron que estaban cooperando con los federales.

Pike no lo sabía, pero ya no importaba. Azzara le daba un objetivo, y si veía el objetivo podía apuntar hacia él.

Cole imprimió la foto de Azzara cuando de pronto sonó su teléfono y le dijo a Pike que la que llamaba era Lucy Chenier. Salió con el teléfono a la galería para atender la llamada, y Pike siguió viendo la grabación.

Lo veía a alta velocidad, pero la imagen aun así se movía a cámara lenta, porque pensaba en Azzara y en cómo podía encontrarle. Más corredores iban y venían, pero la mayoría eran mujeres, y los pocos hombres que salían no parecían posibles candidatos a asesinos curtidos con cuchillos. Pike se vio a sí mismo llegar, y luego irse, pero no apareció nadie más en la calle. Había examinado otra hora y veinte minutos del lapso de tres horas cuando Cole volvió de la terraza, muy serio. Detuvo la grabación.

—¿Qué pasa?

—Era el detective de Lucy. El tipo del que te hablé, Terry Babinette.

Pike esperó, sabiendo por la expresión de Cole que las noticias no eran buenas.

—Después del huracán, el ayuntamiento montó unas webs para que la gente pudiera poner el nombre de amigos y familiares evacuados o dados por perdidos. Terry solo ha podido trabajar con nombres, de modo que esto no es definitivo, ¿vale?

—Suéltalo.

—Los nombres de Drusilla Rayne y Wilson Smith están en la lista de los muertos. Drusilla Rayne era una mujer cau-

201

cásica de cuarenta y dos años que murió como indigente en un hospital benéfico tres días después del huracán. Wilson Smith era un varón afroamericano de setenta y seis años que murió de un ataque al corazón cuando lo evacuaban de Natchez, Misisipi. No tenían parientes conocidos ninguno de los dos. Eso es todo.

Pike se sentía dolorido y entumecido. El hombre y la mujer a los que conocía como Wilson Smith y Dru Rayne habían cogido sus nombres de unos muertos, y probablemente usaban también el número de seguridad de los fallecidos para suplantar su identidad. No sabía qué decir, y Cole parecía incómodo.

—¿Quieres ver más vídeos?

—No tiene sentido.

—¿Y qué quieres hacer ahora?

Pike miró la pantalla congelada y se puso de pie.

—Los tiene Azzara. Voy a darme una ducha y luego a buscar a Azzara.

Dejó a Cole ante el ordenador y volvió a la habitación de invitados.

30

Daniel

*D*aniel dijo:

—Si la información que tenemos del mexicano es correcta, sabré cuál es su situación antes de mediodía.

El boliviano parecía más emocionado que nunca, al menos desde que lo conocía Daniel, y eso significaba que «todos» los bolivianos estaban emocionados. Daniel se los imaginó sentados en sus casas, meneándosela y pensando que finalmente habían conseguido su venganza. No había nada que les gustase más a esos hijos de puta que la venganza, y ahora ya la tendrían. Gracias a él.

—No se retire, señor…

Daniel esperó a que el trueno de un *jet* de negocios Hawker se desvaneciese y luego continuó. Esos Hawkers eran guapos.

—Lo siento, señor; estoy en el aeropuerto. ¿Podemos confirmar que el vuelo sale esta mañana?

Bla, bla, bla.

—Está bien, sí, perfecto. ¿Tenemos el número de registro del avión, o su modelo y marca?

Bla, bla.

Cleo dijo:

—Bla, bla.

Tobey dijo:

—Bla, bla.

Daniel los hizo callar.

—Chist.

Daniel escuchaba con mucha atención mientras el boliviano iba soltando los últimos informes de México. El flujo de información entre México y Nueva Orleans durante los dos últimos días había sido valiosísimo, pero no habría habido información alguna sin Daniel, y los bolivianos lo sabían. Daniel finalmente había encontrado a los cabrones, y los muy hijos de puta habían intentado hacer un trato en lugar de salir huyendo, y ahora ese trato los estaba matando.

El hombre lobo sonríe de nuevo.

—Sí, señor, le mantendré informado... Desde luego.

Daniel quería dejar ya el teléfono, pero el boliviano seguía y seguía, diciendo lo encantados que estaban todos con él, con su lealtad y su decisión, bla, bla, bla.

—Gracias, señor. No, realmente... agradezco la confianza que me ha demostrado. Muchas gracias.

Colgó al fin.

—Gilipollas.

Cleo dijo:

—Vaya imbécil.

Tobey dijo:

—Payaso, payaso, payaso.

Daniel entrecerró los ojos y miró hacia la pista, a la torre de control, y luego hacia arriba, a un neblinoso cielo blanco. Se echó hacia atrás y miró arriba, disfrutando del cielo matutino, de aquel lugar y de aquel momento. Había asesinado a gente en aeropuertos como aquel en toda América del Sur y Central. También había secuestrado gente, volado aviones, robado carga y casi todas las malditas cosas que puede hacer una persona.

—Ha sido una larga caza, chicos.

Tobey dijo:

—Demasiado larga.

Cleo dijo:

—Sí, demasiado larga.

El aeropuerto de Santa Mónica era una sencilla pista con hangares y locales comerciales alineados, junto con una zona de observación donde se sentó Daniel. La gente podía ver desde allí despegar y aterrizar todo tipo de aparatos, desde Cessnas hechos polvo hasta *jets* de empresas, y él podría ver aterrizar el *jet* y tener tiempo suficiente para colocarse en su posición. Ya sabía dónde pararía el avión que llegaba. Una limusina, un SS396 color dorado y un Monte Carlo recortado aparecieron pocos minutos antes de que llamase al boliviano, y esperaron directamente en la pista. Montar un comité de bienvenida era una idea estúpida, desde luego, pero la limusina era una cucaracha negra y gorda que le conduciría hasta la tierra prometida.

Daniel miró su reloj. Si el boliviano decía la verdad, el mexicano aterrizaría al cabo de menos de una hora y se dirigiría hacia el lugar de su reunión.

—Chicos, ¿preparados para matar a alguien?

Tobey dijo:

—Joder, sí.

Cleo dijo:

—Matarlos, sí, qué bien.

Daniel soltó una risita.

—Yo también, chicos, pero no hasta que consigamos lo que queremos.

—¿Entonces podremos matarlos?

—¿Matarlos?

—Desde luego que sí.

—¿Matarlos y comerlos?

—¿Comerlos, comerlos?

—Chicos, estáis locos…

—¿Locos?

—¿… cos?

Daniel disfrutó del sol en su cara y de la agradable compañía de sus voces, sus ecos.

31

Elvis Cole

Cole vio alejarse a Pike en su coche, y luego volvió a su escritorio para mirar las fotos de Dru y Wilson, que en realidad no eran Dru Rayne ni Wilson Smith. La gente se cambia de nombre para esconderse, pero ¿esconderse de qué y quién? Cole era detective desde hacía mucho tiempo, y sabía que la gente a veces tiene buenos motivos para esconderse, pero la mayor parte de las veces los motivos son malos. Tenía un mal presentimiento con aquella gente y, cuanto más sabía del caso, peor se volvía aquella sensación.

La foto de la mujer era la mejor. Se había vuelto hacia la izquierda, como si estuviera hablando con Mendoza o Azzara, de modo que estaba de frente a la cámara. Wilson miraba por encima del volante, ofreciendo una imagen en tres cuartos, con parte de su rostro bloqueado por el espejo retrovisor de un lado.

Algo en la expresión de ambos preocupaba a Cole, pero no sabía el qué. Al cabo de unos pocos minutos dejó a un lado las fotos y llamó a Bree Sloan, de la compañía telefónica, para preguntar por los móviles. A veces le devolvían la llamada enseguida, y otras veces en cambio tenía que insistir.

Ella le dijo:

—Me has leído el pensamiento. Estaba a punto de llamarte.

—¿Tienes buenas noticias?

—No, no te gustarán nada, pero aun así me darás las entradas, ¿no?

—Claro que sí.

Cole conseguía excelentes entradas para ver a los Dodgers

de un antiguo cliente, y se las daba a la gente que le ayudaba. Especialmente a personas como Bree, que era jefa regional de una compañía de telecomunicaciones local de tamaño mediano. Unos asientos exclusivos en el Dodgers Dugout Club funcionaban mejor que una orden judicial.

—¿Estás en tu ordenador?

—Mirándolo. No es tan sexy como tú.

Bree se echó a reír. Tenía una risa estupenda.

—Ay, cómo eres.

—Increíble, ¿verdad?

—Vale, dejémoslo ya y escucha. Esos tres números que me diste... 8272, 3563 y 3502...

Cole miró sus notas. Eran los cuatro últimos dígitos de los números del local de Wilson, el móvil de Wilson y el móvil de Dru.

—Sí. Dime.

—8272 es una línea terrestre de ATT facturada a la empresa hostelera de Wilson. Te voy a mandar los registros entrantes y salientes de los últimos cuarenta y cinco días, ¿vale? Es todo lo que tenemos.

—Entiendo.

Las empresas proveedoras de servicios telefónicos normalmente guardaban el historial de llamadas solamente durante cuarenta y cinco días, aunque seguían guardando la información de facturación más tiempo. Cole esperaba que fuera así cuando examinó las facturas que encontró en el archivador de Wilson.

—Y ahora las malas noticias. El 3563 y el 3502 son de prepago, de un proveedor pequeño establecido en Phoenix. Me debes una buena por estos dos... El tío con el que hablé de allí es un auténtico gilipollas.

—¿Son esos los números de móvil?

—Sí. El proveedor es una empresa llamada Electrotelepathy. Alquilan espacio en su antena a compañías más importantes como nosotros, pero a una escala mucho más reducida. Están especializados en opciones prepago. Así se ahorran la infraestructura.

—¿Y has conseguido el historial?

—Te lo envío por e-mail, pero aquí viene la parte que no te

207

va a gustar: los números fueron activados hace solo doce días. No hay demasiada historia, que digamos.

Cole se echó atrás en la silla. Wilson y Dru usaban teléfonos de usar y tirar, y eso probablemente significaba que cambiaban de número a menudo. Números falsos, imposibles de rastrear. ¿Podía ser más perfecta la cosa?

—¿Y existe algún historial de mensajes de texto?

—Electrotelepathy no guarda los mensajes ni los correos electrónicos. Eso es bastante habitual; algunas de las compañías grandes tampoco los guardan. Y antes de que me preguntes (porque leo la mente también, y sé lo que me vas a preguntar) esos teléfonos no permiten el rastreo por GPS. Electrotelepathy es una empresa de poca categoría, y sus productos son de gama baja.

—¿Son muy recientes los historiales?

—Hasta esta mañana. Que es cuando he hablado con él. Por tercera vez.

—Vale, gracias, amiga. Te lo agradezco de verdad.

—Un partido de los Giants, ¿eh?

—Los Giants.

Bree era fan de los Dodgers, pero su novia, Estelle, era fan de los Giants de San Francisco. El suyo era un matrimonio mixto.

—Eres mi héroe, Elvis. A Estelle le encantará.

—Dile que es la mujer más afortunada de la tierra.

—Eso hago. Todas las noches.

—¡Bien por los azules!

—¡Bien!

Cole se echó a reír mientras colgaba.

Cuando apareció el mensaje de correo de Bree, lo abrió y se encontró tres documentos adjuntos, uno para cada uno de los tres números de teléfono. Los dos historiales de llamadas de móviles eran breves, tal y como le había dicho Bree. Cole no supo cuál era el de Dru y cuál el de Wilson hasta que los fue examinando y encontró el número de móvil de Pike en el historial del 3502. Ese tenía que ser el móvil de Dru. Su última llamada la hizo al número de Pike, casi tres días antes, a las 23.32. Cole supuso que aquella era la llamada perdida de la que le había hablado Pike. Ya no había ninguna más desde aquel número a partir de ese momento. Comprobó el 3563 y no encontró registro alguno desde aquel mismo día más temprano, cosa que significaba que Wilson no había hecho tampoco ninguna llamada en los últimos tres días. Eso coincidía con el secuestro, pero Cole sabía que Wilson había llamado al detective Button después de ver el estropicio de su tienda, y esa llamada no había quedado registrada en la lista. Comprobó si se había hecho desde el local de Wilson, pero tampoco se había telefoneado desde allí aquella mañana. Se quedó muy sorprendido y desconcertado. Si la llamada a Button no aparecía en ninguno de los tres registros, ¿cuántos teléfonos tenía Wilson Smith?

Cole imprimió los tres documentos, y luego se quedó de nuevo mirando las fotos. Era como si estas intentaran decirle algo que él no era capaz de oír.

Frustrado las dejó a un lado, se sirvió otra taza de café y se dedicó a los historiales de llamadas buscando números recurrentes. Estaba elaborando una lista de los números a los que se había llamado más frecuentemente cuando sonó su teléfono.

—¿Puedes hablar? —preguntó John Chen.

—Sí. ¿Dónde estás?

—De camino hacia Los Feliz. Algún idiota ha perdido al juego de la ruleta rusa. Es la única vez que puedo tener algo de intimidad, yendo hacia la escena de un crimen. Llevo toda la mañana esperando para llamarte.

—¿Tienes alguna huella?

—¿Acaso no soy Chen? Once muestras distintas, y estoy bastante seguro de que algunas pertenecen a mujeres. Lo digo basándome en el tamaño; es solo una suposición, pero quienquiera que sea no está fichada. No tienes que preocuparte por ella. El otro tío es muy distinto.

—¿Has encontrado algo sobre el hombre?

—Más o menos.

—¿Cómo que más o menos, John? Venga, ¿quién es?

—No lo sé. Por eso digo que más o menos. Tengo un expediente sellado. Lo único que he podido conseguir es un número de expediente y una indicación que dice con quién hay que ponerse en contacto.

—¿Y qué quiere decir eso?

—Puede significar cualquier cosa. El tío puede ser un policía, un agente federal, quizás alguien en un programa de protección de testigos, algo por el estilo. Vemos esas cosas también con el personal militar, cuando se trata de un tío de las Delta, los SEAL o una de esas cosas de alto secreto.

—¿Me estás diciendo que el hombre es un agente secreto?

—No, solo eran ejemplos. Puede ser un criminal o un policía.

—¿Por qué?

—Por la indicación. Dice que hay que ponerse en contacto con el FBI o el Departamento de Justicia de Luisiana para pedir información. Eso le descarta como agente secreto.

—¿Y has llamado?

—¡No, demonios! Sabrían que estoy implicado. Solo me faltaba eso, ya temo que investiguen mi ordenador por mirar la huella... Quizá vengan husmeando a ver por qué nosotros tenemos sus huellas.

Cole notó un pinchazo de preocupación.

—¿Te vas a meter en un lío por esto?

—No. Usé la contraseña de Harriet cuando entré. No pueden rastrearme. —Harriet era la jefa de John—. Siento no poder conseguirte la información, tío, pero yo no puedo ir más lejos. Quería ayudarte, de verdad. Díselo a Joe, ¿vale?

—Has ayudado mucho, John. De verdad. ¿Qué número tiene el expediente?

Cole copió el número de expediente, e inmediatamente llamó a Lucy Chenier. Estaba en una reunión, pero había dejado instrucciones de que la interrumpiesen si llamaba Cole. Cuando se puso al teléfono, le explicó lo que necesitaba.

—¿Tiene Terry un contacto en el Departamento de Justicia de Luisiana?

—Probablemente más de uno. ¿Por qué?

Cole le contó lo del expediente sellado con su indicación de ponerse en contacto con Justicia de Luisiana.

Lucy suspiró, pensativa.

—El Departamento de Justicia y el FBI. No me gustan las cosas que nos estamos encontrando.

—A mí tampoco. ¿Puedo darte el número de expediente?

Cole se lo leyó, esperó a que ella lo copiase y confirmó cuando ella se lo repitió para asegurarse de que lo había apuntado correctamente.

—Bien. A ver cómo quiere enfocar esto Terry.

—Gracias, Luce.

—Una cosa...

Él esperó.

—Estos expedientes sellados pueden ser cualquier cosa, pero siempre significan que es importante para alguien que la identidad de ese individuo esté protegida. En cuanto Terry haga la gestión (aunque sea a través de una de sus fuentes) no podremos volver a meter al genio en la botella. La gente que está ocultando a ese hombre pueden resultar unos genios con muy mala leche.

—Ya, lo entiendo.

—¿Estás seguro de que quieres seguir adelante?

—Sí.

—Nos pondremos en contacto contigo cuando podamos.

Cole dejó el teléfono con cierta intranquilidad, notando que le estaba levantando los pies del suelo un río frenético de acontecimientos desconocidos y gente extraña, y el río se lo estaba llevando. Se desperezó hasta que le crujieron los hombros, luego recordó las fotos y finalmente se dio cuenta de lo que le había estado incordiando.

Puso las dos fotos en el teclado y examinó de nuevo las caras. Los ojos de Wilson y Dru no mostraban la ansiosa tensión de la gente que tiene un cañón apuntándoles a la espalda. No parecían asustados. Se preguntó por qué.

32

Pike bajó a toda velocidad por el cañón desde la casa de Elvis Cole hasta que se vio libre de las altas crestas. Llamó a Arturo Alvarez al entrar en terreno llano. El teléfono sonó tantas veces que Pike pensó que nadie contestaría, pero finalmente lo cogió una joven con la voz tan apagada que Pike no estaba seguro de si era la misma que había conocido en la casa de Ojos de Ángel.

—Diga.

—¿Marisol?

—Sí, ¿qué quiere?

—Soy Joe Pike. ¿Puedo hablar con Artie?

Hubo un silencio tan largo al otro lado de la línea que Pike se preguntó si ella le habría dejado en espera.

—¿Hola?

—Váyase a la mierda.

Ella colgó sin decir nada más, y Pike supo por su rabia que a Art le había ocurrido algo malo.

La casa de estuco recién pintada estaba tan apagada como la voz de Marisol cuando llegó Pike. La multitud de niños que había visto durante su última visita había desaparecido, y el patio estaba desierto, excepto por un monitor que estaba subido en el tejado, sin camisa, cambiando las tejas bajo el sol de final de la mañana.

La puerta delantera estaba abierta para que entrase el aire, de modo que Pike no llamó. Entró y encontró el salón vacío.

—¿Hay alguien?

Oyó una voz en la parte de atrás y apareció Marisol en el

vestíbulo, con los brazos cruzados y muy apretados encima del pecho, y sus ojos furiosos como negras bocas de cañón.

—Largo de aquí.

—¿Dónde está Art?

—Usted los atrajo aquí. Váyase.

Pike llamó hacia la casa.

—¿Art?

Un murmullo bajo que reconoció como la voz de Art llegó de la habitación de atrás, pero Marisol habló más fuerte.

—No le queremos aquí. Váyase.

Pike la empujó a un lado y encontró al padre Art en un pequeño dormitorio frente a su despacho, una de las diminutas habitaciones que usaban los chicos cuando no tenían otro lugar adonde ir. Ya hacía bastante calor, pero las ventanas estaban abiertas y un pequeño ventilador eléctrico removía el aire. Art estaba echado en una cama individual con unos cojines como apoyo. Tenía el ojo izquierdo tan hinchado que era solo una rendija; ambos ojos de color morado y negro. Unas contusiones como los montes Verdugo le atravesaban la frente. Tenía la nariz de dos veces su tamaño normal y torcida hacia la derecha, señalando hacia su labio superior partido, y un moretón en la mejilla. Con la camiseta blanca y suelta que llevaba parecía muy flaco.

—Azzara —dijo Pike.

No era una pregunta sino una afirmación.

Llegó Marisol por detrás y le dio un puñetazo en la espalda.

—No quiere verle. Lárguese de aquí. —Le dio otro—. ¿Me oye, hijo de puta?

Art levantó la mano y habló con dificultad:

—Marisol. Así no.

Pike la ignoró, mirando hacia el ojo bueno de Art.

—Te llevaré a un hospital.

—Ni hablar, hermano. Nada de hospital.

Pike se acercó más y el ojo bueno de Art le siguió.

—¿Esto es por mi culpa?

Marisol volvió a hablarle por detrás.

—¿Qué le parece? Le echaron la culpa por lo que fuera que usted hizo en el taller de chapa. Y vinieron aquí buscando a Art. No tendría que haberle ayudado.

Pike levantó la camisa de Art. Tenía el pecho y el abdomen lleno de manchas con hematomas morados y verdes de puñetazos y patadas. Le habían pegado tan fuerte que las patadas y puñetazos salieron de Art y fueron hacia Pike. Se bajó la camiseta para cubrir las marcas.

—Es lo que les enseño a estos chicos. ¿Veis cómo se extiende la violencia? Me has decepcionado, hombre.

—¿Tienes las costillas rotas?

—Estoy bien.

—Déjame que te lleve a un médico.

—No, ya está. Olvídalo.

Pike miró a Marisol.

—Tendría que haberme llamado.

—Iba a hacerlo pero él no me dejó: ni a usted, ni a la policía, ni a nadie.

Art levantó la mano otra vez.

—Ya estaba hecho. Ahora tengo que reconstruir la confianza que se ha perdido.

Marisol dijo algo en español que Pike no entendió, pero era duro y furioso.

—¿Dónde puedo encontrarle, Artie? Dime dónde vive.

—¿Para que vayas a matarle? No.

Pike sacó la foto de Azzara y Mendoza en el coche detrás de Wilson y Dru.

—Para salvar a esta gente o encontrar sus cuerpos. Azzara me mintió. Me dijo que detendría a Mendoza y que no sabía lo que les había ocurrido, pero aquí está con ellos dos y con Mendoza. Miguel me va a decir dónde están, Art. Él lo sabe.

—No, ya basta. Si no puedo seguir con esto, ¿quién ayudará a esos chicos? ¿Quién les tenderá una mano? Vete, Joe... vete de aquí.

Pike observó a Arturo Alvarez y se dio cuenta de que no había nada más que decir. Era un tío duro, de la vieja escuela, a pesar de todos sus títulos universitarios. En su mundo la dureza no se juzgaba por lo bien que se podía dar una paliza, sino por lo bien que se encajaba.

—Déjame que te lleve al hospital.

Art se volvió hacia la ventana.

Pike miró a Marisol y se alejó. Lo siguió como un furibundo perro guardián, pero él se detuvo en el salón y bajó la voz.

—¿Tiene fiebre?

—No lo sé. ¿Por qué?

—Compruébalo. Si tiene fiebre o empieza a sudar mucho, llámame.

—¿Eres médico ahora?

—O si tiene sangre en la orina.

—Lleva dos días meando sangre. Lo veo cuando le ayudo a ir al baño.

—¿De un rojo intenso o rosa?

Ella miró hacia la habitación de Art, preocupada.

—Rosa, creo. Era rojo, pero ahora ya no tanto. ¿Es bueno?

—Mejor que si fuera rojo, pero no es bueno. Lo que sea que tiene roto se está curando, pero todavía está tocado.

Ella cruzó los brazos de nuevo y sus ojos se endurecieron.

—Ojalá hubiera estado yo aquí. Le encontré a la mañana siguiente, cuando ya era demasiado tarde.

—Te habrían pegado a ti también.

Los ojos negros se clavaron en los suyos.

—¿Usted cree? A lo mejor les habría pegado un tiro y los habría matado.

Los ojos se desplazaron de nuevo hacia el salón, sin perder nada de su fuego.

—Habría llamado a la policía, pero él no me ha dejado. Ni siquiera a la ambulancia. Estúpido idiota, preocupado por su confianza.

—Habla con él, Marisol.

—¿De qué?

—Quiero a Miguel.

—¿Qué cree, que se envían postales por Navidad? Art no sabe dónde vive. Quizá dónde se crio sí, pero Miguel nos abandonó hace años. Ahora es un ejecutivo. Es mejor que nosotros.

Pike notó algo más aparte del desdén en su voz, y notó que tenía el rabillo del ojo algo descolorido. La miró más de cerca y vio que tenía la piel del cuello moteada por el láser, de una forma muy parecida a la decoloración que había observado en Miguel Azzara.

Pike oyó al monitor que estaba en el tejado, partiendo una teja.

215

—¿Erais malevos?

La chica se irguió, una chica de barrio que había crecido entre las bandas.

—De un grupo diferente, pero de la Trece. Mi hermano y yo. A él lo mataron.

«Quizás habría cogido una pistola y les habría pegado un tiro.»

—¿Conoces a Miguel?

Ella apartó la vista y volvió a mirar hacia Artie.

—Antes. Ya no.

—¿Sabes dónde vive?

—Lo sabía.

—Tengo que encontrarlo. Por mis amigos, por Art.

Marisol asintió, pero le costó un poco hablar.

—Quizá. Conozco a chicas que lo conocen. Que han estado en su casa nueva, tan chula.

Apartó la vista y Pike se preguntó si una de esas chicas era ella.

Marisol hizo una llamada y unos minutos más tarde Pike tenía una dirección. Se detuvo en la puerta mientras él se iba.

—Vigila su temperatura. Si sube mucho traeré a un médico, tanto si quiere como si no.

—No quiere gastarse nada. No lo admitiría nunca, pero yo lo sé. Paga Ojos de Ángel con su dinero, y nunca hay suficiente. Siempre necesita más.

—No te preocupes por el dinero. Yo pago.

—No te dejará.

—No tiene por qué saberlo.

Ella cruzó los brazos de nuevo, pero ya no estaba tan enfadada como antes. Pike oía al monitor en el tejado, partiendo la teja, intentando reforzar el tejado.

33

*P*ike creía que Miguel Azzara disfrutaba mirándose. Probablemente ensayaba poses delante del espejo, pensando que era mucho más guapo que los modelos masculinos de las revistas o los jóvenes actores que interpretaban a vampiros y hombres lobo. Tenía que ser así, porque Mikie Azzara había hundido tanto los dientes en el glamour de Hollywood que se había trasladado a Sunset Strip, lo más lejos que un pandillero podía llegar desde Ghost Town. Pike se preguntaba qué dirían los veteranos si se enteraban, hombres ancianos llenos de cicatrices de mil combates que llevaban La Eme desde prisión, viviendo y muriendo a la manera antigua, en el mismo barrio, durante generaciones. Probablemente al principio no les gustaría mucho, pero decidirían seguir adelante, suponiendo que los jóvenes retoños universitarios como Miguel eran el futuro.

El problema es que, cuando Mikie abandonó Ghost Town, dejó a las chicas que se habían entregado a su carisma y su aspecto de estrella de cine, y las sustituyó por universitarias de UCLA, aspirantes a actrices y esas chicas delgadas como un huso que iban de caza por los clubes del Strip. Eso significaba que había dejado atrás a más de una muchacha resentida, incluyendo la prima y mejor amiga de Marisol, Annabel Reynoso, que había visitado la casa varias veces antes de que Miguel la dejara.

Azzara tenía alquilada una casa moderna y pequeña, de un solo piso, en una calle al sur de Sunset, detrás de una serie de clubes, bares, restaurantes y edificios de apartamentos. La vivienda de Azzara era la primera al sur de una calle estrecha que iba paralela a Sunset Boulevard, en el extremo sur de un muro de hormigón que separaba la calle de los propietarios que vivían junto a ella. Este estaba cubierto por enredaderas y bordeado por una hilera de ficus moribundos, detrás de los cuales quedaba la casa de Azzara.

La calle, como todas las calles residenciales cerca de Sunset, estaba llena de coches aparcados y atascada por los conductores que bloqueaban el tráfico mientras maniobraban para intentar salir y entrar de los aparcamientos. Pike no quería arriesgarse a quedar retenido allí y que le vieran frente a la casa de Azzara, de modo que aparcó en Sunset, a dos manzanas de distancia, y se acercó a pie.

Cuando dobló la esquina y se dirigió hacia la casa vio a dos guardias, de modo que siguió y dobló la otra esquina. La casa de Azzara quedaba oculta por la pared, pero el Monte Carlo estaba aparcado junto a la acera, con Hector dentro. Un segundo hombre merodeaba por la boca del callejón, apoyado contra la pared. El Tercel plateado de Dru estaba detrás del Monte Carlo.

Pike cruzó la calle con una multitud de peatones cuando cambió el semáforo, y siguió por Sunset hasta la calle siguiente. Quería acercarse a Azzara desde detrás, pero cuando se dirigió hacia el callejón se detuvo de nuevo. Dos hombres estaban sentados en una furgoneta Chevy aparcada delante. Había más guardias cubriendo la parte trasera de la casa.

Volvió a la primera esquina y examinó la calle de Azzara desde una posición detrás de un estanco. Notó un zumbido de alarma no muy alto, pero sí continuo, como si estuviese a punto de ser alcanzado por un proyectil que se acercaba, pero ninguno de los guardias parecía haberle visto.

Se dijo que debía tener calma. Todo iba bien. Todo estaba controlado.

La pared le impedía la visión de la casa de Azzara, y no veía ninguna forma adecuada de acercarse sin que le reconocieran. Sabía que podía acercarse más en cuanto oscureciera, pero no quería esperar: el Tercel indicaba que Dru y Wilson estaban dentro, y vivos. Pike no quería arriesgarse a perderles.

Examinó los edificios a lo largo de Sunset y notó que el que estaba justo por encima de la casa de Azzara era un espacio comercial más antiguo, de dos pisos, con un letrero enorme de Regency en el tejado. Este estaba frente a Sunset para que los conductores vieran el anuncio, pero la parte trasera del letrero arrojaba sombra sobre la casa de Azzara.

Dieciséis minutos más tarde Pike subía por una escalera de servicio y trepaba al borde del tejado que daba al callejón. El extremo más alejado del tejado de Azzara era visible entre los ficus, pero nada más.

Retrocedió y pensó de nuevo en el letrero. La parte trasera era un marco de vigas de acero apoyadas en unas enormes patas hechas también de grueso tubo de acero. Una escalera enjaulada trepaba por la pata central hasta una pasarela que se extendía de un extremo del letrero al otro, y pasaba en torno a la parte delantera.

Pike se subió al marco y fue recorriendo la pasarela. Se fue escondiendo detrás del letrero hasta que encontró una vista mucho mejor, y luego se introdujo entre las vigas de acero. Vio entonces gran parte del jardín trasero y la parte de atrás de la casa. Con el jardín le bastaba.

219

Unas puertas de cristal que iban del techo al suelo, a lo largo de la parte trasera de la casa, daban a las líneas limpias de una piscina rectangular y un patio. Dru Rayne estaba echada en una tumbona frente a la piscina, con unas enormes gafas de sol que le ocultaban el rostro. A poca distancia de ella, Wilson Smith estaba de pie con Azzara y otros tres hombres latinos, uno de los cuales era el vaquero que Pike había visto en el taller de chapa. Los cinco hombres se reían. Otro vaquero estaba sentado solo en una silla de lona al otro lado del patio, y otro más estaba dentro, en el sofá del salón.

Ping.

Pike se tensó al notar aquella sensación, pero ninguno de los hombres gritó ni se echó a correr.

Ping.

Comprobó el tejado por debajo del letrero, pero no vio a nadie. Verificó si se veía el callejón y la calle frente a la casa de Azzara, pero los guardias no le habían visto.

Hizo un esfuerzo para relajarse. Un hombre robusto, con la cara como una piña y unos tatuajes muy sofisticados, salió de

la casa con una botella de cerveza, y Azzara inmediatamente
dejó el círculo para hacer lugar al hombre. Era obvio que le trataba con deferencia. Se fue hacia la casa y pronto volvió con
tres botellas marrones. Le dio una a uno de los vaqueros, más
viejo y bajo, otra a Smith y le llevó la tercera a Dru. Ella le
dedicó una sonrisa muy cordial al darle las gracias, y Azzara
volvió con los demás. El buen anfitrión.

Nadie parecía secuestrado.

Pike se sintió hueco, como una burbuja que flotase en el
agua. Iba a la deriva, exactamente igual que una burbuja; un
vacío cubierto por una piel muy fina, sin peso, sin sustancia.
Se concentró en la burbuja: la obligó a menguar hasta que
desapareció. La sensación de vacío seguía ahí, pero no se podía
ver sin la piel que la cubría. Sin burbuja solo quedaba la nada,
y Pike ya no sentía nada.

Ping.

El hombre robusto del tatuaje estrechó la mano del vaquero mayor y más bajo. Se sonrieron el uno al otro y volvieron
a reír. Se trataban entre sí como iguales. Pike pensó que el
hombre robusto era un veterano de La Eme de alto rango, pero
se preguntó quiénes serían los vaqueros.

Era obvio que Dru y Wilson estaban allí porque querían, y
no se hallaban ante ningún peligro inmediato. Pike pensó en
llamar a Straw, Button y Elvis, pero decidió esperar a ver cómo
se desarrollaban las cosas.

Veintidós minutos después, una limusina negra y larga se
acercó por delante a la casa de Azzara. Wilson, el vaquero más
bajo y el hombre robusto siguieron al anfitrión hacia la casa,
pero Dru y el tipo que estaba sentado permanecieron fuera.
Pike tenía que decidir si quedarse en la casa o seguir a la limusina, y tenía que hacerlo antes de saber lo que harían Wilson
y Dru. Llegar hasta su Jeep podía costarle varios minutos, de
modo que, si iba a seguirles, tenía que salir ya. Si esperaba a
verlos partir, no llegaría a su Jeep hasta después de que la
limusina se hubiese ido.

Decidió seguirles.

Recorrió ágilmente las vigas y corrió a toda velocidad por
Sunset hasta su Jeep, pensando que la limusina ya se habría
ido, pero cuando apareció ante la calle de Azzara, la parte tra-

sera asomaba todavía de la casa de Azzara. Pike retrocedió y aparcó en una zona roja frente al estanco. Cinco minutos más tarde la limusina retrocedió y salió colina arriba, hacia él. Pike bajó los visores y se agachó detrás del volante. La limusina se detuvo justo frente a él, esperando al tráfico. Distinguió la oscura silueta del chófer, pero las ventanillas traseras, tintadas, ocultaban a los que iban en el asiento posterior. Cuando apareció un hueco en el tráfico la limusina dio la vuelta. Pike dejó pasar dos coches y luego fue tras ellos.

La limusina atravesó la ciudad por La Cienaga Boulevard, deslizándose lenta y segura, como suelen hacer ese tipo de vehículos. La siguió hasta la autopista I-10 y luego hacia el oeste, hacia Santa Mónica. Cuando hubieron cruzado la 405, Pike pensó que se dirigían hacia Venice, pero salieron por Bundy y dieron la vuelta hacia Ocean Park. Tres minutos después iban hacia el lado norte del aeropuerto de Santa Mónica, y Pike se vio obligado a quedarse mucho más atrás. La limusina se dirigió hacia una cancela que se apartó para dejarlos entrar en la zona de hangar, y luego se detuvo junto a un *jet* de negocios blanco Citation. La puerta del *jet* estaba abierta y la escalera bajada y esperando.

Pike aparcó y observó la escena.

El chófer de la limusina saltó a abrir las portezuelas, pero la gente que estaba dentro no esperó. Wilson, Miguel Azzara, el hombre robusto y el vaquero más bajito salieron de sus asientos. Dru se había quedado en la casa.

Los cuatro hombres se reunieron junto al *jet*, y una vez más se estrecharon las manos. El vaquero dio unas palmadas a Wilson en el hombro como si fueran los mejores amigos del mundo, y luego subió a bordo. Tiró de las escaleras, las subió él mismo y cerró la puerta como si lo hubiese hecho ya cien veces, mientras los demás volvían a la limusina.

Pike observó el número de matrícula: XB-CCL. El prefijo XB significaba que aquel avión estaba registrado en México.

Azzara, el hombre robusto y Wilson se quedaron junto a la limusina mientras el avión ponía en marcha sus motores. Pike vio al piloto y copiloto accionando interruptores mientras iniciaban la maniobra de despegue. Les costó unos minutos, pero Azzara, el hombre robusto y Wilson esperaron. Cuando el *jet* finalmente se alejó, agitaron la mano como lacayos, cosa que le dijo a Pike que el vaquero achaparrado era un hombre muy importante.

En cuanto el avión se hubo ido, el hombre robusto pasó el brazo alrededor de los hombros de Azzara y lo abrazó como si hubiera hecho algo muy bueno. El joven sonrió como si fuera una estrella de cine, y luego sujetó la portezuela para que entrase en el coche el hombre robusto.

Pike ya había visto bastante. Dio la vuelta en redondo, se alejó y llamó a Elvis Cole.

34

Daniel

*D*aniel miró al idiota del Monte Carlo al pasar andando junto a la casa, un tío tan bobo y gilipollas que se había quedado dormido.

Cleo dijo:

—Idiota, idiota.

Tobey dijo:

—Mira ese idiota, se ha dormido.

A Daniel le encantaban los putos aficionados, tan fáciles de matar, pero los pandilleros tenían mucha gente alrededor de la casa y entorpecían su estilo.

Siguió colina abajo hasta la calle siguiente, y luego se subió a su camión. El letrero del camión era de una empresa llamada Hero-Rooter, y decía: ¡LLAMA A UN HÉROE PARA QUE TE SALVE! ¡DESAGÜES LIMPIOS LAS VEINTICUATRO HORAS! Había cogido aquel camión porque no tenía ventanas en los paneles laterales y quedaría disimulado en cualquier parte. Había dejado al conductor en unos contenedores de basura detrás de un restaurante nigeriano, en Long Beach.

Tobey dijo:

—¿Qué estamos haciendo?

Cleo dijo:

—Dar por el saco, saco.

Daniel dijo:

—Callad. Estoy intentando pensar.

—Pensar.

—Pensar.

Daniel había seguido al mexicano y su séquito de estúpidos

pandilleros desde el aeropuerto, de modo que sabía que estaba dentro con el cocinero y la camarera. Los bolivianos habían acertado de pleno en su pronóstico sobre el mexicano, pero alcanzar sus objetivos había resultado un problema.

Daniel dio la vuelta a la manzana subiendo por Sunset, y planeaba ir por el callejón hasta la casa de Azzara, pero entonces vio al tipo alto que salía del Jeep Cherokee rojo. Daniel sabía muy bien que era él, y le asaltó un brote de miedo.

Tobey dijo:

—Mira, mira esas flechas.

Cleo dijo:

—El tío del puente, puente.

Con esta eran dos veces, y dos veces era mala señal. Daniel le había visto en el canal y ahora ahí estaba de nuevo, a una manzana del cocinero y la camarera.

Fue aminorando con el camión para coger el semáforo en rojo. El hombre llegó a la calle de Azzara, dobló la esquina, luego dio un rápido giro de ciento ochenta grados y se mezcló con una multitud de peatones.

Tobey dijo:

—Los está buscando.

Cleo dijo:

—Será mejor que le matemos, matemos.

Daniel negó con la cabeza, intentando ver qué se proponía el hombre, incapaz de entender nada.

Tobey dijo:

—Parece un poli.

Cleo dijo:

—Huele como un poli, poli.

Cuando cambió el semáforo el tío de las flechas cruzó con la multitud y fue caminando por Sunset como la cosa más normal del mundo. Daniel examinó al tipo al pasar. Un tío alto, fuerte, que se movía como si fuera flotando. Las manos eran feas, sin embargo, con unos nudillos grandes y ásperos y las venas que sobresalían de su piel como si fueran sarmientos.

Un poli especialista en bandas de incógnito, o incluso un federal.

Pero ¿vendría solo un policía?

Daniel giró en la calle siguiente, y luego dio la vuelta a la manzana y volvió a Sunset, buscando el Jeep. Lo encontró rápidamente, apuntó el número de matrícula y luego hizo una maniobra hasta un aparcamiento para llamar al boliviano.

Lo primero que este le preguntó era si había cazado a los objetivos.

—No, señor, todavía no, pero los tengo localizados. El mexicano me ha llevado hasta ellos.

Maldiciones y gritos, las habituales mierdas bolivianas. Daniel levantó las cejas.

—Señor, la situación está controlada, pero necesito su ayuda para un asunto. Tenemos a un hombre en la escena que quizá sea oficial de policía o agente federal.

Más bla, bla, bla.

—No, señor; no afectará al resultado, pero me gustaría saber quién es. Tengo su número de matrícula.

Daniel leyó el número, y luego colgó antes de que el hijo de puta pudiera seguir gritando más mierdas. Ahora estaba oficialmente preocupado por el tío de las flechas, y no le gustaba no saber dónde estaba y qué andaba haciendo. El tío de las flechas era un imponderable, y estos pueden morderte en el culo. Daniel decidió que mataría a ese cabrón si lo volvía a ver, aunque fuese un poli, para que no le jodiera el asunto a la hora de coger al cocinero y la camarera. Daniel no quería matarlos. Necesitaba cogerlos vivos y dejar lo de matarlos para más tarde.

Tobey dijo:

—Mátalos.

Cleo dijo:

—Córtales la cabeza, cabeza, cabeza.

Ese era el plan, cortarles la cabeza y mandárselas a los bolivianos. Les gustaban esas cosas macabras.

Dio la vuelta de nuevo hacia la calle de Azzara y aparcó por debajo de la casa, mirando al norte, hacia Sunset, para mantener vigilado todo el asunto. Examinó las casas de los alrededores y el tráfico que subía por Sunset. Los guardias ignoraron su camión. Estúpidos. Daniel comprobó a los peatones que cruzaban Sunset, pensando que igual veía de nuevo al tío de las flechas. Se preguntó dónde estaría ese cabronazo, y si vigilaría a Azzara, o si no sería todo más que una simple coinci-

225

dencia y el tío habría acudido a Sunset a hacerse otro tatuaje. Miró el letrero publicitario mucho rato. Gran parte estaba oculto por los árboles, pero Daniel había pensado en usarlo antes, y ahora lo pensaba de nuevo.

Daniel miraba al idiota del Monte Carlo cuando pasó una limusina negra y se metió en la entrada de Azzara. Recordaba la matrícula: era el mismo coche que había traído al mexicano del aeropuerto, cosa que significaba que ahora iban a llevarle allí de vuelta.

Daniel pensó: «Adiós, muchacho».

Contemplaba la limusina cuando captó un movimiento en el letrero publicitario, entre los árboles. Alguien bajaba de allí, y él sabía que era el tío de las flechas.

—¡Hijo de puta! ¡Estaba vigilando la casa!

—Hostia, hostia, hostia.

Treinta segundos más tarde el tío alto corría por la calle, dirigiéndose hacia su Jeep. Tenía que haber visto también la limusina. Y ahora iba a seguirles.

Tobey dijo:

—Ahí está, mátalo, mátalo.

Cleo dijo:

—Ahí está, cógelo, cógelo.

—¡Ya lo sé, ya lo sé, pero no podemos! ¡Tenemos que quedarnos en la casa!

Daniel olía la sangre en el agua, y sabía que estaba cerca.

El mexicano, Azzara, un pandillero gordo y el cocinero salieron y entraron en la limusina. El corazón de Daniel latía acelerado, y se incorporó en su asiento.

—¡No! ¡Tú no! ¡Quédate! ¡No te vayas con ellos!

Estaba furioso. Apretó el volante hasta que pareció que los huesos iban a salirse a través de la piel. El cocinero y la camarera se estaban separando: él se iba con el mexicano y ella se quedaba en la casa. ¡Le habían jodido!

Tobey dijo:

—Tranquilo.

Cleo susurró:

—Tranquilo, tío; tranquilo.

—¡Tranquilo los cojones! ¿Y el policía? ¿Y si coge la limusina?

La limusina retrocedió en la entrada y se dirigió hacia Sunset.

Tobey dijo:

—Sigamos a esos cabrones.

Cleo dijo:

—Coge a la camarera, Daniel. Ya pensaremos algo, algo, algo.

Daniel sentía que tiraban de sus brazos y sus piernas por las articulaciones; el cocinero en una dirección y la camarera en otra, pero las voces le tranquilizaban. Las voces le ayudaban a pensar.

Tobey susurró:

—La camarera está aquí, coge a la camarera.

Cleo murmuró:

—Coge a la camarera; el cocinero irá después, después, después.

Daniel sabía que tenía razón. Vio desaparecer la limusina al dar la vuelta hacia Sunset.

Primero cogería a la camarera y luego al cocinero, y así los tendría a todos.

227

35

Elvis Cole

Cole se metió el teléfono bajo el oído, intentando asimilar lo que le estaba diciendo Pike. Parecía que le estaba describiendo una realidad mientras que Cole intentaba captar otra.

—Lo que me estás diciendo es que no tratan a esa gente como prisioneros.

—Había cuatro guardias fuera de la casa, y al menos dos más dentro. Si pones guardias fuera no es para evitar que se escape alguien, sino para evitar que entren.

—No lo entiendo. ¿Cómo pasó la gente de la Trece de dar una paliza a Smith a ser sus anfitriones en solo tres días?

Pike no contestó.

—No respondas, si no quieres.

—Por la forma que han tenido de estrecharse las manos me da que son negocios. El avión privado desde México me indica que son negocios a lo grande.

—¿Tienes el número de matrícula? —Copió el número cuando se lo dictó Pike—. Bien. Intentaré averiguar de quién es. ¿Adónde vas ahora?

—Vuelvo a casa de Azzara.

—Ven aquí primero. Quiero ir contigo.

Cole pensó un momento, intentando asimilar los nuevos acontecimientos.

—Alguien está persiguiendo a esa gente. Eso lo sabemos con toda seguridad. Pensábamos que eran Mendoza y Gomer, pero no eran ellos, y ahora Miguel Azzara es su mejor amigo.

—Sí.

—¿Los está protegiendo?

—Si haces negocios con una gente, cuidas de ellos.

—No puedo evitar preguntarme por qué una banda callejera de la Trece y unos vaqueros mexicanos con avión privado necesitan hacer negocios con un hombre que fríe ostras.

—Estaré ahí muy pronto. Lo averiguaremos.

Cole pasó los diez minutos siguientes intentando identificar a los propietarios del *jet* Citation XB-CCL, pero no tuvo suerte. Todavía estaba a la espera con la Administración Federal de Aviación cuando recibió el aviso de que le llamaba Lucy Chenier. Colgó a la AFA y cogió la llamada de Lucy.

Su voz estaba plenamente sintonizada en el modo profesional.

—¿Puedes hablar?

—Desde luego. ¿Qué has averiguado?

—Voy a ponerlo sin manos. Terry está aquí.

La calidad del sonido pasó de aguda a hueca cuando ella conectó el altavoz.

—Hola, Terry. Gracias por ayudarnos en esto.

—De nada, hombre; no importa. ¿Me oyes bien?

—Estupendo.

Terry tenía una voz melodiosa, con un acento silvestre de Luisiana. Se había criado en una familia de policías, y él mismo también fue policía antes de retirarse y trabajar como detective para la empresa de Lucy.

—Bueno, estamos en mi despacho, solos. Nadie puede oír lo que digamos excepto Terry, tú y yo —explicó Lucy.

—Bien.

—¿Tú estás solo?

—Sí, solo nosotros.

—¿No está ahí Joe?

—No, todavía no. Está de camino.

Cole se preguntó por qué tomaban todas aquellas precauciones.

—Bien. Voy a enviarte dos fotos por correo electrónico. ¿Estás delante del ordenador?

—Ahora mismo. Voy hacia allá.

—Dime si estas son las personas a las que conoces como Dru Rayne y Wilson Smith.

229

El correo de ella ya le esperaba cuando Cole llegó a su ordenador.

—Espera. Las estoy abriendo.

Cole no se sorprendió al ver que la imagen de Wilson Smith era la de una ficha policial, pero aun así sintió una vaga decepción. La imagen de Dru Rayne en cambio era una instantánea en la que aparecía detrás de una barra de bar, con el pelo recogido, la sonrisa torcida y pulseras baratas con todos los colores del arcoíris en las muñecas. Llevaba una camiseta negra muy ajustada en la que ponía: DALE PROPINA A LA CAMARERA O TE ESCUPIRÁ EN LA BEBIDA.

—Sí. Son ellos.

Terry parecía complacido.

—Maldita sea, tío.

Lucy dijo:

—Lo que estamos a punto de contarte viene de una investigación importante con el Departamento de Justicia de Luisiana. ¿Recuerdas lo que te dije de que no se podía volver a meter al genio dentro de la botella?

—¿Acaso me van a llamar a mí?

Terry volvió a hablar.

—Me presionó mucho, tío. No le di tu nombre ni tu situación, pero apuesto lo que quieras a que ha llamado al FBI. Te has metido en algo que está al rojo vivo, colega. Están investigando una serie de asesinatos ligados a este caso, y el número va creciendo.

Cole notó una sensación plomiza, como de «ya sabía yo que esto iría a peor», mirando la foto de Smith.

—¿Smith es un asesino?

—Sí, seguramente, pero no hablamos de él. Se han cometido al menos ocho asesinatos, o probablemente nueve, por una persona o personas que intentaban encontrar al hombre al que conoces como Wilson Smith.

Cole notó un cosquilleo frío en el centro del pecho. Pike tenía razón... A los canales de Venice había llegado algo mucho más peligroso que los miembros de unas bandas callejeras.

—Los ha encontrado. Está aquí —dijo.

Lucy y Terry hablaron los dos a la vez, mezclando las palabras hasta que Lucy se impuso.

—¿Cómo sabes que los ha encontrado?

Cole les habló de Mendoza y Gomer.

—No estamos seguros de por qué estaban vigilando la casa, pero los encontraron asesinados a la mañana siguiente. Joe cree que los asesinó alguien que iba buscando a Wilson y Dru.

La voz baja de Terry se dirigió a Lucy.

—Esto no me gusta nada. Si es ese tío, tenemos que poner a nuestros colegas a seguir ese rastro mientras todavía siga caliente.

—Elvis y yo lo comprendemos, Terry. Cuéntale lo de Rainey.

A Cole le pareció que oía a Terry coger aliento, casi como si estuviera intentando recuperar la compostura antes de volver al asunto que tenían entre manos.

—El nombre auténtico de Smith es William Allan Rainey. Sacaba dinero de contrabando del país para unos tíos de aquí conectados con un cártel boliviano. Mi informador dice que, en conjunto, probablemente habrá transportado unos seis o siete millones de dólares antes de dejarlo.

—¿Dinero de las drogas?

—¿Dónde si no se ve tanto dinero en efectivo?

Las drogas eran un negocio de dinero en efectivo, y el problema para los proveedores extranjeros era sacar el efectivo del país. Policías curtidos que Cole conocía le habían dicho que era mucho más fácil para los proveedores meter las drogas que sacar el dinero. No podían depositarlo en bancos ni transferirlo en cantidades sustanciales, porque el gobierno controla los bancos y transferir varios miles por aquí y por allá era inútil para una organización que generaba cientos de millones en efectivo.

—El contrabando de dinero en efectivo no merece un expediente cerrado —dijo Cole.

—Fue la DEA, la agencia antidrogas. Le ablandaron, hicieron un trato con Rainey a cambio de información sobre el negocio de los cárteles.

—Era un informador.

—Sí, lo fue durante un par de años, y quizá por eso hizo lo que hizo. Rainey y la mujer desaparecieron dos semanas antes

231

del Katrina con doce millones de dólares de dinero boliviano. Desde entonces van huyendo.

Cole se echó atrás en el asiento.

—Doce millones. Nada menos.

—Eso sí que es dinero —apuntó Lucy.

—Los chicos del cártel daban un millón de dólares de recompensa por la cabeza de Rainey y enviaron a un especialista a buscarle.

—¿Un especialista significa un asesino?

—Un especialista en encontrar a personas que los bolivianos querían hallar, para hacer lo que ellos quisieran que hiciera. En el Departamento de Justicia lo apodaban el Ejecutor. A ese es al que habéis estado persiguiendo por ahí.

Cole notó otro escalofrío y siguió escuchando a Terry.

Según el contacto de este, William Allan Rainey había pasado toda su vida envuelto en pequeñas actividades criminales y aventuras empresariales dudosas. Había abierto varios restaurantes y bares que fracasaron, pero al final creó un negocio estable como proveedor de marisco al por mayor, comprando gambas y pescado a los pescadores locales para vendérselo a los restaurantes. Los pescadores con los que trataba Rainey pertenecían a empresas con un solo barco que pescaban en el Golfo, con base en ciudades pequeñas de los pantanos, recorriendo la costa de Luisiana. Los investigadores creían que fue durante ese periodo cuando Rainey se vio implicado con personas que tenían negocios con el cártel boliviano; él, que siempre se había sentido atraído por el dinero fácil, vio una forma de sacar provecho de su asociación. Los bolivianos necesitaban un modo de sacar su dinero en efectivo del país, y Rainey les proporcionó el método. Su contacto diario con pescadores le permitía reclutar gente abierta a llevar cargas cuestionables, especialmente si estaban un poco atrasados en el pago del alquiler y necesitaban el dinero.

Cole detuvo la explicación.

—¿Sabía esa gente lo que llevaba?

—El trato era que no se hicieran preguntas, pero Rainey les dijo al menos a dos pescadores que llevaban marihuana de camino a Miami. Se embalaba en unos paquetes negros, impermeables, y funcionaba así: Rainey y un par de guardias entregaban los paquetes a un pescador cuando salía, junto con las coordenadas para que se reuniese con un barco más allá de las plataformas petrolíferas. Lo único que tenían que hacer era entregar los paquetes y seguir pescando.

—¿Y Rainey le contó todo esto a la agencia antidrogas?

Terry se echó a reír.

—No. Les daba los datos de algún envío que entraba, de vez en cuando, o delataba a algunos jugadores de poca monta; justo lo suficiente para mantener a la agencia apartada. No sabían que estaba sacando dinero de contrabando hasta que todo saltó por los aires.

—¿Qué ocurrió?

Contestó Lucy:

—La mujer. El verdadero nombre de Dru Rayne es Rose Marie Platt. Rainey la conoció cuando ella trabajaba en un restaurante en el Quarter para un hombre llamado Tolliver James. Ella y James vivían juntos.

Terry volvió a intervenir.

—James compraba pescado y gambas a Rainey, así que imaginamos que fue así como se conocieron Rainey y Platt. Un par de meses después ella rompió con James y se fue a vivir con él. Y un par de meses más tarde, cosa que nos sitúa dos semanas antes del huracán, ambos desaparecieron con el dinero de los bolivianos. El mismo día más o menos, un pescador de gambas llamado Mike Fourchet se fue a pescar pero no volvió. Encontraron a Mike y su barco en un embarcadero en Quarantine Bay. Le habían pegado un tiro en la nuca.

—¿Fourchet era uno de los pescadores de Rainey?

—Así fue como estableció la conexión la agencia antidrogas. Encontraron el nombre de Fourchet entre los documentos comerciales de Rainey. Luego se quedaron muy intrigados cuando averiguaron que el antiguo novio de la mujer, Tolliver James, fue asesinado durante el huracán.

—¿Lo hizo Rainey?

—Ni de lejos. La agencia cree que lo mató nuestro especialista. Lo mataron a golpes; le dieron una paliza espantosa, realmente; lo torturaron a conciencia. Tenía los huesos de las piernas rotos de tal manera que no quedaban más que astillas entre la carne.

233

Terry hizo una pausa como si se diera cuenta de que aquello era demasiado gráfico, ya que Lucy estaba presente.

—Lo siento, señora Chenier.

—Terry, por favor.

—De todos modos, todo esto que le cuento le costó a los federales y al Departamento de Justicia dos o tres años deducirlo. Ya sabe cómo funcionan las investigaciones... uno va encontrando una pieza cada vez.

—Dice que Rainey está acusado de un asesinato.

—El de Fourchet. Los polis del caso se enteraron de que le entregó los doce millones la mañana que se fue. Creen que Rainey volvió más tarde sin los guardias, o quizá le dijo a Fourchet que se reuniese con él yendo de camino; de cualquier manera, Fourchet acabó muerto y Rainey y Platt huyeron con el dinero.

—¿De modo que ambos mataron a Fourchet?

—Aquí todo el mundo lo cree así, incluidos los bolivianos. Por eso ofrecieron una recompensa y mandaron a su hombre aquí. Ese tipo lleva años detrás de ellos.

—¿Sabe quién es?

—Lo único que sé es lo que le he dicho. Es su ejecutor de confianza.

—Ejecutor...

—Así es como me lo han descrito antes de que se marchara: un ejecutor. ¿Cómo llamaría si no a un animal que acumula nueve asesinatos?

Terry se corrigió.

—Once.

Nadie habló durante un momento, y luego Terry recordó algo.

—Espere, creo que hay algo más. Toda esa gente a la que ha matado estaban relacionados con Rainey o Platt: era alguien de la familia, alguien con quien trabajaban, alguien que quizá sabía cómo encontrarlos. Ha estado abriéndose camino entre sus amigos y su familia. Igual que con Tolliver James.

Se hizo el silencio entre los tres, y nadie parecía ansioso por llenarlo. Finalmente Cole dijo:

—Si el FBI vuelve a preguntarle, deles mi nombre.

Lucy dijo:

—¿Estás seguro? Podemos retrasar esto, o pararlo. No quiero que te veas en peligro.

Elvis sonrió, y por primera vez durante la entrevista sintió un cierto consuelo.

—Eres la mejor, Lucille.

—A veces…

—Sí, lo eres, pero de todos modos dales mi nombre. Terry, se lo agradezco mucho, de verdad, pero si llaman hábleles de mí. Tendremos que meter a los locales, de todos modos. Tendrán que saber esto.

Cole le dijo a Lucy que llamaría más tarde, y luego imprimió las nuevas fotos de Wilson y Dru. Se corrigió: William Rainey y Rose Platt.

—Esto va cada vez mejor… —dijo.

Oyó que Pike aparcaba fuera cuando la segunda foto iba saliendo de la impresora, y fue a encontrarse con él en la cocina. Vio que Pike parecía cansado. Su rostro esbelto estaba demacrado y arrugado bajo las brillantes gafas oscuras. Pike se bebió una botella entera de agua antes de respirar de nuevo.

—¿Cuánto tiempo llevas despierto? —preguntó Elvis.

—Estoy bien.

Se imaginó que igual eran cuarenta y ocho horas.

—Coge algo de comer.

—Estoy bien, vámonos.

—Bueno, al final tenemos algo. Lucy ha averiguado quiénes son. Las noticias no son buenas.

Pike se apoyó en el mostrador mientras Cole se lo contaba, con los brazos cruzados, como si fuera una estatua de secuoya. Solo se movió una vez mientras Cole le contaba lo que sabía.

—Los nombres —dijo.

Cole no lo comprendía, y le preguntó qué quería decir.

—Rainey. Rayne. ¿Crees que ella eligió ese nombre porque se parecía mucho al de él? Quizás él lo eligió para ella.

Cole miró a Pike, pero rápidamente siguió para aliviar su propio corazón dolorido.

—¿Qué quieres hacer?

—Llamar a la policía.

—Bien. Creo que es lo correcto. ¿Tienes el número de Button?

235

Pike buscó su teléfono en el bolsillo, pero el aparato zumbó con una llamada entrante antes de que pudiera hacer nada. Volvió a hacerlo mientras miraba la identificación de la llamada, y Cole se preguntó por qué lo observaba con tanta intensidad. Al tercer zumbido Pike levantó la vista.

—Es Dru.

Abrió el teléfono y contestó la llamada.

QUINTA PARTE

El centinela

centinela m. *Mil.* Soldado que vela guardando
el puesto que se le encarga. (DRAE)

36

*E*lla no había usado aquel teléfono desde hacía tres días, pero allí estaba su nombre, DRU, en la diminuta ventanita. Así había guardado su número en la memoria.

Pike abrió el aparato con delicadeza y respondió de la misma manera, pensando que podía ser Smith, o Azzara, o uno de los matones de Azzara que andaba por allí. Miró a Cole al responder.

—¿Sí?

—¡Willie, por favor, dale el dinero; por favor, dáselo; me tiene y dice que va a…!

Las palabras salieron de su boca de forma explosiva, pero enseguida se calló, como si su llamada hubiese acabado cortada por un hacha.

Cole se acercó a él.

—¿Era ella?

Pike se preguntó si aquello era verdad o era otra mentira incomprensible.

—Háblame, Joseph. ¿Qué ha dicho?

—No lo sé…

Pike levantó un dedo, como diciéndole «espera» mientras volvía a llamar, pero la llamada fue directa al buzón de voz.

—¿Qué ha dicho?

—Me ha llamado Willie, como si estuviera hablando con Rainey. Le ha suplicado a Rainey que le diera a alguien el dinero. Que la tiene a ella. Y ya está.

—¿Quién la tiene, el Ejecutor?

—Eso parecía.

Pike volvió a repetir mentalmente la llamada, la voz de ella tensa como un alambre a punto de romperse. Parecía auténtica, pero podía haberla hecho perfectamente desde la piscina de Azzara, rodeada de espectadores vaqueros que alabasen luego su habilidad interpretativa.

—Llamemos a Button. Tenemos que llamarle de todos modos —propuso Cole.

Pike ya estaba saliendo.

—Dru no sabe que les hemos desenmascarado. Veamos si todavía está con Azzara.

—Rose.

Pike se detuvo en la puerta, sin comprender.

—Se llama Rose. No Dru.

—Si esa llamada es real, entonces él la tiene secuestrada... Vamos a ver a casa de Azzara. Podemos llamar a Button cuando lo sepamos.

Cole no veía ningún conflicto, pero fueron en el Jeep de Pike, a toda velocidad por Laurel Canyon hacia Sunset y luego al oeste hacia la casa de Azzara. Pike describió el diseño de la casa y la posición de los guardias mientras iban conduciendo. Aparcó a una manzana de distancia del letrero de Regency y dirigió a Cole hacia la esquina, para que observara la calle de Azzara.

—Había un guardia en el callejón y otro en el Monte Carlo. ¿Los ves?

—El coche sí. No veo ningún guardia.

—No están.

El Monte Carlo y el Tercel todavía seguían frente a la casa de Azzara, pero el callejón y el coche estaban vacíos.

Cole dijo:

—Esos chicos no me conocen. Espera aquí y echaré una ojeada más de cerca.

Fue andando por la acera como si fuera un peatón más.

Pike observó los coches de los alrededores y del callejón en busca de movimiento, pero no apareció nadie mientras Cole llegaba a la casa. Se detuvo en la acera junto al Monte Carlo, lo miró un momento e hizo señas a Pike de que se acercara.

Este fue trotando, sabiendo que algo iba mal por la expresión vacua de Cole.

—Mira.

Pike vio el cuerpo y luego se acercó al coche para echar un vistazo más de cerca. Un hombre estaba acurrucado de costado en el asiento delantero, como si estuviese durmiendo encima de una almohada de raso rojo. Era Hector.

Inmediatamente se volvió hacia la casa.

—Puertas laterales. Tú a la derecha, yo a la izquierda. La parte de atrás es de cristal.

Se movieron sin decir una palabra más, Cole corriendo por el jardincito delantero mientras Pike subía por el camino. Este pasó por la cancela lateral y corrió hacia atrás, sacando su 357 de debajo de la sudadera. Cole salió por el extremo más alejado del patio mientras su amigo entraba por un lado de la casa.

La piscina estaba vacía. La botella de Dru, todavía medio llena, se encontraba en la terraza de cemento, junto a la tumbona. El vaquero que antes estaba sentado al lado de ella estaba caído en el patio, con su sombrero inmaculado color crema vuelto del revés, a un metro de distancia. Los grandes ventanales de cristal estaban igual que antes, abiertos de par en par, de modo que Pike y Cole veían sin obstáculo alguno la carnicería del interior de la casa.

Cole emitió un suave susurro.

—Esto es malo.

El vaquero del taller de chapa estaba sentado en un sofá, todavía con el sombrero puesto, pero tenía la cabeza muy echada hacia atrás, como si mirase al techo. Un hombre más joven, tatuado como si fuera de una banda, estaba tirado en el suelo junto a una mesa de centro cuadrada y grande, con los ojos abiertos pero sin ver.

Cole fue desplazándose por la casa a través del lado izquierdo de la abertura y Pike entró por el derecho. Otro pandillero muerto se encontraba junto a la isla de la cocina, y otro vaquero tirado junto a la puerta del tocador. El vaquero tenía los pantalones desabrochados y una pistola negra Heckler & Koch se hallaba en el suelo junto a su cuerpo. Sus intestinos se habían salido, produciendo un olor intenso que le quemaba los ojos a Pike.

Cole susurró de nuevo:

—Ninguna de estas personas ha recibido un disparo. No me extraña que le llamen el Ejecutor.

Pike pasó junto a Cole, hacia el vestíbulo.

—Yo me ocuparé del dormitorio, tú mira en el garaje. Azzara lleva un Prius negro.

Pike pasó por una sala pequeña y llegó a un dormitorio donde encontró ropas de Rainey y Dru. La siguiente habitación era de los guardias, con futones y sacos de plumas llenando el suelo. El último dormitorio era el de Azzara. Pike pasó por las habitaciones con rapidez, y luego volvió hacia el salón. Cole levantó la vista desde el vaquero caído en el sofá.

—¿Alguien más?

Pike negó con la cabeza.

—No. ¿El garaje?

—Vacío. Si Azzara estuvo aquí, se ha ido, pero mira esto...

Cole cogió la cartera del vaquero y la abrió, y entonces se vio una estrella azul y dorada y una foto de identificación. En la inscripción ponía: POLICÍA FEDERAL, MÉXICO.

—Los federales. ¿Qué te parece que estaban haciendo aquí estos tíos?

Pike examinó la tarjeta.

—¿Crees que son unos impostores?

—No lo sé. El tío de ahí fuera y el hombre del lavabo tienen placas también, y todos ellos llevan pistolas HK. Los Federales llevan Hecklers.

Pike meneó la cabeza, pensando que no le importaba quiénes eran, ni por qué estaban ahí, ni cuántos habían muerto. La única persona que le importaba era Dru.

—Probablemente la limusina ha traído a Azzara, Rainey y el veterano. Al ver este desaguisado se han ido. El Tercel todavía esta aquí, de modo que Rainey se ha tenido que ir con Azzara.

Cole no parecía muy convencido.

—No sabemos nada, Joe. Quizá no hayan vuelto. Igual están comiendo en la playa. Tal vez Rainey se haya ido con el veterano.

Pike sabía que Cole tenía razón, pero la última oportunidad que tenían era Azzara. Este sabía lo que había ocurrido allí, y podía saber cómo encontrar a Dru.

—¿Qué quieres hacer? —preguntó Cole.

—Llamar a la policía. Encontraremos más rápido a Azzara con la policía.

Llamaron a Button desde la casa. Cole le explicó lo fundamental de William Allan Rainey y Rose Marie Platt, y le dijo que le contarían el resto cuando llegasen. Button se lo tomó muy bien, excepto una pequeña parte de la información.

—Porque lo hemos averiguado hace solo una hora, Button. Deja de perder el tiempo y ven a verlo tú mismo.

—Cuelga —dijo Pike.

Esperaron en el Jeep a que llegase la policía. No querían estar en la casa cuando a los primeros uniformados se les salieran los ojos de las órbitas al ver la sangre y los cuerpos.

El tiempo que transcurría era como hormigas corriendo por las venas de Pike. Cole habló una vez o dos durante el rato que estuvieron esperando, pero Pike no le respondió. Pensaba en Dru, y en que le había llamado a él en busca de ayuda.

37

Daniel

*D*aniel cogió el teléfono de la mujer, la hizo rodar boca abajo y le unió las manos a la espalda con cinta adhesiva. Gran cosa robar un camión de fontaneros Rooter, ya que estaba lleno de materiales muy útiles: cinta adhesiva, cuerdas, alambres... un montón de cosas cortantes.

La mujer no le hablaba ni le miraba, cosa que a Daniel le parecía muy bien. Cuando tuvo sus muñecas seguras, le dio la vuelta y le tapó también la boca con un rectángulo plateado grande que hizo que pareciese un robot. Le gustaba mucho más así.

Estaban en Wilshire Boulevard, en un aparcamiento al otro lado de los pozos de alquitrán de La Brea. A Daniel le gustaba mucho el mamut moribundo. Había una estatua enorme de un mamut atrapado en el alquitrán, como si lo estuviese succionando hasta la muerte. Le gustaba pensar en ese enorme hijo de puta ahogándose en el alquitrán. Se preguntó si el calor sería lo que te mataría primero, quizás hervir hasta morir antes de ahogarse. Eso sería mucho mejor aún.

El teléfono por satélite sonó mientras él subía al asiento delantero. Era el boliviano. Daniel respondió con el tono más profesional y lameculos que pudo.

—Daniel al habla. ¿Sabemos algo de la matrícula?

En lugar de responder a la pregunta de Daniel, el puto boliviano se puso a chillar no sé qué mierdas sin sentido que acabaron con la inevitable pregunta.

—Sí, tengo a la señorita Platt. Sí, señor, está en mi posesión. Está ahora mismo a un metro de distancia de mí. No, señor, no tengo al señor Rainey. Él está con su amigo mexicano, pero lo tendré dentro de unos pocos minutos y conseguiremos lo que queremos.

Bla, bla bla, quejas. Bla, bla, bla, más quejas. Madre mía, ese tío no paraba nunca.

Tobey dijo:

—A tomar por culo.

Cleo dijo:

—Cuélgale a ese mamón.

Daniel se estaba cabreando.

—Señor, ¿ha podido sacar algo en limpio con la matrícula? Me gustaría saber con quién estoy tratando.

El cabrón todavía no tenía repuesta. Ahora quería saber por qué preguntaba por la matrícula y en qué sentido estaba implicado el hombre del Jeep. Daniel se sentía acorralado.

—No sé cómo está implicado, señor. Ha estado en casa de Rainey al menos una vez, y hoy le vi en casa de Azzara. Está claro que sabe quién es esa gente, y eso significa que es un problema.

Más gilipolleces bolivianas. Aquel tío tenía para dar y tomar.

—No, señor. Creo que siguió al mexicano y al señor Rainey desde el aeropuerto, pero no puedo estar seguro de ello. He preferido coger a la señorita Platt.

El puto boliviano chillaba como un grano a punto de estallar, diciendo que el mexicano quizás hubiese llevado al pescador a México. Por eso Daniel no quería hablar con esos hijos de puta, todos unos histéricos chillones.

—Señor, el señor Rainey todavía está en Los Ángeles. La señorita Platt acaba de hablar con él. ¿Puede decirme si se ha enterado de algo? Tengo que moverme con rapidez.

El boliviano vomitó cierta información sobre el tío de las flechas. Se llamaba Pike. Era exmarine, luego oficial de policía. Oyendo esto a Daniel le preocupó que ahora el tío fuese un federal, pero el boliviano le dijo algo interesante.

—Perdón, señor, querría aclarar este asunto. ¿Ya no está en las fuerzas del orden?

Bla, bla bla.

—¿Es un mercenario? ¿Lo sabemos con toda seguridad?

245

Daniel escuchó con mucha atención. Al hombre de las flechas lo echaron a patadas de la policía, luego se convirtió en soldado de fortuna y trabajó para empresas de seguridad privada muy importantes en todo el mundo, incluida Centroamérica. Daniel pensó que eso era estupendo, y se preguntó si alguna vez sus caminos se habrían cruzado. Los cárteles contrataban mercenarios de vez en cuando, y también los gobiernos que combatían a esos cárteles. Daniel nunca conoció a ninguno de esos chicos a quien no pudiera cargarse.

—¿Sabemos para quién está trabajando?

El boliviano no tenía mucho más que decir. Estaban investigando, aún intentaban averiguarlo, bla, bla, bla. Daniel se preguntó si no le estaría dando largas.

—Tengo que irme, señor. La próxima vez que hablemos tendré mejores noticias. Se lo prometo.

Más alabanzas rimbombantes y efusivas hacia el trabajo de Daniel.

—Gracias, señor. De verdad. Es usted muy amable.

Payaso.

Daniel colgó el teléfono.

Tobey lanzó una risita, entre susurros.

—«Es usted muy amable», esa sí que es buena.

Cleo se unió a él.

—Muy amable, qué pedazo de burro.

Parecían unas putas cotorras.

—¿Queréis hacer el favor de callaros?

—Callaros...

—Callaros, callaros...

Daniel miró el mamut metido en el alquitrán, con la cabeza levantada y los colmillos muy altos, como si rogase a Dios que le sacara del pozo. Se preguntó si el boliviano le habría mentido sobre el tío de las flechas. Si aquel tipo era un mercenario, quizá los bolivianos lo hubiesen contratado para encontrar a Rainey y Platt, igual que le habían contratado a él. Quizá les hubiesen dado a los dos la misma información y le hubiesen dado al hijo de puta toda la mierda que habían sabido por Daniel. Era posible que hicieran algo así, y a Daniel le daba dolor de cabeza. Le dolía de lo lindo.

La tranquila voz de Tobey le calmó.

—Para, Daniel.

La suave voz de Cleo también le consoló.

—Para, para, para.

—Vale.

Daniel se concentró en el mamut, intentando imaginar qué se debía de sentir al acabar hirviendo en alquitrán caliente. Probablemente no te ponía caliente.

Tobey se reía como un loco.

—Esa sí que es buena, Daniel; esa sí que es buena.

Cleo también se reía.

—Me matas de risa, Daniel; me matas, me matas.

Daniel dejó a un lado la paranoia. O bien los bolivianos le estaban intentando joder o bien no era así, y probablemente no era así. Ni siquiera los bolivianos eran tan tontos como para joder a un hombre lobo.

El tío de las flechas probablemente había oído hablar de la recompensa y trabajaba por su cuenta. A Daniel le parecía muy bien. Si era mercenario significaba que estaba en esto por el dinero, cosa que significaba que se le podría comprar llegado el momento, pero Daniel no sabía nada; el muy zopenco había perdido a Rainey y se había parado a comerse una hamburguesa. Quizá no volviese a ver en la vida al tatuado con las gafas de sol vestido con ropa de mierda.

Tobey le reprendió suavemente.

—No seas estúpido, Daniel.

—Estúpido, estúpido.

Los chicos tenían razón. Si los bolivianos no habían dado información al tío de las flechas, entonces es que el tío era rematadamente bueno. Apareció en el canal, apareció en el letrero luego... Era peligroso. Daniel tendría que tener mucho cuidado.

Tobey dijo:

—Vigilar nuestras espaldas.

Cleo dijo:

—Vigilar, vigilar.

Daniel dijo:

—No os preocupéis, chicos. Yo os cubro.

Daniel cogió el teléfono de la mujer y la miró. Estaba allí echada como si estuviera muerta. Le gustaba mucho así.

247

—Tu puto novio será mejor que llame pronto. Me estoy poniendo nervioso.

Ella no se movió. Ni un estremecimiento. Sencillamente se le quedó mirando con aquellos ojos estrechos, vigilantes, como si estuviera pensando.

Daniel sacudió el teléfono y le sonrió.

Cuánto más muerta, mejor.

38

Ambos extremos de la calle de Azzara estaban bloqueados por coches patrulla negros y blancos cuando llegaron Button y Futardo. Por aquel entonces había barreras de la policía y cintas amarillas para sellar la escena del crimen desde la casa hasta la calle, y el Monte Carlo de Hector estaba escondido tras una pantalla plegable. El crimen correspondía a la comisaría de Hollywood, pero los Malevos Pacíficos y la Trece de Venice pertenecían a Button.

Este asaeteó a preguntas a Pike y Cole mientras iban andando por la escena del crimen, pero Joe quería que se concentrase en Azzara.

—Creemos que ha vuelto aquí desde el aeropuerto porque no está su coche. Lleva un Prius negro. Consigue su matrícula y notifícalo a las patrullas.

—¿Mató Azzara a esta gente?

Cole habló:

—Ya te hemos dicho quién los mató. Azzara probablemente tiene a Rainey, y uno de ellos o los dos tal vez puedan ayudar a encontrar a Rose Platt. —Les enseñó la foto de la ficha policial de William Rainey—. He escrito detrás el número de expediente de Rainey. Llamad al Departamento de Justicia de Luisiana. Respaldarán lo que os estamos diciendo.

Button apretó la mandíbula al mirar la foto, pero al final se la tendió a Futardo.

—Llama aquí y a ver si puedes encontrar a alguien que sepa de esto. —La agente se alejó, pero Button la detuvo—. Espera... Antes de llamar, saca el número de matrícula de

Azzara y dáselo al comandante de la patrulla. Dile que se sospecha que Azzara está implicado en un homicidio múltiple. Que le llamaré en cuanto pueda. —Fue a alejarse por fin, pero volvió a detenerla—: Futardo... Si te dicen cualquier cosa, lo que sea, de Luisiana, tráeme el teléfono. —Esta vez dejó que se fuera y se volvió hacia Pike—. ¿Doce millones de dólares y el tío está haciendo bocadillos en Venice?

—Bocadillos no, *po'boys*.

Al irse Futardo, un detective de la comisaría de Pacific especializado en bandas, Eduardo Valenti, señaló hacia el pandillero que se encontraba junto a la mesa de centro.

—Yo sé quién es este tío. Bobby Ruiz, más conocido como Lil Rok.

—¿De la gente de Azzara?

—Desde luego. Nacidos y criados como malevos en Ghost Town.

Valenti ya había identificado al pandillero junto a la isla de la cocina como un malevo condenado a la perpetua llamado Trejo Hermanos, más conocido como Crazy T.

A Pike no le importaba quiénes eran. Toda la división de patrulleros de Los Ángeles estaría por aquel entonces buscando el Prius de Azzara, que era lo que quería Pike. Deseaba continuar la búsqueda. Si Azzara estaba con Rainey, encontrándole tendría a Rainey, que era a quien quería.

Dejó a Cole con Button y Valenti y salió para llamar a Marisol.

—¿Cómo está Artie?

—Espera...

Probablemente estaba con Artie y debía salir a otra habitación para poder hablar con más libertad. Al cabo de unos segundos volvió a aparecer en línea, hablando bajito para que Artie no la oyese.

—Creo que está mejor. Le he mirado la temperatura como me dijo. Está bien.

—¿Y la sangre en la orina?

—Algo rosa, pero no mucho. Le he dado zumo de arándanos. ¿Cree que le irá bien el zumo de arándanos?

—Sí, suena bien.

Pike esperó mientras un funcionario forense seguía su

camino hacia un federal muerto. Mientras esperaba, vio que Straw entraba en el salón. Este enseñó la placa a un oficial de uniforme, que le señaló hacia Button. Luego el forense se fue y Pike siguió hablando con Marisol.

—Estoy en casa de Azzara. Es una dirección buena la que me diste. Me ha ayudado.

—¿Está con Miguel?

—No. Azzara no está aquí, pero han asesinado a seis personas, tres de ellos malevos. Probablemente saldrá en las noticias, de modo que quería que lo supieras primero por mí.

—Ya, comprendo. Muchas gracias.

—Azzara se fue con uno de mis amigos cuando encontró los cuerpos, un hombre de Luisiana. Tengo que encontrarle.

—No sé qué decirle.

—La gente se va a casa cuando se siente asustada, y Miguel supongo que lo estará. Si te enteras de algo, ¿me llamarás?

—¿Puedo preguntarle una cosa?

—Sí.

—¿Los ha matado usted?

—No.

—¿Ha sido Miguel?

—No. Un hombre que quiere matar a ese amigo mío ha sido quien lo ha hecho. Por eso tengo que encontrarles yo primero. ¿Me llamarás?

—Sí. Claro, le llamaré.

—Quédate con Artie. Vigila su temperatura.

—Es usted un hombre extraño...

Pike cerró el teléfono, y luego se dirigió hacia la tumbona donde había estado Dru Rayne echada al sol. Se sentó allí y miró su botella. Seguía todavía en el suelo, era una Dos Equis. Pike sacó su teléfono y la llamó. Buzón de voz. Lo dejó y pensó en las opciones que tenía mientras miraba a Cole, Button, Straw y Valenti hablando entre sí. Straw lo vio y levantó una mano, pero Pike no le respondió.

La llamada de Dru le dijo que el asesino la mantendría viva hasta que tuviese a Rainey. Al dejarle hacer la llamada la estaba usando como cebo, pero eso no significaba que se quedara tranquilo hasta que Rainey apareciese. Era un depredador, así que saldría a cazar. Probablemente ya estaba buscando a

251

Rainey mientras Pike estaba allí sentado al sol en la tumbona de Azzara. Confiaba en acertar con lo que haría el asesino, pero estaba menos seguro con Rainey.

Se preguntó si este negociaría con el asesino o saldría huyendo. La llamada de Dru sugería que era Rainey quien tenía el dinero, de modo que pensó que probablemente saldría huyendo. Aunque quisiera quedarse, Azzara quizá no le diese la oportunidad. Fuera cual fuese el asunto que Rainey tenía con Azzara y los mexicanos, podían obligarle a meterse en un avión privado.

Button salió mientras Pike seguía pensando, y le llamó.

—¡Deja de tomar el sol y ven aquí! Valenti tiene una pregunta.

Cuando se dirigió al interior Valenti le dijo:

—El tipo que parecía un veterano, ¿dijiste que tenía un fantasma en el brazo? ¿Era Casper, el fantasma simpático? ¿Conoces los dibujos?

—Sí. Era Casper.

Valenti se volvió hacia Button.

—José Eschuara llevaba un dibujo de Casper. Lo llamaban el fantasma porque iba a hurtadillas por detrás de la gente y les disparaba... Sus víctimas nunca le veían.

—Creativo —señaló Cole.

—Eschuara es un pez gordo... un miembro importante de la estructura de mando de La Eme en California. Si estuvo aquí con los federales (si es que esos vaqueros eran realmente federales), esta fue una reunión al más alto nivel. Muy por encima del nivel de Azzara.

—Gracias, Eddie. Consíguenos una foto suya. Haremos que Pike le eche un vistazo —dijo Button.

Mientras Valenti se alejaba, Straw examinó al vaquero muerto en el sofá.

—¿La persona que hizo esto es la misma que mató a Mendoza y Gomer?

—Eso parece por las pistas. Cole dice que es un asesino boliviano. Rainey hacía negocios con un cártel boliviano.

Straw miró ceñudo a Pike.

—¿Esa gente son Rainey y quién más?

—Rainey y Platt.

Straw miró a Pike y luego a Cole, como si no les pudiese creer.

—¿Están seguros de eso?

—Afirmativo. Tuvimos una visión —respondió Elvis.

Button se rio, pero Straw parecía enfadado.

—¿Y su visión les dijo dónde se encuentra el señor Rainey?

Button intervino, como si estuviese cansado de tanta pregunta.

—Eso es lo que estamos haciendo aquí, Straw. Tratamos de encontrar a esa gente. Estas noticias son de última hora; sabremos más cuando hablemos con la oficina de Luisiana del FBI. Ellos llevan el caso.

Straw levantó las cejas.

—¿Luisiana? Bien. Yo les llamaré. Se moverán más rápido por un compañero.

—Gracias, ya nos las arreglaremos.

Cole recibió una llamada en su móvil y se alejó para poder hablar. Straw le vio alejarse.

—Hablaré con ellos de todos modos. Quizá les guste oír lo de la visión de Cole. Tal vez también tengan la identificación del lunático que hizo esto.

—¿Les has preguntado a tus hombres si recordaban a alguien? —preguntó Pike.

—Sí lo he hecho. Y no lo recordaban.

Button frunció el ceño, sospechando que habían tenido una conversación de la que él no sabía nada.

—¿De qué estáis hablando?

—Una foto del asesino. Si él fue a reconocer el terreno en el local de bocadillos, Straw quizá lo tenga grabado en vídeo.

—Haré que lo comprueben mis chicos, pero ya os he dicho que nos centrábamos en los pandilleros. A menos que ese tipo entrara en la tienda cuando la gente de Azzara estaba allí, no tendremos nada. Y no sé cómo podríamos reconocerle aunque lo tuviésemos.

Pike había pensado en ello y creía que sabía cómo.

—Elvis tiene un vídeo de seguridad de uno de los vecinos de Rainey. Hay que mirarlos los dos. Si aparece la misma persona en ambos vídeos, es nuestro hombre.

253

—Es una idea bastante buena, Straw. Igual funciona —señaló Button.

Straw se alejó para llamar a sus hombres, y Cole tocó el brazo de Pike y le hizo señales para que saliera.

—Vienen Poitras y Starkey.

Lou Poitras llevaba la unidad de homicidios de la comisaría de Hollywood, es decir que la escena del crimen estaba bajo su control. Era uno de los mejores amigos de Cole, pero odiaba a Pike.

—Nos irá bien. Lou me mantendrá informado, pero querrá que me quede —dijo Elvis.

—Yo voy a buscar a Dru.

Cole asintió.

—¿Dónde?

—En Venice. Empezaré por el taller de chapa.

—De acuerdo. Ya te diré si consigo algo.

Pike se alejó y luego se detuvo.

—Gracias por no decirme que su nombre es Rose.

Pike se fue antes de que Cole le respondiera.

39

*P*ike no pensaba que Azzara fuera al taller de chapa, pero era el último lugar probable donde mirar. Las bandas de La Eme eran familias; si Azzara quería un coche distinto o que le ayudasen a salir del país, tendría que acudir a alguien en quien confiase.

Pike pasó treinta y cinco minutos en su coche hasta llegar a Venice, y estaba todavía a cinco minutos del taller de chapa cuando le llamó Elvis Cole.

—¿Dónde estás?

Pike le contó adónde iba y por qué.

—No te preocupes. Azzara y Eschuara están muertos.

Quitó el pie del acelerador y giró hacia la parte lateral de la calle.

—¿Y Rainey?

—Ni rastro de Rainey. Los han encontrado a cinco minutos de aquí, en una callejuela lateral de Doheny. Tiroteados.

—¿El boliviano?

—Me dirijo hacia allí ahora con Lou para echar un vistazo, pero parece que les ha matado Rainey. Les han disparado con un arma de un calibre grande, al menos una nueve milímetros. Las víctimas de Azzara recibieron disparos del veintidós. Espera… —Pike oyó una voz al fondo que probablemente era la de Poitras, y luego Cole volvió al teléfono—. Supongo que Rainey y los pandilleros no se pusieron de acuerdo al final. Parece que les ha pegado un tiro, los ha sacado del coche y ha salido disparado. No hay ni rastro del Prius.

Pike pensó un momento, sin saber qué hacer.

—¿Ha conseguido Button hablar con los investigadores de Luisiana?

—Sí. Van a enviarle algunas cosas por correo electrónico. Ha vuelto a su despacho.

—¿Tienen la foto del Ejecutor?

—Pues no. Enviarán lo que tienen, pero no hay foto.

—Ve informándome.

Pike cerró su teléfono. Había sido razonable pensar que alguien del taller podía haber oído hablar de Azzara, pero ahora este estaba muerto, de modo que se concentró en Rainey. Con doce millones de dólares podía tener casas, apartamentos y coches en toda la ciudad. Quizás incluso pudiera salir en barco por el puerto, mientras él estaba allí sentado en un lado de la calle.

Recordó que Dru le había llamado a él, pero fingiendo que llamaba a Rainey. Si ella no había conseguido contactar con este, quizás él no supiera que el boliviano la había secuestrado.

Sacó el número de móvil de Rainey y probó suerte. El teléfono sonó una sola vez e inmediatamente fue al buzón de voz. Cerró el móvil, pero luego se le ocurrió otra idea y volvió a marcar el número.

Esta vez, cuando contestó el buzón de voz, Pike dejó un mensaje:

—Él la tiene secuestrada.

Dejó su número de teléfono y luego llamó a Cole.

—¿Está todavía Straw en casa de Azzara?

—Se ha ido antes que nosotros. Va a comprobar lo del vídeo, y a compararlo con el disco que sacamos de Laine. Ha sido una buena idea, tío.

—¿Lo está haciendo ahora mismo?

—Sí. Le va a costar bastante tiempo. Quería empezar ya.

Pike pensó en ofrecer su ayuda. Fue directamente al puesto de vigilancia de Straw, frente a la tienda de Rainey. Estaba llena de policías, pero los ignoró. Pasó a través del salón de tatuajes como había hecho antes y una vez más subió por las escaleras de atrás.

Nadie respondió cuando llamó. Tocó más fuerte, luego probó el picaporte y encontró que no estaba cerrado. La oficina estaba vacía. Las camas y las bolsas de basura y todo el equipo habían desaparecido. Ni siquiera estaba la lámina negra con sus cortes rectangulares. La gente del puesto de vigilancia se había ido y se habían llevado con ellos el vídeo.

Pike corrió de vuelta a su Jeep en busca del número de Straw y llamó.

—Jack Straw.

—¿Dónde está?

—¿Quién es...? Pike, ¿es usted?

—¿Qué pasa con el vídeo?

—Tengo a un hombre ocupándose de eso.

—Straw, estoy en su puesto de vigilancia. Está vacío.

—Relájese, Pike. Hemos cerrado ese puesto. La operación de vigilancia ha terminado. La mayoría de mis hombres ya están de camino hacia casa.

—Luisiana no tiene ninguna foto del boliviano.

Straw se quedó callado un momento, y cuando volvió a hablar su voz era comedida.

—Ya sé que no la tienen. He hablado con un agente hace veinte minutos. Kenny está examinando las grabaciones ahora mismo; si ve algo que le parezca sospechoso, cualquiera que pueda remotamente parecerse a nuestro hombre, me lo hará saber. Será mejor que se tranquilice. Parece que está algo confundido.

Colgó.

Kenny. Un hombre solo mirando cientos de horas de vídeo.

Pike se echó atrás en el asiento y examinó los edificios de los alrededores y a los mirones que se encontraban en las aceras, junto a la tienda de Rainey. Este probablemente no volvería, pero nunca se sabe... Llevaba años huyendo, pero esta vez no lo había hecho; había roto su costumbre, y la gente no cambia nunca sin un buen motivo. En lugar de salir corriendo de nuevo, Rainey y Dru se habían mudado a casa de Azzara, pero se habían dejado algunas cosas en casa de Brown, cosa que indicaba que pensaban que aquel desplazamiento sería temporal y que planeaban volver. Quizá Rainey se hubiese dejado algo en la casa que necesitaba antes de irse.

Pike fue a la casa. La policía había bloqueado las calles de los alrededores, de modo que dejó su Jeep en el bulevar e intentó cruzar por el puente peatonal. También habían blo-

257

queado todos los puentes peatonales a ambos extremos del callejón, de modo que se encontró con tres mujeres del barrio y seis niños en la obra donde habían asesinado a Gomer. Contemplaban la actividad mientras policías de uniforme y de paisano registraban la casa de Brown.

Pike pasó un rato mirando a la policía. Los mirones se habían reunido en los puentes y los carriles de bicicleta, y los residentes que tenían vistas a la escena estaban en sus jardines. Examinó los rostros buscando a Rainey, pero sabía que el asesino boliviano también podía estar entre ellos. Si este todavía buscaba a Rainey, quizá volviese a la casa por los mismos motivos que Pike.

Encontró la tarjeta de Lily Palmer en su cartera, y la llamó.

Jared respondió, con la voz baja y apagada.

—Hola.

—Soy Pike. ¿Te acuerdas de mí?

Jared se animó.

—Hala, tío, tendrías que ver cómo está esto. Hay policías por todas partes.

—Ya lo sé. Estoy al otro lado del canal.

—¿De verdad? ¡No jodas! Tío, ¿no lo sabías? Wilson y Dru son criminales. ¿Lo sabías o qué?

Jared salió por un lado de su piscina y saludó cuando vio a Pike.

—¡Eh, tío, ahí estás! ¡Te veo!

—¿Ha entrado alguien en la casa de al lado? —preguntó Pike.

—¿Donde Steve?

—Sí.

—Ya lo ves, tío. Parece un festival de policías.

—No, no me refería a ahora. Antes de la policía.

—Los polis también me lo han preguntado. Pues no, no he visto a nadie.

—No solo hoy. ¿Y ayer, o anoche?

—Nada, tú.

—¿Y no has oído nada tampoco?

—Pues no, colega... Y ya sabes... Yo estoy siempre de guardia. Nadie se escapa a mi vista.

—Coge algo para escribir. Te voy a dar mi número.

—Claro, tío. Espera.

Jared fue corriendo a casa y reapareció unos momentos más tarde.

—Vale, ya estoy preparado para copiar, Houston.

Pike le dio su número.

—Si ves a alguien en la casa de al lado después de irse la policía, quiero que me llames. ¿Lo harás?

—Claro, hombre. También tenemos que llamar a la policía.

—Me parece muy bien. Hazlo, pero llámame a mí también.

—Que sí, colega. No problemo.

—Y una cosa, Jared... ¿tienes alarma en tu casa?

—Sí.

—Pues ponla esta noche. No dejes abierta ninguna puerta ni ventana. Ciérralo todo bien.

—Ay, tío, me estás acojonando. Wilson se enrollaba conmigo. Hacíamos bromas.

Pike no pensaba en Rainey.

—Cierra bien, Jared. Si ves u oyes algo llama a la policía, y luego a mí. Y díselo a tu madre. Dale mi número.

La emoción abandonó la voz de Jared.

—Sí, señor. Se lo diré.

Pike cerró el teléfono.

El chico se le quedó mirando un momento, luego le saludó de nuevo y se dirigió lentamente de vuelta al interior de la casa.

Pike examinó los puentes cercanos y las casas de los alrededores. Si aparecía Rainey para entrar en la casa, se iría y volvería más tarde, cuando se hubiese ido la policía. Pike no tenía otra cosa, así que se dispuso a esperar.

Cuarenta minutos más tarde, la atención de Pike se vio atraída hacia dos hombres que se separaron de la multitud en un lado del puente peatonal. Los agentes especiales Straw y Kenny enseñaron sus insignias al oficial que cerraba el puente, que inmediatamente les dejó pasar. Desaparecieron al llegar al final, pero Kenny reapareció unos minutos más tarde en el jardín de Rainey. Pike se preguntó por qué estaría allí con Straw, en lugar de estar comprobando el vídeo.

Kenny fue andando hasta la verja y luego se volvió hacia la casa. Unos segundos más tarde Straw se unió a él. Hablaron un momento y Straw fue al kayak que estaba sujeto al muelle. Lo hizo oscilar distraídamente adelante y atrás y se dirigió a Kenny, que se limitó a menear la cabeza como respuesta. Miraron los dos a la casa, como si intentaran resolver un enigma irresoluble, y ninguno de los dos parecía dispuesto a alejarse.

Pike se preguntó si Kenny habría acabado de comprobar el vídeo o si Straw sencillamente le habría mentido.

Llamó a este a su móvil. Oyó cómo sonaba, lo vio comprobar la ventanita de la llamada entrante y cómo volvía a meterse el teléfono en el bolsillo sin contestar.

—Mmm —dijo Pike.

Marcó de nuevo el móvil y vio otra vez a Straw comprobar la llamada entrante y no responder. En esta ocasión dijo algo a Kenny, que meneó la cabeza mientras se alejaba.

Marcó de nuevo de inmediato, y esta vez Straw se cansó. Respondió al móvil.

—¿Hola?

—Soy Pike. ¿Qué tal va lo del vídeo?

—Se está poniendo usted muy pesado, ¿sabe? Vamos adelantando.

—Me acercaré yo también. Quizá Kenny necesite algo de ayuda.

—Le va muy bien sin usted.

—¿Ha encontrado algo ya?

—No, Pike; ya le dije que le llamaría, pero usted no para de telefonearme y nos retrasa. No me vuelva a llamar.

Pike vio que Straw bajaba el teléfono. Le decía algo a Kenny que le hizo reír.

Volvió corriendo a su Jeep y fue a lo largo de Venice Boulevard hasta que encontró el Malibu verde. Si Straw no iba a comprobar el vídeo, Pike lo haría por sí mismo.

Pike no sabía lo que encontraría, ni siquiera si encontraría algo, pero el asiento trasero del Malibu estaba lleno de sacos de dormir y bolsas de deporte. Comprobó que nadie miraba y luego, con una ganzúa, abrió el coche.

Quería solo la cinta de la cámara, pero no la veía, de modo que registró las bolsas de deporte. La que quedaba encima contenía un revoltijo de ropas y artículos de tocador. Rápidamente buscó la cámara, cerró la cremallera de la bolsa y la dejó a un lado. Trabajaba deprisa, pero cuando abrió la segunda bolsa vio un sobre grueso de papel marrón con la palabra «Rainey» escrita a mano.

El nombre lo detuvo.

Pike dedujo por el estado de desgaste del sobre y la tinta desvaída que no contenía nada nuevo. Parecía viejo y usado, y tan pronto como lo vio supo que había algo raro en Jack Straw.

El sobre contenía fotocopias de lo que parecían ser informes y documentos sobre William Allen Rainey escritos en unos formularios con encabezamiento de la agencia antidrogas de Estados Unidos. Los documentos parecían oficiales, y contenían unas fotocopias borrosas en blanco y negro de fotos de vigilancia. Como el sobre, los documentos mostraban su desgaste con los bordes desgarrados, círculos hechos por tazas de café y notas escritas a mano en los márgenes. Pike hojeaba aquellas páginas sin leerlas cuando encontró una foto algo borrosa de Rose Marie Platt con un cartel del Jazz Fest al fondo. La calidad de la foto era tan mala que ella resultaba casi irreconocible, pero supo que era ella.

Volvió a meter aquellas páginas en el sobre y siguió buscando la cámara. La encontró unos segundos después, cerró las bolsas de deporte y las dejó en el asiento de atrás, donde las había encontrado.

Pike no buscaba archivos y documentos, pero ahora quería ver lo que tenía Straw. Cogió la cámara y el sobre y se fue a una calle residencial a tres manzanas de distancia.

Comprobó primero el vídeo. Pasó unos cuantos minutos averiguando cómo funcionaba la cámara, luego contempló varios segundos de la grabación de Straw. La pasó con rapidez y saltó entre las diversas pistas, para ver algo más. El nudo duro que tenía entre los omoplatos se hacía más grande con cada escena que contemplaba, y pronto se extendió también por su espalda.

El equipo de vigilancia de Straw no había registrado a Azzara ni a los miembros de la banda de este. Había registrado a Rainey y Dru. Entrando y saliendo de la tienda. Entrando y saliendo de la casa del canal. Dru en el jardín. Rainey en el kayak. Conduciendo el Tercel.

261

El vídeo confirmó lo que había sospechado Pike desde el momento en que vio el gastado sobre con el nombre auténtico de Wilson Smith.

El agente especial Jack Straw le había mentido. A Straw y su equipo no les importaba nada Miguel Azzara. Sabían quiénes eran Wilson y Dru desde el principio. Estaban persiguiendo a Rainey y Platt.

40

Pike dejó a un lado la cámara y fue hojeando los informes. La mayor parte de los documentos eran notas del caso que explicaban reuniones o conversaciones de Rainey y un agente de la agencia antidrogas llamado Norman Lister, que al parecer era el que estaba a cargo de Rainey. La mayor parte de los informes se habían escrito mientras este todavía servía como informador, aunque muchos estaban fechados cuando los agentes ya investigaban su desaparición. Pike pasó por alto esas partes, ya que no le preocupaba Rainey. Lo que quería era leer algo sobre Dru.

Buscó entre las páginas hasta que encontró la foto de Rose Marie Platt y descubrió una serie de documentos grapados. El primero era un resumen de las notas de Lister con las declaraciones hechas por los socios de Rainey, que describían cómo conocieron a Rose Platt y lo que sabían, si es que sabían algo, de su relación con Rainey. Sus nombres estaban subrayados con rotulador amarillo, y sus direcciones escritas a mano en el margen.

La mayor parte de los entrevistados se identificaban como compañeros de trabajo y no tenían nada incriminador. Uno de los entrevistados era la madre de Rose Platt, y dos se identificaban como hermanos suyos. Esos resúmenes eran tan breves como los demás, y no contenían ninguna información útil para la investigación de Lister. Los hermanos aseguraban que hacía seis años que no veían a su hermana, y la madre se quejaba de que no había sabido nada de Rose desde hacía casi diez años. Describían a Rose como rebelde, pirada, egoísta y golfa.

Pike hojeó las demás declaraciones, pero hizo una pausa de nuevo cuando encontró una copia de la orden de arresto emitida para Rose Marie Platt. Contenía una hoja de información con una segunda foto de Dru, su descripción física e información de su entorno que podría resultar útil para los investigadores. Los nombres de amigos y parientes, anteriores direcciones, escuelas a las que había asistido y antiguos patronos estaban perfectamente mecanografiados en las casillas correspondientes.

Pike leyó ese documento cuidadosamente. Una casilla diminuta en la parte superior de la página estaba marcada, indicando que no tenía antecedentes. En otra casilla se especificaba que sus huellas dactilares no estaban fichadas.

Según la investigación, Rose Marie Platt nació en Biloxi, Misisipi. Estuvo casada tres veces, la primera cuando tenía diecisiete años, la segunda a los diecinueve y una tercera vez cuando tenía veintidós. Los dos primeros matrimonios se celebraron en Biloxi; el último, en Slidell, Luisiana. Los nombres y últimas direcciones conocidas de los tres hombres aparecían a continuación, junto con las breves descripciones DV, NO HJ. Divorciado, sin hijos.

Pike pensó en la niña de la foto que le había enseñado Dru. Recordaba perfectamente a la pequeña Amy. Una niña muy guapa, con una sonrisa feliz, de pie junto a un sofá. «El amor de mi vida.»

En el formulario aparecían padres y hermanos. Pike lo examinó. Salían el nombre de la madre y del padre, pero junto al de este se había marcado una casilla: fallecido. Los nombres de los dos hermanos estaban mecanografiados debajo de los de los padres. Debajo de estos se encontraba otra casilla también marcada y un sencillo y descriptivo «Hermanas: ninguna».

Pike miró aquella línea más rato que las demás. Hermanas, ninguna. Dru le había dicho que Amy vivía con su hermana.

Pike miró hacia fuera por la ventana, a la nada, consciente de los coches que pasaban y de la luz que manchaba los olmos torturados, pero sin verlos. Veía perfectamente la escena, y recordaba todos los matices de la expresión de ella. La sombra de extraña indecisión al sacar la foto de su billetera. Cómo se encogió de hombros cuando se la enseñó, como si esperase que él la rechazara. La sonrisa que relampagueó, radiante como la luz del verano, cuando él le preguntó igualmente si quería salir con él.

Pero si no había hermana eso significaba que tampoco había ninguna Amy, lo cual quería decir que nada era verdad.

Pike cogió aliento, luego juntó las páginas y las metió de nuevo en el sobre. Pensó un momento, puso en marcha el Jeep y dio la vuelta hacia la comisaría de Pacific. Estaba solo a cinco minutos de distancia. Sacó el teléfono mientras iba conduciendo y llamó a Jerry Button.

—¿Quién es Straw, y qué está haciendo? —preguntó.

—¿Qué quieres decir con eso de quién es?

—¿Estás metido en esto con él?

—Pike, estoy muy ocupado. ¿De qué coño estás hablando?

Juzgó que la furia de Button era real, cosa que significaba que Straw le había mentido a él también.

—Straw no vino aquí a trincar a Azzara. Estaban vigilando a Rainey. Sabían que Wilson era Rainey desde el principio.

La respuesta de Button parecía indecisa.

—¿Te lo ha dicho él?

Describió los informes de la agencia antidrogas y el vídeo de Straw, pero Button no quería creerle.

—No me cuentes trolas.

—Sal a verme dentro de cinco minutos. Podrás ver la cámara y los informes. Te los daré.

Button se quedó callado, y Pike sabía por qué. Estaba violento.

—Ahora tengo que irme, Jerry. Tendrías que haberlo comprobado.

—Esos putos federales. Esos gilipollas creídos, siempre con sus mierdas y sus cosas turbias.

—Si hubieras hecho las gestiones que tenías que hacer habrías sabido qué era lo que llevaban entre manos. Podríamos haber detenido al boliviano.

Button se aclaró la garganta, ansioso de cambiar de tema.

—Contacté con los agentes de Nueva Orleans. ¿No te lo ha dicho Cole?

—Sí. ¿No tienen ninguna foto?

—No, pero sé que se trata de un americano llamado Gregg Daniel Vincent. No es ningún boliviano.

—¿Y ellos qué saben?

—No mucho, y la mayor parte no pueden confirmarlo. Hizo la prueba de iniciación a la banda protegiendo granjas de la droga en Honduras de las redadas del gobierno. Se ganó una reputación matando chivatos y polis que los bolivianos querían quitarse de enmedio. Los tortura hasta la muerte. Los bolivianos cuentan ese rollo de que el tío se ha escapado de un manicomio para psicópatas, pero seguramente son chorradas que usan para asustar a la gente.

A Pike no le importaba en absoluto nada de todo aquello, y no estaba impresionado.

—¿Hay una descripción?

—Sabemos que es un tío blanco, pero eso es todo. No tienen descripción ni foto.

Pike se colocó junto a la bandera que había en la fachada de la comisaría de Pacific. Aparcó el coche, pero no apagó el motor.

—Aquí estoy, Button. Junto a la bandera, delante. Ven a ver lo de Straw.

Button parecía angustiado.

—¿De verdad lo tienes?

—Ven a verlo. Lo dejo delante de la puerta.

Pike cerró su teléfono, salió con el sobre y la cámara y los dejó en la acera. Menos de un minuto después ya se estaba alejando cuando sonó su teléfono. Pensaba que era Button que le devolvía la llamada, pero no era así.

—¿Pike? ¿Es usted Joe Pike?

Pike reconoció la voz.

—Soy Bill Rainey. Usted me conoce como Wilson Smith.

41

Sargento detective Jerry Button,
departamento de policía de Los Ángeles,
comisaría de Pacific

*L*as manos de Button temblaban cuando volvió a su despacho con la cámara y el expediente. Intentó detenerlas, pero tuvo que metérselas debajo de los brazos. Miró a Futardo, que estaba escribiendo a máquina en su cubículo al otro lado de la sala, junto a la puerta. A los nuevos siempre les daban el escritorio de al lado de la puerta. Button tenía el mejor despacho en la parte de atrás, justo al lado del del teniente. La distancia entre ambos escritorios era mucho más larga de lo que parecía.

Button se sentía furioso, humillado y asustado. Straw, el arrogante capullo federal, había hecho el típico movimiento poco limpio del FBI mintiendo sobre aquel caso. Como todos los cabrones de Quantico, pensaba que los policías de la ciudad eran unos incompetentes, que solo valían para usarlos, abusar de ellos y dejarlos de lado.

Y Button había demostrado que tenía razón.

Hola, Jerry Button, ahora eres el «burro del año» de la comisaría de Pacific.

Fue hojeando los documentos de la agencia antidrogas y vio unos cuantos minutos de la cámara de vídeo para asegurarse de que Pike no lo había toqueteado. Pero Pike, claro, nunca toqueteaba nada ni dejaba que se lo hicieran a él.

Button se sintió mucho más angustiado aún cuando dejó la cámara. Cogió su teléfono móvil para llamar a Straw, pero luego se lo pensó mejor. Desde luego iba a enfrentarse a aquel hijo de puta, por supuesto que sí, pero quería tener todos los hechos bien claros antes de hacerlo. Se proponía presentar una queja oficial.

Llamó a Sale Springer, de la oficina de Nueva Orleans del FBI. Springer era el agente con el que había hablado Button del caso Rainey menos de una hora antes.

—Agente especial Springer.

A Button incluso le daba cien patadas como respondían el teléfono esos cabrones condescendientes.

—Jerry Button de Los Ángeles otra vez. Tengo una información aquí y me gustaría preguntarles algo.

—Desde luego. ¿De qué se trata?

Button notó que Futardo le miraba, cosa que hizo que se le encogiera el estómago. Tendría que contarle lo de su cagada en cuanto soltase el teléfono.

—¿Conocen a un agente llamado Jack Straw?

—Claro. Jack es amigo mío.

—Ya. Bien. ¿Quién es su supervisor?

—¿Qué quiere decir?

—Me gustaría hablar con su supervisor. Su señor Straw se presentó con falsedades ante el departamento de policía de Los Ángeles y está actuando como un capullo solapado. Me gustaría arreglar este asunto.

Springer se aclaró la garganta.

—Espere, sargento. Le pondré con él.

Unos segundos más tarde una voz masculina distinta se puso al teléfono.

—Soy Jack Straw. ¿Quién es?

Button notó una calma extraña que se aposentaba en su vientre.

—Jerry Button, del departamento de policía de Los Ángeles. ¿Se llama usted Jack Straw?

—Así es. ¿Nos conocemos?

—¿Trabaja usted en el caso de William Rayne?

—Soy uno de los agentes originales del caso, detective. ¿Puedo preguntarle qué ocurre?

—¿Y no hay otro Jack Straw en el caso?

El Jack Straw de Nueva Orleans se echó a reír.

—No, la última vez que miré no lo había. ¿Qué ocurre, detective?

—Tenemos a un caballero aquí que se identificó como agente Jack Straw, de su oficina. Tiene credenciales del FBI.

—Eso no es posible…

—Ya le volveré a llamar.

Button se echó atrás en la silla y se miró las manos, tan quietas como coches aparcados. Miró a Futardo, que había vuelto a su ordenador y estaba tecleando. Era una buena chica. Se levantó y se dirigió hacia ella. La mujer se puso de pie de un salto cuando vio que se acercaba, pero él le hizo señas de que se sentara y cogió una silla cercana.

—Siéntate, Nancy.

—¿He hecho algo malo?

Los ojos de la agente eran tan oscuros como el chocolate negro, pero los tenía tan abiertos como platos de postre. Probablemente pensaba que iba a echarle una bronca, cosa que hacía a menudo, pero ahora lo que quería era enseñarle algo.

—No, no has hecho nada malo. He sido yo. La he cagado de mala manera. Ese gilipollas que vino aquí del FBI, Straw… Tenía las credenciales, sabía qué decir, pero es un impostor. El auténtico Jack Straw está chupando cabezas de cangrejo allá en Nueva Orleans en este preciso momento. Yo tendría que haber comprobado al tipo, pero no lo hice. Fue un error estúpido, muy torpe, y quizás haya puesto en peligro la vida de una mujer. —Futardo lo miró como si uno de los dos, o los dos, fueran a tener un ataque—. No cometas nunca el mismo error que yo, Nancy. Durante el resto de tu carrera y toda tu vida cuestiónate todo lo que te diga cualquiera, y comprueba siempre lo que dicen. ¿Queda claro?

—Sí, señor.

—Prométemelo.

—Dios mío, Jerry, ¿qué vamos a hacer?

Button no respondió. Retornó a su escritorio y volvió a llamar al auténtico Jack Straw. Le explicó la situación y le proporcionó una descripción detallada del falso Jack Straw lo mejor que supo. Cuando el auténtico Jack Straw empezó a decirle cómo quería que manejase al impostor, Button colgó. Aspiró aire con fuerza, lo dejó escapar y luego marcó el número que tenía del falso Jack Straw.

—Jack Straw.

—Aquí Jerry Button. Hemos tenido suerte. Vamos a coger a Rainey, salimos ahora mismo. ¿Quiere venir?

269

—¿Le han encontrado?

—Un policía motorizado ha visto el Prius. Yo voy para allá. ¿Quiere venir o no?

—Sí, claro. ¿Dónde nos reunimos?

—¿Dónde está?

—En Santa Mónica.

—Vale, está cerca. Ya le recojo de camino.

Button le dio un emplazamiento y luego se guardó el teléfono. Comprobó la pistola y se la sujetó al cinturón. Ya no quedaban muchos polis que llevasen las antiguas Snubbies del 38, pero él no veía razón alguna para cambiar. Era pequeña, ligera y nunca la había disparado contra otro ser humano.

Button se puso la chaqueta y salió. Vio que Futardo cogía el bolso y saltaba a interceptarle.

—¿Qué hace? —preguntó ella.

—Voy a empaquetar a ese hijo de puta, Nancy. Es mi trabajo.

—Quiero ir. ¿Puedo ir? Por favor.

270

Como una niña. Ansiosa, quizás un poco asustada. Button pensó en dejarle que fuera con él, pero al final negó con la cabeza.

—Acaba tus informes.

Se fue a atrapar al falso Jack Straw, y no vio que ella le seguía.

El impostor estaba apoyado en su coche a un lado de un aparcamiento Ralph, en Wilshire Boulevard. Button lo vio mientras ponía el intermitente para girar y tocó un poco el claxon. Straw se alejó de su coche, dispuesto a salir.

Se preguntó qué pretendería aquel tío, fingiendo ser un agente federal, pero supuso que probablemente tenía algo que ver con el dinero de Rainey.

Dio la vuelta en el aparcamiento y paró junto a Straw, con la puerta del pasajero en el otro lado del coche.

Straw empezó a dar la vuelta hacia el asiento del pasajero, pero Button le detuvo.

—Espere un segundo. Tengo que darle un chaleco antibalas antes de que nos separemos. Está en el maletero.

Straw dudó al ver que Button salía.

—No necesito chaleco.

—Son las normas de la policía de Los Ángeles, hombre. Ya sé que es una tontería, pero...

Button levantó las manos para medir los hombros de Straw, y sonrió como si todo fuera una broma.

—Es talla única, va bien a todo el mundo, pero tengo que hacerlo. Espero que no tenga demasiados agujeros de bala...

Al medir los hombros de Straw Button se le acercó bastante. Le agarró la muñeca, le retorció el brazo a la espalda y lo empujó contra el coche.

—Quieto ahí. Quieto en el coche.

Le puso las esposas en la muñeca derecha y luego en la izquierda. Cuando el falso Straw estaba bien seguro, Button retrocedió y le registró en busca de un arma.

—Quédate en el coche, hijo de puta. Estás arrestado. No te vuelvas.

—¿Qué es esto, Button? ¿Qué está haciendo?

—Jack Straw... Una mierda. Yo sé que no es el puto Jack Straw. Acabo de hablar con ese cabrón.

El detective Jerry Button atisbó un movimiento entre dos coches cercanos, pero no vio al hombre a tiempo porque un claxon que sonaba distrajo su atención. Parecía un gemido largo, angustioso.

Algo duro le golpeó dos veces con tanta fuerza que se tambaleó, y entonces Kenny le disparó de nuevo. Button cayó apoyando una rodilla y buscó precipitadamente la Snubbie, mientras un Crown Victoria color tostado se metía entre el tráfico, levantando un abanico de chispas al saltar el bordillo y entrar en el aparcamiento. Button vio a Futardo, sus ojos color chocolate negro, tan enormes, que venían a salvarlo.

—No, cariño... —le dijo.

Kenny le disparó a través del parabrisas, y rápidamente se dirigió hacia su ventanilla y le volvió a disparar.

Button ya tenía la Snubbie por entonces, pero el falso Jack Straw gritaba:

—¡A Button! ¡Coge a Button!

Jerry esquivó una andanada, y Kenny le volvió a disparar, dándole tan fuerte que notó como si le atravesaran con una jabalina. La Snubbie se le cayó de la mano.

271

Straw dijo:

—Cógele la llave. Quítame estas cosas.

Kenny cogió su arma e hizo rodar a Button de espaldas, buscando las llaves.

El sol era horriblemente brillante, le daba justo en los ojos, pero ya estaban los dos encima, Kenny quitándole las esposas a Straw.

—Cabrones… —dijo.

Straw bajó la vista y Button vio el miedo en sus ojos.

—Lo saben, tío. Se acabó.

—Que no te entre el pánico. Ya estamos cerca.

—Tenemos que irnos. Estamos jodidos.

—No, no es verdad…

Kenny apuntó con el arma justo hacia abajo, bloqueando el sol, y Button miró hacia el negro y tenso esfínter de su cañón.

—Jódete.

Entonces sonó un disparo, y Button pensó que estaba muerto, pero fue Kenny quien se tambaleó hacia un lado y cayó. Al caer, su arma le golpeó en la nariz.

Button vio a Futardo, con la cara roja, apoyándose en la ventanilla mientras intentaba volver a disparar.

El falso Jack Straw recogió con toda calma el arma de Kenny y disparó dos veces más a la agente a través del cristal.

Button trató de agarrar por las piernas al impostor, pero no podía mover los brazos. Intentó gritar pidiendo ayuda, pero lo único que consiguió emitir fue un gruñido gorgoteante.

Entonces el falso Straw lo miró de nuevo, apuntó su arma y disparó.

42

—Soy Bill Rainey. Usted me conoce como Wilson Smith.

Pike arrancó el Jeep, dispuesto a salir.

—Ya sé quién es. ¿Dónde está ella?

—Necesito su ayuda.

—¿Dónde está ella?

—¿Sabe quién soy de verdad?

—William Allan Rainey. El nombre de ella es Rose Platt. ¿Dónde está?

—No lo sé.

—¿Está viva?

—Sí, supongo que sí, pero él la matará.

Rainey hipó, pero luego Pike se dio cuenta de que era un sollozo. Estaba llorando.

—No lo suponga. ¿Sabe si está viva o no?

—¿Tengo a la policía detrás?

—Sí.

—¡Mierda!

—¿Está viva?

—¡Mierda, joder!

Pike regaló a Rainey diez segundos de silencio. Se estaba desmoronando, pero necesitaba que se calmase y pensase.

—¿Quiere que le llame Bill o Wilson?

—Me importa una mierda. Lo que quiera. La tiene secuestrada.

—¿Cómo es él?

—No lo sé. En todos estos años no le hemos visto nunca.

273

Huíamos, tío. Mató al antiguo novio de Rosie. Mató a mi hermana, a mi exmujer… y sigue.

—¿Por qué yo?

—¿Cómo?

—¿Por qué me ha llamado a mí?

Ahora Rainey se quedó callado, pero el silencio era bueno: significaba que estaba pensando.

—No puedo llamar a la policía.

—Llámeles.

—No puedo. ¿No ve cómo son esos bolivianos? ¿Cuánto tiempo duraría yo en prisión? Y ella, ¿cuánto duraría? Si llamo a la policía ahora, nos matarán a los dos luego.

Pike siguió en silencio, de modo que Rainey lo llenó.

—Es usted un mercenario, ¿no? Pues yo le pagaré.

—¿Doce millones de dólares?

Rainey se echó a reír.

—¿Quién le ha dicho eso, la policía? ¿Es lo que piensan que nos llevamos?

—Sí.

—Son unos idiotas. Fueron solo 8 200 000 mil.

—Está bien. ¿Me dará 8 200 000 dólares?

—Nos los hemos gastado. Le daré lo que queda: 342 000 dólares y algo de suelto.

—No lo quiero.

—En efectivo. Libre de impuestos. Es suyo.

—No lo quiero.

Rainey cayó en un silencio más profundo aún.

—No puedo hacerlo yo. No puedo. Tenía que pedírselo…

—¿Por qué mató a Azzara y Eschuara?

—Mierda, lo sabe todo…

—Le vi en casa de Azzara. Le seguí hasta el avión.

—Ella tenía razón con usted.

Pike se preguntó qué querría decir, pero siguió presionándole.

—¿Por qué les mató? ¿No le ayudaban?

—Querían que me fuera. Me iban a llevar a México o algún sitio asqueroso de esos. No podía irme sin ella. La quiero, tío.

Pike respiró lentamente. Rainey ahora estaba tranquilo y

controlado, cómodo con la conversación, de modo que se lo volvió a preguntar.

—¿Sabe con toda seguridad que ella está viva?

—Estaba viva hace... vamos a ver... dieciséis minutos. Fue cuando dejó el último mensaje.

Pike comprobó la hora. Eran las 16.22.

—¿Le ha dejado mensajes?

—Supongo que él no quiere que sepa qué voz tiene. No respondo al maldito teléfono. Tengo miedo. Es la única forma que tengo de pararlo. Él no sabe si estoy recibiendo los mensajes o no. Pero tengo que llamar pronto...

—¿Por qué?

—Rose ha dicho que llamase a las seis. Debe de estar muy cabreado por no poder hablar conmigo. Dice que, si no llamo a las seis, la matará.

Faltaba una hora y treinta y ocho minutos.

—Si llama a las seis, ¿qué ocurrirá?

—Probablemente me dirá qué quiere.

Pike recordó la llamada que había recibido cuando Dru fingía que estaba llamando a Rainey. Ella le había rogado que entregase el dinero.

—Quiere el dinero.

—Dice eso, pero son gilipolleces. Los bolivianos nos quieren muertos. Es lo único que les preocupa.

Pike miró la hora. Faltaba una hora y treinta y siete minutos.

—¿Cuántos mensajes ha dejado Rose?

—Tres. Ha llamado tres veces.

—¿Los tiene?

—Sí.

Pike quería oír su voz.

—¿Dónde está?

—¿Ahora mismo? Pues en Hollywood. Estoy detrás de un restaurante; ¿cómo se llama?, Musso y Frank.

Pike pensó que comprendía cómo querría organizarlo todo el asesino, y urdió un plan. Calculó el tiempo que necesitaría para el trayecto entre el sitio donde estaba y donde quería estar, y luego le dijo a William Allan Rainey dónde reunirse con él exactamente a las 17.30. Así tendría tiempo para recoger unas pocas cosas y llamar a Elvis Cole. Cuando se movieran, tenían que moverse rápido, y estar preparados.

—¿Me va a ayudar? —preguntó Rainey.

—Sí.

—¿Qué va a hacer?

—Venderle.

43

Sesenta y dos minutos más tarde Pike salió de su Jeep. Rainey, a su vez, salió del Prius. Estaban en el aparcamiento detrás de un restaurante de Sunset Boulevard, atrapado entre una colina reforzada y el establecimiento, a menos de cinco minutos de la casa de Miguel Azzara.

Rainey parecía encogido y débil, como si su cuerpo se estuviese desmoronando, junto con su vida.

Pike le retorció el brazo por detrás de la espalda y lo apretó fuerte contra el Jeep.

—Las manos cruzadas detrás de la cabeza. Separe los pies.

Hizo lo que le decían sin resistirse.

—Está en el coche. Debajo del asiento.

—Cállese.

—Tuve que dispararles, ya se lo he dicho.

—¿Como a Michael Fourchet?

Pike no encontró otra cosa que llaves, una cartera y un teléfono. Abrió la puerta del pasajero del Jeep, empujó dentro a Rainey y luego fue hacia el asiento del conductor y se sentó detrás del volante. Cuando cerró la puerta, Cole se inclinó hacia adelante desde el asiento trasero y dio unos golpecitos a Rainey en el hombro.

—Si Pike no coge el dinero, yo sí.

Rainey saltó.

—¿Quién es usted?

—El gemelo malvado de Pike.

Este levantó el teléfono de Rainey.

—¿Es este el teléfono al que le llama ella?

—Sí.

—¿De modo que este es el número en el que ella responderá cuando la llamemos? —preguntó Cole.

—Supongo... ¿Qué vamos a hacer? ¿Qué era esa mierda de venderme?

Pike le dio el teléfono.

—Ponga sus mensajes en el altavoz.

Rainey toqueteó hasta poner el buzón de voz y reproducir su contenido con el altavoz. Resultaba difícil entenderla con aquel teléfono barato, pero finalmente lo consiguieron.

El primer mensaje era casi idéntico al que ella le había dado a Pike: decía que el hombre la había secuestrado, y rogaba a Rainey que le entregara el dinero. Pike no escuchaba tanto a Dru como los ruidos de fondo, pero no oyó nada que le resultase útil. Los micrófonos condensadores introducidos en los teléfonos móviles estaban diseñados para reducir el ruido ambiental.

El segundo mensaje era más de lo mismo, pero con una pequeña diferencia: ahora Dru decía que él quería todo el dinero y le rogaba a Rainey que la llamase. Aquella vez dejaba el número.

Cole detuvo a Rainey antes de que pusiera el último mensaje.

—¿Sabe ella que solo les quedan trescientos?

—Sí, claro, claro que lo sabe. Me ayudó a gastarlos.

—Es que parece como si tuvieran los ocho millones...

—Me está diciendo que a él no se lo ha contado. Ya le he dicho a ese —miró hacia Pike— que esos bolivianos no quieren el dinero. Lo sé porque intenté dárselo, más un extra.

—¿Cómo pensaba pagarles, si no lo tenía? —inquirió Pike.

Cole vio primero el asunto.

—Los federales y La Eme. Hizo un trato con ellos.

—Ya pueden apostar a que lo hice. Esos federales trabajan para un cártel allá en Baja. Pasan droga a sus mexicanos de aquí...

—No son «mis» mexicanos.

—Y sabe lo que yo hacía antes, ¿no?

—Sí. Pasaba dinero de contrabando por la costa, en barcos de pesca.

—Ese follón del petróleo derramado creó muchísimas

oportunidades. La gente aún no puede pescar como antes. Y a mí se me ocurrió. —Se enfrentó de nuevo a Pike—. Hablé con los mexicanos de aquí y ellos hablaron con los de México para que metiera aquí su mierda y sacara su dinero igual que hacía antes en casa. A los mexicanos de México les gustó, y ofrecieron un trato a la gente de Nueva Orleans. Esos putos bolivianos fingieron que estaban de acuerdo, pero era todo mentira, así que aquí estamos. Jodidos.

Pike echó una mirada a Cole y luego examinó a Rainey. Algo en su historia no cuadraba.

—Si estaba negociando con esa gente, ¿por qué fueron a pegarle Mendoza y Gomer?

—Porque entonces todavía no teníamos negocios. Esos dos gilipollas intentaron robarme, como usted pensaba. Azzara vino entonces a presionarme y a amenazarme con todas esas gilipolleces, que si La Eme esto, que si La Eme lo otro, y así fue como se me ocurrió la idea.

—Azzara.

—Sí. Yo he tenido asuntos con traficantes de drogas durante años, y sé que todos tienen los mismos problemas. Así que lo ideé todo: «Esto es lo que puedo hacer por vosotros, pero esto es lo que tenéis que hacer por mí».

—Que los bolivianos se retirasen.

—Sí.

Rainey pensó un momento y luego meneó la cabeza.

—Cómo me odian esos hijos de puta. Ahora tienen una guerra con un cártel de Baja, y no les importa una mierda nada de nada.

Pike le cortó.

—Ponga el último mensaje.

El tercer y último mensaje de Dru era más desesperado. Su voz mostraba el estrés creciente, respiraba con agitación, y Pike notaba su miedo.

«Para ya, Willie; ¿me oyes? Debes llamarme a las seis en punto. Te lo suplico. Por favor, soluciona las cosas. Sabes cómo hacerlo. Si no llamas, dice que me matará.»

Su llamada terminó abruptamente.

Ninguno de ellos habló durante un momento, luego Rainey miró a Pike.

—Usted me preguntó por qué le llamé. Cuando ella dice «hazlo», se entiende lo que quiere decir: que le llame a usted. Y por eso le llamé.

Pike no entendía nada.

Rainey frunció el ceño, mostrando una debilidad en los ojos que ponía de manifiesto que estaba algo violento.

—Cuando empezó todo este asunto con los pandilleros y apareció usted, ella me dijo que era el tipo de tío que podía solucionar las cosas. Eso le gustaba.

Pike le miró hasta que Rainey apartó la vista, y entonces cogió el teléfono y comprobó la hora. Eran las seis menos diez. El tiempo se estaba acabando.

—¿Rose tiene una hermana? —preguntó.

—¿Cómo?

—Tiene dos hermanos. ¿Tiene también una hermana?

Rainey guiñó los ojos como si Pike le estuviese hablando en clave.

—No. ¿Qué tiene que ver eso?

—¿Dónde está el dinero? —preguntó Cole.

—Tengo un almacén en Van Nuys. Si lo quieren, es suyo. Los trescientos cuarenta y dos.

Cole miró a Pike.

—A esta hora del día son dos horas de ida y vuelta. Mal.

—No lo necesitamos.

Rainey miró a Cole, luego a Pike.

—¿Y qué vamos a hacer, pues?

—El boliviano, el que le quiere muerto, ¿cómo se llama?

—Uf, madre mía, es todo un cártel. Un montón de tíos.

Cole se inclinó hacia delante y le dio unos golpecitos en la cabeza a Rainey.

—Piense. ¿A quién estafó? ¿Quién es el macho alfa?

—Pues será Hugo Joaquín. Era el que lo llevaba todo. ¿Qué más da? ¿Qué vamos a hacer?

Pike miró la hora. Tres minutos. Ya tenía lo que necesitaba.

—Estoy preparado.

—¿Preparado para qué?

Cole dio unos golpecitos a Rainey otra vez.

—Salga. Esperaremos fuera.

—¿Para qué? ¿Qué es lo que va a hacer?

Pike comprobó de nuevo la hora. Faltaba un minuto.

—Este es el momento en que le vendo.

Cole salió, sacó a Rainey y lo empujó hacia delante. Cerró la puerta y dejó a Pike solo con el teléfono.

Al otro lado del aparcamiento, una familia salía de un monovolumen y entraba en el restaurante. El padre llevaba sobre los hombros a una niñita pequeña con el pelo rizado. A unos quince metros de distancia, los coches iban reptando por Sunset Boulevard, embotellados en la hora punta. Pike apartó de su mente todo aquello y llamó a Dru Rayne.

44

Ella respondió al tercer timbrazo. Pike imaginó que a Gregg Daniel Vincent le costó un timbrazo enseñarle el número entrante, otro que Rose confirmase que era Rainey, y el tercero para que pulsara el botón de la respuesta y sujetara el teléfono junto al oído de ella. La voz de la mujer sonaba dubitativa.

—¿Hola?

—¿Está escuchando él?

Lo decía por Vincent.

Pasaron veinte segundos completos antes de que ella respondiera, seguramente porque Vincent estaba decidiendo qué hacer.

—Sí, está escuchando. ¿Dónde está Willie? Se suponía que tenía que llamar Willie.

—Willie no puede llamar. ¿Estás bien?

—Sí, sí, estoy bien. No me ha hecho daño.

—Dale el teléfono.

—Él, bueno... no quiere hablar. Si Willie no llama, me hará daño.

—No, no lo hará. Tengo a Rainey y tengo el dinero, pero sobre todo tengo a Rainey.

—Ah, quiere saber quién eres.

—Díselo.

Pike oyó que le decía su nombre. Vincent decía algo, pero demasiado bajo para que lo entendiera. Todavía estaban hablando cuando Pike habló de nuevo.

—¿Y él, cómo se llama?

—¿Qué?

—Que cómo se llama.

Otro murmullo al fondo antes de que Rose contestara.

—Se llama David.

La comisura de los labios de Pike tembló.

—Es usted un mentiroso, señor Vincent. Su nombre es Gregg Daniel Vincent. Déjese ya de chorradas y póngase al teléfono. Si no quiere a Rainey, se lo venderé a los bolivianos.

Treinta segundos de silencio esta vez, y ya bordeaban los cuarenta cuando se oyó al teléfono una voz masculina.

—¿Qué quieres negociar, chico? ¿Cómo sabes mi nombre?

—Me lo dijo un amigo.

—Mataré a tu puto amigo, a ti, a tu familia y a todos los hijos de puta que conozcas. ¿Te ha dicho eso tu amigo?

—Mi amigo me ha dicho que tú eres el tipo que envían los bolivianos para asustar a la gente. Ya sé quién eres. Pero nada de eso importa.

—Tengo amigos también. ¿Trabajas en Nicaragua o en Honduras? ¿Trabajas en Ecuador o Colombia? ¿Acaso crees que nos hemos enfrentado antes?

La comisura de los labios de Pike tembló de nuevo. No le había dicho a Dru dónde había trabajado, de modo que ella no podía haberle dicho nada a Vincent. Su nombre sí, y que había sido contratista militar, pero nada más. Vincent lo habría investigado, cosa que significaba que veía a Pike como una amenaza.

—Está bien. Los dos tenemos amigos. Quizá sean las mismas personas.

—¿Y eso qué significa?

—Que yo tengo a Rainey y el dinero. Te lo vendo.

—¿Vendérmelo? Una mierda. Tienes que traerlo y esperar que yo no salga a por ti.

—Si tengo que ir, se lo venderé a Hugo. Ya me han ofrecido un millón. Quizá pueda sacar más.

El silencio pareció distinto esta vez, y cuando habló Vincent su voz era pensativa y cautelosa.

—Pero estás aquí, hablando conmigo. Debo de tener algo que quieres.

—La chica.

—Ah.

—La chica y la mitad del dinero que queda. Tú te quedas con Rainey y con la otra mitad.

—Vete a la mierda, tío. Cortaré por la mitad a la puta esta.

—Y yo seguiré teniendo a Rainey.

Vincent gritó.

—¡Y te cortaré a ti por la mitad también, hijo de puta, cuando os tenga a los dos!

Pike sabía que estaba ganando. Era bueno que gritase. Siguió hablando en voz baja y tranquila.

—Mira, así están las cosas. Tú solo conseguirás a uno de ellos para el señor Joaquín, ¿a cuál de los dos quieres? ¿Cuál de los dos quiere más? Rainey le estafó. Rose simplemente iba de acompañante.

Pike dejó que aquello penetrara bien. Fuera, en el mundo exterior, Cole y Rainey le miraban. La familia volvió a su monovolumen con cajas desbordantes de perritos calientes y patatas fritas. Los coches se iban moviendo como un pulso letárgico.

—¿Trabajas para los bolivianos? —preguntó Vincent.

A Pike le sorprendió aquella pregunta. Vincent estaba preocupado por su posición con los bolivianos.

—Nunca digo para quién trabajo.

Pike dejó que aquello también fuera penetrando, sabiendo que la inseguridad de Vincent iría en aumento. Dejando las cosas vagas, podría pensar que el amigo de Pike era un boliviano. También sabía que intentaría averiguar cómo podía conseguir a ambos, a Rainey y a Rose.

Finalmente tomó una decisión.

—De acuerdo. ¿Cómo queréis hacerlo?

—Como te parezca. Podemos encontrarnos en alguna parte. Tú me das a la chica, yo te doy a Rainey y ya está.

Vincent se echó a reír, como esperaba Pike. Lo había comentado con Cole cuando esperaban a Rainey: Vincent nunca se expondría. Nunca dejaría que la chica saliera ante Pike y Rainey para hacer un intercambio, porque así podría convertirse en objetivo.

—De ninguna manera, tío. Venga ya, ¿hablas en serio?

—Pon la chica donde pueda verla. Tengo que ver que está viva. Si parece que está bien, te enviaré a Rainey con tu mitad del dinero. Se cruzarán a mitad de camino, ella vendrá hacia mí y él hacia ti. ¿Te parece mejor así?

—Espera, espera un momento... ¿Y si el hijo de puta se echa a correr?

—Pégale un tiro.

Era un montaje estúpido y lleno de agujeros, pero eso era precisamente lo que quería Pike. Vincent vería aquellos huecos como oportunidades. La única preocupación de Pike era forzar a Vincent para que le enseñara a Dru Rayne. Este no se expondría, sino que estaría cerca de la chica y la vigilaría desde una posición oculta, con una vía de escape clara. Pike sabía que querría que fuese así porque es lo que él mismo habría querido. Podría observarlo todo desde su escondite e intentar matar a Pike. Casi le oía pensarlo.

—De acuerdo. Nos reunimos en alguna parte —dijo finalmente Vincent.

—¿Qué tal en casa de Rainey, en el canal? Está vacía.

—Demasiado cerrado.

Por eso lo había sugerido Pike, empujando así a Vincent a pensar en rutas de escape y campos de visión más amplios.

—Donde tú quieras, Vincent. ¿Quieres pensarlo y llamarme más tarde?

Se quedó callado de nuevo, y luego murmuró algo que Pike no pudo oír. Pensó que estaba hablando con Dru, y luego se dio cuenta de que hablaba consigo mismo.

Dos minutos más tarde tenían ya un momento, un lugar, y habían acordado todos los detalles.

Pike bajó la ventanilla del Jeep e hizo una seña a Cole.

—Ya estamos. Vamos.

285

45

Daniel

Daniel bajó el teléfono y miró a la camarera. Habían vuelto de nuevo a la parte de atrás del camión, los cuatro.

Daniel dijo:

—¿Te estás follando a ese tío?

Tobey sonrió, lascivo:

—Sí, se lo está follando.

Cleo soltó una risita:

—Sí, follándoselo bien.

Tenía los ojos achinados y duros, como una puta correosa de Bogotá que quisiera robar una cartera. Pero también parecía asustada. Mucho, mucho mejor.

—No, no es nada de eso.

—¿Por qué quiere recuperarte, si no te está follando?

Ella apartó la vista, abajo y arriba, abajo y arriba.

—No lo sé. No hace mucho que le conozco.

Tobey se burló:

—Se lo está follando, la muy puta.

Cleo siseó:

—Puta, puta, puta.

Daniel esperaba que tuviesen razón. El tío de las flechas quizá fuese un mercenario muy machote, pero si se le ponía dura con la camarera la cosa ya no iba de dinero. Los hombres se mantienen firmes en lo que respecta al dinero, y se vuelven idiotas en lo que respecta a las mujeres.

Daniel arrancó un trozo nuevo de cinta plateada y se lo puso a ella encima de la boca.

—¿Sabes lo que eres?

Tobey dijo:

—Una golfa.

Cleo dijo:

—Puta, puta, puta.

Ella negó con la cabeza, ya que ahora no podía hablar.

—Eres una cabra atada a una estaca. Esos suajilis de África atan una cabra a una estaca debajo de un árbol como cebo para un león. La cortan toda, para que sangre, y luego esperan arriba, en el árbol. El león lo único que huele es la sangre. Y esa es una forma bastante buena de cazar a un zombi también.

Daniel la dejó atrás y subió delante, poniéndose al volante. Revisó de nuevo lo que el boliviano le había dicho de Pike, que era muy impresionante para los estándares de cualquier persona, y pensó que tenía una idea muy precisa de cómo acudiría a él. Daniel no tenía duda alguna de que Pike intentaría matarle, y se imaginó que este sabía que él intentaría matarle también. No había ni que decirlo. No tenía que hacer otra cosa que ir un poco por delante de él en el aspecto de la planificación.

Daniel salió entre los coches, considerando las variables de su inminente reunión. Quería llegar a la ubicación lo más rápidamente posible, pero antes tenía que recoger un par de cosas.

Fue recorriendo Hollywood, pensando en distintas situaciones tácticas, hasta que encontró una que le gustó.

Tres minutos después pasó bajo el paso elevado de Vine y vio a un hombre viejo sentado tranquilamente en una parada de autobús, con la barba gris y sucia y el pelo canoso. No hablaba con voces como los esquizos. Este era un simple borracho patológico en un mal momento. Hasta llevaba un letrero de cartón donde ponía: TRABAJO POR COMIDA.

Tobey dijo:

—Ese me parece bien.

Cleo dijo:

—Servirá.

Daniel aparcó junto al banco y llamó por la ventanilla del pasajero.

—Eh. ¿Es verdad lo que pone en el cartel? Tengo un trabajito para dos horas.

El tío miró la camioneta Hero-Rooter y luego negó con la cabeza.

—No soy fontanero.

Tonto del culo.

—Yo tampoco soy fontanero. Lo único que necesito que hagas es que sujetes una linterna. Mi empleado está enfermo.

El jodido perezoso apenas se movió.

—¿Qué linterna?

—Pues una puta linterna normal y corriente. Necesito un ayudante que me enfoque con una linterna. Cuarenta pavos para ti. Dos horas de trabajo. ¿Lo quieres o no?

—¿Cuarenta dólares?

—El curro es por ahí, colina arriba. Vamos, tío. Ya llego tarde. ¿Quieres los cuarenta?

Tobey dijo:

—¿Pero qué le pasa a este tío?

Cleo dijo:

—Chist, chist...

Finalmente, el tipo se levantó del banco.

—Quiero veinte por adelantado.

—Ni hablar. Cuarenta cuando acabes el trabajo, o si no me voy. Vamos.

El tipo le dirigió una mirada como si le estuviera haciendo un favor al mundo, pero al final subió. Olía a repollo podrido. Cerró la puerta de golpe, examinó la furgoneta mientras se instalaba y miró hacia atrás, pero por aquel entonces ya era demasiado tarde.

Daniel le empujó entre los asientos justo encima de la camarera.

Tobey dijo:

—Mátale.

Cleo dijo:

—Mátale.

Daniel dijo:

—Más tarde.

46

Pike examinó la furgoneta a la desfalleciente luz color latón. Hero-Rooter. ¡LLAMA A UN HÉROE PARA QUE TE SALVE! ¡DESAGÜES LIMPIOS LAS VEINTICUATRO HORAS! Basándose en lo poco que sabía de Gregg Daniel Vincent, Pike juzgó que la ubicación estaba cerca de la perfección. Él habría elegido un sitio idéntico.

La furgoneta Hero-Rooter estaba aparcada entre la maleza, en una cresta no urbanizada a un centenar de metros de Mulholland Drive, dominando el valle de San Fernando. En el lado sur de Mulholland se había cortado la montaña, dejando una cuesta empinada salpicada de pinos moribundos. No era un buen sitio para salir corriendo. El lado del valle estaba mejor. Vincent tendría una visión despejada en ambas direcciones, a lo largo de Mulholland y de las casas que llenaban el cañón que quedaba más abajo. Mulholland era la única vía para entrar o salir, pero, si aparecía la policía, un hombre con la habilidad de Vicent podría escabullirse fácilmente por entre los arbustos y desaparecer entre las serpenteantes calles y casas.

Pike bajó los binoculares y susurró en su móvil:

—Es listo. Es un buen sitio para matar.

—¿Ves a alguien? —preguntó Cole.

—Solo la camioneta. Está en una cresta, donde están despejando la colina. Rainey se ocupará.

Cole y Rainey estaban aparcados en un apartadero a unos quinientos metros al este, a poco más de un kilómetro de la furgoneta.

—Espera…

Pike examinó de nuevo la furgoneta. Probablemente Dru estaba dentro, pero Vincent estaría en la colina. El plan era fácil: cuando Rainey apareciese en la cresta, Dru saldría de la furgoneta, de modo que Pike pudiese ver que estaba sana y salva. Rainey entonces saldría de su coche y avanzaría a mitad de camino con el dinero. Dru saldría para encontrarse con él, comprobaría el dinero, y luego Rainey continuaría hasta la furgoneta mientras Dru iba hacia el Prius.

Ese era el plan que habían tramado Pike y Vincent, pero no ocurriría nada de eso. Pike lo sabía perfectamente, y Vincent también. Este buscaría a Pike, igual que él estaría buscando a Vincent. Si ganaba Vincent mataría a Rose Platt, luego torturaría a Rainey hasta que sacara el resto del dinero y después lo mataría. Todo en la historia de Vincent confirmaba aquella posibilidad. Le gustaba torturar y matar.

Pike examinó la zona de matorrales junto a Mulholland donde se detendría Rainey, y luego una suave elevación detrás de la furgoneta. Vincent estaría en uno de esos dos lugares. Cuando Rainey se volviera hacia la cresta, estaría de cara a la furgoneta y Vincent tras él, en una posición elevada, donde podría verlo y también vigilar a Pike. Este examinó las dos zonas, pero no vio nada, y volvió al teléfono.

—Me voy. Dame ocho minutos y avanza. Diez, y estaremos allí.

Pike se deslizó detrás de un retorcido matorral de roble y bajó por la colina que se iba desmoronando. Llevaba su Python, una Kimber del 45 y un rifle Remington modelo 700 con cerrojo que él mismo había modificado, junto con una bolsa para sus prismáticos y una cámara de imagen térmica FLIR, de barrido frontal. La FLIR leía imágenes de calor por infrarrojos. Cuando Pike estuviera más cerca, la FLIR le permitiría ver a Vincent entre los arbustos.

Se movió rápidamente bajando la empinada cuesta y deslizándose entre resecos arbustos a la carrera, y luego trepó por la siguiente lengua. Anduvo agachado en torno al repecho exterior, manteniendo Mulholland y la furgoneta por encima de él.

Dio la vuelta al repecho en el siguiente cañón, e hizo una

pausa para orientarse. La siguiente lengua estaba delante y por encima de él, con Mulholland a su izquierda. Cogió dos robles achaparrados como puntos de navegación, bajó atravesando un mar de arbustos grises y subió por un barranco causado por la erosión hasta alcanzar el borde de la cresta. No veía todavía la furgoneta, pero sabía que estaba a mitad de camino entre esta y Mulholland. Comprobó la hora: nueve minutos. Rainey y Cole iban avanzando.

Pike subió los últimos metros, agachado entre los arbustos hasta que coronó la cresta. La furgoneta estaba a treinta metros de distancia. Abrió la FLIR y examinó toda la zona. La máquina no podía detectar a ningún ser humano a través del metal, pero Pike quería ver si Vincent estaba debajo del camión.

La imagen en el visor era un paisaje de grises y negros. Cuanto más frío estaba algo, más oscura era su imagen. Cuanto más caliente, más clara. La furgoneta era una sombra gris brillante, más clara que el fondo por el calor que absorbía del sol. El cielo por encima del horizonte se veía negro.

Nadie se escondía debajo de la furgoneta ni junto a ella.

Pike paseó la FLIR por el apartadero. Nada. Esperaba encontrar a Vincent en la elevación que había por encima, pero no había nadie entre las hierbas.

Cogió su móvil y susurró de nuevo.

—Dame tres más.

Cambió de posición y probó un ángulo nuevo, pero de nuevo obtuvo una lectura fría. No había nadie en los arbustos junto a la carretera, ni a lo largo del apartadero.

Lentamente, examinó la loma circundante. Comprobó la cresta desde Mulholland hasta el camión y luego la colina que se alzaba detrás, y allí fue donde le encontró. El visor mostraba la forma brillante y gris de un hombre echado bajo un matojo de salvia, de cara hacia abajo, en la posición prona de un tirador. Bajó la FLIR y comprobó la salvia con sus prismáticos. El hombre resultaba invisible tras los arbustos, pero Pike pronto encontró el borde recto y poco natural del cañón de un rifle que sobresalía detrás de las ramas. Un lugar perfecto para una emboscada.

Pike cogió de nuevo su teléfono.

—Está en la subida que hay por encima de la furgoneta. Rifle.

Cole susurró a su vez.

—¿Cuánto tiempo necesitas?

—Dos minutos.

—Ya casi estamos allí. Si paramos ahora nos verá y se preguntará por qué nos detenemos.

—Dos minutos.

Pike se dejó caer por la pendiente abajo y avanzó de lado rápidamente a lo largo de la lengua, más allá de la furgoneta, y por el lado de atrás de la loma. Echó un vistazo al Prius que daba la vuelta en la cresta mientras él mismo la coronaba, pero bajó el ritmo para mantener el silencio.

El matojo gris de salvia ahora estaba justo delante de él. Pike bajó el rifle y la bolsa y sacó el 357. Se acercó más y finalmente vio una pierna vestida de camuflaje detrás del arbusto.

«Estoy aquí.»

Pike cubrió la distancia silenciosamente hasta que se encontró justo detrás del hombre, y luego empujó con la Python el costado de Vincent.

Se dio cuenta al momento de que estaba muerto por la quietud del cuerpo, y comprendió al instante que aquel hombre no era Vincent.

Se puso tenso, con los músculos rígidos contra la bala que esperaba, pero el disparo no llegó.

El cadáver era el de un viejo con el pelo gris enmarañado y un agujero de bala de pequeño calibre en la sien. Recién muerto, todavía caliente. Un cebo.

Entonces oyó gritar a Dru, y William Rainey la llamó por su nombre.

Daniel

Daniel examinó el promontorio distante a través de la mirilla de su rifle, susurrando para sí.

—Ya te tengo, hijo de puta. Vamos. Déjame ver tu culo lisiado.

La furgoneta se encontraba a ciento sesenta y dos metros

ante él. Los había contado paso a paso. Estaba metida entre dos árboles moribundos en el extremo sur de Mulholland, en una alta loma donde no había otra cosa que rocas a la espalda y una pendiente larga y empinada por abajo. Pike nunca se metería en un lugar jodido y sin salida como aquel, de modo que se había imaginado que Daniel también lo evitaría. Y por eso precisamente lo había elegido.

Tobey dijo:

—Has sido más listo que el gilipollas.

Cleo dijo:

—No nos verá llegar, gar, gar.

Daniel sabía que Pike estaba en algún lugar del arbusto. Ocho minutos antes había captado un destello de movimiento gris en la cresta de al lado, aparecido y desaparecido en un segundo. De modo que ahora examinaba el arbusto, y la cresta, y la zona en torno al tipo muerto. Daniel quería que Pike encontrase al tipo muerto. Pike vería el rifle, dispararía quizá, y entonces lo tendría. A lo mejor intentaba acercarse más, y captaría su movimiento. Pero hasta el momento, nada.

Daniel había dejado el maldito rifle sobresaliendo tanto del arbusto que un explorador novato lo habría encontrado ya por aquel entonces. Empezaba a pensar que quizás ese Joe Pike no fuese tan listo como él había creído.

Tobey dijo:

—Enséñale a la camarera, Daniel. Eso le hará salir.

Cleo dijo:

—A lo mejor se mueve, eve, eve.

Tobey y Cleo eran un par de pesados, pero a veces se ganaban el pan. Si sacaba a la camarera, Pike a lo mejor cambiaba de posición. *Bang.*

Sacó su *walkie-talkie* y la llamó, tal y como había dicho.

—¿Me oyes?

La voz de ella se volvió metálica, llena de interferencias.

—Te oigo. ¿Está aquí Willie?

—Sal. Te vas a casa.

Tobey dijo:

—Ay, ay. Aquí viene.

Cleo dijo:

—Aquí está, está, está.

Daniel pensó que hablaban de Pike, pero no era así.

El Prius tomó una curva muy cerrada a menos de quinientos metros de distancia. Daniel pensó que quizá debería decirle a la mujer que se quedase en la maldita furgoneta, pero decidió dejar que viniese.

Apretó de nuevo el botón de hablar.

—Sal de la maldita furgoneta, mujer. No voy a hacerte daño.

La puerta de atrás se abrió y Daniel examinó los arbustos en busca de movimiento.

Elvis Cole

Cole estaba apelotonado y tan metido en el asiento trasero del Prius que no veía nada, ni siquiera la nuca de Bill Rainey.

—¿Ves la furgoneta?

—Sí, casi estamos allí. No te preocupes.

El criminal que tenía un cártel boliviano tras él le decía a Cole que no se preocupase. Perfecto.

—Asegúrate de llevar escondida el arma. Si la ve, estás listo.

—Relájate, por el amor de Dios. Estoy bien.

Le habían dado un arma a Rainey y le habían puesto un chaleco antibalas. No pensaban colocarlo ante la mirilla de Gregg Daniel Vincent sin nada.

—Ya estamos. Doy la vuelta —dijo Rainey.

Fueron rebotando en el pavimento hasta la cresta. Una nube de polvo entró formando remolinos por las ventanillas abiertas, bajas por si Cole tenía que disparar.

Entonces Rainey pisó el freno.

—¿Qué es esta mierda? Ella ya ha salido. Se suponía que tenía que salir yo primero...

Cole vio la cabeza de Rainey girando a derecha e izquierda, como si pensase que Vincent iba a saltar de detrás de un arbusto. Cole quiso mirar, pero sabía que Vincent estaría observando su coche.

—Calma. ¿Qué hace ella?

—Me mira. Me saluda con las manos.

—¿Hay alguien en la furgoneta?

—No lo veo.

—Mira por los lados. Busca a Vincent.

—¡Joder! ¡Rose se ha echado a correr! ¡Está intentando escapar!

Rainey de repente abrió su portezuela de golpe y salió del coche.

—¡Rose! ¡Ro...!

Cole oyó el primer disparo.

Pike se puso de pie cuando les oyó gritar. Por debajo de él, Rose Platt corría hacia el Prius mientras Rainey corría hacia ella, los dos separados por casi cien metros.

Pike se dejó ver junto a una salvia, intentando atraer el fuego de Vincent. Atravesó rápidamente el matorral mientras un estampido agudo rompía el silencio del atardecer, corriendo por los cañones amoratados. Oyó pasar la bala, luego se agachó detrás de las rocas; rodó y siguió corriendo, zigzagueando a derecha e izquierda al bajar la pendiente.

Rose Platt y Rainey se detuvieron al oír el disparo. Entonces Elvis Cole salió del Prius y ella se volvió hacia la furgoneta.

El segundo disparo dio en la pendiente a los pies de Pike, pero este vio el destello y corrió más aún mientras le gritaba a Cole:

—¡Al otro lado, los árboles por encima!

Pike disparó tres veces, disparos a larga distancia hacia el destello, esperando hacerlo salir. Cole y Rainey se volvieron a mirar a Vincent. Pike vio otro destello, solo que esta vez Vincent no le disparaba a él.

La bala dio a Rainey en la pierna izquierda y surgió un surtidor rosa. El hombre giró con los brazos y las piernas extendidos como una marioneta, y no chilló hasta que cayó al suelo.

Rose Platt gritó una sola vez y se arrojó detrás de la furgoneta, mientras otro disparo daba en el guardabarros.

Rainey se incorporó, gritó algo que Pike no entendió y luego disparó la pistola hacia los árboles. Vincent disparó a su vez. La bala atravesó el hombro de Rainey formando otra

295

nube roja, pero Cole ya había localizado el destello y descargó cinco balas.

Pike captó un parpadeo entre los árboles: era Vincent, que se movía colina abajo y se iba.

Pike gritó de nuevo:

—¡Se va colina abajo!

Cole corrió a través de Mulholland y desapareció bajando por el promontorio más alejado. Pike se volvió hacia Dru y la vio arrodillada junto a la furgoneta. En aquel momento se sentía desgarrado, no sabía si irse o quedarse, pero ella estaba a salvo, así que corrió a ayudar a Cole. Corrió pasando junto a Rainey y luego subió la empinada pendiente que conducía al extremo más alejado de Mulholland, hacia los árboles.

47

Daniel

*T*obey susurró al oído de Daniel, haciéndole cosquillas con sus labios peludos, suplicante, urgente.

—Puedes hacerlo, chico. Todavía puedes cogerlos.

Cleo salió disparada dando vueltas y girando como un derviche.

—Puedes hacerlo, Daniel, el, el. Igual que un zombi, ombi, ombi.

—Abre los ojos, chico. ¡Abre los ojos, os, os!

Cleo giraba más deprisa.

—Ábrelos y mata, mata, mata.

Las rocas y ramas podridas le daban a Daniel en la espalda. Intentó respirar y notó un chasquido húmedo en el pecho. Tosió, pero no salió más que vómito.

Se miró la sangre en las manos.

—Me han dado.

Tobey djo:

—Hace falta algo más que esto para matar a un hombre-lobo, amigo, igo, igo.

Daniel se tocó el pecho de nuevo y miró la sangre. No se encontraba mal. Ni siquiera recordaba que le hubiesen dado. Sabía que estaban disparando y que volaban las balas, pero no notaba nada. Quizás hubiese algo de verdad en el rollo ese del hombre-lobo, al final.

Tobey dijo:

—Encuentra tu arma, Daniel. Coge el arma.

—Arma, arma, arma.

Daniel tocó a su alrededor hasta que la encontró. El rifle

había desaparecido, pero todavía llevaba la pistola en el bolsillo. Quitó el seguro.

—Creo que todavía puedo trincar a ese cabrón, chicos.

Tobey dijo:

—Seguro que puedes, des.

Cleo dijo:

—Seguro, guro, guro.

Se encontraba mejor. Cogió aire otra vez y se sintió mucho
mejor. Aunque no pudiera trincar a aquel cabrón, pensaba que
igual conseguía librarse. Muchas casas alrededor. Muchos
coches. Lo único que tenía que hacer era atravesar Mulholland
y entrar en el cañón.

Daniel escuchó. Oyó movimiento en la loma, pero estaba
lejos, y abajo. Probablemente pensaban que se había ido
mucho más abajo de lo que estaba en realidad.

Daniel se puso de pie, apoyándose en el árbol.

Entonces vio al tío de las flechas que le miraba. No decía ni
una sola palabra, solo estaba allí, de pie, a un metro de distancia, con el arma en el costado.

48

*P*ike sabía que Cole estaba en algún lugar de la loma, abajo. Le oía avanzar entre los arbustos, y el ruido de las rocas al deslizarse mientras bajaba colina abajo, de lado. Había visto a Vincent colina abajo, de modo que bajar era lo adecuado, pero decidió quedarse un poco rezagado por si a Vincent se le ocurría darse la vuelta.

Dejó que Cole se alejara. Cuanto más se alejara, más tranquilo se quedaría todo, y la tranquilidad estaba bien.

Escuchó casi un minuto entero y luego oyó ruido de guijarros entre los árboles, en la pendiente, en algún lugar por delante. Una suave tos siguió a los guijarros.

Pike se desplazó entre los árboles y vio a Vincent en las rocas entre dos nogales moribundos a menos de veinte metros de la carretera. Pensaba que estaba muerto, pero se movió y se puso en pie con mucho esfuerzo. Vincent era delgado pero de constitución fuerte, con la cara esbelta, marcas de viruela y ojeras. No parecía ningún loco, pero ¿qué otro tipo de persona tortura y mata para unos traficantes de droga lunáticos?

Pike vio que Vincent llevaba un arma, pero esperó a ver qué hacía. Tenía una herida en el pecho, pero estaba situada baja, en un costado. Él había visto luchar y ganar a algunos hombres con el cuerpo vuelto del revés.

Entonces Vincent lo vio y sus ojos se afilaron como tachuelas.

—Mirad, chicos. Ya le tenemos.

Pike se preguntó con quién hablaría.

—¿Eres Pike?

Asintió.

—No has sido tú el que me ha dado. Ha sido el otro tío. ¿Llamas a una ambulancia?

—No.

—¿No? Me estoy desangrando, tío. Ayúdame.

Pike meneó la cabeza.

Vincent se lo quedó mirando un momento y luego se encogió de hombros. No quería ninguna ambulancia, y se habría largado antes de que viniera. Lo que esperaba era coger por sorpresa a Pike mientras sacaba el teléfono o hacía la llamada. Quería esa ventaja.

—No has respondido a mi pregunta —dijo Vincent.

—¿Qué pregunta era?

—En el sur. ¿Crees que nos enfrentamos antes, tú y yo?

—No.

—¿Y cómo lo sabes tan seguro?

—Porque estarías muerto.

—Qué gracia. Los chicos me han dicho lo mismo de ti.

Pike dijo:

—¿De quién estás hablando?

Vincent levantó el arma. Era rápido, pero no le dio tiempo.

Pike le disparó tres veces en el pecho, las balas muy agrupadas, del tamaño de un trébol. Luego se acercó a él, recogió su arma y llamó a Cole en voz alta.

—Ya ha caído. Está más arriba, a veinte metros de la carretera.

Registró el cuerpo antes de apartar su 357.

Cole lo llamó desde abajo.

—¿Estás bien?

—Bien. Voy a por Dru.

Dru. Pike dijo su nombre real, bajito, para sí.

—Rose.

Bajó corriendo atravesando Mulholland y encontró a Rose Platt agachada junto a Rainey. Intentaba dilucidar lo que sentía por ella, pero la verdad es que apenas sentía nada.

Rose se puso de pie al llegar él, y Pike fue aminorando la marcha y llegó andando. Ella seguía teniendo aquellos mismos ojos. Inteligentes, complicados, muy vivos. Quizá fue eso lo que le atrajo: la vitalidad que había en sus ojos.

—Está muerto —dijo Rose.

—Lo siento.

Rose recogió la pistola de Rainey, pasó por encima de su cuerpo y abrió el Prius.

—Rose. —Ella sonrió con los ojos inteligentes, brillantes—. No vas a ir a ninguna parte. —Pike se detuvo, esperando que ella lo dejara—. Baja el arma.

—No puedo dejar todo ese dinero, Joe. He vivido como una rata por ese dinero. ¿No lo entiendes? Es mío.

—Trescientos mil dólares no es mucho.

Ella inclinó la cabeza y algo jugueteó en sus ojos que le puso furioso.

—Ay, si supieras…

Se volvió hacia el coche, y Pike se dirigió hacia ella.

—Rose.

Ella sacó el arma y Pike fue a sacar la suya, pero sonaron dos disparos que pasaron a su lado antes de que pudiera hacerlo.

Pike vio que las balas le daban a ella, que su camisa se arrugaba y agujereaba. Vio que sus ojos vacilaban y que abría la boca, como si no entendiera lo que había ocurrido. Levantó las manos para tocar algo que no existía, y luego cayó.

301

Ni se acercó a ella. Se volvió y vio a Elvis Cole, que seguía con el arma en la mano. Vio que por la cara de Cole corrían las lágrimas. Vio llorar a su amigo y ninguno de los dos se movió.

49

Daniel

*D*aniel vio luces que bailaban y pensó que era Cleo, pero las luces corrían hacia él, hacia su cara, y luego se alejaban a toda velocidad, como una bala, y chasqueaban, concentrándose en un foco cristalino absolutamente nítido. Veía las ramas. Ramas, agujas de pino, ramas de roble enano retorcidas, nudosas, deformadas, como dedos artríticos con hojas.

Tobey dijo:

—¿Daniel?

Cleo dijo:

—¿Daniel?

Notó que se encogía, como si el mundo se fuese haciendo más grande y él más pequeño, y Tobey y Cleo estuvieran muy, muy lejos.

Daniel dijo:

—¿Chicos?

Tobey dijo:

—Te estamos buscando, tío; ¿dónde estás?

Cleo dijo:

—¿Daniel, el, el?

Intentaba ponerse de pie. Luchaba como un hombre lobo con un zombi que le mordía el cuello, pero el zombi iba ganando.

—¿Tobey? ¿Cleo? ¿Dónde estáis, dónde…?

Daniel intentaba mantener los ojos abiertos, pero la luz, que antes era tan brillante, ahora se había vuelto negra.

Tobey chilló:

—¡Daniel, vuelve!

Cleo chilló:
—¿Dónde está, está, está…?
Tobey dijo:
—¿Cleo?
Cleo dijo:
—¿Tobey?
—Me voy.
—Me he ido.
—…

—…

Daniel iba flotando. Ya no sentía su cuerpo, ni la tierra que tenía debajo, ni el aire que besaba su piel. Se sentía como nada dentro de la nada, y sabía que echaría de menos a los chicos, a Cleo y Tobey, sus únicos queridos y fieles amigos.

303

50

*P*ike se sentó en el puente de Venice Boulevard, mirando hacia Grand Canal y la casa. Se sentó en la base de cemento de una farola con los pies colgando, cosa que se suponía que no se podía hacer, pero la oficial Hydeck estaba apoyada en la barandilla a su lado.

—Lleva mucho rato aquí —le dijo.

Pike asintió.

—Le he visto desde hace mucho rato. ¿Está bien?

—Sí, estoy bien.

Hydeck se ajustó la pistola.

—¿Qué cree que ocurrió con el dinero?

—Rainey dijo que se lo había gastado.

—¿Quién sabe? ¿Recuerda el robo del banco de North Hollywood, aquellos idiotas con las ametralladoras? Esos tíos robaron tres cuartos de millón de dólares, y nadie sabe dónde fueron a parar. Esas cosas ocurren. El dinero del crimen desaparece.

Pike no respondió. Le caía bien Hydeck, pero quería que le dejara solo.

—Ah, ¿sabe una cosa? No sé si se ha enterado. Los cabrones que mataron a Button y Futardo, ¿sabe? ¿Ha oído hablar de ellos?

Pike sabía que Futardo había matado a uno de los hombres, pero que el otro había desaparecido.

—No. ¿Qué ocurre con ellos?

—Pues que antes eran agentes de la agencia antidrogas. El que se hacía llamar Straw en realidad era Norm Lister. El otro se llamaba Carbone. Trabajaban en el caso Rainey cuando empezó todo. Lister fue despedido, y el otro dimitió. Supongo que decidieron ir a por el oro...

Pike recordó los expedientes que él había cogido del Malibu. La mayor parte de los informes los había redactado Lister.

—Lo siento por Jerry. Y por Futardo también —dijo.

—Era una chica muy agradable. Medalla póstuma al valor.

Hydeck acabó por alejarse de la barandilla y se guardó el arma.

—Bueno, amigo, ya me voy. Nos vemos.

Pike la miró.

—Oficial, gracias por su ayuda.

—No debería estar ahí con los pies colgando hacia fuera...

Hydeck sonrió y se fue andando hacia el coche.

Pike siguió mirando la casa.

Los investigadores federales y estatales de Luisiana vinieron y luego se fueron. Entrevistaron a Pike y le contaron lo que sabían. Negaron lo que decía Rainey de que había robado solo 8 200 000 dólares y contaron varias versiones que decían que Rainey había robado un mínimo de doce millones y un máximo de dieciocho a los bolivianos. Pike les creía. Rainey era de naturaleza mentirosa, así que no tenía ninguna duda de que siguió mintiendo hasta el final.

Rose Platt lo convenció.

Pike subió las piernas, se apartó del puente y fue andando hasta el Sidewalk Café. Se sentó en la terraza exterior, a dos mesas de distancia de la que compartió un día con Rose Platt.

La joven camarera, la de los hoyuelos, sonrió cuando le vio. Ya era cliente habitual.

—¿Té verde?

Pike asintió.

Se bebió el té y miró hacia el océano entre la gente que pasaba, sin verlos a ellos, ni ver el agua, ni ver nada. No pensaba en nada excepto en lo caliente que estaba el té y lo fresca que era la brisa del océano, y la sensación tan agradable que producía el sol fundido en el horizonte.

Cuando el cielo se volvió oscuro, Pike pagó su cuenta y volvió a los canales. Siguió por la acera a lo largo del canal, más allá de la casa de los Palmer, y comprobó la ventana de Jared.

Estaba allí, con los cascos puestos y retorciéndose al compás de un ritmo desconocido.

Siguió adelante y entró en el diminuto muelle que se encontraba en la parte de atrás de la casa de Steve Brown, donde colgaba el kayak en dos postes de madera idénticos.

Jared le dijo que Steve Brown volvería a finales de aquella semana. También le contó otras cosas, como que Rainey se sentaba en el pequeño muelle por la noche y salía en el kayak de noche también, y que lo había visto dos veces vadeando el canal por la noche.

Siempre de noche.

Pero fue Rose quien lo convenció por las cosas que dijo al final, eso de no dejar todo ese dinero, de que había vivido como una rata por eso. La forma que tuvo de mirarle cuando pensó que lo iba a perder. «Ay, si supieras…»

Pike se preguntó si ella ya sabía dónde estaba o si Rainey se lo dijo justo antes de morir. De cualquier manera parecía que hablaba de mucho más que 342 000 dólares.

Pike pasó la mano por la suave piel del kayak y lo levantó de los ganchos donde estaba colgado. Sabía que el dinero no estaba en el barquito porque lo había comprobado ya hacía dos días, pero le gustaba la sensación de su peso.

Colocó de nuevo el kayak en sus ganchos, y luego se sentó en el muelle. La noche era bonita, fresca, y el agua estaría fría.

Ochenta y cinco bloques de hormigón se alineaban en la orilla, de un extremo de la propiedad al otro, colocados en cinco capas escalonadas de diecisiete bloques cada una. Pike lo sabía porque los había contado cuando había marea baja. Volvió dos veces por la noche y vadeó hasta el centro del canal, donde, en el punto más profundo, cuando la marea estaba alta, el agua le llegaba al cuello. Fue hurgando en el fondo y las plantas que crecían allí formando plumosas nubes y no encontró nada, y luego empezó a comprobar los bloques para ver si alguno estaba suelto o se podía mover.

Sin motivo alguno, solo porque tenía que empezar por algún sitio, Pike empezó a examinar primero los bloques que quedaban justo debajo y alrededor del muelle. Era lo más obvio, pero no encontró nada. Cada bloque estaba bien firme y seguro en su fila.

Quedaban por comprobar dos bloques más.

Se quitó las zapatillas deportivas y la pistola, los pantalones y la sudadera, envolvió la pistola con los pantalones y luego puso encima los zapatos y se metió silenciosamente en el agua. Se le contrajeron los músculos con el primer contacto frío, pero esa conmoción, como todos los dolores, se fue desvaneciendo.

Siguió por donde lo había dejado, comprobó once bloques más, y ya iba vadeando entre las plantas acuáticas cuando golpeó con la pierna en un objeto duro. Lo palpó con el pie y se dio cuenta de que había tropezado con una tubería de veinticinco centímetros. Había visto tuberías como aquella en los canales cuando la marea estaba baja y su fondo quedaba expuesto. Eran desagües para la lluvia y los residuos líquidos recogidos de calles y jardines.

Las tuberías que había visto estaban tapadas con una pesada rejilla metálica para que no se metieran las aves y otros animales cuando el agua bajaba, pero cuando dio con el pie contra aquella, notó que la rejilla se movía.

307

Pike cogió aliento, se metió bajo el agua y encontró cuatro sacos de nailon metidos en la tubería y atados entre sí con una cuerda. No salieron con facilidad, pero al cabo de un rato Pike los había conseguido soltar.

En cuanto los tuvo fuera del agua se puso la camiseta y los pantalones, se sujetó la pistola al cinturón y se dirigió hacia su Jeep con las bolsas. Mientras iba subiendo por el pequeño puente peatonal, una pareja mayor se detuvo en el otro extremo para dejarle pasar.

—Gracias —dijo.

—Qué noche más bonita —comentó la señora.

El Jeep de Pike estaba en Venice Boulevard, no lejos del puente. Dejó las bolsas en la sombra, en la acera, y abrió la puerta de atrás. Cuando volvió a por las bolsas, el antiguo agente de la agencia antidrogas Norm Lister le esperaba apuntándole con un arma.

—Buen trabajo, Pike. Muy bueno. Excelente.

Lister parecía andrajoso y sucio, como si hubiera estado viviendo en un coche. Hizo un gesto hacia delante con el arma, como si esperase que Pike retrocediera. «Ay, si supieras...»

—Ponga las llaves ahí en el parterre, y aléjese.

Pike no se movió.

—¿Sabía dónde estaba el dinero?

—No, pero conocía a Rainey. Yo soy el tipo que le hizo salir. Tenía que estar cerca.

Pike recordó el vídeo. Cómo habían seguido a Rainey y Platt, observando todos sus movimientos, quizás esperando que Rainey echara un vistazo al dinero.

Lister empujó de nuevo.

—Váyase, Pike. Esta es su oportunidad.

Miró el cañón tembloroso del arma de Lister, y luego sus ojos nerviosos. Pensó en Jerry Button y en la pobre Futardo, y en Rainey y Dru Rayne, que resultó ser Rose Platt.

—Lister, si me conociera tan bien como conocía a Rainey no estaría aquí.

Le disparó dos veces en el pecho, y luego se acercó y le pegó un tiro en la cara, exactamente igual que él había hecho con Jerry Button.

Cargó el dinero en el coche y dejó a Norman Lister en la acera.

51

*P*ike se llevó las bolsas a casa, pero no las abrió hasta al cabo de tres días. Las puso en la bañera la primera noche, suponiendo que chorrearían. Al día siguiente las trasladó al dormitorio, a los pies de su cama.

Al tercer día se las llevó abajo y las abrió por primera vez desde que las sacó del agua. Cortó los envoltorios de plástico y amontonó las pilas de dinero en el suelo. Había unos pocos paquetes de billetes de cincuenta y de veinte, y la mayoría de los paquetes de diez centímetros solo tenían billetes de cien dólares.

Le costó cuatro horas y treinta y cinco minutos contar todo el dinero, anotando la cantidad que había en cada montón en un bloc. Cuando acabó, Pike se echó atrás en el sofá y pensó en la ciudad en miniatura con sus rascacielos que se extendía en su salón.

William Rainey había mentido al final, diciéndole que solo le quedaban 342 000 dólares.

«Si supieras…»

Pike contó 6 755 000 dólares.

Se preguntó cuánto dinero permanecería oculto en otras ubicaciones, pero no le importaba demasiado, en ningún sentido. Se quedó mirando el dinero un rato, intentando decidir qué hacer con él, y luego puso la tele y vio las noticias deportivas de última hora.

Más tarde apagó la luz y se fue a dormir. No recogió el dinero. Dejó aquellas montañas en el suelo como lo que eran, trozos de papel sin sentido.

52

Marisol Rivera
Ojos de ángel

El padre Art estaba mejor, excepto por la fiebre. La orina ya era más clara, pero todavía tenía unas décimas. No demasiado, solo una o dos, pero se le agarraba como una deuda pendiente, dejándole debilitado. Marisol estaba preocupada, de modo que venía temprano y se iba tarde, e intentaba en lo posible hacer llamamientos para recoger más dinero.

Aquella mañana, cuando llegó, mucho antes que los consejeros o los niños, Marisol encontró una bolsa de nailon azul en el suelo, ante la puerta delantera.

Que aquella bolsa estuviese allí ya era raro, pero más raro aún era que hubiese una tarjeta sujeta a la bolsa. Era una sencilla tarjeta blanca en la que estaba escrito su nombre.

Miró a su alrededor para ver si alguien miraba, quizás alguien que quisiera gastarle una broma para ver lo que hacía, pero no vio a nadie.

Metió la bolsa dentro y la puso encima de su mesa. La bolsa abultaba y pesaba mucho, quizá cuatro o cinco kilos, como si estuviera llena de chocolate.

El padre Art la llamó desde dentro.

—¿Eres tú?

—Sí, ¿quién iba a ser?

—No entres. Estoy en el baño.

—Acaba lo tuyo. Llama cuando estés preparado.

Marisol pasó detrás de su escritorio, examinó la bolsa y luego dejó a un lado sus sospechas y la abrió. Lo primero que vio fue otra tarjeta blanca. Y la nota que llevaba escrita era sencilla.

«Alguien te vigila.»

53

Elvis Cole

Cole vio la niebla roja. El sueño le despertó aquella mañana, como había ocurrido la noche anterior, y la anterior a la anterior, y muchas más noches de las que recordaba. Ahora estaba de pie ante su escritorio, un día luminoso y tranquilo, pensando en lo cerca que habían estado.

Destellos en la boca del cañón de un arma, en una habitación lúgubre. La sombra de una mujer proyectada en la pared. Unas gafas de sol que dan vueltas en el aire. Joe Pike se derrumba entre una horrible niebla roja.

Cole no había visto a Joe ni hablado con él desde que dejaron Mulholland Drive once días antes. Ya incluso entonces, mientras hablaban con la policía, Pike le había parecido más distante, como si se hubiese retirado más aún a un lugar secreto que solo él conocía.

Cole le había dejado mensajes, pero Pike no le había devuelto las llamadas. Había acudido a casa de Pike, pero no le había encontrado allí. A veces Pike desaparecía durante semanas, pero aquella vez era distinto.

Dos halcones de cola roja flotaban describiendo lentos círculos por encima del cañón. Cole los contempló, preguntándose qué buscarían. Llevaba horas mirándolos. Su gato estaba sentado al borde de la terraza, observando a Cole, que a su vez observaba a las aves. Aburrido.

—¿No tienes nada mejor que hacer? —dijo Cole.

El gato entrecerró los ojos, se quedó dormido y luego se despertó de repente y entró corriendo en la casa.

—Gracias a Dios.

Fue a las puertas correderas mientras Joe Pike entraba por la puerta delantera. Quedó un momento enmarcado en la puerta, rodeado por la luz, y luego cerró la puerta y salió a la terraza.

Se quedaron cara a cara, ninguno de los dos habló, y luego Pike le atrajo hacia sí y le abrazó. No dijo una sola palabra, simplemente le abrazó y fue a la barandilla.

Al cabo de un rato Cole salió también a la barandilla, mirando hacia el cañón que se extendía ante ellos como un cuenco de un color verde neblinoso.

—Me alegro de verte.

Pike asintió.

—¿Quieres algo para beber?

—No, estoy bien.

Cole se agarró fuerte a la barandilla para sujetarse.

—He pensado que teníamos que hablar…

—No hace falta.

—Ella iba a matarte.

—Ya lo sé.

—Tuve que hacerlo. No quería, pero tuve que hacerlo. ¿Lo comprendes?

Pike apretó el hombro de Cole, y luego miró hacia el cielo.

—Halcones.

—Llevan ahí todo el día.

—Es donde deben estar.

Cole asintió y notó que fluían las lágrimas. Contemplaron juntos a los gavilanes. Donde debían estar.

313

Agradecimientos

*E*scribir es un acto solitario, pero dar vida a un libro requiere un equipo. Al autor le gustaría dar las gracias a Patricia Crais por su duro trabajo y sus largas horas mejorando el manuscrito, y a Lauren Crais por su investigación legal y su información.

Gracias también a Steve Brown por compartir sus conocimientos sobre los canales de Venice, y por proporcionar visitas comentadas y diversas aportaciones a la historia.

Marylin Ducksworth, Michael Barson y Matthew Venzon estuvieron fantásticos. Su trabajo y sus innovadoras ideas resultaron muy importantes e inspiradoras. Gracias.

Lo mismo para Kate Stark y Lydia Hirt, por impulsar al autor y su trabajo al reino de lo emergente, y a Ivan Held y Neil Nyren por su fe y su compromiso.

En Gran Bretaña, gracias a Tim Healy Hutchinson, Jon Wood, Juliet Ewers, Helen Richardson, Susan Lamb y Malcolm Edwards.

Y también debo agradecimiento y respeto a Aaron Priest y su equipo de la agencia literaria Aaron Priest (Lucy Chields, Nicole James, John Richmond y Lisa Vance) por alimentar mis sueños y hacerlos realidad.

Y para mi amigo David Thompson, un libro y un cóctel margarita.

Robert Crais

Nació en el estado de Luisiana y creció a orillas del río Misisipi, en una familia humilde en la que varios de sus miembros son agentes de policía. A los quince años compró un ejemplar de segunda mano de *La hermana pequeña* de Raymond Chandler, que le inspiró su amor por la escritura. Otras influencias declaradas de Crais son Dashiell Hammett, Ernest Hemingway, Robert B. Parker y John Steinbeck.

Es autor de la reconocida serie de novelas protagonizada por Elvis Cole que ha sido publicada en más de 42 países y de la que han surgido personajes memorables como Joe Pike, protagonista de *El centinela*.

En la actualidad reside en las montañas de Santa Mónica con su esposa, tres gatos y varios miles de libros.

ESTE LIBRO UTILIZA EL TIPO ALDUS, QUE TOMA SU NOMBRE
DEL VANGUARDISTA IMPRESOR DEL RENACIMIENTO
ITALIANO ALDUS MANUTIUS. HERMANN ZAPF
DISEÑÓ EL TIPO ALDUS PARA LA IMPRENTA
STEMPEL EN 1954, COMO UNA RÉPLICA
MÁS LIGERA Y ELEGANTE DEL
POPULAR TIPO
PALATINO

* * *
* *
*

EL CENTINELA
SE ACABÓ DE IMPRIMIR
EN UN DÍA DE OTOÑO DE 2012,
EN LOS TALLERES GRÁFICOS DE LIBERDÚPLEX, S.L.U.
CRTA. BV-2249, KM 7,4, POL. IND. TORRENTFONDO
SANT LLORENÇ D'HORTONS
(BARCELONA)

* * *
* *
*